The Brief McGraw-Hill Handbook

Second Edition

Elaine P. Maimon
Governors State University

W9-BTH-617

Janice H. Peritz
The City University of New York, Queens College

Kathleen Blake Yancey
Florida State University

McGraw Hill

Connect
Learn
Succeed™

Published by McGraw-Hill, an imprint of The McGraw-Hill Companies, Inc., 1221 Avenue of the Americas, New York, NY 10020. Copyright © 2012, 2010 by the McGraw-Hill Companies, Inc. All rights reserved. Printed in the United States of America. No part of this publication may be reproduced or distributed in any form or by any means, or stored in a database or retrieval system, without the prior written consent of The McGraw-Hill Companies, Inc., including, but not limited to, in any network or other electronic storage or transmission, or broadcast for distance learning.

This book is printed on acid-free paper.

5 6 7 8 9 0 DOC/DOC 1 0 9 8 7 6 5 4

ISBN: 978-0-07-338398-9
MHID: 0-07-338398-8

Executive Sponsoring Editor:
Christopher Bennem
Senior Marketing Manager:
Kevin Colleary
Senior Development Editor:
Carla Kay Samodulski
Executive Market Development Manager:
Nanette Giles
Managing Editor: *Anne Fuzellier*
Production Editor: *Margaret Young*
Interior and Cover Designer:
Preston Thomas, Cadence Design
Photo Researcher: *Judy Mason*
Buyer II: *Louis Swaim*
Production Service: *Alma Bell,*
Thompson Type

Composition: *Thompson Type*
Printing: *45# New Era Thin Plus*

Vice President Editorial: *Michael Ryan*
Publisher: *David S. Patterson*
Senior Director of Development:
Dawn Groundwater

Cover image: © Lisa Thornberg

Credits: *The credits section for this book is on page C-1 and is considered an extension of the copyright page.*

Library of Congress Cataloging-in-Publication Data
Maimon, Elaine P.
    The brief McGraw-Hill handbook / Elaine Maimon, Janice Peritz, Kathleen Yancey.—2nd ed., [brief ed.].
        p. cm.
    Includes bibliographical references and index.
    Previous ed.: 2008.
    ISBN-13: 978-0-07-338398-9 (acid-free paper)
    ISBN-10: 0-07-338398-8 (acid-free paper)
    1. English language—Rhetoric—Handbooks, manuals, etc.   2. Academic writing—Handbooks, manuals, etc.   3. Report writing—Handbooks, manuals, etc.   I. Peritz, Janice.   II. Yancey, Kathleen Blake, 1950-   III. Title.
    PE1408.M3363 2011b
    808'.042--dc23

                                                                    2011025109

The Internet addresses listed in the text were accurate at the time of publication. The inclusion of a website does not indicate an endorsement by the authors or McGraw-Hill, and McGraw-Hill does not guarantee the accuracy of the information presented at these sites.

www.mhhe.com

Preface for Students and Tutorials

The Brief McGraw-Hill Handbook will help you improve your writing in any situation you may encounter, whether you are taking a composition class or applying for a job. It offers help with writing in all of your courses, including developing a topic, working with print and online sources, and mastering tricky grammar rules. It also includes chapters on community service writing, business writing, and multimedia presentations, as well as help for multilingual writers.

The first part, "Writing and Designing Texts," focuses on the writing process, from defining a topic to incorporating visuals, revising, and creating a portfolio. Part 2, "Writing in College and Beyond College," provides advice for dealing with common writing assignments, oral presentations, Web site creation, business letters, and service learning projects. Part 3, "Researching," offers a complete guide to finding and evaluating sources and avoiding plagiarism. Parts 4 and 5 present two widely used documentation systems: the Modern Language Association (MLA) system, used in the humanities, and the American Psychological Association (APA) system, used in the social sciences. The next three sections cover the details of usage and grammar conventions, as well as sentence punctuation, mechanics, and spelling. Part 9 provides a quick review of grammar basics.

We've designed this handbook for your ease of use as a quick reference. Read on to learn how to find the information you need.

Brief Contents

The Brief Contents inside the front cover lists the topics covered in this handbook. If you need help preparing a list of works cited in MLA style, you can scan the contents and find Part 4, "MLA Documentation

Style," Chapter 22, "MLA Style: List of Works Cited." You can look up the page number or use the shaded tabs on the pages to flip to "22."

Detailed Contents

For a more specific question, use the detailed contents inside the back cover. Maybe you want to find out when to use *who* vs. *whom*. If you know both are pronouns, you can find Chapter 46, "Problems with Pronouns," section d. Look up the section by page number, or find section 46d with the tabs on the pages.

Index

If you don't know that *who* and *whom* are pronouns, you can look in the index and find *who, whom*. The index will point you to pages 478–79. Use the index to find specific subjects quickly (such as blogs, pp. 167-68).

Glossary of Usage

The Glossary of Usage on pages 414-24 defines words or phrases that are commonly confused or misused (*farther* vs. *further*, *different than* vs. *different from*).

Documentation Directories and Flowcharts

Find out how to cite a source in MLA or APA format by using the directories (on pages 269 and 277–78 for MLA and pages 322 and 328–29 for APA) or the foldout charts at the beginning of Parts 4 or 5. For proper in-text citation of a government publication in MLA style, look up "Government publication" in the directory at the beginning of Chapter 21. You will be directed to the appropriate section and page. Alternately, by answering the questions posed in the charts on the back of the foldout for MLA style at the beginning of Part 4, you can usually find the model you are looking for. By looking at the examples of different types of sources and the documentation models on the front of the foldouts, you can determine where to find the information you need to document a source.

Grammar Foldout

At the beginning of Part 6, a foldout provides a chart of the most common errors students make (for example, sentence fragments). Each error includes an example and a reference to the section and page number where you can find a more detailed explanation and examples. Checkmark icons mark these sections within the text. On the opposite side of the foldout is a quick reference guide for multilingual writers.

Connect Composition
(www.mhconnectcomposition.com)

Connect, McGraw-Hill's online writing resource, provides individualized instruction and practice with all aspects of writing and research, with immediate feedback on every activity. In addition, a digital version of the handbook gives you the ability to build your own personalized online writing resource.

Resources for Multilingual Writers

If English is not your first language, look for the following helpful sections and features:

- Chapter 48, "Special Editing Topics for Multilingual Writers": This chapter covers a broad range of topics, including article use, verbs, and idioms.
- Quick Reference for Multilingual Writers: As noted above, this handy reference guide on the back of the grammar foldout includes common trouble spots for multilingual writers.
- Index for Multilingual Writers: When you look up a term or phrase in this index, it will direct you to spots throughout the text that focus on the concerns of multilingual writers.
- "For Multilingual Writers" boxes throughout the text: These boxes offer advice on culture, learning in college, writing, research, and grammar.

(Preface continues on p. vi.)

Features at a Glance

The sample pages to the right show the key features of this text. These features will help you find the advice you need:

- The **chapter number and title** give the topic of the chapter.
- The **running head** gives the topic covered on the page.
- The **main heading** includes the chapter number and section letter as well as the title of the section.
- **Examples,** many of them with hand corrections, illustrate typical errors and how to correct them.
- **Shaded thumb tabs,** each containing the number and letter of the last section on the page and an abbreviation or symbol for that section, help you find the topic you are looking for.
- **Exercises** test your understanding of the material with a range of activities. Answers to the first three questions of each set appear in the back of the book.
- **Identify and Edit** boxes in Parts 6, 7, and 8 help you recognize and correct errors and problems with grammar, style, and punctuation.

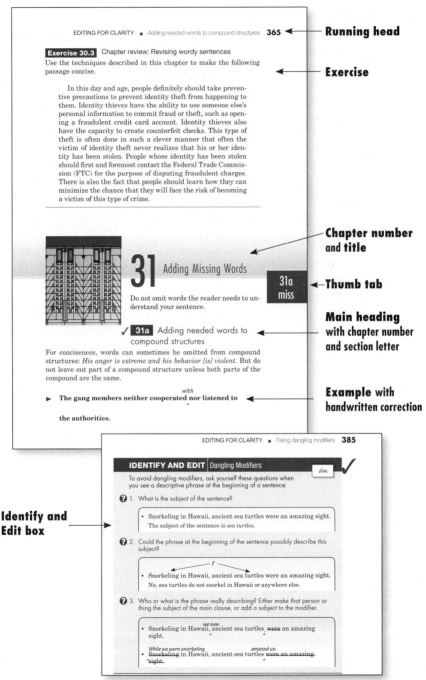

Running head

EDITING FOR CLARITY ■ Adding needed words to compound structures **365**

Exercise

Exercise 30.3 Chapter review: Revising wordy sentences
Use the techniques described in this chapter to make the following passage concise.

In this day and age, people definitely should take preventive precautions to prevent identity theft from happening to them. Identity thieves have the ability to use someone else's personal information to commit fraud or theft, such as opening a fraudulent credit card account. Identity thieves also have the capacity to create counterfeit checks. This type of theft is often done in such a clever manner that often the victim of identity theft never realizes that his or her identity has been stolen. People whose identity has been stolen should first and foremost contact the Federal Trade Commission (FTC) for the purpose of disputing fraudulent charges. There is also the fact that people should learn how they can minimize the chance that they will face the risk of becoming a victim of this type of crime.

Chapter number and title

31 Adding Missing Words

Do not omit words the reader needs to understand your sentence.

31a miss

Thumb tab

✓ **31a** Adding needed words to compound structures

Main heading with chapter number and section letter

For conciseness, words can sometimes be omitted from compound structures: *His anger is extreme and his behavior [is] violent.* But do not leave out part of a compound structure unless both parts of the compound are the same.

with
▶ The gang members neither cooperated nor listened to

the authorities.

Example with handwritten correction

EDITING FOR CLARITY ■ Fixing dangling modifiers **385**

IDENTIFY AND EDIT Dangling Modifiers   *dm* ✓

Identify and Edit box

To avoid dangling modifiers, ask yourself these questions when you see a descriptive phrase at the beginning of a sentence:

❓ 1. What is the subject of the sentence?

• Snorkeling in Hawaii, ancient sea turtles were an amazing sight.
The subject of the sentence is *sea turtles.*

❓ 2. Could the phrase at the beginning of the sentence possibly describe this subject?

• Snorkeling in Hawaii, ancient sea turtles were an amazing sight.
No, sea turtles do not snorkel in Hawaii or anywhere else.

❓ 3. Who or what is the phrase really describing? Either make that person or thing the subject of the main clause, or add a subject to the modifier.

• Snorkeling in Hawaii, ancient sea turtles *we saw* were an amazing sight.

While we were snorkeling   amazed us.
• Snorkeling in Hawaii, ancient sea turtles were an amazing sight.

Tutorials

Before you begin using this book, take a moment to complete the following tutorials. They will give you practice navigating through *The Brief McGraw-Hill Handbook* via the Brief Contents, Contents, Index, Glossary of Usage, and MLA directory or documentation flowchart. Answers appear at the back of the book.

Tutorial A: Brief Contents and Contents

Joe Green is a first-year college student assigned to write about plagiarism in college. As he writes, he wonders whether the following sentences are correct. Using the Brief Contents in the front of this book or the expanded Contents in the back, find the section of the book with the answer, and correct the sentence if necessary. List the chapter or section of the book that contains the answer.

1. Student's today face many pressures that can lead to plagiarism. [Should the first word in the sentence be *Student's, Students,* or *Students'* ?]

2. If a student paraphrases another writer's work too closely without giving the source, they have plagiarized. [Is *they* the correct pronoun to use in this sentence?]

3. Although many students do not realize it. They can plagiarize by using their own words in another writer's sentence structure. [Are these complete and correct sentences?]

4. Colleges deal with plagiarism in different ways, some expel students caught plagiarizing. Others issue warnings first. [Are these complete and correct sentences?]

5. The Internet have made a variety of sources available to students. [Does the subject of this sentence agree with the verb?]

6. Students often copy source material from the Internet, but then they may confuse it with their own notes. [Is the comma in this sentence used correctly?]

7. Plagiarism-detection software be helpful to teachers. [Is there a complete verb in this sentence?]

Tutorial B: Index

Maria Hernandez is peer-reviewing the first draft of Joe's paper. She has questions about each of the following sentences. Using the index at the back of the book, find the information needed and edit the sentences appropriately.

1. The reason some students plagiarize is because they feel pressured to keep a high GPA. [Does *is because* go with *the reason*?]
2. Of the students accused of plagiarism at our school this year, none have been expelled. [Does *none* agree with *have* or should the verb be changed to *has*?]
3. In our honor code, it says students must report others who plagiarize. [Is *it* used correctly here?]
4. A student who lets other students turn in his/her work for an assignment is guilty of plagiarism. [Is the use of *his/her* acceptable?]
5. A teacher once accused my friend and I of copying material from Wikipedia. [Should it be *my friend and I* or *my friend and me*?]
6. Turning in someone else's writing as your own is no different than any other type of cheating. [Is *different than* correct, or should it be changed to *different from*?]
7. Many students do not understand plagiarism because our society excepts many forms of borrowing, such as music samples and Web site mashups. [Is *excepts* the correct word to use here?]

Tutorial C: Glossary of Usage

Joe is revising his paper based on Maria's peer review. He wants to add the following sentences. Using the Glossary of Usage, check to see if the italicized words are used correctly, and fix any incorrect usage.

1. The *amount* of prominent authors accused of plagiarism has increased recently.
2. Instructors must ensure that *everyone* of their students knows how to use sources appropriately.
3. Schools should *adapt* a program of educational seminars about integrating and documenting sources.
4. Students who *flaunt* school policy by failing to document sources must be *censured*.
5. Even when unintentional, plagiarism has a negative *affect* on the academic community.
6. When writing research papers, students have to *site* their sources.

Tutorial D: MLA Documentation Directory and Flowchart

Joe is preparing the list of works cited for his paper. For each of the following sources, create an entry in MLA style using the flowchart at the beginning of Part 4 (after p. 265) or the directory at the beginning of Chapter 22 (pp. 277–78). Arrange the entries into an appropriately formatted list of works cited.

1. A book by Ann Lathrop and Kathleen Foss titled *Student Cheating and Plagiarism in the Internet Era: A Wake-Up Call*. The book was published by Libraries Unlimited in Englewood, Colorado, in 2000.

2. An article in the online magazine *Slate* by Ann Hulbert titled "How Kaavya Got Packaged and Got into Trouble." The article was published on April 27, 2006, at http://www.slate .com/id/ 2140683/. Joe found this article on March 15, 2010.

3. A posting to the blog *The Wired Campus* by Brock Read titled "Are Professors to Blame for Plagiarism?" The posting was published on October 18, 2006, at http://chronicle.com/ wiredcampus/ index.php?id=1644. Joe read this article on March 5, 2010.

Tutorial E: Contents and Index

1. Joe wants to know what typeface and point size he should use for his paper. Where can he find this information in *The Brief McGraw-Hill Handbook*? What are the answers?

2. Joe plans to use a visual to show the increase in the reported instances of plagiarism at his school over the last three years. Would a pie chart, flowchart, or line graph illustrate this data most effectively? Which section of this book should he consult?

3. Joe's professor has asked him to create a wiki for the class on the topic of plagiarism and how to avoid it. Which section of this book should he consult?

4. What is the best way for Joe to find library books on the topic of his research project? Which section of this book should he consult to find the answer?

5. Joe has found a Web site advocating use of a particular type of anti-plagiarism software, which is also sold on that site. The site's URL ends in ".com." Should Joe incorporate information from this site into his paper? Which section of this book should he consult to help him decide?

Preface for Instructors

A Letter from the Authors

Even though the audiences, tools, and occasions for writing today may seem more varied than ever, the fundamental goals of composition courses persist. Instructors strive to motivate and coach students to think critically, recognize rhetorical situations, communicate clearly and effectively, compose in a variety of genres, and edit their own work. They create learning environments where students can practice writing and do research that is discerning and ethical, representing the contributions of others fairly and using and documenting sources appropriately.

Composition courses ultimately aim to help students build a solid set of writing skills that will transfer into other courses and support their effort within their communities and in their professional lives. In revising this text, we have dedicated ourselves to making *The Brief McGraw-Hill Handbook* an even stronger, more practical, and more versatile resource for achieving excellence in college. In this edition, we have paid special attention to helping students understand, navigate, and master common writing situations. This situational approach to writing will help students think about the writing opportunity and then move forward to achieve their purposes.

Thanks in advance for taking a moment to browse through the pages that follow to sample our suggestions.

Sincerely,

Elaine P. Maimon
Janice H. Peritz
Kathleen Blake Yancey

A Resource

McGraw-Hill's commitment to research is unique in higher education publishing. In-depth, multi-campus research studies like our SCORE (Southern California Outcomes Research in English) program yield critical information that helps us understand your needs and test the efficacy of our products. Among our findings:

Students' core challenges—and opportunities—are rhetorical. Whether students are trying to understand an assignment or turn a topic into a thesis, their core challenges are chiefly related to getting started and mastering the writing situation. Our research also shows that their success in addressing these rhetorical issues correlates most highly with their success as writers overall.

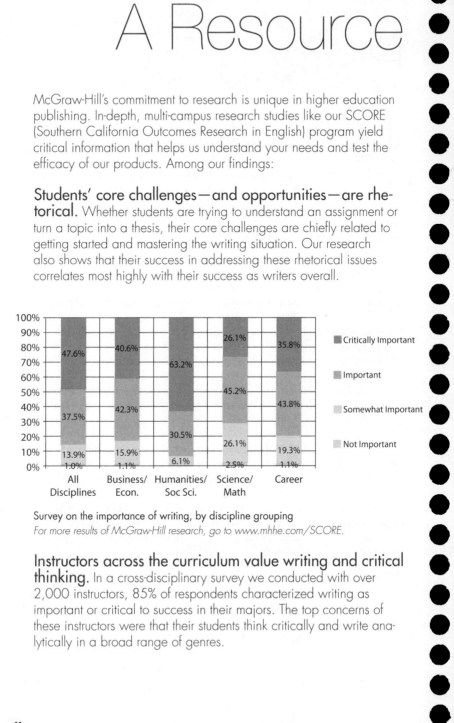

Survey on the importance of writing, by discipline grouping
For more results of McGraw-Hill research, go to www.mhhe.com/SCORE.

Instructors across the curriculum value writing and critical thinking. In a cross-disciplinary survey we conducted with over 2,000 instructors, 85% of respondents characterized writing as important or critical to success in their majors. The top concerns of these instructors were that their students think critically and write analytically in a broad range of genres.

Based on Research

Students don't always "know what they know." Our research shows that students are often inaccurate in their assessments of their writing abilities, especially in the areas of grammar, usage, and critical thinking (see below). Our studies show that the more students used *Connect*—getting help they didn't always know they needed—the better they performed.

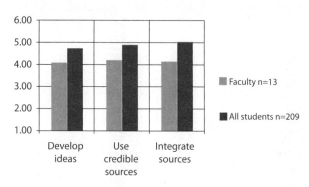

Instructor vs. student assessments of critical thinking aptitude
For more results of McGraw-Hill research, go to www.mhhe.com/SCORE.

Students assigned digital materials made greater gains than those assigned only print. Our research showed that instructors who incorporated digital elements into their coursework generally had more positive results among their students than those who did not.

A Resource for

Whether in print or online, *The Brief McGraw-Hill Handbook* presents the writing situation as a framework for beginning any type of composition across the curriculum and beyond college:

Start Smart: Addressing the Writing Situation In print or online, the *Start Smart* foldout helps students begin assignments and locate appropriate print and online handbook resources with ease, guiding them through a simple series of steps that encourage clear and critical thinking as they move through the writing process.

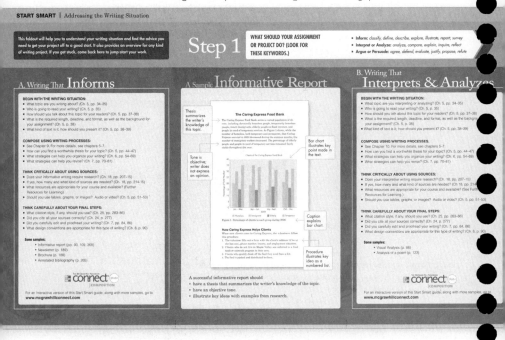

Source Smart boxes offer specific tips on key skills and strategies for incorporating sources.

SOURCE SMART

Planning Your Search

Your research plan should include where you expect to find your sources. For example, you may have to visit the library to view print materials that predate 1980; you will need to consult a subscription database online or at the library for recent scientific discoveries; you may need to access archives for historical research; and you may need to conduct field research, such as interviewing fellow students. Set priorities to increase your efficiency in each location (library, archive, online).

Navigating the Writing Situation

A new section in the Introduction devoted to the writing situation: A section in the Introduction introduces students to five essential elements (purpose, audience, stance, genre, medium), framing these variables as a way to manage the writing process and produce stronger, more effective work.

Consider Your Situation identifies the key elements of the writing situation in each of the print text's five student compositions. Each includes comments that reflect on choices the student author made based on the writing situation. A *Consider Your Situation* template is available online for students to manage and work through their own assignments.

CONSIDER YOUR SITUATION

Author: John Terrell, a political science major, interested in a career in international relations

Type of writing: Informative report

Purpose: To inform readers about Sisters in Islam (SIS)

Stance: Reasonable, informed, objective

Audience: Classmates and instructor standing in for U.S. general public

Medium: Print, computer file, part of e-portfolio

Terrell writes: After writing this informative paper, I know a great deal more about possibilities for women in Muslim countries, and I am eager to share that information with readers.

Common Writing Situations: Six chapters in Part 2 offer guidelines for writing that informs, analyzes, and argues in academic, business, and community settings. Three full student academic compositions appear in these chapters, with numerous interactive examples online representing a range of genres and media.

A Resource that

With *Connect Composition,* course management and assessment can be easily implemented in a writing course. *Connect* provides a wide range of tools that can all be seamlessly accessed by your local course management system.

Market-leading integration with course management: With McGraw-Hill Campus, instructors enjoy single sign-on access to *Connect Composition* through any learning management system. Seamless interoperability of all *Connect* assets allows students to access all the features and functionalities of McGraw-Hill's digital tools directly from their instructor's course management site.

The **Best** of **Both Worlds**

Outcomes Based Assessment of Writing. *Connect*'s assessment tools allow instructors to provide students with the feedback they need when they need it. Pre-built, customizable grading rubrics make the set-up, management, and reporting of outcomes-based assessment efficient and professional. Finally: an affordable, easy to use, and statistically valid assessment solution—for a single course or for an entire program.

Visit *Connect Composition 3.0* <www.mhconnectcomposition.com>.

Makes Course Management and Assessment Easy

Adaptive Diagnostics develop customized learning plans to individualize instruction, practice, and assessment, meeting the needs of individual students in core skill areas. Students get immediate feedback on every exercise, and results are sent directly to the instructor's grade book.

A full digital handbook gives students the ability to build their own personalized online writing resource using state-of-the-art annotation and search tools. Students and instructors may highlight, bookmark, and create notes in context to collect the content they need the most.

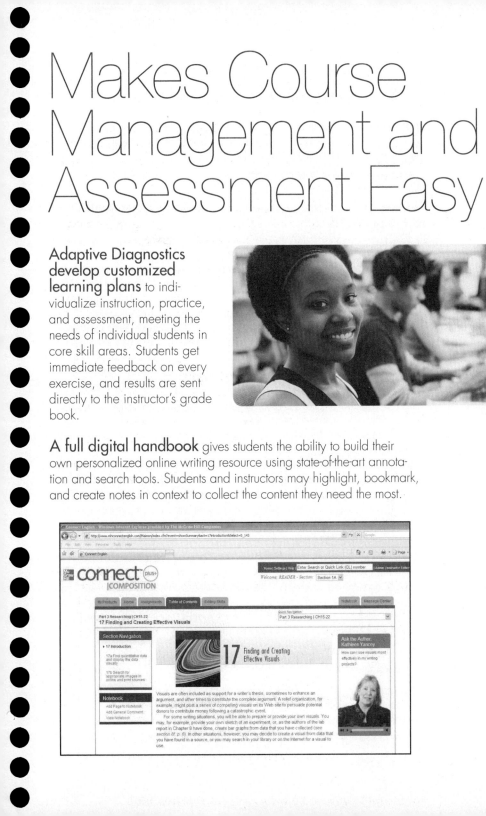

WPA Outcomes Statement for First-Year Composition

Adopted by the Council of Writing Program Administrators (WPA), April 2000, amended July 2008. For further information about the development of the Outcomes Statement, please see http://comppile.tamucc.edu/ WPAoutcomes/continue.html

For further information about the Council of Writing Program Administrators, please see http://www.wpacouncil.org

A version of this statement was published in *WPA: Writing Program Administration* 23.1/2 (Fall/Winter 1999): 59-66.

Introduction

This statement describes the common knowledge, skills, and attitudes sought by first-year composition programs in American postsecondary education. To some extent, we seek to regularize what can be expected to be taught in first-year composition; to this end the document is not merely a compilation or summary of what currently takes place. Rather, the following statement articulates what composition teachers nationwide have learned from practice, research, and theory. This document intentionally defines only "outcomes," or types of results, and not "standards," or precise levels of achievement. The setting of standards should be left to specific institutions or specific groups of institutions.

Learning to write is a complex process, both individual and social, that takes place over time with continued practice and informed guidance. Therefore, it is important that teachers, administrators, and a concerned public do not imagine that these outcomes can be taught in reduced or simple ways. Helping students demonstrate these outcomes requires expert understanding of how students actually learn to write. For this reason we expect the primary audience for this document to be well-prepared college writing teachers and college writing program administrators. In some places, we have chosen to write in their professional language. Among such readers, terms such as "rhetorical" and "genre" convey a rich meaning that is not easily simplified. While we have also aimed at writing a document that the general public can understand, in limited cases we have aimed first at communicating effectively with expert writing teachers and writing program administrators.

These statements describe only what we expect to find at the end of first-year composition, at most schools a required general education course or sequence of courses. As writers move beyond first-year composition, their writing abilities do not merely improve. Rather, students' abilities not only diversify along disciplinary and professional lines but also move into whole new levels where expected outcomes expand, multiply, and diverge. For this reason, each statement of outcomes for first-year composition is followed by suggestions for further work that builds on these outcomes.

Rhetorical Knowledge

By the end of first year composition, students should
- Focus on a purpose
- Respond to the needs of different audiences
- Respond appropriately to different kinds of rhetorical situations

- Use conventions of format and structure appropriate to the rhetorical situation
- Adopt appropriate voice, tone, and level of formality
- Understand how genres shape reading and writing
- Write in several genres

Faculty in all programs and departments can build on this preparation by helping students learn

- The main features of writing in their fields
- The main uses of writing in their fields
- The expectations of readers in their fields

Critical Thinking, Reading, and Writing

By the end of first year composition, students should

- Use writing and reading for inquiry, learning, thinking, and communicating
- Understand a writing assignment as a series of tasks, including finding, evaluating, analyzing, and synthesizing appropriate primary and secondary sources
- Integrate their own ideas with those of others
- Understand the relationships among language, knowledge, and power

Faculty in all programs and departments can build on this preparation by helping students learn

- The uses of writing as a critical thinking method
- The interactions among critical thinking, critical reading, and writing
- The relationships among language, knowledge, and power in their fields

Processes

By the end of first year composition, students should

- Be aware that it usually takes multiple drafts to create and complete a successful text
- Develop flexible strategies for generating, revising, editing, and proof-reading
- Understand writing as an open process that permits writers to use later invention and re-thinking to revise their work
- Understand the collaborative and social aspects of writing processes
- Learn to critique their own and others' works
- Learn to balance the advantages of relying on others with the responsibility of doing their part
- Use a variety of technologies to address a range of audiences

Faculty in all programs and departments can build on this preparation by helping students learn

- To build final results in stages
- To review work-in-progress in collaborative peer groups for purposes other than editing
- To save extensive editing for later parts of the writing process
- To apply the technologies commonly used to research and communicate within their fields

Knowledge of Conventions

By the end of first year composition, students should
- Learn common formats for different kinds of texts
- Develop knowledge of genre conventions ranging from structure and paragraphing to tone and mechanics
- Practice appropriate means of documenting their work
- Control such surface features as syntax, grammar, punctuation, and spelling

Faculty in all programs and departments can build on this preparation by helping students learn
- The conventions of usage, specialized vocabulary, format, and documentation in their fields
- Strategies through which better control of conventions can be achieved

Composing in Electronic Environments

As has become clear over the last twenty years, writing in the 21st-century involves the use of digital technologies for several purposes, from drafting to peer reviewing to editing. Therefore, although the kinds of composing processes and texts expected from students vary across programs and institutions, there are nonetheless common expectations.

By the end of first-year composition, students should
- Use electronic environments for drafting, reviewing, revising, editing, and sharing texts
- Locate, evaluate, organize, and use research material collected from electronic sources, including scholarly library databases; other official databases (e.g., federal government databases); and informal electronic networks and internet sources
- Understand and exploit the differences in the rhetorical strategies and in the affor-dances available for both print and electronic composing processes and texts

Faculty in all programs and departments can build on this preparation by helping students learn
- How to engage in the electronic research and composing processes common in their fields
- How to disseminate texts in both print and electronic forms in their fields

[http://www.wpacouncil.org/positions/outcomes.html, accessed 9/13/2010]

Acknowledgments

When we wrote *The Brief McGraw-Hill Handbook,* we started with the premise that it takes a campus to teach a writer. It is also the case that it takes a community to write a handbook. This text has been a major collaborative effort for all three of us. And over the years, that ever-widening circle of collaboration has included reviewers, editors, librarians, faculty colleagues, and family members.

Let us start close to home. Mort Maimon brought to this project his years of insight and experience as a writer and as a secondary and postsecondary English teacher. Gillian Maimon, Ph.D., first-grade teacher and writing workshop leader, and Alan Maimon, journalist and author, inspired and encouraged their mother in this project. Elaine also drew inspiration from her young granddaughters, Dasia and Madison Stewart and Annabelle Elaine Maimon, who already show promise of becoming writers. Rudy Peritz and Lynne Haney reviewed drafts of a number of chapters, bringing to our cross-curricular mix the pedagogical and writerly perspectives of, respectively, a law professor and a sociologist. Jess Peritz, a recent college graduate, was consulted on numerous occasions for her expert advice on making examples both up-to-date and understandable. David, Genevieve, and Matthew Yancey—whose combined writing experience includes the fields of biology, psychology, medicine, computer engineering, and information technology—helped with examples as well as with accounts of their writing practices: completing many kinds of classroom assignments, applying to medical and graduate schools, writing for internships and jobs both inside and outside of the academy.

At Governors State University, Diane Dates Casey and Penny Perdue provided research support. At Arizona State University West, Beverly Buddee worried with us over this project for many years. Our deepest gratitude goes to Lisa Kammerlocher and Dennis Isbell for the guidelines on critically evaluating Web resources in Chapter 16, as well as to Sharon Wilson. Thanks, too, go to C. J. Jeney and Cheryl Warren for providing assistance. ASU West professors Thomas McGovern and Martin Meznar shared assignments and student papers with us. In the Chancellor's Office at the University of Alaska Anchorage, Denise Burger and Christine Tullius showed admirable support and patience.

Several colleagues at Queens College and elsewhere not only shared their reflections on teaching and writing, but also gave us valuable classroom materials to use as we saw fit. Our thanks go to Fred Buell, Stuart Cochran, Jane Collins, Nancy Comley, Ann Davison, Joan Dupre, Hugh English, Sue Goldhaber, Marci Goodman, Jane Hathaway, Steve Kruger, Eric Lehman, Norman Lewis, Charles Molesworth, Beth Stickney, Jan Tecklin, Christine Timm, Amy Tucker, Stan Walker, Scott Zaluda, Diane Zannoni, and Richard

Zeikowitz. The Queens College librarians also gave us various kinds of help with the researching and documentation chapters, and we thank them, especially Sharon Bonk, Alexandra DeLuise, Izabella Taler, and Manny Sanudo.

We want to give special thanks to the students whose papers we include in full: Diane Chen, McKenna Doherty, Rebecca Hollingsworth, Bud Littleton, Tina Schwab, and Jon Paul Terrell. We also want to acknowledge the following students who allowed us to use substantial excerpts from their work: Diane Chen, Ilona Bouzoukashvili, Lara Deforest, Baz Dreisinger, Sheila Foster, Jacob Grossman, Jennifer Koehler, Holly Musetti, and Umawattie Roopnarian.

From Florida State University, we thank the Rhetoric and Composition program and the many good ideas that come from students and faculty alike. Specifically, we thank Liane Robertson, now at William Paterson University of New Jersey, and Kara Taczak, now at the University of Denver, who brought their experiences as excellent teachers of writing to many pages of this book.

Our thanks also go to Judy Williamson and Trent Batson for contributing their expertise on writing and computers as well as for sharing what they learned from the Epiphany Project. Our thanks go out as well to Casey Furlong of Glendale Community College and Santi Buscemi of Middlesex County College for their excellent contributions to *Connect*. We are grateful to Harvey Wiener and the late Richard Marius for their permission to draw on their explanations of grammatical points in the *Brief McGraw-Hill Handbook*. We also appreciate the work of Andras Tapolcai and Charlotte Smith of Adirondack Community College, who collected many of the examples used in the documentation chapters, and of Maria Zlateva, Boston University, our ESL consultant. Thanks also go to librarians Debora Person, University of Wyoming, and Ronelle K. H. Thompson, Augustana College, who provided us with helpful comments on Part 3, "Researching." Our colleague Don McQuade has inspired us, advised us, and encouraged us throughout the years of this project.

Within the McGraw-Hill organization, many wonderful people have been our true teammates. Tim Julet believed in this project initially and signed us on to what has become a major life commitment. From 1999, Lisa Moore, first as executive editor for the composition list, then as publisher for English, creatively, expertly, and tirelessly led the group of development editors and in-house experts who helped us find the appropriate form to bring our insights as composition teachers to the widest possible group of students. Thanks also to Christopher Bennem, our sponsoring editor, who extended Lisa's legacy with his own creativity, imagining, for example, how pages of prose could be presented in concise visual form. Crucial support also came from Beth Mejia, editorial director; David Patterson, publisher for English; Dawn Groundwater, director of development for English;

and Nanette Giles, market development manager. Kudos go to Bruce Thaler, Karen Mauk, Anne Stameshkin, Suzy Spivey, and Diana Puglisi George for their tireless work on this project. Thanks as well to Janet Smith, Paul Banks, Andrea Pasquarelli, Paula Kepos, and Jesse LaBuff, all of whom worked diligently on *Connect Composition.* Rachel Castillo, Margaret Young, and Alma Bell, lead project managers, monitored every detail of production; Preston Thomas, lead designer, supervised every aspect of the striking text design and cover; and Robin Mouat, art editor, was responsible for the stunning visuals that appear throughout the book. Allister Fein worked diligently to produce the helpful foldouts. Kevin Colleary, senior marketing manager, and Ray Kelley, field publisher, have worked tirelessly and enthusiastically to market *The Brief McGraw-Hill Handbook.* We also appreciate the hands-on attention of McGraw-Hill senior executives Mike Ryan, vice president and editor-in-chief of the Humanities, Social Sciences, and World Languages group, and Steve Debow, president of the Humanities, Social Sciences, and World Languages group.

This book has benefited enormously from three extraordinary development editors: Anne Kemper, David Chodoff, and the remarkable Carla Samodulski. Carla joined *The Brief McGraw-Hill Handbook* in medias res and guided our progress with expertise and poise. Even in the middle of Hurricane Irene, when she called on an old technology—candles!—to provide enough light to proofread by—Carla was our beacon. We are in her debt.

Finally, many, many thanks go to the reviewers who read chapters from the new edition of one of our handbooks, generously offered their perceptions and reactions to our plans, and had confidence in us as we shaped our texts to address the needs of their students. We wish to thank the following instructors:

Content Consultants and Reviewers

Alamance Community College
  Susan Dalton

Alvin Community College
  Ann H. Guess

Arizona Western College, Yuma
  Stephen Moore

Baruch College
  Paula Berggren
  Harold Brent
  Cheryl Smith

Black Hawk College
  Torria Norman

Blinn College
  Becky Renee Almany
  Alicia Clay

Bluefield State College
  Tamara Lynn Ferguson

Bossier Parish Community College
  Holly French-Hart

Bowie State University
  Stephanie Johnson
  Nicole Wilson

Bowling Green State University
  Abigail Cloud
  Dawn Hubbell-Staeble

Brazosport College
  Brenda Dillard

Bridgewater State University
  Michelle Cox

Brown Mackie College,
Fort Wayne
  Julia Clark

California University of
Pennsylvania
  Carole Waterhouse

Campbell University
  Elizabeth Rambo

College of Central Florida
  Sandra Cooper

College of Southern Nevada
  Shelley Kelly

Columbia College
  Jean Petrolle

Community College of
Allegheny County
  Pamela J. Turley

Community College of Baltimore
County, Catonsville
  Evan Balkan
  Christine Gray
  Carol Joseph

Cumberland County College
  John Lore

Delaware State University
  Andrew Blake

Eastern Washington University
  Polly Buckingham
  Justin Young

Ferrum College
  Katherine Grimes

Fullerton College
  Bruce Henderson

Georgia Highlands College
  Nancy Applegate
  Jesse Bishop
  Rachel Wall
  Cindy Wheeler

Holy Family University
  Janice Showler

Houston Community College,
Central College
  Alan Ainsworth
  Robert Ford
  Syble Simon

Houston Community College,
Northwest College
  Melissa Miller-Waters
  Ritu Raju

Houston Community College,
Southeast College
  Carlton Downey

Houston Community College,
Southwest College
  Amy Harris Tan

Itawamba Community College
  Larry Armstrong

Ivy Tech Community College,
Indianapolis
  Judith Lafourest
  David Soots

Jackson State Community College
  Melina Baer
  Mark Walls

Jacksonville State University
  William Hug
  Deborah Prickett
  Susan Sellers

Jefferson College
  Shanie Latham
  Shirley Dubman
  John Pleimann

Kishwaukee College
  Nathan Gordon
  Tina Hultgren

Lake Michigan College
  Karen Johnson-McWilliams
  Galina Sundberg
  Jean Ann Yakshaw

Lamar University
  James Sanderson
  Steven Zani

Lincoln College
  Judith Cortelloni

McNeese State University
  Rita Costello
  Keagan Lejeune
  Molly A. Martin

Mississippi State University
  Tennyson O'Donnell
  Ann Spurlock

Moberly Area Community College
  Michael Barrett

Nicholls State University
  Keri Turner
  Shana Walton

Normandale Community College
  Terri Symonds

North Lake College
  Ulanda Forbess

Northwest Arkansas
Community College
  Audley Hall

Ocean County College
  David Bordelon
  Bob Kleinschmidt

Old Dominion University
  Dana Heller
  Matt Oliver

Owens Community College
  Ann-Marie Paulin
  Ellen Sorg

Ozarks Technical Community
College
  Dane K. Galloway

Pace University, Pleasantville
  Betty Kirschstein

Palm Beach Atlantic University
  Susan Jones

Pearl River Community College
  Martha Willoughby

Pima Community College,
Downtown Campus
  Kristina Beckman-Brito
  Jo Ann Little
  William Scurrah

Point Park University
  Robert Alexander
  Portia Weston

Polk State College
  Rebecca Heintz
  Howard Kerner

Richard Bland College
  Lejeanna Raymond

Sacred Heart University
  Anita August

Santa Barbara City College
  Sheila Wiley

Scottsdale Community College
  Jamie Moore

Seminole State College of Florida
  Kate Kellen

Somerset Community College
  Wanda Fries

Southeastern Louisiana
University
  Michelle Bellavia
  Natasha Whitton
  Jeff Wiemelt

Southern Methodist University
  Diana Grumbles

Southwestern Illinois College
  Nicole Hancock
  Monica Hatch
  Cory Lund
  Steven Moiles
  Linda Schink

Sussex County Community
College
  Frank Ancona
  James Rawlins
  Mary Thompson

Texas Southern University
  Lana Reese

Tidewater Community College
  Joseph Antinarella

Troy University
  Elaine Bassett
  Catherine Hutcheson

Connect Editorial Board of Advisors

Helping us with the digital development of *Connect Composition* has been of pivotal importance in this edition:

North Central Texas College
Rochelle Gregory

Old Dominion University
Matt Oliver

The Pennsylvania State University
Dan Tripp

Pima Community College,
Downtown Campus
Kristina Beckman-Brito

Santa Ana College
Gary Bennett

University of California, Irvine
Lynda Haas

Freshman Composition Symposia

We are deeply indebted to the following sixty-seven instructors who participated in one of the several composition symposia we hosted in the fall of 2010, spring of 2011, and fall of 2011. Representing the needs and goals of their writing programs and students, they provided vision and guided the McGraw-Hill English editors as they made critical decisions concerning *Connect Composition*. Their contributions will result in a rich *Connect Composition* platform for years to come. Thank you.

Abraham Baldwin Agricultural College
Jeff Newberry

Angelina College
Diana Throckmorton

Arapahoe Community College
Sallie Wolf

Brevard Community College
Heather Elko

Brigham Young University
Brett McInelly

Broome Community College
David Chirico

Broward College
Sandra Stollman

Cedar Valley College
Elsie Burnett

Chattanooga State Community College
Joel Henderson

Clayton State University
Mary Lamb

Coastal Bend College
Anna Green

College of the Canyons
Jia-Yi Cheng-Levine

Dutchess Community College
Angela Batchelor

Eastern Washington University
Justin Young

Ferrum College
Margaret Katherine Grimes

Florida A & M University
Nandi Riley

Glendale Community College
Alisa Cooper

Heartland Community College
Jennifer Cherry

Ithaca College
Susan Adams Delaney

Indiana University—Purdue University Indianapolis
Mel Wininger

Kapi'olani Community College
Georganne Nordstrom

Lake Sumter Community College
Patricia Campbell

Lehigh Carbon Community
College
Douglas Rigby

Lindenwood University
Ana Schnellmann

Loyola Marymount University
K. J. Peters

Mercer County Community
College
Noreen Duncan

Michigan State University
Bill Hart-Davidson

Montgomery County
Community College
Diane McDonald

Naugatuck Valley
Community College
Anne Mattrella

North Central Texas College
Rochelle Gregory

North Idaho College
Lloyd Duman

Northern Illinois University
Eric Hoffman

Oakland Community College
Subashini Subbarao

Old Dominion University
Matt Oliver

Oregon State University
Susan Meyers

Pearl River Community College
Greg Underwood

Pima Community College,
Downtown Campus
Kristina Beckman-Brito

Quinnipiac University
Glenda Pritchett

Sacramento City College
Jeff Knorr

Saint Louis Community College
James Sodon

Salt Lake Community College
Brittany Stephenson

Santa Ana College
Gary Bennett

Savannah State University
Gwendolyn Hale

Seminole State College of Florida
Ruth Reis-Palatiere

Sinclair Community College
Kate Geiselman

Southeastern Louisiana
University
Jeff Wiemelt

Southern Illinois University,
Carbondale
Ronda Dively

Southwestern Illinois College
Winnie Kenney

Southwestern Oklahoma
State University
Jill Jones

Spokane Community College
Andrea Reid

St. Louis University
Janice McIntire-Strasburg

Sussex County Community
College
James Rawlins

Tarrant County College
Jim Schrantz

Tidewater Community College
Joe Antinarella

Truman State University
Monica Barron

University of California, Irvine
Lynda Haas

University of Florida
Creed Greer

University of Idaho
Jodie Nicotra

University of Missouri, St. Louis
Suellynn Duffey

University of Nevada, Las Vegas
Ruby Fowler

University of North Florida
  Jeanette Berger

University of Rhode Island
  Libby Miles

University of Texas, El Paso
  Beth Brunk-Chavez

University of the District of
Columbia
  La Tanya Reese Rogers

University of Wisconsin,
Eau Claire
  Shevaun Watson

University of Wisconsin, Stout
  Andrea Deacon

Wilbur Wright College
  Phillip Virgen

Research Study Partners and Participants

Our research studies included the Southern California Outcomes
Research in English project (SCORE) and The Writing Situation
Study. Neither would have been possible without the close collaboration and assistance of our instructor-participants and site partners,
to whom we owe special thanks:

Bowling Green State University
  Amanda McGuire
  Donna Nelson-Beene
  Angela Zimmann

Chattanooga State University
  Allison Fetters
  Brian Hale
  Joel Henderson
  Jennifer Ontog

Loyola Marymount University
  Celeste Amos
  Karen Feiner
  Wendy Kozak
  Ruth Lane
  K. J. Peters
  Lauren Redwine
  Erica Steakley
  Shelby Schaefer

Owens Community College
  Anita Flynn
  Laurence Levy
  Ellen Sorg

Santa Ana College
  Gary Bennett
  Francisco Gomez
  Noha Kabaji

  Jayne Munoz
  Dianne Pearce
  Stacey Simmerman
  Rachel Sosta

University of California, Irvine
  Chieh Chieng
  Alberto Gullaba
  Lynda Haas
  Greg McClure
  Ali Meghdadi
  Ryan Ridge

University of California, Merced
  Cheryl Finley

University of California,
Santa Cruz
  Nirshan Perera

University of Toledo
  Sheri Benton
  Anthony Edgington
  Charles Kell

Elaine P. Maimon
Janice H. Peritz
Kathleen Blake Yancey

About the Authors

Elaine P. Maimon is president of Governors State University in the south suburbs of Chicago, where she is also professor of English. Previously she was chancellor of the University of Alaska Anchorage, provost (chief campus officer) at Arizona State University West, and vice president of Arizona State University as a whole. In the 1970s, she initiated and then directed the Beaver College writing-across-the-curriculum program, one of the first WAC programs in the nation. A founding executive board member of the national Council of Writing Program Administrators (CWPA), she has directed national institutes to improve the teaching of writing and to disseminate the principles of writing across the curriculum. With a PhD in English from the University of Pennsylvania, where she later helped to create the Writing Across the University (WATU) program, she has also taught and served as an academic administrator at Haverford College, Brown University, and Queens College.

Janice Haney Peritz is an associate professor of English who has taught college writing for more than thirty years, first at Stanford University, where she received her PhD in 1978, and then at the University of Texas at Austin; Beaver College; and Queens College, City University of New York. From 1989 to 2002, she directed the Composition Program at Queens College, where in 1996, she also initiated the college's writing-across-the-curriculum program and the English department's involvement with the Epiphany Project and cyber-composition. She also worked with a group of CUNY colleagues to develop The Write Site, an online learning center, and more recently directed the CUNY Honors College at Queens College for three years. Currently, she is back in the English department doing what she loves most: full-time classroom teaching of writing, literature, and culture.

Kathleen Blake Yancey is the Kellogg W. Hunt Professor of English, a Distinguished Research Professor, and director of the Graduate Program in Rhetoric and Composition at Florida State University. She is past president of the Council of Writing Program Administrators (CWPA), past chair of the Conference on College Composition and Communication (CCCC), and past president of the National Council of Teachers of English (NCTE). Currently, she co-directs the Inter/National Coalition on Electronic Portfolio Research, which has brought together teachers and researchers from over 60 institutions around the world to learn together how to use eportfolios to foster learning. She also edits *College Composition and Communication,* the flagship journal for writing studies. She has led many institutes and workshops—focused on electronic portfolios, on service learning and reflection, and on writing and composing with digital technologies. Previously, she taught at UNC Charlotte and at Clemson University, where she directed the Pearce Center for Professional Communication and was the founding director of the Class of 1941 Studio for Student Communication, both of which are dedicated to supporting communication across the curriculum.

College is a place for exploration, opening new pathways for your life. You will travel through many courses, participating in numerous conversations—oral and written—about nature, society, and culture. As you navigate your college experience, use this book as your map and guide:

- As a map, this text will help you understand different approaches to knowledge and see how your studies relate to the larger world.
- As a guide, this text will help you write in college and in the other areas of your life: exams, research reports, résumés, brochures, letters of complaint, and business correspondence.

As a permanent part of your library, this text can take you where you need to go in college and beyond.

1a Studying a range of academic disciplines

Each department in your college represents a specialized field of academic study, or area of inquiry, called a **discipline.** Each discipline has its own history, terminology, and concerns. Sociology, for example, is concerned with the conditions, patterns, and problems of people in groups and societies. Sociologists collect, analyze, and interpret data connected to that focus; sociologists also debate questions of reliability and interpretation. These debates occur in classrooms with students; in conferences with colleagues; in journals and books that reach national and international academic audiences; and in conversations, presentations, and publications addressing members of the public, including elected officials.

Your college curriculum is likely to include distribution requirements that will expose you to a range of disciplines. You may be asked to take one or two courses in the humanities (the disciplines of literature, music, and philosophy, for example), the social sciences (sociology, economics, and psychology, for example), and the natural sciences (physics, biology, and chemistry, for example). When you write in each discipline—taking notes, writing papers, answering essay-exam questions—you will deepen your understanding of how knowledge is constructed. In doing so, you will join the academic conversation, learning to see and think about the world from different vantage points.

1b Using writing as a tool for learning

Writing is a great aid to learning. Think of the way a simple shopping list jogs your memory once you get to the store, or recall the last time you were asked to take the minutes of a meeting. Because of your heightened attention, you undoubtedly knew more about what happened at that meeting than did anyone else in the room. Writing helps you remember, understand, and create.

- **Writing aids memory.** From taking class notes *(see Figure I.1)* to jotting down ideas for later development, writing helps you to retrieve important information. Many students use an informal outline for lecture notes and then go back to fill in the details after class. Write down ideas inspired by your course work— in any form or order. These ideas can be seeds for a research project or other types of critical inquiry, or you can apply them to your life outside the classroom.

- **Writing sharpens observations.** When you record what you see, hear, taste, smell, and feel, you increase the powers of your senses. Note the smells during a chemistry experiment, and you will more readily detect changes caused by reactions; record how the aroma of freshly popped popcorn makes you feel, and you will better understand your own moods.

- **Writing clarifies thought.** After composing a draft, carefully reading it helps you pinpoint what you really want to say. The last paragraph of a first draft often becomes the first paragraph of the next draft.

- **Writing uncovers connections.** Maybe a character in a short story reminds you of your neighbor, or an image in a poem makes you feel sad. Writing down the reasons you make these connections can help you learn more about the work and more about yourself.

- **Writing improves reading.** When you read, annotating—or taking notes on the main ideas—and drafting a brief summary of the writer's points sharpen your reading skills and help you remember what you have read. Because memories are often tinged with emotion, writing a personal reaction to a reading can connect the material to your own life, thereby enhancing both your memory and your understanding. *(For a detailed discussion of critical reading and writing, see Chapter 1.)*

- **Writing strengthens argument.** In academic projects, an argument is not a fiery disagreement, but rather a path of reasoning to a position. When you write an argument supporting a claim, you work out *the connections linking your ideas—*

```
3/17
MEMORY

3 ways to store memory
 1. sensory memory —everything sensed
 2. short term memory STM —15-25 sec.
     —stored as meaning
     —5-9 chunks
 3. long term memory LTM —unlimited
     —rehearsal
     —visualization
 * If long term memory is unlimited, why do we forget?
Techniques for STM to LTM
     —write, draw, diagram
     —visualize
     —mnemonics
```

FIGURE I.1 An outline for lecture notes. Jotting down the main ideas of a lecture and the questions they raise helps you become a more active listener.

uncovering both flaws that force you to rethink your position and new connections that make your position stronger. Through writing, you also address your audience and the objections they might raise. Success in life often depends on understanding opposing points of view and arguing for your own ideas in ways that others can hear. *(For a detailed discussion of argument, see Chapter 8.)*

Ic Taking responsibility for reading, writing, and research

The academic community assumes that you are an independent learner, capable of managing your workload without supervision. For most courses, the syllabus will be the primary guide to what is expected of you, serving as a contract between you and your instructor. It will tell you what reading you must do in advance of each class, when tests are scheduled, and when formal assignments or stages of projects (for example, topic and research plan, draft, and final project) are due. Use the syllabus to map out your weekly schedule for reading, research, and writing. *(For tips on how to schedule a research paper, see Chapter 13, pp. 195–96.)*

NAVIGATING THROUGH COLLEGE AND BEYOND

Study Skills and Dealing with Stress

Whether academic pursuits are a struggle or come easily to you, whether you are fresh out of high school or are returning to school after many years, college, like all new and challenging experiences, can be stressful. Here are some strategies for dealing with the stress of college and achieving success:

- **Make flexible schedules.** Schedules help you control your time and avoid procrastination by breaking big projects into manageable bits. Be sure to build some flexibility into your schedule, so that you can manage the unexpected.
- **Make the most of your time by setting clear priorities.** Deal with last-minute invitations by saying "no," getting away from it all, and taking control of phone, text, and e-mail interruptions.
- **Take good notes.** The central feature of good note taking, in college and in life, is listening and distilling the important information—not writing down everything that is said.
- **Build reading and listening skills.** When you read, identify and prioritize the main ideas, think critically about the arguments, and explain the writer's ideas to someone else. Listen actively: focus on what is being said, pay attention to nonverbal messages, listen for what is *not* being said, and take notes.
- **Improve your memory.** Repetition and making connections are key strategies in remembering important information. Repeat the information, summarize it, and associate it with other memories.
- **Evaluate the information you gather.** Consider how authoritative the source is, whether the author has potential biases, how recent the information is, and what facts or other evidence is missing from the research. In college, as in life, critical thinking is essential.
- **Take care of yourself.** Eating healthful food, exercising regularly, and getting plenty of sleep are well-known stress relievers. Some people find meditation to be effective. Stopping for a few seconds to take some deep breaths can do wonders.
- **Reach out for support.** If you find it difficult to cope with stress, seek professional help. Colleges have trained counselors on staff as well as twenty-four-hour crisis lines.

Source: Based partly on Robert S. Feldman, *P.O.W.E.R. Learning: Strategies for Success in College and Life,* 2nd ed., New York: McGraw-Hill, 2003.

Id Achieving the core outcomes of successful writing

As you write, you will communicate your ideas more effectively if you keep these five outcomes in mind. Although they are presented separately here, these outcomes work together as you compose. For example, you will use critical thinking (part of one outcome) as you revise your project (part of another outcome):

- **Rhetorical knowledge** includes focusing on your purpose for writing and the specific audience you are addressing. It also means using the most appropriate genre and medium to achieve that purpose, employing conventions necessary to the genre, and taking an appropriate rhetorical stance. *(See Section Ie and Chapter 2.)*
- **Critical thinking, reading, and writing** include using writing for inquiry, for thinking about ways to approach a project, and for developing that project, especially as you work with sources. *(See Chapters 1, 8b, and 16.)*
- **Processes** are flexible strategies for drafting and revising as well as working with others on a writing task, whether through peer review or collaborative writing. *(See Chapters 2–4.)*
- **Knowledge of conventions** includes working within the formats that characterize different genres (for example, a résumé or a literary analysis) and using the correct requirements— governing syntax, punctuation, and spelling, for example— expected in every writing project. *(See Chapters 5 and 12 and Parts 6–8.)*
- **Composing in electronic environments** includes composing electronically and publishing your work digitally (for example, on a blog) as well as using electronic sources like scholarly databases for researched projects. *(See Chapter 11 and Connect Composition.)*

Throughout this handbook, Outcomes boxes (like the one that appears on page 16) will keep you focused on the concerns you are most likely to encounter at each point in the writing process.

Ie Exploring the writing situation as a means of approaching any writing task

Composition courses will help you learn to write at the college level, but your development as a writer does not end there. Writing in all your courses will enable you to mature as a writer while preparing you for more writing after college.

The **rhetorical situation**—also known as the **writing situation**—includes the considerations that all writers take into account, both before writing and as they compose. When writers think about their situation, they reflect on the following:

- The primary **purpose**
- Which **audience(s)** to address
- The **context**
- The **stance,** or authorial tone
- What **genre** and **medium** are most appropriate for the purpose, audience, and writing task

Martin Luther King Jr., for example, wrote "A Letter from Birmingham Jail" to achieve a specific purpose, persuading others to rethink their views of the best way to achieve racial justice in the South in the 1960s; for a specific audience, those who disagreed with his approach of nonviolent civil disobedience; in a given genre, an *open letter* addressed to a particular group but intended for publication. A student composing an essay evaluating a recent film for a newspaper has a different purpose, to provide a recommendation about whether the film is worth seeing; to a given audience, the readers of the newspaper; in the form of a review, another genre. The context for Martin Luther King Jr. was very different from the context for the student reviewer, of course. A writer's context includes the means of communication, current events, and the environment in which the communication takes place. See an illustration of how these elements are related in Figure I.2.

All writing tasks are framed by a rhetorical situation. By keeping your rhetorical situation in mind, you will find the writing process easier to manage, making the project that results stronger and more effective.

1. Understanding your purpose   You write to achieve many different purposes. Sometimes, as when you make a grocery list, your purpose may seem trivial: to be sure that you identify all the items you need so you have to make only one trip to the store. At other times, you write for a more important purpose, such as when you compose a job application letter or send an e-mail or a text to let a family member know that you have arrived at your destination safely. Whether your writing **informs** your readers by telling them what you know about a topic or issue, **interprets** and **analyzes** by exploring the meaning of your subject, **argues** or **persuades** by proving a point or supporting an opinion through logic and concrete evidence, or simply **expresses** your feelings, it is always keyed to achieving a given purpose.

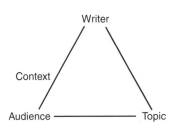

FIGURE I.2 Elements of a writing situation.

le

2. Thinking about audience A second, equally important feature of the writing situation is the audience, the readers you are writing to and for. Thinking of your potential readers can help you shape your writing. An exercise program, for example, would look very different if you were to write it as a journal entry for a health class, post it on a personal blog, or craft it as a press release for a business enterprise or community organization. If you were writing about possible changes to Social Security, the examples you would share might vary depending on whether your audience included mostly senior citizens, who are the main beneficiaries of the program now, or people in their 20s, most of whom will not benefit from it for many years. Thinking about the needs of your audience can help you decide what to include in your writing project as you compose—and what you might leave out.

3. Considering your context Context, or the larger circumstances surrounding a text, exerts a major influence on the rhetorical situation. Consider how the meaning of a single word can change, depending on the context. For example, a *chair* can be a piece of furniture or someone who leads a committee or department. Likewise, because the contexts differ, writers discussing immigration patterns in an academic context know that their readers expect a balanced and informed discussion of this controversial issue, whereas writers in the context of an online environment in the blogosphere may address the same issue in a more personal and impassioned way. Although it is impossible to know the full context of any situation, it is important to identify what you do know and keep that information in mind as you write.

4. Choosing an appropriate stance A *rhetorical stance* is the attitude a writer takes in relation to a topic and the tone used in addressing the audience. A dignitary giving a commencement address tries to inspire the audience, for example, while a friend consoles another friend on a loss. When you are exploring an issue that could divide your audience, you might take the stance of someone who inquires rather than someone who argues. When creating a résumé, most people take the stance of a competent future employee. Considering your stance carefully is an important part of writing well.

5. Deciding on the best medium   When you know your composition's rhetorical situation and have decided on your stance, you can select an appropriate medium to support your purpose and communicate with your audience. A **medium** is a means of communication—you can communicate with your audience via print, screen, or network. Print can take various forms: a letter to the editor of a newspaper can be a simple word-processed text, whereas a poster for a science presentation will probably be printed in large type, with images as well as text. A screen composition might consist of a set of Power-Point slides detailing election results, or it might be a digital photo essay. A composition posted on a computer network could be a blog on athletes' salaries or a Web site on the issue of abandoned children. Increasingly, all disciplines require that students write in each of these three media. In some cases, the medium will be determined by the rhetorical situation: a scientific poster session requires print posters. In other cases, you can decide which medium is best.

These questions can help you decide which medium to select:

1. Does the rhetorical situation provide guidance for which medium to use? What will the audience expect?

2. Does your composition require or make use of other electronic sources, such as an animated graphic or streaming video? Consider a digital or networked medium such as a Web site.

3. How widely will your project be distributed? If you plan a small distribution, consider print. For a larger distribution, consider a networked medium such as a Web page or social network site.

4. How large is your audience, and where is it located? You can reach a small, local audience with a print text such as a flyer. In general, consider a print or digital medium for preselected and previously identified readers. If your audience is large and diversified, consider a networked medium such as a blog.

6. Making effective use of multimedia elements and genres
All writers today have access to digital technologies that widen the possibilities for composing and sharing texts. Through the use of electronic media, people are communicating more than ever before. On Web sites and blogs, writers combine their texts with photos, videos, and audio files—using all of these options to achieve a variety of

purposes. Social networking sites like Facebook and YouTube facilitate connections across time and space.

As you plan to compose for a specific writing situation, consider two issues that can help you decide what kind of text to create:

1. Whether your text will include *multimedia elements* (for example, graphs, hyperlinks, video or audio clips)
2. What *genre* best suits your purpose

Incorporating multimedia elements Digital technology allows you to include sound files, hyperlinks, and other **multimedia elements** in digital projects to convey ideas more efficiently and powerfully. You can create these elements yourself or import them from other sources. Use multimedia to serve your overall purpose, placing a photo, sound file, or link strategically and always citing the source of any item you import into your work. *(See Chapters 18 and 19 for information on how to do so.)*

Posting your text online enables you to include an even greater variety of media. You could help your reader hear the music you analyzed by providing a link to an audio file. You could supplement a project about political speeches with a link to a video clip of a politician giving a speech. (Connect Composition offers guidelines for constructing effective digital compositions.)

Presentation software such as *PowerPoint* allows you to integrate audio and visual features into your oral presentations or stand-alone presentations posted online on a site like SlideShare. Strategically selected effects like animation can enliven your presentation. *(For details on creating effective visuals and other multimedia elements, see Chapter 2: Planning and Shaping; Chapter 3: Drafting; and Chapter 4: Revising and Editing. For information on creating oral and multimedia presentations, see Chapter 10: Oral Presentations, and Chapter 11: Multimedia Writing. For help with finding appropriate visuals, see Chapter 15: Finding and Creating Effective Visuals, Audio, and Video.)*

Choosing the best genre When you understand your rhetorical situation, you can select an appropriate genre. **Genre** simply means kind of writing. Poems, stories, and plays are genres of literature, and audiences have different expectations for each. Most of the writing you do in college is nonfiction, that is, writing about real events, people, and things for the purpose of argument, information, or interpretation. Within nonfiction, however, there are many additional genres of writing: for example, letters, brochures, case studies, lab reports, and literary analyses. Some types of writing, like the case study, are common in a particular field such as sociology. *(Chapter 2* *has additional information on how to choose an appropriate genre for an academic assignment—see pp. 28–29.)*

Here are some typical genres for the three purposes you will be using most commonly in academic writing:

- **Informative:** research report, newsletter, lab report, design study, medical record

- **Interpretive:** literary analysis, case study, data analysis, feasibility study, film/music/restaurant review

- **Argument:** editorial, letter to the editor, proposal

If Recognizing audience and academic English in a multilingual world

To some extent, all college students, indeed all people, must navigate multiple cultures and languages. To solve a problem with your computer software in Dallas, you may be speaking to a tech support person in India. As you stock shelves in a toy store in Omaha, you may be interacting with a supply chain that originates in Shanghai.

The college environment will introduce you to a wide range of cultural contexts that may be new to you. Each of these contexts challenges you with a rhetorical situation you will learn how to navigate:

- **Social contexts:** Whether you are attending a full-time campus residential program, commuting to classes at a local community college, or taking classes online, college provides you with opportunities to join new social groups. These groups may be connected by social action within a community, a shared cultural heritage, a common interest, or simply the residence hall in which you live. Whatever context you find yourself in, be aware that colleges are generally gathering places for people from a wide range of cultures and backgrounds, with differences in language, communication practices, and social conventions. Learning to respect and accommodate these differences is an essential part of the college experience.

- **Workplace contexts:** Whether you are working as a barista at the local Starbucks, a home health aide for seniors, or an assistant in the campus library, your job will likely come with new demands and expectations, and you will have an advantage if you are able to communicate effectively. Chapter 12 will help you navigate some of the situations you may encounter when trying to get or keep a job.

- **Academic contexts:** Disciplines have distinctive languages and cultural expectations. The language of statistics or anthropology, for example, probably sounds strange and new at first to most students who take those courses. Academic English in general has a range of conventions and forms to which students must become accustomed in order to succeed in college. This text focuses on these conventions, and, although it cannot cover the terminology of every academic discipline, it will prepare you to be aware of specialized vocabulary, contexts, and expectations.

In the ways just described, all students are language learners and cultural explorers. In college, however, students who know two or more languages and cultures may find that they have an advantage over those who know only one. Multilingual students can contribute insights about other cultures in a world that is interconnected in ever more complex and sophisticated ways.

This book uses the term *multilingual* to address students from varied cultural, national, and linguistic backgrounds. You may be an international student learning to speak and write English. You may have grown up speaking standard American English at school and another language or dialect at home. Perhaps your family has close ties to another part of the world. You may have moved between the United States and another country more than once. If you came to the United States when young, you may read and write English better than you do your parents' native language. You may speak a blended language such as "Spanglish," a mixture of English and Spanish.

Because the way we talk influences the way we write, blended and other nonstandard forms of English often appear in college students' writing. There is no single "correct" English, but Standard Written English is expected in academic contexts. Academic language is formal, with an expanded vocabulary as well as complex grammatical patterns and culturally specific usage patterns. In addition, disciplines have their own language patterns. You will find that interacting with classmates has many benefits as you study these patterns. Monolingual and multilingual speakers have much to learn from each other.

1. Becoming aware of your audience and joining the academic conversation
If you are familiar with at least two languages and cultures, you already know about multiple ways to interact politely and effectively with other people. All students must carefully assess the classroom situation as a special culture. What does the instructor expect? What counts as evidence? What is polite, and what is not?

In some cultures, asking a question indicates that the student has not done the homework or has not been paying attention. In contrast, instructors in the United States and Great Britain generally encourage students to ask questions and participate in class discussion. The American philosopher Richard Rorty makes the point that the history of philosophy is all about sustaining a lively intellectual conversation, and classrooms often reflect that principle. Students are usually encouraged to approach the instructor or fellow students outside class to keep the conversation going.

2. Finding out what instructors expect Just as students are not all the same, neither are instructors. Take advantage of your instructor's office hours—a time designated for further conversation on material discussed in class—to ask questions about assignments as well as other matters.

Instructors in the United States sometimes ask students to form small groups to talk over an issue or solve a problem. All members of such groups are expected to contribute to the conversation and offer ideas. Students usually speak and interact much more informally in these groups than they do with the instructor in class. (For example, you would not raise your hand before speaking in a small group.)

Peer study groups, whether assigned or formed spontaneously, can be excellent resources for interpreting assignments. Instructors in different disciplines may use key words in different ways. When biology professors ask for a description of "significant" results, for example, that term means something different from what English professors mean when they compare two "significant" fictional characters. The terms *analyze, critique,* and *assess* can all be used variously. Terms such as these are discussed in this book *(see p. 27),* but it also helps to talk about assignments with your instructor and with peers.

3. Determining what your audience expects Colleges in the United States and Great Britain, and English-speaking culture more generally, emphasize openly exchanging views, clearly stating opinions, and explicitly supporting judgments with examples, observations, and reasons. Being direct is highly valued. Audiences in the United States expect speakers and writers to come to the point and will feel impatient without an identifiable thesis statement. *(See Section 2c on thesis statements.)* On the other hand, to communicate successfully in a global context, you need to be aware of differing expectations. If, for example, you are sending business correspondence to a Japanese company, you may accomplish your goals more successfully by spending more time on courteous opening remarks. Everything depends on the cultural situation.

4. Choosing evidence with care Different cultures, as well as different academic disciplines, expect varying forms of evidence.

Most scientists and mathematicians, for example, are convinced by the application of the scientific method. In that sense, science and math are universal languages, but scientists from different fields rely on various types of methods and evidence. Some scientists compare the results from experimental groups and control groups, while others emphasize close observation and qualitative analysis. Likewise, different cultures assign varying degrees of importance to firsthand observations, expert opinion, and quotations from sacred or widely respected sources. Once again, it's essential to figure out the context and what you are trying to achieve within it.

5. Considering the organization your audience expects A laboratory report is organized according to expectations determined by the scientific method. But the organization of most other texts varies greatly. In the classroom, careful study of the assignment and the advice provided in this book will assist you in organizing your project effectively. Practicing this kind of analysis should help in writing to multiple, international audiences as well. Seek guidance by studying effective communication in a particular culture. In addition, it never hurts to ask those familiar with the expectations of readers and listeners in a given situation how to communicate politely and successfully.

6. Choosing an appropriate tone Writing to strangers is different from writing to friends. Whether you are communicating by e-mail or by formal, letterhead stationery, you should use a level of formality when addressing professors and others who are not your close friends that you might not use in other writing situations. That attention to tone means typing "Dear Professor Maxell:" even in an e-mail, using full paragraphs, and avoiding abbreviations. "Texting," on the other hand, is the ultimate shorthand used by people who know each other very well and can literally finish each other's sentences. Once in a while, a professor may invite you to send a text on a simple matter, to confirm, for example, that you have received a message about a classroom relocation. In general, however, texting is an option to be used only among friends. *(See Chapter 39 for more on tone.)*

PART

1

I like to do first drafts at night, when I'm

tired, and then do the surgical work in the

morning when I'm sharp.

—ALEX HALEY

Writing and Designing Texts

1   Writing and Designing Texts

1. Reading and Writing: The Critical Connection
2. Planning and Shaping
3. Drafting
4. Revising and Editing
5. Designing Academic Texts and Portfolios

WRITING OUTCOMES

Rhetorical Knowledge

- What is a rhetorical situation, and how can understanding this term help me now and as a writer throughout college and life? **(2a)**
- How do I respond appropriately to different writing situations? **(2a)**
- How might I integrate visuals such as images, photographs, and graphs into my writing to achieve my purpose? **(2e)**

Critical Thinking, Reading, and Writing

- What is a thesis statement, and how do I create one? **(2c)**
- How do I provide constructive feedback to my classmates? **(4a)**

Processes

- How do I determine what writing processes are appropriate for my purpose in a given rhetorical situation? **(2, 3, 4)**

Knowledge of Writing Conventions

- How do I frame my writing task? What patterns and conventions, keyed to readers' expectations, should I consider as I work within a particular genre or type of writing? **(2b, 3a, 4c)**
- How can I write effective, organized paragraphs? **(3b)**
- What features of document design can help me to communicate more effectively? **(5c)**

Composing in Electronic Environments

- How can I work with multimedia elements? **(2e, 3c, 4g)**
- How do I create an electronic portfolio? **(5d)**

For a general introduction to writing outcomes, see Id, page 5.

C. Writing That
Argues/Persuades

BEGIN WITH THE WRITING SITUATION:
- What topic are you writing about? (Ch. 2, p. 25)
- Who is going to read your writing? (Ch. 2, p. 27)
- How should you talk about this topic for your readers? (Ch. 2, pp. 27–28)
- What is the required length, deadline, and format, as well as the background for your assignment? (Ch. 2, p. 28)
- What kind of text is it; how should you present it? (Ch. 2, pp. 28–29)

COMPOSE USING WRITING PROCESSES:
- See Chapter 8. For more details, see chapters 2–4.
- How can you find a thesis for your topic? (Ch. 2, pp. 35–37)
- What strategies can help you organize your writing? (Ch. 3, pp. 47–61)
- What strategies can help you revise? (Ch. 4, pp. 63–75)

THINK CRITICALLY ABOUT USING SOURCES:
- Does your argument require research? (Ch. 13, pp. 189–97)
- How many and what kind of sources are needed? (Ch. 13, p. 197)
- Should you use tables, graphs, or images? Audio or video? (Ch. 2, pp. 42–46)

THINK CAREFULLY ABOUT YOUR FINAL STEPS:
- What citation style, if any, should you use? (Ch. 20, pp. 263–64)
- Did you cite all your sources correctly? (Ch. 19, p. 254)
- Did you edit and proofread your writing? (Ch. 4, pp. 79, 82)
- What design conventions are appropriate for this type of writing? (Ch. 5, p. 86)
    - **Some samples:**
    - ▸ Arguments (pp. 134, 306)
    - ▸ Persuasive PowerPoint/Oral presentation (p. 154)
    - ▸ Job application letter (p. 180)

McGraw-Hill Guide Online²·⁰

|COMPOSITION

For an interactive version of this Start Smart guide, along with more samples, go to **www.mcgrawhillconnect.com**

Resources for Writers

A Sample Visual Analysis

> Topic is identified, followed by statement of a focused, powerful thesis.

Diane Chen
Professor Bennet
Art 258: History of Photography
5 December 2009

The Caring Eye of Sebastião Salgado

Photographer Sebastião Salgado spent seven years traveling along migration routes to city slums and refugee camps in order to document the lives of people uprooted from their homelands. A selection of his photographs can be seen in the exhibit *Migrations: Humanity in Transition*. Like a photojournalist, Salgado brings us images of newsworthy events, but he goes beyond objective reporting, imparting his compassion for refugees and migrants to the viewer.

Many of the photographs in Salgado's show are certain to touch viewers. Whether capturing the thousands of refugee tents in Africa that seem to stretch on for miles or the disheartened faces of immigrant children, the images in *Migrations* suggest that Salgado does so much more than point and shoot.

Salgado's photograph of the most vulnerable among these refugees illustrates the power of his work. "Orphanage attached to the hospital at Kibumba, Number One Camp, Goma, Zaire" (see fig.1) depicts three infants who are victims of the genocidal war in neighboring Rwanda. The label for the photograph reveals that there were 4,000 orphans at this camp and an estimated 100,000 Rwandan orphans overall. Those numbers are mind-numbing abstractions, but this picture is not.

> Uses a thoughtful tone.

The orphanage photograph is shot in black and white, as are the others in the show, giving it a documentary feel that emphasizes that this is a real situation deserving our attention. But Salgado's choice of black-and-white photography is also an artistic decision. He uses the contrasts of light and dark to create a dramatic image of the three babies.

The vertical black-and-white stripes of the blanket direct our eyes to the infants' faces and hands, which are framed by a horizontal white stripe. The whites of their eyes in particular stand out against the darkness created by the shell of the blankets. The camera's lens also seems to be in sharper focus on the faces than on the blankets, again focusing our attention on the babies' expressions.

> A description of the image that illustrates the main point.

> Caption gives the title of the photograph.

Fig.1. Sebastião Salgado, *Migrations*, "Orphanage attached to the hospital at Kibumba, Number One Camp, Goma, Zaire."

A successful visual analysis should
- have a focused and purposeful thesis.
- have a thoughtful tone.
- include a description of image illustrating main point.

Full analysis is available (in draft form) on pages 83–86.

A Sample Argument

Bud Littleton

Professor Robertson

English 102

1 June 2010

Cyberbullying: An Alarming Trend for the Digital Age

[Introduces issue of cyberbullying using a reasonable tone.]

In childhood, many of us learned that it was best to stand up to a bully; we were told that a bully would back down if challenged. But in our digital society, standing up to a bully is infinitely more difficult. Cyberbullying, defined broadly as the use of electronic means to harm someone else (Trolley and Hanel 33), is an alarming trend in online behavior with significant consequences for its victims. Cyberbullying is destructive to victims because of its immediacy, its circulation, and its permanence: the humiliation is easily inflicted and can continue indefinitely before a wide audience. If this new form of bullying for the digital age is ever to be conquered, students, parents, and educators must work together to instill guidelines for online behavior.

[Thesis statement.]

Cyberbullying is commonly carried out through social networking sites, text messaging, instant messaging, or blogging (Shariff 30) and targets those who are different or isolated (34). Cyberbullying can be done in various ways, but most of the time it involves the posting of hurtful comments or rumors online, as shown in fig. 1. Often cyberbullying is simply a matter of teasing carried too far, but the digital nature of the messages means they cannot be retracted easily. This permanent and potentially uncontrollable content is often disseminated far and wide before the victim can do anything to mitigate its effects.

[Presents definition of cyberbullying; refers to a visual that supports key point by defining issue.]

A successful argument should

- have a reasonable tone.
- include a thesis that clearly states the writer's position.
- identify key points that support and develop the thesis, with evidence for each point.
- use a structure that is appropriate for the content and context of the argument.
- conclude by emphasizing the importance of the position and its implications and by answering the "So what?" question.

Full argument is available on pages 134–39.

- **Inform:** *classify, define, describe, explore, illustrate, report, survey*
- **Interpret or Analyze:** *analyze, compare, explain, inquire, reflect*
- **Argue or Persuade:** *agree, defend, evaluate, justify, propose, refute*

B. Writing That
Interprets & Analyzes

BEGIN WITH THE WRITING SITUATION:
- What topic are you interpreting or analyzing? (Ch. 2, p. 25)
- Who is going to read your writing? (Ch. 2, p. 27)
- How should you talk about this topic for your readers? (Ch. 2, pp. 27–28)
- What is the required length, deadline, and format, as well as the background for your assignment? (Ch. 2, p. 28)
- What kind of text is it; how should you present it? (Ch. 2, pp. 28–29)

COMPOSE USING WRITING PROCESSES:
- See Chapter 7. For more details, see chapters 2–4.
- How can you find a worthwhile thesis for your topic? (Ch. 2, pp. 35–37)
- What strategies can help you organize your writing? (Ch. 3, pp. 47–61)
- What strategies can help you revise? (Ch. 4, pp. 63–75)

THINK CRITICALLY ABOUT USING SOURCES:
- Does your interpretive writing require research? (Ch. 13, pp. 189–97)
- If yes, how many and what kind of sources are needed? (Ch. 13, p. 197)
- Should you use tables, graphs, or images? Audio or video? (Ch. 2, pp. 42–46)

THINK CAREFULLY ABOUT YOUR FINAL STEPS:
- What citation style, if any, should you use? (Ch. 20, pp. 263–64)
- Did you cite all your sources correctly? (Ch. 19, p. 254)
- Did you carefully edit and proofread your writing? (Ch. 4, pp. 79, 82)
- What design conventions are appropriate for this type of writing? (Ch. 5, p. 86)

Some samples:
- ▶ Visual Analysis (p. 83)
- ▶ Analysis of a poem (p. 115)

McGraw-Hill Guide Online²·⁰

connect plus+

|COMPOSITION

For an interactive version of this Start Smart guide, along with more samples, go to
www.mcgrawhillconnect.com

A Sample Persuasive Web Site

Highlights key point of article.

Text has a reasonable tone.

Link to an expert who supports the writer's position.

A successful Web site should
- include pages that capture and hold interest.
- be readable, with a unified look.
- be easy to access and navigate.

A successful persuasive Web site should
- have a reasonable tone.
- include links to authoritative sources that support the writer's position.
- highlight key points so that readers can spot them quickly.
- use visual cues to establish credibility. Don't use clip art or images/ patterns that are cluttered or "cute."

A Sample Informative Report

> **Thesis summarizes the writer's knowledge of this topic.**

> **Tone is objective; writer does not express an opinion.**

> **Bar chart illustrates key point made in the text.**

> **Caption explains bar chart.**

> **Procedure illustrates key idea as a numbered list.**

The Caring Express Food Bank

The Caring Express Food Bank serves a varied population of clients, including chronically homeless people, temporarily homeless people, recent immigrants, elderly people on fixed incomes, and people in need of temporary services. As Figure 1 shows, while the number of homeless, both temporary and permanent, that Caring Express assisted in 2008 decreased during the summer months, the number of immigrant workers increased. The percentage of elderly people and people in need of temporary services remained fairly stable throughout the year.

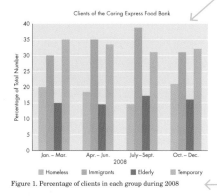

Clients of the Caring Express Food Bank

Figure 1. Percentage of clients in each group during 2008

How Caring Express Helps Clients

When new clients come to Caring Express, the volunteers follow this procedure:

1. The volunteer fills out a form with the client's address (if he or she has one), phone number, income, and employment situation.
2. Clients who do not live in Maple Valley are referred to a food bank or outreach program in their area.
3. Clients who qualify check off the food they need from a list.
4. The food is packed and distributed to them.

A successful informative report should

- have a thesis that summarizes the writer's knowledge of the topic.
- have an objective tone.
- illustrate key ideas with examples from research.

This foldout will help you to understand your writing situation and find the advice you need to get your project off to a good start. It also provides an overview for any kind of writing project. If you get stuck, come back here to jump-start your work.

A. Writing That Informs

BEGIN WITH THE WRITING SITUATION:
- What topic are you writing about? (Ch. 2, p. 25)
- Who is going to read your writing? (Ch. 2, p. 27)
- How should you talk about this topic for your readers? (Ch. 2, pp. 27–28)
- What is the required length, deadline, and format, as well as the background for your assignment? (Ch. 2, p. 28)
- What kind of text is it; how should you present it? (Ch. 2, pp. 28–29)

COMPOSE USING WRITING PROCESSES:
- See Chapter 6. For more details, see chapters 2–4.
- How can you find a worthwhile thesis for your topic? (Ch. 2, pp. 35–37)
- What strategies can help you organize your writing? (Ch. 3, pp. 47–61)
- What strategies can help you revise? (Ch. 4, pp. 63–75)

THINK CRITICALLY ABOUT USING SOURCES:
- Does your informative writing require research? (Ch. 13, pp. 189–97)
- If yes, how many and what kind of sources are needed? (Ch. 13, p. 197)
- Should you use tables, graphs, or images? Audio or video? (Ch. 2, pp. 42–46)

THINK CAREFULLY ABOUT YOUR FINAL STEPS:
- What citation style, if any, should you use? (Ch. 20, pp. 263–64)
- Did you cite all your sources correctly? (Ch. 19, p. 254)
- Did you carefully edit and proofread your writing? (Ch. 4, pp. 79, 82)
- What design conventions are appropriate for this type of writing? (Ch. 5, p. 86)

Some samples:
- ▸ Informative report (pp. 89, 102, 347)
- ▸ Newsletter (p. 173)
- ▸ Brochure (p. 172)
- ▸ Annotated bibliography (p. 244)

McGraw-Hill Guide Online²·⁰

|COMPOSITION

For an interactive version of this Start Smart guide, along with more samples, go to
www.mcgrawhillconnect.com

PowerPoints for a
Persuasive Oral Presentation

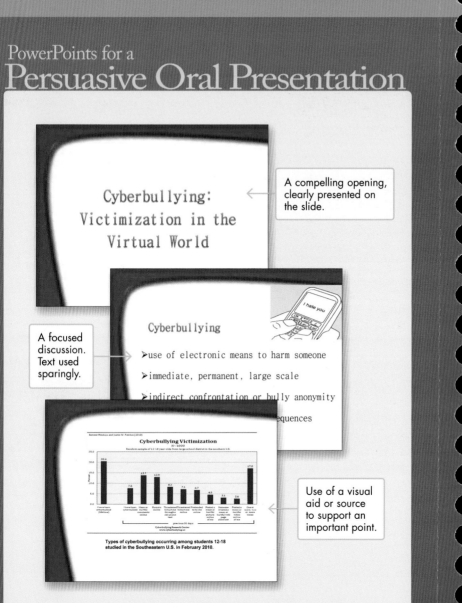

Cyberbullying:
Victimization in the
Virtual World

A compelling opening, clearly presented on the slide.

Cyberbullying

➤ use of electronic means to harm someone

➤ immediate, permanent, large scale

➤ indirect confrontation or bully anonymity

➤ ...quences

A focused discussion. Text used sparingly.

Cyberbullying Victimization
N = 4000
Random sample of 12-18 year-olds from large school district in the southern U.S.

Types of cyberbullying occurring among students 12-18 studied in the Southeastern U.S. in February 2010.

Use of a visual aid or source to support an important point.

A persuasive oral presentation should
- have a compelling opening.
- have a clear focus and organization.
- be delivered extemporaneously (avoid reading the slides).
- use visual aids and sources to support key points
  and highlight content (with text used sparingly).
- conclude memorably.

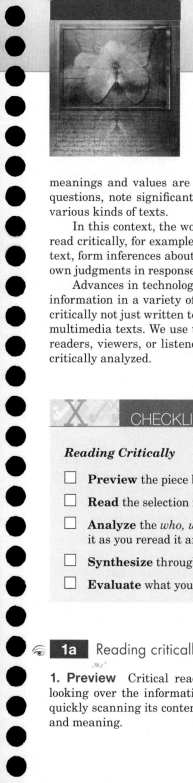

Reading and Writing: The Critical Connection

Like writing, critical reading is a process that involves moving back and forth, rather than in a straight line. Critical readers, thinkers, and writers get intellectually involved. They recognize that meanings and values are made, not found, so they pose pertinent questions, note significant features, and examine the credibility of various kinds of texts.

In this context, the word *critical* means "thoughtful." When you read critically, for example, you recognize the literal meaning of the text, form inferences about unstated meanings, and then make your own judgments in response.

Advances in technology have made it easier than ever to obtain information in a variety of ways. It is essential to be able to "read" critically not just written texts but visuals, sounds, videos, and other multimedia texts. We use the word *text,* then, to refer to works that readers, viewers, or listeners invest with meaning and that can be critically analyzed.

CHECKLIST

Reading Critically

- [ ] **Preview** the piece before you read it.
- [ ] **Read** the selection for its topic and point.
- [ ] **Analyze** the *who, what,* and *why* of the piece by **annotating** it as you reread it and **summarizing** what you have read.
- [ ] **Synthesize** through making connections.
- [ ] **Evaluate** what you've read.

1a Reading critically

1. Preview Critical reading begins with **previewing a text**—looking over the information about its author and publication and quickly scanning its contents to gain a sense of its context, purpose, and meaning.

Previewing written texts   As you preview a text, ask questions about the approach and claims in the text, and assess the credibility of its evidence and arguments:

- **Author:** Who wrote this piece? What are the writer's credentials? Who is the writer's employer? What is the writer's occupation? Age? What are his or her interests and values?

- **Purpose:** What do the title and first and last paragraphs tell you about the purpose of this piece? Do the headings and visuals provide clues to its purpose? What might have motivated the author to write it? Is the main purpose to inform, to interpret, to argue, to entertain, or is it something else?

- **Audience:** Who is the target of the author's information or persuasion? Is the author addressing you or readers like you?

- **Content:** What does the title tell you about the piece? Does the first paragraph include the main point? What do the headings tell you about the gist of the piece? Does the conclusion sharpen the author's focus and show its significance?

- **Context:** Is the publication date current? Does the date matter? What kind of publication is it? Where and by whom was it published? Does the publisher have biases about the topic? If it was published electronically, was it posted by the author or by an organization with a special interest? Did it undergo a peer review process?

Previewing visuals   You can use most of the previewing questions for written texts to preview visuals. You should also ask some additional questions, however. For example, suppose you were asked to preview the public service advertisement shown in Figure 1.1. Here are some preview questions with possible answers:

- **In what context does the visual appear?** Was it intended to be viewed on its own or as part of a larger work? Is it part of a series of images (for example, a graphic novel, a music video, or a film)? This public service advertisement appeared in several publications targeted to college students. As the logo in the lower right-hand corner indicates, the ad was produced by the Peace Corps to recruit volunteers.

- **What does the visual depict? What is the first thing you notice in the visual?** The scene is a bare schoolroom in Botswana. *(Look at the world map in Resources for Writers to find Botswana in Africa.)* As sun streams from a window, one young man in the foreground looks on as a younger boy erases a black-

FIGURE 1.1 Peace Corps advertisement. The text superimposed on this photograph reads: **What happens in Botswana doesn't stay in Botswana.** When you help make a better life for others abroad, you also develop skills and experience that will serve your community back home. Life is calling. How far will you go?

board. On the blackboard, a handwritten poster appears with points of advice, for example, "Accept responsibility for your decision." The sunlight shining directly on the boy at the black-board draws the viewer's attention to him.

- **Is the visual accompanied by audio or printed text?** Bold text appears in the center of the image, followed by smaller print directly addressed to the viewer. The phone number and Web address for the Peace Corps are printed in the lower left, and another appeal to the viewer, followed by the Peace Corps logo, is printed in the lower right.

2. Reading and recording initial impressions Read the selection for its literal meaning. Identify the topic and the main point. Note difficult passages to come back to as well as ideas that grab your attention. Look up unfamiliar terms. Record your initial impressions:

- If the text or image is an argument, what opinion is being expressed? Were you persuaded by the argument?

NAVIGATING THROUGH COLLEGE AND BEYOND

Evaluating Context in Different Kinds of Publications and Disciplines

Nothing can be understood in isolation. We evaluate meaning in terms of surrounding conditions, including types of publications and academic disciplines:

■ **For a book:** Are you looking at the original publication or a reprint? What is the publisher's reputation? University presses, for example, are very selective and usually publish scholarly works. A vanity press—one that requires authors to pay to publish their work—is not selective at all.

■ **For an article in a periodical:** Look at the list of editors and their affiliations. What do you know about the journal, magazine, or newspaper in which this article appears? Are the articles reviewed before publication by experts in a particular field?

■ **For a Web page:** Who created the page? A Web page named for a political candidate, for example, may actually have been put on the Web by opponents. *(See the box on p. 229.)*

Whether you are studying a book, an article, or a Web page, be aware of how the same topic is handled from the perspective of different disciplines. A book, article, and Web page on the fall of the Berlin Wall (1989), for example, will differ depending on whether the author addresses the topic from an historical, a political, or an economic point of view.

■ Did you have an emotional response to the text or image? Were you surprised, amused, or angered by anything in it?

■ What was your initial impression of the writer or speaker?

■ What key ideas did you take away from the work?

Exercise 1.1 Preview and first reading of an essay

Find an article that interests you in a newspaper or magazine, preview it using the questions on page 18, then read through it in one sitting and record your initial impressions using the preceding questions.

Exercise 1.2 First reading of a visual

Spend some time looking at the image and text for the Peace Corps ad in Figure 1.1. Record your responses to the following questions:

1. Did you have an emotional response to the ad?
2. What opinion, if any, did you have of the Peace Corps before you read the ad? Has your opinion changed in any way as a result of the ad?
3. What key ideas does the ad present?

1a crit

3. Using annotation and summary to analyze a text Once you understand the literal or surface meaning of a text, you can analyze and interpret it. To **analyze** a text you must break it down into significant parts and examine how those parts relate to each other. Critical readers analyze a text in order to **interpret** it and come to a better understanding of its meaning.

Using annotation and summary **Annotation** combines reading with analysis. To annotate a text, read through it slowly and carefully while asking yourself the *who, what, how,* and *why* questions. As you read, underline or make separate notes about words, phrases, and sentences that strike you as significant or puzzling—even if you don't know why at this point—and write down your questions and observations.

SAMPLE ANNOTATED PASSAGE

Opens with a story about his childhood

Establishes his authority—he's experienced multiculturalism.

Both my parents were immigrants from Russia. In my neighborhood, Yiddish was a first and second language. I grew up in the depths of the Great Depression. There were weeks when my father came home with $5 or less. My mother walked blocks to save a few cents on food.

I went to public school. Some of my friends were sent to the yeshiva—an Orthodox Jewish religious school—but my parents, having experienced the vicious, pervasive anti-Semitism in the Old Country, wanted me to learn what America was all about.

Essential??

At Boston Latin School and Northeastern University—a working-class college—I took classes that taught a great deal about the fundamental rights and liberties that had to be fought for during this still "unfinished American revolution," as Thurgood Marshall called it. These were required courses, and inspired my lifelong involvement in civil rights and civil liberties.

Supreme Court Does he assume they would inspire everyone?

—NAT HENTOFF, "Misguided Multiculturalism"

A **summary** conveys the basic content of a text. When you summarize an essay or article, your goal is to condense, without commentary, the text's main points into one paragraph. Even when you are writing a summary of a longer work, use the fewest words possible. A summary should be clear and brief. A summary requires getting to the essence of the matter without oversimplification and misrepresentation. *(For specific instructions on how to write a summary, see Chapter 19: Working with Sources and Avoiding Plagiarism, pp. 250–52.)*

Here are some suggestions for approaching the task:

- **Write down the text's main point.** Compose a sentence that identifies the text, the writer, the approach (reports, explores, analyzes, argues), and the key point the writer makes about the topic.
- **Divide the text into sections.** To develop the main point, writers move from one subtopic to another or from the statement of an idea to the reasons, evidence, and examples that support it. If you own the book or article, annotate it to indicate where sections begin and end.
- **In one or two sentences, sum up what each of the text's sections says.** When you summarize, you in effect compose your own topic sentence for each major section of the text. If you own the book or article, highlight key sentences in each section to help focus your summary.
- **Combine your sentence stating the writer's main point with the sentences summarizing each of the text's major sections.** Now you have a summary of your source. *(For specific examples of summaries, see Chapter 19, pp. 250–52.)*

Questioning the text   Analysis and interpretation require a critical understanding of the *who, what, how,* and *why* of a text:

- **What is the writer's *stance,* or attitude toward the subject?** Does the writer appear to be objective, or can you identify expressions of personal feelings about the subject?
- **What is the writer's *voice?*** Is it like that of a reasonable judge, an enthusiastic preacher, or a reassuring friend?
- **What assumptions does the writer seem to be making about the audience?** Does the writer assume that readers agree, or does the writer try to build agreement? Does the writer choose examples and evidence with a certain audience in mind?
- **What is the writer's primary purpose?** Is it to present findings, offer an objective analysis, or argue for a particular action or opinion?

- **How does the writer develop ideas?** Does the writer define key terms? Include supporting facts? Tell relevant stories? Provide logical reasons?

- **Does the text appeal to emotions?** Does the writer use words, phrases, clichés, images, or examples that are emotionally charged?

- **Is the text fair?** Does the writer consider opposing ideas, arguments, or evidence? Does he or she deal with them fairly?

- **Is the evidence strong?** Does the writer provide sufficient evidence?

- **Where is the argument** strongest and weakest?

- **Is the text effective?** Have your beliefs on this subject been changed by the text?

Visuals, too, can be subjected to critical analysis, as the comments a reader made on the Peace Corps ad indicate *(see Figure 1.2).*

Composition of the photograph like Vermeer's paintings of sunlight illuminating an indoor scene. Subtle appeal to students of art history?

Reference to Las Vegas slogan, "What happens here stays here." Secrets of Las Vegas (superficial fun) stay there because of shame. Working with the Peace Corps (worthwhile life direction) in Botswana illuminates your life—and the world (Reference to sunlight?).

The boy is reaching up to erase or wash something from the blackboard. An older boy watches—also "reaching"? A poster covering part of the board lists principles valuable in Botswana and in the U.S.A.

Smaller print elaborates on win/win opportunity of the Peace Corps vs. odds of losing games in Las Vegas.

The Peace Corps logo combines the globe with the American flag—a global view of patriotism. How far will you go geographically and personally?

FIGURE 1.2 Sample annotations on the Peace Corps ad.

4. Synthesizing your observations in a critical-response paper

To **synthesize** means to bring together, to make something out of different parts. In the last stage of critical reading, you pull your summary, analysis, and interpretation together into a coherent whole to support a claim. Whether you realize it or not, you synthesize material every day. When you hear contrasting accounts of a party from two different people, you assess the reliability of each source; you select the information that is most pertinent to you; you evaluate the story that each one tells; and, finally, you create a composite, or synthesis, of what you think really went on. When you synthesize information from two or more texts, you follow the same process.

Exercise 1.3   Analyzing and summarizing a visual

Add to the annotated analysis of the Peace Corps ad in Figure 1.2, focusing on the text as well as the photograph. Summarize the content and message of the ad. Using this summary and analysis, write a critical response to the Peace Corps ad.

1b Writing critically

In college, you will gain practice in addressing issues that are important in the larger community. Selecting a topic that you care about will give you the energy to think matters through and to make cogent arguments. Of course, you will have to go beyond your personal feelings to make the most convincing case. You will also have to empathize with potential readers who may disagree with you about something that is important to you. *(For more help with writing arguments, see Chapter 8, pp. 117–39.)*

Sharpening your ability to think critically and to express your views effectively is one of the main purposes of undergraduate study. When you write critically, you gain a voice in the important discussions and decisions of our society. Writing can make a difference.

In college and beyond, you will apply critical-thinking skills to different writing purposes. Part 2 of this book *(Writing in College and beyond College)* focuses on writing to **inform** *(Chapter 6, pp. 99–107),* to **analyze** *(Chapter 7, pp. 107–17),* and to **argue** *(Chapter 8, pp. 117–39).* In each case, you will present evidence that supports a central point, or **thesis.** For your writing to be convincing and effective, consider your rhetorical situation: your purpose, audience, and the context of your assignment.

2 Planning and Shaping

This chapter will help you determine the kind of writing a particular assignment requires and offer strategies for writing a first draft. After reviewing an assignment, be sure to seek clarification from your instructor. It is far better to ask questions early rather than having to start over later or, even worse, turning in something that does not do the job.

2a Learning how to approach assignments

Because college assignments are a special type of writing situation, you will be more successful if you take some time to understand this particular type of communication.

1. Understanding the writing situation Writers respond to **writing situations.** When you write a lab report for a science class, create a flyer for a candidate for student government, or send an e-mail inviting a friend for coffee, you shape the communication **(message)** to suit the purpose, audience, and context. The results for each situation will differ. All communication arises because something is at stake (the **exigence**). *(For more on the writing situation, or rhetorical situation, see the Introduction, pp. 5–10.)*

2. Writing about a question Most of your academic writing will be in response to assignments that pose a question or ask you to formulate one. The particular course you are taking defines a range of questions that are appropriate within a given discipline. Here are examples of the way your course would help define the questions you might ask if, for example, you were writing about Thomas Jefferson:

- **U.S. history:** How did Jefferson's ownership of slaves affect his public stance on slavery?
- **Political science:** To what extent did Jefferson's conflict with the courts redefine the balance of power among the three branches of government?
- **Education:** Given his beliefs about the relationship between democracy and public education, what would Jefferson think about contemporary proposals for a school voucher system?

25

CHECKLIST

Understanding the Writing Situation

Ask yourself these questions as you approach a writing assignment:

Topic *(see 2a.2)*

☐ What are you being asked to write about?

☐ Have you narrowed your topic to a question that interests you?

☐ What kinds of visuals, if any, would be appropriate for this topic?

☐ What types of sources will help you explore this topic? Where will you look for them?

Purpose *(see 2a.3)*

☐ What do you want your writing to accomplish? Are you trying to inform, analyze, or argue? (What key words in your assignment indicate the purpose?)

☐ Do you want to intensify, clarify, complicate, or change your audience's assumptions or opinions?

Audience, Stance, and Tone *(see 2a.4 and 2a.5)*

☐ What are your audience's demographics (education level, social status, gender, cultural background, and language)? How diverse is your audience?

☐ What does your audience know about the topic?

☐ What common assumptions and different opinions do audience members bring to the issue? Are they likely to agree with you, or will you have to persuade them?

☐ What is your relationship to them? How does that relationship influence your rhetorical stance?

☐ What tone would appeal to this audience: informal, entertaining, reasonable, or forceful? Why?

Context *(see 2a.6)*

☐ Does your topic deal with issues of interest to the public or to members of an academic discipline?

☐ What have other writers said recently about this topic?

☐ How much time do you have to complete the assignment?

☐ What is the specified number of pages?

Genre and Medium *(see 2a.7)*

☐ What genre would best support your purpose?

☐ What medium are you using (print essay, video podcast, Web site, presentation software) and why?

3. Being clear about your purpose What kind of assignment are you doing? Think beyond the simple statement, "I have to write an essay." Are you expected to inform, interpret, or argue?

**2a
plan**

- **Informing:** writing to transmit knowledge. Terms like *classify, describe, illustrate, report,* and *survey* are often associated with the task of informing.

- **Interpreting:** writing to produce understanding. Terms like *analyze, compare, explain,* and *reflect* are more likely to appear when the purpose is interpreting.

- **Arguing:** writing to assert and negotiate matters of public debate. Terms like *agree, assess, critique, defend,* and *refute* go with the task of arguing.

Some terms, such as *comment, consider,* and *discuss,* do not point to a particular purpose, but many others do. If you are not clear about the kind of work you are expected to do, ask your professor.

4. Asking questions about your audience Who makes up your audience? In college, instructors are usually your primary readers, of course, but they represent a larger group who have an interest or a stake in your topic. An education professor reads and evaluates a text as a representative of several groups—other students in the course, experts in educational policy, school board members, public school principals, and parents of school-age children, among others. See the box on page 26 for questions to answer about your audience.

5. Determining an appropriate rhetorical stance and tone
Your **stance** is determined by the position you take in relationship to your audience. In other words, you might take one stance in your workplace writing as an employee and another stance when you assume leadership responsibilities. As a college student, your stance is seldom that of an expert. Instead, you will usually want to inspire trust by sounding informed, reasonable, and fair.

The identity, knowledge level, and needs of your audience will determine the tone of your writing as expressed in content, style, and word choice. Consider the differences in **tone** in the following passages on the subject of a cafeteria makeover.

SARCASTIC "I am special," the poster headline under the smirking face announces. Well, good for you. And I'm specially glad that cafeteria prices are up because so much money was spent on motivational signs and new paint colors.

SERIOUS   Although the new colors in the cafeteria are elec-
tric and clashing, color in general does brighten
the space and distinguish it from the classrooms.
But the motivational posters are not inspiring and
should be removed.

The tone in the first passage is sarcastic and obviously intended for
other students. An audience of school administrators probably would
not appreciate the slang or the humor. The second passage is more serious and respectful—the appropriate tone for most college writing—
while still offering a critique. *(For more on appropriate language, see
Chapter 39.)*

Exercise 2.1   Analyzing audience, stance, and tone

Find an article from one of the following sources and rewrite a paragraph in the article for the specified audience.

1. An article on a diet or exercise program that appears in a maga-
    zine for teenagers (thirty- to forty-year-old adults)
2. An article on a celebrity's court trial that appears in a super-
    market tabloid (the audience of a highly respected newspaper
    such as the *New York Times* or the *Wall Street Journal*)
3. A discussion of clinical depression from a psychology journal
    (your classmates)

---

6. Considering the context   The context, or surrounding circumstances, influence how an audience receives your communication.
Your assignment goes a long way toward establishing the context
in which you write. Your instructor probably has specified length,
due date, and genre. Context also involves broader conversations
about your topic. Your course gives you background on what others
in the discipline have said and what issues have been debated. Current events, on campus and in society as a whole, provide a context
for public writing. You may wish, for example, to e-mail the student
newspaper in response to a new school policy or on an issue of general
concern.

7. Selecting the appropriate genre and medium   **Genre** simply means kind of writing. Poems, stories, and plays are genres of
literature.

Sometimes an assignment will specify the kind of work, or genre,
you are being asked to produce. For example, you may be asked to
write a report (an informative genre), a comparative analysis (an

interpretive genre), or a critique (an argumentative genre). Some genres, like the case study, are common in a particular field such as sociology but not in other disciplines. Understanding the genre that is called for is important in successfully completing an assignment.

Writers today have wide choices in **medium,** whether in print or online, and many instructors will encourage you to use technology to exercise those choices. You can ask yourself, for example, what might be the best medium to persuade your college administration to repave the parking lot with materials that protect the environment. Would the print medium available in your student newspaper be best, or would it be more persuasive to use presentation software at a Student Senate meeting? Or perhaps a Web page or YouTube video might be more effective.

2b plan

2b Exploring your ideas

The following **invention techniques** or **prewriting activities** are designed to help you begin. Remember that what you write at this stage is for your eyes only—no one will be judging your work. You can explore ideas in either a print or digital journal, which is simply a place to record your thoughts on a regular basis. *(For more on journals, see pp. 32–33.)* Your class notes constitute a type of academic journal, as do the notes you take on your reading and research.

CHECKLIST

Activities for Exploring Your Ideas

Try one or several of the following when you begin an assignment:

☐ Freewriting *(See 2b.1.)*
☐ Listing *(See 2b.2.)*
☐ Clustering *(See 2b.3.)*
☐ Questioning *(See 2b.4.)*
☐ Reviewing your notes and annotations *(See 2b.5.)*
☐ Keeping a journal *(See 2b.6.)*
☐ Browsing in the library *(See 2b.7.)*
☐ Searching the Internet *(See 2b.7.)*
☐ Exchanging ideas *(See 2b.8.)*

As you explore, turn off your internal critic, and generate as much material as possible.

1. Freewriting To figure out what you are thinking, try **freewriting,** typically for a limited period of time (five minutes, for example). Just write whatever occurs to you about a topic. If nothing comes to mind, then write "nothing comes to mind" until you think of something else. The trick is to keep pushing forward without stopping or worrying about spelling, punctuation, or grammar rules. Usually, you will discover some implicit point in your seemingly random writing. You might then try doing some **focused freewriting,** in which you begin with a point or a specific question. The following is a portion of Diane Chen's freewriting about Sebastião Salgado's exhibit *Migrations: Humanity in Transition* in response to an assignment to analyze one or more photographs from an exhibit or archive.

> I want to talk about what it's like to look at all these pictures of people suffering, but to also admire how beautifully the photographs have been composed. Those two things feel like they shouldn't go together. But it's also what makes the photographs so great—because you're feeling two different emotions at the same time. It makes it harder to stop looking at what it is he's trying to show us.

(You can read the second draft of Chen's essay in Chapter 4 on pp. 83–86.)

2. Listing Another strategy is to **brainstorm** by starting with a topic and listing all the words, phrases, images, and ideas that come to mind; again, limiting the time to five minutes or so can "force" ideas. When you brainstorm in this way, don't worry about whether the in-

TEXTCONNEX

Digital Tools for Exploring Ideas

Some students write their ideas on a computer screen—desktop, laptop, or iPad; these ideas can then be copied and pasted into a draft. Web sites such as <https://bubbl.us> allow individuals and groups to generate ideas and link them in a visual cluster, which can be e-mailed to one or more recipients.

dividual thoughts or ideas are "right." Just get them down on paper or on screen.

Once you have completed your list, go through it looking for patterns and connections. Highlight or connect related ideas or group related material together. Move apparently extraneous material or ideas to the end of the list or to a separate page. Now zero in on the areas of most interest, and add any new ideas that occur to you. Arrange the items into main points and subpoints if necessary. Later, this material may form the basis of an outline for your paper.

Here is part of a list that Diane Chen produced for her paper about a photography exhibit:

> Migrations—still photographs, dynamic subject why migrate/ emigrate?
>
> my family—hope of a better life fear & doubt in new places; uprooting beautiful photos but horrible reality
>
> Sebastião Salgado as photojournalist black & white pictures strong vertical & horizontal lines lighting choices are meaningful

3. Clustering   **Clustering,** sometimes called **mapping,** is a brainstorming technique that generates categories and connections from the beginning. To make an idea cluster, do the following:

- Write your topic in the center of a piece of paper, and circle it.

- Surround the topic with subtopics that interest you. Circle each, and draw a line from it to the center circle. You may also connect the circles to each other.

- Brainstorm more ideas, connecting each one to a subtopic already on the sheet or making it into a new subtopic.

Web sites such as bubbl.us allow you to use this technique on the computer, on your own or in groups. *(See the TextConnex box on p. 30.)*

As she explored her ideas about the Sebastião Salgado exhibit, Diane Chen prepared the cluster that appears in Figure 2.1 on page 32.

4. Questioning   The journalist's five *w*'s and an *h (who? what? where? when? why?* and *how?)* can help you find specific ideas and details. For example, here are some questions that would apply to the photography exhibit:

- Who is the photographer, who are his subjects, and who is his audience?

- What is the photographer's attitude toward his subjects?

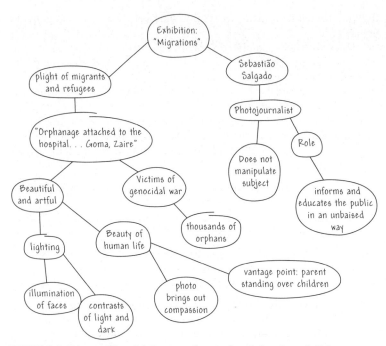

FIGURE 2.1 Diane Chen's cluster about the Salgado exhibit.

- Where were these pictures shot and first published?
- When did these events take place?
- Why are the people in these pictures migrating?
- How did I react to these images?

For other examples of what to question and how, take note of the problems or questions your professor poses in class discussions. If you are using a textbook in your course, check out the study questions.

5. Reviewing your notes and annotations   Review your notes and annotations on your reading or research. *(For details on annotating, see Chapter 1. For details on keeping a research journal, see Chapter 19.)* If you are writing about something you have observed, review your notes and sketches. These immediate comments and reactions are excellent sources for ideas.

6. Keeping a journal or notebook   Record ideas and questions in a journal or notebook. You might write about connections between

---

NAVIGATING THROUGH COLLEGE AND BEYOND

2b plan

Different Questions Lead to Different Answers

Pose the questions that make the most sense in the context of the course you are taking:

- **Sociology:** How do recent immigrants interact with more established immigrants from the same country?
- **History:** How and why has immigration to the United States changed over the past century?
- **Economics:** What effect do immigrants have on the economy of their host country?

---

your personal life and your academic subjects, connections among your subjects, or ideas touched on in class that you would like to know more about. Jotting down one or two thoughts at the end of class and exploring those ideas at greater length later in the day will help you build a store of ideas for future projects.

> My economics textbook says that moving jobs to companies overseas ultimately does more good than harm to the economy, but how can that be? When the electronics factory closed, it devastated my town.

Exercise 2.2   Keeping an academic journal

Start a print or electronic journal, and write in it daily for two weeks. Using your course work as a springboard, record anything that comes to mind, including personal reactions and memories. At the end of two weeks, reread your journal, and write about the journal-keeping experience. Does your journal contain any ideas or information that might be useful for the papers you are writing? Has the journal helped you gain insight into your courses or your life as a student?

---

7. Browsing in the library or searching the Internet   Your college library is filled with ideas—and it can be a great inspiration when you need to come up with your own. Browse the bookshelves containing texts that relate to a topic of interest. Exploring a subject on the Web is the electronic equivalent of browsing in the library. Type keywords related to your topic into a search engine such as Google, and visit several sites on the list that results. *(See Chapter 14, pp. 205–8.)*

For MULTILINGUAL WRITERS

Using Another Language to Explore Ideas

Consider exploring your topic using your native language. You won't have to worry about grammar, spelling, or vocabulary, so these issues won't interfere with your creative thought. Once you have some ideas, it is best to work with them in English.

8. Exchanging ideas Writing is a social activity. Most authors thank family members, editors, librarians, and colleagues for help on work in progress. Talking about your writing with classmates, friends, and family can also be a source of ideas.

Online tools offer additional opportunities for collaboration. Discuss your assignments by exchanging e-mail. If your class has a Web site, you might exchange ideas in chat rooms. Other options include instant messaging (IM), text messaging, and blogs. *Facebook* and *Twitter* provide additional opportunities to discuss your work with friends. Keep a list of your interactions so that you can write a page of acknowledgments for the help and encouragement you receive.

Writing e-mail When you work on papers with classmates, you can use e-mail in the following ways:

- To check your understanding of the assignment
- To try out various topics
- To ask each other questions
- To share freewriting, listing, and other exploratory writing
- To respond to each other's ideas

Chatting about ideas You can also use online chat rooms as well as other virtual spaces to share ideas. You can exchange ideas in virtual worlds such as SecondLife.com. **Instant messaging (IM)** permits real-time online communication. Exchanging ideas with other writers via IM can help you clarify your thinking on a topic.

Exchanging text messages **Text messaging**—the exchange of brief messages between cell phones—can be useful to writers in two ways. First, you can text your ideas for an assignment to a classmate (or—with permission—your instructor) for response. Second, you can use abbreviations commonly used in texting for speedier note taking

FIGURE 2.2
Exchanging ideas
via texting.

2c
plan

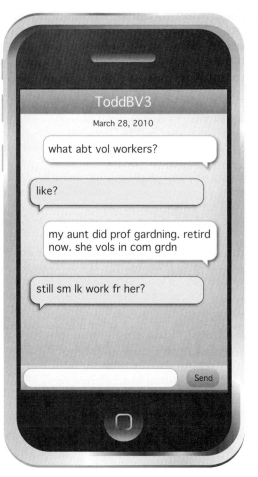

both in class and for research projects. Such shorthand should *never* be used in assignments. In the exchange shown in Figure 2.2, for example, two students share ideas about volunteerism.

2c Developing a working thesis

The **thesis** or **claim** is the central idea of your paper. It needs to communicate a specific point about your topic and suit the purpose of the assignment. As you explore your topic, ideas for your thesis will begin to emerge. You can focus these ideas by drafting a preliminary or working **thesis statement,** which is typically one or two sentences long. As you draft and revise your project, you may change your thesis several times to make it stronger.

To develop a thesis, answer a question posed by your assignment. *(For more about questions, see pp. 31–32.)* For example, an assignment in a political science class might ask you to defend or critique "The Limits of the Welfare State," an article by George Will on the conflict between limited government and unlimited human rights. The question your thesis must answer is, "Is George Will's position that government should not be responsible for the economic welfare of its citizens correct?"

To create a strong thesis, you will need to think critically, developing a point of view based on reading course materials and doing research. Not all theses can be stated in one sentence, but all strong theses are suitable, specific, and significant.

1. Making sure your thesis is suitable

All theses make an assertion about a topic, but these assertions differ. A thesis for an argument will take a clear position on an issue or recommend an action; a thesis for an informative or interpretive project will often preview the content or express the writer's insight into the topic. All the following theses are on the same topic, but each is for a project with a different purpose.

THESIS TO INFORM

James Madison and Woodrow Wilson had different views on the government's role in the economic well-being of its citizens.

THESIS TO INTERPRET

The economic ideas George Will expresses in "The Limits of the Welfare State" are politically conservative.

THESIS TO ARGUE

George Will's contention that government should not be responsible for the economic well-being of its citizens does not adequately take into account the economic complexities of twenty-first-century society.

2. Making sure your thesis is specific

Vague theses usually lead to weak, unfocused papers. Watch out in particular for thesis statements that simply announce your topic, state an obvious fact about it, or offer a general observation.

ANNOUNCEMENT

I will discuss the article "The Limits of the Welfare State" by George Will. *[What is the writer's point about the article?]*

STATEMENT OF FACT

The article "The Limits of the Welfare State" by George Will is about the need for limited government. *[This thesis gives us information about the article, but it does not make a specific point about it.]*

2c
plan

GENERAL OBSERVATION

George Will's article "The Limits of the Welfare State" is interesting. *[While this thesis makes a point about the article, the point could apply to many articles. What makes this article worth reading?]*

In contrast, a specific thesis signals a focused, well-developed composition.

SPECIFIC

George Will, in his article "The Limits of the Welfare State," is wrong about the government's lack of responsibility for the economic welfare of its citizens. His interpretation of the Constitution is questionable. His reasoning about history is flawed. Above all, his definition of limits is too narrow.

In this example, the thesis expresses the writer's particular point—there are three reasons to reject Will's argument. It also forecasts the structure of the whole argument.

Note: A thesis statement can be longer than one sentence (if necessary) to provide a framework for your main idea. All of the sentences taken together, though, should build to one specific, significant point that fits the purpose of your assignment and of the rhetorical situation. (Some instructors may prefer that you limit your thesis statements to one sentence.)

---

3. Making sure your thesis is significant   A topic that makes a difference to you is much more likely to make a difference to your readers, though you should be sure to connect your interest to theirs. When you are looking for possible theses, be sure to challenge yourself to develop one that you care about.

Exercise 2.3   Evaluating thesis statements

Evaluate the thesis statements that accompany each of the following assignments. If the thesis statement is inappropriate or weak, explain why, and suggest how it could be stronger.

1. *Assignment:* For a social ethics course, find an essay by a philosopher on a contemporary social issue, and argue either for or against the writer's position.
   Thesis: In "Active and Passive Euthanasia," James Rachels argues against the standard view that voluntary euthanasia is always wrong.

2. *Assignment:* For an economics course, find an essay on the gap between rich and poor in the United States, and argue either for or against the writer's position.
   Thesis: George Will's argument that economic inequality is healthy for the United States depends on two false analogies.

3. *Assignment:* For a nutrition course, report on recent research on an herbal supplement.
   Thesis: Although several researchers believe that echinacea supplements may help reduce the duration of a cold, all agree that the quality and the content of these supplements vary widely.

4. *Assignment:* For a literature course, analyze the significance of setting in a short story.
   Thesis: William Faulkner's "A Rose for Emily" is set in the fictional town of Jefferson, Mississippi, a once-elegant town that is in decline.

5. *Assignment:* For a history course, describe the factors that led to the fall of the Achaemenid Empire.
   Thesis: Governments that attempt to build far-flung empires will suffer the same fate as the Achaemenids.

2d Planning structure

Every composition needs the following components:

- A beginning, or **introduction,** that hooks readers and usually states the thesis
- A middle, or **body,** that develops the main idea in a series of paragraphs—each making a point supported by specific details
- An ending, or **conclusion,** that gives readers a sense of completion, often by offering a final comment on the thesis

Typically, you will state your thesis in the introduction. However, in personal, narrative, or descriptive writing, you may instead imply the thesis through the details and evidence you present. Or you may begin with background and contextual material leading up to the thesis. In other cases, the thesis may be most effective at the end of the text. This tactic works well when you are arguing for a position that your audience is likely to oppose.

It is not essential to prepare an outline before you start drafting; indeed, some writers prefer to discover how to connect and develop ideas as they compose. However, an outline of your first draft can help you spot organizational problems or places where the support for the thesis is weak.

**2d
Plan**

For MULTILINGUAL WRITERS

State Your Thesis Directly

In U.S. academic and business settings, readers usually expect the statement of the main idea to appear early in the text. Some other cultures may prefer a more indirect style, telling stories and giving facts but not stating the central idea in an obvious way. Assess the rhetorical situation, considering your readers' expectations and values.

1. Preparing an informal plan   A **scratch outline** is a simple list of points, without the levels of subordination found in more complex outlines. Scratch outlines are useful for briefer papers. Here is a scratch outline for a paper on an exhibit of photographs by Sebastião Salgado:

- Photojournalism should be informative, but it can be beautiful and artful too, as Salgado's *Migrations* exhibit illustrates.
- The exhibit overall—powerful pictures of people uprooted, taken in 39 countries over 7 years. Salgado documents a global crisis; over 100 million displaced due to war, resource depletion, overpopulation, natural disasters, poverty.
- Specific picture—"Orphanage"—describe subjects, framing, lighting, emotions it evokes.
- Salgado on the purpose of his photographs. Quote.

A **do/say plan** is a more detailed type of informal outline. To come up with such a plan, review your notes and other relevant material. Then write down your working thesis, and list what you will say for each of the following "do" categories: introduce, support and develop, and conclude. Here is an example.

Thesis: George Will is wrong about the government's lack of responsibility for the economic welfare of its citizens.

1. **Introduce** the issue and my focus.
   - Use two examples to contrast rich and poor: in the recession of 2007–2009, the poverty rate increased to 14.3% in 2009,

TEXTCONNEX

Using Presentation Software as a Writing Process Tool

Presentation-software slides provide a useful tool for exploring
and organizing your ideas before you start drafting. They also
can prompt feedback from peer reviewers and others. Here is a
way to begin:

- Far in advance of the due date, create a brief, three- to five-
  slide presentation—with visuals if appropriate—that previews
  the key points you intend to make in the paper.
- Present the preview to an audience of friends, classmates, or
  perhaps even your instructor. Ask for suggestions for improvement and advice for developing the presentation into a completed text.

a 15-year high (Eckholm). During the same period, the
income levels of the wealthiest Americans continued to increase; for example, the top 0.1% had 8% of the total income
in the United States in 2008, up from 2% in 1973 (Noah).

- Say that the issue is how to evaluate increasing economic
  inequality, and introduce Will's article "The Limits of the
  Welfare State." Summarize Will's argument.
- Give Will credit for raising issue, but then state thesis: he's
  wrong about limited government when it comes to citizens'
  economic well-being.

2. **Support and develop** thesis that Will's argument is wrong.

   - Point out that Will relies on a strict construction of the
     Constitution in his defense of natural economic rights.
   - Point out one thing that Madison and Wilson—two U.S.
     presidents Will cites—would agree on: government should
     be limited in the exercise of "untrammeled power" over its
     citizens.
   - Show that government's actions for the well-being of its
     citizens is appropriate to the natural right of "the pursuit
     of happiness."
   - Say that Will makes fun of those who see the Constitution
     as a living document in response to the evolving times.
     Will's idea of limited government is too narrow. If govern-
     ment does not focus on economic well-being, then how will
     U.S. society thrive in times of economic hardship?

3. **Conclude** that Will doesn't ask or answer such key questions because he believes, quoting former British prime minister Margaret Thatcher, that government "always runs out of other people's money." Follow with quotation from political analyst James Carville, "It's the economy, stupid!"?

**2d
plan**

In outlining his plan, this student has already begun drafting because as he works on the outline, he gets a clearer sense of what he thinks is wrong with Will's argument. He starts writing sentences that he is likely to include in the first complete draft.

2. Preparing a formal outline A **formal outline** classifies and divides the information you have gathered, showing main points, supporting ideas, and specific details by organizing them into levels of subordination.

A **topic outline** uses single words or phrases; a **sentence outline** states every idea in a sentence. Because the process of division always results in at least two parts, in a formal outline, every *I* must have a *II;* every *A,* a *B;* and so on. Also, items placed at the same level must be of the same kind; for example, if *I* is London, then *II* can be New York City but not the Bronx or Wall Street. Items at the same level should also be grammatically parallel; if *A* is "Choosing screen icons," then *B* can be "Creating away messages" but not "Away messages."

Here is a formal sentence outline for a paper on Salgado's *Migrations* exhibit.

Thesis: Like a photojournalist, Salgado brings us images of newsworthy events, but he goes beyond objective reporting, imparting his compassion for refugees and migrants to the viewer.

 I. The images in *Migrations,* an exhibit of his work, suggest that Salgado does more then simply point and shoot.
 II. Salgado's photograph "Orphanage attached to the hospital at Kibumba, Number One Camp, Goma Zaire" illustrates the power of his work.
   A. The photograph depicts three infants who are victims of the war in Rwanda.
     1. The label indicates that there are 4,000 orphans in the camp and 100,000 orphans overall.
     2. The numbers are abstractions that the photo makes real.
   B. Salgado's use of black and white gives the photo a documentary feel, but he also uses contrasts of light and dark to create a dramatic image of the babies.

    1. The vertical black-and-white stripes of the blanket direct viewers' eyes to the infants' faces and hands.

    2. The whites of their eyes stand out against the darkness of the blankets.

    3. The camera's lens focuses sharply on the babies' faces, highlighting their expressions.

       a. The baby on the left has a heart-wrenching look.

       b. The baby in the center has a startled look.

       c. The baby on the right has a glazed and sunken look and is near death.

  C. The vantage point of this photograph is one of a parent standing directly over his or her child.

    1. The infants seem to belong to the viewer.

    2. The photo is framed so that the babies take up the entire space, consuming the viewer with their innocence and vulnerability.

III. Salgado uses his artistic skill to get viewers to look closely at painful subjects, illustrating a big, complex topic with a collection of intimate, intensely moving images.

Exercise 2.4 Reflecting on your own work: Outlining

Try making an outline in response to one of your current assignments. Freewrite about your experience with outlining. Were you able to generate an outline before you started drafting paragraphs? If so, did you stick with your outline, or did you deviate from it? What kind of outline are you most comfortable with? If you were not able to create an outline before you started drafting, why not?

2e Considering using visuals and multimedia, depending on your purpose and audience

Technology makes it easy to go beyond words to pictures, graphs, sounds, and videos—all with the goal of improving a specific project. Before deciding whether to include multimedia materials, be sure to ask what they contribute to the project.

    When you use graphs to visualize data, images, audio files, or videos, always credit your source, and be aware that most visuals and other multimedia elements are protected by copyright. If you plan to use a photograph as part of a Web page, for example, you will usually need to obtain permission from the copyright holder. *(For information about finding visuals, audio, and video, see Chapter 15, pp. 214–21.)*

1. Using visuals effectively Visuals such as tables, charts, and graphs clarify complex data or ideas. Effective visuals are used for a specific purpose, and each type of visual illustrates particular types of material better than others. For example, compare the table on this page and the line graph on page 44. Both present similar types of data, but do both have the same effect? Does one strike you as clearer or more powerful than the other?

**2e
Plan**

> *Caution:* Because the use of visual elements is more acceptable in some fields than in others, you may want to ask your instructor for advice before planning to include visuals in your project.

TEXTCONNEX

Preparing Tables

You can usually create and edit tables using your word-processing software. You can also create tables using database, spreadsheet, presentation, and Web site construction software.

TYPES OF VISUALS AND THEIR USES

Tables

Tables organize precise data for readers. Because the measurements in the example include decimals, it would be difficult to plot them on a graph. Consider this example taken from the Web site of the Environmental Protection Agency.

Emissions from Waste (Tg CO_2 Eq.)

Gas/Source	1990	1995	2000	2001	2002	2003	2004	2005
CH_4	185.8	182.2	158.3	153.5	156.2	160.5	157.8	157.4
Landfills	161.0	157.1	131.9	127.6	130.4	134.9	132.1	132.0
Wastewater treatment	24.8	25.1	26.4	25.9	25.8	25.6	25.7	25.4
N_2O	6.4	6.9	7.6	7.6	7.7	7.8	7.9	8.0
Domestic wastewater treatment	6.4	6.9	7.6	7.6	7.7	7.8	7.9	8.0
Total	192.2	189.1	165.9	161.1	163.9	168.4	165.7	165.4

Note: Totals may not sum due to independent rounding.
SOURCE: U.S. Environmental Protection Agency. *Inventory of U.S. Greenhouse Gas Emissions and Sinks: 1996–2006.* U.S. Environmental Protection Agency, Apr. 2008. Web. 9 June 2008. p. 8-1.

Bar graphs

Bar graphs highlight comparisons between two or more variables, such as the percentage of men and women employed in various jobs in the nation's newsrooms. Bar graphs allow readers to see relative sizes quickly.

NEWSROOM EMPLOYMENT BY GENDER, 2009

Pie charts

Pie charts show the size of parts in relation to the whole. The segments must add up to 100 percent of something, as shown here. Differences in segment size must be noticeable, and there should not be too many segments.

U. S. HOUSEHOLDS BY FAMILY TYPE, 2010

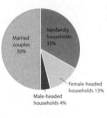

SOURCE: Estimate based on Bureau of the Census.

Married couples 50%

Nonfamily households 33%

Female-headed households 13%

Male-headed households 4%

Line graphs

Line graphs show changes in one or more variables over time, such as how the life goals of U.S. college students have changed over a span of forty-three years.

LIFE GOALS OF FIRST-YEAR COLLEGE STUDENTS IN THE UNITED STATES, 1966–2009

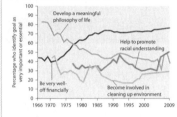

Percentage who identify goal as very important or essential

Develop a meaningful philosophy of life

Help to promote racial understanding

Be very well-off financially

Become involved in cleaning up environment

1966 1970 1975   1980   1985   1990 1995 2000   2009

Diagrams

Diagrams show processes or structures visually. Common in technical writing, they include timelines, organization charts, and decision trees. This diagram shows the factors involved in the decision to commit a burglary.

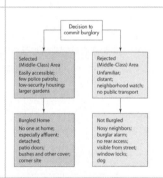

Decision to commit burglary

Selected (Middle-Class) Area
Easily accessible; few police patrols; low-security housing; larger gardens

Rejected (Middle-Class) Area
Unfamiliar; distant; neighborhood watch; no public transport

Burgled Home
No one at home; especially affluent; detached; patio doors; bushes and other cover; corner site

Not Burgled
Nosy neighbors; burglar alarm; no rear access; visible from street; window locks; dog

Photographs

Photos can reinforce your point by showing readers what your subject actually looks like or how it has been affected. This image could support a portrayal of Eminem as a talented but controversial artist.

Maps

Maps highlight locations and spatial relationships, and they show relationships between ideas. This one shows the routes followed by slaves escaping to freedom in the nineteenth century, prior to the Civil War.

ROUTES TO FREEDOM ON THE UNDERGROUND RAILROAD

2e plan

Illustrations

Like photographs, illustrations make a point dramatically. (A larger version of this image appears on p. 126.)

Exercise 2.5   Using visuals

For each of the following kinds of information, decide what type of visual would be most effective. (You do not need to prepare the visual itself.)

1. For an education paper, show the percentage of teaching time per week devoted to math, language arts, science, social studies, world languages, art, music, and physical education using a _____ .

2. For a business paper, compare the gross domestic product for ten leading industrial countries using a _____.

3. For a criminal justice paper, compare the incidence of three different types of crime in one precinct during a three-month period using a _____.

4. For a health paper, chart the number of new cases of AIDS in North America and Africa over a ten-year period in order to show which continent has had the greater increase, using a

_____.

2. Using audio and video effectively You might use audio elements such as music, interviews, or speeches to present or illustrate your major points. Video elements—clips from films, TV, YouTube, or your personal archive—are likewise valuable for clear explanation or powerful argument. No matter how entertaining, audio and video should not be used as mere decoration.

3 Drafting

Think of drafting as an attempt to discover a beginning, a middle, and an end for what you have to say, but remember that a draft is preliminary. Avoid putting pressure on yourself to make it perfect.

The following tips will make this process go smoothly:

■ **Save your work.** Always protect your creativity and hard-won drafts from power surges and other electronic hiccups. Save often, and make backups.

■ **Label revised drafts with different file names.** Use a different file name for each successive version of your text. For example, you might save drafts of a paper on work as Work1, Work2, Work3, and so on.

NAVIGATING THROUGH COLLEGE AND BEYOND

3a
draft

Avoiding Writer's Block

Use these tips to get an early start on a first draft:

- **Resist the temptation to be a perfectionist.** For your first draft, do not worry about getting the right word, the stylish phrase, or even the correct spelling.
- **Take it "bird by bird."** Writer Anne Lamott counsels students to break down writing assignments into manageable units and to finish each unit in one session. She passes along her father's advice to her brother, who had procrastinated on a report about birds and was paralyzed by the enormity of the project: "Bird by bird, buddy. Just take it bird by bird."
- **Start anywhere.** If you are stuck on the beginning, select another section where you know what you want to say. You can go back later and work out the transitions. Writers often compose the introduction after drafting a complete text.
- **Generate more ideas.** If you hit a section where you are drawing a blank, you may need to do more reading, research, or brainstorming. Be careful, though, not to use reading and research as a stalling tactic.
- **Set aside time and work in a suitable place.** Many writers find that working undisturbed for at least half an hour at a stretch is helpful.

TEXTCONNEX

Using Internet Links as a Writing Process Tool

As you compose, add links to supplemental material that you may—or may not—decide to use in a later draft. For example, you might include a link to additional research, to a source that refutes an argument, or to interesting information that is not directly relevant to the primary subject. Readers can be helpful in advising you on whether to include the linked material in the next draft. Before the final draft, be sure to remove all links.

3a Developing ideas using patterns of organization and visuals

The following strategies can help you develop the ideas that support your thesis into a complete draft. Depending on the purpose of your composition, you may use a few of these patterns throughout or a mix of all of them.

Photographs, tables, graphs, and audio and video clips can also support your ideas, so long as they serve the overall purpose of the work and are not used just for fun or decoration. Regardless of the type of visual you use, be sure to discuss it in the body of your text. *(See pp. 43–45 for more on types of visuals and their purposes.)*

1. Illustration   To appeal to readers, you should show as well as tell. Detailed examples and well-chosen visuals *(see Figure 3.1)* can make abstractions more concrete and generalizations more specific, as the following paragraph illustrates.

> As Rubin explains, "for much of the Accord era, the ideal-typical family . . . was composed of a 'stay-at-home-mom,' a working father, and dependent children. He earned wages; she cooked, cleaned, cared for the home, managed the family's social life, and nurtured the family members" (97). Just such an arrangement characterized my grandmother's married life. My grandmother, who had four children, stayed at home with them, while her husband went off to work as a safety engineer. Sadly, when he died, she was left with nothing. She needed to support herself, yet had no work experience, no credit, and little education. But even though society frowned

FIGURE 3.1 Visuals that illustrate. This advertisement shows an idealized version of the lives of many women in the 1950s and 1960s.

Why you need a kitchen extension phone

BELL TELEPHONE SYSTEM

on her for seeking employment, my grandmother eventually found a clerical position—a low-level job with few perks.

—JENNIFER KOEHLER, "Women's Work in the United States: The 1950s and 1990s," student text

2. Narration When you narrate, you tell a story. *(See Figure 3.2 for an example of a narrative visual.)* The following paragraph comes from a personal essay on the goods that result from "a lifetime of production."

> My dad changed too. He had come to that job feeling—as I do now—that everything was still possible. He'd served his time in the Air Force during the Korean War. Then, while my mother worked as a secretary to support them, he earned a college degree courtesy of the GI Bill. After graduation, my father painted houses for a season until he was offered a position scheduling the production of corrugated board. He

FIGURE 3.2 Visuals that narrate. Images that narrate can reinforce a message or portray events you discuss in your paper. Images like this one help tell one of many stories about work in the United States in the twenty-first century.

took it, though he has told me that he never planned to stay. It was not something he envisioned as his life's work. I try to imagine what it is like suddenly to look up from a stack of orders and discover that the job you started one December day has watched you age.

—MICHELLE M. DUCHARME, "A Lifetime of Production"

Notice that Ducharme begins with two sentences that state the topic and point of her narration. Then, using the past tense, she recounts in chronological sequence some key events that led to her father's taking a job in the box manufacturing business.

3. Description To make an object, person, or activity vivid for your readers, describe it in concrete, specific words that appeal to the senses of sight, sound, taste, smell, and touch. *(See Figure 3.3 for an example of a descriptive visual.)* In the following paragraph, Diane Chen describes her impression of a photograph.

The vertical black-and-white stripes of the blanket direct our eyes to the infants' faces and hands, which are framed

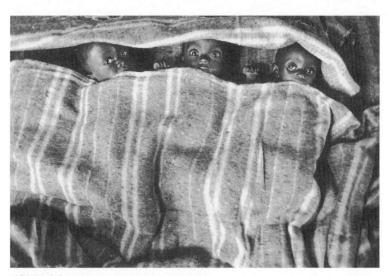

FIGURE 3.3 Visuals that describe. Pay careful attention to the effect your selection will have on your paper. This photograph by Sebastião Salgado, for example, appeals to the viewer's emotions, evoking sympathy for the refugee children's plight.

by a horizontal white stripe. The whites of their eyes in particular stand out against the darkness created by the shell of the blankets. The camera's lens also seems to be in sharper focus on the faces than on the blankets, again focusing our attention on the babies' expressions.

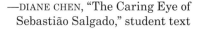

—DIANE CHEN, "The Caring Eye of Sebastião Salgado," student text

4. Classification   Classification is a useful way of grouping individual entities into identifiable categories. *(See Figure 3.4.)* Classifying occurs in all academic disciplines and often appears with its complement—**division,** or breaking a whole entity into its parts.

In the following passage, Robert Reich first classifies kinds of future work into two broad categories: complex services and person-to-person services. Then, in the next paragraph, he develops the idea of complex services in more detail, in part by dividing that category into more specific—and familiar—categories like engineering and advertising.

[M]ost of America's traditional, routinized manufacturing jobs will disappear. So will routinized service jobs that can be done from remote locations, like keypunching of data transmitted by satellite. Instead, you will be engaged in one of two broad categories of work: either complex services, some of which will be sold to the rest of the world to pay for whatever Americans want to buy from the rest of the world, or person-to-person services, which foreigners can't provide

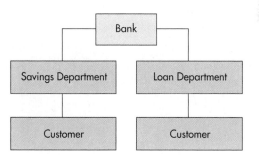

FIGURE 3.4 Visuals that classify or divide. An image can help make the categories in or parts of complex systems or organizations easier to understand. The image shown here, for example, helps readers comprehend the structure of a business.

for us because (apart from new immigrants and illegal aliens) they aren't here to provide them.

Complex services involve the manipulation of data and abstract symbols. Included in this category are insurance, engineering, law, finance, computer programming, and advertising. Such activities now account for almost 25 percent of our GNP, up from 13 percent in 1950. They have already surpassed manufacturing (down to about 20 percent of GNP).

—ROBERT REICH, "The Future of Work"

5. Definition   Define concepts that readers need to follow your ideas. *(See Figure 3.5 for an example of a visual that defines.)* Interpretations and arguments often depend on one or two key ideas that cannot be quickly and easily defined. In the following example, an online encyclopedia defines the Ionic column.

Unlike the Greek Doric order, Ionic columns normally stand on a base . . . which separates the shaft of the column from the stylobate or platform. The capital of the Ionic column has characteristic paired scrolling volutes that are laid on the molded cap ("echinus") of the column, or spring from within it. The cap is usually enriched with egg-and-dart. Originally the volutes lay in a single plane . . . ; then it was seen that they could be angled out on the corners. This feature of the Ionic order made it more pliant and satisfactory

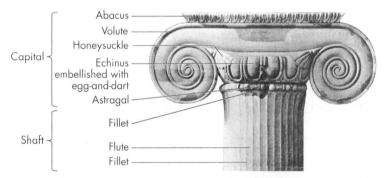

FIGURE 3.5 Visuals that define. Visuals can be effective when used to support a written definition or to identify parts of a whole. This image uses labels and leader lines to identify the characteristics of an Ionic column.

than the Doric to critical eyes in the 4th century BCE: angling the volutes on the corner columns ensured that they "read" equally when seen from either front or side facade. The 16th-century Renaissance architect and theorist Vincenzo Scamozzi designed a version of such a perfectly four-sided Ionic capital, which became so much the standard, that when a Greek Ionic order was eventually reintroduced, in the later 18th century Greek Revival, it conveyed an air of archaic freshness and primitive, perhaps even republican, vitality.

—wordiq.com

6. Analogy An **analogy** compares topics that at first glance seem quite different. *(See Figure 3.6.)* A well-chosen analogy can make new or technical information appear more commonplace and understandable. In the following passage, the writer compares the human eye to a traditional camera.

The human eye provides a good starting point for learning how a camera works. The lens of the eye is like the *lens* of the camera. In both instruments the lens focuses an image of the surroundings on a *light-sensitive surface*—the *retina* of the eye and the *film* in the camera. In both, the light-sensitive material is protected within a light-tight container—the *eyeball* of

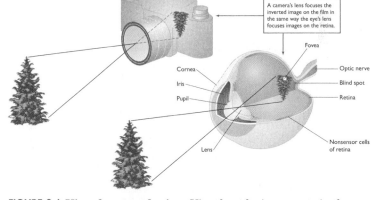

A camera's lens focuses the inverted image on the film in the same way as the eye's lens focuses images on the retina.

Fovea

Cornea

Iris

Pupil

Optic nerve

Blind spot

Retina

Nonsensor cells of retina

Lens

FIGURE 3.6 Visuals as analogies. Visual analogies operate in the same way as written analogies. This figure uses the image of a traditional camera to illustrate how the human eye works.

the eye and the *body* of the camera. Both eye and camera have a mechanism for shutting off light passing through the lens to the interior of the container—the *lid* of the eye and the *shutter* of the camera. In both, the size of the lens opening, or *aperture,* is regulated by an *iris diaphragm.*

—MARVIN ROSEN, *Introduction to Photography*

7. Process When you explain how to do something or show readers how something is done, you use process analysis *(see Figure 3.7),* explaining each step in the process in chronological order, as in the following example.

The scientific method requires precise preparation in developing useful research. Otherwise, the research data collected

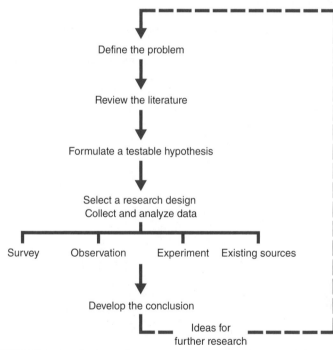

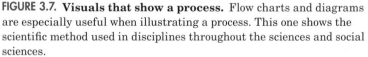

FIGURE 3.7. Visuals that show a process. Flow charts and diagrams are especially useful when illustrating a process. This one shows the scientific method used in disciplines throughout the sciences and social sciences.

may not prove accurate. Sociologists and other researchers follow five basic steps in the scientific method: (1) defining the problem, (2) reviewing the literature, (3) formulating the hypothesis, (4) selecting the research design and then collecting and analyzing the data, and (5) developing the conclusion.

—RICHARD T. SCHAEFER, *Sociology*

8. Cause and effect   This strategy can help you trace the causes of an event or situation, describe its effects, or both. *(See Figure 3.8.)* In the following example, Eric Klinenberg explains the possible reasons for the deaths of 739 Chicagoans in a 1995 heat wave.

> On July 12, 1995, a dangerous hot-air mass settled over Chicago, producing three consecutive days of temperatures over 99 degrees Fahrenheit, heat indices (which measure the heat experienced by a typical person) around 120, high humidity, and little evening cooling. The heat wave was not the most extreme weather system in the city's history, but

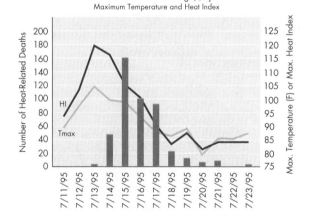

This graph tracks maximum temperature (Tmax), heat index (HI), and heat-related deaths in Chicago each day from July 11 to 23, 1995. The light blue line shows maximum daily temperature, the dark blue line shows the heat index, and the bars indicate number of deaths for the day.

FIGURE 3.8 Visuals that show cause and effect. Visuals can provide powerful evidence when you are writing about causes and effects. Although graphs like this one may seem self-explanatory, you will still need to analyze and interpret them for your readers.

it proved to be Chicago's most deadly environmental event. During the week of the most severe weather, 485 city residents, many of whom were old, alone, and impoverished, died of causes that medical examiners attributed to the heat. Several hundred decedents were never autopsied, though, and after the event the Chicago Department of Public Health discovered that 739 Chicagoans in excess of the norm had perished while thousands more had been hospitalized for heat-related problems.

—ERIC KLINENBERG, "Heat Wave of 1995"

9. Comparison and contrast When you *compare,* you explore the similarities and differences among various items. When the term *compare* is used along with the term *contrast, compare* has a narrower meaning: "to spell out key similarities." *Contrast* always means "to itemize important differences." *(See Figure 3.9.)*

In the following example, the student writer uses a **subject-by-subject** pattern to contrast the ideas of two social commentators, Jeremy Rifkin and George Will.

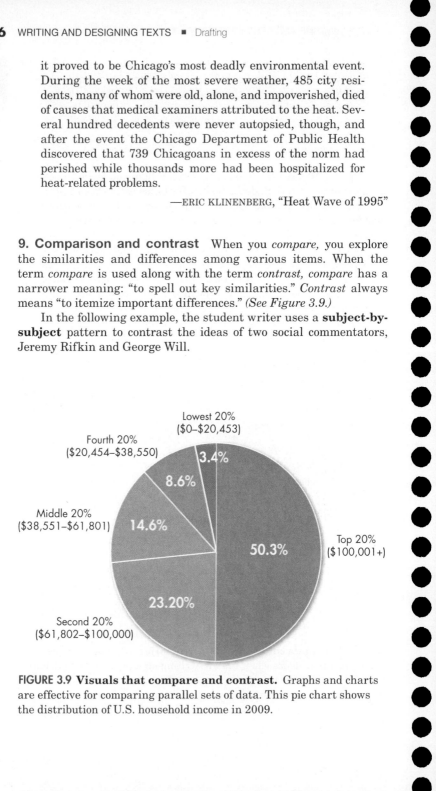

FIGURE 3.9 Visuals that compare and contrast. Graphs and charts are effective for comparing parallel sets of data. This pie chart shows the distribution of U.S. household income in 2009.

Rifkin and Will have different opinions about unemployment due to downsizing and the widening income gap between rich and poor. Rifkin sees both the decrease in employment and the increase in income disparity as evils that must be immediately dealt with lest society fall apart: "If no measures are taken to provide financial opportunities for millions of Americans in an era of diminishing jobs, then . . . violent crime is going to increase" (3). Will, on the other hand, seems to believe that both unemployment and income differences are necessary to the health of American society. Will writes, "A society that chafes against stratification derived from disparities of talents will be a society that discourages individual talents" (92). Apparently, the society that Rifkin wants is just the kind of society that Will rejects.

> —JACOB GROSSMAN, "Dark Comes before Dawn,"
> student text

Notice that Grossman comments on Rifkin first and then turns to his second subject, Will. To ensure paragraph unity, he begins with a topic sentence that mentions both subjects.

In the following paragraph, the student writer organizes her comparison **point by point** rather than subject by subject. Instead of saying everything about Smith's picture before commenting on the AP photo, she moves back and forth between the two images as she makes and supports two points: (1) that the images differ in figure and scene and (2) that they are similar in theme.

> Divided by an ocean, two photographers took pictures that at first glance seem absolutely different. W. Eugene Smith's well-known *Tomoko in the Bath* and the less well-known AP photo *A Paratrooper Works to Save the Life of a Buddy* portray distinctively different settings and people. Smith brings us into a darkened room where a Japanese woman is lovingly bathing her malformed child, while the AP staff photographer captures two soldiers on the battlefield, one intently performing CPR on his wounded friend. But even though the two images seem as different as women and men, peace and war, or life and death, both pictures figure something similar: a time of suffering. It is the early 1970s—a time when the hopes and dreams that modernity promoted are being exposed as deadly to human beings. Perhaps that is why the bodies in both pictures seem humbled. Grief pulls you down onto your knees. Terror impels you to crawl along the ground.

> —ILONA BOUZOUKASHVILI, "On Reading Photographs,"
> student text

Exercise 3.1 Developing paragraphs

Experiment with the development strategies just discussed—illustration, narration, description, classification, definition, analogy, process, cause and effect, and comparison and contrast—in a text you are currently drafting. Are some strategies inappropriate to your assignment? Have you combined any of the strategies in a single paragraph?

3b Writing focused, clearly organized paragraphs

Paragraphs break the text into blocks for your readers, allowing them to see how your essay builds step by step and providing a rhythm for their reading. Introductory and concluding paragraphs have special functions, but all paragraphs should have a single, clear focus and a clear organization. (Paragraphs on the Web tend to be short, with links at the ends so readers do not navigate away.)

1. Focusing on one main point or example In a strong paragraph, the sentences form a unit that explores one main point or elaborates one main example. When you are drafting, start a new paragraph when you introduce a new reason in support of your thesis, a new step in a process, or a new element in an analysis. New paragraphs also signal shifts in time and place, changing speakers in dialogue, contrasts with earlier material, and changes in level of emphasis. As you draft, bear in mind that each paragraph develops a main point or example.

In the following excerpt, the paragraph focuses on a theory that the writer will refer to later in the essay. The main idea is highlighted.

> Current thinking on the topic of loss and mourning rests on foundations constructed by the British psychiatrist John Bowlby. Using examples from animal and human behavior, Bowlby (1977) posited "attachment theory" as a means of understanding the powerful bonds between humans and the disruption that comes when the bonds are jeopardized or destroyed. The bonds are formed because of a need for security and safety, are developed early in life, are long enduring, and are directed toward a few special individuals. In normal maturation, the child becomes ever more independent, moving away from the figure of attachment, and returning periodically for safety and security. If the bonds are threatened, the individual will try to restore them through crying, clinging, or other types of coercion; if they are destroyed, withdrawal, apathy, and despair will follow.
>
> —JONATHAN FAST, "After Columbine: How People Mourn Sudden Death"

Details of attachment theory are developed in the rest of the paragraph.

2. Signaling the main idea of your paragraph with a topic

sentence   A topic sentence can be a helpful starting point as you draft a paragraph. In the following paragraph, the topic sentence (highlighted) provides the writer with a launching point for a series of details.

3b
draft

> The excavation also revealed dramatic evidence for the commemorative rituals that took place after the burial. Four cattle had been decapitated and their skulls symbolically placed in a ditch enclosing the burial pit. In the soil above the skulls archaeologists found the butchered bones of at least 250 slaughtered cattle, evidence for a huge ceremonial feast. Clearly this was an expensive way to commemorate a leader. Indeed, the huge quantity of meat suggests that the entire tribe may have gathered at the grave to take part in a ritual feast. Perhaps this was one way the bonds between scattered communities were strengthened.

The topic sentence announces that the paragraph will focus on a certain kind of evidence.

> —DAMIAN ROBINSON, "Riding into the Afterlife"

Sometimes the sentences in a paragraph will lead to a unifying conclusion (highlighted), as in this example.

> The nation's community colleges are receiving much deserved attention, from the Oval Office to the family living room. Community colleges in Indiana and Illinois offer great value: high quality at an affordable price. As the academic year moves forward and high school students complete college applications, I recommend that those who intend to continue their education close to home take a look at pathways that lead from the community college to university graduation.

> —ELAINE MAIMON,
> "Students Must Focus on Degree Completion"

If a topic sentence would simply state the obvious, it can be omitted. In the following example, it is not necessary to state that the paragraph is about Igor Stravinsky's preprofessional life.

> Stravinsky was born in Russia, near St. Petersburg, grew up in a musical atmosphere, and studied with Nikolai Rimsky-Korsakov. He had his first important opportunity in 1909, when the great impresario Sergei Diaghilev heard his music.

> —ROGER KAMIEN, *Music: An Appreciation*

Exercise 3.2   Paragraph unity

Underline the topic sentences in the following paragraphs. If there is no topic sentence, state the main idea.

1. Based on the results of this study, it appears that a substantial amount of bullying by both students and teachers may be occurring in college. Over 60% of the students reported having observed a student being bullied by another student, and over 44% had seen a teacher bully a student. More than 6% of the students reported having been bullied by another student occasionally or very frequently, and almost 5% reported being bullied by a teacher occasionally or very frequently, while over 5% of the students stated that they bullied students occasionally or very frequently.

   —MARK CHAPELL ET AL., "Bullying in College by
   Students and Teachers"

2. ARS [the Agricultural Research Service] launched the first area-wide IPM [Integrated Pest Management] attacks against the codling moth, a pest in apple and pear orchards, on 7,700 acres in the Pacific Northwest. Other programs include a major assault against the corn rootworm on over 40,000 acres in the Corn Belt, fruit flies in the Hawaiian Islands, and leafy spurge in the Northern Plains area. In 2001, an areawide IPM project began for fire ants in Florida, Mississippi, Oklahoma, South Carolina, and Texas on pastures using natural enemies, microbial pesticides, and attracticides.

   —ROBERT FAUST, "Integrated Pest Management
   Programs Strive to Solve Agricultural Problems"

---

3. Writing paragraphs that have a clear organization The sentences in your final draft should be clearly related to one another. As you are drafting, move your writing forward by making connections among the ideas, using strategies in Section 3b. Another way to make your ideas work together is to use one of the common organizational schemes for paragraphs. These organizational patterns can also be used for essays as a whole (for advice on using repetition, pronouns, and transitions to relate sentences to one another, see Chapter 4, pp. 72–75):

- **Chronological organization:** The sentences in a paragraph with a chronological organization describe a series of events, steps, or observations as they occur in time: this happened, then that, and so on.

- **Spatial organization:** The sentences in a paragraph with a spatial organization present details as they appear to a viewer: from top to bottom, outside to inside, east to west, and so on.

▪ **General-to-specific organization:** Paragraphs often start with a general topic sentence that states the main idea and then proceed with specifics that elaborate on that idea. The general topic sentence can include a question that the paragraph then answers or a problem that the paragraph goes on to solve.

▪ **Specific-to-general organization:** The general topic sentence can come at the end of the paragraph, with the specific details leading up to that general conclusion *(see the paragraph from "Students Must Focus on Degree Completion," p. 59)*. This organization is especially effective when you are preparing readers for a revelation.

Exercise 3.3   Paragraph organization

Go back to the paragraphs in Exercise 3.2 *(pp. 59–60),* and identify the organizational strategy used in each one.

4. Drafting introductions and conclusions   As you begin your first draft, you may want to focus on the body of your text. Later, you can go back and sketch out the main ideas for your introduction.

To get readers' attention, show why the topic matters. The opening of your text should encourage readers to share your view of its importance. Except for essay exams, it's best not to refer directly to the assignment or to your intentions ("In this paper I will . . ."). Avoid vague general statements ("Jane Austen is a famous author"), and try instead to find a way to arouse readers' interest. Here are some opening strategies:

▪ Tell a brief story related to the issue your thesis raises.

▪ Begin with a relevant, attention-getting quotation.

▪ Begin with a paraphrase of a commonly held view that you immediately question.

▪ State a working hypothesis.

▪ Define a key term, but avoid the tired opener that begins, "According to the dictionary . . ."

▪ Pose an important question.

For informative reports, arguments, and other types of essays, your opening paragraph or paragraphs will include a thesis statement, usually at the beginning or near the end of the introduction. If your purpose is interpretive, however, you may instead choose to build up to your thesis. For some types of writing, such as narratives, an explicitly stated thesis may not be needed if the main idea is clear without it.

Just as the opening makes a first impression and motivates readers to continue reading, the closing makes a final impression and motivates readers to think further. While you should not merely repeat the main idea that you introduced at the beginning of the text, also avoid overgeneralizing or introducing a completely new topic. Your conclusion should remind readers of your text's significance and satisfy those who might be asking, "So what?" Here are some good strategies for concluding:

- Refer to the story or quotation you used in your introduction.
- Answer the question you posed in your introduction.
- Summarize your main point.
- Call for some action on your readers' part.
- Present a powerful image or forceful example.
- Suggest implications for the future.

Exercise 3.4   Analyzing introductions and conclusions

Find an essay that has an introduction or a conclusion that engaged you and one with an introduction or conclusion that failed to draw you in. What strategies did the successful essay employ? What strategies could the writer of the unsuccessful essay have used? Next look at the introduction and conclusion of an essay you are currently writing. Do these paragraphs use any of the strategies discussed in this section? If not, try one of these strategies when you revise.

3c   Integrating multimedia elements effectively

If you decide to use a table, chart, diagram, photograph, or video or audio file, keep this general advice in mind:

- **Number tables and other figures** consecutively throughout your text, and label them appropriately: Table 1, Table 2, and so on. Do not abbreviate *Table*. *Figure* may be abbreviated as *Fig*.

- **Refer to the visual element in your text** before it appears, placing the visual as close as possible to the discussion where you state why you are including it. If your project contains complex tables or many other visuals, however, you may want to group them in an appendix. Always refer to a visual by its label—for example, "See Fig. 1."

- **Give each visual a title and caption** that clearly explains what the visual shows. A visual with its caption should be clear without the discussion in the text, and the discussion of the visual in the text should be clear without the visual itself.

- **Include explanatory notes below the visuals.** To explain a specific element within the visual, use a superscript letter (not a number) both after the specific element and before the note. The explanation should appear directly beneath the graphic, not at the foot of the page or at the end of your text.

4a
edit

- **Credit sources for visuals and multimedia.** You must credit all "cited" visuals and multimedia elements. Unless you have specific guidelines to follow, you can use the word *Source*, followed by a colon and complete documentation of the source, including the author, title, publication information, and page number if applicable.

Note: The Modern Language Association (MLA) and the American Psychological Association (APA) provide guidelines for figure captions and crediting sources of visuals that differ from the preceding guidelines. *(See Chapter 24: MLA Style: Format, p. 303, and Chapter 28: APA Style: Format, p. 345.)*

4 Revising and Editing

To revise means to see something again. In the **revising** stage of the writing process, you review the entire composition, adding, deleting, and moving text as necessary. After you are satisfied with the substance of your draft, **editing** begins. When you edit, you refine sentences so that you say what you want to say as effectively as possible, and you correct grammatical and mechanical errors.

This chapter focuses on revising and introduces the principles of editing, which are addressed in greater detail in Parts 6–8.

4a Getting comments from readers

Asking actual readers to comment on your draft is the best way to get fresh perspectives. (Most professors encourage peer review, but it is wise to check.) Always acknowledge this help, in an endnote, a cover note, a preface, or an acknowledgments page.

1. Using peer review **Peer review** involves critiquing your classmates' work while they review yours. You can send your draft to your peer reviewers electronically (also print out a hard copy for yourself) or exchange drafts in person.

Help your readers help you by giving them information and identifying areas where you want help. When you share a draft with readers, provide answers to the following questions:

- **What is your assignment?** Readers need to understand the context for your project—especially your intended purpose and audience.

- **How close are you to being finished?** Your answer lets readers know where you are in the writing process and how best to assist you in taking the next step.

- **What steps do you plan to take to complete the project?** If readers know your plans, they can either question the direction you are taking or give you more specific help, such as the titles of additional sources you might consult.

- **What kind of feedback do you need?** Do you want readers to summarize your main points so you can determine if you have communicated clearly? Do you want a response to the logic of your argument or the development of your thesis?

NAVIGATING THROUGH COLLEGE AND BEYOND

Re-Visioning Your Work

Revising is a process of "re-visioning"—of looking at your work through the eyes of your audience. Here are some tips for getting a fresh perspective:

- **Get feedback from other readers.** Candid, respectful feedback can help you discover strengths and weaknesses. See Section 4a for advice on making use of readers' reactions to your drafts.

- **Let your draft cool.** Try to schedule a break between drafting and revising. A good night's sleep, a movie break, or some physical exercise will help you view your draft with new eyes.

- **Read your draft aloud.** Some find that reading aloud helps them "hear" their words the way their audience will.

- **Use revising and editing checklists.** The checklists on pages 65, 68, 76, 79, and 82 will assist you in evaluating your work systematically. Even better, create your own checklist based on the changes you make to final drafts.

CHECKLIST

Giving Feedback

☐ **Don't forget strengths.** Let writers know what you think works well, so that they can build on that in their next draft and try similar approaches in another writing task.

☐ **Be specific.** Give examples to back up your general reactions.

☐ **Be constructive.** Instead of saying that an example is a bad choice, explain that you did not understand how the example was connected to the main point, and, if you can, suggest a way to clarify the connection.

☐ **Ask questions.** Jot down any questions that occur to you while reading. Ask for clarification, or note an objection that readers of the final version might make.

Guidelines for Receiving Feedback

☐ **Resist being defensive.** Keep in mind that readers are discussing your draft, not you; their feedback offers a way to see your writing from another angle. Be respectful of their time and effort. You will be the one to decide how to proceed.

☐ **Ask for more feedback if you need it.** Some readers may be hesitant to share all of their reactions, and you may need to do some coaxing.

Reading other writers' drafts will help you view your own work in a larger context, and comments from readers will help you see your own writing as others see it. As you gain more objectivity, you will become more adept at revising your work. In addition, the approaches that you see your classmates taking to the assignment will give you ideas for new directions in your own writing.

2. Responding to readers   While you should consider your readers' suggestions, you are under no obligation to do what they say. Sometimes you will receive contradictory advice: one reader may like a particular sentence that a second reader suggests you eliminate. Is there common ground? Yes. Both readers stopped at that sentence. Ask yourself why—and whether you want readers to pause there.

For MULTILINGUAL WRITERS

Peer Review

Respectful peer review will challenge you to see your writing critically as you present ideas to an American audience. It also will show you that everyone benefits from the process of revising. You may comment on points that English speakers may too easily take for granted, while your classmates can assist you in mastering idioms.

Also look for patterns in readers' comments, which might indicate areas to address.

4b Using electronic tools for revising

Even though word-processing programs can make a first draft look finished, it is still a first draft. Check below the surface for problems in content, structure, and style. Move paragraphs around, add details, and delete irrelevant sentences. You may find it easier to revise if you have a printed copy so that you can see the composition as a whole.

To work efficiently, become familiar with the revising and editing tools in your word-processing program:

- **Comments:** Many word-processing programs have a "Comments" feature allowing you to add notes to sections of text. This feature is useful for giving feedback on someone else's draft. Some writers also use it to make notes to themselves.

- **Track changes:** The Track Changes feature allows you to revise and edit a piece of writing while also maintaining the original text. Usually, marginal notes or strike-through marks show what you have deleted or replaced. Because you can still see the original text, you can judge whether a change has improved the draft. If you change your mind, you can restore the deleted text. When collaborating with another writer, save the Track Changes version as a separate file.

You can see the Track Changes and Comments features in the second draft of Diane Chen's analysis on pages 83–86. In addition, many Web-based tools such as Google Docs enable work to be shared, edited, and revised online.

4c Focusing on the writing situation
(topic, purpose, audience, medium, genre)

As you revise your draft within your selected rhetorical situation, be sure to consider your purpose, rhetorical stance, and audience. Is your primary purpose to inform, to interpret, to analyze, or to argue? *(For more on purpose, see the Introduction, p. 6.)*

Clarity about your rhetorical situation and writing purpose is especially important when an assignment calls for interpretation. A description is not the same as an interpretation. With this principle in mind, Diane Chen read over her first draft interpreting the *Migrations* photography exhibit. Here is part of her description of the photograph she chose to discuss in detail.

FIRST DRAFT

The photograph is black and white, as are the others in the show. The faces of the babies are in sharp focus while the blanket is a bit defocused. Light, which is essential to photography, is disseminated from a single source coming from the upper left-hand corner of the picture. The light source is not too bright as to bathe the babies in light, but just bright enough to illuminate their faces, which have expressions of interest and puzzlement. Perhaps they are wondering who Salgado is or what is that strange contraption he is holding.

Keeping the writing situation in mind, Chen realized that she needed to discuss the significance of her observations—to interpret and analyze the details for readers who would see a copy of the photograph incorporated into her online text. Within the genre of a review, she revised to demonstrate how the formal elements of the photograph function.

REVISION

The orphanage photograph is shot in black and white, as are the other images in the show, giving it a documentary feel that emphasizes the truth of the situation. But Salgado's choice of black-and-white photography is also an artistic decision. He uses the contrasts of light and dark to create a dramatic image of the three babies.
The vertical black-and-white stripes of the blanket direct our eyes to the infants' faces and hands, which are framed by a horizontal white stripe. . . .

4d   Making sure you have a strong thesis

Remember that a thesis makes an assertion about a topic. It links the *what* and the *why*. Is your thesis evident on the first page of your draft? Before readers get very far along, they expect an answer to the question, "What is the point of all this?" If you do not find the point on the first page, its absence is a signal to revise, unless you are deliberately waiting until the end to share your thesis. *(For more on strong theses, see Chapter 2, pp. 36–38.)*

Many writers start with a working thesis, which often evolves into a more specific, complex assertion as they develop their ideas. One of the key challenges of revising is to compose a clear statement of this revised thesis. When she began her draft on Germany's economic prospects, Jennifer Koehler stated her working thesis as follows.

WORKING THESIS

Germany is experiencing a great deal of change.

During the revision process, Koehler realized that her working thesis was weak. A weak thesis is predictable: readers read it, agree, and that's that. A strong thesis, on the other hand, stimulates thoughtful inquiry. Koehler's revised thesis provokes questions.

4e
edit

REVISED THESIS

With proper follow-through, Germany can become one of the world's primary sources of direct investment and maintain its status as one of the world's preeminent exporters.

Sometimes writers find that their ideas change altogether, and the working thesis needs to be completely revised.

Your thesis should evolve throughout the draft. Readers need to see a statement of the main idea on the first page, but they also expect a more complex or general statement near the end. After presenting evidence to support her revised thesis, Koehler concludes by stating her thesis in a more general way.

If the government efforts continue, the economy will strengthen over the next decade, and Germany will reinforce its position as an integral nation in the global economy.

Exercise 4.1   Revising thesis statements

Examine some of your recent writing to see whether the thesis is clearly stated. Is the thesis significant? Can you follow the development of this idea throughout the draft? Does the version of your thesis in the conclusion answer the "So what?" question?

4e   Reviewing the structure of your draft

Does the draft have a beginning, a middle, and an end, with bridges between those parts? When you revise, you can refine and even change this structure so that it supports what you want to say more effectively.

One way to review your structure is by outlining your first draft. *(For help with outlining, see Chapter 2, pp. 39–42.)* Try listing the key points in sentence form; whenever possible, use sentences that actually appear in the draft. Ask yourself whether the key points are arranged effectively or if another arrangement would work better. The following structures are typical ways of organizing texts:

- **Informative:** Presents the key points of a topic.

- **Problem-Solution:** Begins with a question or problem and works step-by-step to discover an answer or a solution.

- **Argumentative:** Presents a set of linked reasons plus supporting evidence.

▪ **Analytic:** Shows how the parts come together to form a coherent whole and makes connections.

4f Revising for paragraph development, unity, and coherence

As you revise, examine each paragraph, asking yourself what role it plays—or should play—in the work as a whole. Keeping this role in mind, check each paragraph for development and unity. You should also check each paragraph for coherence—and consider whether all of the paragraphs together contribute to the work as a whole. Does the length of sections reflect their relative importance? *(For more on paragraphs, see Chapter 3: Drafting, pp. 58–62.)*

1. Paragraph development   Paragraphs in academic texts are usually about a hundred words long. Consider dividing any that exceed two hundred words or that are especially dense, and develop or combine paragraphs that seem very short. Would more information make the point clearer? Perhaps a term should be defined. Do generalizations need to be supported with examples? Make stylistic choices about paragraph length. In many cases, similar length sets a rhythm for the reader, although you may sometimes use a short paragraph for emphasis.

Note how this writer developed one of her draft paragraphs, adding details and examples to make her argument more effective.

FIRST DRAFT

A 1913 advertisement for Shredded Wheat illustrates Kellner's claim that advertisements sell self-images. The ad suggests that serving Shredded Wheat will give women the same sense of accomplishment as gaining the right to vote.

REVISION

According to Kellner, "advertising is as concerned with selling lifestyles and socially desirable identities . . . as with selling the products themselves" (193). A 1913 ad for Shredded Wheat shows how the selling of self-images works. At first glance, this ad seems to be promoting the women's suffrage movement. In big, bold letters, "Votes for Women" is emblazoned across the top of the ad. But a closer look reveals that the ad is for Shredded Wheat cereal. Holding a piece of the cereal in her hand, a woman stands behind a large bowlful of Shredded Wheat biscuits that is made to look like a ballot box. The text claims that "every biscuit is a vote for health, happiness, and domestic freedom." Like the rest of the advertisement, this claim suggests that serving Shredded Wheat will give women the same sense of accomplishment as gaining the right to vote.

—HOLLY MUSETTI, "Targeting Women," student text

4f
edit

2. Paragraph unity A unified paragraph has a single, clear focus. To check for **unity,** identify the paragraph's topic sentence *(see pp. 59–61),* and make sure everything in the paragraph is clearly and closely related to it. Ideas unrelated to the topic sentence should be deleted or developed into separate paragraphs. Alternatively, revise the topic sentence.

Compare the first draft of the following paragraph with its revision, and note how the addition of a topic sentence (in bold in the revision) sharpens the focus, making it easier for the writer to revise further. Note also that the writer deleted the underlined ideas because they did not directly relate to the paragraph's main point.

FIRST DRAFT

Students today volunteer for their own personal benefit, motivated partly by the desire for money or fame. One study of college-aged Americans, for instance, reported that for 81% of participants, getting rich was their highest priority in life, and 51% sought fame as a primary goal (Pew Research Center for the People and the Press, 2007). The pursuit of wealth is encouraged by parents, teachers, and the media. People who are working for a cause today usually integrate the common good with their own personal aspirations; those of college age do not take for granted that programs like Social Security will survive the coming decades, and therefore they do all they can to enhance their future earning power by keeping an eye out for opportunities as they are volunteering. Social Security is currently projected to run out of money by the year 2037.

REVISION

In fact, the economic realities of our society have much to do with the perceptions of how volunteering is different for today's student than it was in times past. Students today volunteer for their own personal benefit, motivated partly by the desire for money or fame. One study of college-aged Americans, for instance, reported that for 81% of participants, getting rich was their highest priority in life, and 51% sought fame as a primary goal (Pew Research Center for the People and the Press, 2007). People who are working for a cause today usually integrate the common good with their own personal aspirations; those of college age do not take for granted that programs like Social Security will survive the coming decades, and therefore they do all they can to enhance their future earning power by keeping an eye out for opportunities as they are volunteering.

—TINA SCHWAB, "The New Volunteer: College Students' Involvement in Community Giving Grows"

3. Coherence A coherent paragraph flows smoothly, with an organization that is easy to follow and with each sentence clearly related to the next. *(See Chapter 3, pp. 58–62, for tips on how to develop well-organized paragraphs.)* You can improve coherence both within and among the paragraphs in your draft by using repetition, pronouns, parallel structure, synonyms, and transitions:

- Repeat key words to emphasize the main idea and provide a transition.

  A photograph displays a unique *moment*. To capture that *moment* . . .

- Use pronouns and antecedents to form connections between sentences and avoid unnecessary repetition. In the following example, *it* refers to *Germany* and connects the two sentences.

  Germany imports raw materials, energy sources, and food products. *It* exports a wide range of industrial products, including automobiles, aircraft, and machine tools.

- Repeat sentence structures to emphasize connections.

  Because the former West Germany lived through a generation of prosperity, its people developed high expectations of material comfort. *Because the former East Germany* lived through a generation of deprivation, its people developed disdain for material values.

- Use **synonyms**—words that are close in meaning to words or phrases that have preceded them—to link ideas.

  In the world of photography, critics *argue* for either a scientific or an artistic approach. This *controversy* . . .

- Use transitional words and phrases. One-word transitions and **transitional expressions** link one idea with another, helping readers see the relationship between them. *(See the list of common transitional expressions in the box on p. 74.)* Compare the following two paragraphs, the first version without transitions and the revised version with transitions (in bold type and highlighted).

FIRST DRAFT

Blogs have turned citizens into novice reporters. What do they mean for mainstream news outlets? Traditional forms of reporting, such as newspapers and televised news broadcasts, have always depended on the objectivity and credibility of their journalists, the reliability of their sources, and the extensive research and fact-checking that inform every news story. Blogs are a fast and easy way to publicize current issues and events. Many wonder if they can offer information that is as reliable as that provided by traditional news organizations and their carefully researched news. A seventeen-year-old high school graduate can report on the *New York Times* blog *The Choice* about her experience applying for college financial aid. Her report will not be backed by the comprehensive, objective research that would inform a *Times* newspaper article about the broader financial aid situation throughout the country.

4f
edit

REVISION

Blogs have turned citizens into novice reporters, **but** what do they mean for mainstream news outlets? Traditional forms of reporting, such as newspapers and televised news broadcasts, have always depended on the objectivity and credibility of their journalists, the reliability of their sources, and the extensive research and fact-checking that inform every news story. Blogs are a fast and easy way to publicize current issues and events; **however,** many wonder if they can offer information that is as reliable as that provided by traditional news organizations and their carefully researched news. **For example,** a seventeen-year-old high school graduate can report on the *New York Times* blog *The Choice* about her experience applying for college financial aid, **but** her report will not be backed by the comprehensive, objective research that would inform a *Times* newspaper article about the broader financial aid situation throughout the country.

—REBECCA HOLLINGSWORTH, "Breaking News: Blogging's Impact on Traditional and New Media"

■ Use repetition, pronouns, parallelism, transitions, and **transitional sentences,** which refer to the previous paragraph and move your essay on to the next point, to show how paragraphs in an essay are related to one another.

The vertical black-and-white stripes of the blanket direct our eyes to the infants' faces and hands, which are framed by a horizontal white stripe. The whites of their eyes in particular stand out against the darkness created by the shell of the

TRANSITIONAL EXPRESSIONS

- **To show relationships in space:** above, adjacent to, against, alongside, around, at a distance from, at the . . . , below, beside, beyond, encircling, far off, forward, from the . . . , in front of, in the rear, inside, near the back, near the end, nearby, next to, on, over, surrounding, there, through the, to the left, to the right, up front
- **To show relationships in time:** afterward, at last, before, earlier, first, former, formerly, immediately, in the first place, in the meantime, in the next place, in the last place, later on, meanwhile, next, now, often, once, previously, second, simultaneously, sometime later, subsequently, suddenly, then, third, today, tomorrow, until now, when, years ago, yesterday
- **To show addition or to compare:** again, also, and, and then, besides, further, furthermore, in addition, last, likewise, moreover, next, too
- **To give examples that intensify points:** after all, as an example, certainly, clearly, for example, for instance, indeed, in fact, in truth, it is true, of course, specifically, that is
- **To show similarities:** alike, in the same way, like, likewise, resembling, similarly
- **To show contrasts:** after all, although, but, conversely, differ(s) from, difference, different, dissimilar, even though, granted, however, in contrast, in spite of, nevertheless, notwithstanding, on the contrary, on the other hand, otherwise, still, though, unlike, while this may be true, yet
- **To indicate cause and effect:** accordingly, as a result, because, consequently, hence, since, then, therefore, thus
- **To conclude or summarize:** finally, in brief, in conclusion, in other words, in short, in summary, that is, to summarize

---

blankets. The camera's lens also seems to be in sharper focus on the faces than on the blankets, again focusing our attention on the babies' expressions.

Each baby has a different response to the camera. The baby on the left returns our gaze with a heart-wrenching look. . . .

Exercise 4.2   Revising paragraphs

Revise the paragraphs below to improve their unity, development, and coherence:

1. Vivaldi was famous and influential as a virtuoso violinist and composer. Vivaldi died in poverty, having lost popularity in

the last years before his death. He had been acclaimed during his lifetime and forgotten for two hundred years after his death. Many composers suffer that fate. The baroque revival of the 1950s brought his music back to the public's attention.

4g edit

2.   People who want to adopt an exotic pet need to be aware of the consequences. Baby snakes and lizards can seem fairly easy to manage. Lion and tiger cubs are playful and friendly. They can seem as harmless as kittens. Domestic cats can revert to a wild state quite easily. Adult snakes and lizards can grow large. Many species of lizards and snakes require carefully controlled environments. Big cats can escape. An escaped lion or tiger is a danger to itself and to others. Most exotic animals need professional care. This kind of care is available in zoos and wild-animal parks. The best environment for an exotic animal is the wild.

Exercise 4.3   Writing well-developed, coherent paragraphs

Using the strategies for paragraph development and coherence discussed in Section 4f, write a paragraph for one of the following topic sentences. Working with two or more classmates, decide where your paragraph needs more details or improved coherence:

1. Awards shows on television often fail to recognize creativity and innovation.

2. Most people learn only those aspects of a computer program that they need to use every day.

3. First-year students who also work can have an easier time adjusting to the demands of college life than nonworking students.

4. Tweets and e-mail messages that circulate widely can be broken down into several categories.

Exercise 4.4   Revising your paragraphs

Review the paragraph you wrote in Exercise 4.3, and revise it using the strategies in this section.

4g   Revising visuals, images, and multimedia

If you have used visuals to display data in your paper, return to them during the revision stage to eliminate what scholar Edward Tufte calls **chartjunk,** or distracting visual elements. The checklist on page 76 contains Tufte's suggestions for editing visuals so that your readers will focus on your data rather than your "data containers." Likewise, review images (for example, photographs or drawings) to

CHECKLIST

Revising Visuals

☐ **Are grid lines needed in tables?** Eliminate grid lines or, if the lines are needed for clarity, lighten them. Tables should not look like nets with every number enclosed. Vertical rules are needed only when space is extremely tight between columns.

☐ **Are there any unnecessary 3D renderings?** Cubes and shadows can distort the information in a visual. For most charts, including pie charts, a flat image makes it easier for readers to compare parts.

☐ **Are data labeled clearly,** avoiding abbreviations and legends if possible? Does each visual have an informative title?

☐ **Do bright colors focus attention on the key data?** For example, if you are including a map, use muted colors over large areas and save strong colors for areas you want to emphasize.

☐ **Do irrelevant elements distract from the visual's purpose?** Clip art and other decorative elements seldom make data more interesting or appear more substantial.

☐ **Are data distorted?** In the first graph in Figure 4.1 on page 77, each month gets its own point, except for January, February, March, and April. This presentation creates a misleading impression of hurricane activity by month. The revision corrects this distortion.

be sure that they illustrate the points made in the text. Be sure that the specific image provides evidence for your claim. Do you need the full portrait of a historical figure to make a point, or would a close-up of one part of the portrait better serve your purpose? Also, review multimedia—like slides, audio files, and video—to be sure that you have included only what you need to provide sufficient context for the viewer.

4h Editing sentences

Parts 6 and 7 of this handbook address the many specific questions writers have when they are editing for clarity, word choice, and grammatical conventions.

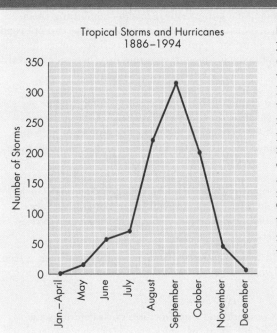

Tropical Storms and Hurricanes
1886–1994

**FIGURE 4.1
Misleading
(top) and re-
vised graphs.**
In the graph at
the top, the activ-
ity in the first
part of the year
is combined into
one point on the
axis, mislead-
ing readers.
The chart at the
bottom has been
revised to correct
this problem.

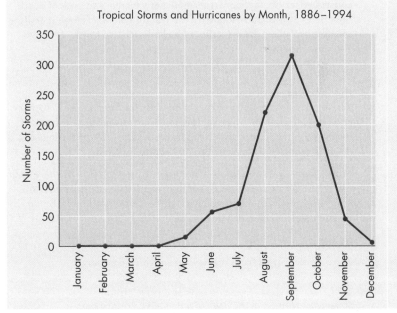

Tropical Storms and Hurricanes by Month, 1886–1994

1. Editing for clarity

As you edit, concentrate on sentence style, aiming for focused and interestingly varied writing. A series of short, choppy sentences is like a bumpy ride. Consider combining them.

An unbroken stream of long, complicated sentences can put readers to sleep. Vary sentence openings and structure. Notice how the revised passage connects ideas and, consequently, is easier to read.

DRAFT

My father was a zealous fisherman. He took his fishing rod on every family outing. He often spent the whole outing staring at the water, waiting for a nibble. He went to the kitchen as soon as he got home. He usually cleaned and cooked the fish the same day he caught them.

REVISED

A zealous fisherman, my father took his fishing rod on every family outing. He would often spend the whole afternoon by the shore, waiting for a nibble, and then hurry straight to the kitchen to clean and cook his catch.

Condense and focus sentences that are wordy and lack a clear subject and vivid verb.

DRAFT

Although both vertebral and wrist fractures cause deformity and impair movement, hip fractures, which are one of the most devastating consequences of osteoporosis, significantly increase the risk of death, since 12%–30% of patients with a hip fracture die within one year after the fracture, while the mortality rate climbs to 40% for the first two years postfracture.

REVISED

Hip fractures are one of the most devastating consequences of osteoporosis. Although vertebral and wrist fractures cause deformity and impair movement, hip fractures significantly increase the risk of death. Within one year after a hip fracture, 12%–20% of the injured die. The mortality rate climbs to 40% within two years.

More often than not, sentences beginning with *it is* or *there is* or *there are* (*it was* or *there was*)—called **expletive constructions**—are weak and indirect. Using a clear subject and a vivid verb usually makes such sentences more powerful.

DRAFT

There are stereotypes from the days of a divided Germany.

REVISED

Stereotypes formed in the days of a divided Germany persist.

| X✓ CHECKLIST | **4h**
edit |

Editing Your Draft for Style and Grammar

To create a personalized editing checklist, fill in the boxes next to your trouble spots, as determined from any other personalized checklists you have, your instructor's comments on your writing, and any diagnostic tests you have taken:

☐ **Clarity** *(Part 6, Chapters 30 through 38, pp. 361–401)*: Does every sentence communicate your meaning in a clear, direct style? Does the text contain any of the following common causes of unclear sentences? Note sections that could be clearer:
  ☐ Wordiness
  ☐ Missing words
  ☐ Mixed constructions
  ☐ Confusing shifts
  ☐ Faulty parallelism
  ☐ Misplaced and dangling modifiers
  ☐ Problems with coordination and subordination
  ☐ Other: _____

☐ **Word choice** *(Part 6, Chapters 39–41, pp. 401–24)*: How could the choice of words be more precise, especially given your rhetorical situation? Does the text include slang, biased language, clichés, or other inappropriate usages? Does it misuse any commonly confused words (for example, *advice* vs. *advise*) or use any nonstandard expressions (for example, *could of*)?

☐ **Grammar conventions** *(Part 7, Chapters 42–48, pp. 427–506)*: Does the draft contain common errors that may confuse or distract readers?
  ☐ Sentence fragments
  ☐ Comma splices
  ☐ Run-on sentences
  ☐ Subject-verb agreement problems
  ☐ Incorrect verb forms
  ☐ Inconsistent verb tenses
  ☐ Pronoun-antecedent agreement problems
  ☐ Incorrect pronoun forms
  ☐ Problems with use of adjectives or adverbs
  ☐ Other: _____

If you are in the process of developing fluency in English, consult Chapter 48.

2. Editing for word choice

Different disciplines and occupations have their own vocabularies. The word *significant,* for example, has a mathematical meaning for the statistician and a different meaning for the literary critic. When taking courses in a discipline, you should use its terminology accurately.

As you review your draft, look for general terms that should be more specific.

DRAFT

Foreign direct investment (FDI) in Germany will probably remain low because of several *factors. [*Factors *is a general word. To get specific, answer the question* "What *factors?"]*

REVISED

Foreign direct investment (FDI) in Germany will probably remain low because of *high labor costs, high taxation, and government regulation.*

Your search for more specific words can lead you to a dictionary and thesaurus. *(For more on using a dictionary and a thesaurus, see Chapter 40.)*

3. Editing for grammatical conventions

Sometimes, writers will construct a sentence or choose a word form that violates the rules of standard written English.

DRAFT

Photographs of illegal immigrants being captured by the U.S. Border Patrol, of emotional immigrants on the plane to their new country, and of villagers fleeing rebel gangs. *[This is a sentence fragment because it lacks a verb; it also omits the writer's point about these images.]*

EDITED SENTENCE

Photographs of illegal immigrants being captured by the U.S. Border Patrol, of emotional immigrants on the plane to their new country, and of villagers fleeing rebel gangs exemplify the range of migration stories.

A list of common abbreviations and symbols used to note errors in a manuscript can be found at the end of this text. Your instructor and other readers may use these.

Exercise 4.5   Editing sentences

Type the following sentences into your word processor, and activate the grammar and spell-checker feature. Copy the sentence suggested by the software, and then write your own edited version of the sentence:

TEXTCONNEX

You Know More Than Grammar and Spell Checkers

4i edit

Grammar and spell checkers can help you spot some errors, but they miss many others and may even flag a correct sentence. Consider the following example.

> Thee neighbors puts there cats' outsider.

Neither a spelling nor grammar checker detected the five errors in the sentence. (Correct version: *The neighbors put their cats outside.*)

As long as you are aware of the limitations of these checkers, use them as you edit your manuscript. Be sure, however, to re-view your writing carefully yourself.

1. Lighting affects are sense of the shape and texture of the objects depict.
2. A novelist's tells the truth even though he invent stories and characters.
3. There are the question of why bad things happen to good people, which story of Job illustrate.
4. A expensive marketing campaign is of little value if the product stinks.
5. Digestive enzymes melt down the nutrients in food so that the body is able to put in effect a utilization of those nutrients when the body needs energy to do things.

4i Proofreading carefully

Once you have revised your draft at the paragraph and sentence levels, it is time to give it one last check to make sure that it is free of typos and other mechanical errors.

Even if you are submitting an electronic version of your project, you may still prefer to proofread a printed version. Placing a ruler under each line can make it easier to focus. You can also start at the end and proofread your way backward to the beginning, sentence by sentence. Some students read their drafts aloud. Do not at this stage read for content but for form and correctness.

CHECKLIST

Proofreading

☐ Have you included your name, the date, your professor's name, and the title of your text? *(See Chapters 21–29 for the formats to use for MLA or APA style.)*

☐ Are all words spelled correctly? Be sure to check the spelling of titles and headings. *(See Chapter 60, pp. 566–70.)*

☐ Have you used the words you intended, or have you substituted words that sound like the ones you want but have a different spelling and meaning, such as *too* for *to, their* for *there,* or *it's* for *its*? *(See Chapter 41, pp. 414–24.)*

☐ Are all proper names capitalized? Have you capitalized titles of works correctly and either italicized them or put them in quotation marks as required? *(See Chapter 55, pp. 550–54, and Chapter 58, pp. 560–63.)*

☐ Have you punctuated your sentences correctly? *(See Part 8.)*

☐ Are sources cited correctly? Is the works-cited or references list in the correct format? *(See Parts 4 and 5.)*

☐ Have you checked anything you retyped—for instance, quotations and tables—against the original?

4j Using campus, Internet, and community resources

You can call on a number of resources outside the classroom for feedback on your writing.

1. Using the campus writing center Tutors in the writing center can read and comment on drafts of your work. They can also help you find and correct problems with grammar and punctuation.

2. Using online writing labs (OWLs) Most OWLs offer information about writing, including lists of useful online resources that you can access anytime. *CONNECT* offers Net Tutor: opportunities for off-site writing tutors to read and comment on your drafts. (You can have up to an hour of a tutor's time per semester.) Always check with your instructor before accessing this help, and be sure to acknowledge the assistance. OWLs with tutors can be useful in the following ways:

- You can submit a draft via e-mail for feedback. OWL tutors will return your work, often within forty-eight hours.
- You can post your draft in a public access space where you will receive feedback from more than just one or two readers.
- You can read others' drafts online and learn how they are handling writing issues.

You can learn more about what OWLs have to offer by checking out Purdue University's Online Writing Lab: <http://owl.english.purdue.edu>.

3. Working with experts and instructors In addition to sharing your work with classmates, through e-mail, or in online environments, you can consult electronically with your instructor or other experts. Your instructor's comments on an early draft are especially valuable. Be sure to think long and hard about the issues your instructor raises and revise your work accordingly.

4k Learning from one student's revisions

In the second draft of Diane Chen's review of an exhibit of photographs by Sebastião Salgado, you can see how she revised her draft to tighten the focus of her descriptive paragraphs and edited to improve clarity, word choice, and grammar. The photograph Chen discusses appears on p. 85.

The Caring Eye of Sebastião Salgado

Photographer Sebastião Salgado spent seven years ~~of his life~~ traveling along migration routes to city slums and refugee camps, and migration routes in order to document the lives of people uprooted from their homelands. A selection of his photographs can be seen in the exhibit, "*Migrations: Humanity in Transition.*" Like a photojournalist, Salgado brings us images of newsworthy events, but he goes beyond objective reporting, imparting his compassion for refugees and migrants to the viewer.

~~So m~~ Many of the photographs in Salgado's show are certain to touch viewers~~the viewer with their subject matter and sheer beauty~~. Whether capturing the ~~millions~~ thousands of refugee tents in Africa that seem to stretch on for miles or the disheartened faces of ~~small~~ immigrant children, the images in *Migrations* ~~Salgado brings an artistic element to his pictures that~~suggest that ~~he~~ Salgado does so much more with his camera than ~~just~~ point and shoot.

Salgado's photograph of the most vulnerable of these refugees illustrates the power of his work. "Orphanage attached to the hospital at Kibumba, Number One Camp, Goma Zaire," (Fig. 1) depicts three infants ~~apparently newborn or several month old babies,~~ who are victims of the genocidal war in neighboring Rwanda. The label for the photograph reveals ~~tells us~~ that there were 4,000 orphans at this camp and an estimated 100,000 Rwandan orphans overall. Those numbers are mind-numbing abstractions, but this picture is not.

The orphanage photograph is shot in black and white, as are the others in the show, ~~and provides the audience with a very~~ giving it a documentary~~, newspaper type of~~ feel that emphasizes that this is a real~~, newsworthy~~ situation ~~that we need to be aware of~~ deserving our attention. But Salgado's choice of black-and-white photography is also an artistic decision. He uses the contrasts of light and dark to create a dramatic image of the three babies.

The vertical black-and-white stripes of the blanket direct our eyes to the infants' faces and hands, which are framed by a horizontal white stripe. The whites of their eyes in particular stand out against the darkness created by the shell of the blankets. The camera's lens also seems to be in sharper focus on the faces than on the blankets, again focusing our attention on the babies' expressions. Each baby has a different response to the camera. The center baby, with his or her extra-wide eyes, appears startled and in need of comforting. The

Diane Chen 4/22/2010
Reorganize—move from left to right across the picture for a more dramatic conclusion.

baby to the right is oblivious to the camera and in fact seems to be starving or ill. The healthy baby on the left returns our gaze.

The vantage point ~~that~~ of this photograph ~~was taken from~~ is one of a ~~mother or father~~ parent standing over ~~the~~ his or her child. In this sense the infants become our own. Salgado also ~~makes an interesting point with the framing of~~ frames this picture strategically. The babies in their blanket consume the entire space, so that their innocence and vulnerability consume the viewer.

Salgado uses his skills as an artist to get us to look at these difficult subjects~~, but also to feel compassion for them~~. He is able to bring a story as big and complex as the epic displacement of the world's people to us through a collection of intimate and intensely moving images. As he says in his introduction to the exhibit catalog, "We hold the key to humanity's future, but for that we must understand the present. We cannot afford to look away."

> Diane Chen 4/22/2010
> Add citation to work cited.

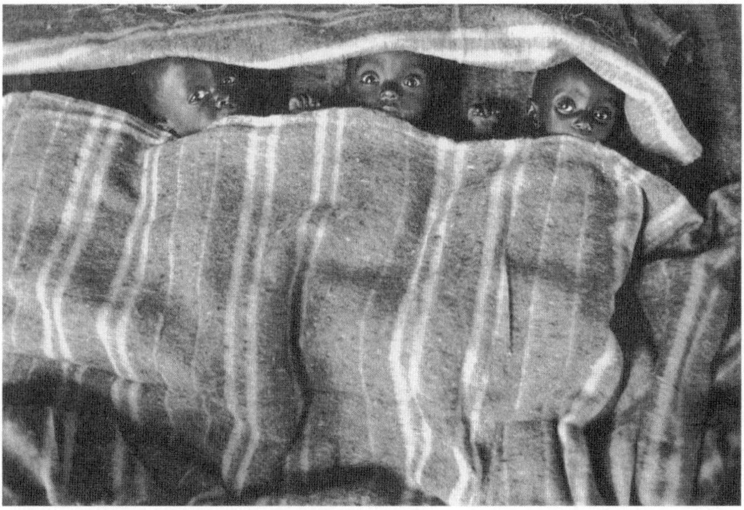

Fig. 1. Sebastião Salgado, *Migrations,* "Orphanage attached to the hospital at Kibumba, Number One Camp, Goma, Zaire."

---[new page]-----------------------------------

Work Cited

Salgado, Sebastião. *Migrations*. New York: Aperture, 2000. Print.

5 Designing Academic Texts and Portfolios

A crucial writing task is to format your text so that readers can "see" your ideas clearly. In this chapter, we focus on designing responses to academic writing assignments. *(Multimedia presentations, posters, and Web sites can be found in Chapter 11 and brochures, newsletters, résumés, and other documents in Chapter 12.)*

In college and in your professional life, you may wish to showcase your writing and related work in a print or an online portfolio. This chapter offers guidelines for designing effective portfolios.

5a Considering audience and purpose

As you plan your document, consider your purpose and the needs of your audience. If you are writing an informative project for a psychology class, your instructor—your primary audience—will probably prefer that you follow the guidelines provided by the American Psychological Association (APA). However, interpretive analyses for language and literature courses usually use the style recommended by the Modern Language Association (MLA). *(For help with these documentation styles, see Parts 4 and 5.)*

5b Using the tools available in your word-processing program

Most word-processing programs provide a range of options for editing, sharing, and, especially, designing your documents. For example, if you are using Microsoft Word 2010, you can access groups of commands by clicking on the various tabs at the top of the screen. Figure 5.1 shows the Home tab, which contains basic formatting and editing commands. You can choose different fonts and sizes; add

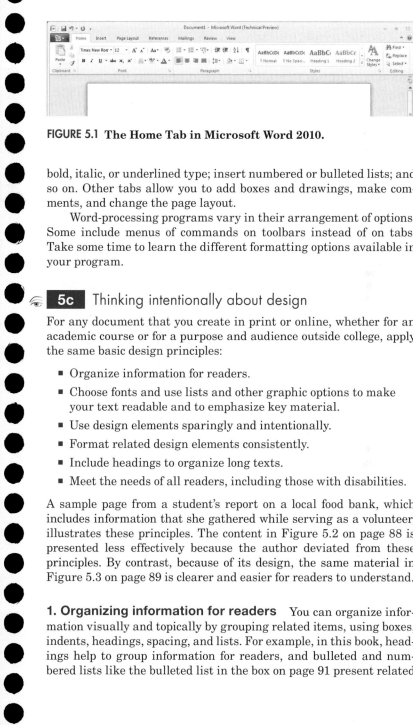

FIGURE 5.1 **The Home Tab in Microsoft Word 2010.**

bold, italic, or underlined type; insert numbered or bulleted lists; and so on. Other tabs allow you to add boxes and drawings, make comments, and change the page layout.

Word-processing programs vary in their arrangement of options. Some include menus of commands on toolbars instead of on tabs. Take some time to learn the different formatting options available in your program.

5c   Thinking intentionally about design

For any document that you create in print or online, whether for an academic course or for a purpose and audience outside college, apply the same basic design principles:

- Organize information for readers.
- Choose fonts and use lists and other graphic options to make your text readable and to emphasize key material.
- Use design elements sparingly and intentionally.
- Format related design elements consistently.
- Include headings to organize long texts.
- Meet the needs of all readers, including those with disabilities.

A sample page from a student's report on a local food bank, which includes information that she gathered while serving as a volunteer, illustrates these principles. The content in Figure 5.2 on page 88 is presented less effectively because the author deviated from these principles. By contrast, because of its design, the same material in Figure 5.3 on page 89 is clearer and easier for readers to understand.

1. Organizing information for readers   You can organize information visually and topically by grouping related items, using boxes, indents, headings, spacing, and lists. For example, in this book, headings help to group information for readers, and bulleted and numbered lists like the bulleted list in the box on page 91 present related

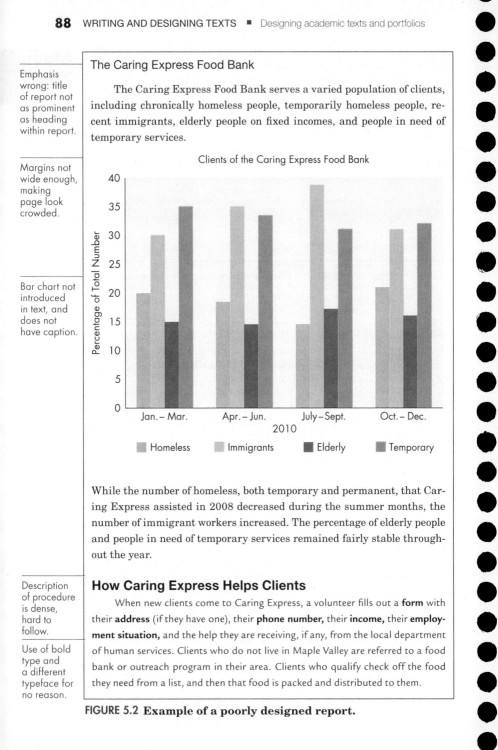

Emphasis wrong: title of report not as prominent as heading within report.

Margins not wide enough, making page look crowded.

Bar chart not introduced in text, and does not have caption.

The Caring Express Food Bank

The Caring Express Food Bank serves a varied population of clients, including chronically homeless people, temporarily homeless people, recent immigrants, elderly people on fixed incomes, and people in need of temporary services.

Clients of the Caring Express Food Bank

While the number of homeless, both temporary and permanent, that Caring Express assisted in 2008 decreased during the summer months, the number of immigrant workers increased. The percentage of elderly people and people in need of temporary services remained fairly stable throughout the year.

Description of procedure is dense, hard to follow.

Use of bold type and a different typeface for no reason.

How Caring Express Helps Clients

When new clients come to Caring Express, a volunteer fills out a **form** with their **address** (if they have one), their **phone number,** their **income,** their **employment situation,** and the help they are receiving, if any, from the local department of human services. Clients who do not live in Maple Valley are referred to a food bank or outreach program in their area. Clients who qualify check off the food they need from a list, and then that food is packed and distributed to them.

FIGURE 5.2 Example of a poorly designed report.

The Caring Express Food Bank

The Caring Express Food Bank serves a varied population of clients, including chronically homeless people, temporarily homeless people, recent immigrants, elderly people on fixed incomes, and people in need of temporary services. As Figure 1 shows, while the number of homeless, both temporary and permanent, that Caring Express assisted in 2010 decreased during the summer months, the number of immigrant workers increased. The percentage of elderly people and people in need of temporary services remained fairly stable throughout the year.

Title centered and in larger type than text and heading.

Bar chart introduced and explained.

Wider margins and white space above and below figure make report easier to read.

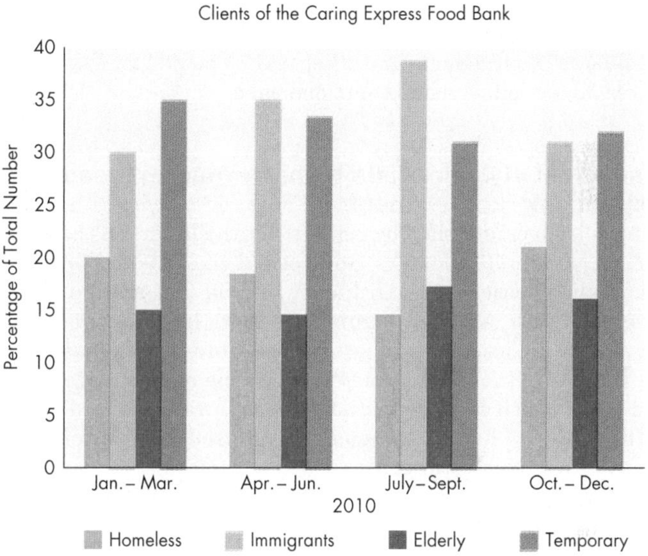

Figure 1. Percentage of clients in each group during 2008

Caption explains figure.

How Caring Express Helps Clients

Heading subordinate to title.

When new clients come to Caring Express, the volunteers follow this procedure:

1. The volunteer fills out a form with the client's address (if he or she has one), phone number, income, and employment situation.
2. Clients who do not live in Maple Valley are referred to a food bank or outreach program in their area.
3. Clients who qualify check off the food they need from a list.
4. The food is packed and distributed to them.

Procedure is explained in numbered list. Parallel structure is used for list entries.

FIGURE 5.3 Example of a well-designed report.

points. These features help readers scan material, locate important information, and dive in when they need to know more about a topic. If a color printer is available to you and your instructor allows you to use color, you have an additional tool for organizing information. For instance, in this text, headings and subheadings are in blue type. Use color with restraint, and choose colors that display well for all readers, bearing in mind that colors may look different on screen and on paper *(pp. 93–94).*

White space, areas of a document that do not contain type or graphics, also helps organize information for your audience. Generous margins and plenty of white space above headings and around other elements make the text easier to read.

You should also introduce any visuals within your text and position them so that they appear near—but never before—the text reference. Balance your visuals and other text elements; for example, don't try to cram too many visuals onto one page.

2. Using font style and lists to make your text readable and to emphasize key elements Fonts, or *typefaces,* are designs that have been established by printers for the letters in the alphabet, numbers, punctuation marks, and special characters. For most academic texts, choose a standard, easy-to-read font and an eleven- or twelve-point size. You can manipulate fonts for effect: for example, twelve-point Times New Roman can be **boldfaced,** *italicized,* and underlined. Serif fonts have tiny lines at the ends of letters such as *n* and *y;* sans serif fonts do not have these lines. Standard serif fonts like the following have traditionally been used for basic printed text because they are easy to read:

Times New Roman	Courier
Bookman Old Style	Palatino

Sans serif typefaces like the following are often used for headings because they offer a contrast or for electronic documents because they are more readable on screen. (Some standards may be changing. Calibri, the default font in Microsoft Word 2010, is a sans serif font.)

Calibri
Arial
Verdana

Usually, if the main text of a document is in a sans serif font, headings should be in a serif font, and vice versa. In general, you should not use more than two fonts in a single text.

Many fonts available on your computer are known as *display fonts,* such as the following:

Curlz **Bauhauſ 93**
Lucida Sans *Monotype Corsiva*

5c
design

These should be used rarely, if ever, in academic texts, on the screen, or in presentations. They can be effective, however, in other kinds of documents, such as brochures, flyers, and posters.

Numbered or bulleted lists help you cluster large amounts of information, making the information easier for readers to reference and understand. Because they stand out from your text visually, lists also help readers see that ideas are related. You can use lists to display steps in a sequence, present checklists, or suggest recommendations for action.

Format text as a numbered or bulleted list by choosing the option you want from your word-processing program's formatting commands.

NAVIGATING THROUGH COLLEGE AND BEYOND

The Basics: Margins, Spacing, Type, and Page Numbers

Here are a few basic guidelines for formatting academic texts:

- **First page:** In an assignment under five pages, you can usually place a header with your name, your professor's name, your course and section number, and the date on the first page, above the text. *(See the first page of Rebecca Hollingsworth's project on p. 306.)* If your text exceeds five pages, page 1 is often a title page. *(See the first page of Tina Schwab's project on p. 347.)*

- **Type:** Select a common font and choose the eleven- or twelve-point size.

- **Margins:** Use one-inch margins on all four sides of the text. Adequate margins make your document easier to read and give your instructor room to write comments and suggestions.

- **Margin justification:** Line up, or justify, the lines of your document along the left margin but not along the right margin. Leaving a "ragged right"—or uneven right margin, as in this box—enables you to avoid odd spacing between words.

- **Spacing:** Double-space unless you are instructed to do otherwise, and indent the first line of each paragraph five spaces. (Many business documents are single-spaced, however, with an extra line space between paragraphs, which are not indented.)

- **Page numbers:** Place page numbers in the upper or lower right-hand corner of the page. Some documentation styles require a header next to the page number. *(See Chapters 24 and 28 for the requirements of the style you are following.)*

Introduce the list with a complete sentence followed by a colon, use parallel structure in your list items, and put a period at the end of each item only if the entries are complete sentences.

Putting information in a box emphasizes it and also makes it easier for readers to find for future reference. Most word-processing programs offer several ways to enclose text within a border or box.

3. Using design elements sparingly and intentionally If you use too many graphics, headings, bullets, boxes, or other elements in a document, you risk making it as "noisy" as a loud radio. Standard fonts have become standard because they are easy on the eye. Bold type, italic type, underlining, and other graphic effects should not continue for more than one sentence at a time.

4. Formatting related design elements In design, the key words are simplicity, contrast, and consistency. If you emphasize an item by putting it in italic or bold type or in color, or if you use a graphic element such as a box to set it off, consider repeating this effect for similar items so that your document has a unified look. Even a simple horizontal line can be a purposeful element in a long document when used consistently to help organize information.

5. Using headings to organize long documents In short texts, headings can be disruptive and unnecessary. In longer texts, though, they can help organize complex information. *(For headings in APA style, see Chapter 28.)*

Effective headings are brief, descriptive, and consistent in grammatical structure and formatting:

PHRASES BEGINNING WITH *–ING* WORDS

Fielding Inquiries
Handling Complaints

NOUNS AND NOUN PHRASES

Customer Inquiries
Complaints

QUESTIONS

How Do I Field Inquiries?
How Do I Handle Complaints?

IMPERATIVE SENTENCES

Field Inquiries Efficiently
Handle Complaints Calmly and Politely

Headings at different levels can be in different forms. For example, the first-level headings in a book might be imperative sentences, while the second-level headings might begin with *–ing* words.

Place and emphasize headings consistently throughout the text. If you have not already done so, preparing a formal topic outline will help you decide what your main points and second-level points are and where headings should go. *(See Chapter 2, pp. 41–42.)* You might center all first-level headings, which correspond to the main points in your outline. If you have second-level headings—your supporting points—you might align them at the left margin and underline them. Third-level headings, if you have them, could be aligned at the left margin and set in plain type:

First-Level Heading

<u>Second-Level Heading</u>

Third-Level Heading

If a heading falls at the very bottom of a page, move it to the top of the next page.

6. Meeting the needs of readers with disabilities   If your potential audience might include the visually or hearing impaired, take a few simple principles into account:

- **Use a large, easily readable font.** The font should be fourteen point or larger. Use a sans serif font such as Arial, as readers with poor vision find these fonts easier to read. Make headings larger than the surrounding text (rather than relying on a change in font, bold, italics, or color to set them apart).

- **Use ample spacing between lines.** The American Council of the Blind recommends a line space of 1.5.

- **Use appropriate, high-contrast colors.** Black text on a white background is best. If you use color for text or visuals, put light material on a dark background and dark material on a light background. Use colors from different families (such as yellow on purple). Avoid red and green because color-blind readers may have trouble distinguishing them. Do not use glossy paper.

- **Include narrative descriptions of all visuals.** Describe each chart, map, photograph, or other visual in your text. Indicate the key information and the point the visual makes. (This is most important when writing for the Web because individuals may use screen-reader software; *see Chapter 11, p. 166.*)

- **If you include audio or video files in an electronic document, provide transcripts.** Also include narrative descriptions of what is happening in the video.

For further information, consult the American Council of the Blind (<http://acb.org/accessible-formats.html>), Lighthouse International (<http://www.lighthouse.org/accessibility/design/accessible-print -design/making-text-legible>), and the American Printing House for the Blind (<www.aph.org/edresearch/lpguide.htm>).

👁 **5d** Compiling an effective print or electronic portfolio

Students, job candidates, and professionals are often asked to collect their writing in a portfolio. Although most portfolios consist of a collection of texts in print form, many writers create electronic portfolios incorporating a variety of media.

Portfolios, regardless of medium, share at least three common features:

- They are a *collection* of work.
- They are a *selection*—or subset—of a larger body of work.
- They are introduced, narrated, or commented on by a text (for example, print or video) that offers *reflections* on the work.

Like any type of writing, portfolios serve a purpose and address an audience—to demonstrate your progress in a course for your instructor, for example, or to present your best work for a prospective employer. Portfolios also allow writers to assess their work and set new writing goals.

1. Assembling a print portfolio

Gathering your writing   Create a list, or inventory, of the items that you might include. For a writing course, consider providing exploratory writing, notes, and comments from peer reviewers as well as all drafts for one or more of the selections. Make sure all items include your name and that your final drafts are error-free.

Reviewing written work and making appropriate selections   As you consider selections, keep the purpose of the portfolio in mind as well as the criteria that will be used to evaluate it. If you are assembling a presentation portfolio, select your very best work. If you are demonstrating your improvement as a writer in a process portfolio, select work showing your development and creativity.

Even if no criteria have been provided, consider the audience for the portfolio when deciding which selections will be most appropriate. Who will read it, and what qualities will they be looking for?

CHECKLIST

Assembling a Print Portfolio

☐ Gather all your written work.

☐ Make appropriate selections.

☐ Arrange the selections.

☐ Write a reflective essay or letter.

☐ Polish your portfolio.

Arranging the selections deliberately If you have not been told how to organize your portfolio—for instance, in the order in which you wrote the pieces—think of it as if it were a single text, and decide on an arrangement that will serve your purpose: from weakest to strongest? from a less important project to a more important one? How will you determine importance?

Explain your rationale for this arrangement in a letter to the reader, in a brief introduction, or in annotations in the table of contents.

Writing a reflective essay or letter The reflective statement may take the form of an essay or a letter, depending on purpose and requirements. Sometimes the reflective essay will be the last one in a portfolio, so the reader can review all the work first and then read the writer's interpretation at the end. Alternatively, a reflective letter can open the portfolio. Regardless of its genre or placement, the reflective text gives you an opportunity to explain something about your writing or about yourself as a writer:

- How you developed various assignments
- Which projects you believe are particularly strong and why
- What you learned as you worked on these assignments
- Who you are now as a writer

Follow the stages of the writing process in preparing your reflective essay or letter. Once you have completed it, assemble all the components of your portfolio in a folder or notebook.

Polishing your portfolio In the process of writing the reflective letter or essay, you might discover a better way to arrange your work.

Or, as you arrange the portfolio, you might want to review all your work again. Do not be surprised if you find yourself repeating some of these tasks. As with any writing, peer review will help you revise your portfolio to be most effective.

Most students learn about themselves and their writing as they compile their portfolios and write reflections on their work. The process makes them better writers and helps them learn how to demonstrate their strengths to others.

2. Preparing an electronic portfolio   For some courses or professional purposes, you will present your work in an electronic format. Electronic portfolios can be saved on a CD, DVD, or flash drive, or they can be published on the Web. Here are some brief guidelines for preparing electronic portfolios:

- Use your opening screen to establish your purpose, appeal to your audience, provide links to help readers navigate your portfolio, and suggest who you are as a writer.

- Use links to help readers move within your portfolio. You can link to texts from your table of contents, from other texts, and from your reflective letter or essay.

- Consider using links to connect to related files that are external to the work in the portfolio but relevant to it, such as audio files and video clips.

- Before releasing it, make sure your portfolio works—both conceptually and structurally—by navigating all the way through it yourself. Ask a friend to do so from a different computer. Sometimes links fail to work, or files stored on one machine do not open on another.

Auguste Rodin's sculpture The Thinker *evokes the psychological complexity of human thought and suggests the spirit of critical inquiry common to all disciplines across the curriculum.*

Anybody who is involved in working across the disciplines is much more likely to have a lively mind and a lively life.

—MARY FIELD BELENKY

Writing in College and beyond College

2

Writing in College and beyond College

WRITING OUTCOMES

Rhetorical Knowledge

- How can I argue persuasively? **(8c)**
- How can I keep my audience interested in my oral presentation? **(10b)**

Critical Thinking, Reading, and Writing

- How do I analyze a literary work? **(7b)**
- How can I defend my thesis against counterarguments? **(8c)**

Processes

- What is the best way to prepare for essay exams? **(9b)**
- How can I use presentation software (such as PowerPoint) effectively? **(10c)**

Knowledge of Conventions

- What conventions should I use for a personal essay? **(9a)**

Composing in Electronic Environments

- What should I *not* put on my blog or social networking page? **(11c)**
- What steps should I take in planning my Web site? **(11b)**

(For a general introduction to writing outcomes, see Id, page 5.)

6 Informative Reports

Imagine what the world would be like without records of what others have learned. Fortunately, we have many sources of information to draw on, including informative reports.

6a Understanding the assignment

An **informative report** passes on what someone has learned about a topic or issue; it teaches. An informative report gives you a chance to do the following:

- Learn more about an issue that interests you.
- Make sense of what you have read, heard, and seen.
- Teach others what you have learned.

6b Approaching writing an informative report as a process

1. Selecting a topic that interests you The major challenge in writing informative reports is engaging readers' interest. Selecting a topic that interests you makes it more likely that your report will interest your readers.

Connect what you are learning in one course with a topic you are studying in another course or with your personal experience. For example, student John Terrell, a political science major, aspired to a

KNOW THE SITUATION

Informative Reports

Purpose: To inform

Audience: Classmates and instructor, representing the general public

Stance: Reasonable, informed, objective

Genre: Informative report

Medium: Print, computer file, Web page, video, audio, poster

Commonly used: In most disciplines, the workplace, and public life

career in international relations. For his topic, he decided to investigate how one Muslim organization was pursuing human rights for women. *(Terrell's essay begins on p. 102.)*

2. Considering what your readers know about the topic Assume that your readers have some familiarity with the topic but that most of them do not have clear, specific knowledge of it. In his essay on Sisters in Islam, Terrell assumes that his readers probably have seen images of Afghan women in burqas but may not know much more about their lives.

NAVIGATING THROUGH COLLEGE AND BEYOND

Informative Reports

Informative reports are commonly written by members of humanities, social sciences, and natural sciences disciplines, as these examples indicate:

- In a published article, an anthropologist surveys and summarizes a large body of material on indigenous warfare among the Pueblos before the arrival of the Spanish explorers.
- For an encyclopedia of British women writers, a professor of literature briefly recounts the life and work of Eliza Fenwick, a recently rediscovered eighteenth-century author.
- In an academic journal, two biochemists summarize the findings of more than two hundred recently published articles on defense mechanisms in plants.

3. Developing an objective stance A commitment to objectivity gives your report its authority. Present differing views fairly, and do not take sides in a debate.

4. Composing a thesis that summarizes your knowledge of the topic An informative thesis typically reports the results of the writer's study. Before you decide on a thesis, review the information you have collected. Compose a thesis statement that presents the goal of your paper and forecasts its content.

In the paper about Sisters in Islam (SIS), Terrell develops a general thesis that he supports in the body of his report with information about how the group does its work.

Based in Malaysia, SIS has developed three key ways to promote women's rights within the context of the Muslim religion and its holy book, the Qur'an.

Notice how the phrase "three key ways" forecasts the body of Terrell's report. We expect to learn something about each of the three key ways, and the report is structured to give us that information, subtopic by subtopic.

5. Providing context in your introduction Informative reports usually begin with a relatively simple introduction to the topic and a straightforward statement of the thesis. Provide some relevant context or background, but get to your specific topic as quickly as possible, and keep it in the foreground.

6. Organizing your report by classifying and dividing information Develop ideas in an organized way by classifying and dividing information into categories, subtopics, or the stages of a process.

7. Illustrating key ideas with examples Use specific examples to help readers understand your ideas. In his paper on Sisters in Islam, Terrell provides many specific examples, including pertinent quotations from the Qur'an, a discussion of the attempt to establish the Domestic Violence Act, and descriptions of SIS educational programs. Examples make his report interesting as well as educational.

8. Defining specialized terms and spelling out unfamiliar abbreviations Specialized terms (such as foreign words or discipline-specific terminology) will probably not be familiar to most readers. Concisely explain these terms. For example, Terrell provides a synonym and a brief definition of the term *sharia* in the third paragraph of his informative report on Sisters in Islam. *(For more on definition, see Chapter 3, pp. 52–53.)* Unfamiliar abbreviations like SIS (Sisters in Islam) and NGO (nongovernmental organization) are spelled out the first time they are used, with the abbreviation in parentheses.

9. Concluding by answering "So what?" Conclude with an image that suggests the information's value. The conclusion reminds readers of the topic and thesis. It then answers the "So what?" question.

At the end of his report on Sisters in Islam, Terrell answers the "So what?" question by contrasting press stereotypes of the status of women in Islam with the more encouraging view his paper presents.

> But their efforts show that the situation of women in Islamic countries is actually much more complex and encouraging than many recent newspaper images and stories have led us to believe.

**6b
info**

6c Student paper: Informative report

In the informative paper that follows, John Terrell reports what he has learned about a Muslim nongovernmental organization dedicated to promoting women's rights. As you read his report, notice how Terrell provides a context for his topic, cites various sources (using APA documentation style), divides the information into subtopics, and illustrates his ideas with examples, all hallmarks of a clear, carefully developed paper. The annotations in the margin of this paper point out specific features of the informative report.

CONSIDER YOUR SITUATION

Author: John Terrell, a political science major, interested in a career in international relations

Type of writing: Informative report

Purpose: To inform readers about Sisters in Islam (SIS)

Stance: Reasonable, informed, objective

Audience: Classmates and instructor standing in for U.S. general public

Medium: Print, computer file, part of e-portfolio

Terrell writes: After writing this informative paper, I know a great deal more about possibilities for women in Muslim countries, and I am eager to share that information with readers.

Note: For details on the proper formatting of a paper in APA style, see Chapter 28 and the sample paper that begins on page 347.

Following APA style, Terrell includes a separate title page. He does not include an abstract because his instructor did not require one for this assignment.

SAMPLE STUDENT INFORMATIVE REPORT

Sisters Redefining the Divine

John Terrell

Governors State University

---------------------------------- [new page] ----------------------------------

The rights of women in Islamist and majority-Muslim nations have recently become an issue of concern and contention. Images of women in burqas, along with news stories describing forced marriages, public executions by flogging, and virtual house arrest for women without chaperones have led many Americans to assume that Muslim women have no rights and no way to change that situation. But that is not the whole picture. In many parts of the Islamic world, nongovernmental organizations (NGOs) are working hard to make sure that women and their interests have a political voice. Sisters in Islam (SIS) is just such an organization. Based in Malaysia, SIS has developed three key ways to promote women's rights within the context of the Muslim religion and its holy book, the Qur'an.

One way that SIS works to promote women's rights is to show how those rights are rooted in the origins of Islam and the Qur'an. Members note that women fought side by side with the prophet Muhammad in the early struggle to establish Islam's rule and point out that allowing some degree of choice in marriage, permitting divorce, and granting inheritance rights for women were revolutionary concepts when Muslims first introduced them to the world 1,400 years ago (Othman, 1997). Furthermore, they argue that the Qur'an mandates "the principles of equality, justice and freedom" and does not specifically prohibit women from assuming leadership roles or contributing to public service. But they also recognize that the revolutionary possibilities of Islam were curtailed when a small group of men claimed "exclusive control over the interpretation of the Qur'an" (Sisters in Islam, 2007).

According to Coleman (2006), the Qur'an contains almost 80 sections on legal issues, but neither it nor the secondary texts and oral traditions of Islam contain instruction on everyday matters. To make matters even more complex, the Qur'an includes many seemingly contradictory passages. Its statements on polygamy are a prime

Annotations (right margin):

Topic introduced.

6c info

First use of unfamiliar abbreviation spelled out.

Thesis stated.

First way—introduces subtopic.

Source information summarized.

Voices of Muslim women are important to this topic, so are quoted directly.

Source named in signal phrase.

Example given for clarity and interest.

example. One verse in the text says, "Marry those women who are lawful for you, up to two, three, or four, but only if you can treat them equally" (Qur'an 4:3), while a later verse reads, "No matter how you try you will never be able to treat your wives equally" (Qur'an 4:129). In the early years following the death of the prophet Muhammad, legal scholars were called upon to examine issues in need of clarification. They were also encouraged to apply independent thinking and then make non-binding rulings. This practice lasted until the 11th century, at which time Sunni religious scholars consolidated legal judgments into strict schools of thought and placed a ban on independent

Unfamiliar term defined.

interpretation. The result was *sharia,* or Muslim law. Over the next 900 years, this approach to the law changed little. In application, however, sharia does vary according to regional traditions. In Tunisia, for example, taking more than one wife is banned altogether, while India provides few restrictions upon polygamy (Women Living Under Muslim Laws, 2003). Likewise, rules concerning dress and moral codes vary from state to state, with headscarves for women being obligatory in Iran and optional in Egypt.

Second way— introduces subtopic.

National diversity in applying sharia accounts for the second way that SIS promotes women's rights within the framework of Islam: It focuses its work for change on one country, Malaysia. Before 1957, Malaysia was a British colony with a court system divided between the federal and the local levels. Local Islamic leaders were allowed to establish courts to preside over cases of family law, while most other legal matters went to the federal courts.

After Malaysia gained independence, Article 3 of its constitution named Islam as the state religion, although a clause in the same article guaranteed non-Muslims the right to practice their faiths (Mohamad, 1988). The court system, however, remained the same, meaning that the 60% of the population who are Muslim are still subject to local

Source given for data.

Islamic family courts, while the 40% who do not follow Islam are not (U.S. Department of State, 2005).

Malaysia's legal system complicates the work of SIS, as the 1995 campaign to pass a domestic violence act shows. In matters of violence against women, Muslim family law provides little legal recourse. The usual response by Islamic judges is to send the woman home to reconcile with her husband. So in 1995 SIS campaigned to pass the Domestic Violence Act, which aimed to provide basic legal protections for women. After a vigorous lobbying campaign, the law was passed. Yet the response from Malaysia's Islamic religious establishment was to say that the law would only apply to non-Muslims (Othman, 1997). Even though this interpretation of the law has not been successfully reversed, SIS continues to work on family law reform, submitting to the government memoranda and reports on such issues as divorce, guardianship, and polygamy. In 2005, for example, SIS and five other NGOs formed a Joint Action Group on Gender Equality (JAG) and prepared a memorandum requesting a review and withdrawal of parts of a bill that was intended to improve the Islamic Family Law Act of 1984. While praising the new requirement that in cases of contracting polygamous marriages, both the existing and future wives must be present in the court, the JAG (2005) objected to other parts of the bill such as a change in wording that would make it easier for men to practice polygamy; instead of having to show that the new marriage was both "just and necessary," the men would only have to show that it was "just or necessary."

Although advocating for changes in the law is certainly important, SIS has developed another key way of promoting women's rights: public research-backed education. Using surveys and interviews, the group began a pilot research project in 2004 on the impact of polygamy on the family institution; that research project has recently gone national. As its website documents, SIS also sponsors numerous public lectures and forums on such issues as Islam and the political participation of women, the challenges of modernity, the use of fatwa, and the emergence of genetic engineering. There

6c info

Objective stance.

Example given for clarity and interest.

Third way—introduces subtopic.

Examples given for clarity and interest.

are also seminars and workshops for specific groups such as single parents, study sessions with visiting writers, and a rich array of printed material, including newspaper columns that answer women's questions as well as pamphlets on such concerns as family planning, Qur'an interpretation, and domestic violence. Clearly SIS takes a very public approach to reform, an approach that Zainah Anwar (2004), the executive director, contends is necessary to ensure that Islam does not "remain the exclusive preserve of the *ulama* [traditionally trained religious scholars]" (para. 2).

Quotation integrated into writer's sentence.

Instead of waiting patiently for Islamic scholars and judges to work issues out in closed sessions, SIS has developed an activist approach to reform. It is not surprising, therefore, that its key ways of effecting change sometimes get as much criticism from conservative Islamists as the proposed changes themselves do (Anwar, 2004). It remains to be seen whether SIS, along with other NGOs working for human rights in Muslim countries, will succeed in moderating what they see as harmful expressions of their faith. Their efforts show, however, that the situation of women in Islamic countries is actually much more complex and encouraging than many recent newspaper images and stories have led us to believe.

Interpre-tation provided without biased opinion.

Point and purpose restated in conclusion.

---------------------------------- [new page] ----------------------------------

References list follows APA style and begins on a new page.

References

Anwar, Z. (2004, September–October). Sisters in Islam: A voice for everyone. *Fellowship Magazine, 70*(5). Retrieved from http://www .forusa.org/fellowship

Coleman, I. (2006, January–February). Women, Islam, and the new Iraq. *Foreign Affairs, 85*(1). Retrieved from http://www .foreignaffairs.org

Joint Action Group on Gender Equality. (2005, December). *Memorandum to Ahli Dewan Negara to review the Islamic Family Law (Federal Territories) (Amendment) Bill 2005.* Retrieved from Sisters in Islam website: http://www.sistersinislam.org.my/memo /08122005.htm

Mohamad, M. (1988). *Islam, the secular state, and Muslim women in Malaysia.* Retrieved from Women Living Under Muslim Laws website: http://www.wluml.org/english/pubsfulltxt .shtml?cmd[87]=i-87-2615

Othman, N. (1997). Implementing women's human rights in Malaysia. *Human Rights Dialogue, 1*(9). Retrieved from http://www.cceia.org /resources/publications/dialogue/1_09 /articles/567.html

Sisters in Islam. (2007). *Mission.* Retrieved from http://www .sistersinislam.org.my/mission.htm

U.S. Department of State, Bureau of Democracy, Human Rights, and Labor. (2005). *Malaysia: International religious freedom report 2005.* Retrieved from http://www.state.gov/g/drl/rls /irf/2005/51518.htm

Women Living Under Muslim Laws. (2003). *Knowing our rights: Women, family, laws, and customs in the Muslim world.* Retrieved from http://www.wluml.org/english/pubsfulltxt .shtml?cmd[87]=i-87-16766

7a
lit

7 Interpretive Analyses and Writing about Literature

Interpretation means working to understand a written document, literary work, cultural artifact, social situation, or natural event and then explaining what you understand in a meaningful and convincing way.

7a Understanding the assignment

When an assignment asks you to compare, explain, analyze, or discuss something, you are expected to study that subject closely. An **interpretive analysis** moves beyond simple description and examines or compares particular items for a reason: to enhance your readers' understanding of people's conditions, actions, beliefs, or desires.

7b Approaching writing an interpretive analysis as a process

Writing an interpretive analysis typically begins with critical reading.

1. Discovering an aspect of the subject that is meaningful to you   Think about your own feelings and experiences while you read, listen, or observe. Connecting your own thoughts and experiences to what you are studying can help you develop fresh interpretations.

KNOW THE SITUATION

Interpretive Analyses

Purpose: To enhance understanding
Audience: Classmates and instructor, representing the general public
Stance: Thoughtful, inquisitive, open minded
Genres: Review, critique, blog
Medium: Print, computer file, Web page, video, audio
Commonly used: In the arts, humanities, and many other disciplines

2. Developing a thoughtful stance   Think of yourself as an explorer. Be thoughtful, inquisitive, and open minded as you discover possible meanings. When you write your analysis, invite your readers to join you on an intellectual journey, saying, in effect, "Come, think this through with me."

3. Using an intellectual framework   To interpret your subject effectively, use a relevant perspective or intellectual framework. For example, the elements of a work of fiction, such as plot, character, and setting, are often used to analyze stories.

   In the student essay that begins on page 115, McKenna Doherty develops a thesis about the poem "Testimonial," reprinted in Section 7c. Attempting to discover the poem's theme, Doherty bases her analysis on her knowledge of other poems by Rita Dove. Doherty focuses on how four poetic devices give the theme its emotional impact.

No matter what framework you use, analysis often entails taking your subject apart, figuring out how the parts make up a cohesive whole, and then putting it all back together. Because the goal of analysis is to create a meaningful interpretation, treat the whole as more than the sum of its parts. Determining meaning is a complex problem with multiple solutions.

7b
lit

NAVIGATING THROUGH COLLEGE AND BEYOND

Interpretive Analyses

You can find interpretive analyses like the following in professional journals like *PMLA (Publications of the Modern Language Association)* as well as popular publications like the *New Yorker* and the *Atlantic Monthly*. For example, a cultural critic might contrast the way AIDS and cancer are talked about, imagined, and therefore treated, or a musicologist might compare the revised endings of two pieces by Beethoven to figure out what makes a work complete.

Students are often called on to write interpretive analyses such as the following:

- A student in an English course analyzes the poetic techniques in Rita Dove's "Testimonial."
- A student majoring in music outlines the emotional implications of the tempo and harmonic progression in Schubert's *Der Atlas*.
- A student in an economics course demonstrates that, according to an econometric model of nine variables, deregulation has not decreased the level of airline safety.

4. Listing, comparing, questioning, and classifying to discover your thesis   To figure out your thesis, it is often useful to explore separate features of your subject. If you are analyzing literature, you might consider the plot, the characters, the setting, and the tone before deciding to focus your thesis on one character's personality.

Try one or more of the following strategies:

- Take notes about what you see or read, and if it helps, write a summary.
- Ask yourself questions about the subject you are analyzing, and write down any interesting answers. Imagine what kinds of questions your instructor or classmates might ask about the artifact, document, or performance you are considering. In

answering these questions, try to figure out the thesis you will present and support.

■ Name the class of things to which the item you are analyzing belongs (for example, memoirs), and then identify important features of that class (for example, scene, point of view, friends, and turning points).

5. Making your thesis focused and purposeful To make a point about your subject, focus on one or two key questions. Resist the temptation to describe everything you see. Consider this example of a focused, purposeful thesis for an interpretive analysis of Rita Dove's poem, "Testimonial."

QUESTIONS FOR ANALYZING LITERATURE

Fiction

Plot and Structure
What events take place over the course of the work? What did you think and feel at different places? How do the parts of the work relate to one another?

Characters
What and how are the relationships among the people portrayed? How do they change? What does dialogue reveal about their motivations?

Setting
What is the significance of the time and place? What associations does the writer make with the location?

Point of View
Is there a first-person narrator ("I"), or is the story told by a third-person narrator who reveals what one, all, or none of the characters is thinking?

Tone
Is the work's tone stern or playful, melancholy, or something else?

Language
Does the work conjure images that appeal to the senses? Does it use **simile** to compare two things directly using *like* or *as (his heart is sealed tight like a freezer door)?* Does it use **metaphor** to link two things implicitly *(his ice-hard heart)?* What feelings or ideas do individual words suggest?

Theme
What is at issue in the work? What statement is the author making about the issue?

QUESTIONS FOR ANALYZING LITERATURE
(continued)

Poetry

Speaker and Tone
Who is speaking? Is it a parent, a lover, an adult or a child, a man or a woman? What is the speaker's tone—is it stern or playful, melancholy or elated, nostalgic or hopeful?

7b
lit

Connotations
What feelings or ideas do individual words in the poem connote? Although both *trudge* and *saunter* mean "walk slowly," their connotations (associative meanings) are very different.

Imagery
Does the poem evoke images that appeal to any of your senses—for example, the shocking feeling of a cold cloth on feverish skin or the sharp smell of a gas station? How do the images shape the mood of the poem? What ideas do they suggest?

Figurative Language
Does the poem use **simile** to directly compare two things using *like* or *as?* Does it use **metaphor** to implicitly link one thing to another? How does the comparison enhance meaning?

Sound, Rhythm, and Meter
What vowel and consonant sounds recur through the poem? Do the lines of the poem resemble the rhythms of ordinary speech, or do they have a more musical quality? Consider how the sounds of the poem create an effect.

Structure
Notice how the poem is organized into parts or stanzas, considering spacing, punctuation, capitalization, and rhyme schemes. How do the parts relate to one another?

Theme
What is the subject of the poem? What does the poet's choice of language and imagery suggest about his or her attitude toward that subject?

Although the poem seems ambiguous on first reading, repeated readings reveal many common and cleverly used poetic techniques that are employed to express a common literary theme: the difference between adult knowledge and childhood innocence.

6. Introducing the general issue, a clear thesis or question, and relevant context In interpretive analyses, it often takes more than one paragraph to do what an introduction needs to do:

- Identify the general issue, concept, or problem at stake. You can also present the intellectual framework that you are applying.
- Provide relevant background information.
- Name the specific item or items you will focus on.
- State the thesis or pose the main question(s) your analysis will address.

You need not do these things in the order listed. Sometimes it is a good idea to introduce the specific focus of your analysis before presenting either the issue or the background information. Even though you may begin with a provocative statement or a stimulating example, make sure that your introduction does the four things in the preceding list.

NAVIGATING THROUGH COLLEGE AND BEYOND

Ideas and Practices for Writing in the Humanities

- **Base your analysis on the work itself.** Works of art affect each of us differently, and any interpretation has a subjective element. Interpreting art within the context of differing critical theories will lead to differing interpretations. But not all interpretations are equally valid. Your reading of the work needs to be grounded in details from the work itself.
- **Consider how the concepts you are learning in your course apply to the work you are analyzing.** If your course focuses on the formal elements of art, for example, you might look at how those elements function in the painting you have chosen. If your course focuses on the social context of a work, you might look at how the poem or story shares or subverts the belief system and worldview that was common in its time.
- **Use the present tense when writing about the work and the past tense when writing about its history.** Use the present tense to talk about the events that happen within a work: "In Aristophanes' plays, characters frequently *step* out of the scene and *address* the audience directly." Use the past tense, however, to relate historical information about the work or creator: "Kant *wrote* about science, history, criminal justice, and politics as well as philosophical ideas."

7. Planning your analysis so that each point supports your thesis   Organize your points to answer the question you pose or to support the thesis you present. Readers must be able to follow your train of thought and see how each point is related to your thesis.

As you guide readers through your analysis, you will integrate source material, including important quotations, as McKenna Doherty does in her analysis of Rita Dove's "Testimonial" on p. 115. When you are writing about a painting or photograph, your pointed description of visual elements will enhance effective communication.

7c
lit

8. Concluding by answering the "So what?" question   Anticipate the "So what?" question and set up an interesting context for your interpretation. Unless you relate your specific thesis to some more general issue, idea, or problem, your interpretive analysis may seem pointless to readers.

7c   Student paper: Interpretive analysis

Although literary analysis can never tell us exactly what a poem is saying, it can help us think more deeply about possible meanings.

First read the complete poem without stopping, and then note your initial thoughts and feelings. Reread the poem several times, paying close attention to the rhythms of the lines (reading aloud helps) and the poet's choice of words. Think about how the poem develops. Do the last lines represent a shift from or fulfillment of the poem's opening? Look for connections among the poem's details, and think about their significance. The questions in the box on page 111 may help guide your analysis.

Use the insights you gain from your close reading to develop a working thesis about the poem. In the student essay that begins on page 115, McKenna Doherty develops a thesis about the poem "Testimonial," reprinted below. Doherty focuses on how four poetic devices give the theme its emotional impact.

Testimonial

RITA DOVE

Back when the earth was new
and heaven just a whisper,
back when the names of things
hadn't had time to stick;

> back when the smallest breezes   5
> melted summer into autumn,
> when all the poplars quivered
> sweetly in rank and file . . .
>
> the world called, and I answered.
> Each glance ignited to a gaze.   10
> I caught my breath and called that life,
> swooned between spoonfuls of lemon sorbet.
>
> I was pirouette and flourish,
> I was filigree and flame.
> How could I count my blessings   15
> when I didn't know their names?
>
> Back when everything was still to come,
> luck leaked out everywhere.
> I gave my promise to the world,
> and the world followed me here.   20

CONSIDER YOUR SITUATION

Author: McKenna Doherty

Type of writing: Literary analysis

Purpose: To analyze a poem and illuminate its themes

Stance: Reasonable, appreciative, clarifying

Audience: Classmates and instructor representing a general public interested in understanding poetry

Medium: Print, computer file, part of e-portfolio

Doherty writes: Writing an analysis of Rita Dove's poem "Testimonial," has helped me understand the theme of adult knowledge contrasted with childhood innocence. I also have a better understanding of the techniques of poetry and how they work to express ideas and emotions.

Note: For details on the proper formatting of a paper in MLA style, see Chapter 24 and the sample paper that begins on page 306.

SAMPLE STUDENT ANALYSIS OF A POEM

Rita Dove's "Testimonial": The Music of Childhood

Rita Dove rarely uses obvious, rigid rhyme schemes or strict metrical patterns in her poetry, and her subtle use of language often obscures both the subject and themes of her poetry. However, careful analysis of her work is rewarding, as Dove's poems are dense with ideas and figurative language. Her poem "Testimonial" is a good example of this complexity. Although the poem seems ambiguous on first reading, repeated readings reveal many common and cleverly used poetic techniques that are employed to express a common literary theme: the difference between adult knowledge and childhood innocence.

> Thesis of the paper identified.

The first two lines refer to a time when "the earth was new / and heaven just a whisper." At first, these lines appear to refer to the biblical origins of earth and heaven; however, the title of the poem invites us to take the poem as a personal account of the speaker's experience. The time when "the earth was new" could refer to the speaker's youth. Youth is also the time of life when heaven is "just a whisper," since matters of death and religion are not present in a child's awareness. Thus, Dove's opening lines actually put the reader in the clear, familiar context of childhood.

> Examples provided to illustrate theme.

The lines that follow support the idea that the poem refers to youth. Dove describes the time period of the poem as "when the names of things / hadn't had time to stick" (lines 3–4). Children often forget the names of things and are constantly asking their parents, "What is this? What is that?" The names of objects do not "stick" in their minds. The second stanza, describing a scene of trees and breezes, seems childlike in its sensitivity to nature, particularly to the change of seasons. The trees swaying "sweetly in rank and file" (8) suggest an innocent, simplistic worldview, in which everything, even the random movement of trees in the wind, occurs in an orderly, nonthreatening fashion.

> More examples given and interpreted.

7c
lit

Writer presents four poetic techniques, which she explains in the following paragraphs.

Notice that Dove does not state "when I was a child" at the beginning of the poem. Instead, she uses poetic language—alliteration, rhyme, uncommon words, and personification—to evoke the experience of childhood. Figurative language may make the poem more difficult to understand on first reading, but it ultimately makes the poem more personally meaningful.

Discussion of first poetic technique: alliteration.

In line 12, "swooned between spoonfuls of lemon sorbet" not only evokes the experience of childhood, a time when ice cream might literally make one swoon, but the alliteration of "swooned," "spoonfuls," and "sorbet" also makes the poem musical. Dove also uses alliteration in lines 12, 14, and 18. This conventional poetic technique is used relatively briefly and not regularly. The alliteration does not call attention to itself—the music is quiet.

Discussion of second poetic technique: rhyme.

"Testimonial" also uses the best-known poetic technique: rhyme. Rhyme is used in many poems—what is unusual about its use in this poem is that, as with alliteration, rhyme appears irregularly. Only a few lines end with rhyming words, and the rhymes are more suggestive than exact: "whisper" and "stick"(2 and 4), "gaze" and "sorbet" (10 and 12), "flame" and "names" (14 and 16), and "everywhere" and "here" (18 and 20). These rhymes, or consonances, stand out because they are isolated and contrast with the other, unrhymed lines.

Discussion of third technique: uncommon words.

Dove occasionally uses words that children would probably not know, such as "swooned" (12), "sorbet" (12), "pirouette" (13), "flourish" (13), and "filigree" (14). These words suggest the central theme, which is underscored in the final question of the stanza when the narrator of the poem asks, "How could I count my blessings / when I didn't know their names?" The adult words emphasize the contrast between the speaker's past innocence and present knowledge.

Discussion of fourth poetic technique: personification.

The poem ends with the mysterious lines, "I gave my promise to the world / and the world followed me here" (19–20). The world is personified, given the characteristics of a man or woman capable of accepting a promise and following the speaker. As with the opening lines, these final lines are confusing if they are taken literally, but the lines become clearer when one considers the perspective of the speaker. It is as if the speaker has taken a journey from childhood to adulthood. Just as the speaker has changed during the course of this journey, so too has the world changed. The childhood impressions of the world that make up the poem—the sorbet, the trees swaying in the breeze—do not last into adulthood. The speaker becomes a different person, an adult, and the world also becomes something else. It has "followed" the speaker into adulthood; it has not remained static and unchanging.

> Analysis of poem con-cluded with interpretation of entire poem.

8
arg

In "Testimonial," Dove presents a vision of childhood so beautifully, so musically, that we can experience it with her, if only for the space of a few lines.

> Paper concluded briefly, neatly.

-------------------------------------- [new page] ----------------------------------

Work Cited

Dove, Rita. "Testimonial." *Literature: Approaches to Fiction, Poetry, and Drama.* Ed. Robert DiYanni. New York: McGraw-Hill, 2004. 738. Print.

> Works-cited list follows MLA style and begins on a new page.

8 Arguments

In the college classroom and in countless situations outside the classroom, an **argument** makes a reasoned assertion about a debatable issue. In this chapter, we look at how to evaluate arguments presented by others and how to construct arguments on important issues.

8a Understanding the assignment

In college, opinions based on personal feelings have less weight than reasoned positions expressed as written arguments. When you write an argument, your purpose is not to win but to state and support your position on an issue. Written arguments appear in various forms, including critiques, reviews, and proposals:

- **Critiques:** Critiques address the question, "What is true?" A critique fairly summarizes someone's position before either refuting or defending it. *Refutations* expose the reasoning as inadequate or present evidence that contradicts the position. *Defenses* clarify the author's key terms and reasoning, present new arguments to support the position, and show that criticisms are unreasonable or unconvincing.

- **Reviews:** Reviews address the question, "What is good?" In a review, the writer evaluates an event, artifact, practice, or institution, judging by reasonable principles and criteria. Diane Chen's consideration of a photograph from an exhibit of Sebastião Salgado's work in Chapter 4 *(pp. 83–86)* can be seen as an example of this genre.

- **Proposals, or policy papers:** Proposals, sometimes called policy papers, address the question, "What should be done?" They are designed to cause change in the world. Readers are encouraged to see a situation in a specific way and to take action.

NAVIGATING THROUGH COLLEGE AND BEYOND

Arguments

Arguments are central to American democracy and its institutions of higher learning because they help create common ground. Both outside and inside the academy, reason and arguments such as the following are welcome:

- The board of a national dietetic association publishes a position statement identifying obesity as a growing health problem that dieticians should be involved in preventing and treating.
- An art critic praises a museum's special exhibition of modern American paintings for its diversity and thematic coherence.
- A sociologist proposes four policies to improve the prospects of people living in poverty in rural and suburban areas.

8b Learning how to evaluate verbal and visual arguments

Critical thinkers never simply gather information. They inquire about what they see, hear, and read, evaluating a text's argument to identify strengths and weaknesses.

1. Recognizing an argument An **argument** means a path of reasoning aimed at persuading people to accept or reject an assertion. The assertion must be arguable: it must be on an issue about which reasonable people can disagree. For example, the assertion that women should be allowed to try out for all college sports teams is arguable.

2. Analyzing and evaluating an argument Three common ways to analyze verbal and visual arguments are (1) to concentrate on the type of reasoning the writer is using; (2) to question the logical relation of a writer's claims, grounds, and warrants, using the Toulmin method; and (3) to examine an argument's appeal to its audience.

Types of reasoning When writers use **inductive reasoning** to make an argument, they do not prove that the argument is true; instead, they convince reasonable people that it is probable by presenting evidence (facts and statistics, anecdotes, and expert opinion). When writers use **deductive reasoning,** they are making the claim that a conclusion follows necessarily from a set of assertions, or premises—in other words, that if the premises are true, the conclusion must be true.

For example, a journalism student writing for the school newspaper might make the following assertion.

> As Sunday's game shows, the Philadelphia Eagles are on their way to the playoffs.

Reasoning inductively, the student presents a number of facts—her evidence—that support her claim but do not prove it conclusively.

FACT **1**   With three games remaining, the Eagles have a two-game lead over the second-place New York Giants.

FACT **2**   The Eagles' final three opponents have a combined record of fifteen wins and twenty-four losses.

FACT **3**   The Giants lost their first-string quarterback to a season-ending injury last week.

FACT **4**   The Eagles will play two of the last three games at home, where they are undefeated.

A reader would evaluate this student's argument by judging the quality of her evidence, using the criteria listed in the "Navigating through College and Beyond" box.

Inductive reasoning is a feature of the **scientific method.** Scientists gather data from experiments, surveys, and careful observations to formulate hypotheses—arguments that explain the data. Then they test their hypotheses by collecting additional information.

NAVIGATING THROUGH COLLEGE AND BEYOND

Assessing Evidence in an Inductive Argument

- **Is it accurate?** Make sure that any facts presented as evidence are correct and not taken out of context.
- **Is it relevant?** Check to see if the evidence is clearly connected to the point being made.
- **Is it representative?** Make sure that the writer's conclusion is supported by evidence gathered from a sample that accurately reflects the larger population (for example, it has the same proportion of men and women, older and younger people, and so on). If the writer is using an example, make sure that the example is typical and not a unique situation.
- **Is it sufficient?** Evaluate whether there is enough evidence to satisfy questioning readers.

Now suppose the journalism student is using deductive reasoning in an article about great baseball teams; in that case, the truth of her conclusion will depend on the truth of her premises:

PREMISE   Any baseball team that wins the World Series more than twenty-five times in a hundred years is one of the greatest teams in history.

PREMISE   The New York Yankees have won the World Series more than twenty-five times in the past hundred years.

CONCLUSION   The New York Yankees are one of the greatest baseball teams in history.

This is a deductive argument: if its premises are true, its conclusion must be true. To challenge the argument, a reader has to evaluate the premises. Do you think, for example, that the number of

World Series wins is a proper measure of a team's greatness? If not, then you could claim that the first premise is false and does not support the conclusion.

The Toulmin method Philosopher Stephen Toulmin's analysis of arguments is based on claims (assertions about a topic), grounds (reasons and evidence), and warrants (assumptions or principles that link the grounds to the claims).

Consider the following sentence from an argument by a student.

8b
arg

> The death penalty should be abolished because if it is not abolished innocent people could be executed.

This example, like all logical arguments, has three facets:

CLAIM	The death penalty should be abolished.
GROUNDS	Innocent people could be executed. (related stories and statistics).
WARRANT	It is not possible to be completely sure of a person's guilt.

- **The argument makes a claim.** A **claim** is the same thing as a point or a thesis: it is an assertion about a topic. A strong claim responds to an issue of real interest to an audience in clear, precise terms. It also allows for some uncertainty by including qualifying words such as *might* or *possibly*. A weak claim is merely a statement of fact or a statement that few would argue with. Personal feelings are not debatable and thus are not an appropriate claim for an argument:

WEAK CLAIMS	The death penalty is highly controversial. The death penalty makes me sick.

- **The argument presents grounds for the claim.** Here, **grounds** consist of the reasons and evidence (facts and statistics, anecdotes, and expert opinion) that support the claim. A strong argument relies on evidence that is varied, relevant to the claim, and sufficient to support the claim. As grounds for the claim in the example, the student would present anecdotes and statistics related to innocent people being executed. The following box should help you assess the evidence supporting a claim.

- **The argument depends on assumptions that link the grounds to the claim.** When you analyze an argument, be aware of the unstated assumptions, or **warrants,** that underlie both the claim and the grounds that support it. The warrants underlying the example argument against the death penalty include the idea that it is not possible to be completely sure of a person's guilt.

As you read the writings of others and as you write yourself, look for unstated assumptions. What does the reader have to assume—take for granted—to accept the evidence in support of the claim? In particular, hidden assumptions sometimes show **bias**—positive or negative inclinations that can manipulate unwary readers.

TYPES OF EVIDENCE FOR CLAIMS

- **Facts and statistics:** Facts and statistics can be convincing support for a claim. Be aware, however, that people on different sides of an issue can interpret the same facts and statistics differently or can cite different facts and statistics to support their point.
- **Anecdotes:** An anecdote is a brief story used as an illustration to support a claim. Stories appeal to the emotions as well as to the intellect and can be very effective in making an argument. Be especially careful to check anecdotes for logical fallacies *(see pp. 123–24)*.
- **Expert opinion:** The views of authorities in a given field can also be powerful support for a claim. Check that the expert cited has proper credentials to comment on the issue.

Analyzing appeals   Arguments support claims by way of three types of appeals to readers, categorized by the Greek words **logos** (logic), **pathos** (emotions), and **ethos** (character):

- Logical appeals offer facts, including statistics, as well as reasoning, such as the inductive and deductive arguments on pages 119–20.
- Emotional appeals engage an audience's feelings and invoke beliefs that the author and audience share.
- Ethical appeals present authors as fair, reasonable, and trustworthy, backed up with the testimony of experts

Most arguments draw on all three appeals. A proposal for more nutritious school lunches might cite statistics about childhood obesity (a logical appeal). The argument might address the audience's emotions by describing overweight children feasting on junk food available in the cafeteria (an emotional appeal). It might quote a doctor explaining that healthful food aids concentration (a logical appeal) and that all children deserve to have nutritious food available at school (an ethical appeal). When writing an argument, tailor the type and content of appeals to the specific audience you are addressing. For example, school administrators, charged with making decisions about cafeteria food, might be persuaded by statistics demonstrating the relationship of the cost of food to its nutritional value (logical appeal) and the impact of good nutrition on learning.

8b arg

3. Recognizing common logical fallacies In their enthusiasm to make a point, writers sometimes commit errors called fallacies, or mistakes in logic. Use the box below to help you identify fallacies when you read and avoid them when you write.

COMMON LOGICAL FALLACIES

- **Non sequitur:** A conclusion that does not logically follow from the evidence presented or one that is based on irrelevant evidence: "Students who default on their student loans have no sense of responsibility." [*Students who default on loans could be faced with high medical bills or prolonged unemployment.*]
- **False cause or post hoc:** An argument that falsely assumes that because one thing happens after another, the first event was a cause of the second event: "I drank green tea, and my headache went away: therefore, green tea makes headaches go away." [*How do we know that the headache didn't go away for another reason?*]
- **Self-contradiction:** An argument that contradicts itself: "No absolute statement can be true." [*The statement itself is an absolute.*]
- **False analogy:** A comparison in which a surface similarity masks a significant difference: "Governments and businesses both work within a budget to accomplish their goals. Just as business must focus on the bottom line, so should government." [*Is the goal of government to make a profit? Does government have different goals?*]
- **Red herring:** An argument that diverts attention from the true issue by concentrating on an irrelevant one: "Hemingway's book *Death in the Afternoon* is not successful because it glorifies the brutal sport of bullfighting." [*Why can't a book about a brutal sport be successful? The statement is irrelevant.*]
- **Begging the question:** A form of circular reasoning that assumes the truth of a questionable opinion: "The president's poor relationship with the military has weakened the armed forces." [*Does the president really have a poor relationship with the military?*]

(continued on next page)

COMMON LOGICAL FALLACIES (continued)

- **Hasty generalization:** A conclusion based on inadequate evidence: "It took me over an hour to find a parking spot downtown. Therefore, the city should build a new parking garage." [*Is this evidence enough to prove this very broad conclusion?*]
- **Sweeping generalization:** An overly broad statement made in absolute terms. When made about a group of people, a sweeping generalization is a **stereotype:** "College students are carefree." [*What about students who work to put themselves through school?*]
- **Bandwagon:** An argument that depends on going along with the crowd, on the false assumption that truth can be determined by a popularity contest: "Given the sales of that book, its claims must be true." [*Sales volume does not indicate the truth of the claim. How do we know that a popular book presents accurate information?*]
- **Ad hominem:** A personal attack on someone who disagrees with you rather than on the person's argument: "The district attorney is a lazy political hack, so naturally she opposes streamlining the court system." [*Even if the district attorney usually supports her party's position, does that make her wrong about this issue?*]
- **Guilt by association:** Discrediting a person because of problems with that person's associates, friends, or family: "Smith's friend has been convicted of fraud, so Smith cannot be trusted." [*Is Smith responsible for his friend's actions?*]
- **False authority:** Presenting the testimony of an unqualified person to support a claim: "As the actor who plays Dr. Fine on *The Emergency Room,* I recommend this weight-loss drug because . . ." [*Is an actor qualified to judge the benefit and dangers of a diet drug?*]
- **Circular reasoning:** An argument that restates the point rather than supporting it with reasonable evidence: "The wealthy should pay more taxes because taxes should be higher for people with higher incomes." [*Why should wealthy people pay more taxes? The rest of the statement doesn't answer this question; it just restates the position.*]
- **Either/or fallacy:** The idea that a complicated issue can be resolved by resorting to one of only two options when in reality there are additional choices: "Either the state legislature will raise taxes or our state's economy will falter." [*Are there really only two possibilities?*]

Exercise 8.1 Recognizing warrants

For each of the following claims, identify one or more underlying warrants (assumptions).

1. College students should have fewer required courses and more electives because they should have more control over their own education.
2. The drinking age should be lowered to eighteen because that is the legal age for voting and serving in the military.
3. The United States should intervene in areas of the world where humanitarian crises exist because we are the strongest country in the world and should set an example for other nations.
4. To reduce the rate of global warming, the government should offer tax credits to consumers who buy hybrid cars.
5. The new sports arena should not be built because it will reduce the amount of parkland in the community.

8b arg

5. Reading visual arguments Like written arguments, visual arguments support claims with reasons and evidence, rely on assumptions, and may contain fallacies. They make logical appeals, such as a graph of experimental data; emotional appeals, such as a photograph of a hungry child; and ethical appeals, such as a corporate logo. Like written works, visual arguments are created by an author to achieve a purpose and to address an audience within a given context.

Recall that Toulmin's system analyzes arguments based on the claims they make, the grounds (evidence and reasons) for those claims, and the warrants (underlying assumptions) that connect the grounds with the claims. *(See the explanation of Toulmin analysis on pp. 121–22.)* While these elements function similarly in verbal and visual arguments, unstated assumptions play a larger role in visual arguments because we are not used to "reading" visuals and interpreting the implicitly stated claims and grounds.

For example, consider a photograph of a politician with her family members. The image makes a claim (she is a good public servant) and implicitly offers grounds (because she cares for her family). The warrant is that a person's family life indicates how she will perform in office. This assumption may be false.

Advertisements combine text and images to promote a product or message to an audience in a social context. They use the resources of visual design: type of image, position, color, light and shadows, fonts, and white space. *(See the questions on previewing a visual in Chapter 1, pp. 18–19, and the discussion of design in Chapter 5, pp. 87–94.)* The public-service ad in Figure 8.1 was developed by the nonprofit advocacy group Adbusters.

The ad's text and format evoke a popular series of ads for a brand of vodka. Its uncluttered design focuses the viewer's attention on the

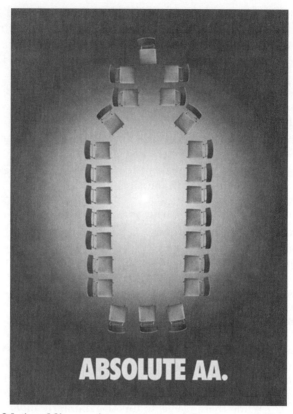

FIGURE 8.1 A public-service argument: Adbusters public-service advertisement.

shape of a bottle, the outline of which consists of chairs. The text at the bottom refers to AA (Alcoholics Anonymous). By association, the text and images in this public-service ad remind readers that liquor consumption can lead to alcoholism (and then to AA). In contrast with those it spoofs, this ad evokes an unexpected threat, creating a powerful emotional appeal.

What claims do you think this ad makes? One might be "alcohol is dangerous." The evidence is supplied by the reader's prior knowledge about alcoholism. The argument's assumptions include the viewer's familiarity with both the original liquor campaign and the initials "AA" for Alcoholics Anonymous.

Fallacies frequently occur in visual arguments. For example, celebrity endorsements of products rely on our respect for the celebrity's character. However, a photo of an athlete driving a particular type of

CHECKLIST

Reading Visual Arguments Critically

Review the questions for previewing a visual from Chapter 1, pages 18–19, and add the following:

☐ What can you tell about the visual's creator or sponsor?

☐ What seems to be the visual's purpose? Does it promote a product or message?

☐ What features of the visual suggest the intended audience? How?

☐ How do aspects of design such as the size and position of the elements, the colors, and shapes of images affect the visual's message?

☐ What is the effect of accompanying text, audio, or video?

car demonstrates false authority, unless the athlete also happens to be an expert on cars. *(See p. 124.)*

8c Approaching writing your own argument as a process

Selecting a topic that you care about will give you the energy to think matters through and make cogent arguments. Of course, you will have to go beyond your personal emotions to make the most convincing

TEXTCONNEX

Blogs

Weblogs, or blogs for short—the continually updated sites linking an author's comments to other sites on the Web—frequently function as vehicles for public debate and discussion. For example, online editions of many newspapers include blogs that invite readers to comment on the news of the day and to present dissenting opinions. While online debate can be freewheeling, it's important to search for common ground with your readers. *(For more on blogs, see Chapter 11, pp. 167–68.)*

case. You will also have to empathize with potential readers who may disagree with you about a subject that is important to you.

1. Figuring out what is at issue

Before you can take a position on a topic like air pollution or population growth, you must figure out what is at issue. Ask questions about your topic. Do you see indications that all is not as it should be? Have things always been this way, or have they changed for the worse? From what different perspectives— economic, social, political, cultural, medical, geographic—can problems like world food shortages be understood? Do people interested in the topic disagree about what is true, what is good, or what should be done?

Based on your answers to such questions, identify the issues your topic raises, and decide which of these issues you think is most important, interesting, and appropriate to write about.

2. Developing a reasonable stance that negotiates differences

When writing arguments, you want your readers to respect your intelligence and trust your judgment. By influencing readers to trust your character, you build **ethos.** Conducting research on an issue can make you well informed; reading other people's views can enhance your thoughtfulness. Pay attention to the places where you disagree with the opinions of others, but also note what you have in common—topical interests, key questions, or underlying values. *(For more on appeals to your audience, see pp. 122–23.)*

KNOW THE SITUATION: ARGUMENTS

Purpose: To persuade

Audience: Audience members can be close to a writer (for example, classmates) or distant from him or her (for example, citizens of an unfamiliar country), but, in either case, keying in on members of that audience is important because reasons, examples, and stories should speak to them.

Stance: Reasonable

Genres: Arguments appear as stand-alone genres and inside other genres like reviews, critiques, and proposals.

Medium: Print, digital, or networked depending on the audience and the topic. (A proposal for a new bridge might be more compelling in a visual medium, for example.)

Commonly used: In most disciplines, the workplace, and public life

Avoid language that may promote prejudice or fear. Misrepresentations of other people's ideas reduce your ethos, as do personal attacks. Write arguments to expand thinking, your own and that of others. *(See the box on blogs on p. 127.)*

Trying out different perspectives can also help you figure out where you stand on an issue. *(Also see the next section on stating your position.)* Make a list of the arguments for and against a specific position; then compare the lists, and decide where you stand, perhaps on one side or the other or somewhere in between. Does one set of arguments seem stronger than the other? Do you want to change or qualify your initial position?

8c arg

3. Composing a thesis that states your position   A successful argument requires a strong, engaging, arguable thesis. As noted in the section on the Toulmin model of argument, personal feelings and accepted facts cannot serve as an argument's thesis because they are not debatable *(see 8b, pp. 121–22).*

PERSONAL FEELING, NOT A DEBATABLE THESIS

I feel that developing nations should not suffer food shortages.

ACCEPTED FACT, NOT A DEBATABLE THESIS

Food shortages are a growing problem in many developing nations.

DEBATABLE THESIS

Current food shortages in developing nations are in large part caused by climate change and the use of food crops in biofuels.

In proposals, the thesis presents a solution in terms of the writer's definition of the problem. The logic behind a thesis for a proposal can be stated like this.

Given these key variables and their underlying cause, one solution to the problem would be . . .

Because this kind of thesis is both complex and qualified, you will often need more than one sentence to state it clearly. Draw on numerous well-supported arguments to make it credible. Readers finally want to know that the proposed solution will not cause more problems than it solves.

4. Supporting and developing your thesis   A strong, debatable thesis needs to be supported and developed with sound reasoning and carefully documented evidence. You can think of an argument as a dialogue between writer and readers. The writer states a debatable thesis, and one reader wonders, "Why do you believe that?" Another reader wants to know, "But what about this factor?" Anticipate readers' questions, and answer them by presenting reasons that are substantiated with evidence and by refuting opposing views. Define any abstract terms, such as *freedom,* that figure importantly in your arguments. In his proposal for eliminating cyberbullying, Bud Littleton defines cyberbullying and shows how it both compares to bullying and differs from it *(pp. 134–39).*

Usually, a well-developed argument paper includes more than one type of claim and more than one kind of evidence. Employ generalizations based on empirical data or statistics, authoritative reasons based on the opinions of experts, and ethical reasons based on the application of principle. In his argument, Littleton provides data from the Cyberbullying Research Center showing the types and extent of cyberbullying of teens in the Southeast as well as anecdotal evidence on a teen suicide that led to a new law.

As you conduct research, note evidence—facts, examples or anecdotes, and expert testimony—that can support each argument for or against your position. Demonstrate your trustworthiness by properly quoting and documenting the information you have gathered from your sources. Bud Littleton adds credibility to his argument by quoting experts on his topic.

> Heirman and Walrave believe that victims of online abuse often remain quiet in part because they "don't believe that adult intervention can ameliorate their painful situation, especially when the identity of the perpetrator is unknown."

Littleton integrates the quotation seamlessly into his own argument.

Also build your credibility by paying attention to **counterarguments,** substantiated claims that do not support your position. Consider whether a reader could reasonably draw different conclusions from your evidence or disagree with your assumptions. Use one of the following strategies to address potential counterarguments:

- Qualify your thesis in light of the counterargument by including a word such as *most, some, usually,* or *likely:* "Students with credit cards *usually* have trouble with debt" recognizes that some do not.

- Add to the thesis a statement of the conditions for or exceptions to your position: "Businesses *with over five hundred employees* saved money using the new process."

- Choose at least one or two counterarguments, and refute their truth or their importance.

5. Creating an outline that includes a linked set of reasons
Arguments are most effective when they present a chain—a linked set—of reasons. Littleton states his thesis in the introductory paragraph and then demonstrates two types of cyberbullying and ways to combat them. Your outline should include these parts:

- An introduction to the topic and the debatable issue
- A thesis stating your position on the issue
- A point-by-point account of the reasons for your position, including the evidence (facts, examples, authorities) you will use to substantiate each major reason
- A fair presentation and refutation of one or two key counter-arguments to your thesis
- A response to the "So what?" question—why your argument matters

6. Emphasizing your commitment to dialogue in the introduction
To promote dialogue with readers, look for common ground—beliefs, concerns, and values you share with those who disagree with you and those who are undecided. Sometimes called **Rogerian argument** after the psychologist Carl Rogers, the common-ground approach is particularly important in your introduction, where it can build bridges with readers who might otherwise become too defensive or annoyed to read further. Keep the dialogue open throughout your essay by maintaining a reasonable tone and acknowledging opposing views. If possible, return to that common ground at the end of your argument.

7. Concluding by restating your position and emphasizing its importance
After presenting your reasoning in detail, remind readers of your thesis. To encourage readers to appreciate your argument's importance, make the version of your thesis in your conclusion more complex and qualified than in your introduction. Readers may not agree with you, but they should know why the issue and your argument matter.

8. Reexamining your reasoning
After you have completed the first draft of your argument, take time to reexamine your reasoning for errors. Answer the following questions:

- Have you given a sufficient number of reasons to support your thesis, or should you add one or two more?
- Have you made any mistakes in logic? *(See the list of common logical fallacies, pp. 123–24.)*

For MULTILINGUAL WRITERS

Learning about Cultural Differences through Peer Review

In some cultures, writing direct and explicit arguments is discouraged, but not so in the United States. When you share your work with peers raised in the United States, you may learn that the way in which you have expressed certain ideas and values— the vocabulary or the style of presentation you have used—makes it difficult for them to understand and accept the point you are making. Ask your peers to suggest different words and approaches, and then decide if their suggestions would make your ideas more accessible to others.

■ Have you clearly and adequately developed each claim presented in support of your thesis? Is your supporting evidence sufficient? Have you quoted or paraphrased from sources accurately and documented them properly? *(For more on quoting, paraphrasing, and documenting sources, see Chapter 19, pp. 240–58, and Parts 4 and 5.)*

8d Sample Student Argument

In an English course, Bud Littleton did research on cyberbullying and then constructed a policy paper (sometimes called a proposal) to address the question, "What should be done?" In the humanities, as well as in other disciplines, arguments like Bud Littleton's are de-

CONSIDER YOUR SITUATION

Author: Bud Littleton

Type of writing: Argument in the form of a proposal

Purpose: To show (1) that cyberbullying is a new form of bullying and (2) that if it is to be stopped, students, parents, and educators must work together to instill guidelines for online behavior

Stance: Informed and reasonable

Audience: Students, parents, and educators

Medium: This argument is developed in two media: print and slides.

Littleton writes: As I worked on this argument, I was at first dismayed that the wonders of technology have opened up new opportunities for emotional violence. But then I realized the importance of calling on students, parents, and educators to address the issue.

CHECKLIST

Reviewing Your Own and Other Writers' Arguments

First identify what the text is doing well, and find ways to build on that. Then identify parts in the text that are confusing, underdeveloped, or inaccurate, and share ways of addressing those problems:

☐ **What makes the thesis strong and arguable?**

☐ **Is the thesis supported with a sufficient number of reasons, or are more needed?**

☐ **Are the reasons and evidence appropriate for the purpose, audience, and context?**

☐ **Does the argument contain mistakes in logic?** Refer to pages 123–24 to check for logical fallacies.

☐ **How is each reason developed?** Is the reason clear? Where are its key terms defined? Is the supporting evidence sufficient?

☐ **Does the argument quote or paraphrase from sources accurately and document them properly?** *(For more on quoting, paraphrasing, and documenting sources, see Chapter 19, pp. 246–58 and Parts 4 and 5.)*

☐ **Has at least one significant counterargument been addressed?** How have opposing views been treated?

☐ **In what way does each visual support the thesis?** How are the visuals tailored to the audience?

☐ **Are logical, ethical, and emotional appeals used consistently and effectively?**

signed to bring about change. Bud Littleton documents the impact of cyberbullying, evaluates its negative consequences, and then argues that students, parents, and educators must take action.

Note: For details on the proper formatting of a paper in MLA style, see Chapter 24 and the sample paper that begins on page 306.

SAMPLE STUDENT ARGUMENT

Cyberbullying: An Alarming Trend for the Digital Age

In childhood, many of us learned that it was best to stand up to a bully; we were told that a bully would back down if challenged. But in our digital society, standing up to a bully is infinitely more difficult.

Introduces issue of cyber-bullying.

Cyberbullying, defined broadly as the use of electronic means to harm someone else (Trolley and Hanel 33), is an alarming trend in online behavior with significant consequences for its victims. Cyberbullying is destructive to victims because of its immediacy, its circulation, and its permanence: the humiliation is easily inflicted and can continue indefinitely before a wide audience. If this new form of bullying for the digital age is ever to be conquered, students, parents, and educators must work together to instill guidelines for online behavior.

Thesis statement.

Presents definition of cyber-bullying, along with a visual that indicates the extent of the problem.

Cyberbullying is commonly carried out through social networking sites, text messaging, instant messaging, or blogging (Shariff 30) and targets those who are different or isolated (34). Cyberbullying can be done in various ways, but most of the time it involves the posting of hurtful comments or rumors online, as shown in fig. 1. Often cyberbullying is simply a matter of teasing carried too far, but the digital nature of the messages means they cannot be retracted easily. This permanent and potentially uncontrollable content is often disseminated far and wide before the victim can do anything to mitigate its effects.

Establishes the nature of the prob-lem with examples and dem-onstrates its seriousness.

Some common cyberbullying tactics include *flaming* (using angry language in an online "fight"), *harassment* (repeated online messages that insult or offend), *outing* (sharing secrets online, including embarrassing images or information), *trickery* (deliberate deception or tricking someone into sharing secrets widely), *denigration* (malicious spreading of gossip or a rumor), *cyber stalking* (aggressive online behavior that intimidates or threatens a person's safety), and *exclusion* (from online groups, lists, or activities) (Kowalski, Limber, and Agatston 47). For example, a cyberbully might engage in *denigration*

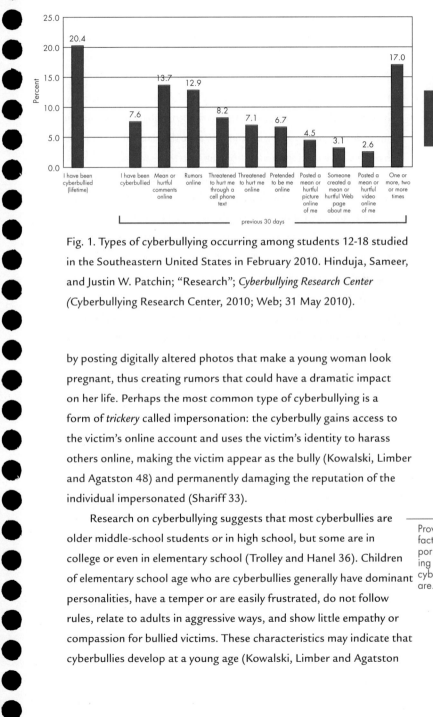

8d
arg

Fig. 1. Types of cyberbullying occurring among students 12-18 studied in the Southeastern United States in February 2010. Hinduja, Sameer, and Justin W. Patchin; "Research"; *Cyberbullying Research Center* (Cyberbullying Research Center, 2010; Web; 31 May 2010).

by posting digitally altered photos that make a young woman look pregnant, thus creating rumors that could have a dramatic impact on her life. Perhaps the most common type of cyberbullying is a form of *trickery* called impersonation: the cyberbully gains access to the victim's online account and uses the victim's identity to harass others online, making the victim appear as the bully (Kowalski, Limber and Agatston 48) and permanently damaging the reputation of the individual impersonated (Shariff 33).

Research on cyberbullying suggests that most cyberbullies are older middle-school students or in high school, but some are in college or even in elementary school (Trolley and Hanel 36). Children of elementary school age who are cyberbullies generally have dominant personalities, have a temper or are easily frustrated, do not follow rules, relate to adults in aggressive ways, and show little empathy or compassion for bullied victims. These characteristics may indicate that cyberbullies develop at a young age (Kowalski, Limber and Agatston

Provides factual support indicating who the cyberbullies are.

58). However, researcher Shaheen Shariff suggests that an imbalance in power between perpetrator and victim—rather than individual characteristics—is the cause of digital abuse within any age group. By relentlessly victimizing the target, the perpetrator gains power; at the same time the victim, who is often randomly chosen, is socially isolated and thus disempowered (Shariff 16). Cyberbullying may be most destructive to younger teens because they lack the maturity to handle such situations and rarely seek help from adults.

Summarizes research on the causes of the problem of cyberbullying.

Cyberbullies may consider their actions to be harmless practical jokes. A student at Ohio State University who was expelled from on-campus housing for repeatedly cyber stalking his former girlfriend, also a resident in the same dormitory, continues the same behavior off campus. "I don't see what the big deal is about pranking somebody on *Facebook*. Everyone knows it's a joke; those pictures were obviously photoshopped" (Warren). However, mounting evidence indicates the serious consequences of cyberbullying. Belgian researchers recently found that victims of cyberbullying were three times as likely as victims of face-to-face bullying to report that they suffer from depression, loneliness, hopelessness, and humiliation (Heirman and Walrave). Although research in this area is relatively new, and the long-term effects of cyberbullying are unknown, scholars believe that cyberbullying creates significant and prolonged anxiety in victims because of the permanence and wide reach of online communication.

Presents quotation from a person engaged in this behavior.

Provides factual support (logical appeal).

At their most severe, incidents of cyberbullying have led victims to take dire action. Researchers at the Cyberbullying Research Center have termed the recent phenomenon of "suicide indirectly or directly influenced by experiences with online aggression" as *cyberbullicide* (Hinduja and Patchin). In 2006, Megan Meier, a 13-year-old Missouri girl, was the victim of an online hoax perpetrated by a friend and the friend's mother; the mother impersonated a 14-year-old boy by using a false profile on a *MySpace* page. Meier was deceived for months into believing she had an online boyfriend. When the "boyfriend" suddenly turned on her, she was so hurt and humiliated that she committed

Provides support by expert opinion (ethical appeal).

suicide (Tresniowski et al. 73-74). The cyberbully in this instance, Lori Drew, was prosecuted in this country's first cyberbullying case. Drew was ultimately convicted of fraud (the conviction was later overturned); her trial brought national attention to the issue. Missouri eventually passed "Megan's Law" making cyberbullying a crime, and federal legislation is now pending in Congress ("Megan's law" 32).

Provides anecdotal support (emotional appeal).

8d arg

While students may not appreciate the potential tragedy of "pranks" leading to tragedy, parents, educators, and other adults are starting to comprehend the dangers. For example, a principal in Charlotte, North Carolina, recently reacted to a *Facebook* "burn" page about some of his students and took decisive action. A burn page is a social networking page designed specifically to spread rumors with immediacy and vast circulation for maximum humiliation. When Barry Bowe, principal of Northwest School of the Arts, became aware of the burn page, he sent a broadcast voicemail to all parents alerting them to the incident and then contacted *Facebook* to get the page taken down (Frazier). More broadly, in 2010 MTV.com launched its "A Thin Line" campaign to raise awareness about teen digital abuse and to help teens recognize and handle it. MTV partnered with the Associated Press to conduct a survey of 14- to 24-year-olds and found that over half had been the victims of digital abuse, one in ten of those a victim of online impersonation ("MTV-AP Digital Abuse Study"). Campaigns such as this one are particularly needed given the scope of the danger to children. A 2008 study reported that one in four Americans between the ages of 11 and 19 had been threatened online (Shariff 45).

Establishes that parents and educators are becoming aware of the problem and the need to take action.

If cyberbullying is ever to be conquered, however, students, parents, and educators must work together to confront this serious problem and establish guidelines for proper online behavior, or "netiquette." The line between appropriate and inappropriate online behavior is indeed thin, and this distinction is further complicated by the trend toward increasing use of technology by younger and younger students. A 2008 study reported that 84 percent of children in the

Restates thesis: solution to the problem of cyberbullying.

United States ages 10 to 14 carried cell phones (Shariff 45). When unsupervised, technology use among young children breeds the digital behaviors of questionable appropriateness that researchers warn us about. Trolley and Hanel caution that, beyond guidelines, young people also need to develop a healthy balance of online and offline activities to change the social nature of cyberbullying: "Prevention, primarily through education and process communication, as well as therapeutic intervention, is essential to achieve this proper use of technology" (82). Families can begin to achieve that cyber balance by placing the computer in a common area and establishing guidelines for behavior when a family member is using the computer or a cell phone.

Some might object that young people will resist sharing information about their use of technology with adults, and there is research to back up this concern. Heirman and Walrave believe that victims of online abuse often remain quiet in part because they "don't believe that adult intervention can ameliorate their painful situation, especially when the identity of the perpetrator is unknown." They also cite several studies that indicate students do not report cyberbullying to parents or teachers for fear their Internet access will be restricted, allowing abuse to go on for longer periods of time unchecked. The stealthy nature of cyberbullying and the reluctance by victims to report it contribute to the accumulation of emotional and psychological damage (Heirman and Walrave). Although these concerns are warranted, the experience of Principal Bowe and others demonstrates that adult involvement can make a difference.

The "Stop, Save, and Share" approach (Trolley and Hanel 79), for example, offers simple tips that families can implement: children should stop and consider consequences before reacting to a cyberbully attack, save the information as proof, and share the information with a trusted adult. With increasing awareness of the impact of cyberbullying on its victims, families and schools can mitigate those effects by paying attention to balancing technology

---

Margin annotations:

Integrates expert testimony to support the argument.

Acknowledges counterargument: young people, and particularly victims of abuse, will resist sharing information with adults about cyberbullying.

Emphasizes common ground ("these concerns are warranted") but provides evidence that adult intervention can work to refute the counterargument.

use with common sense and by preparing children to understand and report incidents of cyberbullying before they result in tragedy.

------------------------------------ [new page] ------------------------------------

Works Cited

Frazier, Eric. "Principal Fuming over *Facebook* 'Burn' Page." *Charlotte Observer*. Charlotte Observer, 31 March 2010. Web. 31 March 2010.

Heirman, Wanness, and Michel Walrave. "Assessing Concerns and Issues about the Mediation of Technology in Cyberbullying." *Cyberpsychology: Journal of Psychosocial Research on Cyberspace 2.2* (2008): n.pag. Web. 31 March 2010.

Hinduja, Sameer, and Justin W. Patchin. "Cyberbullying Research Summary: Cyberbullying and Suicide." *Cyberbullying Research Center*. Cyberbullying Research Center, 2009. Web. 31 May 2010.

Kowalski, Robin M., Susan P. Limber, and Patricia W. Agatston. *Cyber Bullying: Bullying in the Digital Age*. Malden: Blackwell, 2008. Print.

"Megan's Law." Economist 11 July 2009: 32. Print.

"MTV-AP Digital Abuse Study" *A Thin Line*. MTV.com. January 2010. Web. 31 May 2010.

Shariff, Shaheen. *Cyber-Bullying: Issues and Solutions for the School, the Classroom and the Home*. Oxon: Routledge, 2008. Print.

Tresniowski, Alex, Jeff Truesdell, Siobhan Morrissey, and Howard Breuer. "A Cyberbully Convicted." *People* 15 December 2008: 73-74. Print.

Trolley, Barbara C., and Constance Hanel. *Cyber Kids, Cyber Bullying, Cyber Balance*. Thousand Oaks: Corwin, 2010. Print.

Warren, James. Personal Interview. 31 May 2010.

8d arg

List of works cited begins on a new page and is formatted according to MLA style.

9 Other Kinds of Assignments

This chapter helps you to respond to three common writing situations: one requiring a personal essay, another requiring an essay exam, and another requiring a coauthored project.

In your studies—and in your life—you will encounter situations requiring writing from personal experience. Responding efficiently to a question, whether on an essay exam or under deadline on the job, is another important skill. In both classroom and workplace, you will frequently be asked to cooperate with others on a project.

9a Personal essays

The **personal essay** is a literary form. Like a poem, a play, or a story, it should feel meaningful to readers and relevant to their lives. A personal essay should speak in a distinctive voice and be both compelling and memorable.

1. Making connections between your experiences and those of your readers   When you write a personal essay, you are exploring your experiences, clarifying your values, and composing a public self. Since the writing situation involves an audience of strangers who will be more interested in your topic than in you, it is important to make distinctions between the personal and the private. Whether you are writing a personal essay about a tree in autumn, a trip to Senegal, or an athletic event, your purpose is to engage readers in what is meaningful to you—and potentially to them—in these objects and experiences.

TEXTCONNEX

Personal Writing and Social Networking Web Sites

In addition to writing personal essays for class, you may use the Web sites like *Facebook* and your own weblog for personal expression and autobiographical writing. Since these sites are networked, it is important to remember that strangers, including prospective employers, may have access to your profiles and comments.

When we read a personal essay, we expect to learn more than the details of the writer's experience; we expect to see the connections between that experience and our own.

2. Turning your essay into a conversation   Personal essayists usually use the first person (*I* and *we*) to create a sense of open-ended conversation between writer and reader. Your rhetorical stance— whether you appear shy, belligerent, or friendly in this conversation, for example—will be determined by the details you include in your essay as well as the connotations of the words you use. Consider how Meghan Daum represents herself in relation to both computer-literate and computer-phobic readers in the following excerpt from her personal essay "Virtual Love," which appeared in a 1997 issue of the *New Yorker:*

9a

> The kindness pouring forth from my computer screen was bizarrely exhilarating, and I logged off and thought about it for a few hours before writing back to express how flattered and "touched"—this was probably the first time I had ever used that word in earnest—I was by his message.
>
> I am not what most people would call a computer person. I have no interest in chat rooms, news groups, or most Web sites. I derive a palpable thrill from sticking a letter in the United States mail.

Besides Daum's conversational tone, notice the emotional effect of her remark on the word *touched* and her choice of words connoting excitement: *pouring forth, exhilarating,* and *palpable thrill.*

3. Structuring your essay like a story   There are three common ways to narrate events and reflections:

- **Chronological sequence:** uses an order determined by clock time; what happened first is presented first, followed by what happened second, then third, and so on.
- **Emphatic sequence:** uses an order determined by the point you want to make; for emphasis, events and reflections are arranged either from least to most or most to least important.
- **Suspenseful sequence:** uses an order determined by the emotional effect the writer wants the essay to have on readers. To keep readers hanging, the essay may begin in the middle of things with a puzzling event, then flash back or go forward. Some essays may even begin with the end and then flash back to recount how the writer came to that insight.

4. Letting details tell your story

A story takes shape through the details you emphasize, the words you choose, and the characters you create.

Consider, for example, the following passage by Gloria Ladson-Billings.

> Mrs. Harris, my third-grade teacher, was quite a sharp dresser. She wore beautiful high-heeled shoes. Sometimes she switched to flats in the afternoon if her feet got tired, but every morning began with the click, click, click of her high heels as she greeted us up and down the rows. I wanted to dress the way Mrs. Harris did. I didn't want to wear old-lady comforters like Mrs. Benn's, and I certainly didn't want to wear worn-out loafers like those of my first-grade teacher, Miss Schwartz. I wanted to wear beautiful, shiny, high-heeled shoes like Mrs. Harris's. That was the way a teacher should look, I thought.
>
> —GLORIA LADSON-BILLINGS, *The Dreamkeepers: Successful Teachers of African-American Children*

Ladson-Billings uses details to make her idea of a good teacher come alive for the reader. At one level—the literal—the "click, click, click" refers to the sound of Mrs. Harris's shoes. At another level, it represents the glamorous teacher. And at the most figurative level, the "click, click, click" evokes the kind of feminine power that the narrator both longs for and admires.

5. Connecting your experience to a larger issue

To demonstrate the significance of a personal essay to readers, writers usually connect their individual experience to a larger issue. Here, for example, are the closing lines of Daum's essay on "virtual love":

> The world had proved to be too cluttered and too fast for us, too polluted to allow the thing we'd attempted through technology ever to grow on the earth. PFSlider and I had joined the angry and exhausted living. Even if we met on the street, we wouldn't recognize each other, our particular version of intimacy now obscured by the branches and bodies and falling debris that make up the physical world.

Notice how Daum relates the disappointment of her failed Internet romance with "PFSlider" to a larger social issue: the general contrast between cyberspace and material realities. Her point, however, is quite surprising; most people do not think of cyberspace as more "intimate"—or touching—than their everyday, earthly world of "branches and bodies."

9b Essay exams

Spending time in advance thinking about writing essay exams will reduce stress and increase success.

1. Preparing with the course and your instructor in mind

Consider the specific course as your writing context and the course's instructor as your audience (standing in for general readers, of course, since your instructor already knows what you are telling her on the exam):

- What questions or problems did your instructor explicitly or implicitly address?
- What frameworks did your instructor use to analyze topics?
- What key terms did your instructor repeatedly use during lectures and discussions?

2. Understanding your assignment

Essay exams are designed to test your knowledge and understanding, not just your memory. Make up some essay questions that require you to:

- **Explain** what you have learned in a clear, well-organized way. *(See question 1 in the box on page 144.)*
- **Connect** what you know about one topic with what you know about another topic. *(See question 2 in the box.)*
- **Apply** what you have learned to a new situation. *(See question 3 in the box.)*
- **Interpret** the causes, effects, meaning, value, or potential of something. *(See question 4 in the box.)*
- **Argue** for or against some controversial statement about what you have learned. *(See question 5 in the box.)*

Almost all these directions require you to synthesize what you have learned from your reading, class notes, and projects.

3. Planning your time

At the beginning of the exam, quickly look through the whole exam to determine how much time to spend on each part. Move as quickly as possible through the questions with lower point values and spend the bulk of your time responding to those that are worth the greatest number of points.

NAVIGATING THROUGH COLLEGE AND BEYOND

Essay Exam Questions across the Curriculum

During finals week, you may be asked to respond to essay questions like the following:

1. Discuss the power of the contemporary presidency as well as the limits of that power. [*from a political science course*]
2. Compare and contrast the treatment of labor supply decisions in the economic models proposed by Greg Lewis and Gary Becker. [*from an economics course*]
3. Describe the observations that would be made in an alpha-particle scattering experiment if (a) the nucleus of an atom were negatively charged and the protons occupied the empty space outside the nucleus and (b) the electrons were embedded in a positively charged sphere. [*from a chemistry course*]
4. Examine the uses of caesura and enjambment in the following poem, and analyze their effect on the poem's rhythm. [*from a literature course*]
5. In 1800, was Thomas Jefferson a "dangerous radical," as the Federalists claimed? Define key terms, and support your position with evidence from specific events and documents. [*from an American history course*]

4. Responding to short-answer questions by showing the significance of the information   The most common type of short-answer question is the identification question: Who or what is *X*? In answering questions of this sort, present just enough information to show that you understand *X*'s significance within the context of the course. For example, if you are asked to identify "Federalists" on an American history exam, don't just write, "political party that opposed Thomas Jefferson." Instead, craft one or two sentences that identify the Federalists as a party that supported the Constitution over the Articles of Confederation but then evolved, under the influence of Alexander Hamilton, into support for an elite social establishment.

5. Making tactical responses to essay questions   Keep in mind that essay questions usually ask you to do something specific. Begin by determining precisely what you are being asked to do. Before you write anything, read the question—all of it—and circle key words.

Explain two ways in which Picasso's *Guernica* evokes war's terrifying destructiveness.

To answer this question, you need to focus on two of the painting's features, such as coloring and composition, not on Picasso's life.

6. Using the essay question to structure your response   Usually, you can transform the question itself into the thesis of your answer. If you are asked to agree or disagree with the Federalists' characterization of Thomas Jefferson in the election of 1800, you might begin with this thesis.

9b

> In the election of 1800, the Federalists characterized Jefferson as a dangerous radical. Although Jefferson's ideas were radical for the times, they were not dangerous to the republic.

Take a minute or two to list evidence for each of your main points, and then write the essay.

7. Checking your work   Save a few minutes to read quickly through your completed answer, looking for words you might have omitted or key sentences that make no sense. Make corrections neatly.

SAMPLE ESSAY TEST RESPONSE

A student's response to an essay question in an art appreciation course follows. Both the question and the student's notes are provided.

QUESTION

Both of these buildings (Figure 1 and Figure 2) feature dome construction. Identify the buildings, and discuss the differences in the visual effects created by the different dome styles.

STUDENT'S NOTES

Fig 1: Pantheon. Plain outside—concrete, can barely see dome. Dramatic inside—dome opens up huge interior space. Oculus to sky: light, air, rain. Coffered ceiling.

Fig 2: Taj Mahal. Dramatic exterior—dome set high, marble, reflecting pool, exterior lines go up. Inside not meant to be visited.

STUDENT'S ANSWER

The Pantheon (Figure 1) and the Taj Mahal (Figure 2) are famous for their dome construction. The styles of the domes are dramatically different, however, resulting in dramatically different visual effects.

The Pantheon, which was built by the Romans as a temple to the gods, looks very plain on the exterior. The dome is barely visible from the outside, and it is made of a dull grey concrete. Inside the building, however, the dome

Answers identification question and states thesis.

FIGURE 1

FIGURE 2

produces an amazing effect. It opens up a huge space within the building, unobstructed by interior supports. The sides of the dome are coffered, and those recessed rectangles both lessen the weight of the dome and add to its visual beauty. Most dramatically, the top of the dome is open to the sky, which allows sun or rain to pour into the building. This opening is called the oculus, meaning "eye" (to or of Heaven).

    The Taj Mahal, which was built by a Muslim emperor of India as a tomb for his wife, is the complete opposite of the Pantheon—dazzling on the outside and plain on the inside. The large central dome is set up high on the base so that it can be seen from far away. It is made of white marble, which reflects light beautifully. The dome is surrounded by other structures that frame it and draw attention to its exterior—a long reflecting pond and four minarets. Arches and smaller domes on the outside of the building repeat the large dome's shape. Because the Taj Mahal's dome is tall and narrow, however, it does not produce the kind of vast interior space of the shorter, squatter Pantheon dome. Indeed, the inside of the Taj Mahal is not meant to be visited. Unlike the Pantheon, the dome of the Taj Mahal is intended to be admired from the outside.

> Key points supported by details and specialized terms from the course.

> Key point supported by details.

> Overall comparison as brief conclusion.

9c   Coauthored projects

A project is coauthored when more than one person is responsible for producing it. In many fields, working collaboratively is essential. Here are some suggestions to help you make the most of this challenge:

- Working with your partners, decide on some ground rules, including meeting times, deadlines, and ways of reconciling differences. Will the majority rule, or will some other principle prevail? Is there an interested and respected third party who can be consulted if the group's dynamics break down?
- Will the group meet primarily online or in person? See the box on page 148 for guidelines for online communication.
- Divide the work fairly so that everyone has a part to contribute to the project. Keep in mind that each group member should do some researching, drafting, revising, and editing. Responsibility for taking notes at meetings should rotate.
- In your personal journal, record, analyze, and evaluate the intellectual and interpersonal workings of the group as you see and experience them. If the group's dynamics begin to break down, seek the assistance of a third party.
- After each group member has completed his or her assigned part or subtopic, gather the whole group face to face or online to weave the parts together and create a focused piece of writing

with a consistent voice. At this point group members usually need to negotiate with one another. Although healthy debate is good for a project, tact is essential.

TEXTCONNEX

For Coauthoring Online

Computer networks make it easy for two or more writers to coauthor texts. Wikis allow writers to contribute to a common structure and edit one another's work, a type of writing environment that is sometimes referred to as *cloud technology*. Other cloud technologies like google.docs may be available to make coauthoring even easier. Most courseware (such as Blackboard) includes chat rooms and public space for posting and commenting on drafts. Word-processing software also allows writers to make tracked changes in files.

If your group meets online, make sure a transcript of the discussion is saved. If you exchange ideas via e-mail, you automatically will have a record of how the piece developed and how well the group worked together. Archive these transcripts and e-mails into designated folders. In all online communications, be especially careful with your tone. Without the benefit of facial expression and other cues, writers can easily misinterpret even the most constructive criticism.

10 Oral Presentations

When preparing an oral presentation, consider your rhetorical situation—your audience, purpose, and context—as you determine your focus and level of communication. Gather information, decide on the main idea, think through the organization, and choose visuals that support your points.

10a Planning and shaping your presentation

Effective oral presentations seem informal, but that effect is the result of careful planning and strategic shaping of the material.

1. Considering the interests, background knowledge, and attitudes of your audience Find out as much as you can about your listeners before you prepare the speech. What does the audience already think about your topic? Do you want to intensify your listeners' commitment to already existing views, provide new and clarifying information, provoke more analysis and understanding, or change listeners' beliefs?

    If you are addressing an unfamiliar audience, ask the people who invited you to fill you in on the audience's interests and expectations. You also can adjust your speech once you get in front of the actual audience, making your language more or less technical, for example, or offering additional examples to illustrate points.

2. Working within the time allotted to your presentation
Gauge how many words you speak per minute by reading a passage aloud at a conversational pace (about 120 to 150 words per minute is ideal). Be sure to time your presentation when you practice it.

10b Drafting your presentation with the rhetorical situation in mind

1. Making your opening interesting A strong opening puts the speaker at ease and gains the audience's confidence and attention. During rehearsal, try out several approaches to your introduction to see what gets the best reactions. Stories, brief quotations, striking statistics, and surprising statements are good attention getters. Try crafting an introduction that lets your listeners know what they have to gain from your presentation—for example, new information or new perspectives on a subject of common interest.

2. Making the focus and organization of your presentation explicit Select two or three ideas that you most want your audience to hear—and remember. Make these ideas the focus of your presentation, and let your audience know what to expect by previewing the content of your presentation—"I will make three points about fraternities on campus"—and then listing the three points.

10b
oral

The phrase "to make three points" signals a topical organization. Other common organizational patterns include chronological *(at first . . . later . . . in the end)*, causal *(because of that . . . then this follows)*, and problem-solution *(given the situation . . . then this set of proposals)*. A question-answer format also works well, either as an overall strategy or as part of another organizational pattern.

3. Being direct   What your audience hears and remembers has as much to do with how you speak as it does with what you say. Use a direct, simple style:

▪ Choose basic sentence structures.

▪ Repeat key terms.

▪ Pay attention to the pace and rhythm of your speech.

▪ Don't be afraid to use the pronouns *I, you,* and *we.*

Notice how applying these principles transforms the following written sentence into a group of sentences appropriate for oral presentation.

WRITTEN

Although the claim that the position of the stars can help people predict the future has yet to be substantiated by either an ample body or an exemplary piece of empirical research, advocates of astrology persist in pressing the claim.

ORAL

Your sign says a lot about you. So say advocates of astrology. But what evidence do we have that the position of the stars helps people predict the future? Do we have lots of empirical research or even one really good study? The answer is, "Not yet."

4. Using visual aids: Posters and presentation software   Although slides, posters, objects, video clips, and music can help make your focus explicit, you should avoid oversimplifying your ideas to fit them on a slide. Make sure the images, videos, or music fit your purpose and audience. Presentation software such as PowerPoint can help you stay focused while you are speaking. *(For more on using presentation software to incorporate multimedia elements into a presentation, see Section 10c.)*

When preparing a poster presentation, keep the poster simple with a clear title, bullets listing key points, and images that support your purpose. Be sure that text can be read from several feet away. *(For more on design principles, see Chapter 5: Designing Academic Texts and Portfolios, pp. 87–94.)*

5. Concluding memorably Make your ending memorable: return to that surprising opener, play with the words of your opening quotation, look at the initial image from another angle, or reflect on the story you have told. Make sure your listeners are aware that you are about to end your presentation, using such signal phrases as "in conclusion" or "let me end by saying," if necessary. Keep your conclusion short to hold the audience's attention.

10c Using presentation software to create multimedia presentations

Presentation software makes it possible to incorporate audio, video, and animation into a talk and to create a multimedia composition that viewers can review on their own.

1. Using presentation software for an oral presentation

Presentation slides that accompany a talk should identify major points and display information in a visually effective way.

Remember that slides support your talk, but they do not replace it. Limit the amount of information on each slide to as few words as possible, and plan to show each slide for about one minute. Use bulleted lists and phrases keyed to your major points rather than full sentences. Make fonts large enough to be seen by the person in the last row of your audience: titles should be in forty-four-point type or larger, subheads in thirty-two-point type or larger. High-contrast color schemes and sufficient blank space between slide elements will also increase the visibility of your presentation.

2. Using presentation software to create independent projects

With presentation software, you can also create compositions that run on their own or at the prompting of the viewer. This capability is especially useful in distance-learning settings, in which students attend class and share information electronically.

3. Preparing a slide presentation

The following guidelines will help you prepare effective slides.

Decide on a slide format Begin thinking about slides right away. As you write the words for your talk, you will think of visuals that support your points, and as you work out the visuals, you will discover additional points to make. Every feature of your slides—fonts, images, and animations—should support your purpose and appeal to your audience.

Before you create your slides, establish their basic appearance. What background color will they have? What typeface or typefaces? What design elements, such as borders and rules? Will the templates provided by the software go well with your talk, or should you modify a template to suit your needs? Since the format you establish will be the canvas for all your slides, avoid distractions and make sure that it complements the images and words you intend to display.

Incorporate images into your presentation Include images when appropriate. To summarize quantitative information, you might use a chart or graph. To show geographical relationships, you would likely use a map. You can also add photographs that illustrate your points. In all cases, select appropriate, relevant images that support your purpose. *(For more on choosing visuals, see Chapter 2, pp. 42–45.)*

Incorporate relevant audio, video, and animation Slides can also include audio files, which can record background information for each slide in an independent composition project. For a presentation on music, you might insert audio files to show how a type of music has developed over time.

Slides can also include video files and **animation**—visuals that have moving parts or that change over time. An animated diagram of the process of cell division, for example, could help illustrate a presentation on cellular biology. (As you would for any other source, provide documentation if you are using files that belong to others.)

Incorporate hypertext links A presenter might use an internal link within a slide sequence to jump to another slide that illustrates or explains a particular point or issue. For instance, for a presentation on insects, you might include a hyperlink to a slide about insects specific to the part of the country in which you live, complete with an image of one of them. You can also create external links to resources on the Web. Be careful not to rely too much on external links, however, because they can undermine the coherence of a presentation and can sometimes take a long time to load.

Caution: If you plan to make external links part of your presentation, make sure that you have a functioning Web browser on your computer and that a fast connection to the Internet is available where you will be giving the presentation.

---

4. Reviewing the presentation   Once you have the text of your presentation in final form and the multimedia elements in place, carefully review your slides to make sure they work together coherently:

- **Check how the slides in your software's slide sorter window proceed from one to the next.** Do you have an introductory slide? Should you add transitional effects that reveal the content of a slide gradually or point by point? Some transitions permit audio; would that support your purpose? Use transitional effects to support your rhetorical situation. Do you have a concluding slide?

- **Make sure that the slides are consistent with the script of the talk you plan to deliver.** If the slides are to function independently, do they include enough information in the introduction, an adequate explanation of each point, and a clear conclusion?

- **Check the arrangement of your slides.** Try printing them and spreading them out over a large surface, rearranging them if necessary, before implementing needed changes on the computer.

- **Be sure the slides have a unified look.** For example, do all the slides have the same background? Do they all use the same fonts in the same way? Are headers and bullets consistent?

For an example of a slide presentation created to accompany a talk about the issue of cyberbullying, see Figure 10.1 on page 154.

10d   Preparing for your presentation

Your oral presentation will have the appropriate effect on an audience if you make certain crucial decisions in advance.

1. Deciding whether to use notes or a written script   When giving your talk, make eye contact with your listeners to monitor their responses and adjust your message accordingly. For most occasions, it is inappropriate to write out everything you want to say and then read it word for word, nor do you want to read from the slides. Instead, speak from an outline or bullet points, and write out only those parts of your presentation where precise wording counts, such as quotations.

   In some scholarly or formal settings, precise wording may be necessary, especially if your oral presentation is to be published or if your remarks will be quoted by others. Sometimes the setting for

FIGURE 10.1 Sample PowerPoint slides for a presentation on the topic of cyberbullying.

Cyberbullying:
Victimization in the Virtual World

CYBERBULLYING

➢Victims are attacked using electronic means.
➢Results are immediate and can be permanent and large scale.
➢Confrontations are indirect and anonymous.
➢Consequences can be devastating.

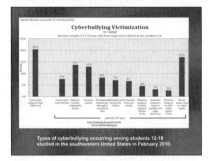

Types of cyberbullying occurring among students 12-18 studied in the southeastern United States in February 2010.

How Does It Occur?

➢Can occur on social networking sites or via text messaging or IMing
➢Often starts as school-related gossip
➢Can involve mean, hurtful comments or the spreading of rumors
➢Sometimes involves threats to safety or impersonation of another person online

UR UGLY !
WE ALL HATE YOU
UR GONNA DIE

Who Is Involved?

➢More than 20% of students age 12-18.
➢17% of those more than once.
➢Many instances go unreported because victims think no one can help.
➢Sometimes identity of cyberbully is unknown (adds to victims' feelings of futility).

Impact of Cyberbullying

➢Embarrassment of having secrets shared online
➢Loss of self-esteem
➢Depression
➢Feeling of helplessness, in some cases leading to suicide

Cyberbullying Resources

www.athinline.org
www.cyberbullying.us
www.isafe.org
www.stopcyberbullying.org

your presentation may be so formal or the audience may be so large that a script feels necessary. In such instances, do the following:

- Triple-space the typescript of your text.
- Avoid carrying sentences over from one page to another.
- Mark your manuscript for pauses, emphasis, and the pronunciation of proper names.

2. Rehearsing, revising, and polishing Whether you are using an outline or a script, practice your presentation aloud. Revise transitions that don't quite work, points that need further development, and sections that are too long. After you have settled on the content of your speech and can project it comfortably, focus on polishing your style of delivery. Ask your friends to watch and listen to your rehearsal. Check that your body posture is straight but relaxed, that your voice is loud and clear, that you keep your hands away from your face, and that you are making eye contact around the room. Time your final rehearsals, adding and cutting material as necessary.

3. Accepting nervousness as normal The adrenaline surge you feel before a presentation can actually invest your talk with positive energy. Practice and revise your presentation until it flows smoothly, and make sure that you have a strong opener to get you through the first, most difficult moments. Remember that other people cannot always tell that you are nervous.

11 Multimedia Writing

Multimedia writing combines words with images, video, or audio into a single composition. Done well, multimedia writing can be both dynamic and memorable, repaying the considerable time and effort involved. The most common form of multimedia writing—discussed in many chapters of this handbook—is a combination of words and still visuals (photographs, maps, charts, or graphs). Another form is an oral presentation with any kind of visual support from a diagram on a blackboard or Smart Board to a *PowerPoint* slide show *(see Chapter 10, Oral Presentations)*. Digital technology also allows writers to combine written words with sound, video, and animation. On social networking Web sites such as *Facebook,* users integrate text, images, and other multimedia elements.

Like any form of composition, multimedia writing is governed by the rhetorical situation; you use multimedia resources to convey a message effectively to a particular audience for a particular purpose: to inform, to interpret, or to persuade. A video or audio segment—like a photograph, map, or recording—must support your purpose and be appropriate for the audience to whom you are writing.

11a Learning about tools for creating multimedia texts

Multimedia writing can take a variety of forms and can be created with a variety of software tools. Here are a few options:

- Most word-processing programs permit you to integrate still images into a text document, and many also make it possible to create a composition that links to various files—including audio, image, and video files *(see Section 11b)*.
- Most presentation software allows you to include audio and video files in your presentation as well as still visuals *(see Section 10c)*.
- A variety of programs and Web-based tools allow you to create your own **Web pages** and **Web sites,** which can include a wide range of multimedia features *(see Section 11c)*.

TEXTCONNEX

Some Key Concepts in Multimedia Writing

- **File:** A computer file is a collection of information in computer-readable form. Text files store words, image files store pictures, audio files store sounds, and video files store video.
- **Link:** A link is a connection from one file to another or to another place in the same file. You can link to files stored on your own computer or, through the Internet and World Wide Web, to files stored on other computers.
- **Hypertext:** Hypertext is text with links. (In a sense, the Web is one vast hypertext document with countless links to a nearly endless variety of files.)

- You can create a **Weblog** (**blog** for short), on which, in addition to your written entries, you can post your own multimedia files and link to files on other blogs and Web sites *(see Section 11d).* You also can collaborate with other writers on a **wiki.** *(See section 11d.)*

11b Interpreting and analyzing multimedia

Texts that combine words and images are the most common form of multimedia writing. Two types of assignments you might be given are image analyses and a narrative that explains an image.

1. Composing image analyses You may be asked to analyze a single image such as a painting from a museum (possibly viewed online), as Diane Chen does in her analysis of the Salgado photograph. In an image analysis, you have two tasks: (1) describe the picture as fully as possible, using adjectives, comparisons, and words that help readers focus on the picture and the details that compose it; and (2) analyze the argument the picture seems to be making.

Exercise 11.1 Image interpretations

1. In a local museum or on a museum Web site, find a painting created by an artist whose work is new to you. (Some examples of museum Web sites include <www.moma.org/collection/> for the Museum of Modern Art (New York), <www.artic.edu/aic/> for the Art Institute of Chicago, and <www.louvre.fr/ louvrea.htm> for the Louvre in Paris.)

   Take notes on your response to the painting, and write an initial analysis of it. As you do, consider the following:

   - Who or what is in the painting?
   - If there are people in the painting, are they active or passive? Rich or poor? Old or young?
   - Are the people central to the painting, or are they peripheral? If peripheral, what is the painting's central focus?
   - How does the artist represent the subjects of the painting— in other words, what does the artist's presentation of people, objects, buildings, or landscapes say about his or her attitude toward them?
   - What in your own experience may be affecting your response? What personal associations do you make with the subject of the painting? How might your own position—for

example, as a student, daughter or son, member of a political party—influence the way you interpret the painting? Now read a short biography of the artist in a book or on the Web, and add that information to your analysis. Point out whether and how the biographical information either reinforces your interpretation or leads you to alter it.

2. Find an image in a current newspaper or magazine or an image of historical interest. For example, you might look at the collection maintained by the Library of Congress (<http://www.loc .gov/pictures/>), where you can find a treasure trove of historical photographs. First outline two possible arguments that the picture might be making. Then decide which is the more likely of the two arguments, and explain why.

2. Narrating a story behind an image   Sometimes a writer tries to imagine the story behind an evocative photograph. Often, this is as much an expression of the writer as it is a statement about the photograph.

Some photographs, like the one in Figure 11.1, taken on September 11, 2001, by photojournalist Thomas Hoepker, connect private life and public events. On the morning of the catastrophe, Hoepker drove across New York City's East River from Manhattan to Brooklyn, with the intention of shooting a panoramic view of the burning World Trade Center towers. He took this photo of five young people who, in the photographer's opinion, "didn't seem to care." When David Plotz, deputy editor of the online magazine *Slate,* saw the photo, he disagreed and called for a response from any of the people in the photograph <http://www.slate.com/id/2149508>. Walter Sipser, one of the photograph's subjects, wrote to *Slate,* saying "we were in a profound state of shock" <http://www.slate.com/id/2149578/>. What story do you see in this photograph?

Exercise 11.2   Photographic stories

1. Find one photograph from at least fifty years ago in a magazine or book, on a Web site, or in a family collection. (The Library of Congress's online repository is an excellent source <www .loc.gov/rr/print/catalog.html>.) For the photograph, create two short, specific stories and one more general story. Explain the "logic" of each story using evidence from the photograph. As you imagine possibilities, ask yourself these questions:

   ■ Who or what is in the photograph?

FIGURE 11.1 New York City, September 11, 2001.
SOURCE: © Thomas Hoepker/Magnum.

- How is the photograph composed? What first draws your attention?
- If you think of the photograph as having a center, where would it be, and what would be in it?
- If you think of the photograph as being divided into quadrants, what is in each one?
- What emotional reaction do you have to the photograph?
- If the photograph is in color, what do the colors in the photograph suggest? What do they contribute to the photograph? If the photograph is in black and white, what effect does that convey to you?
- What details in the picture evoke a mood?
- What is left out of the photograph, and why? Can you imagine other items or people who, if included, would help tell a different story?
- Is the photograph telling a short, specific story, a longer story, or both kinds of stories?
- How might your own position—for example, as a student, daughter or son, member of a community group or political party—influence your view of the photo?

2. Take several photographs that allow for rich interpretations. Choose two of the photos, and interpret them. Bring them to class, and ask two classmates to provide you with a narrative for each. Do their stories match yours? Do their stories seem more interesting than yours? Why or why not?

11c Creating a Web site

Thanks to Web editing software, it is now almost as easy to create a Web site and post it on the Internet as it is to write a print text using word-processing software. Many Web-based businesses like Google provide free server space for hosting sites and offer tools for creating Web pages. Many schools also make server space available for student Web sites.

To be effective, a Web site must be well designed and serve a well-defined purpose for its audience. In creating a Web site, plan the site, draft its content and select its visuals, and then revise and edit as you would for any other composition. However, each stage involves decisions and requirements that are unique to this medium; the following sections offer guidelines for making some of these decisions.

KNOW THE SITUATION

Purpose: To inform or persuade

Audience: Audience members for the Web can be people who need information about your topic (and may be knowledgeable themselves) or those who are only mildly interested.

Stance: Knowledgeable

Genres: Web sites often host several genres, for instance reports, reviews, and opinion pieces.

Medium: Digital and networked

1. Planning a structure for your site Like most print documents, a Web site can have a hierarchical, linear structure, where one page leads to the next. Because of the hyperlinked nature of this medium, however, a site can also be organized in a hub-and-spoke structure, with a central page leading to other pages. The diagrams in Figure 11.2 illustrate these two possible structures.

To choose the structure that will work best for your site, consider how you expect visitors to use it. The structure of each site accommodates its users' needs.

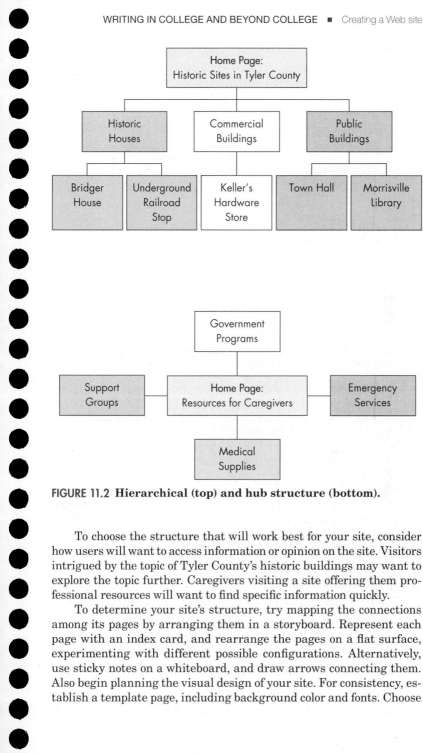

11c
media

FIGURE 11.2 Hierarchical (top) and hub structure (bottom).

To choose the structure that will work best for your site, consider how users will want to access information or opinion on the site. Visitors intrigued by the topic of Tyler County's historic buildings may want to explore the topic further. Caregivers visiting a site offering them professional resources will want to find specific information quickly.

To determine your site's structure, try mapping the connections among its pages by arranging them in a storyboard. Represent each page with an index card, and rearrange the pages on a flat surface, experimenting with different possible configurations. Alternatively, use sticky notes on a whiteboard, and draw arrows connecting them. Also begin planning the visual design of your site. For consistency, establish a template page, including background color and fonts. Choose a uniform location (for example, at the top, in the middle) for material that will appear on each page, such as site title, page title, navigation links, and your contact information. *(See pp. 162–64 on designing a site with a unified look.)*

2. Gathering content for your site The content for a Web site will usually consist of written work along with links and graphics. Depending on your situation, you might also provide audio files, video files, and even animation.

Follow these special requirements for written content on a Web site:

- Usually readers do not want lengthy text explanations; they expect chunks of information—short paragraphs—delivered quickly.

- Chunks for each topic or point should fit on one screen. Avoid long passages that require readers to use the scroll bar.

- Use links to connect your interests with those of others and to provide extra sources of credible and relevant information. Integrate links into your text, and give them descriptive names, such as "Historic Houses" for one of the Web pages in Figure 11.2. Place links at the end of a paragraph so readers do not navigate away in the middle.

As you prepare your written text, gather the graphics, photographs, and audio and video files that you plan to include. Some sites allow you to download images, and some images, including many of the historical photographs available through the Library of Congress, are in the public domain. Another useful site for visual, audio, and video files is *Creative Commons* (search.creativecommons.org), which directs you to material licensed for specific types of use. Check the license of the material to see what is permitted, and always provide acknowledgments.

Whether or not an image is in the public domain, be sure to give proper credit for material that you have not generated yourself and, if necessary, request permission for its use. *(See Chapter 18, pp. 234–40 for guidelines on what requires permission.)*

3. Designing Web pages to capture and hold interest On good Web sites, you will also find such easy-to-follow links as "what you'll find here" or FAQs (frequently asked questions). In planning the structure and content of your site, keep your readers' convenience in mind.

4. Designing a readable site with a unified look Because the Web is a visual medium, readers appreciate a site with a unified look. "Sets" or "themes" are readily available at free graphics sites offering banners, navigation buttons, and other design elements. You also can

CHECKLIST

Planning a Web Site

When you begin your Web composition, consider these questions about this writing situation:

☐ What is your purpose?

☐ Who are your viewers, and what are their needs? Will the site be limited by password protection to a specific group of viewers, or should you plan for a broader audience?

☐ What type of content will you include on your site: images, audio files, video files?

☐ Will you need to get permission to use visuals or other files that you obtain from outside sources?

☐ What design elements will appeal to your audience and complement your purpose and content?

☐ Given your technical knowledge, amount of content, and deadline, how much time should you allot to each stage of building your site?

☐ Will the site be updated, and if so, how frequently?

11c
media

create visuals with a graphics program, scan your own art, and scan or upload personal photographs. Design your home page to complement your other pages, or your readers may lose track of where they are in the site—and lose interest in staying:

- Use a design template—a preformatted style with structure and headings established—to keep elements of page layout consistent across the site.
- Align items such as text and images.
- Consider including a site map—a Web page that serves as a table of contents for your entire site.
- Select elements such as buttons, signs, animations, sounds, and backgrounds with a consistent design suited to your purpose and audience. Use animations and sounds sparingly.
- Use colors that provide adequate contrast, white space, and sans serif fonts to make text easy to read. Pages that are too busy are not visually compelling. *(For more on design, see Chapter 5, pp. 86–94.)*
- Limit the width of your text; readers find wide lines of text difficult to process.

TEXTCONNEX

Understanding Web Jargon

- **Browser:** software that allows you to access and view material on the Web. When you identify a site you want to see on the Web by typing in a URL (see the following), your browser (*Microsoft Internet Explorer, Mozilla Firefox,* or *Google Chrome,* for example) tells a distant computer—a **server**—to send that site to you.

- **JPEG and GIF:** formats for photographs and other visuals that are recognized by browsers. Photographs that appear on a Web site should be saved in JPEG (pronounced *"jay-peg"*) format, which stands for Joint Photographic Experts Group. The file extension is .jpg or .jpeg. Clip art should be saved as GIF files (Graphics Interchange Format, pronounced like *"gift"* without the *t*).

- **Home page:** the opening page of a Web site. A home page typically includes general information about the site as well as links to various parts of it.

- **HTML/XML:** hypertext markup language/extensible markup language. These languages tag or code text so that your browser can rebuild a document from the compressed files that travel through the Internet. It is not necessary to learn HTML or XML to publish on the Web. Programs such as *FrontPage, PageMill, Dreamweaver, Nvue,* and *Mozilla* provide a WYSIWYG (What You See Is What You Get) interface for creating Web pages. In addition, most word-processing programs have a "Save as HTML" option.

- **URL:** uniform resource locator or Web address. When you type or paste a URL into your Web browser, you are sending a request through your browser to another computer, asking it to transfer data to your computer.

- Leave time to find appropriate image, audio, and video files created by others and to obtain permission to use them.
- Always check your Web site to be sure all the pages and links load as planned.

The home page and interior page shown in Figure 11.3 illustrate some of these design considerations.

5. Designing a Web site that is easy to access and navigate

Help readers find their way to the areas of the site they want to visit. Make it easy for them to take interesting side trips without wasting their time or losing their way:

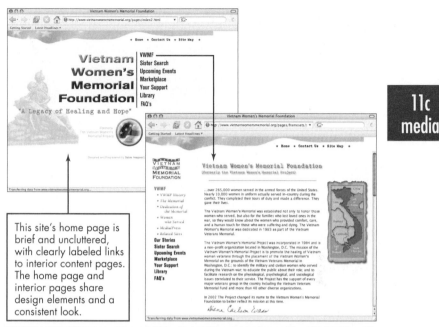

This site's home page is brief and uncluttered, with clearly labeled links to interior content pages. The home page and interior pages share design elements and a consistent look.

11c media

FIGURE 11.3 Home page and an interior page from the Web site of the Vietnam Women's Memorial Foundation.

- **Identify your Web site on each page, and provide a link to the home page.** Remember that readers will not always enter your Web site through the home page. Give the title of the site on each page, and provide an easy-to-spot link to your home page as well.

- **Provide a navigation bar on each page.** A **navigation bar** can be a simple line of links that you copy and paste at the top or bottom of each page. A navigation bar on each page makes it easy for visitors to move from the site's home page to other pages and back again.

- **Use graphics that load quickly.** Limit the size of your images to no more than forty kilobytes so that they will load faster.

- **Use graphics judiciously.** Your Web site should not depend on graphics alone to make its message clear and interesting. Graphics should be used to reinforce your message. The designers of the Library of Congress Web site *(see Figure 11.4)* use icons such as musical notation and a map to help visitors navigate the site. Avoid clip art, which often looks unprofessional.

- **Be aware of the needs of visitors with disabilities.** Provide alternative ways of accessing visual and auditory information.

FIGURE 11.4 The home page of the Web site of the Library of Congress.

For MULTILINGUAL WRITERS

Designing a Web Site Collaboratively

If you are asked to create a Web site as part of a class assignment, ask your instructor if you can work with a partner or a small group. Alternatively, you can invite peers to look over your writing and make suggestions. At the same time, you will be able to provide your peers with the benefit of your unique multicultural viewpoint, which is especially important in our increasingly globalized world.

Include text descriptions of visuals, media files, and tables (for users of screen-reader software or text-only browsers). All audio files should have captions and full transcriptions. For more information, visit *Webmonkey* at *<www.webmonkey.com>*. (See Chapter 5, pp. 93–94.)

Exercise 11.3 Web site critique

Identify an example of a well-designed Web site and an example of one that is poorly designed. Compare and contrast features of the two designs.

6. Using peer feedback to revise your Web site   Before publishing your site, to be read by anyone in the world, proofread your text carefully, and ask friends to look at your site in different browsers and share their responses with you. Make sure your site reflects favorably on your abilities.

11d   Creating and interacting with blogs and wikis

Weblogs or **blogs** are Web sites that can be continually updated. Some blogs are the exclusive creations of one writer; others provide a group of writers a space for sharing ideas and discussing each other's work. You can include images in a blog and link to other blogs and Web pages *(see Figure 11.5)*.

A **wiki** is another kind of Web-interfaced database that can be updated easily. One well-known wiki is the online encyclopedia *Wikipedia (see Chapter 14, p. 202)*. Many instructors do not consider Wikipedia a credible source for research because almost anyone can create or edit its content. Although changes are reviewed before appearing on the site, the reviewers may not have the requisite expertise. Verify that the information provided is correct by confirming it with another source. Some other wikis, such as *Citizendium,* rely on experts in a discipline to write and edit articles.

1. Creating your own blog   To begin blogging, set up a blog site with a server such as www.blogger.com or wordpress.com. Be sure about your writing situation, especially regarding purpose, which may

FIGURE 11.5 The blog for a writing course.

be very specifically focused on a single issue; alternatively, provide space for a range of opinions.

Some social networking sites such as *NING,* will, for a charge, allow users to create blogs. These blogs can sometimes be used to explore a topic or find an expert on a particular subject. For example, if school policy permits, you might informally survey your friends on a campus issue or set up a group to discuss the topic.

CHECKLIST

Setting up a Blog

When you begin your blog, consider the following questions about your writing situation:

☐ What is your purpose? How will your blog's visual design reflect that purpose? What other multimedia elements can contribute to your purpose?

☐ To whom will you give access? Will the blog be public, for all to see? Or will it be limited to specific viewers?

☐ Do you want to allow others to post on your blog, comment on your posts, or just comment?

☐ Do you want to set up a schedule of postings or a series of events that will cue you to post?

☐ Do you want to link to other blogs?

Caution: Blogs and profiles on social networking sites are more or less public depending on the level of access they allow. Do not post anything (including photographs and videos) that you would not want family members, teachers, and prospective employers to view.

---

2. Setting up a wiki A wiki is an updatable Web site for sharing and coauthoring content. In addition to using wikis to conduct research together, students often use them simply to share their

TEXTCONNEX

11d media

Blog Resources

Blogs 101—The New York Times—directory of blogs by topic
<www.nytimes.com/ref/technology/blogs_101.html>

Technorati—search engine for blogs <http://technorati.com
/blogs/directory/>

writing and various kinds of information—for instance relevant videos or Web sites related to a common research topic. Coauthors and peer reviewers find wikis useful because they provide a history of the revisions in a document. To create a wiki, begin by identifying the writing situation and the platform you will use, probably one like wikispaces.com that provides set-up tools and direction.

Like blogs, wikis can have a limited number of participants or be open to the world.

CHECKLIST

Setting up a Wiki

When you begin your wiki, consider these questions related to your writing situation:

☐ What is your purpose?

☐ Who is the audience, and to whom will you give access? Will the wiki have broad participation, or is it designed for a specific group of participants?

☐ Given the tasks that participants will work on, do you want to set up a schedule of deadlines or post reminders to the group?

☐ What design elements will appeal to the participants and to your audience?

☐ Do you have a preference for the specific content? Should participants contribute images? Audio files? Video files?

Exercise 11.4 Blogs

1. Examine a variety of blogs, and identify their purpose and audience. How do features of the visual design and the writing support the purpose?

2. Create your own blog with three of your classmates, and use it as a peer-review forum for your next paper assignment. How does this kind of peer review compare with a face-to-face review?

3. Choose a current-events blog to read for several days, and then post a comment on an issue. If the blog author or another reader responds to your comment, write in your print or electronic journal or blog about the resulting exchange.

4. Using the questions for previewing text and visuals in Chapter 1 *(pp. 18–19),* write a short rhetorical analysis of a blog.

Exercise 11.5 Wikis

Review two entries on the same topic in two different kinds of reference materials: Wikipedia and a print encyclopedia. How do the entries compare? For instance, which one is longer? Which one has more references? Which one is more credible, and how do you know?

12 Writing beyond College

Many students work on or off campus as employees, as interns, or as volunteers for community organizations. Writing is one way to connect your work, your other activities, and your studies. Your ability to research and write can be of great value to organizations that serve the community, such as homeless shelters, tutoring centers, and environmental groups. Strong writing skills will also help you to find a good job once you leave college and advance in your chosen career.

12a Addressing the community

When you are writing for a community group, consider these questions:

- What do community members talk about?
- How do they talk about these issues, and why?
- Who is an outsider (member of the community), and who is an insider (member of the organization)?
- How can you best write from the inside to the outside?

Your answers will help you shape your writing so that it reaches its intended audience and moves that audience to action.

Writing on behalf of a community organization almost always involves negotiation and collaboration. A community organization may revise your draft to fit its needs, and you will have to live with those revisions. In these situations, having a cooperative attitude is as important as having strong writing skills.

12b Designing brochures, posters, and newsletters

If you are participating in a service learning program or an internship, you may have opportunities to design brochures and newsletters for wide distribution, as well as posters to create awareness and promote events. To create an effective poster, brochure, or newsletter, you will need to integrate your skills in document design with what you have learned about purpose and audience.

Here are a few tips:

- Consider how readers will access the pages of the brochure or newsletter. Will it be mailed or distributed electronically or in person?
- Sketch the design in pencil or on a whiteboard before using the computer.
- Make decisions about photographs, illustrations, type fonts, and design in general to convey the sponsoring organization's overall image.
- If the organization has a logo, include it; if not, suggest designing one. A **logo** is a small visual symbol, like the Nike "swoosh" or the distinctive font used for Coca-Cola.
- Create a template for the brochure, poster, or newsletter so that you can easily produce future editions. In word-processing and document design programs, a **template** is a blank document that includes all the necessary formatting and codes. When you use a template, you just "plug in" new content and visuals—the format and design are already done.

The brochure "Stopping (Cyber)bullies in Their Tracks" *(Figure 12.1)* carefully defines terms *(bully, cyberbullying),* reviews consequences, and suggests countermeasures.

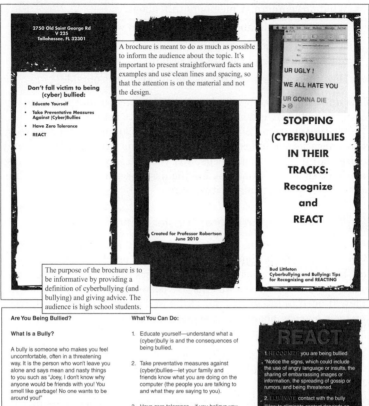

2750 Old Saint George Rd
V 225
Tallahassee, FL 32301

A brochure is meant to do as much as possible to inform the audience about the topic. It's important to present straightforward facts and examples and use clean lines and spacing, so that the attention is on the material and not the design.

Don't fall victim to being (cyber) bullied:

- Educate Yourself
- Take Preventative Measures Against (Cyber)Bullies
- Have Zero Tolerance
- REACT

UR UGLY !

WE ALL HATE YOU

UR GONNA DIE
> ☺

STOPPING (CYBER)BULLIES IN THEIR TRACKS: Recognize and REACT

Created for Professor Robertson
June 2010

Bud Littleton
Cyberbullying and Bullying: Tips for Recognizing and REACTING

The purpose of the brochure is to be informative by providing a definition of cyberbullying (and bullying) and giving advice. The audience is high school students.

Are You Being Bullied?

What Is a Bully?

A bully is someone who makes you feel uncomfortable, often in a threatening way. It is the person who won't leave you alone and says mean and nasty things to you such as "Joey, I don't know why anyone would be friends with you! You smell like garbage! No one wants to be around you!"

What Is a Cyberbully?

A cyberbully uses digital technologies like text messaging and Internet communication to threaten or scare someone else. These bullies can be more dangerous than a traditional bully because they have the digital technology to hide behind. An example of a cyberbully on IM—
Crazymadsinger: i hate u!! ☺ u r an ugly person!!

Consequences of Being Bullied

Victims are more likely to feel anxious and depressed. They think that because one person is mean to them, lots of people will be mean to them. And even when the bullying stops, victims can be haunted by negative memories. Do not let yourself become a victim: **REACT!** now.

What You Can Do:

1. Educate yourself—understand what a (cyber)bully is and the consequences of being bullied.

2. Take preventative measures against (cyber)bullies—let your family and friends know what you are doing on the computer (the people you are talking to and what they are saying to you).

3. Have zero tolerance—if you believe you are being bullied, don't wait to take action.

4. REACT.

REACT

1. RECOGNIZE you are being bullied
*Notice the signs, which could include the use of angry language or insults, the sharing of embarrassing images or information, the spreading of gossip or rumors, and being threatened.

2. ELIMINATE contact with the bully
*How to eliminate contact depends on the type of contact you have with the bully. If it is a face-to-face bully, create situations where you are always with other people. If it is a cyberbully, either de-friend the bully or create a new profile.

3. ASK someone in authority for help
*This can be a parent, a teacher, an older brother or sister, or someone you trust.
*Ask this person to give you guidance on how to deal with being bullied and to help you do something about the person who is bullying you.

4. COMPLIMENT yourself for seeking help
*Understanding that you are being bullied is not easy. By getting help, you have taken the first step toward no longer being a victim.

5. TELL others your story.
*By sharing your story, you could help prevent others from becoming victims.

FIGURE 12.1 Example of an effective brochure.

FIGURE 12.2 Example of a well-designed newsletter.

The Coalition for Internet Safety

Volume 13.2   June 2010

Internet Safety: Tips for Keeping Kids Safe Online

- Don't allow kids to have computers in their bedrooms – keep computers in the kitchen or family room where you can supervise their use.

- Have house rules and post them near the computer.

- Go online with kids to see who their "friends" are and what they are viewing regularly.

- Regulate kids' computer time to ensure they enjoy offline activities and friends.

- Beware of late night computer use, which may indicate a child is keeping secrets.

- Watch out for any changes in self-esteem or unusual behavior – it may indicate a problem in kids' virtual life.

- Talk to kids about Internet safety on an ongoing basis.

Internet Safety: It Takes a Village

Staying safe on the Internet isn't always easy; even adults have to watch out for scams, traps that can lead to identity theft, computer viruses, malware, annoying spam, and simple information overload. Kids can be more susceptible to trouble online because they may not be able to distinguish between honest communication, a sales pitch, and predatory behavior. They may mistake someone posing as a friend for a genuine friend and communicate with that person under this misapprehension.

Parents are often way behind their children when it comes to knowledge about the Internet and what dangers can lurk there. Even tech-savvy parents may not realize how kids can inadvertently put themselves at risk. Information or photos posted publicly on social networking sites can give predators clues about a child's interests or after-school activities, for example. Even information shared online with a known friend can end up as public knowledge, an action not easily undone that can sometimes lead to tragic consequences. For example, posting a private photograph online intended only for a friend to see can quickly become an embarrassment if that friend in turn posts it more publicly. Intentionally or not, such public exposure can cause what can feel to its subject like an insurmountable level of anxiety and distress.

Helping young children stay safe online may seem easy to parents at first. Parents and teachers can set rules and monitor children's online activities. But once older children become more familiar with the Internet and begin using social-networking sites, as well as cell phones for texting, protecting them from danger becomes more difficult. Rather than one-time instruction on Internet safety, children need constant mentoring about online behavior. To keep children safe in a digital environment, adults need to make an ongoing commitment to understanding privacy and other concerns for different applications and in a growing variety of situations, and they need to be diligent. Parents, older siblings, and educators can all play a role in fostering appropriate digital behavior.

Parental Online Awareness

The greatest challenge for parents in monitoring their children's online behavior is a lack of familiarity with the Internet itself or with the ways in which their kids interact with others online. The best way to understand and prevent the potential online dangers your child might be exposed to is to use the Internet in the same way they do. Create a profile on the social networking sites they use and go there regularly so that you understand their virtual world and can see their online friends. Monitor text messages and limit cell phone time so that your children are preoccupied with homework rather than texting. Learn the shorthand that young people use online or while texting, such as POS (parent over shoulder), so you won't miss warning signs for potentially dangerous situations, such as inappropriate online communication with an unknown person.

Internet Safety Awareness Seminar
Detective Marc Rivera, Cybercrimes Unit
June 25, 5:00 – 7:00 p.m.
Griffin Middle School Auditorium

Intro to Social Networking Workshop
Collier County Community College
July 1, 6:30 – 9:00 p.m.
Hutchins Building, 230–A

The Coalition for Internet Safety

p. 2

Internet Safety: Online Resources for Parents and Children

- MTV recently launched athinline.org to help teens understand how easily the line between appropriate and inappropriate online behavior can be crossed. Parents will also find this resource helpful in understanding the peer pressures and challenges their children face online (www.athinline.org).
- Worried about cyber bullying? Check out the Cyber Bullying Research Center, which hosts a wealth of information on everything from awareness and prevention to contacting authorities for help (www.cyberbullyingresearchcenter.org).
- The FBI produces an online Parent's Guide to Internet Safety that is updated regularly and describes how to keep your child safe from Internet predators (http://www.fbi.gov/publications/pguide/pguidee.htm).
- i-SAFE Inc. is a nonprofit organization endorsed by Congress that is dedicated to protecting kids online. It features a standard curriculum, community outreach initiatives, and information for students, parents, law enforcement, educators and any others concerned with keeping children safe online (www.isafe.org).
- For parents concerned with monitoring online activity, companies like InternetSafety.com provide products designed to prevent danger, including Internet filters that block selected sites and mobile phone locators (www.internetsafety.com).

Report to Congress Outlines Latest Safety Concerns and Solutions

SafeKids.com recently prepared a report to Congress that advocates civility and respect online. The report also recommends increased media literacy among youth using the Internet and those protecting their interests. *Youth Safety on a Living Internet* "points to the growing importance of online citizenship and media-literacy education, in addition to what has come to be seen as online safety education, as solutions to youth risk online" (Magid).

The report looks at the previous 20 years of online safety, but also considers the newest research on the use of social media among today's youth. The report calls for kids themselves to become more responsible for online actions and to become more aware of the risky behavior that may lead to unfortunate consequences. Today, young people are just as likely to create online content as they are to consume it; this requires responsibility and a respect for "the living entity that is the Internet today" (Magid). The report can be viewed online at SafeKids.com or downloaded in PDF format. The site also features a wide range of helpful tools for encouraging safe online behavior (www.safekids.com).

Magid, Larry. "Study has good news about kids' online behavior." *Safekids.com.* Larry Magid, 26 June 2010. Web. 5 July 2010.

Privacy Settings Workshop Hits Home

Dr. Pat Carroll has been recognized numerous times for her scholarship and teaching excellence at Collier County Community College. In May she hosted a workshop for parents of area students, providing information on the latest trends in online behavior of tweens and teens and helping parents understand how to keep a handle on what kids are doing online.

Photo credit: Emily Baker (2006)

Dr. Carroll's workshop hit home with Lisa Brooks, mother to 14-year-old twin girls, who worries about what her kids do online. "I don't really understand what they're doing most of the time if I'm looking at the screen," she explains. "My girls know much more about using the Internet than I do, but this workshop helped me understand how to better understand what they're up to online." Parents worry that they are invading their children's privacy by closely monitoring online activity. Dr. Carroll advises parents to tell their children that when they use privacy settings or monitor their online activity, it is for their own protection. She compares letting young people use the Internet unsupervised to a parent dropping children off in Times Square at midnight without adult supervision.

On the second page, the visual establishing a No Bully Zone is elegant in its simplicity and impact. The familiar circle with a slash across it suggests "Stop!" to bullying.

The newsletter from The Coalition for Internet Safety also has a simple, clear design *(Figure 12.2)*. The designer uses a shaded area on the left side of the front page to summarize tips for keeping kids safe online. The box with the heading "Internet Safety: Online Resources for Parents and Children" on the second page includes Web addresses for further information.

12c Exploring internships and keeping a portfolio of career-related writing

An internship, in which you do work in your chosen field, is a vital connection between the classroom and the workplace, allowing you to gain academic credit for integrating the theoretical and the practical. Writing and learning go together. During your internship, keep a journal to record and analyze your experiences, as well as a file of writing you do on the job. With permission, your final project for internship credit could be an analysis of that file.

On-the-job writing, clippings of articles and editorials you have written for the school newspaper, brochures you have created for a community organization—these and other documents demonstrate your ability to apply intellectual concepts to real-world demands. Organized into a portfolio, especially into an electronic portfolio (e-portfolio), this material displays your marketable skills. Your campus career resource center may offer assistance, keep your portfolio on file, if it is in print format, and send it to future employers or graduate schools. *(For advice on assembling an e-portfolio, see Chapter 5, p. 96.)*

12d Keeping an up-to-date résumé available on a disk or zip drive or posted online

A **résumé** is a brief summary of your education and your work experience that you send to prospective employers. Expect the person reviewing your résumé to give it no more than sixty seconds. Make that first impression count. Design a document that is easy to read, attractively formatted, and flawlessly edited.

1. Guidelines for writing a résumé Always include the following *necessary* categories in a résumé:

- Heading (name, address, phone number, e-mail address)
- Education (in reverse chronological order; do not include high school)

- Work experience (in reverse chronological order)
- References (often included on a separate sheet; for many situations, you can substitute the line "References available on request" instead)

Include the following *optional* categories in your résumé as appropriate:

12d

- Honors and awards
- Internships
- Activities and service
- Special skills

Some career counselors still recommend that you list a career objective under the heading of your résumé, but others discourage you from including something so specific and counsel you instead to incorporate goals into your cover letter. If you do include an objective or goals, be sure you know what the prospective employer is looking for and tailor your résumé accordingly.

2. Two sample résumés   Laura Amabisca has organized the information in her résumé *(p. 176)* by time and by categories. Within each category, she has listed items from most to least recent. This reverse chronological order gives appropriate emphasis to what she is doing now and has most recently done. Because she is applying for jobs in public relations, she has highlighted her internship in that field by placing it at the top of her experience section.

The résumé on page 176 reflects appropriate formatting for print. Note the use of a line rule, alignment of text, bullet points, and bold and italic type. These elements organize the information visually, directing the reader's eye appropriately.

Amabisca's scannable résumé *(p. 177)* contains no italics, bold, or other formatting so it may be submitted electronically or entered into an employer's database *(see the box on p. 178)*.

Amabisca's entire résumé is just one page. A brief, well-organized résumé is more attractive to potential employers than a rambling, multipage one.

The résumé features active verbs such as *supervise.*

LAURA AMABISCA
20650 North 58th Avenue, Apt. 15A
Glendale, AZ 85308
623-555-7310
lamabisca@peoplelink.com

Education	**Arizona State University West,** Phoenix ▪ Bachelor of Arts, History, Minor in Global Management (May 2010) ▪ Senior Thesis: Picturing the Hopi, 1920–1940: A Historical Analysis **Glendale Community College,** Glendale, AZ (2006–2008)
Experience	**Public Relations Office, Arizona State University West** *Intern* (Summer 2009) ▪ Researched and reported on university external publications. ▪ Created original content for print and Web. ▪ Assisted in planning fundraising campaign and events. **Sears,** Bell Road, Phoenix, AZ *Assistant Manager, Sporting Goods Department* (2008–present) ▪ Assist sales manager in day-to-day operations. ▪ Supervise team of sales associates. ▪ Ensure quality customer service. *Sales Associate, Sporting Goods Department* (2005–2008) ▪ Recommended products to meet customer needs. ▪ Processed sales and returns. *Stock Clerk, Sporting Goods Department* (2003–2005) ▪ Received, sorted, and tracked incoming merchandise. ▪ Stocked shelves to ensure appropriate supply on sales floor.
Special Skills	*Language*: Bilingual: Spanish/English *Computer*: Windows, Mac OS, MS Office, HTML
Activities	**America Reads** *Tutor, Public Relations Consultant* (2009) ▪ Taught reading to first-grade students. ▪ Created brochure to recruit tutors. **Multicultural Festival, Arizona State University West** *Student Coordinator* (2009) ▪ Organized festival of international performances, crafts, and community organizations. **Writing Center, Glendale Community College** *Tutor* (2006–2008) ▪ Met with peers to help them with writing assignments.
References	Available on request to Career Services, Arizona State University West

LAURA AMABISCA
20650 North 58th Avenue, Apt. 15A
Glendale, AZ 85308
623-555-7310
lamabisca@peoplelink.com

EDUCATION
Arizona State University West, Phoenix
* Bachelor of Arts, History, Minor in Global Management (May 2010)
* Senior Thesis: Picturing the Hopi, 1920-1940: A Historical Analysis
Glendale Community College, Glendale, AZ (2006-2008)

EXPERIENCE
Public Relations Office, Arizona State University West (Summer 2010)
Intern
* Researched and reported on university external publications.
* Created original content for print and Web.
* Assisted in planning fundraising campaign and events.

Sears, Bell Road, Phoenix, AZ
Assistant Manager, Sporting Goods Department (2008-present)
* Supervise team of sales associates.
* Ensure quality customer service.

Sales Associate, Sporting Goods Department (2005-2008)
* Recommended products to meet customer needs.
* Processed sales and returns.

Stock Clerk, Sporting Goods Department (2003-2005)
* Received, sorted, and tracked incoming merchandise.
* Stocked shelves to ensure appropriate supply on sales floor.

SPECIAL SKILLS
Language: Bilingual: Spanish/English
Computer: Windows, Mac OS, MS Office, HTML

ACTIVITIES
America Reads (2009)
Tutor, Public Relations Consultant
* Taught reading to first-grade students.
* Created brochure to recruit tutors.

Multicultural Festival, Arizona State University West (2007)
Student Coordinator
* Organized festival of international performances, crafts, and community organizations.

Writing Center, Glendale Community College (2004-2006)
Tutor
* Met with peers to help them with writing assignments.

REFERENCES
Available on request to Career Services, Arizona State University West

Amabisca includes keywords (highlighted) to catch the eye of a potential employer or match desired positions in a database. Amabisca knows that a position in public relations requires computer skills, communication skills, and experience working with diverse groups of people. Keywords such as *sales, bilingual, HTML,* and *public relations* are critical to her résumé.

TEXTCONNEX

Electronic and Scannable Résumés

Many employers now request résumés by e-mail and electronically scan print résumés. Here are some tips for using electronic technology to submit your résumé:

- Contact the human resource department of a potential employer, and ask whether your résumé should be scannable.
- If so, be sure to use a clear, common typeface in an easy-to-read size. Do not include any unusual symbols or characters.
- If the employer expects the résumé as an e-mail attachment, save it in a widely readable form such as rich text format (RTF) or PDF. Use minimal formatting and no colors, unusual fonts, or decorative flourishes.
- Configure your e-mail program to send you an automated reply when your e-mail has been successfully received.
- Include specific keywords that allow employers to locate your electronic résumé in a database. See the résumé section of Monster.com at <http://resume.monster.com> for industry-specific advice on appropriate keywords and other step-by-step advice.

12e Applying for a job: Application letters and interviews

A clear and concise **application letter** should always accompany a résumé. Before drafting the letter, do some research about the organization you are contacting. For example, even though Laura Amabisca was already familiar with the Heard Museum, she found out the name of the director of public relations. *(Amabisca's application letter appears on p. 180.)* If you are unable to identify an appropriate name, it is better to direct the letter to "Dear Director of Public Relations" than to "Dear Sir or Madam."

Here are some additional guidelines:

- **Tailor your letter.** A form letter accompanied by a generic résumé is not an effective way of getting a job interview. Before writing an application letter or preparing a résumé, consider the overall situation. What exactly is the employer seeking? How might you draw on your experience to address the employer's needs?

- **Use business style.** Use the block form shown on page 180. Type your address at the top of the page, with each line starting at the left margin; place the date at the left margin two lines above the recipient's name and address; use a colon (:) after the greeting; double-space between single-spaced paragraphs; use a traditional closing *(Sincerely, Sincerely yours, Yours truly)*; and make sure that the inside address and the address on the envelope match exactly.

- **Be professional.** Your letter should be crisp and to the point. Be direct as well as objective in presenting your qualifications, and maintain a courteous and dignified tone toward the prospective employer. Your résumé should contain only education and work-related information. It is better not to include personal information (such as ethnicity, age, or marital status).

12e

- **Limit your letter to three or four paragraphs.** Focus clearly and concisely on what the employer needs to know. In the first paragraph, identify the position you are applying for, mention how you heard about it, and briefly state that you are qualified. In the following one or two paragraphs, explain your qualifications, elaborating on the most pertinent items in your résumé. Because Amabisca was applying for a public relations job at a museum of Native American culture, she chose to highlight her internship and her thesis. In an application letter for a management position at American Express, however, she emphasized her work experience at Sears.

- **State your expectation for future contact.** Conclude with a one- or two-sentence paragraph informing the reader that you are anticipating a follow-up to your letter.

- **Use *Enc.* if you are enclosing additional materials.** Decide whether it is appropriate to enclose supporting materials other than your résumé, such as samples of your writing. Amabisca decided to do so because she was applying for her ideal job and had highly relevant materials to send. If you have been instructed to send a cover letter and résumé as attachments to an e-mail, include the word *Attachments* after your e-mail "signature."

CONSIDER YOUR SITUATION

Author: Laura Amabisca, a recent graduate and history major

Type of writing: Job application letter

Purpose: To persuade the employer to hire her

Stance: Professional, qualified, and enthusiastic

Audience: Director of public relations at a museum of Native American culture

Medium: Electronic text (word-processing document)

Amabisca writes: Because this museum focuses on Native American culture, my letter emphasized my U.S. history major and my senior thesis on the Hopi. I can say more in an interview.

20650 North 58th Avenue, Apt. 15A
Glendale, AZ 85308
August 17, 2010

Ms. Jaclyn Abel
Director of Public Relations
Heard Museum
2301 North Central Avenue
Phoenix, AZ 85004

Dear Ms. Abel:

I am writing to apply for the position of Public Relations Assistant that you recently advertised in the *Arizona Republic*. I believe that my experience and qualifications fit well with your needs at the Heard, a museum that I have visited and loved all my life.

As the attached résumé indicates, I have experience in the public relations field. While at Arizona State University West, I worked as an intern in the Public Relations Office, where I was responsible for analyzing and reporting on the image projected by the university's external publications. I also had a hand in creating the brochure for the University-College Center and participated in planning ASU West's "Dream Big" campaign. In addition, I assisted in organizing an opening convocation attended by 800 people. This work in the not-for-profit sector has prepared me well for employment at the Heard.

My undergraduate major in U.S. history has also helped me understand the rich heritage of Native Americans. In my senior thesis, which received the Westmarc Writing Award, I studied the history of the relationship between the Hopis and the Anglo population as reflected in photographs taken from 1920 to 1940. Although my thesis focuses on a specific tribe, I have been interested for many years in Native American culture and have often made use of resources in the Heard. I think that I would do a superior job of presenting the Heard as the premier museum of Native American culture.

Confidential reference letters are available from ASU West Career Services. I sincerely hope that we will have an opportunity to talk further about the Heard Museum and its outstanding cultural contributions to the Phoenix metropolitan area. Please contact me at 623-555-7310 or at lamabisca@peoplelink.com.

Sincerely,

Laura Amabisca

Laura Amabisca

Enc.

Amabisca writes to a specific person and uses the correct salutation (*Mr., Ms. Dr.,* and so on). Never use someone's first name in an application letter.

Amabisca sums up her work experience, information that also appears on her résumé. She makes evident why she is applying for the job. Without this explanation, a potential employer might overlook her résumé.

Amabisca demonstrates her familiarity with the museum to which she is applying. This shows her genuine interest in joining the organization.

For MULTILINGUAL WRITERS

Applying for a Job

Before applying for an internship or a job in the United States, be sure that you have the appropriate visa or work permits. American employers are required by law to confirm such documentation before they can hire anyone. (American citizens must prove their citizenship as well.) For more information, visit your campus international student center and the campus career resource center.

12f

Prepare in advance for the job interview. Many campus career centers offer free seminars on interviewing skills and can also arrange for you to role-play an interview with a career guidance counselor.

Here are some additional guidelines for job interviews:

- Call to confirm your interview the day before it is scheduled. Determine how much time you will need to get there. A late appearance at an interview can count heavily against you.

- Dress professionally.

- Bring an additional copy of your résumé and cover letter.

- Expect to speak with several people—perhaps someone from human resources as well as your potential supervisor and other people in the department.

- *Always* send a personalized thank-you note or e-mail to everyone who took the time to meet you. In each, mention an interesting point that the person made and your interest in working with him or her. Send these notes within twenty-four hours of your interview.

12f Applying college writing to writing on the job

Once you get a job, writing establishes and maintains lines of communication with your colleagues and clients. When you write in the workplace, you should imagine a reader who is pressed for time and wants you to get to the point immediately.

1. Writing e-mail and memos in the workplace In the workplace, you will do much of your writing online, in the form of e-mail. Most e-mail programs set up messages in memo format, with "From," "To," "Sent," and "Subject" lines, as in Figure 12.3.

E-mail in the workplace requires a more formal style than the e-mail you send to family and friends. In an e-mail for a business

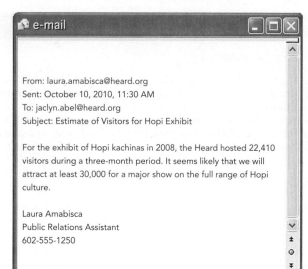

FIGURE 12.3 Sample workplace e-mail.

occasion—communication with colleagues, a request for information, or a thank-you note after an interview—you should observe the same care with organization, spelling, and tone that you would in a business letter:

- Use the subject line to cue the reader to the intent of the e-mail. When replying to messages, replace subject lines that do not clearly reflect the topic.
- Maintain a courteous tone. Avoid joking, informality, and sarcasm since not everyone reading the memo will know you well enough to understand your intent.
- Make sentences brief and to the point. Use short paragraphs.
- Use special formatting such as italics sparingly since not all readers will be able to view it.
- Use standard punctuation and capitalization.
- Close with your name and contact information. *(See Figure 12.3.)*
- Particularly when you do not know the recipient, use the conventions of letter writing, such as opening with "Dear" and ending with "Sincerely."

Business memos are used for communication with others within an organization and are usually sent electronically. Written in a professional tone, memos are concise and formal and may be used to set

TEXTCONNEX

E-mail in the Workplace

Anything you write using a company's or an organization's computers is considered company property. If you want to gossip with a co-worker, do so over a cup of coffee. If you want to e-mail your best friend about your personal life, do so from your home computer. The following guidelines will help you use e-mail wisely:

12f

- When you are replying to an e-mail that has been sent to several people (the term *cc* means "carbon copy"), determine whether your response should go to all of the original recipients or just to the original sender. Avoid cluttering other people's in-boxes.
- File your e-mail as carefully as you would paper documents. Create separate folders in your e-mail program for each client, project, or co-worker.

To: Sonia Gonzalez, Grace Kim, Jonathan Jones
From: Jennifer Richer, Design Team Manager
CC: Michael Garcia, Director, Worldwide Design

Date: March 3, 2010
Re: Meeting on Monday

Please plan to attend a meeting on Monday at 9:00 AM in Room 401. At that time, we'll review our progress on the library project as well as outline future activities to ensure the following:

· Client satisfaction
· Maintenance of the current schedule
· Operation within budget constraints

In addition, we will discuss assignments related to other upcoming projects, such as the renovation of the gymnasium and science lab. Please bring design ideas and be prepared to brainstorm. Thanks.

FIGURE 12.4 Sample business memo.

up meetings, summarize information, or make announcements. *(See Figure 12.4 on p. 183.)* They generally contain the following elements and characteristics:

- A header at the top that identifies author, recipient, date, and subject
- Block paragraphs that are single-spaced within the paragraph and double-spaced between paragraphs
- Bulleted lists and other design elements (such as headers) to set off sections of longer memos
- A professional tone

Consider both the content and the appearance of your memo. For example, presenting your information as a numbered or bulleted list surrounded by white space aids readability and allows you to highlight important points and to emphasize crucial ideas.

2. Writing in other business genres Conventional forms of business writing also increase readability because readers have built-in expectations for the genre and therefore know what to look for. Besides the memo, there are a number of common business genres:

- **Business letters:** Use business letters to communicate formally with people outside an organization. Typically, letters in business format have single-spaced block paragraphs with double spacing between the paragraphs. *(See the example on p. 180.)*
- **Business reports and proposals:** Like college research projects, business reports and proposals can be used to inform, analyze, and interpret. An abstract, sometimes called an **executive summary,** is almost always required. Tables and graphs should be included when appropriate. *(For more on these visual elements, see Chapter 2, pp. 42–43.)*
- **Evaluations and recommendations:** You might need to evaluate a person, or you might be called on to evaluate a product or a procedure and recommend whether the company should buy or use it. Like the reviews and critiques that college writers compose, workplace evaluations should be reasonable as well as convincing. Always support your account of both strengths and weaknesses with specific illustrations or examples.
- **Presentations:** In many professions, information is presented informally and formally to different groups of people. You might suddenly be asked to offer an opinion in a group meeting; or you might be given a week to prepare a formal presentation, with visuals, on an ongoing project.

TEXTCONNEX

12f

Writing Connections

- *Job Central* <http://jobstar.org/tools/resume/samples.cfm>: This site provides samples of résumés for many different situations, as well as sample cover letters.
- *Career Collection: Write a Résumé* <http://owl.english.purdue .edu/owl/resource/564/1/>: This site provides help with preparing cover letters and writing résumés.
- *Résumé services and tips from Monster:* <http://career-advice .monster.com/>: This site includes sample résumés and cover letters in addition to career advice.

The Hubble Space Telescope, which has helped astronomers view the far reaches of the universe, provided this image of a distant galaxy.

For all knowledge and wonder (which is

the seed of knowledge) is an impression

of pleasure in itself.

—FRANCIS BACON

Researching

3

Researching

WRITING OUTCOMES

This section will help you answer questions such as the following:

Rhetorical Knowledge

- What writing situation does my assignment specify? **(13c)**

Critical Thinking, Reading, and Writing

- What is the difference between primary and secondary research? **(13a)**
- How can I tell if sources are worth including? **(16)**
- How do I present my ideas along with those of my sources? **(19d)**

Processes

- How can I think of a topic for my research paper? **(13d)**
- How should I plan my research project? **(13e)**
- When and how should I use visuals in my paper? **(15)**

Knowledge of Conventions

- What is an annotated bibliography, and how do I create one? **(19b)**
- What is a documentation style? Which one should I use? **(20c)**

Composing in Electronic Environments

- How should I evaluate sources that I find on the Web? **(16b)**
- Where can I find appropriate images from online sources? **(15b)**

(For a general introduction to writing outcomes, see Id, page 5.)

13 Understanding Research

Your campus library provides valuable resources for almost any kind of research, offering not only books, magazines, and journals, but also specialized online databases and the expert guidance of research librarians.

Doing research in the twenty-first century includes using the library, but is not limited to it. In seconds, the Internet now offers direct access to an abundance of information unimaginable to earlier generations of students. The results of Internet searches, however, can sometimes yield an overwhelming flood of sources, many of questionable legitimacy.

The goal of the research section of this book *(Chapters 13–20)* is to help you learn about the research process, manage the information you discover within it, and use that information to write research projects.

13a Understanding primary and secondary research

Doing **primary research** means working in a laboratory, in the field, or with an archive of raw data, original documents, and authentic artifacts to make firsthand discoveries. *(For more information about primary research, see Chapter 17, pp. 231–34.)* Doing **secondary research** means looking to see what other people have learned and written about a topic.

Knowing how to identify facts, interpretations, and evaluations is key to good secondary research:

TEXTCONNEX

Types of Sources

- *Research 101—The Basics* <www.lib.washington.edu/UWILL /research101/basic03.htm>: This page from the University of Washington site discusses the difference between primary and secondary research sources, as well as the difference between popular and scholarly periodicals. You can also practice seeing the differences between them on this page: <www.lib .washington.edu/UWILL/research101/Images/primary.swf>
- *Research Papers: Resources* <http://owl.english.purdue.edu/owl /resource/559/1/>: This page from the Purdue Online Writing Lab offers guidelines for conducting primary research.

- **Facts** are objective. Like your body weight, facts can be measured, observed, or independently verified.

- **Interpretations** spell out the implications of facts. Are you as thin as you are because of your genes, because you exercise every day, or both? The answer to this question is an interpretation.

- **Evaluations** are debatable judgments based on a set of facts or a situation. The assertion that "one can never be too rich or too thin" is an evaluation.

Once you are up-to-date on the facts, interpretations, and evaluations in a particular area, you will be able to design a research project that adds your *perspective* on the sources you found and read:

- Given all that you have learned about the topic, what strikes you as important or interesting?

- What patterns do you see, or what connections can you make between one person's work and another's?

- Where is the research going, and what problems still need to be explored?

Putting together the facts, interpretations, and evaluations— **synthesis**—requires time and thought. Since in research writing you are not just stitching sources together but using them to support your own thesis, try beginning the process by focusing on a question you want to answer.

13b Recognizing the connection between research and writing in college and beyond

In many ways, research informs all writing. But some tasks require more rigorous and systematic research than others. These **research projects** require that you go beyond course texts and more casually selected sources—to find and read both classic and current material on a specific issue. A research project constitutes your contribution to the ongoing conversation.

Research is a key component of much workplace and public writing. A sound business proposal will depend on research to identify best practices. A public commentary on the value of charter schools will require research into their performance. Writing academic research projects provides excellent opportunities to prepare for writing situations that you will encounter throughout life.

When you are assigned research writing, the project may seem overwhelming at first. If you break it into phases, however, and allow enough time for each phase, you can manage your work and prepare a project that contributes to an ongoing conversation.

NAVIGATING THROUGH COLLEGE AND BEYOND

Classic and Current Sources

Classic sources are well-known and respected older works that made such an important contribution to a discipline or a particular area of research that contemporary researchers use them as touchstones for further research in that area. In many fields, sources published within the past five years are considered current. However, sources on topics related to medicine, recent scientific discoveries, or technological change must be much more recent to be considered current.

13c
res

13c Understanding the research assignment

Consider the rhetorical situation of the research project. Think about your project's audience, purpose, voice/stance/tone, genre, context, and scope.

1. Audience Although your *audience* may include only your instructor and your classmates, thinking critically about the needs and expectations of practitioners of the discipline will help you to plan a research strategy and create a schedule for writing your project.

Ask yourself the following questions about your audience:

- What do they already know about my subject? How much background information and context should I provide? (Your research should include *facts*.)

- Might they find my conclusions controversial or challenging? How should I accommodate and acknowledge different perspectives and viewpoints? (Your research should include *interpretations*, which balance opposing perspectives.)

- Do I expect the audience to take action based on my research? (Your research should include *evaluations*, carefully supported by facts and interpretations, which demonstrate clearly why readers should adopt a course of action or point of view.)

2. Purpose Your *purpose* for writing a research project depends on both the specifics of the assignment as set by your instructor and your own interest in the topic. Your purpose might be **informative**—to educate your audience about an unfamiliar subject or point of view *(see Chapter 6: Informative Reports, p. 99)*. Your purpose might be **interpretive**—to reveal the meaning or significance of a work of art, an historical document, a literary work, or a scientific study *(see Chapter 7: Interpretive Analyses and Writing about Literature, p. 107)*. Your purpose might be **persuasive**—to convince your audience, with logic and evidence, to accept your point of view on a controversial issue or to act on the information in your project *(see Chapter 8: Arguments, p. 118)*. Review your assignment for keywords that signal its purpose. Here are some examples:

- **Informative:** Explain, describe, define, review
- **Interpretive:** Analyze, compare, explain, interpret
- **Persuasive:** Assess, justify, defend, refute, determine

Note, however, that some terms can signal more than one type of assignment, depending on the context.

3. Voice/stance/tone Your stance in a research project—reflected in your voice and tone—should be that of a well-informed, helpful individual. Even though you will have done extensive work on the topic, it is important to avoid sounding like a know-it-all; instead, you are sharing with others who want to be informed.

4. Genre/medium Research projects prepared for different purposes will reflect characteristics of various genres and may be expressed in different media. Your research on charter schools, for example, may take the form of a proposal or an informative report. Either genre could be communicated in print or on a Web site. Some projects are shared in more than one medium: you may present the findings of your research in class with presentation software, share a brief summary of it on the Web, and submit the full study to the professor in print.

5. Context The overall situation will affect the presentation of your projects. State cuts in public school funding will affect your presentation of a proposal to expand charter schools, even if you have full confidence in the research you have synthesized.

6. Scope A project's scope includes the expected length of the paper, the deadline, and any other requirements such as number and type of sources. Are primary sources appropriate? Should you include visuals, and is any type specified?

13d Choosing an interesting research question for critical inquiry

Approach your assignment in a spirit of critical inquiry. *Critical* in this sense does not mean "fault finding," "skeptical," "cynical," or even "urgent." Rather, it refers to a receptive, but reasonable and discerning, frame of mind. Choosing an interesting topic will make the results of your inquiry meaningful—to yourself and your readers.

1. Choosing a question with personal significance Even though you are writing for an academic assignment, you can still get personally involved in your work. Begin with the wording of the assignment, analyzing the project's required audience, purpose, and scope *(see Chapter 2, pp. 25–29)*. Then browse through the course texts and your class notes, looking for a match between your interests and topics, issues, or problems in the subject area.

13d
res

2. Making your question specific The more specific your question, the more your research will have direction and focus. To make a question more specific, use the "five *w*'s and an *h*" strategy by asking about the *who, what, why, when, where,* and *how* of a topic *(see Chapter 2, pp. 31–32)*.

After you have compiled a list of possible research questions, choose one that is specific, or rewrite a broad one to make it more specific and therefore answerable. For example, as Tina Schwab developed a topic for a sociology course on the reasons young adults volunteer, she rewrote the following broad question.

TOO BROAD	How has the volunteerism of young people affected the United States?
ANSWERABLE	Why do today's college students choose to volunteer?

(Schwab's finished paper appears in Chapter 29, pp. 347–57.)

NAVIGATING THROUGH COLLEGE AND BEYOND

Typical Lines of Inquiry in Different Disciplines

Research topics and questions—even when related to a single broad issue such as volunteerism—differ from one discipline to another. The following examples show the distinctions:

- **History:** How important were volunteers in the creation of lending libraries in nineteenth-century America?
- **Marketing:** What marketing strategies have successfully persuaded busy adults that they should volunteer?
- **Political Science:** What role did volunteers play in the election of national political candidates in the late twentieth century?

3. Finding a challenging question

If a question can be answered with a yes or no, a dictionary-like definition, or a textbook presentation of information, you should choose another question or rework it to make it more challenging.

NOT CHALLENGING	Do college students volunteer?
CHALLENGING	What motivates college students to give of their "time and treasure" when they get no material reward for such efforts?

Exercise 13.1   Creating answerable, challenging questions

For each of the following broad topics, create at least three answerable, challenging questions:

1. Internet access is becoming as important as literacy in determining how a nation's people will earn their livelihood.
2. Genetically modified organisms (GMOs) and biotechnology are controversial approaches to addressing the world's food problems.
3. The problem of terrorism requires a multilateral solution.

---

4. Speculating about answers

Sometimes it can be useful to speculate on the answer to your research question so that you have a **hypothesis** to work with during the research process. Don't forget, though, that a hypothesis is a tentative answer that must be tested and revised based on the evidence you turn up in your research. Be aware of the assumptions embedded in your hypothesis or research question. Consider, for example, the following.

HYPOTHESIS	College students volunteer for more than one reason.

This hypothesis assumes that because college students differ from one another in many ways, they have more than one reason for volunteering. But assumptions are always open to question. Researchers must be willing to adjust their ideas as they learn more about a topic.

As the preceding example demonstrates, your research question must allow you to generate testable hypotheses. Assertions about your personal beliefs and feelings cannot be tested.

NAVIGATING THROUGH COLLEGE AND BEYOND

Scheduling Your Research Project

Task	Date

Phase I

- Complete general plan for research. _____
- Decide on topic and research question. _____
- Consult reference works and reference librarians. _____
- Make list of relevant keywords for online searching
  (see Chapter 14, p. 199). _____
- Compile **working bibliography**
  (see Chapter 19, p. 241). _____
- Sample some items in bibliography. _____
- Make arrangements for primary research
  (if necessary). _____

Phase II

- Locate, read, and evaluate selected sources. _____
- Take notes, write summaries and paraphrases. _____
- Cross-check notes with working bibliography. _____
- Conduct primary research (if necessary). _____
- Find and create visuals. _____
- Confer with instructor or writing center (optional). _____
- Develop thesis and outline or plan organization
  of paper. _____

Phase III

- Write first draft, deciding which primary and
  secondary source materials to include. _____
- Have peer review (optional). _____
- Revise draft. _____
- Confer with instructor or writing center (optional). _____
- Do final revision and editing. _____
- Create works-cited or references page. _____
- Proofread and check spelling. _____

Due date _____

13e
res

13e Creating a research plan

Your research will be more productive if you create both a general
plan and a detailed schedule immediately after you receive your assignment. A general plan ensures that you understand the full scope

of the assignment. A detailed schedule helps you set priorities and meet deadlines.

Use the "Navigating through College and Beyond" box on page 195, which outlines the steps in a research project, as a starting point, adjusting the time allotments based on the amount of time you have to complete the assignment. Consider what you already know about the topic as well as what you must learn through your research.

Exercise 13.2 Research plan

Think through the situation for the research you will be doing. What is your purpose? Describe your audience. Will the research be the basis of an informative report or a proposal? Will your medium be print, a word-processed text with visuals, or a Web page? As you think through these questions, make notes below.

The context for the research is _____.

My interest in the research is _____.

The writing situation:

My purpose is _____.

My audience is _____.

My rhetorical stance is _____.

The medium (or media) I will use is (are) _____.

I will use it because _____.

If I succeed, my audience will know or believe _____

_____.

Exercise 13.3 Research schedule

Adapt the worksheet in the box on page 195 to create a research schedule whenever you have a research assignment. If you use a smartphone or other digital tool, type in this schedule—you can also access it online from *Connect*—and set reminders or alarms for key dates (such as completing library research, completing a first draft, and conferring with the campus Writing Center).

SOURCE SMART

Planning Your Search

Your research plan should include where you expect to find your sources. For example, you may have to visit the library to view print materials that predate 1980; you will need to consult a subscription database online or at the library for recent scientific discoveries; you may need to access archives for historical research; and you may need to conduct field research, such as interviewing fellow students. Set priorities to increase your efficiency in each location (library, archive, online).

14a
res

14 Finding and Managing Print and Online Sources

To conduct a meaningful search through the vast amount of available information, focus on the following three activities:

- Collecting keywords from reference works
- Using library databases
- Finding material in the library and on the Web

14a Using the library in person and online

Librarians know what is available at your library and how to get material from other libraries. They can also show you how to access the library's computerized book catalog, periodical databases, and electronic resources, and how to use the Internet to find information relevant to your research. At many schools, reference librarians are available for online chats, and some even take queries via text message. Your library's Web site may also have links to subscription databases or important reference works available on the Internet, as shown in Figure 14.1 on page 198.

In addition, **help sheets** or online tutorials at most college libraries give the location of both general and discipline-specific periodicals and noncirculating reference books, along with information

FIGURE 14.1 A page from the Web site of Governors State University. The Web page provides links to a variety of Web-based reference sources. SOURCE: Reprinted with permission from Governors State University.

about the book catalog, special databases, indexes, Web resources, and library policies.

Exercise 14.1 Finding information at your library

Choose anyone born between 1910 and 1960 whose life and accomplishments interest you. You could select a politician, a film director, a rock star, a Nobel Prize–winning economist—*anyone*. At your library, find at least one of each of the following resources with information about or relevant to this person:

■ A directory of biographies
■ An article in a pre-1990 newspaper
■ An article in a scholarly journal

- An audio or video recording, a photograph, or a work of art
- A printout of the search results of your library's electronic catalog
- A printout of an article obtained via a subscription database
- An obituary (if your subject has died)
- A list of your subject's accomplishments, including, for example, prizes received, books published, albums released, or movies made

14b Consulting various kinds of sources

You should always consult more than one source, and usually more than one *kind* of source. Your assignment may specify how many print and electronic sources you are expected to consult and cite. Here are some of the available resources:

14c
res

- **General reference works (for overview and keywords)**
  Encyclopedias, annuals, almanacs
  Computer databases, bibliographies, abstracts
- **Specialized reference works (for overview and keywords)**
  Discipline-specific encyclopedias, almanacs, and dictionaries
- **Books**
- **Periodical articles**
  In newspapers
  In magazines
  In scholarly and technical journals
  On the Web
- **Web sites**
- **Other online sources**
- **Virtual communities**
  MUDs (multiuser dimensions)
  MOOs (multiuser object-oriented dimensions)
- **Government documents, pamphlets, census data**
- **Primary sources**
  Original documents like literary works, art objects, performances, manuscripts, letters, and personal journals
  Museum collections; maps; photo, film, sound, and music archives
  Field notes, surveys, interviews
  Results of observation and lab experiments

14c Understanding keywords and keyword searches

Most online research—whether conducted in your library's catalog, in a specialized database, or on the Web—requires an understanding of **keyword searches.** In this context, a **keyword** is a term (or

NAVIGATING THROUGH COLLEGE AND BEYOND

Sources: Popular or Scholarly?

A source's audience and purpose determine whether it should be considered *popular* or *scholarly*. You may begin your inquiry into a research topic with popular sources, but to become fully informed, you must consult scholarly sources.

Popular sources:

- Are widely available on newsstands and in retail stores (print)
- Are printed on magazine paper with a color cover (print)
- Accept advertising for a wide range of consumer goods or are themselves widely advertised (in the case of books)
- Are published by a commercial publishing house or media company (such as Time Warner)
- May include a wide range of topics in each issue, from international affairs to popular entertainment
- Usually do not contain bibliographic information
- Have a URL that likely ends in .com (online)

Scholarly sources:

- Are usually found in libraries, not on newsstands (print)
- List article titles and authors on the cover (print)
- Have few advertisements
- Are published by a scholarly or nonprofit organization, often in association with a university press
- Focus on discipline-specific topics
- Include articles mostly by authors who are affiliated with colleges, museums, or other scholarly institutions
- Include articles with extensive citations and bibliographies
- Have a URL that likely ends in .edu or .org (online)
- Are **refereed** (peer reviewed), which means that each article has been reviewed, commented on, and accepted for publication by other scholars in the field

terms) you enter into a **search engine** (searching software) to find sources that have information about a particular subject.

As you focus more sharply on your topic, you must also refine your search terms. The "Navigating through College and Beyond" box on page 201 describes a variety of techniques that work in most search engines. Look for advanced search features that help with the refining process.

NAVIGATING THROUGH COLLEGE AND BEYOND

Refining Keyword Searches

Although search engines vary, the following guidelines should work for many:

- **Group words together.** Put quotation marks or parentheses around the specific phrase you are looking for—for example, "traditional news media."
- **Use Boolean operators.**

  AND (+) Use **AND** or **+** when you need sites with both of two or more words: New York Times + blogs.

  OR Use **OR** when you want sites with either of two or more terms: blogs OR "online journalism."

  NOT Use **NOT** in front of words that you do not want to appear together in your results: Cass NOT John.

- **Use truncation plus a "wildcard."** For more results, combine part of a keyword with an asterisk (*) used as a wildcard: blog* (for "blogger," "blogging," "blogs," and so forth).
- **Search the fields.** Some search engines permit you to search within fields, such as the title field of Web pages or the author field of a library catalog. Thus, TITLE + "news media" will give you all pages that have "news media" in their title.

14d res

Exercise 14.2 Finding information online

Look at the sample research topics listed in the "Navigating through College and Beyond" box on page 193, and conduct a keyword search for each on at least three search engines. Experiment with the phrasing of each keyword search, and compare your results with those of your classmates.

EXAMPLE   **What marketing strategies have successfully persuaded busy adults that they should volunteer?**

"marketing strategies" AND "adult volunteers"

14d Using printed and online reference works for general information

Reference works provide an overview of a subject area and typically are less up-to-date than the specialized knowledge found in academic journals and scholarly books. If your instructor approves, you may

TEXTCONNEX

Wikipedia

The online encyclopedia Wikipedia offers information on almost any subject, and it can be a good starting place for research. However, you should evaluate its content critically and use other sources to verify information you find there. Volunteers (who may or may not be experts) write Wikipedia's articles, and almost any user may edit any article. Although the site has some mechanisms to maintain accuracy, always verify findings with another, more authoritative source (and cite that source, if you use the information).

start your research by consulting a general or discipline-specific encyclopedia, but for college research, you must explore your topic in more depth. Often, the list of references at the end of an encyclopedia article can lead you to useful sources on your topic.

Reference books do not circulate, so take notes and make photocopies of the pages you may need to consult later. Check your college library's home page for access to online encyclopedias.

Here is a list of some other kinds of reference materials available in print, on the Internet, or both:

ALMANACS	*Almanac of American Politics* *Information Please Almanac* *World Almanac*
BIBLIOGRAPHIES	*Bibliographic Index* *Bibliography of Asian Studies* *MLA International Bibliography*
BIOGRAPHIES	*African American Biographical Database* *American Men and Women of Science* *Dictionary of American Biography* *Dictionary of Literary Biography:* *Chicano Writers* *Dictionary of National Biography* *Webster's New Biographical Dictionary* *Who's Who*
DICTIONARIES	*American Heritage Dictionary of the* *English Language* *Concise Oxford Dictionary of Literary Terms* *Dictionary of American History* *Dictionary of Philosophy* *Dictionary of the Social Sciences* *Oxford English Dictionary (OED)*

For MULTILINGUAL WRITERS

Researching a Full Range of Sources

Your mastery of a language other than English can give you access to important non-English sources. Do not limit yourself to sources in your first language, however. Even if you find researching in English challenging, it is important to broaden your search as soon as you can to include a range of print and Internet resources written in English.

14e Using print indexes and online databases to find articles in journals and other periodicals

14e
res

Indexes and online databases are essential tools for researching in journals and other periodicals.

1. Periodicals Newspapers, magazines, and scholarly journals that are published at regular intervals are classified as **periodicals.** The articles in scholarly and technical journals, written by experts and based on up-to-date research, are more credible than articles in popular newspapers and magazines. Ask your instructor or librarian which periodicals are considered important in the discipline you are studying.

2. Indexes and databases Articles published in periodicals are cataloged in general and specialized **indexes.** Indexes are available on subscription-only **databases** and as print volumes. If you are searching for articles that are more than twenty years old, you may use print indexes, or an appropriate electronic index. Print indexes can be searched by author, subject, or title. Electronic databases can also be searched by date and keyword and will provide a list of articles that meet your search criteria. Each entry in the list will include the information you need to find and cite the article.

You can find databases on your library's Web site (and on CD-ROMs in the library). When selecting a database, consult its description on your library's site (often labeled "Info") to see the types of sources included, subjects covered, and number of periodicals from each subject area. Would your topic be best served by a general database (such as EBSCO Academic Search Premier) or one that is discipline specific (such as PsycINFO)? Also consider the time period the database spans.

The "Navigating through College and Beyond" box on page 205 lists common formats for database information. The "TextConnex" box on pages 206–7 lists some of the major online databases, and the

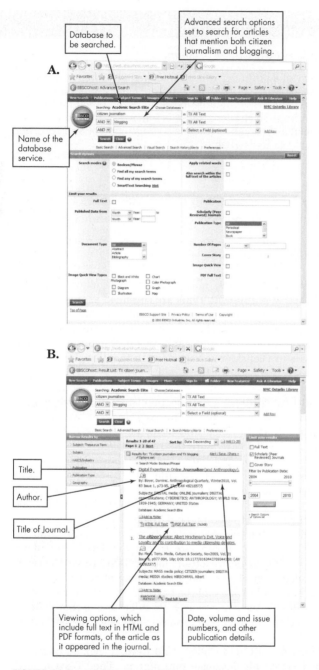

FIGURE 14.2 EBSCOhost's Advanced Search page (A) and partial results of a search (B). SOURCE: © EBSCO Publishing, Inc. All rights reserved.

NAVIGATING THROUGH COLLEGE AND BEYOND

Formats for Database Information

When searching a database, you will encounter both abstracts and full-text articles, and full-text articles may be available in either PDF or HTML format:

- **Abstract:** An abstract is a brief summary of a full-text article. Abstracts appear at the beginning of articles in some scholarly journals and are used in databases to summarize complete articles. (Do not mistake an abstract for a full-text source.)
- **Full text:** When an article is listed as "full text," the database provides a link to the complete text. Full-text articles accessed through databases do not always include accompanying photographs or other illustrations, however.
- **PDF** and **HTML:** Articles in databases and other online sources may be in either PDF or HTML format (or both). Documents in HTML (hypertext markup language) have been formatted to read as Web pages and may directly link to related sources. PDF (portable document format) documents appear as a facsimile of the original pages. To read a PDF document, download *Adobe Acrobat Reader,* available free of charge from <www.adobe.com>.

**14f
res**

screen images on page 204 in Figure 14.2 illustrate a search on one of them, EBSCOhost. Keep in mind that not all libraries subscribe to all databases.

14f Using search engines and subject directories to find Internet sources

To find information that has been published in Web pages, use more than one Internet search engine, because each searches the Web in its own way. Each search engine's home page provides a link to advice on efficient use as well as help in refining a search. *(See the box on p. 209 for a list of popular Internet search engines.)* Look for a link labeled "search help," "about us," or something similar.

Some Internet search engines allow you to conduct specialized searches—for images, for example *(see Chapter 15). Google Book Search* can help you locate books on your topic. *Google Scholar* locates only scholarly sources in response to a search term. At this point, it offers incomplete information, so you should not rely on it alone.

Many Internet search engines also include sponsored links—links that a commercial enterprise has paid to make appear in response to specific search terms. These are usually clearly identified.

TEXTCONNEX

Some Online Databases

- **ABC-CLIO:** This service offers access to numerous history-related databases, including *American History* and *American Government,* as well as databases on African American, American Indian, and Latino American experience, pop culture, war, social history, geography, and world history.
- **EBSCOhost:** The Academic Search Premier database provides full-text coverage for more than eight thousand scholarly publications and indexes articles in all academic subject areas.
- **ERIC:** This database lists publications in the area of education.
- **Factiva:** This database offers access to the Dow Jones and Reuters news agencies, including newspapers, magazines, journals, newsletters, and Web sites.
- **General Science Index:** This index is general (rather than specialized). It lists scholarly and popular articles by biologists, chemists, and other scientists.
- **GPO Monthly Catalogue:** Updated monthly, the Government Printing Office Catalogue contains records of all publications printed by the U.S. Government Printing Office since 1976.
- **Humanities Index:** This index lists articles from journals in language and literature, history, philosophy, and similar areas.
- **InfoTrac Web:** This Web-based service searches bibliographic and other databases such as the *General Reference Center Gold, General Business File ASAP,* and *Health Reference Center.*
- **JSTOR:** This archive provides full-text access to recent issues of journals in the humanities, social sciences, and natural sciences, typically from two to five years before the current date.
- **LexisNexis Academic:** Updated daily, this online service provides full-text access to around six thousand newspapers, professional publications, legal references, and congressional sources.

To find relevant results, carefully select the words for Internet keyword searches. For example, a search of *Google* using the keywords *citizen journalism* yields a list of more than 2,380,000 Web sites. Altering the keywords to make them more specific narrows the results significantly (*see Figure 14.3 on p. 208*). The most relevant matches will appear at the beginning of the results page.

Most search engines have an Advanced Search option. This allows you to search for exact phrases, to exclude a specific term, to

TEXTCONNEX *(continued)*

- *MLA Bibliography:* Covering 1963 to the present, the *MLA Bibliography* indexes journals, dissertations, and serials published worldwide in the fields of modern languages, literature, literary criticism, linguistics, and folklore.
- *New York Times Index:* This index lists major articles published by the *Times* since 1913.
- *Newspaper Abstracts:* This database provides an index to fifty national and regional newspapers.
- *PAIS International:* Produced by the Public Affairs Information Service, this database indexes literature on public policy, social policy, and the social sciences from 1972 to the present.
- *Periodical Abstracts:* This database indexes more than two thousand general and academic journals covering business, current affairs, economics, literature, religion, psychology, and women's studies from 1987 to the present.
- *ProQuest:* This database provides access to dissertations; newspapers and journals; information on sources in business, general reference, the social sciences, and humanities; and historical sources dating back to the nineteenth century.
- *PsycInfo:* Sponsored by the American Psychological Association (APA), this database indexes and abstracts books, scholarly articles, technical reports, and dissertations in psychology and related disciplines since the 1800s.
- *PubMed:* The National Library of Medicine publishes this database, which indexes and abstracts fifteen million journal articles in biomedicine and provides links to related databases.
- *Sociological Abstracts:* This database indexes and abstracts articles from more than 2,600 journals, as well as books, conference papers, and dissertations.
- *Social Science Index:* This index lists articles from such fields as economics, psychology, political science, and sociology.
- *WorldCat:* This is a catalog of books and other resources available in libraries worldwide.

14f
res

search only for pages in a certain language, and to refine searches in many other ways.

In addition to keyword searches, many Internet search engines offer a **subject directory**—a listing of broad categories. Clicking through this hierarchy of choices eventually brings you to a list of sites related to a specific topic.

Some Web sites, such as *the Internet Public Library* (<www.ipl .org>), provide content-specific subject directories designed for research

FIGURE 14.3 Refining the search. Adding the key terms *blogging, social media, newspapers,* and *reporting* reduces the number of hits in this Google search to 307,000 from more than two million.

in a particular field. These sites are often reviewed or screened and are excellent starting points for academic research.

Other online tools can help organize sources and keep track of your Web research. Save the URLs of promising sites to your browser's Bookmarks or Favorites. Your browser's history function can allow you to retrace your steps if you forget how to find a particular site. The box on page 212 includes additional online resources.

14g Using your library's catalog to find books

Books in most libraries are shelved by **call numbers** based on the Library of Congress classification system. In this system, books on the same topic have similar call numbers and are shelved together. You will need the call number to locate the actual book on the library's

TEXTCONNEX

Popular Internet Search Engines

General search engines: These sites allow for both category and keyword searches:

- *AltaVista* <www.altavista.com>
- *Ask* <www.ask.com/>
- *Bing* <www.bing.com>
- *Google* <www.google.com>
- *Yahoo!* <www.yahoo.com>

Meta search engines: These sites search several different search engines at once:

- *Dogpile* <www.dogpile.com>
- *Internet Public Library* <www.ipl.org>
- *Ixquick* <www.ixquick.com>
- *Library of Congress* <http://loc.gov>
- *MetaCrawler* <www.metacrawler.com>
- *WebCrawler* <www.webcrawler.com>

Mediated search engines: These sites have been assembled and reviewed by people who sometimes provide annotations and commentary about topic areas and specific sites:

- *About.com* <www.about.com>

14g
res

shelves. Therefore, when consulting a library catalog, be sure to jot down (or print out) the call numbers of books you want to consult.

You can conduct a keyword search of most library catalogs by author, by title, or by subject. Subject terms appear in the *Library of Congress Subject Headings (LCSH),* which provides a set of key terms that you can use in your search for sources. Keyword searches available in many catalogs also include publisher, notes, and other fields.

Card catalogs are rarely used except by archives and specialized libraries. Cards are usually filed by author, title, and subject (based on the *Library of Congress Subject Headings*).

The results of a keyword search of a library's catalog will provide a list composed mostly of books. As shown in the examples in Figures 14.4 and 14.5 of a search of the Governors State University's online catalog on pages 210 and 211, you can alter the terms of a search to restrict the formats to a specific medium.

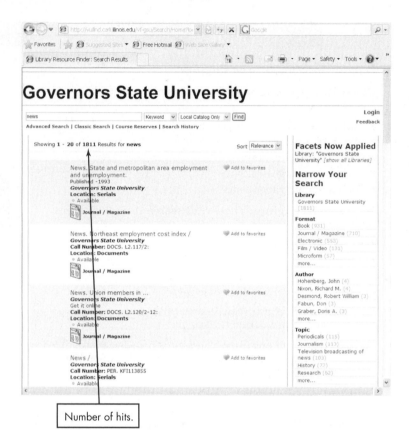

Number of hits.

FIGURE 14.4 Searching an online catalog. Using the word *news* as a keyword in a subject search produces 1,811 sources. SOURCE: Reprinted with permission from Governors State University.

SOURCE SMART

Organizing Your Sources

List your sources alphabetically. For each source, include citation information *(see pp. 241–42),* its relevance to your topic, and key points. Does the source support or detract from your claim? Is it an early source or a more recent one? Does it agree or disagree with other sources you have read? Do other sources refer to this one? You might color-code your list to indicate related ideas that appear in a number of your sources. Include useful quotations and their page numbers.

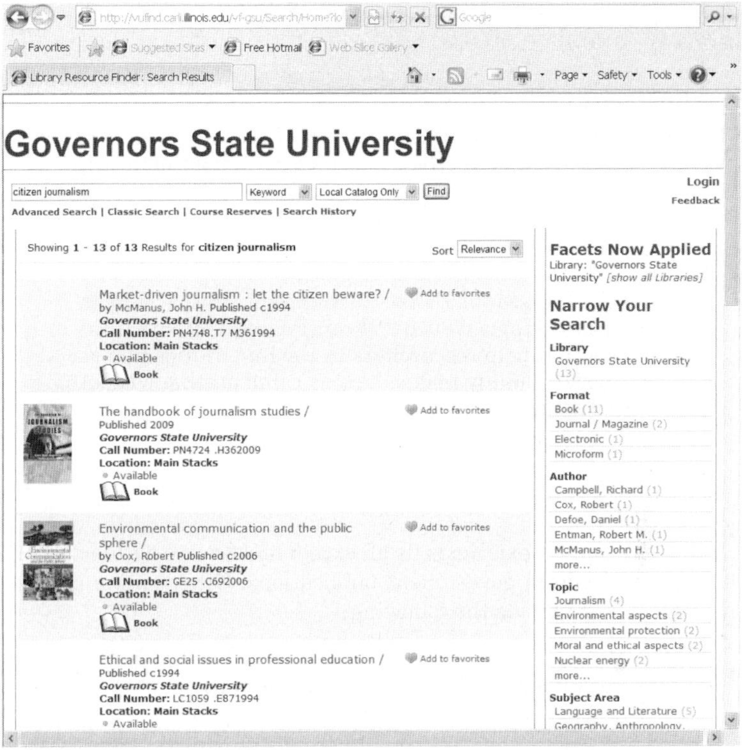

FIGURE 14.5 Changing a search term. A keyword search using the search term *citizen journalism* produces thirteen results, a manageable number. SOURCE: Reprinted with permission from Governors State University.

As with any keyword search, getting what you really need—a manageable number of relevant sources—depends on your choice of keywords. If your search terms are too broad, you will get too many hits; if they are too narrow, you will get few or none.

14h Taking advantage of printed and online government documents

The U.S. government publishes an enormous amount of information and research every year, most of which is available online. The *GPO Monthly Catalogue* and the *U.S. Government Periodicals Index* are available as online databases. The Government Printing Office's own Web site, *The Federal Digital System* <www.gpo.gov/fdsys/>,

TEXTCONNEX

Online Tools for Research

■ *Zotero* <www.zotero.org>: Compatible with the *Mozilla Firefox* browser (version 2.0 and higher), this program automatically saves citation information for many types of online sources (text and images) via your browser. It creates formatted references in multiple styles and helps you organize your sources by assigning tags (categories based on keywords) to them.

■ *DiRT (Digital Research Tools)* <https://digitalresearchtools .pbworks.com/w/page/17801672/FrontPage>: This site links to online tools that help researchers in the humanities and social sciences perform many tasks, such as collaborating with others, finding sources, and visualizing data.

available through LexisNexis, is an excellent resource for identifying and locating federal government publications. Other online government resources include the following:

■ *FedWorld Information Network* (maintained by the National Technical Information Service)

■ *FirstGov* (the U.S. government's "Official Web Portal") <http:// firstgov.gov/>

■ *The National Institutes of Health* <www.nih.gov>

■ *U.S. Census Bureau* <www.census.gov>

14i Exploring online communication

Usenet news groups, electronic mailing lists, blogs, and social networking offer opportunities to converse regularly with people who have common interests. Carefully evaluate information from these sources *(see Chapter 16: Evaluating Sources, pp. 224–27)*. Participants will have different levels of expertise—or possibly no expertise at all. Online forums can help you with research in the following ways:

■ You can get ideas for your writing by identifying topics of general concern and becoming aware of general trends in thinking about the topic.

■ You can zero in on a very specific or current topic.

■ You can query an expert in the field about your topic via e-mail or a social networking site.

> *Caution:* Since the credibility of online forums varies widely, use your library or department Web site to find scholarly forums for purposes of comparison and assessment.

Social networking sites like *Facebook* and *Twitter* help people form online communities. **Blogs** *(see Chapter 11)* can be designed to allow readers to post their own comments and questions. Blogs can convey a wide range of positions on a topic under debate. However, many blog postings consist of unsupported opinion, and they may not be monitored closely for accuracy. **Wikis,** sites designed for online collaboration, allow people both to comment on and to modify one another's contributions. When evaluating information from a wiki, check to see who can update content and whether experts review the changes. If content is not monitored by identified experts, check your findings with another source. *(See the box on* Wikipedia *on p. 202.)*

14i

res

Usenet news groups are posted to a **news server**—a computer that hosts the news group and distributes postings to participating servers. You must subscribe to read postings, which are not automatically distributed by e-mail.

Podcasts are downloadable digital audio or video recordings, updated regularly. The Smithsonian produces reliable podcasts on many topics: <www.si.edu/Connect/podcasts>.

RSS (Really Simple Syndication) **feeds** deliver the latest content from continuously updated Web sites to your e-mail address. You can use RSS feeds to keep up with information on your topic, once you identify relevant Web sites.

Synchronous communication includes **chat rooms** organized by topic, where people can carry on real-time discussions. **Instant messaging (IM)** links only those who have agreed to form a conversing group. Other formats include virtual worlds such as *Second Life,* multiuser dimensions (MUDs), and object-oriented multiuser dimensions (MOOs). These can be used for collaborative projects.

For a list of discipline-specific resources, go online to www.mhhe.com/bmhh2.

15 Finding and Creating Effective Visuals, Audio Clips, and Videos

Visuals can support a writer's thesis, enhance an argument, and sometimes constitute the complete argument. Relief organizations, for example, may post a series of compelling visuals on their Web sites to persuade potential donors to contribute money following a catastrophic event.

For some writing situations, you will prepare or provide your own visuals. You may, for example, make your own sketch of an experiment or create a bar graph from data that you have collected. In other situations, however, you may decide to create a visual from data that you have found in a source, or you may search in your library or on the Internet for a visual to use.

In an online text, an audio clip or a video can provide support for an argument or add an engaging note to a personal Web site.

15a Finding quantitative data and displaying it visually

Research writing in many disciplines—especially in the sciences, social sciences, business, math, engineering, and other technical fields—almost always requires reference to quantitative information. That information generally has more impact when it is displayed visually in a chart, graph, or map than as raw numbers alone. Visual displays of information are also tools of analysis.

Think through the writing situation as you decide about when to include visuals or multimedia and what types are appropriate to include. Consider your readers' expectations for presentations of numerical relationships that words alone cannot convey. *(For examples of graphs and charts, and a discussion of what situations to use them in, see Chapter 2, pp. 42–45.)*

1. Finding existing graphs, charts, and maps   As you search for print and online sources *(see Chapter 14),* take notes on useful graphs, charts, or maps that you might incorporate (with proper

> *Caution:* Whether you are using data from a source to create an image or incorporating an image made by someone else, you must give credit to the source of the data or image, just as you do when you paraphrase or quote the work of others. Furthermore, if you plan to publish this visual on a Web site or in another medium, you must obtain permission to use it from the copyright holder, unless the source specifically states that such use is allowed.

SOURCE SMART

Citing Data

Make citations of data specific. Indicate the report and page number or Web address(es) where you found the information, as well as any other elements required by your documentation style. If you analyze the data, refer to any analysis in the source before presenting your own interpretation.

15a
visual

acknowledgment) into your text. If your source is available in print only, you may be able to use a scanner to capture and digitize it.

2. Creating visuals from quantitative data Sometimes you may find data presented in writing or in tables that would be more effective as a chart or graph. Using the graphics tool available in spreadsheet or other software, you can create your own visual.

For example, suppose you are drafting a research project about population trends in the United States in the nineteenth century and want to illustrate the country's population growth in that period with a line graph, using U.S. Census Bureau data, which is in the public domain. Most census data, however, appears in tables like the one shown in Figure 15.1 on page 216. If you transfer the data from a table to a spreadsheet program or a word-processing program, you can use it to create graphs that you can insert into a project, as in Figure 15.1.

3. Displaying the data accurately Display data in a way that is consistent with your purpose and not misleading to viewers. For example, Nancy Kaplan has pointed out distortions in a graph from a National Endowment for the Arts report on reading practices (Figure 15.2 on page 217). The NEA graph presents the years 1984 to 2004, showing a sharp decline in reading. However, the source for the graph, the National Center for Educational Statistics (NCES), presents a less alarming picture in Figure 15.3 on page 217. Here, reading levels are plotted over a longer period of time, from 1971 to 2004. In addition, the NEA graph is not consistent in its units: the four-year period from 1984 to 1988 takes up the same amount of space as the two-year period from 1988 to 1990. In selectively displaying and distorting data, the NEA graph stacks the deck to argue for the reality of a reading crisis.

Avoid intentionally or unintentionally distorting data. Do not use photo-editing software to alter photographs. Plot the axes of line and bar graphs so that they do not misrepresent data.

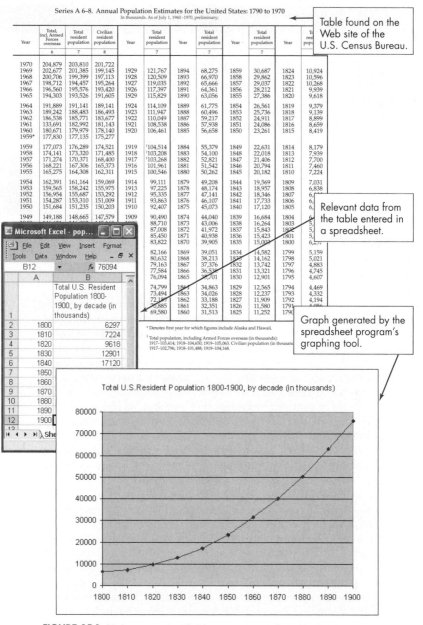

FIGURE 15.1 Using a spreadsheet program to create a graph from data in a table.

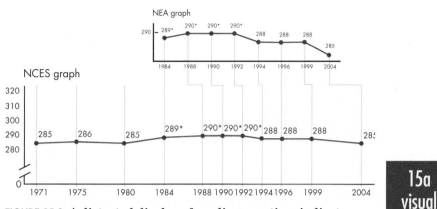

FIGURE 15.2 A distorted display of reading practices indicates a decline.

FIGURE 15.3 An accurate display of reading practices shows only mild fluctuations.

15a
visual

CHECKLIST

Deciding What Kind of Chart or Graph to Use

In deciding the kind of chart or graph to use, consider these questions:

☐ Who are my readers, and what are their expectations?

☐ What information is most important to show, and why?

☐ What options do I have for displaying the information?

☐ How much context is necessary to include, and why?

☐ How many charts or graphs will contribute to achieving my purpose, based on readers' expectations, academic discipline, medium, and genre?

☐ How detailed should each visual be, and why?

☐ Will my visual project into the future or report on the past?

☐ What information will be left out or minimized, and how important is that omission?

☐ What other information—an introduction, an explanation, a summary, an interpretation—will readers need to make sense of the visual information?

15b Searching for appropriate images in online and print sources

Photographs, pictures of artwork, drawings, diagrams, and maps can provide visual support for many kinds of texts, particularly in subjects like history, English and other languages, philosophy, music, theater, and other performing arts. As with the display of quantitative data, you might *choose* an image from another source, or you might *create one*. If you were doing a report comparing the way different corporations are organized, for example, you might use organizational charts that appear in corporate reports. Alternatively, you could use your word processor's drawing feature to create your own organizational charts based on information you find in the corporate reports. When using an image from another source, be sure to cite it correctly. If the image will appear on a public Web site, consult the copyright holder for permission.

The following are three sources of images that you can use:

- **Online library and museum image collections and subscription databases:** Several libraries and other archives maintain collections of images online. See the TextConnex box on page 220 for the URLs of image collections. Follow the guidelines for usage posted on these sites. Your library also may subscribe to an image database such as the Associated Press *AP Multimedia Archive.*

- **Images on the Internet:** Many search engines have the ability to search the Web for images. You can conduct an image search on Google, for example, by clicking on the "images" option, entering the key term, and then clicking "search." Image- and media-sharing sites such as Flickr and YouTube can serve as sources as well. Read the information on the site carefully to see what uses of the material are permitted. The *Creative Commons* site (www.creativecommons.org) lets you search for material with a Creative Commons license, which describes allowed uses of the content. The material shown can be used or altered for noncommercial purposes, as long as it is cited. All the images accompanying *Wikipedia* are licensed through *Creative Commons,* so that is another source you can use. Assume that copyright applies to material on the Web unless the site says otherwise. If your project will be published or placed on a public Web site, you must obtain permission to use this material. *(See Chapter 18: Plagiarism, Copyright Infringement, and Intellectual Property, pp. 234–40.)*

- **Images scanned from a book or journal:** You can use a scanner to scan some images from books and journals, but, as

always, only if you are sure your use is within fair-use guidelines. Also, be sure to credit the source.

Caution: The results of Internet image searches, like those
of any Internet search, need to be carefully evaluated for relevance and credibility. *(See Chapter 16, pp. 224–27.)* Make sure
you have proper source information for any images that you
find in this way.

NAVIGATING THROUGH COLLEGE AND BEYOND

**15c
visual**

Deciding When to Use an Image in Your Project

Consider these questions as you look for visuals:

- What contribution will each image make to the text?
- What contribution do the images taken as a whole make to the
  text?
- How many images do you need?
- Where will each image appear in the text?
- Does the audience have enough background information to
  interpret each image in the way you intend?
- If not, what additional information should you include?
- What information should be in the caption?
- Have you reviewed your own text (and perhaps asked a friend
  to review it as well) to see how well the image is working in
  terms of appropriateness, location, and context?

15c Searching for or creating appropriate audio clips and videos

Some writing situations call for audio or video clips. A history of the
ways that Franklin Delano Roosevelt managed his paralyzed legs
might include a video showing him leaning against a podium to give
a talk. Video of the *Challenger* explosion in 1986 could underscore
the constant danger faced by astronauts. The sounds made by locusts
would help explain how quickly these insects consume everything in
their path.

When deciding to use a video or audio clip, you have two choices:
you can use material that is available elsewhere, crediting it appropriately, or create your own. A rich stock of material is available on

TEXTCONNEX

Some Online Image Collections

- *Art Institute of Chicago* (selected works from the museum's collection) <www.artic.edu/aic/collections/>
- *The Library of Congress* (various images and documents from American history)
- *National Archives Digital Classroom* (documents and photographs from American history) <www.archives.gov/ digital _classroom/index.html>
- *National Aeronautics and Space Administration* (images and multimedia features on space exploration) <www.nasa.gov /multimedia/imagegallery/index.html>
- *National Park Service Digital Image Archive* (thousands of public domain photographs of U.S. national parks) <www.nps .gov/photosmultimedia/photogalleries.htm>
- *New York Public Library* (maps, posters, photographs, and documents) <www.nypl.org/digital/>
- *Schomburg Center for Research in Black Culture* (articles, books, and images representing the African diaspora and African American history) <www.nypl.org/research/sc/sc.html>
- *VRoma: A Virtual Community for Teaching and Learning Classics* (images and other resources related to ancient Rome) <www.vroma.org/images/image_search.html>

the Web *(see the TextConnex box on p. 221)*. You can begin by searching in general categories such as Google Video Search or Yahoo video search or in more specific categories like CNN video or the National Science Foundation's *NSF Science Nation*. Likewise, you can find audio clips at large databases like the Library of Congress American Memory Web site and on DIY (Do It Yourself) Web sites like *Pandora,* where you can create your own playlist.

For some projects, you might include video and audio clips that you create yourself. Audio interviews with students engaged in volunteer activities can allow them to "speak" to the experience and provide details supporting your claim about student volunteerism. A video of a student discussing his or her award-winning artwork— with the artwork visible—helps your reader see both the artist and the art. Whenever you create an audio or video file, be sure to ask your subjects for permission.

TEXTCONNEX

Online Sources of Audio and Video Clips

Sources of audio and video clips, from the University of Illinois library's Web site:

- **Google Video Search** <http://video.google.com/?ie=UTF-8&hl=enj&tab=wv> A good place to search for videos on a wide range of subjects.
- **CNN Video** <www.cnn.com/video/> Provides free video news about national and international events.
- **MTV Music Videos** <www.mtv.com/music/videos/#/music/video> Allows you to search for your favorite artist or music video; however, will play a short MTV ad before the video.
- **Research Channel** <www.researchchannel.org/> Created by a group of research and academic institutions to share their researchers' work with the public.
- **American Memory Project** <http://memory.loc.gov/ammem/browse/index.html> Provided by the Library of Congress; provides access to historical materials that document the American experience. Select "Motion Pictures" in the Browse Collections Containing section.

16
eval

16 Evaluating Sources

Never before in the history of the planet has information been more readily available. The catch is that a good deal of this information is misleading or downright false. Your major task is to evaluate the information that you find for credibility, accuracy, reasonableness, and support (CARS).

Digital technologies give you fast access to a tremendous variety of sources, but it is up to you to pose questions. Is the source relevant, and does it pertain to your research topic? Is the source trustworthy: does it provide credibility, accuracy, reasonableness, and support?

16a Questioning print sources

Just because something is in print (or on the Web) does not make it relevant or true. How can you determine whether a print source is likely to be both credible and useful? Before assessing a source's credibility, make sure it is relevant to your topic. The box on the following pages provides some questions to ask about any source you are considering.

Relevance can be a tricky matter, requiring careful analysis of the writing situation. What sources will be particularly meaningful or persuasive to your anticipated audience? For an audience opposed

CHECKLIST

Relevance and Credibility of Sources

Here are some questions to ask about any source you are considering:

Relevance

☐ **Do the source's title and subtitle indicate that it addresses your specific research question?**

☐ **What is the publication date?** Is the material up to date, classic, or historically pertinent? The concept of "up to date" depends on discipline and topic. Ask your instructor how recent sources should be for your project.

☐ **Does the table of contents of a book indicate that it contains useful information?**

☐ **If the source is a book, does it have an index?** Scan the index for keywords related to your topic.

☐ **Does the abstract at the beginning or the summary at the end of an article suggest it will be useful?** An abstract or summary presents the main points made in the article.

☐ **Does the work contain headings?** Skim the subheadings to see whether they indicate that the source contains useful information.

to gun control legislation, an acknowledgment that certain types of weapons should be regulated will be more relevant and persuasive from a source that usually supports the NRA (National Rifle Association). Relevance is also associated with the academic discipline that forms the context for your work. Your sociology instructor will expect you to give special preference to sociological sources in a project on the organization of the workplace. Your business management instructor will expect you to use material from that field in a project on the same topic. Be prepared to discover that some promising sources turn out to be less relevant than you first thought.

16a
eval

CHECKLIST *(continued)*

Credibility

☐ **What information can you find about the writer's credentials?** Obtain biographical information about the writer by checking the source itself, consulting a biographical dictionary, or conducting an Internet search of the writer's name. Is the writer affiliated with a research institution that contributes knowledge about an issue? Is the writer an expert on the topic? Is the writer cited frequently in other sources about the topic?

☐ **Who is the publisher?** University presses and academic publishers are considered more scholarly and therefore more credible than the popular press.

☐ **Does the work include a bibliography of works consulted or cited?** Trustworthy writers cite a variety of sources and document their citations properly. Does this source do so? Does the source include a variety of citations?

☐ **Does the work argue reasonably for its position and treat opposing views fairly?** What tone does the author use? Is the work objective or subjective? Are the writer's arguments clear and logical? What is the author's point of view? Does he or she present other views fairly? *(For more on evaluating arguments, see Chapter 8: Arguments, pp. 119–27.)*

TEXTCONNEX

Evaluating Sources

- **"Evaluating Web Pages: Techniques to Apply & Questions to Ask"** <www.lib.berkeley.edu/TeachingLib/ Guides /Internet/Evaluate.html>: This site from the UC Berkeley Library provides a step-by-step guide to evaluating online sources.
- **"Evaluating sources of information"** <http://owl.english .purdue.edu/owl/resource/553/1/>: From the Purdue Online Writing Lab, this page provides guidelines for evaluating print and online sources.

For MULTILINGUAL WRITERS

Questioning Sources

Although some cultures emphasize respect for established authors, U.S. universities follow an intellectual tradition that values careful questioning even of so-called expert opinion. Carefully consider a source's claim to expertise. A respected scientist's statement about global warming should be considered more credible than that of a Hollywood celebrity whose name might be familiar but who has no background relevant to the topic. Consider the pertinence and credibility of all sources.

16b Questioning Internet sources

Although the questions in the Checklist box on pages 222–23 should be applied to online sources, Web resources also require additional methods of ensuring the credibility of information presented. Most of the material in the library has been evaluated to some extent for credibility. Editors and publishers have reviewed the content of books, magazines, journals, and newspapers, and journals, and many books are reviewed by scholars as well. Some presses and publications are more reputable than others. Subscription databases generally compile articles that originally appeared in print, and librarians try to purchase the most reliable databases. While you should still evaluate all sources, you can have some confidence that most of the material you find in a college library is credible, at least to some degree.

In contrast, anyone can create a Web site that looks attractive but contains nonsense. Similarly, the people who post to blogs, discussion lists, and newsgroups may not be experts or even marginally well informed. Some information on the Web is valuable and timely, but much of it is not, so you must assess its credibility carefully.

Consult the Checklist box on pages 222–23, and consider the following questions when determining whether online information is reliable:

1. Who is hosting the site? Is the site hosted by a university or by a government agency (like the National Science Foundation or the National Endowment for the Humanities)? In general, sites hosted by institutions with scholarly credentials are more likely to be trustworthy. However, they remain open to critical inquiry (as exemplified by the NEA graph on page 217).

2. Who is speaking on the site? A nationally recognized biologist is likely to be more credible on biological topics than a politician with no scientific background. If you cannot identify the author, who is the editor or compiler? If you cannot identify an author, editor, compiler, or sponsoring organization, do not use the source.

3. What links does the site provide? If it is networked to sites with obviously biased or inaccurate content, you must question the credibility of the original site.

4. Is the information on the site supported with documentation from scholarly or otherwise credible sources (for example, government reports)?

16b
eval

Consider the following factors as well:

■ **Authority and credibility:** Are the author and sponsor of the Web site identifiable? Does the author include biographical information? Is there any indication that the author has relevant expertise on the subject? Look for information about the individual or organization sponsoring the site. The following extensions in the Web address, or uniform resource locator (URL), can help you determine the type of site (which often tells you something about its purpose):

.com commercial (business)	**.edu** educational	**.mil** military
.org nonprofit organization	**.gov** U.S. government	**.net** network

A tilde (~) followed by a name in a URL usually means the site is a personal home page not affiliated with any organization.

■ **Audience and purpose:** How does the appearance of the site, along with the tone of any written material, suggest its intended audience? A site's purpose also influences the way it presents information and the credibility of that information. Is the site's main purpose to promote a cause, raise money, advertise a product or service, deliver factual information, present research results, provide news, share personal information, or offer entertainment? Always try to view the site's home page; delete everything after the first slash in the URL to do so.

- **Objectivity and reasonableness:** Look carefully at the purpose and tone of the text. Nearly all sources express a point of view or bias. You should consult sources that represent a range of opinions on your topic. However, unreasonable sources have no place in academic debate. Clues that indicate a lack of reasonableness include an intemperate tone, broad claims, exaggerated statements of significance, conflicts of interest, no recognition of opposing views, and strident attacks on differing opinions. *(For more on evaluating arguments, see Chapter 8: Arguments, pp. 119–27.)*

- **Relevance and timeliness:** In what ways does the information from an online source specifically support (or refute) your thesis or topic? Do the site's intended audience and purpose include an academic audience? Does the site indicate how recently it has been updated, and are most of the included links still working?

- **Context:** Do others' comments on a blog or posts to a discussion list make your source appear more credible, or do they undermine the writer's credibility?

Consider a student writing a report on the reintroduction of gray wolves in the western United States following their near-extinction. Many environmentalists have favored this program, while farmers and ranchers have worried about the impact of wolves on livestock.

The student conducts an online keyword search and finds the site in Figure 16.1. This site focuses on the gray wolf population in the United States and its status under the Endangered Species Act, making it relevant to the student's topic. The URL indicates that the site belongs to a U.S. government agency, suggesting its credibility (although such sites are not immune to politics and bias). Information on the site appears in a simple, easy-to-follow format, indicating an educational purpose. It links to other government sites. Scrolling down, the student sees the site has been updated recently. This site's apparent authority, credibility, and purpose make it a good candidate for use as a source.

Next, the student finds the site in Figure 16.2 on page 228. Following the link that says "About us," the student learns that the site is sponsored by Wolf Park, a nonprofit organization in Indiana dedicated to the preservation and study of wolves. The site's purpose appears to be educational and persuasive; it includes information about

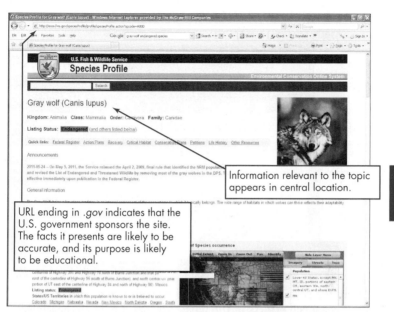

Information relevant to the topic appears in central location.

URL ending in .gov indicates that the U.S. government sponsors the site. The facts it presents are likely to be accurate, and its purpose is likely to be educational.

16c
eval

FIGURE 16.1 U.S. Fish & Wildlife Service Endangered Species Program site on the gray wolf. This government site provides information on the efforts to preserve and rebuild the gray wolf population in the United States.

wolves and conservation efforts on their behalf. The page shown in Figure 16.2 on page 228 describes research at the park and includes a link to papers with clearly documented sources, suggesting that the site is credible.

After further research the student reaches the site in Figure 16.3 on page 228, which presents apparently accurate and impartial information about wolves. Scrolling down, the student sees that the site also features advertisements, which do not appear in most scholarly sources. The site does not state the author's credentials, nor does it include documentation for its information. For these reasons, the student should confirm its statements with another source before using them in an academic report.

16c Evaluating a source's arguments

As you read the sources you have selected, continue to assess their credibility. Look for arguments that are qualified, supported with evidence, and well documented. Avoid sources that appeal mostly to emotions or promote one-sided agendas instead of inquiry and discussion.

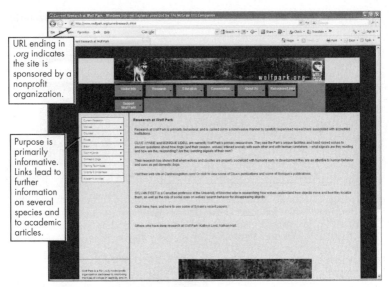

URL ending in *.org* indicates the site is sponsored by a nonprofit organization.

Purpose is primarily informative. Links lead to further information on several species and to academic articles.

FIGURE 16.2 A page from Wolf Park's Web site, with information about research efforts at the park. The list of links on the left side of the page includes a link to academic articles. SOURCE: Reprinted with permission from Wolf Park, www.wolfpark.org.

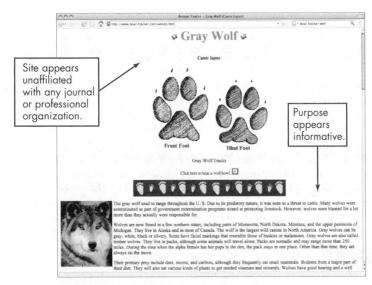

Site appears unaffiliated with any journal or professional organization.

Purpose appears informative.

FIGURE 16.3 Animal Tracks gray wolf site. This site's information appears to be accurate, but it does not document its sources or present the author's credentials. SOURCE: Screenshot from Gray Wolf page at http://bear-tracker.com/wolves. Reprinted with permission from Kim Cabrera.

A fair-minded researcher must read and evaluate sources on many sides of an issue, including relevant primary sources if they exist.

Exercise 16.1 Evaluating Web sites

Working alone or in groups, choose one of the following topics:

1. The cost of prescription drugs in the United States
2. Alternative energy sources
3. Immigration
4. Global warming
5. The role of private and charter schools in a democracy

For your topic, find at least three Web sites that clearly demonstrate at least one of the following characteristics:

Bias	Conflict of interest
Objectivity	Timeliness
Authority	Quality control (or lack thereof)
Fallacy	Obvious audience and purpose

Be prepared to share example Web pages with your class (either print them out or use a projection screen) and to point out how they demonstrate the characteristics you have identified.

16c eval

CHECKLIST

Using the CARS Checklist to Evaluate Web Sites

A Web site that is **C**redible, **A**ccurate, **R**easonable, and **S**upported (CARS) should meet the following criteria:

Credibility

☐ The source is trustworthy; you would consider a print version to be authoritative (for example, an online edition of a major newspaper or news magazine).

☐ The argument and use of evidence are clear and logical.

☐ The author's or sponsor's credentials are available.

☐ Quality control is evident (for example, spelling and grammar are correct, and links are functional).

(continued)

CHECKLIST *(continued)*

☐ The source is a known or respected authority; it has organizational support (such as a university, a research institution, or a major news publication).

☐ The source appears at or near the top of a Google search. (Google.com ranks sites according to their popularity; sites near the top of a list of "hits" are the most frequently accessed by people looking for the same information you seek.)

Accuracy

☐ The site is updated frequently, if not daily (and includes "last updated" information).

☐ The site provides evidence for its assertions.

☐ The site is detailed; text appears in full paragraphs.

☐ The site is comprehensive, including archives, links, and additional resources. A search feature and table of contents or tabs allow you to quickly find the information you need.

☐ The site's purpose includes completeness and accuracy.

Reasonableness

☐ The site is fair, balanced, and objective.

☐ The site makes its purpose clear. (Is it selling something? Prompting site visitors to sign a petition? Promoting a new film?)

☐ The site contains no conflict of interest.

☐ The site does not include fallacies or a slanted tone. *(For more on fallacies, see Chapter 8, pp. 123–24.)*

Support

☐ The site lists scholarly or otherwise reliable sources for its information, providing links where available.

☐ The site clarifies the content it is responsible for and which links are created by unrelated authors or sponsors.

☐ The site provides contact information for its authors and/or sponsors.

☐ If the site is an academic resource, it follows the conventions of a specific citation style (MLA, APA, or another accepted style).

17 Doing Research in the Archive, Field, and Lab

Often, research involves more than finding answers to questions in books and other print and online resources **(secondary research)**. When you conduct **primary research**—looking up old maps, consulting census records, polling community members about a current issue—you participate in the discovery of knowledge.

17a Adhering to ethical principles when doing primary research

In the archive, field, or lab, you are working directly with something precious and immediate: an original record, a group of people, or special materials. An ethical researcher shows respect for materials, experimental subjects, fellow researchers, and readers. Here are some guidelines for ethical research:

- Handle original documents and materials with great care, always leaving sources and data available for other researchers.
- Accurately report your sources and results.
- Follow proper procedures when working with human participants.

Researchers who work with human participants should also adhere to the following basic principles:

- **Confidentiality:** People who fill out surveys, participate in focus groups, or respond to interviews should be assured that their names will not be used without their permission.
- **Informed consent:** Before participating in an experiment, all participants must sign a statement affirming that they understand the general purpose of the research.
- **Minimal risk:** Participants in experiments should not incur any risks greater than they do in everyday life.
- **Protection of vulnerable groups:** Researchers must be held strictly accountable for research done with the physically disabled, prisoners, mentally impaired or incompetent, minors, the elderly, and pregnant women.

17b Preparing yourself for archival research

An **archive** is a cataloged collection of documents, manuscripts, and other materials, possibly including receipts, wills, photographs, sound recordings, and other kinds of media. Archives are found in libraries,

231

museums, other institutions and private collections, and on video- and audiotape. Your own attic may contain family archives—letters, diaries, and photographs that could have value to a researcher and that may or may not be organized. Some archival collections are accessible through audio- and videotape as well as the Internet; others you must visit in person. The more you know about your area of study, the more likely you will be to see the significance of an item in an archival collection.

Archives generally require that you call or e-mail to arrange a time for your visit, and some are restricted. If you find out about an archive on the Internet that you would like to visit in person, phone or e-mail well in advance to find out if you will need references, a letter of introduction, or other qualifying papers. Archives often will not allow you to browse; instead, use finding aids (often available online) to determine which records you need to see.

Archives also generally require you to present a photo identification and to leave personal items in a locker or at a coat check. They have strict policies about reproducing materials and rarely allow anything to leave the premises. The more you know about the archive's policies and procedures before you visit, the more productive your visit will be. When you are finished, thank the archivist for the help you have received.

17c Planning your field research carefully

Field research involves recording observations, conducting interviews, and administering surveys. To conduct field research at a particular site, such as a place of business or a school, you must obtain permission. Explain the nature of your project, the date and time you would like to visit, and how much time you will need. Will you be observing? Interviewing people? Taking photographs? Also ask for a confirming letter or e-mail. Always write a thank-you note after you have concluded your research.

1. Observing and writing field notes College assignments offer opportunities to conduct systematic observations. For a sociology class, you might observe the behavior of students in the cafeteria, taking notes on who sits with whom in terms of race, class, and social status. Such primary research will help you to look and really see throughout your life.

When you use direct observation, keep careful records in order to retain the information you gather. Whenever you can, count or measure, and take down word for word what is said as objectively as possible—describe, don't evaluate. Use frequency counts—the number of occurrences of specific, narrowly defined instances of behavior. If you are observing a classroom, for example, you might count the number of teacher-directed questions asked by several children. Be systematic in your observations, but be alert to unexpected behavior. Take more notes than you think you will need.

2. Conducting interviews Interviews are useful in a wide variety of writing situations: finding out what students think about the university logo, gathering ideas to promote recycling on campus, talking with a family member about memories of a historical figure. Interviews can be conducted in person, by phone, or online. Like other research tools, interviews require systematic preparation and implementation:

- Identify appropriate people for your interviews.
- Do background research, and plan a list of open-ended questions.
- Take careful notes, and, if possible, make an audio recording of the interview. (Be sure to obtain your subject's permission if you use audiotape or videotape.)
- Follow up on vague responses with questions that get at specific information. Do not rush interviewees.
- Politely probe inconsistencies and contradictions.
- Write thank-you notes to interviewees, and later send them copies of your report.

3. Taking surveys Conducted either orally or in writing, **surveys** are made up of structured questions. Written surveys are called **questionnaires.** Many colleges have offices that must review and approve student surveys. Check to see what guidelines your school may have. The following suggestions will help you prepare informal surveys:

- Define your purpose and your target population—the people who are relevant to the purpose of your survey. Are you trying to gauge attitudes, learn about typical behaviors, or both?
- Write clear directions and questions. For example, if you are asking multiple-choice questions, make sure that you cover all possible options and that your options do not overlap.
- Make sure that your questions do not suggest a preference for one answer over another.
- Make the survey brief and easy to complete.

17d Keeping a notebook when doing lab research

Every science course you take will most likely involve a laboratory component. In the laboratory, you work individually or in a team to carefully record each step of an experiment. Such firsthand observations in the controlled environment of the laboratory are at the heart of the scientific method and define the situation for scientific research. To provide a complete and accurate account of your laboratory work, keep careful records in a notebook. The following guidelines will help you take accurate notes on your research:

■ Record immediate, on-the-spot, accurate notes on what happens in the lab. Write down as much detail as possible. Measure precisely; do not estimate. Identify major pieces of apparatus, unusual chemicals, and laboratory animals in detail. Use drawings, when appropriate, to illustrate complicated equipment setups. Include tables, when useful, to present results.

■ Follow a basic format. Present your results in a format that allows you to communicate all the major features of an experiment. The five basic sections that must be included are title, purpose, materials and methods, results, and conclusions.

■ Write in complete sentences, even if you are filling in answers to questions in a lab manual. Resist the temptation to use shorthand to record your notes. Later, the complete sentences will provide a clear record of your procedures and results. Highlight connections in your sentences by using the following transitions: *then, next, consequently, because,* and *therefore.* Cause-and-effect relationships should be clear.

When necessary, revise and correct your laboratory notebook in visible ways. If you make a mistake in recording laboratory results, correct it as clearly as possible, either by erasing or by crossing out and rewriting on the original sheet. If you make an uncorrectable mistake in your notebook, simply fold the sheet lengthwise and mark *omit* on the face side. Unanticipated results often occur in the lab, and you may find yourself jotting down notes on a convenient piece of scrap paper. Attach these notes to your notebook.

18 Plagiarism, Copyright Infringement, and Intellectual Property

When we draw on the words and ideas of others, integrity and honesty require us to acknowledge their contributions. Otherwise, we are committing **plagiarism.** Some forms of plagiarism are obvious, such as buying a term paper from an online paper mill or "borrowing" a friend's completed assignment. Others are more subtle and may even be inadvertent. Since ignorance is no excuse, it is important to learn appropriate ways to paraphrase or summarize another writer's material *(See Chapter 19: Working with Sources and Avoiding Plagiarism, pp. 246–52, for more on paraphrasing and summarizing.)*

Penalties for plagiarism are serious. Journalists who are caught plagiarizing are publicly exposed and fired by the publications they write for. Scholars who fail to acknowledge the words and ideas of others lose their professional credibility, and often their jobs. Students who plagiarize might receive a failing grade for an assignment or course and face other disciplinary action—including expulsion. Be sure to read your campus's written policy on plagiarism and its consequences.

The Internet has made many types of sources available, and it can be unclear what, when, and how to cite. Although the line between "original" and "borrowed" appears to be blurring in our society, you should review the following guidelines for crediting sources appropriately.

18a
plag

18a Understanding how plagiarism relates to copyright and intellectual property

Copyright is the legal right to control the reproduction of any original work—a piece of writing, a musical composition, a play, a movie, a computer program, a photograph, a work of art. A copyrighted work is the **intellectual property** of the copyright holder, whether that entity is a publisher, a record company, an entertainment conglomerate, or the individual creator of the work. Here is some additional information on these legal concepts:

▪ **Copyright:** A copyrighted text cannot be reproduced legally (in print or online) without the written permission of the copyright holder. The copyright protects the right of authors and publishers to benefit from their productions.

▪ **Fair use:** The concept of **fair use** protects most academic use of copyrighted sources. Under this provision of copyright law, you can legally quote a brief passage from a copyrighted text for an academic purpose without infringing on copyright. Of course, to avoid plagiarism, you must identify the passage as a quotation and cite it properly. Always ask permission of the author in the case of blog entries and newsgroup postings.

▪ **Intellectual property:** In addition to works protected by copyright, intellectual property includes patented inventions, trademarks, industrial designs, and similar intellectual creations that are protected by other laws.

TEXTCONNEX

Learning More about Plagiarism, Copyright and Fair Use, and Intellectual Property

▪ **Plagiarism:** For more information about plagiarism, see the Council of Writing Program Administrators' "Defining and Avoiding Plagiarism: The WPA Statement on Best Practices," <http://wpacouncil.org/positions/WPAplagiarism.pdf>. Educators at Indiana University offer tips on avoiding plagiarism at <www.indiana.edu/~wts/pamphlets/plagiarism.shtml>.

▪ Georgetown University's Honor Council offers an example of a campus honor code pertaining to plagiarism and academic ethics at <http://gervaseprograms.georgetown.edu/honor /system/53377.html>.

▪ **Copyright and fair use:** For information and discussion of fair use, see *Copyright and Fair Use* at <http://fairuse .stanford.edu>, and the U.S. Copyright Office at <www .copyright.gov>. The University of Texas posts guidelines for fair use and multimedia projects at <http://copyright.lib .utexas.edu/ccmcguid.html>.

▪ **Intellectual property:** For information about what constitutes intellectual property and related issues, see the World Intellectual Property Organization Web site at <www.wipo .int/>. For a legal perspective, the American Intellectual Property Law Association offers information on and overviews of recent cases at <www.aipla.org/>.

18b Taking steps to avoid plagiarism

When people are under pressure, they sometimes make poor choices. Inadvertent plagiarism occurs when busy students take notes carelessly, forgetting to record the source of a paraphrase or accidentally inserting material downloaded from a Web site into a paper. Deliberate plagiarism occurs when students wait until the last minute and then "borrow" a paper from a friend or copy and paste portions of an online article into their own work. Even though you may be tired or pressured, careful planning and adherence to the following guidelines can help you avoid plagiarism:

▪ When you receive an assignment, write down your thoughts and questions before you begin looking at sources. Use this record to keep track of changes in your ideas.

▪ As you proceed with your research, record your ideas in one color and those of others in a different color.

- As you continue researching and taking notes, keep accurate records. If you do not know where you got an idea or a piece of information, do not use it until you find out.

- When you take notes, be sure to put quotation marks around words, phrases, or sentences taken verbatim from a source, and note the pages. If you use any of those words, phrases, or sentences when summarizing or paraphrasing the source, put them in quotation marks. Changing a word here and there while keeping a source's sentence structure or phrasing constitutes plagiarism even if you credit the source for the ideas. *(See p. 248 for an example.)*

- Do not rely too much on one source, or you may easily slip into using that person's thoughts as your own.

- Cite the source of all ideas, opinions, facts, and statistics that are not common knowledge.

**18b
plag**

SOURCE SMART

Determining What Is "Common Knowledge"

Information that an audience could be expected to know from many sources is considered common knowledge. For example, the structure of DNA and the process of photosynthesis are considered common knowledge among biologists. However, a recent scientific discovery about genetics would not be common knowledge, and so you would need to cite the source of this information. You do not need to cite common knowledge if you use your own wording and sentence structure. Common knowledge can take various forms, including at least these four:

- Folktales with no particular author (for example, Little Red Riding Hood outsmarted the wolf)

- Common sense (for example, property values in an area fall when crime rises)

- Historical facts and dates (for example, the United States entered World War II in 1941)

- Information found in many general reference works (for example, the heart drives the body's circulation system)

Maps, charts, graphs, and other visual displays of information are not considered common knowledge. Even though everyone knows that Paris is the capital of France, if you reproduce a map of France in your text, you must credit the map's creator.

- Choose an appropriate documentation style, and use it consistently and properly. *(See Parts 4 and 5 for information about the most common documentation styles for academic writing.)*

When working with information on the Web, it's important to take notes, just as you do with print sources, and to acknowledge that information—by paraphrasing, summarizing, and citing—just as you do with print sources. *(For more on taking notes, paraphrasing, and summarizing, see Chapter 19, pp. 240–52. For more on citations, see Parts 4 and 5.)*

When working with electronic sources, keep in mind the following guidelines:

- Print or save to your computer any online source you consult. Note the date on which you viewed it, and be sure to keep the complete URL in case you need to view the source again. Some documentation styles require you to include the URL in your citation.
- If you copy and paste a passage from a Web site into a word-processing file, use a different font to identify that material as well as the URL and the access date.
- Acknowledge all sites you use as sources, including those you access via links on another site.
- As a courtesy, request the author's permission before quoting from blogs, newsgroup postings, or e-mails.
- Acknowledge any audio, video, or illustrated material that has informed your research.

It may be tempting to copy and paste material from the Internet without acknowledgment, but instructors can easily detect that form of plagiarism by using a search engine to locate the original.

Posting material on a publicly accessible Web site is usually considered the legal equivalent of publishing it in print format. (Password-protected sites generally are exempt.) Before posting on a public site, seek copyright permission from all your sources. *(See the following guidelines for fair use and the box on p. 237.)*

18c Using copyrighted materials fairly

All written materials, including student projects, graphics, and videos, are covered by copyright even if they do not bear an official copyright symbol. A copyright grants its owner—often the creator—exclusive rights to the use of a protected work, including reproducing, distributing, and displaying the work. The popularity of the Web as a venue for publication has led to increased concerns about the fair use of copy-

---

X✓ CHECKLIST

Avoiding Inadvertent Plagiarism: Some Questions to Ask Yourself

☐ Is my thesis my own idea, not something I found in one of my sources?

☐ Have I used a variety of sources, not just one or two?

☐ Have I identified each source clearly?

☐ Do I fully understand and explain all words, phrases, or ideas?

☐ Have I acknowledged all ideas that are based on neither my original thinking nor common knowledge?

☐ Have I properly integrated material from sources, using either paraphrases, summaries, or quotations *(see Chapter 19, pp. 246–53)?*

☐ If I am planning to publish my text online, have I received all necessary permissions?

18c plag

---

righted material. Before you publish your work on the Web or produce a multimedia presentation that includes audio, video, and graphic elements copied from a Web site, make sure that you have used copyrighted material fairly by considering the following four questions:

- **What is the purpose of the use?** Educational, nonprofit, and personal uses are more likely to be considered fair than is commercial use.

- **What is the nature of the work being used?** In most cases, imaginative and unpublished materials can be used only if you have the permission of the copyright holder.

- **How much of the copyrighted work is being used?** The use of a small portion of a text for academic purposes is more likely to be considered fair than the use of a whole work for commercial purposes. While no clear legal definition of "a small portion" exists, one conservative guideline is that you can quote up to fifty words from an article (print or online) and three hundred words from a book. It is safest to ask permission to quote an entire work or a substantial portion of a text (be cautious with poems, plays, and songs). Images and multimedia clips are considered entire works. Also, you may need permission to link your Web site to another.

- **What effect would this use have on the market for the original?** The use of a work is usually considered unfair if it would hurt sales of the original.

When in doubt, ask permission.

For MULTILINGUAL WRITERS

Cultural Assumptions and Misunderstandings about Plagiarism

Respect for ownership of ideas is a core value of Western society. Your culture may consider the knowledge in classic texts a national heritage and, therefore, common property. As a result, you may have been encouraged to incorporate words and information from those texts into your writing without citing their source. American academic culture, however, requires you to identify any use you make of someone else's original work and to cite the work properly in an appropriate documentation style *(see Parts 4 and 5)*. You must similarly credit the source of ideas that are not considered common knowledge. You should accept these rules as nonnegotiable and apply them conscientiously to avoid plagiarism and its serious consequences. When in doubt about citation rules, ask your instructor.

19 Working with Sources and Avoiding Plagiarism

Once you have a research question to answer, an idea about what the library and Internet have to offer, and some reliable, appropriate sources in hand, you are ready to begin working with your sources. If you pay attention to detail and keep careful records at this stage, you will stay organized, save time, and credit sources appropriately.

19a Maintaining a working bibliography

As you research, compile a **working bibliography**—a list of those books, articles, pamphlets, Web sites, and other sources that seem most likely to help you answer your research question. Maintain an accurate and complete record of all sources you consult. For each source, record the following information:

- Call number of the book, reference work, or other print source; the complete URL of each Web site
- All authors, editors, and translators
- Title and subtitle of the chapter, article, or Web page
- Title and subtitle of the book, periodical, or Web site in which the chapter, article, or page appears
- For books, the date of publication, place, and publisher as well as the edition or volume number, if applicable
- For periodical articles, the date, edition or volume number, issue, and page numbers if applicable
- For a Web source, the date you consulted it, the sponsor of the site, and the following additional information, if available: publication information, including any information about a version in another medium (such as print, radio, or film), the date the online material was published or most recently updated, and other identifying numbers, such as a Digital Object Identifier (DOI)
- For an article from an online database, the name of the database and the URL of the database's home page
- For music, film, multimedia, photographs, paintings, and so on, name of author or creator
- Medium (for example, print, Web, CD-ROM, or DVD-ROM) or format (for example, photograph, lecture)

(See the foldouts at the beginning of Chapters 21 and 26 for examples of these elements.)

You can record bibliographic information on note cards or in a word-processing file; you can print out or e-mail to yourself bibliographic information obtained from online searches in databases and library catalogs; you can use an app on your cell phone to send a citation to yourself; or you can record bibliographic information directly on photocopies or printouts of source material. You can also save most Web pages and other online sources to your own computer. Many professional researchers use bibliographic software such as *Endnote, ProCite,* and *Reference Manager* to help them keep track of sources and format bibliographic information. Ask your instructor before using any bibliographic software, and always review your citations carefully.

19a
plag

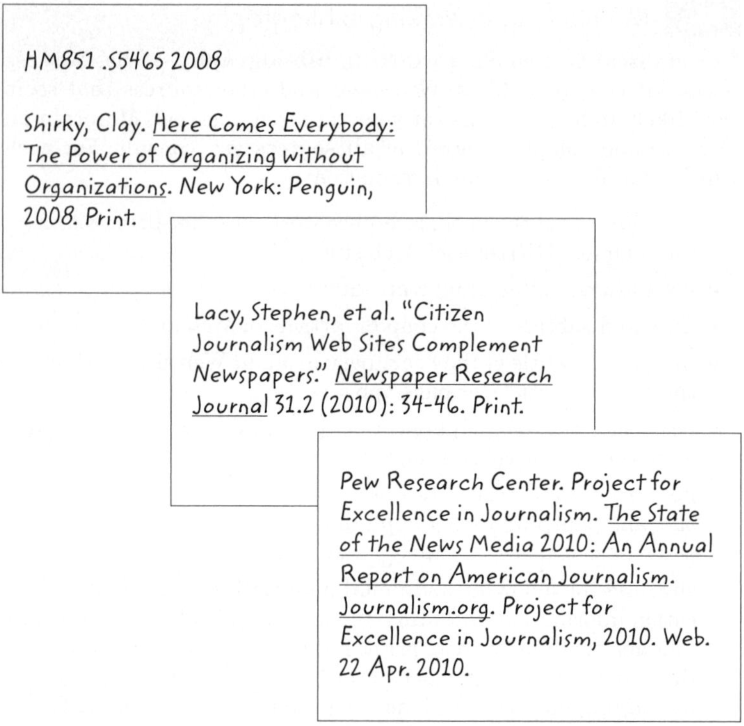

HM851 .S5465 2008

Shirky, Clay. <u>Here Comes Everybody:</u>
<u>The Power of Organizing without</u>
<u>Organizations</u>. New York: Penguin,
2008. Print.

Lacy, Stephen, et al. "Citizen
Journalism Web Sites Complement
Newspapers." <u>Newspaper Research</u>
<u>Journal</u> 31.2 (2010): 34-46. Print.

Pew Research Center. Project for
Excellence in Journalism. <u>The State</u>
<u>of the News Media 2010: An Annual</u>
<u>Report on American Journalism</u>.
Journalism.org. Project for
Excellence in Journalism, 2010. Web.
22 Apr. 2010.

**FIGURE 19.1 Three sample bibliography note cards in MLA
style.** The cards are for a book (top), a journal article (middle), and a
Web site (bottom).

1. Using note cards or a word processor One classic method
for taking notes is still useful: using three-by-five-inch note cards to
compile the working bibliography, with each potential source getting
a separate card. *(see Figure 19.1 above)*. You can also use the cards to
record brief quotations from or comments on those sources. Instead
of handwriting on cards, you can record bibliographic information in
a computer file.

**2. Printing the results of online searches in databases and
library catalogs** The results of searches in online indexes and
databases usually include complete bibliographic information about
the sources they list. You can print these results directly from your
browser, or, in some cases, save them to a flash drive and transfer

---

SOURCE SMART

The Uses and Limits of Bibliographic Software

Programs such as *Microsoft Word 2010* allow you to store source data, automatically insert citations in common documentation styles, and generate a list of references. These programs might not incorporate the most recent updates to documentation styles, however, nor do they accommodate all types of sources. Talk to your instructor before using bibliographic software, and check your citations carefully against the models in the foldouts at the beginning of Chapters 21 and 26. Also check references that a database creates for you.

**19b
plag**

> *Caution:* If you download the full text of an article from a database and refer to it in your paper, your citation may require information about the database (depending on your documentation style) as well as bibliographic information about the article itself. *(See the foldouts at the beginning of Chapters 21 and 26.)*

---

them to a Word file. Be sure also to record the name of the database and the date of your search.

You can similarly print out or save bibliographic information from the results of searches in online library catalogs. Some college libraries make it possible for you to compile a list of sources and e-mail it to yourself.

3. Using photocopies and printouts from Web sites

If you photocopy articles, essays, or pages of reference works from a print or a microfilm source, noting the bibliographic information on the photocopy can save you time later. Similarly, if you print out a source you found on a Web site or copy it to your computer, be sure to note the site's author, name, sponsor, date of publication, complete URL, and the date you visited the site.

19b Creating an annotated bibliography

An annotated bibliography can be useful to you in your research. You will need the full citation, correctly formatted, for your works-cited or references list. The annotation for each source should include a summary of major points, your evaluation of the source's relevance

Lacy, Stephen, et al. "Citizen Journalism Web Sites Complement Newspapers." *Newspaper Research Journal* 31.2 (2010): 34-46. Print.
This scholarly study compares the purpose of citizen journalism websites to that of newspaper websites. It includes a discussion of the theoretical framework behind the study, a review of the literature on citizen journalism, and extensive notes on the research that informed the study. The article concludes that citizen journalism sites cannot sufficiently replace, but should instead accompany, newspaper sites.

Shirky, Clay. *Here Comes Everybody: The Power of Organizing without Organizations.* New York: Penguin, 2008. Print.
Aimed at a popular audience, Shirky's book describes the impact of group communications, such as blogs, and predicts the far-reaching benefits of such forms of social media. Shirky also compares traditional media to new media and explains how and why this transition is necessary. Shirky's book supports my ideas about the need for journalists to adopt forms of new media.

FIGURE 19.2 Sample annotated bibliography. A section of Rebecca Hollingsworth's annotated bibliography. *(To read "Breaking News: Blogging's Impact on Traditional and New Media," Hollingsworth's final research report on this topic, see Chapter 25.)*

and credibility, and your thoughts on what the material contributes to your project and where it might fit in. *(See Figure 19.2, above.)*

19c Taking notes on your sources

Taking notes helps you think through your research question and read both digital and print sources more systematically. Consult a table of contents or other introductory material to find the most relevant sections. You can take notes on your sources by annotating photocopies or printouts or by noting useful quotations and ideas on paper, on note cards, or in a computer file. See whether categories emerge that can help you organize your project.

1. Annotating   One way to take notes is to annotate photocopied articles and printouts from online information services or Web sites. *(See Figure 19.3 on p. 245 for an annotated Web site printout.)* As you read, write the following notes directly on the page:

- On the first page, write down complete bibliographic information for the source.
- Record questions, reactions, and ideas in the margins.

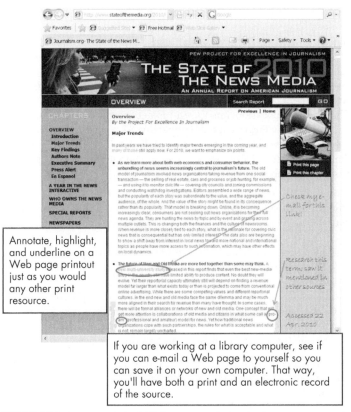

19c plag

Annotate, highlight, and underline on a Web page printout just as you would any other print resource.

If you are working at a library computer, see if you can e-mail a Web page to yourself so you can save it on your own computer. That way, you'll have both a print and an electronic record of the source.

FIGURE 19.3 An annotated Web page printout.

- Comment on ideas that agree with or differ from those you have already learned about.
- Put important and difficult passages into your own words by paraphrasing or summarizing them in the margins. *(For help with paraphrasing and summarizing, see pp. 246–49.)*
- Highlight statements that you may want to quote because they are especially well expressed or are key to readers' understanding of the issue.

2. Taking notes in a research journal or log   A **research journal** or **research log** is a tool for keeping track of your research. It can be a spiral or loose-leaf notebook, a box of note cards, a word-processing document on a laptop computer, or a blog—whatever form you are most comfortable with. Use the journal to write down leads for sources and to record ideas and observations about your topic as they occur to you. If you use a blog, you can use it to link to potential sources.

When you have finished annotating a photocopy, printout, or electronic version of an article, use your research journal to explore the comments, connections, and questions you recorded. If you do not have a copy of the material to annotate, take notes directly in your research journal.

Enclose in quotation marks any exact words from a source. If you think you may forget that the phrasing, as well as the idea, came from someone else, label the passage a "quote" and note the page number, as Rebecca Hollingsworth did in the following excerpt from her research notebook:

> Notes on Pew Research Center. Project for Excellence in Journalism. The State of the News Media 2010: An Annual Report on American Journalism. Journalism.org. Project for Excellence in Journalism, 2010. Web. 22 Apr. 2010.
> - Similar struggles faced by both traditional and new forms of journalism. Hard to raise funds, esp. from advertising. New relationships developing between old and new.
> - One such relationship is betw. expert and novice reporters. Quote: "One concept that will get more attention is collaborations of old media and citizens in what some call a 'pro-am' (professional and amateur) model for news."

Unless you think you might use a particular quotation in your paper, express the author's ideas in your own words by using a paraphrase or a summary.

19d Taking stock of what you have learned as you paraphrase, summarize, quote, and synthesize your sources

When you take stock, remember your writing situation. As you synthesize what you have learned from the sources you are consulting, think about how these sources relate to one another: where do they agree, and where do they disagree? Where do you stand relative to these sources? Did anything you read surprise or disturb you, and how will it affect your audience? Writing down your responses to such questions can help you clarify what you have learned and decide how that information fits in with your own claim as you are developing it.

The credibility of your work depends on the relevance and credibility of your sources as well as the scope and depth of your reading and observation. College research projects usually require multiple sources and viewpoints. A project on the impact of blogging on traditional news, for example, is unlikely to be credible if it relies on only one source of information. An argument about an issue in the social sciences will not be taken seriously if it cites research on only one side of the debate.

As the context and kind of writing change, so too do the requirements for types and numbers of sources. As a general rule, however, you should consult more than two sources and use only sources that are both credible and respected by people working in the field. To determine whether you have located appropriate and sufficient sources, ask yourself the following questions:

- Are your sources trustworthy? *(See Chapter 16, pp. 221–30, for more on evaluating sources.)*
- If you have started to develop a tentative answer to your research question, have your sources provided you with a sufficient number of facts, examples, and ideas to support that answer?
- Have you used sources that examine the issues from several different perspectives?

19d
plag

1. Paraphrasing information from sources

When you **paraphrase,** you put someone else's statements into your words and sentence structures. Paraphrase when a passage's details are important to your topic but its exact words are not memorable or when you need to reorder a source's ideas or clarify complicated information. A paraphrase should be about the same length and level of detail as the original. Cite the original writer, and put quotation marks around any exact phrasing from the source. See the Source Smart box on page 250 for advice on approaching the task.

In the first unacceptable paraphrase that follows, the writer has done a word-for-word translation, using synonyms for some terms but retaining phrases from the original (highlighted) and failing to enclose them in quotation marks ("few-to-few, one-to-one, and many-to-many," "attentive publics"). Notice also how close the sentence structures in the first faulty paraphrase are to the original.

SOURCE

The media used to work in a one-to-many pattern—that is, by broadcasting. The Internet, though it can be used for one-to-many transmission, is just as well suited for few-to-few, one-to-one, and many-to-many patterns. Traditionally, the media connected audiences "up" to centers of power, people of influence, and national spectacles. The Internet does all that, but it is equally good at connecting us laterally—to peers, to colleagues, and to strangers who share our interests. When experts and power players had something to communicate to the attentive publics they wished to address, they once had to go through the media. Now they can go direct.

—JAY ROSEN, "The New News"

UNACCEPTABLE PARAPHRASE: PLAGIARISM

The news was previously transmitted from one to many. Online media, although they can function in this way, can also follow a few-to-few, one-to-one, and many-to-many pattern. In the past, traditional news outlets connected audiences up to those in a position of power. Online media can do that as well, but they also succeed in connecting us laterally to others who share our interests. If those in a position of power wanted to reach their attentive publics, traditional news outlets used to be their only method. Currently, they can communicate directly with their audiences (Rosen).

In the second example of a faulty paraphrase (following), the writer has merely substituted synonyms for the original author's words (such as "individual-to-individual" instead of "one-to-one") and kept the source's sentence structure. Because it relies on the sentence structure of the original source, the paraphrase is too close to the original and constitutes **plagiarism.**

UNACCEPTABLE PARAPHRASE (SENTENCE STRUCTURE OF SOURCE): PLAGIARISM

The news was previously transmitted from single corporations to several individuals. Online media, although they can function in this way, can also follow a group-to-group, organization-to-organization, and individual-to-individual model. In the past, traditional news outlets linked consumers upward to those in a position of authority. Online media can do that as well, but they also succeed in linking us to one another, including others with whom we have something in common. If those in a position of authority wanted to reach their captive audiences, traditional news outlets used to be their only method. Currently, they can communicate right with their audiences (Rosen).

The third unacceptable paraphrase (following) alters the sentence structure of the source but plagiarizes by using some of the original wording (highlighted) without quotation marks.

UNACCEPTABLE PARAPHRASE (WORDING FROM SOURCE): PLAGIARISM

In contrast to traditional news outlets, which functioned in a one-to-many pattern, online media use other patterns to engage audiences, such as few-to-few, one-to-one, and many-to-many (Rosen).

In contrast, the acceptable paraphrase expresses all ideas from the original using different words and phrasing. Although it quotes a few words from the source, the writer has used quotation marks and indicates where the paraphrase begins.

ACCEPTABLE PARAPHRASE

According to Rosen, the shift away from expert reporting to citizen journalism has opened doors for those who both produce and consume the news. No longer at the mercy of those in a position to seek out and select what makes the news, citizens now have more authority, through the power of blogging, to investigate and publicize the events that matter to us. As a result, we are linked to other informed citizens like never before.

Note that all paraphrases require a citation.

In the following two paraphrases of a podcast, note that the unacceptable version copies words and phrasing from the source.

SOURCE

I think it's great for journalism. I think the more people there are writing, and the easier it is to publish writing of all kinds, the more likely we are to find the information we need and the more likely we are to get a clearer picture of an event or a situation.

—MATHEW INGRAM, interview by Eric Berlin

UNACCEPTABLE PARAPHRASE: PLAGIARISM

In an interview with Eric Berlin, Mathew Ingram noted that the more bloggers there are, the more likely we are to get the information we need in a clear and complete way.

ACCEPTABLE PARAPHRASE

In an interview by Eric Berlin, Mathew Ingram explains that blogging has given us greater access to and broader coverage of the issues that matter to us.

19d
plag

Exercise 19.1 Paraphrasing

Read the following passage, annotating as necessary. Write a paraphrase of the passage, and then compare your paraphrase with those of your classmates. What are the similarities and differences among your paraphrases? Are they all acceptable? If one is not acceptable, why not? How can it be changed to make it acceptable?

SOURCE

The origins of jazz, an urban music, stemmed from the countryside of the South as well as the streets of America's cities. It

SOURCE SMART

Guidelines for Writing a Paraphrase

- **Read the passage carefully.** Focus on its sequence of ideas and important details.
- **Be sure you understand the material.** Look up any unfamiliar words.
- **Imagine addressing an audience that has not read the material.**
- **Without looking at the original passage, write down its main ideas and key details.**
- **Use clear, direct language.** Express complicated ideas as a series of simple ones.
- **Check your paraphrase against the original.** Make sure your text conveys the source's ideas accurately without copying its words or sentence structures. Add quotation marks around any phrases from the source, or rewrite them.
- **Note the citation information.** List author and page number after every important point.

resulted from two distinct musical traditions, those of West Africa and Europe. West Africa gave jazz its incessant rhythmic drive, the need to move and the emotional urgency that has served the music so well. The European ingredients had more to do with classical qualities pertaining to harmony and melody.

— JOHN EPHLAND, "Down Beat's Jazz 101: The Very Beginning" (from downbeat.com)

2. Summarizing information from sources When you **summarize,** you state the main point of a piece, condensing paragraphs into sentences, pages into paragraphs, or a book into a few pages. As you work with sources, you will summarize more frequently than you will quote or paraphrase. Summarizing works best when the passage is very long and the central idea is important but the details are not. *(For specific guidelines on writing summaries, see Chapter 1, pp. 21–22. as well as the Source Smart box on p. 251.)*

Here are two summaries of a passage on journalism by Clay Shirky, which is reprinted below.

SOURCE

For the next few decades, journalism will be made up of overlapping special cases. Many of these models will rely on amateurs as researchers and writers. Many of these models will rely on sponsorship or grants or endowments instead of revenues. Many of these models will rely on excitable 14-year-olds distributing the results. Many of these models will fail. No one experiment is going to replace what we are now losing with the demise of news on paper, but over time, the collection of new experiments that do work might give us the journalism we need.

—CLAY SHIRKY, "Newspapers and Thinking the Unthinkable," p. 29

The unacceptable summary is simply a restatement of Shirky's thesis using much of his phrasing (highlighted).

UNACCEPTABLE SUMMARY: PLAGIARISM

**19d
plag**

The journalism of the future will be made up of overlapping special cases, some of which will rely on novice reporters and new revenue models. Although many of these models will fail, they will, collectively, help to give us the journalism we need (Shirky, "Newspapers" 29).

SOURCE SMART

Guidelines for Writing a Summary

- **Read the material carefully.** Locate relevant sections.
- **If the text is longer than a few paragraphs, divide it into sections, and sum up each section in one or two sentences.** Compose a topic sentence for each of these sections.
- **Be sure you understand the material.**
- **Imagine explaining the points to an audience that has not read this content.**
- **Identify the main point of the source, in your own words.** Compose a sentence that names the text, the writer, what the writer does (reports, argues), and the most important point.
- **Note any other points that relate to your topic.** State each one (in your own words) in one sentence or less. Simplify complex language.
- **Combine your sentence stating the writer's main point with your sentences about secondary points or those summarizing the text's sections.**
- **Check your summary against the original** to see whether it makes sense, expresses the source's meaning, and does not copy any wording or sentence structure.
- **Note all the citation information for the source.**

The acceptable summary states Shirky's main point in the writer's own words. Note that the acceptable summary still requires a citation. Because more than one work by Shirky is being cited, a shortened version of the title is included in the in-text citation in MLA style. *(For more on MLA style for in-text citations, see pp. 267–75.)*

ACCEPTABLE SUMMARY

According to Shirky, partnerships between traditional and citizen journalism will take several forms. Although many wonder whether new forms can offer information that is as reliable as traditional news, as these forms evolve they may usher in a new era of journalism that is better able to serve our needs ("Newspapers" 29).

Exercise 19.2 | Summarizing

Read the following passage, and write a summary of it. Compare your summary with those of your classmates. What are the similarities and differences among your summaries? How does writing a summary compare with writing a paraphrase? Which task was more difficult, and why?

SOURCE

Male musicians dominated the jazz scene when the music first surfaced, making it difficult for women to enter their ranks. The fraternity of jazzmen also frowned upon women wind instrumentalists. However, some African American women, in the late 19th century, played the instruments that were barred from the "opposite sex." . . . Many of their names have been lost in history, but a few have survived. For example, Mattie Simpson, a cornetist, performed "on principal and prominent streets of each city" (10) in Indianapolis, in 1895; Nettie Goff, a trombonist, was a member of The Mahara Minstrels; and Mrs. Laurie Johnson, a trumpeter, had a career that spanned 30 years. They all broke instrumental taboos.

—MARIO A. CHARLES, "The Age of a Jazzwoman:
Valaida Snow, 1900–1956"

---

3. Quoting your sources directly Sometimes a writer will say something so eloquently and perceptively that you will want to include that writer's words as a **direct quotation** in your work.

In general, quote these types of sources:

- Primary sources (for example, in a text about Rita Dove, a direct quotation from her or a colleague)
- Sources containing very technical language that cannot be paraphrased

- Literary or historical sources, when you analyze the wording
- An authority in the field whose words support your thesis
- Debaters explaining their different positions on an issue

To avoid inadvertent plagiarism, be careful to indicate that the content is a direct quotation when you copy it onto your note cards or into your research notebook. Try to keep quotations short, and always place quotation marks around them. You might also use a special color to indicate direct quotations or deliberately make quotation marks oversized.

When referring to most secondary sources, paraphrase or summarize instead of quoting. Your readers will have difficulty following a text with too many quotations, and your text will lose your voice and ideas. In some instances you may use paraphrase, summary, and quotation together. You might summarize a long passage, paraphrase an important section of it, and directly quote a short part of that section.

19e
plag

> *Note:* If you have used more than one quotation every two or three paragraphs, convert most of the quotations into paraphrases *(see pp. 246–49)*.

19e Integrating quotations, paraphrases, and summaries properly and effectively

Ultimately, you will use some of the paraphrases, summaries, and quotations you have collected during the course of your research to support and develop the ideas you present in your paper. Here are some guidelines for integrating them properly and effectively into the body of your text. (Examples in this section represent MLA format for in-text citations and block quotations. *See Part 4 for guidelines on using this style.*)

1. Integrating quotations Be selective about the quotations you include. Brief quotations can be effective if they are especially well phrased and make a significant point. But take a moment to think about your own interpretation, which might actually be better than the exact wording of the source.

Short quotations should be enclosed in quotation marks and well integrated into your sentence structure. Set off longer quotations in blocks *(see p. 257)*. The following example from Rebecca Hollingsworth's paper on the impact of blogging on traditional news shows the use of a short quotation.

EFFECTIVE QUOTATION

According to Stephen Cass, *we media* is "a term that encompasses a wide range of mostly amateur activities—including

CHECKLIST

Paraphrasing, Summarizing, and Quoting Sources

Paraphrases

☐ Have I used my own words and sentence structure for all paraphrases?

☐ Have I maintained the original meaning?

Summaries

☐ Do all my summaries include my own wording and sentence structure? Are they shorter than the original text?

☐ Do they accurately represent the content of the original?

Quotations

☐ Have I enclosed in quotation marks any uncommon terms, distinctive phrases, or direct quotations from a source?

☐ Have I checked all quotations against the original source?

☐ Do I include ellipsis marks and brackets where I have altered the original wording and capitalization of quotations?

Documentation

☐ Have I indicated my source for all quotations, paraphrases, summaries, statistics, and visuals either within the text or in a parenthetical citation?

☐ Have I included page numbers as required for all quotations, paraphrases, and summaries?

☐ Does every in-text citation have a corresponding entry in the list of works cited or references?

blogging and commentary in online forums—that have been made possible by an array of technologies" (62).

The quotation is effective because it provides a concise, memorable definition of "we media." Hollingsworth integrates the quotation effectively by introducing the name of the source *(Stephen Cass)* and then blending the quotation into the structure of her own sentence. By contrast, the following poorly integrated quotation is not set up to assist the reader in any way.

POORLY INTEGRATED QUOTATION

If the blogging machine makes traditional news outlets defunct, how can we be certain that the news we consume is credible and reliable? "Every citizen can be a reporter, but not every citizen should or will. Every person will get news, but not in the same way, not at the same time, and not with the same perspective" (Goldhammer 13).

When you are integrating someone else's words into your writing, use a **signal phrase** that indicates whom you are quoting. The signal phrase "According to Stephen Cass," identifies Cass as the source of the quotation in the passage on pages 253–54.

A signal phrase clearly indicates where your words end and the source's words begin. The first time you quote a source, include the author's full name and credentials (or authority to describe a topic), such as "New York University professor and media consultant Clay Shirky explains . . ." You may also include the title of the work for context: "Gary Goldhammer tackles this question in his book *The Last Newspaper . . .*"

When you introduce a brief quotation with a signal phrase, you have three basic options:

- You can use a complete sentence followed by a colon.
- You can use a phrase.
- You can make the source's words part of your own sentence structure.

A complete sentence followed by a colon   Introducing a quotation with a complete sentence allows you to provide context for the quote. Use a colon (:) at the end of this introductory sentence, not a semicolon or a comma.

> **COMPLETE SENTENCE**   New York University professor and media consultant Clay Shirky explains how this aspect of blogging is affecting news: "The change isn't a shift from one kind of news institution to another, but rather in the definition of news" (*Here Comes Everybody* 65–66).

More than one work by Shirky is being cited, so a shortened version of the title is included in the in-text citation in MLA style.

**19e
plag**

An introductory or explanatory phrase, followed by a comma
Phrases move the reader efficiently to the quotation.

PHRASE As New York University Professor Clay Shirky
explains, "The change isn't a shift from one
kind of news institution to another, but rather
in the definition of news" (*Here Comes Everybody*
65–66).

Instead of introducing a quotation, the signal phrase can follow
or interrupt it.

FOLLOWS "The change isn't a shift from one kind of news
institution to another, but rather in the definition of news," explains New York University
Professor Clay Shirky (*Here Comes Everybody*
65–66).

INTERRUPTS "The change isn't a shift from one kind of news
institution to another," explains New York University Professor Clay Shirky, "but rather in
the definition of news" (*Here Comes Everybody*
65–66).

Part of your sentence structure When you can, integrate the quotation as part of your own sentence structure without any punctuation between your words and the words you are quoting. By doing so,
you will clearly connect the quoted material with your own ideas.

QUOTATION New York University Professor Clay Shirky
INTEGRATED notes that this transformation "isn't a shift
from one kind of news institution to another,
but rather in the definition of news" (*Here
Comes Everybody* 65–66).

The verb you use in a signal phrase, such as *refutes* or *summarizes,* should show how you are using the quotation in your text. If
your source provides an example that strengthens your argument,
you could say, "Mann *supports* this line of reasoning." *(For more on
varying signal phrases, see the box on p. 258.)*

MLA style places signal-phrase verbs in present tense *(Johnson writes)* while APA uses past tense *(Johnson wrote). (See Parts
4 and 5 for more on these documentation styles.)* When a quotation,
paraphrase, or summary in MLA or APA style begins with a signal
phrase, the ending citation includes the page number (unless the
work lacks page numbers). You can quote without a signal phrase if
you give the author's name in the parenthetical citation.

Brackets and ellipses are important tools for integrating quotations into your text:

- **Brackets within quotations:** Sentences that include quotations must make sense grammatically. Sometimes you may have to adjust a quotation to make it fit your sentence. Use **brackets** to indicate any such minor adjustments. For example, here *over* has been changed to *Over* to make the quotation fit:

"[O]ver time," Shirky writes, "the collection of new experiments that do work might give us the journalism we need" ("Newspapers" 29).

- **Ellipses within quotations:** Use **ellipses** (. . .) to indicate that words have been omitted from the quotation, but be sure that what you omit does not significantly alter the source's meaning.

19e
plag

The Pew Research Center explains, "One concept that will get more attention is . . . what some call a 'pro-am' (professional and amateur) model for news."

(For more on using ellipses, see Chapter 54, pp. 546–47.)

Quotations in block format Quotations longer than four lines should be used rarely because they tend to break up the text and make readers impatient. Research papers should consist primarily of your own analysis of sources. Always tell your readers why you want them to read a long quotation, and afterward comment on it.

If you use a verse quotation longer than three lines or a prose quotation longer than four typed lines, put it in block format *(see Chapter 53, pp. 535–36),* and be careful to integrate it into your paper.

2. Integrating paraphrases and summaries

The principles for integrating paraphrases and summaries into your text are similar to those for including direct quotations. Make a smooth transition between a source's point and your own voice, accurately attributing the information to the source. Use signal phrases to introduce ideas you have borrowed from your sources.

Besides crediting others for their work, signal phrases make ideas more interesting by giving them a human face. Include a citation after the paraphrase or summary. Here are some examples.

As mass communication experts David D. Perlmutter and Misti McDaniel argue, bloggers are exceptionally good at reporting on issues in a way that creates mass appeal (60).

In this passage, Rebecca Hollingsworth uses the signal phrase *As mass communication experts David D. Perlmutter and Misti McDaniel argue* to identify Perlmutter and McDaniel as the source of the paraphrased information about the advantages that bloggers have in reporting on issues.

> According to journalism experts Stephen Lacy, Margaret Duffy, Daniel Riffe, Esther Thorson, and Ken Fleming, citizen journalism websites cannot sufficiently replace, but should instead accompany, newspaper websites (42).

This passage in Hollingsworth's text about blogging uses the signal phrase *According to journalism experts Stephen Lacy, Margaret Duffy, Daniel Riffe, Esther Thorson, and Ken Fleming* to lead into a summary of the source's conclusions about this type of Web site.

> In a recent report, the Pew Research Center points out that traditional and new media face similar challenges in their efforts to generate revenue, particularly from advertising.

In this passage, Hollingsworth uses the phrase *points out* to signal her paraphrase of a report. She directly names the source (the Pew Research Center), so she does not need additional parenthetical documentation. Remember that all summaries and paraphrases must be acknowledged.

NAVIGATING THROUGH COLLEGE AND BEYOND

Varying Signal Phrases

To keep your work interesting, to show the original writer's purpose *(Martinez describes* or *Lin argues),* and to connect the quote to your reasoning *(Johnson refutes),* use appropriate signal phrases such as the following:

according to	contends	points out
acknowledges	denies	proposes
adds	describes	proves
admits	emphasizes	refutes
argues	explains	rejects
asks	expresses	remarks
asserts	finds	reports
charges	holds	responds
claims	implies	shows
comments	insists	speculates
complains	interprets	states
concedes	maintains	suggests
concludes	notes	warns
considers	observes	

20 Writing the Paper

You have chosen a challenging research question and have located, read, and evaluated a variety of sources. It is now time to develop a thesis that will allow you to share your perspective on the issue and make use of all that you have learned.

20a Planning and drafting your paper

Begin planning by recalling the context and purpose of your assignment. If you have an assignment sheet, review it to see if the project is supposed to be primarily informative, interpretive, or argumentative. Think about the academic discipline or disciplines that shape the perspective for your work, and think through the special genres within those disciplines. Consider how much your audience is likely to know about your topic. Keep your overall situation in mind—purpose, audience, and context—as you decide on a thesis to support and develop.

1. Deciding on a thesis Consider the question that guided your research as well as others provoked by what you have learned during your research. Revise the wording of these questions, and summarize them in a central question that is interesting and relevant to your audience *(see Chapter 13, pp. 189–97).* After you write down this question, compose an answer that you can use as your working thesis, as Rebecca Hollingsworth does in the following example.

HOLLINGSWORTH'S FOCAL QUESTION

What are some of the fundamental differences between traditional and new media?

HOLLINGSWORTH'S WORKING THESIS

While traditional journalism uses trustworthy (and time-consuming) methods of reporting, new forms of media get news to the people instantaneously and universally.

(For more on devising a thesis, see Chapter 2, pp. 35–38.)

2. Outlining a plan for supporting and developing your thesis Guided by your tentative thesis, outline a plan that uses your sources in a purposeful way. Decide on the kind of structure you will use—chronological, problem-solution, or thematic—and develop your support by choosing facts, examples, and ideas drawn from a variety of sources. A chronological organization presents examples from earliest to most recent, and a problem-solution structure introduces an issue and a means of addressing it. A thematic organization orders examples from simple to complex, specific to general, or in another logical way.

For her research project on new forms of journalism, Hollingsworth decided on a thematic organization, an approach structured around raising and answering a central question:

- Introduce some of the fundamental differences between traditional and new media.

- State the thesis: In order to survive, journalism must blend traditional and trustworthy forms of reporting with new forms of media that get news to the people instantaneously and universally.

- Offer background information on blogging and how it has changed journalism.

- Introduce the concept of *citizen journalism,* and explain the shift from expert to novice reporting.

- Discuss how mainstream journalism and citizen journalism have merged, and give examples of the benefits of this relationship.

- Illustrate what the relationship between traditional and new media outlets looks like and how it functions.

- Discuss how this relationship will continue to develop as people continue to demand reporting that is both reliable and instantaneous.

- Describe the benefits of blogs to the field of journalism.

- Conclude: The evolution of journalism toward citizen-driven news has led to a more open, more immediate, more widespread, and more emphatic experience of world issues and events.

To develop this outline, Hollingsworth would need to list supporting facts, examples, or ideas for each point, as well as indicate the sources of this information. Each section would need to center on her original thinking, backed by her analysis of sources. *(For more on developing an outline, see Chapter 2, pp. 39–42.)*

3. Organizing and evaluating your information
Your note-taking strategies will determine how you collect and organize your information. Whether you have taken notes in a research journal, in a blog, or on note cards, group them according to topic and subtopic. For example, Rebecca Hollingsworth could have used the following categories to organize her notes:

Characteristics—traditional reporting
Characteristics—blogging
Evolution of journalism—general info
Citizen journalism—benefits
Relationship betw. old and new—examples

Sorting index cards into stacks that match up topics and subtopics allows you to see what you have gathered. A small stack of cards for a particular subtopic might mean that the subtopic is not as important as you originally thought—or that you need to do additional research focused on that specific subtopic.

If your notes are primarily on your computer, you can create a category heading for each topic and subtopic and then copy and paste to move information to the appropriate category.

20a

4. Writing a draft that you can revise, share, and edit   When you have a tentative thesis and a plan, you are ready to write a draft. Many writers present their thesis or focal question at the end of an introductory, context-setting paragraph or two. The introduction should interest readers in your project.

As you write beyond the introduction, be prepared to reexamine and refine your thesis. When drawing on ideas from your sources, be sure to quote and paraphrase properly. *(For advice on quoting and paraphrasing, see Chapter 19, pp. 246–58.)* Make your conclusion as memorable as possible. You may need to review the paper as a whole before writing the conclusion.

5. Integrating visuals   Well-chosen visuals such as photographs, drawings, charts, graphs, and maps can sometimes help illustrate your argument. In some cases, a visual might itself be a subject of your analysis. Rebecca Hollingsworth uses a line graph that illustrates the increasing audience for online news. She integrates this visual into her research project.

When integrating visuals, be sure to give careful attention to figure numbers and captions:

- **Figure numbers:** Both MLA and APA style require writers to number each image in a research paper. In MLA style, the word *figure* is abbreviated to *Fig.* In APA style, the full word *Figure* is written out.

- **Captions:** Each visual that you include in your paper must be followed by a caption that includes the title of the visual (if given; otherwise, a brief description will do) and its source. In MLA style, each caption begins with the figure number and a period after the number (Fig. 1.); in APA style, use italics for the figure number (*Figure 1.*).

20b Revising your draft

You may prefer to revise a hard copy of your draft by hand, or you might find it easier to use the "Track Changes" feature in your word-processing program. Either way, be sure to keep previous versions of your drafts. It is useful to have a record of how your work evolved—especially if you need to hunt down a particular source or want to reincorporate information, ideas, or sources you used earlier in the process. The Checklist box can help you revise your text.

CHECKLIST

Revising and Editing a Research Paper

Consider these questions as you read your draft and gather feedback from your instructor and peers (see also Checklist for Avoiding Inadvertent Plagiarism, Chapter 18, p. 239):

Thesis and structure

☐ How does my draft address the topic and purpose given in the assignment?

☐ Who are my readers, and how much can I assume that they know about the topic?

☐ What are the conventions of the academic discipline or disciplines in which I am working?

☐ Do I communicate in an informed, thoughtful tone, without condescension?

☐ How well does my thesis fit my evidence and reasoning?

☐ Is the central idea of each section based on my own thinking and backed with evidence from my sources?

☐ How have I dealt with the most likely critiques of my thesis?

☐ Do the transitions from section to section assist the reader in moving from one topic to the next?

☐ What evidence do I use to support each point? Is it sufficient?

CHECKLIST *(continued)*

Editing: Use of sources

☐ Do my paraphrases and summaries alter the wording and sentence structure, but not the meaning, of the original text?

☐ Have I checked all quotations for accuracy and used ellipses or brackets where necessary?

☐ Do signal phrases set off and establish context for quotations, paraphrases, and summaries?

☐ Have I provided adequate in-text citation for each source?

☐ Do my in-text citations match my works-cited or references page?

☐ Do all my illustrations have complete and accurate captions?

(See also the checklists Revising Content and Organization, p. 68, Editing for Style and Grammar, p. 79, and Proofreading, p. 82.)

20c

20c Documenting your sources

Be sure to acknowledge information, ideas, or words that are not your own. As noted in the box on page 237, the only exception to this principle is when you use information that is common knowledge, such as the chemical composition of water or the names of the thirteen original U.S. states. When you tell readers what sources you have consulted, they can more readily understand your paper as well as the conversation you are participating in by writing it.

The mode of documentation depends on the overall situation. How sources are documented varies by field and discipline. Choose a documentation style that is appropriate for the particular course you are taking, and use it properly and consistently.

NAVIGATING THROUGH COLLEGE AND BEYOND

Documentation Styles Explained in This Text

TYPE OF COURSE	DOCUMENTATION STYLE MOST COMMONLY USED	WHERE TO FIND THIS STYLE IN THE HANDBOOK
Humanities (English, religion, music, art, philosophy)	MLA (Modern Language Association)	*Pages 265–317*
Social sciences (anthropology, psychology, sociology, education, business)	APA (American Psychological Association)	*Pages 319–57*

Built near the site of the Great Library of Alexandria, Egypt, an ancient storehouse of knowledge that was destroyed by fire in the fourth century CE, the new Bibliotheca Alexandria offers a variety of collections and programs, including books, rare manuscripts, and a science museum.

Next to the originator of a good sentence is

the first quoter of it.

—RALPH WALDO EMERSON

MLA
Documentation
Style

4 MLA Documentation Style

MLA style requires writers to provide bibliographic information about their sources in a works-cited list. To format works-cited entries correctly, you need to know first of all what kind of source you are citing. The directory on pages 278–79 will help you find the appropriate sample to use as your model. As an alternative, you can use the charts on the foldout pages that follow. Answering the questions provided in the charts on the reverse side of the foldout will usually lead you to the sample entry you need. If you cannot find what you are looking for, consult your instructor for help.

WRITING OUTCOMES

Part 4: MLA Documentation Style

This section will help you answer questions such as the following:

Rhetorical Knowledge
- Which disciplines use MLA style? (**21**)
- When should I use explanatory notes in MLA style? (**23**)

Critical Thinking, Reading, and Writing
- Why do I need to document my sources? (**21**)

Processes
- How do I create a works-cited list? (**22**)
- How should I position and label visuals? (**24**)

Knowledge of Conventions
- What are correct formats for in-text citations (**21**), works-cited list entries (**22**), and notes (**23**)?
- How do I cite electronic sources such as databases, Web sites, and podcasts? (**22**)
- What kind of spacing and margins should I use? (**24**)

Composing in Electronic Environments
- How do I cite a Web site or a blog in the text of my paper? (**21**) In my list of works cited? (**22**)

For a general introduction to writing outcomes, see Id, page 5.

The Elements of an MLA Works-Cited Entry:

Journal Article

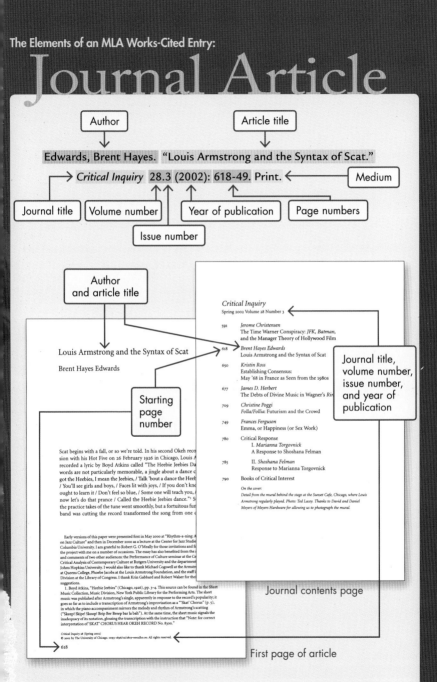

Author

Article title

Edwards, Brent Hayes. "Louis Armstrong and the Syntax of Scat."

Critical Inquiry 28.3 (2002): 618-49. Print. ← **Medium**

Journal title   **Volume number**   **Year of publication**   **Page numbers**

Issue number

Author and article title

Critical Inquiry
Spring 2002 Volume 28 Number 3

591 *Jerome Christensen*
     The Time Warner Conspiracy: *JFK, Batman,*
     and the Manager Theory of Hollywood Film

618 *Brent Hayes Edwards*
     Louis Armstrong and the Syntax of Scat

650 *Kristin Ross*
     Establishing Consensus:
     May '68 in France as Seen from the 1980s

677 *James D. Herbert*
     The Debts of Divine Music in Wagner's *Rin*

709 *Christine Poggi*
     Folla/Folla: Futurism and the Crowd

749 *Frances Ferguson*
     Emma, or Happiness (or Sex Work)

780 Critical Response
        I. *Marianna Torgovnick*
           A Response to Shoshana Felman

785   II. *Shoshana Felman*
           Response to Marianna Torgovnick

790 Books of Critical Interest

     On the cover:
     Detail from the mural behind the stage at the Sunset Cafe, Chicago, where Louis
     Armstrong regularly played. Photo: Ted Lacey. Thanks to David and Daniel
     Meyers of Meyers Hardware for allowing us to photograph the mural.

Journal title, volume number, issue number, and year of publication

Louis Armstrong and the Syntax of Scat

Brent Hayes Edwards

Starting page number

Scat begins with a fall, or so we're told. In his second Okeh reco
sion with his Hot Five on 26 February 1926 in Chicago, Louis A
recorded a lyric by Boyd Atkins called "The Heebie Jeebies Da
words are not particularly memorable, a jingle about a dance c
got the Heebies, I mean the Jeebies, / Talk 'bout a dance the Heeb
/ You'll see girls and boys, / Faces lit with joys, / If you don't kno
ought to learn it / Don't feel so blue, / Some one will teach you, /
now let's do that prance / Called the Heebie Jeebies dance."¹ S
the practice takes of the tune went smoothly, but a fortuitous fur
band was cutting the record transformed the song from one c

Early versions of this paper were presented first in May 2000 at "Rhythm-a-ning: A
on Jazz Culture" and then in December 2000 as a lecture at the Center for Jazz Studie
Columbia University. I am grateful to Robert G. O'Meally for those invitations and for
the project with me on a number of occasions. The essay has also benefited from the r
and comments of two other audiences: the Performance of Culture seminar at the Ce
Critical Analysis of Contemporary Culture at Rutgers University and the department
Johns Hopkins University. I would also like to thank Michael Cogswell at the Armstr
at Queens College, Phoebe Jacobs at the Louis Armstrong Foundation, and the staff i
Division at the Library of Congress. I thank Krin Gabbard and Robert Walser for the
suggestions.
   1. Boyd Atkins, "Heebie Jeebies" (Chicago, 1926), pp. 3-4. This source can be found in the Sheet
Music Collection, Music Division, New York Public Library for the Performing Arts. The sheet
music was published after Armstrong's single, apparently in response to the record's popularity; it
goes so far as to include a transcription of Armstrong's improvisation as a "Skat' Chorus" (p. 5),
in which the piano accompaniment mirrors the melody and rhythm of Armstrong's scatting
("Skeep! Skipe! Skoop! Brip Ber Breep bar la bah"). At the same time, the sheet music signals the
inadequacy of its notation, glossing the transcription with the instruction that "Note: for correct
interpretation of 'SKAT' CHORUS HEAR OKEH RECORD No. 8300."

Critical Inquiry 28 (Spring 2002)
© 2002 by The University of Chicago. 0093-1896/02/2803-0002$10.00. All rights reserved.

→ 618

Journal contents page

First page of article

Some academic journals, like this one, provide most of the information
needed for a citation on the first page of an article as well as, like others,
on the cover or contents page. You will need to look at the article's last
page for the last page number.

Electronic or Other Nonprin

❓ DID YOU FIND YOUR NONPRINT SOURCE ONLINE?

NO   YES   Go to this entry *on page*
↓

Go to next panel.

The Elements of an MLA Works-Cited Entry: Online Database

Journal Article from an

Authors → Article title → Page numbers →

Lacy, Stephen, et al. "Citizen Journalism Web Sites Complement Newspapers." *Newspaper Research Journal* 31.2 (2010): 34-46. *Academic Search Elite*. Web. 5 May 2010.

Database title

Medium

Date of access

Journal title

Volume number

Issue number

Year of publication

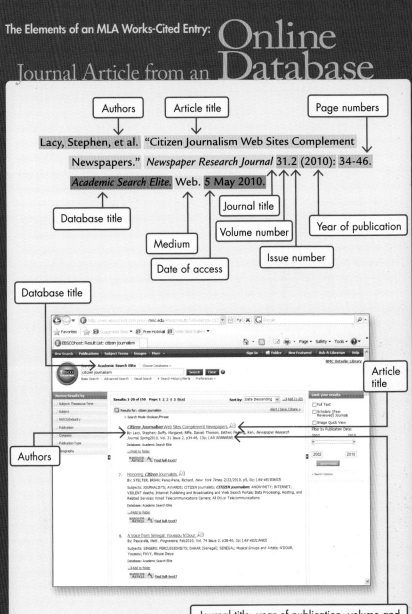

Database title

Article title

Authors

Journal title, year of publication, volume and issue number, and page range information

A citation for an article obtained from an online database includes information about the database, the medium, and the date of access in addition to information about the print version of the article. Information about the date of access comes from the researcher's notes. When a work has more than six authors, you have the option of using the abbreviation *et al.* (meaning "and others") after the first name.

Print Periodicals or Other Print Sources

❓ IS YOUR SOURCE FROM A JOURNAL, A MAGAZINE, OR A NEWSPAPER?

NO　　**YES**　　　　　　　　　　　　　　　**Go to this entry *on page***
　　　　↓

❓ IS IT A PRINT SOURCE BUT NOT A BOOK, A PART OF A BOOK, OR AN ARTICLE IN AN ACADEMIC JOURNAL, A MAGAZINE, OR A NEWSPAPER?

NO　　**YES**　　　　　　　　　　　　　　　**Go to this entry *on page***
　　　　↓

Check the directory on pages 277–78 or consult your instructor.

The Elements of an MLA Works-Cited Entry:

Short Work on a Web Site

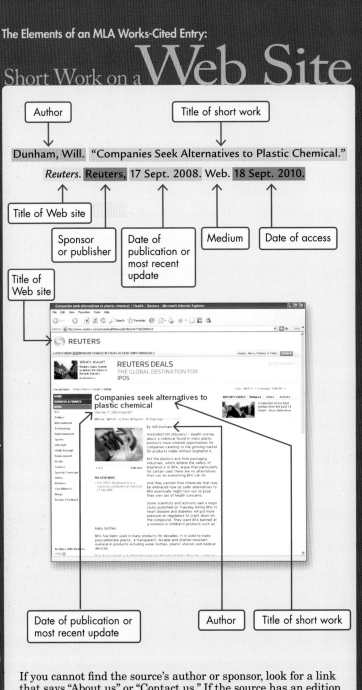

Author → Dunham, Will. "Companies Seek Alternatives to Plastic Chemical."

Title of short work

Reuters. Reuters, 17 Sept. 2008. Web. 18 Sept. 2010.

Title of Web site

Sponsor or publisher

Date of publication or most recent update

Medium

Date of access

Title of Web site

Date of publication or most recent update

Author

Title of short work

If you cannot find the source's author or sponsor, look for a link that says "About us" or "Contact us." If the source has an edition or version number, place it after the site title. See page 297 for online scholarly journals and pages 294-96 for works existing online and in another medium (e.g., print or film).

Entries in a Works-Cited List:

Books

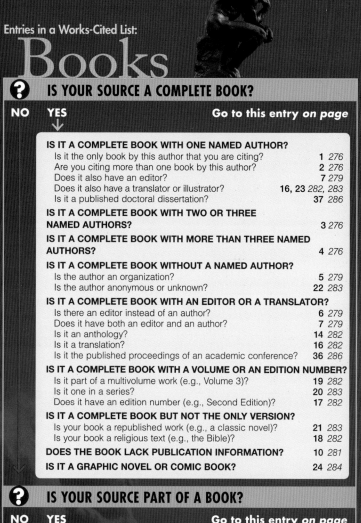

❓ IS YOUR SOURCE A COMPLETE BOOK?

NO **YES** Go to this entry *on page*

❓ IS YOUR SOURCE PART OF A BOOK?

NO **YES** Go to this entry *on page*

Check the next panel or the directory on pages 277–78 or consult your instructor.

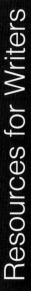

Resources for Writers

The Elements of an MLA Works-Cited Entry:

Book

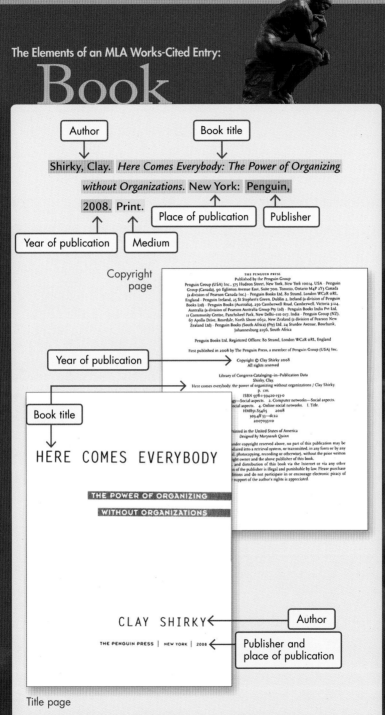

Author

Book title

Shirky, Clay. *Here Comes Everybody: The Power of Organizing without Organizations.* New York: Penguin, 2008. Print.

Place of publication

Publisher

Year of publication

Medium

Copyright page

Year of publication

Book title

HERE COMES EVERYBODY

THE POWER OF ORGANIZING WITHOUT ORGANIZATIONS

CLAY SHIRKY

THE PENGUIN PRESS | NEW YORK | 2008

Author

Publisher and place of publication

Title page

Information for a book citation can be found on the book's title and copyright pages.

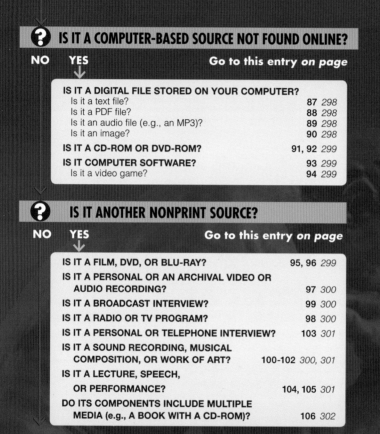

t Sources

Check the directory on pages 277–78 or consult your instructor.

The documentation style developed by the Modern Language Association (MLA) is used by many researchers in the arts and humanities, especially by those who write about language and literature. The guidelines presented here are based on the seventh edition of the *MLA Handbook for Writers of Research Papers* (New York: MLA, 2009).

College papers include information, ideas, and quotations from sources that must be accurately documented. Documentation allows others to see the path you have taken in researching and writing your paper. *(For more on what to document, see Part 3: Researching, pp. 234–40.)*

The MLA documentation style has three parts:

- In-text citations
- List of works cited
- Explanatory notes and acknowledgments

In-text citations and a list of works cited are mandatory; explanatory notes are optional.

21
MLA

21 MLA Style: In-Text Citations

In-text citations let readers know that they can find full bibliographical information about your sources in the list of works cited at the end of your text.

1. Author named in sentence   In your first reference, give the author's full name as the source presents it. Afterward, use the last name only, unless two or more of your sources have the same last name *(see no. 6)* or unless two or more works by the same author appear in your works-cited list *(no. 3)*.

signal phrase

New York University professor and media consultant Clay Shirky explains how this aspect of blogging is affecting news: "The change isn't a shift from one kind of news institution to another, but rather in the definition of news" (65).

The parenthetical page citation comes after the closing quotation mark but before the period.

2. Author named in parentheses If you do not name the source's author in your sentence, then you must provide the name in the parentheses (give the full name if the author of another source has the same last name).

> For many, the term *we media* aptly characterizes the kind of citizen
>
> journalism that blogging represents; it is "a term that encompasses
>
> a wide range of mostly amateur activities—including blogging and
>
> commentary in online forums—that have been made possible by an
>
>   no comma after author's name
> array of technologies" (Cass 62).

There is no comma between the author's name and the page number. If you cite two or more distinct pages, however, separate the numbers with a comma: (Cass 62, 70).

3. Two or more works by the same author If you use two or more works by the same author, you must identify which work you are citing, either in your sentence or in an abbreviated form in parentheses: (Shirky, *Here Comes Everybody* 66).

                      book title is italicized
> In *Here Comes Everybody: The Power of Organizing without Organizations,*
>
> Shirky compares new forms of media, like blogging, to fundamental
>
> advances in human literacy, such as the printing press (66).

4. Two or three authors of the same work If a source has up to three authors, you should name them all either in your text, as the next example shows, or in parentheses: (Perlmutter and McDaniel 60).

> Mass communication experts David D. Perlmutter and Misti McDaniel
>
> argue that bloggers are exceptionally good at reporting on issues in a
>
> way that creates mass appeal (60).

5. More than three authors If a source has more than three authors, either list all the authors or give the first author's last name followed by *et al.,* meaning "and others" (note that *et,* which means "and," is fine as is, but *al.,* which is an abbreviation for *alia,* needs a period). Do the same in your works-cited list.

> Changes in social regulations are bound to produce new forms of
>
> subjectivity (Henriques et al. 275).

MLA IN-TEXT CITATIONS: DIRECTORY TO SAMPLE TYPES

(See pp. 276–302 for works-cited examples.)

21 MLA

6. Authors with the same last name If the authors of two or more of your sources have the same last name, include the first initial of the author you are citing (R. Campbell 63); if the first initial is also shared, use the full first name, as shown in the following example.

> In the late nineteenth century, the sale of sheet music spread rapidly in a Manhattan area along Broadway known as Tin Pan Alley (Richard Campbell 63).

7. Organization as author Treat the organization as the author. If the name is long, put it in a signal phrase.

> The Centre for Contemporary Cultural Studies claims that "there is nothing inherently concrete about historiography" (10).

8. Unknown author When no author is given, cite a work by its title, using either the full title in a signal phrase or an abbreviated

MLA IN-TEXT CITATIONS

- Name the author, either in a signal phrase such as "Shirky compares" or in a parenthetical citation.
- Include a page reference in parentheses. No "p." precedes the page number; if the author is named in the parentheses, there is no punctuation between the author's name and the page number.
- Place the citation as close to the material being cited as possible and before any punctuation marks that divide or end the sentence except in a block quotation, where the citation comes one space after the period or final punctuation mark. See no. 12 for quotations ending with a question mark or an exclamation point.
- Italicize the titles of books, magazines, and plays. Place quotation marks around the titles of articles and short poems.
- For Internet sources, follow the same general guidelines as for print sources. Keep the parenthetical citation simple, providing enough information for your reader to find the full citation in your works-cited list. Cite either the author's name or the title of the site or article. Begin the parenthetical citation with the first word of the corresponding works-cited list entry.
- For works without page or paragraph numbers, give the author or title only. Often it is best to mention them in your sentence, in which case no parenthetical citation is needed.

version in the parentheses. When abbreviating the title, begin with the word by which it is alphabetized in your works-cited list.

title of article

"Squaresville, USA vs. Beatsville" makes the Midwestern small-town home seem boring compared with the West Coast artist's "pad" (31).

The Midwestern small-town home seems boring compared with the West Coast artist's "pad" ("Squaresville" 31).

9. Entire work   Acknowledge an entire work in your text, not in a parenthetical citation. Include the work in your list of works cited, and include in the text the word by which the entry is alphabetized.

Sidney J. Furie's film *Lady Sings the Blues* presents Billie Holiday as a beautiful woman in pain rather than as the great jazz artist she was.

10. Paraphrased or summarized source   If you include the author's name in your paraphrase or summary, include only the page number or numbers in your parenthetical citation. Signal phrases clarify that you are paraphrasing or summarizing.

signal phrase
Shirky cites an example from 2002, when it was the bloggers, not the mainstream reporters, who first publicized former Mississippi senator Trent Lott's controversial remarks at Strom Thurmond's hundredth birthday party, resulting in Lott's decision to step down from his position as majority leader (61).

11. Source of a long quotation For a quotation of more than four typed lines of prose or three of poetry, do not use quotation marks. Instead, indent the material you are quoting by one inch. Following the final punctuation mark of the quotation, allow one space before the parenthetical information.

Shirky describes what this trend toward "pro-am" reporting might

look like:

> For the next few decades, journalism will be made up of
>
> overlapping special cases. Many of these models will rely on
>
> amateurs as researchers and writers. Many of these models
>
> will rely on sponsorship or grants or endowments instead
>
> of revenues. Many of these models will rely on excitable
>
> 14-year-olds distributing the results. Many of these models
>
> ellipses and brackets indicate an omission from the quotation
> will fail. . . . [O]ver time, the collection of new experiments
>
> that do work might give us the journalism we need.

("Newspapers" 29)

12. Source of a short quotation Close the quotation before the parenthetical citation. If the quotation concludes with an exclamation point or a question mark, place the closing quotation mark after that punctuation mark, and place the sentence period after the parenthetical citation.

Encyclopaedia Britannica defines a blog, short for Web log, as an "online journal where an individual, group, or corporation presents a record of activities, thoughts, or beliefs" ("Blog").

Shakespeare's Sonnet XVIII asks, "Shall I compare thee to a summer's day?" (line 1).

13. One-page source   You need not include a page number in the parenthetical citation for a one-page printed source.

14. Government publication   To avoid an overly long parenthetical citation, name within your text the government agency that published the source.

> According to a report issued by the Bureau of National Affairs,
> many employers in 1964 needed guidance to apply new workplace
> rules that ensured fairness and complied with the Civil Rights Act
> of 1964 (32).

15. Photograph, map, graph, chart, or other visual

VISUAL APPEARS IN YOUR PAPER

> An aerial photograph of Manhattan (fig. 3), taken by the United
> States Geographical Survey, demonstrates how creative city planning
> can introduce parks and green spaces within even the most densely
> populated urban areas.

If the caption you write for the image includes all the information found in a works-cited list entry, you need not include it in your list. *(See p. 311 for an example.)*

VISUAL DOES NOT APPEAR IN YOUR PAPER

> An aerial photograph of Manhattan taken by the United States
> Geographical Survey demonstrates how creative city planning can
> introduce parks and green spaces within even the most densely
> populated urban areas (TerraServer-USA).

Provide a parenthetical citation that directs your reader to information about the source of the image in your works-cited list.

16. Web site or other online electronic source   If you cannot find the author of an online source, then identify the source by title or sponsor, either in your text or in a parenthetical citation. Because most online sources do not have set page, section, or paragraph numbers, they must usually be cited as entire works.

> organization cited as author
> In its annual report, the Pew Research Center argues that one model
> in the future will involve partnerships between traditional and newer
> forms of media and, in particular, that one type of relationship will

be a concept known as a "pro-am" (for "professional and amateur")
page number not provided
approach to news.

17. Work with numbered paragraphs or sections instead of pages
To distinguish them from page numbers, use the abbreviation *par(s).* or the type of division such as *section(s)* or *screen(s).*

Rothstein suggests that many German Romantic musical techniques

may have originated in Italian opera (par. 9).

Give the paragraph or section number(s) after the author's name and a comma in a parenthetical citation: (Rothstein, par. 9).

18. Work with no page or paragraph numbers
When citing an electronic or print source without page, paragraph, or other reference numbers, try to include the author's name in your text instead of in a parenthetical citation.

author's name
Mathew Ingram, a technology journalist and blogger, notes that "I think

the more people there are writing, and the easier it is to publish writing

of all kinds, the more likely we are to find the information we need."

19. Multivolume work
When citing more than one volume of a multivolume work in your paper, include with each citation the volume number, followed by a colon, a space, and the page number.

Scott argues that today people tend to solve problems "by turning to

the Web" (2: 5).

If you consult only one volume of a multivolume work, then specify that volume in the works-cited list *(see pp. 282–83),* but not in the parenthetical citation.

20. Literary work

Novels and literary nonfiction books Include the relevant page number, followed by a semicolon, a space, and the chapter number.

Jenkins states that because Harry Potter's fandom involves both

adults and children, it's a "space where conversations could occur

across generations" (216; ch. 5).

If the author is not named in your sentence, add the name in front of the page number: (Jenkins 216; ch. 5).

**21
MLA**

Poem   Use line numbers, not page numbers.

> In "Ode on a Grecian Urn," Keats asks "What men or gods are these?
> What maidens loth? / What mad pursuit? What struggle to escape?"
> (lines 8-9). He can provide no answer, but he notes that the lucky
> lovers pictured on the urn are "for ever young; / All breathing human
> passion far above" (27-28).

Note that the word *lines* (not italicized), rather than "l." or "ll.," is used in the first citation to establish what the numbers in parentheses refer to; subsequent citations need not use the word *lines*.

Plays and long, multisection poems   Use division (act, scene, canto, book, part) and lines, not page numbers. In the following example, notice that Arabic numerals are used for act and scene divisions as well as for line numbers: (*Ham.* 2.3.22-27). The same is true for canto, verse, and lines in the following citation of Byron's *Don Juan:* (*DJ* 1.37.4-8). (The *MLA Handbook* lists abbreviations for titles of certain literary works.)

21. Religious text   Cite material in the Bible, Upanishads, or Koran by book, chapter, and verse, using an appropriate abbreviation when the name of the book is in the parentheses rather than in your sentence. Name the edition from which you are citing.

> As the Bible says, "The wise man knows there will be a time of
> judgment" (*Holy Bible, Rev. Stand. Vers.,* Eccles. 8.5).

Note that titles of scriptural writings are not italicized.

22. Historical document   For familiar documents such as the Constitution and the Declaration of Independence, provide the document's name and the numbers of the parts you are citing.

> Judges are allowed to remain in office "during good behavior," a vague
> standard that has had various interpretations (US Const., art. 3, sec. 1).

23. Indirect source   When you quote or paraphrase a quotation you found in someone else's work, put *qtd. in* (not italicized, meaning "quoted in," with a period after the abbreviation) before the name of your source.

> Advertising agencies try to come up with ways to "interrupt" people
> so that "they pay attention to one-way message[s]" (qtd. in Scott 7).

In your list of works cited, list only the work you consulted, in this case the indirect source by Scott.

24. Two or more sources in one citation   When you credit two or more sources for the same idea, use a semicolon to separate the citations.

> The impact of blogging on human knowledge, communication, and
> interactions has led to improvements in our daily lives. We are not
> only more up to date on the latest goings-on in the world, but are
> also connected to other informed citizens like never before (Ingram;
> Shirky).

25. Two or more sources in one sentence   Include a parenthetical reference after each idea or quotation you have borrowed.

> Ironically, Americans lavish more money each year on their pets
> than they spend on children's toys (Merkins 21), but the feral cat
> population—consisting of abandoned pets and their offspring—is at
> an estimated 70 million and growing (Mott).

26. Work in an anthology   When citing a work in a collection, give the name of the specific work's author, not the name of the editor of the whole collection.

> "Exile marks us like a talisman or tattoo. It teaches us how to endure
> long nights and short days" (Agosin 273).

Here, Agosin is cited as the source even though his work appears in a collection edited by Ringoberto Gonzalez. Note that the list of works cited must include an entry for Agosin.

27. E-mail, letter, or personal interview   Cite by name the person you communicated with, using either a signal phrase or parentheses.

> Blogging is a beneficial tool to use in the classroom because it allows
> students to keep up with new media trends (Carter).

In the works-cited list, after giving the person's last name you will need to identify the kind of communication and its date *(see pp. 288, 298, and 301)*.

22 MLA Style: List of Works Cited

MLA documentation style requires a works-cited page with full bibliographic information about your sources. The list of works cited should appear at the end of your research project, beginning on a new page entitled "Works Cited." Include only those sources you cite, unless your instructor tells you to prepare a "Works Consulted" list.

BOOKS

1. Book with one author Italicize the book's title. Generally only the city, not the state, is included in the publication data. Conclude with the medium (Print). In MLA style, abbreviations are suggested for most publishers, for instance, *Wayne State UP* for *Wayne State University Press,* and *Random* for *Random House.* For books published by a division within a publishing company, known as an imprint, put a hyphen between the imprint and publisher, like so: Knopf-Random.

> Shirky, Clay. *Here Comes Everybody: The Power of Organizing without Organizations.* New York: Penguin, 2008. Print.

2. Two or more works by the same author(s) Give the author's name in the first entry only. For subsequent works authored by that person, replace the name with three hyphens and a period. Alphabetize by title.

> Shirky, Clay. *Here Comes Everybody: The Power of Organizing without Organizations.* New York: Penguin, 2008. Print.
>
> ---. "Newspapers and Thinking the Unthinkable." *Risk Management* May 2009: 24-29. *Academic Search Elite.* Web. 21 Apr. 2010.

3. Book with two or three authors Name the two or three authors in the order in which they appear on the title page, putting the last name first for the first author only.

> Reeder, Joelle, and Katherine Scoleri. *The IT Girl's Guide to Blogging with Moxie.* Hoboken: Wiley, 2007. Print.

4. Book with four or more authors When a work has more than three authors, you may list them all or use the abbreviation *et al.*

MLA WORKS-CITED ENTRIES: DIRECTORY to SAMPLE TYPES

(See pp. 267–75 for examples of in-text citations.)

**22
MLA**

(continued)

MLA WORKS-CITED ENTRIES: DIRECTORY to SAMPLE TYPES *(continued)*

(meaning "and others") to replace the names of all authors except the first.

> Henriques, Julian, et al. *Changing the Subject: Psychology, Social Regulation, and Subjectivity.* New York: Methuen, 1984. Print.

5. Organization as author   Consider as an organization any group, commission, association, or corporation whose members are not identified on the title page.

> Centre for Contemporary Cultural Studies. *Making Histories: Studies in History Writing and Politics.* London: Hutchinson, 1982. Print.

6. Book by an editor or editors   If the title page lists an editor instead of an author, begin with the editor's name followed by the abbreviation *ed.* with a period (not italicized). Use *eds.* when more than one editor is listed. Only the first editor's name should appear in reverse order. When a book's title contains the title of another book (as this one does), do not italicize the title-within-a-title (here, *The Invisible Man*).

> title in title not italicized
> O'Meally, Robert, ed. *New Essays on* The Invisible Man. Cambridge: Cambridge UP, 1988. Print.

7. Book with an author and an editor   Put the author and title first, followed by the abbreviation *Ed.* (not italicized, for "edited by") and the name of the editor. However, if you cite something written by the editor, see no. 15.

> editor's name not in reverse order
> James, Henry. *The Portrait of a Lady.* Ed. Robert D. Bamberg. New York: Norton, 1975. Print.

8. Work in an anthology or textbook or chapter in an edited book   List the author and title of the selection, followed by the title of the anthology, *Ed.* (not italicized) and the editor's name, publication data, page numbers of the selection, and medium. The first example cites a reading from a textbook.

> Brodkey, Linda. "On the Subjects of Class and Gender in 'The Literacy Letters.'" *Cross-Talk in Comp Theory.* Ed. Victor Villanueva. Urbana: NCTE Press, 2003. 677-96. Print.

> Fisher, Walter R. "Narration, Knowledge, and the Possibility of Wisdom." *Rethinking Knowledge: Reflections across the Disciplines.* Ed. Robert F. Goodman and Walter R. Fisher. Albany: SUNY Press, 1995. 169-92. Print.

22
MLA

MLA LIST of WORKS CITED

- Begin on a new page with the centered title "Works Cited."
- Include an entry for every source cited in your text.
- Include author, title, publication data, and medium (such as print, Web, radio) for each entry, if available. Use a period to set off each of these elements from the others. Leave one space after the periods.
- Do not number the entries.
- Put entries in alphabetical order by author's or editor's last name. If the work has more than one author, see nos. 3 and 4 *(pp. 276, 279)*. (If the author is unknown, use the first word of the title, excluding the articles *A, An,* or *The*).
- Italicize titles of books, periodicals, long poems, and plays. Put quotation marks around titles of articles, short stories, and short poems.
- Capitalize the first and last and all important words in all titles and subtitles. Do not capitalize articles, prepositions, coordinating conjunctions, and the *to* in infinitives unless they appear as the first or last word in the title. Place a colon between title and subtitle unless the title ends in a question mark or an exclamation point.
- In the publication data, abbreviate months and publishers' names (Dec. rather than December; Oxford UP instead of Oxford University Press), and include the name of the city in which the publisher is located but not the state (unless the city is obscure or ambiguous): Ithaca: Cornell UP. Use *n.p.* in place of publisher or location information if none is available. If the date of publication is not given, provide the approximate date, enclosed in brackets: [c. 1975]. If you cannot approximate the date, write *n.d.* for "no date."
- Do not use *p., pp.,* or *page(s)*. Use *n. pag.* (not italicized) if the source lacks page or paragraph numbers or other divisions. When page citations over 100 have the same first digit, do not repeat it for the second number: 243-47.
- Abbreviate all months except May, June, and July.
- For articles and other print sources that skip pages, provide the page number for the beginning of the article followed by a plus (+) sign.
- Use a hanging indent: Start the first line of each entry at the left margin, and indent all subsequent lines of the entry five spaces (or one-half inch in a word-processing program).
- Double-space within entries and between them.

9. Two or more items from one anthology

Include a complete entry for the anthology beginning with the name of the editor(s). Each selection should have its own entry in the alphabetical list that includes only the author, title of the selection, editor, and page numbers.

entry for the anthology
Jacobs, Jonathan, Ed. *Open Game Table: The Anthology of Roleplaying in*
    publication information unknown, see no. 10
    Game Blogs. Vol. 2. N.p.: Open Game Table, 2010. Print.
entry for a selection from the anthology
Jones, Jeremy. "Gaming Roots and Reflections." Jacobs 11-35.

10. Book without publication information or pagination

If a book has no page numbers, as in the first example, use *N. pag.* instead. Or, if the place of publication is unknown, as in the second example, indicate *N.p.* (not italicized).

Barber, Tiki, and Ronde Barber. *By My Brother's Side.* New York: Simon,

2004. N. pag. Print.

Goldhammer, Gary. *The Last Newspaper: Reflections on the Future of*

News. N.p.: Lulu, 2009. Print.

11. Signed article in an encyclopedia or another reference work

Cite the author's name, title of the entry (in quotation marks), title of the reference work (italicized), edition, publication information, and medium. Omit page numbers if entries appear in alphabetical order.

Hirsch, E. D. "Idioms." *Dictionary of Cultural Literacy.* 2nd ed. Boston:

Houghton, 1993. 59. Print.

12. Unsigned entry in an encyclopedia or another reference work

Start the entry with the title. For well-known reference works, omit the place and publisher.

"Godiva, Lady." *Dictionary of Cultural Literacy.* 2nd ed. Boston:

Houghton, 1993. 199. Print.

13. Article from a collection of reprinted articles

Haney-Peritz, Janice. "Monumental Feminism and Literature's

Ancestral House: Another Look at 'The Yellow Wallpaper.'"
            abbreviation for "reprinted"
Women's Studies 12.2 (1986): 113-28. Rpt. in *The Captive*

Imagination: A Casebook on "The Yellow Wallpaper." Ed. Catherine

Golden. New York: Feminist, 1992. 261-76. Print.

14. Anthology

Eggers, Dave, ed. *The Best American Nonrequired Reading 2007.* Boston:

Houghton, 2007. Print.

15. Preface, foreword, introduction, or afterword   When the
writer of some part of a book is different from the author of the book,
use the word *By* after the book's title, and cite the author's full name.
If the book's sole author wrote the part and the book has an editor,
use only the author's last name after *By*. If there is no editor and the
author wrote the part, cite the complete book.

name of part of book
Schlesinger, Arthur M. Jr. Introduction. *Pioneer Women: Voices from the*
author of the book
Kansas Frontier. By Joanna L. Stratton. New York: Simon, 1981.

11-15. Print.

16. Translation   The translator's name goes after the title, with
the abbreviation *Trans.* (not italicized).

Freire, Paulo. *Pedagogy of the Oppressed.* Trans. Mara Bergman Ramos.

New York: Continuum, 2005. Print.

17. Edition other than the first   Include the number of the edition: *2nd ed., 3rd ed.* (not italicized), and so on. Place the number
after the title, or if there is an editor, after that person's name.

Jenkins, Henry. *Convergence Culture: Where Old and New Media Collide.*

2nd ed. New York: New York UP, 2008. Print.

18. Religious text   Give the version, italicized; the editor's or
translator's name (if any); and the publication information, including
medium.

New American Standard Bible. La Habra: Lockman Foundation, 1995.

Print.

The Upanishads. Trans. Eknath Easwaran. Tomales: Nilgiri, 1987. Print.

19. Multivolume work   The first example indicates that the researcher used more than one volume of the work; the second shows

that only the second volume was used *(to cite an individual article or chapter in a multivolume work or set of reference books, refer to no. 8 or 11).*

> Manning, Martin J., and Clarence R. Wyatt. *Encyclopedia of Media and Propaganda in Wartime America.* 2 vols. Santa Barbara: ABC-CLIO, 2010. Print.

> Manning, Martin J., and Clarence R. Wyatt. *Encyclopedia of Media and Propaganda in Wartime America.* Vol. 1. Santa Barbara: ABC-CLIO, 2010. Print.

20. Book in a series
After the medium, put the name of the series and, if available on the title page, the number of the work.

> Wimmer, Roger D., and Joseph R. Dominick. *Mass Media Research: An Introduction (with InfoTrac).* Boston: Wadsworth, 2005. Print.
> name of series not italicized
> Contributions in Wadsworth Ser. in Mass Comm. and Journalism.

21. Republished book
Put the original date of publication, followed by a period, before the current publication data.

> original publication date
> Freire, Paulo. *Pedagogy of the Oppressed.* 1970. New York: Continuum, 2005. Print.

22. Unknown author
The citation begins with the title. In the list of works cited, alphabetize the citation by the first important word, excluding the articles *A, An,* and *The.*

> *Webster's College Dictionary.* New York: Random; New York: McGraw, 1991. Print.

Note that this entry includes both of the publishers listed on the dictionary's title page; they are separated by a semicolon.

23. Book with illustrator
List the illustrator after the title with the abbreviation *illus.* (not italicized). If you refer primarily to the illustrator, put that name before the title instead of the author's.

> Carroll, Lewis. *Alice's Adventures in Wonderland and through the Looking-Glass.* Illus. John Tenniel. New York: Modern Library-Random, 2002. Print.

Tenniel, John, illus. *Alice's Adventures in Wonderland and through the
Looking-Glass.* By Lewis Carroll. New York: Modern Library-
Random, 2002. Print.

24. Graphic novel or comic book   Cite graphic narratives created by one person as you would any other book or multivolume work. For collaborations, begin with the person whose work you refer to most, and list others in the order in which they appear on the title page. Indicate each person's contribution *(for part of a series, see no. 20).*

Moore, Alan, writer. *Watchmen.* Illus. David Gibbons. Color by John
Higgins. New York: DC Comics, 1995. Print.

Satrapi, Marjane. *Persepolis.* 2 vols. New York: Pantheon-Random,
2004-05. Print.

PERIODICALS

Periodicals are published at set intervals, usually four times a year for scholarly journals, monthly or weekly for magazines, and daily or weekly for newspapers. Between the author and the publication data are two titles: the title of the article, in quotation marks, and the title of the periodical, italicized. *(For online versions of print periodicals and periodicals published only online, see pp. 292–93 and 297–98.)*

25. Article in a journal with volume numbers   Most journals have a volume number corresponding to the year and an issue number for each publication that year. The issue may be indicated by a month or season. Put the volume number after the title. Follow it with a period and the issue number. Give the year of publication in parentheses, followed by a colon, a space, and the page numbers of the article. End with the medium.

Lacy, Stephen, et al. "Citizen Journalism Web Sites Complement
Newspapers." *Newspaper Research Journal* 31.2 (2010): 34-46. Print.

26. Article in a journal with issue numbers only   Give only the issue number.

Lousley, Cheryl. "Knowledge, Power and Place." *Canadian Literature*
195 (2007): 11-30. Print.

27. Article in a popular magazine   For a monthly magazine, provide the month and year, abbreviating all months except May, June, and July. For a weekly publication, include the complete date (day, month, and year).

Robbins, Sarah. "One Mother's Fierce Love." *Glamour* Feb. 2008: 34.
Print.

Tresniowski, Alex, Jeff Truesdell, Siobhan Morrissey, and Howard Breuer.
"A Cyberbully Convicted." *People* 15 Dec. 2008: 73-74. Print.

28. Article in a newspaper

Provide the day, month, and year. If an edition is named on the top of the first page, specify the edition—*natl. ed.* or *late ed.* (without italics), for example—after the date. If the section letter is part of the page number, see the first example. Give the title of an unnumbered section with *sec.* (not italicized). If the article appears on nonconsecutive pages, put a plus (+) sign after the first page number.

Gillis, Justin. "A Scientist, His Work and a Climate Reckoning." *New York Times* 22 Dec. 2010, natl. ed.: A1+. Print.

Just, Julie. "Children's Bookshelf." *New York Times* 15 Mar. 2009, natl. ed., Book Review sec.: 13. Print.

29. Unsigned article in a magazine or newspaper

The citation begins with the title and is alphabetized by the first word, excluding articles such as *A, An,* or *The.*

"Findings." *Harper's* Jan. 2011: 80. Print.

"Senate Repeals Military Gay Ban." *St. Petersburg Times* 19 Dec. 2010: 1A. Print.

30. Review

Begin with the name of the reviewer and, if there is one, the title of the review. Add *Rev. of* (without italics, meaning "review of") and the title plus the author or performer of the work being reviewed.

Want, Chun-Chi. Rev. of *Convergence Culture: Where Old and New Media Collide,* by Henry Jenkins. *Spectator* Fall 2007: 101-03. Print.

31. Editorial

Treat editorials as articles, but add the word *Editorial* (not italicized) after the title. If the editorial is unsigned, begin with the title.

Shaw, Theodore M. "The Debate over Race Needs Minority Students' Voices." Editorial. *Chronicle of Higher Education* 25 Feb. 2000: A72. Print.

22
MLA

32. Abstract of a journal article Collections of abstracts from journals can be found in the library's reference section. Include the publication information for the original article, followed by the title of the publication that provides the abstract, the volume, the year in parentheses, the item or page number, and the medium.

> Theiler, Anne M., and Louise G. Lippman. "Effects of Mental Practice
>
> and Modeling on Guitar and Vocal Performance." *Journal of*
>
> *General Psychology* 122.4 (1995): 329-43. *Psychological Abstracts*
>
> 83.1 (1996): item 30039. Print.

33. Letter to the editor

> Tyler, Steve. Letter. *National Geographic Adventure* Apr. 2004: 11. Print.

OTHER PRINT SOURCES

34. Government document Either the name of the government and agency or the name of the document's author comes first. If the government and agency name come first, follow the title of the document with *By* for a writer, *Ed.* for an editor, or *Comp.* for a compiler (if any), and give the name. Publication information and medium come last.

> United States. Bureau of Natl. Affairs. *The Civil Rights Act of 1964: Text,*
>
> *Analysis, Legislative History; What It Means to Employers, Businessmen,*
>
> *Unions, Employees, Minority Groups.* Washington: BNA, 1964. Print.

For the format to use when citing the *Congressional Record,* see no. 69.

35. Pamphlet or brochure Treat it as a book. If the pamphlet or brochure has an author, list his or her name first; otherwise, begin with the title.

> *The Digital Derry Strategy.* Donegal: PIKE, 2009.

36. Conference proceedings Cite as you would an edited book, but include information about the conference if it is not in the title.

> Mendel, Arthur, Gustave Reese, and Gilbert Chase, eds. *Papers Read at*
>
> *the International Congress of Musicology Held at New York September*
>
> *11th to 16th, 1939.* New York: Music Educators' Natl. Conf. for the
>
> American Musicological Soc., 1944. Print.

37. Published dissertation Cite as you would a book. After the title, add *Diss.* (not italicized) for "dissertation," the name of the institution, the year the dissertation was written, place of publication and publisher, year, and the medium.

> Fraser, Wilmot Alfred. *Jazzology: A Study of the Tradition in Which Jazz Musicians Learn to Improvise.* Diss. U of Pennsylvania, 1983. Ann Arbor: UMI, 1987. Print.

38. Unpublished dissertation   Begin with the author's name, followed by the title in quotation marks, the abbreviation *Diss.* (not italicized), the name of the institution, the year the dissertation was written, and the medium.

> Price, Deidre Dowling. "Confessional Poetry and Blog Culture in the Age of Autobiography." Diss. Florida State U, 2010. Print.

39. Abstract of a dissertation   Use the format for an unpublished dissertation. After the dissertation date, give the abbreviation *DA* or *DAI* (for *Dissertation Abstracts* or *Dissertation Abstracts International*), then the volume number, the issue number, the date of publication, the page number, and the medium.

> Quinn, Richard Allen. "Playing Together: Improvisation in Postwar American Literature and Culture." Diss. U of Iowa, 2000. *DAI* 61.6 (2001): 2305A. Print.

40. Published interview   Name the person interviewed, and give the title of the interview or the descriptive term *Interview* (not italicized), the name of the interviewer (if known and relevant), the publication information, and the medium.

> Pelosi, Nancy. "Minority Report." Interview by Deborah Solomon. *The New York Times Magazine* 18 Nov. 2010: 18. Print.

41. Map or chart   Cite as you would a book with an unknown author. Italicize the title of the map or chart, and add the word *Map* or *Chart* (not italicized) following the title.

> *Let's Go Map Guide to New Orleans.* Map. New York: St. Martin's, 1997. Print.

42. Cartoon or photograph in a print work   Include the artist's name, the title of the image (in quotation marks for cartoons, italicized for photographs), the publication information, and the medium. Include the word *Cartoon* or *Photograph* (not italicized) after the title.

22
MLA

Dator, Joe. "14 Street." Cartoon. *New Yorker* 10 Jan. 2011: 72. Print.

Wallace, Daniel. *Calvin Johnson Tries to Get by Bucs Cornerback Ronde Barber.* Photograph. *St. Petersburg Times* 20 Dec. 2010: 1C. Print.

43. Reproduction of artwork   Treat a photograph of a work of art in another source like a work in an anthology *(no. 8)*. Italicize the titles of both the artwork and the source, and include the institution or collection and city where the work can be found prior to information about the source in which it appears.

Da Vinci, Leonardo. *Mona Lisa.* N.d. Louvre, Paris. *Gardner's Art through the Ages: A Concise History of Western Art.* By Fred S. Kleiner and Christin J. Mamiya. Belmont: Thomson, 2008. 253. Print.

44. Advertisement   Name the item or organization being advertised, include the word *Advertisement* (not italicized), and indicate where the ad appeared.

Hartwick College Summer Music Festival and Institute. Advertisement. *New York Times Magazine* 3 Jan. 1999: 54. Print.

45. Published letter   Treat like a work in an anthology, but include the date. Include the number, if one was assigned by the editor. If you use more than one letter from a published collection, follow the instructions for cross-referencing in no. 9.

Hughes, Langston. "To Arna Bontemps." 17 Jan. 1938. *Arna Bontemps-Langston Hughes Letters 1925-1967.* Ed. Charles H. Nichols. New York: Dodd, 1980. 27-28. Print.

46. Personal letter   To cite a letter you received, start with the writer's name, followed by the descriptive phrase *Letter to the author* (not italicized), the date, and *MS* (manuscript):

Cogswell, Michael. Letter to the author. 15 Mar. 2008. MS.

To cite someone else's unpublished personal letter, see no. 47.

47. Manuscripts, typescripts, and material in archives   Give the author, a title or description *(Letter, Notebook),* the date, the form *(MS* if handwritten, *TS* if typed), any identifying number, and the name and location of the institution housing the material (do not italicize any part of the citation).

Arendt, Hannah. Thinking and Moral Considerations: A Lecture.

date uncertain

[c. 1971]. TS. Library of Congress Manuscript Div., Washington.

Pollack, Bracha. "A Man ahead of His Time." 1997. TS.

48. Legal source (print or online)   To cite a specific act, give its name, Public Law number, its Statutes at Large number, page range, the date it was enacted, and the medium.

Energy Policy Act of 2005. Pub. L. 109-58. 119 Stat. 594-1143.

8 Aug. 2005. Print.

To cite a law case, provide the name of the plaintiff and defendant, the case number, the court that decided the case, the date of the decision, and the medium.

PRINT

Ashcroft v. the Free Speech Coalition. 535 US 234-73. Supreme Court

of the US. 2002. Print.

WEB

Ashcroft v. the Free Speech Coalition. 535 US 234-73. Supreme Court

of the US. 2002. *Supreme Court Collection.* Legal Information Inst.,

Cornell U Law School, n.d. Web. 20 May 2008.

For more information about citing legal documents or from case law, MLA recommends consulting *The Bluebook: A Uniform System of Citation,* published by the Harvard Law Review Association.

ONLINE SOURCES

The examples that follow are based on guidelines for the citation of electronic sources in the seventh edition of the *MLA Handbook for Writers of Research Papers* (2009).

For scholarly journals published online, see no. 81. For periodical articles from an online database, see no. 84. Cite most other Web sources according to nos. 49 and 50. For works that also exist in another medium (for example, print), the MLA recommends including information about the other version in your citation. See nos. 70–80.

Basic Web sources

49. Web site or independent online work   Begin with the author, editor (*ed.*), compiler (*comp.*), director (*dir.*), performer (*perf.*), or translator (*trans.*), if any, of the site. Give the title (italicized), the

TEXTCONNEX

Web Addresses in MLA Citations

Include the URL (Web address) of an online source in a citation only if your reader would be unable to find the source without it (via a search engine). For example, basic citation information might not sufficiently identify your source if multiple versions of a document exist online without version numbers. Place a URL at the end of your citation in angle brackets, and end with a period.

> Raeburn, Bruce Boyd, ed. *William Ransom Hogan Archive of New Orleans Jazz.* Tulane U, 13 Apr. 2006. Web. 11 May 2008. <http://www.tulane.edu/~lmiller/JazzHome.html>.

If you need to divide a URL between lines, do so after a slash, and do not insert a hyphen. If the URL is long (more than one line of your text), give the URL of the site's search page. Do not make the URL a hyperlink.

version or edition (if any), the publisher or sponsor (or *N.p.*), publication date (or last update, or *n.d.*), medium, and your access date. (Use italics for the title only.) Citations 50–69 follow this format. The following examples are of a government-sponsored Web site, a professional site, and a personal site.

> *Cyber Crimes Center.* U.S. Immigration and Customs Enforcement, 2010. Web. 18 Dec. 2010.

no date
> Garrett, Chris. *The Business of Blogging and New Media.* Headway, n.d. Web. 20 Dec. 2010.

no publisher
> Johnson, Steven. *StevenBerlinJohnson.com.* N.p., 2002. Web. 19 Dec. 2010.

50. Page, selection, or part of a Web site or larger online work   Give the title of the part in quotation marks. If no title is available, use a descriptive term such as "Home page."

> Oliver, Rachel. "All About: Forests and Carbon Trading." *CNN.com.* Cable News Network, 11 Feb. 2008. Web. 14 Mar. 2008.

51. Course Web page   After the instructor's name, list the site title, then the department and school names.

Web site title
> Hea, Kimme. *Spatial and Visual Rhetorics.* Dept. of English, U of Arizona, 4 Jan. 2003. Web. 11 May 2008.

CITING ELECTRONIC SOURCES in MLA STYLE

- Begin with the name of the writer, editor, compiler, translator, director, or performer.
- Put the title of a short work in quotation marks.
- If there is no title, identify the genre of your source, such as *editorial* or *comment* (not italicized).
- Italicize the name of the publication or Web site. The online versions of some print magazines and newspapers have different titles than the print versions.
- Cite the date of publication or last update.
- For an online magazine or newspaper article or a Web original source, give the source (in quotation marks), the site title (italicized), version (if any), publisher or sponsor, date of publication, medium (Web), and access date. *(See p. 292.)*
- You may cite online sources that also appear in another medium with information about the other version *(see pp. 294–96)*. (Do not cite online versions of print newspapers and magazines in this way.)
- For a journal article, include the article title (in quotation marks), periodical title (italicized), volume and issue numbers, and inclusive page numbers or *n. pag.* (not italicized). Conclude with the medium (Web) and access date. *(See p. 297.)*
- To cite a periodical article from an online database, provide the print publication information, the database title (italicized), the medium, and your access date.
- If the source is not divided into sections or pages, include *n. pag.* (not italicized) for "no pagination." Give the medium (Web).
- Include your most recent date of access to the specific source (not the general site).
- Conclude the citation with a URL only if readers may have difficulty finding the source without it *(see the box on p. 290)*.

52. Personal page on a social networking site

Taczak, Joey. "Joey Taczak." *Facebook*. Facebook, 20 Dec 2010. Web. 21 Dec 2010.

53. Blog   The first example cites an entire blog; the second refers to a specific entry from one.

McLennan, Doug. *Diacritical*. ArtsJournal, 2008. Web. 11 May 2008.

McLennan, Doug. "The Rise of Arts Culture." *Diacritical*. ArtsJournal, 21 Nov. 2007. Web. 11 May 2008.

54. Article in an online magazine or newspaper

Castillo, Michelle. "FCC Passes Ruling to Protect Net Neutrality."
Time.com. Time, 21 Dec. 2010. Web. 22 Dec. 2010.

Kang, Cecilia. "FCC's Rules to Protect Internet Access Spark Claims of
sponsor
Violations." *Washington Post*. Washington Post, 24 Jan. 2011. Web.

4 Mar. 2011.

55. Online editorial   Include the word *Editorial* (not italicized) after the published title of the editorial.

sponsor
"Saner Gun Laws." Editorial. *New York Times*. New York Times, 22 Jan.

2011. Web. 23 Jan. 2011.

56. Online letter to the editor   Include the word *Letter* (not italicized) after the name of the letter writer.

sponsor
Dow, Roger. Letter. *SFGate*. San Francisco Chronicle, 10 Jan. 2008.

Web. 12 May 2008.

57. Online review

Kot, Greg. "The Roots Fuel Their Rage into 'Rising Down.'" Rev. of
sponsor
Rising Down, by the Roots. *Chicago Tribune*. Chicago Tribune, 11

May 2008. Web. 12 May 2008.

58. Online interview   See no. 40 for a print interview.

Haddon, Mark. Interview by Dave Weich. *Powells.com*. Powell's, 24 June

2003. Web. 15 May 2008.

59. Article in an online encyclopedia or other reference work   Begin with the author's name, if any is given.

Hosch, William L. "Media Convergence and Podcasting." *Encyclopaedia
Britannica Online*. Britannica, 2007. Web. 20 Dec. 2010.

60. Entry in a wiki   A wiki is a collaborative creation, so no author should be listed. Begin with the title of the entry or file, the wiki name, the sponsor, the date of latest update, the medium, and your access date. Check with your instructor before using a wiki as a source.

"Symphony." *Citizendium.* Citizendium Foundation, 1 Nov. 2007. Web.

12 May 2008.

61. Online visual (map, chart, or photograph—Web only)   Include the genre—*Map, Chart,* or similar term—unless the image is a photograph (do not italicize). Begin with the artist's name, if one is given.

"Denver, Colorado." Map. *Google Maps.* Google, 12 May 2008. Web.

12 May 2008.

Jelonek, Matt. "U2 perform in Perth, Australia." *Rolling Stone.* Rolling

Stone, 21 Dec. 2010. Web. 22 Dec. 2010.

62. Online slideshow

A Look at America's Assassins. Slide program. *Newsweek.* Newsweek, 19

Jan. 2011. Web. 22 Jan. 2011.

63. Online advertisement

Coca Cola. Advertisement. *Pandora Internet Radio.* Web. 21 Dec. 2010.

64. Audio or video podcast

Powell, Padgett. "Padgett Powell: The Interrogative Mood." Interview

by St. John Flynn. *Cover to Cover.* Natl. Public Radio. GPB, Atlanta,

29 Mar. 2010. Web. 4 Mar. 2011.

65. Online video (Web original)

Wesch, Michael. "The Machine Is Us/ing Us." *Digital Ethnography.*

Kansas State U, 31 Jan. 2007. Web. 12 May 2008.

For material posted online from a film, TV series, or other non-Web source, see nos. 77–80.

66. Posting to a news group, electronic forum, or e-mail discussion list   Treat an archived posting as a Web source. Include the author, and use the subject line as the title of the posting. If there is no subject, substitute *Online posting* (not italicized).

Harbin, David. "Furtwangler's Beethoven 9 Bayreuth." *Opera-L*

Archives. City U of New York, 3 Jan. 2008. Web. 12 May 2008.

Pomeroy, Leslie K. Jr. "Racing with the Moon." *Rec.music.bluenote.* N.p.,

4 May 2008. Web. 12 May 2008.

**22
MLA**

67. Synchronous (real-time) communication Cite the online transcript of a synchronous communication as you would an online lecture or shorter work on a Web site.

> Curran, Stuart, and Harry Rusche. "Discussion: Plenary Log 6. Third
>
>   Annual Graduate Student Conference in Romanticism." *Prometheus*
>
>   *Unplugged: Emory MOO.* Emory U, 20 Apr. 1996. Web. 4 Jan. 1999.

68. Online government publication other than the *Congressional Record* Begin with the name of the country, followed by the name of the sponsoring department, the title of the document, and the names (if listed) of the authors.

> United States. National Commission on Terrorist Attacks upon the
>
>   United States. *The 9/11 Commission Report.* By Thomas H. Kean,
>
>   et al. 5 Aug. 2004. Web. 12 May 2008.

69. *Congressional Record* (online or print) The *Congressional Record* has its own citation format, which is the same for print and online (apart from the medium and access date). Abbreviate the title, and include the date and page numbers. Give the medium (print or Web).

> *Cong. Rec.* 28 Apr. 2005: D419-D428. Web. 12 May 2008.

Web sources also available in another medium If an online work also appears in another medium (for example, print), the MLA recommends (but does not require) that your citation include information about the other version of the work. (Information about the editor or sponsor of the Web site or database is optional in this model.) If the facts about the other version of the source are not available, cite it as a basic Web source *(see nos. 49 and 50).* (Articles on the Web sites of newspapers and magazines are never cited with print publication information. *For academic journals, see nos. 81–83 and 85.*)

70. Online or electronic book (e-book) Cite a book you download from a database such as *Bartleby.com* as a print book *(no. 1).* Instead of ending with *Print* (not italicized), give the Web site or database, the medium (Web), and your access date.

> Arter, Jared Maurice. *Echoes from a Pioneer Life.* Atlanta: Caldwell,
>
>   name and location (optional) of Web publisher
>
>   1922. *Documenting the American South.* U of North Carolina,
>
>   Chapel Hill. Web. 21 May 2008.

For an e-book that you download from an online bookseller or library, use the same format as a print book *(no. 1),* but change the medium from *Print* to the kind of e-book (for example, *Kindle e-book file).*

> Schiff, Stacy. *Cleopatra: A Life.* New York: Little, Brown, 2010.
>
> Kindle e-book file.

71. Selection from an online book   Add the title of the selection after the author. If the online version of the work lacks page numbers, use *n. pag.* instead (capitalize the *n* in *n. pag.* when it follows a period).

> Sandburg, Carl. "Chicago." *Chicago Poems.* New York: Holt, 1916.
>
> N. pag. *Bartleby.com.* Web. 12 May 2008.

72. Online dissertation   Give the Web site or database, the medium (Web), and your access date. Or cite as a basic Web source *(see nos. 49 and 50).*

> Kosiba, Sara A. "A Successful Revolt? The Redefinition of Midwestern
>
> Literary Culture in the 1920s and 1930s." Diss. Kent State U,
>
> 2007. *OhioLINK.* Web. 12 May 2008.

73. Online pamphlet or brochure (also in print)   Cite as a book. Give the title of the Web site or database, the medium (Web), and your access date, or cite as a basic Web source *(see no. 49).*

> United States. Securities and Exchange Commission. Division
>
> of Corporate Finance. *International Investing: Get the Facts.*
>
> Washington: GPO, 1999. *US Securities and Exchange Commission.*
>
> Web. 12 May 2008.

74. Online map or chart (also in print)   See no. 41 for a print map. Remove the medium; add the title of the database or Web site, the medium (Web), and your access date. (See no. 67 for a Web-only map.) Or cite as a basic Web source *(see nos. 49 and 50).*

> *MTA New York City Subway.* New York: Metropolitan Transit Authority,
>
> 2008. *MTA New York City Transit.* Web. 12 May 2008.

75. Online cartoon (also in print)   See no. 42 for a cartoon. Remove the medium; add the database or site, the medium (Web), and your access date, or cite as a basic Web source *(see nos. 49 and 50).*

> Ziegler, Jack. "A Viking Funeral for My Goldfish." *New Yorker* 19 May
>
> 2008: 65. *Cartoonbank.com.* Web. 20 May 2008.

22 MLA

76. Online representation of visual artwork Cite as you would the original *(no. 102)*. Remove the medium; add the database or Web site, the medium (Web), and your access date, or cite as a basic Web source *(see nos. 49 and 50)*.

> Seurat, Georges-Pierre. *Evening, Honfleur.* 1886. Museum of Mod. Art,
>
> New York. *MoMA.org.* Web. 8 May 2008.

77. Online video or film (also on film or DVD) See nos. 96 and 97 for a film or video. Remove the medium; add the database or site, the medium (Web), and your access date, or cite as a basic Web source *(see nos. 49 and 50)*.

> *Night of the Living Dead.* Dir. George A. Romero. Image Ten, 1968.
>
> *Internet Archive.* Web. 12 May 2008.

78. Online radio or television program See no. 98 for a radio or television program. Remove the medium; add the database or site, the medium (Web), and your access date, or cite as a basic Web source *(see nos. 49 and 50)*.

> "Bill Evans: 'Piano Impressionism.'" *Jazz Profiles.* Narr. Nancy Wilson.
>
> Natl. Public Radio. WGBH, Boston, 27 Feb. 2008. *NPR.org.* Web.
>
> 16 Mar. 2008.

episode (not series)   director of episode   series   performer in series
> "Local Ad." Dir. Jason Reitman. *The Office.* Perf. Steve Carrell. NBC.
>
> WNBC, New York, 12 Dec. 2007. *NBC.com.* Web. 12 May 2008.

79. Online broadcast interview See no. 99 for a broadcast interview. Remove the medium; add the database or site and the medium (Web), and give your access date. Otherwise, cite as a basic Web source *(see nos. 49 and 50)*.

> Jones, Sharon. Interview by Terry Gross. *Fresh Air.* Natl. Public Radio.
>
> WNYC, New York, 28 Nov. 2007. *NPR.org.* Web. 12 May 2008.

80. Online archival material Provide the information for the original. Add the Web site or database, the medium (Web), and your access date. Otherwise, cite as a basic Web source *(see nos. 49 and 50)*.

date uncertain
> Whitman, Walt. "After the Argument." [c. 1890]. The Charles E.
>
> Feinberg Collection of the Papers of Walt Whitman, Lib. of Cong.
>
> *The Walt Whitman Archive.* Web. 13 May 2008.

Works in online scholarly journals Use the same format for all online journals, including those with print editions.

81. Article in an online journal Give the author, the article title (in quotation marks) or a term such as *Editorial* (not italicized), the journal title (italicized), the volume number, issue number, date, and the inclusive page range (or *n. pag.*—not italicized—if the source lacks page numbers). Conclude with the medium (Web) and your access date.

> Ridolfo, Jim, and Danielle Nicole DeVoss. "Composing for
>
> Recomposition: Rhetorical Velocity and Delivery." *Kairos* 13.2
>
> (2009): n. pag. Web. 25 April 2011.

82. Editorial or letter to the editor in an online journal

> Heitmeyer, Wilhelm, et al. "Letter from the Editors." Editorial.
>
> *International Journal of Conflict and Violence* 1.1 (2007): n. pag. Web.
>
> 14 May 2008.

> Destaillats, Frédéric, Julie Moulin, and Jean-Baptiste Bezelgues. Letter.
>
> *Nutrition & Metabolism* 4.10 (2007): n. pag. Web. 14 May 2008.

83. Review in an online journal

> Friedman, Edward H. Rev. of *Transnational Cervantes,* by William
>
> Childers. *Cervantes: Bulletin of the Cervantes Society of America* 27.2
>
> (2007): 41-43. Web. 13 May 2008.

Works from online databases In addition to information about the print version of the source, provide the title of the database (in italics), the medium (Web), and your access date.

84. Newspaper or magazine article from an online database

> Blumenfeld, Larry. "House of Blues." *New York Times* 11 Nov. 2007:
>
> A33. *Academic Universe.* Web. 31 Dec. 2007.

> Farley, Christopher John. "Music Goes Global." *Time* 15 Sept. 2001:
>
> 4+. *General OneFile.* Web. 31 Dec. 2007.

85. Journal article or abstract from an online database

> Nielson, Aldon Lynn. "A Hard Rain." *Callaloo* 25.1 (2002): 135-45.
>
> *Academic Search Premier.* Web. 17 Mar. 2008.

**22
MLA**

Dempsey, Nicholas P. "Hook-Ups and Train Wrecks: Contextual

Parameters and the Coordination of Jazz Interactions." *Symbolic*

Interaction 31.1 (2008): 57-75. Abstract. *Academic Search Premier.*

Web. 17 Mar. 2008.

86. E-mail   Include the author, the subject line (if any) in quotation marks, the descriptive term Message to (not italicized), and the name of the recipient, the date of the message, and the medium.

Hoffman, Esther. "Re: My Louis Armstrong Paper." Message to

J. Peritz. 14 Apr. 2008. E-mail.

Other Electronic (Non-Web) Sources

87. A digital file stored on your computer   Record the file format as the medium (for example, *XML file*). If the format is unclear, use the designation *Digital file*. Do not italicize the medium. Use the citation format of the most closely related print or nonprint source. Cite local word-processor documents as manuscripts *(see no. 47)*, and note the date last modified if you wish to cite a specific version.

McNutt, Lea. "The Origination of Avian Flight." 2008. *Microsoft*

Word file.

Hoffman, Esther. "Louis Armstrong and Joe Glaser: More Than Meets

the Eye." File last modified on 9 May 2008. *Microsoft Word* file.

88. A PDF   Treat local PDFs as published, and follow the closest print model.

United States. US Copyright Office. *Report on Orphan Works.*

Washington: US Copyright Office, 2006. PDF file.

89. An audio file   Use the format for a sound recording *(see no. 100)*. Record the file format as the medium.

Holiday, Billie. "God Bless the Child." *God Bless the Child.* Columbia,

1936. MP3 file.

90. A visual file   Cite local image files as works of visual art *(see no. 102)*. Record the file format as the medium.

Gursky, Andreas. *Times Square, New York.* 1997. Museum of Mod. Art,

New York. JPEG file.

91. CD-ROM or DVD-ROM published periodically

If a CD-ROM or DVD-ROM is revised on a regular basis, include in its citation the author, title of the work, any print publication information, medium, title of the CD-ROM or DVD-ROM (if different from the original title), vendor, and date of electronic publication.

> Ross, Alex. "Separate Worlds, Linked Electronically." *New York Times*
>
>   29 Apr. 1996, late ed.: A22. CD-ROM. *New York Times Ondisc.*
>
>   UMI-ProQuest. Dec. 1996.

92. CD-ROM or DVD-ROM not published periodically

Works on CD-ROM or DVD-ROM are usually cited like books or parts of books if they are not revised periodically. The medium and the name of the vendor (if different from the publisher) appear after the publication data. For a work that also exists in print, give the print publication information followed by the medium, electronic publisher, and date of electronic publication.

> print publisher omitted for pre-1900 work
> Jones, Owen. *The Grammar of Ornament.* London, 1856. CD-ROM.
>
>   Octavo, 1998.

If there are multiple discs, list the total number of discs at the end of the entry, or give the number of the disc you reviewed if you used only one.

93. Computer software

Include the title, version, publisher, and date in your text or in an explanatory note. Do not include an entry in your works-cited list.

94. Video game

In your entry, include the title, version, publisher, date of publication, and medium.

> *Europa 1400: The Guild.* Vienna: JoWood Entertainment AG, 2002. DVD.

Audiovisual and Other Nonprint Sources

95. Film

Begin with the title (italicized) unless you want to highlight a particular contributor. For a film, cite the director and the featured performer(s) or narrator (*Perf.* or *Narr.*, neither italicized), followed by the distributor and year. Conclude with the medium.

> *Artists and Models.* Dir. Raoul Walsh. Perf. Jack Benny, Ida Lupino, and
>
>   Alan Townsend. Paramount, 1937. Film.

96. DVD or Blu-ray

See no. 95. Include the original film's release date if relevant. Conclude with the medium (DVD, Blu-ray). Do not italicize the medium.

**22
MLA**

> *Casablanca.* Dir. Michael Curtiz. Perf. Humphrey Bogart and Ingrid
> Bergman. 1942. Warner, 2000. DVD.

97. Personal or archival video or audio recording Give the date recorded and the location of the recording.

> Adderley, Nat. Interview by Jimmy Owens. Schomburg Center for
> Research in Black Culture, New York Public Lib. 2 Apr. 1993.
> Videocassette.

98. Radio or television program Give the episode title (in quotation marks), the program title (italicized), the name of the series (if any), the network (call letters), the city, the broadcast date, and the medium (*Radio* or *Television,* neither italicized). Name individuals if relevant.

> "Who's Carl This Time?" *Wait, Wait . . . Don't Tell Me.* Natl. Public
> Radio, WAMU, Washington, 18 Dec. 2010. Radio.

episode (not series)   director of episode   series   performer in series
> "Local Ad." Dir. Jason Reitman. *The Office.* Perf. Steve Carrell. NBC.
> WNBC, New York, 12 Dec. 2007. Television.

99. Broadcast interview Give the name of the person interviewed, followed by the word *Interview* (not italicized) and the name of the interviewer if you know it. End with information about the broadcast and the medium.

> Meacham, Jon. Interview by Jon Stewart. *The Daily Show with Jon
> Stewart.* Comedy Central, 5 May 2010. Television.

100. Sound recording Start with the composer, conductor, or performer, depending on your focus. Include the following information: the work's title (italicized); the artist(s), if not already mentioned; the manufacturer; the date of release; and the medium. In the first example, an individual song on a recording is noted (in quotation marks) before the album title.

> Arcade Fire. "We Used to Wait." *The Suburbs.* Merge/Mercury, 2010.
> MP3 file.

> Yanni. *Truth of Touch.* Virgin Records/EMI, 2011. LP.

101. Musical composition Include only the composer and title, unless you are referring to a published score (see the third example). Published scores are treated like books except that the date of composition appears after the title. Titles of instrumental pieces are not italicized when known only by form and number, unless the reference is to a published score.

> Ellington, Duke. *Satin Doll.*

> Haydn, Franz Josef. Symphony No. 94 in G Major.
> reference to a published score
> Haydn, Franz Josef. *Symphony No. 94 in G Major.* 1791. Ed. H. C.
> Robbins Landon. Salzburg: Haydn-Mozart, 1965. Print.

102. Artwork Provide the artist's name, the title of the artwork (italicized), the date (if unknown, write *N.d.*), the medium, and the institution or private collection and city (or *n.p.*) in which the artwork can be found. For anonymous collectors, write *Private collection,* and omit the city (do not write *n.p.*).

> Warhol, Andy. *Campbell's Soup Can.* 1962. Oil on Canvas. Saatchi
> Collection, London.

103. Personal, telephone, or e-mail interview Begin with the person interviewed, followed by *Personal interview, Telephone interview,* or *E-mail interview* (not italicized) and the date of the interview *(see no. 40 for a published interview).*

> Jacobs, Phoebe. Personal interview. 5 May 2008.

104. Lecture or speech Give the speaker, the title (in quotation marks), the name of the forum or sponsor, the location, and the date. Conclude with a description such as *Speech, Lecture,* or *Presentation* (not italicized). If you access the speech online, include that information, and replace the medium *Speech* with *Web.*

> Beaufort, Anne. "All Talk, No Action? Or, Does Transfer Really Happen
> after Reflective Practice?" Conference on College Composition
> and Communication. Hilton San Francisco. 13 March 2009.
> Presentation.

105. Live performance To cite a play, opera, dance performance, or concert, begin with the title, followed by the authors *(By),* information such as the director *(Dir.)* and major performers, the site, the city, the performance date, and the word *Performance* (not italicized).

> *Ragtime.* By Terrence McNally, Lynn Athrens, and Stephen Flaherty.
>
> Dir. Frank Galati. Ford Performing Arts Center, New York. 11 Nov.
>
> 1998. Performance.

106. Publication in more than one medium If you are citing a publication that consists of several different media, list alphabetically all of the media you consulted. Follow the citation format of the medium you used primarily (which is *print* in the example).

> Sadker, David M., and Karen Zittleman. *Teachers, Schools, and Society:*
>
> *A Brief Introduction to Education.* New York: McGraw, 2007.
>
> CD-ROM, print, Web.

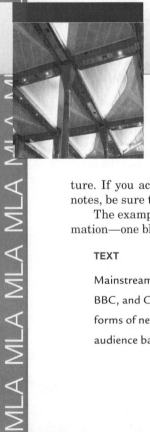

23 MLA Style: Explanatory Notes and Acknowledgments

Explanatory notes are used to cite multiple sources for borrowed material or to give readers supplemental information. You can also use explanatory notes to acknowledge people who helped you with research and writing. Acknowledgments are a courteous gesture. If you acknowledge someone's assistance in your explanatory notes, be sure to send that person a copy of your research project.

The example that follows is a note that provides additional information—one blogger's opinion about the nature of his audience.

TEXT

Mainstream media companies, such as the *New York Times, Newsweek,* BBC, and CNN, have started their own blogs and have adopted other forms of new media, such as *Twitter,* in an effort to expand their audience base.[1]

NOTE

1. Former librarian and public administrator Will Manley notes that, in contrast to face-to-face audiences or print media audiences, his blogging audience is "solid and real" because of the sheer volume of daily traffic on his blog.

24 MLA Style: Format

The following guidelines will help you prepare your research project in the format recommended by the seventh edition of the *MLA Handbook for Writers of Research Papers.* For an example of a research project that has been prepared using MLA style, see pages 306–17.

**24
MLA**

Materials   Back up your final draft on a flash drive, CD, or DVD. Use a high-quality printer and high-quality, white 8½-by-11-inch paper. Put the printed pages together with a paper clip.

Heading and title   Include a separate title page if your instructor requires one. In the upper left-hand corner of the first page of the paper, one inch from the top and side, enter on separate, double-spaced lines your name, your instructor's name, the course number, and the date. Double-space between the date and the title and between the title and the first line of text, as well as throughout your paper. The title should be centered and properly capitalized *(see p. 306).* Do not italicize the title or put it in quotation marks or bold type.

If your instructor requires a title page, prepare it according to his or her instructions. If your instructor requires a final outline, place it between the title page and the first page of the paper.

Margins and spacing   Use one-inch margins all around, except for the top right-hand corner, where the page number goes. Your right margin should be ragged (not "justified," or even).

TEXTCONNEX

Electronic Submission of Assignments

Some instructors may request that you submit your project electronically. Keep these tips in mind:

- Confirm the appropriate procedure for submission.
- Find out in advance your instructor's preferred format for the submission of documents. *Always ask permission before sending an attached document to anyone.*
- If you are asked to send a document as an attachment, save your document as a "rich text format" (.rtf) file or in PDF format.
- As a courtesy, run a virus scan on your file before sending it electronically or submitting it on a disk or CD-ROM.

Double-space lines throughout the paper, including in quotations, notes, and the works-cited list. Indent the first word of each paragraph one-half inch (or five spaces) from the left margin. For block quotations, indent one inch (or ten spaces) from the left.

Page numbers Put your last name and the page number in the upper right-hand corner of the page, one-half inch from the top and flush with the right margin.

Visuals Place visuals (tables, charts, graphs, and images) close to the place in your text where you refer to them. Label and number tables consecutively *(Table 1, Table 2),* and give each one an explanatory caption; put this information above the table. The term *Figure* (abbreviated *Fig.*) is used to label all other kinds of visuals, except for musical illustrations, which are labeled *Example* (abbreviated *Ex.*). Place a figure or an example caption below the visual. Below all visuals, cite the source of the material, and provide explanatory notes as needed. *(For more on using visuals effectively, see Chapter 3: Drafting.)*

As a first-year college student, Rebecca Hollingsworth wrote the following research project for her composition course. She knew very little about blogging before beginning her research.

CONSIDER YOUR SITUATION

Author: Rebecca Hollingsworth

Type of writing: Research report

Purpose: To investigate the effect of blogging on traditional forms of news reporting

Stance: Informed and reasonable

Audience: Students, instructors, consumers of print and online journalism

Medium: Print, part of e-portfolio

Hollingsworth writes: As I worked on this research report, I learned about the effects that blogging has had—and continues to have—on traditional journalism. You can see the impact of my research in the information I have shared.

Hollingsworth 1

Rebecca Hollingsworth

Professor Spaulding

English 120

7 May 2011

Breaking News: Blogging's Impact on

Traditional and New Media

In previous decades, when people wanted to know what was happening in the world, they turned to the daily newspaper and their television sets. Today, many of us are more likely to go online, where a simple *Google* search on any subject can produce thousands of hits and open doors to seemingly limitless sources of information. Much of this information comes from the online journals known as blogs, which have redefined the concept of news and multiplied our ways of obtaining it. In the blogosphere--the vast assortment of these individual Web sites on the Internet--a wide range of diverse voices provides us with news and opinion. Bloggers frame a single event, such as an oil spill or a politician's blunder, according to various political, geographical, economic, and philosophical positions. In fact, the increasing popularity and influence of blogs has changed the very nature of journalism in recent years, creating a movement toward citizen journalism, or news for and by the people. No longer controlled by a few media conglomerates, the news is now deeply influenced by average citizens as well as trained journalists. Multimedia corporations have come to depend on bloggers, from professional journalists to activist citizens, to deliver the most recent developments on the very latest events around the globe. To survive, journalism must blend traditional forms of reporting

---

Annotations (left margin):

Place your name, your professor's name, your course title, and the date at the left margin, double-spaced.

Title centered, not italicized.

Double-spaced throughout.

Establishes context for argument.

Background information on blogging.

Thesis statement.

Measurements: ½", 1", 1"

Hollingsworth 2

with new methods that get news and opinion to the people instantaneously and universally.

Blogging has become an extremely popular activity; many people are doing it for a wide variety of reasons. Arts and crafts, politics, sustainable living, pets, pop music, and astrophysics are just a few of the countless topics currently discussed in the millions of blogs on the Internet. *Encyclopaedia Britannica* defines a *blog*, short for *Web log*, as an "online journal where an individual, group, or corporation presents a record of activities, thoughts, or beliefs" ("Blog"). This definition points out an important aspect of blogs: Some are maintained by companies and organizations, but many are maintained by people not necessarily affiliated with traditional news outlets. New York University professor and media consultant Clay Shirky explains that this aspect of blogging is a fundamental transformation "in the definition of news: from news as an institutional prerogative to news as part of a communications ecosystem, occupied by a mix of formal organizations, informal collectives, and individuals" (*Here Comes Everybody* 65-66). Like *Britannica*'s definition of *blog*, Shirky's definition of *news* emphasizes the range of people producing the news today, from multinational corporations to college students. By noting the interdependence of all news producers, Shirky reveals an important insight about the evolution of journalism: New forms of media, especially blogs and other social media, have allowed average citizens to influence and even create the very news we consume.

Blogs have turned citizens into novice reporters, but what do they mean for mainstream news outlets? Traditional forms of

Thesis statement *(continued).*

Development by illustration (see p. 48).

Online encyclopedia definition cited by title; development by definition (see p. 52).

MLA in-text citation: author (Shirky) is named in signal phrase. Short title identifies which one of two works by Shirky is cited.

Development by definition (see p. 52).

Synthesis of material from two sources.

Focus introduced.

Hollingsworth 3

reporting, such as newspapers and televised news broadcasts, have always depended on the objectivity and credibility of their journalists, the reliability of their sources, and the extensive research and fact-checking that inform every news story. Blogs are a fast and easy way to publicize current issues and events, but many wonder if they can offer information that is as reliable as that provided by traditional news organizations and their carefully researched news. For example, a seventeen-year-old high school graduate can report on the *New York Times* blog *The Choice* about her experience applying for college financial aid, but her report will not be backed by the comprehensive, objective research that would inform a *Times* newspaper article about the broader financial aid situation throughout the country. During an interview about the struggling news industry on *The Daily Show,* Jon Stewart asked Jon Meacham, at the time the editor of *Newsweek,* a central question: "Who exactly is going to be doing the reporting?" Formerly a newspaper reporter and currently a blogger, media consultant, and senior vice president for Edelman Digital, Gary Goldhammer tackles this question in his book *The Last Newspaper*: "every citizen can be a reporter, but not every citizen should or will. Every person will get news, but not in the same way, not at the same time, and not with the same perspective" (13). As Stewart and Goldhammer suggest, blogging and other forms of new media have significantly widened the lens of news reporting throughout the world. For many, the term *we media* aptly characterizes the kind of citizen journalism that blogging represents; it is "a term that encompasses a wide range of mostly amateur activities--including blogging and commentary

Page number provided at the end of quotation; source's name is included in the introduction to the quotation, so there is no need to restate his name in the parenthetical citation.

Hollingsworth 4

in online forums--that have been made possible by an array of technologies" (Cass 62). No longer a specialized field, news reporting is now in the hands of the masses.

As news producers become more widespread and less specialized, news itself becomes a blurry concept. Now a broad range of people (with a broad range of interests) can determine what is important and worth talking about. This development has put significant power in the hands of more citizens, rather than a few media corporations. Goldhammer identifies three spokes of the news media wheel: mainstream journalism, citizen journalism, and their audiences (14). He also allows for a fourth possibility, "the former 'mainstream' journalist who works exclusively online, or the journalism-school trained reporter who has only worked in new media and not for a 'traditional' media outlet" (14). The lines between mainstream journalism and citizen journalism have become fuzzy. Mainstream media companies, such as the New York Times, Newsweek, BBC, and CNN, have started their own blogs and have adopted other forms of new media, such as *Twitter*, in an effort to expand their audience base.[1] Some of these companies encourage their audiences to submit personal videos or photos that they then filter and incorporate into broadcast news (Cass 63). In a 2010 article called "The New News," Jay Rosen argues that patterns of communication have increased:

> The media used to work in a one-to-many pattern--that is, by broadcasting. The Internet, though it can be used for one-to-many transmission, is just as well suited for few-to-few, one-to-one, and many-to-many patterns. Traditionally, the media connected audiences 'up' to

---

Side annotations:

MLA in-text citation: author named in parentheses because his name is not included in a signal phrase.

Presents a claim plus supporting evidence.

Development by classification (see p. 51).

Goldhammer is the source of the second quotation, so it is not necessary to repeat his name in the parenthetical citation.

Superscript number indicates an explanatory note.

Block quotation is introduced by a complete sentence, ending in a colon.

Hollingsworth 5

centers of power, people of influence, and national spectacles. The Internet does all that, but it is equally good at connecting us laterally--to peers, to colleagues, and to strangers who share our interests. When experts and power players had something to communicate to the attentive publics they wished to address, they once had to go through the media. Now they can go direct.

No longer at the mercy of those in a position to seek out and select what makes the news, citizens now have more authority, through the power of blogging, to investigate and publicize the events that matter to us. According to Shirky, this shift away from expert reporting to citizen journalism means that the older definition of "news" as a matter of journalists' and other media experts "professional judgment" has been replaced. Today an event can become news before members of the press begin to cover it, and in fact they may begin to cover it only after their audience has become aware of it in another way (*Here Comes Everybody* 64-65). Shirky cites an example from 2002, when it was the bloggers, not the mainstream reporters, who first publicized former Mississippi senator Trent Lott's controversial remarks at Strom Thurmond's hundredth birthday party, resulting in Lott's decision to step down from his position as majority leader of the Senate (61). More recently, during the 2008 presidential campaign, the candidates battled to create the most online buzz, recognizing the power of blogs and social media to generate campaign support and funding.[2] Blogs not only deliver the news, but they can also determine what makes the news in the first place.

Block quotation is indented one inch; page reference not needed for quotation from one-page work.

Paraphrase of source is mixed with a direct quotation of the phrase "professional judgment."

Support by anecdote (see p. 122).

Development by illustration (see p. 48).

Hollingsworth 6

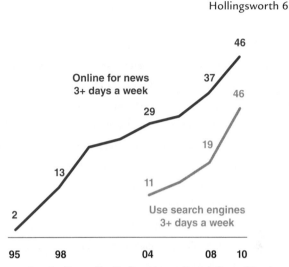

Fig. 1 Increasing Audience for Online News. Graph from "Section 2: Online and Digital News"; *Ideological News Sources: Who Watches What and Why* (The Pew Research Center for the People and the Press, 12 Sept. 2010; Web; 5 May 2011).

Blogging has ushered in a new era of journalism and a new set of consumer expectations for immediate news coverage on a wide range of topics. Now that consumers increasingly go online for news, as shown in fig. 1, traditional media outlets are realizing that they need to adopt blogging and other forms of new media to stay in the race. They understand the need to incorporate blogging and other forms of new media into everyday business.

With the rise of blogs and the abundance of free online information, media corporations are finding it harder and harder to maintain funding for traditional news reporting. In a recent report, the Pew Research Center's Project for Excellence in Journalism points out that traditional and new media face

Hollingsworth 7

similar challenges in their efforts to generate revenue, particularly

from advertising.[3] These challenges are further complicated

as new media and their markets expand (Gillmor). The Pew

Research Center argues that one model in the future will involve

partnerships between traditional and newer forms of media

and, in particular, that one type of relationship will be a concept

known as a "pro-am" (for "professional and amateur") approach

to news. Shirky describes what this trend toward "pro-am"

reporting might look like:

> For the next few decades, journalism will be made up
> of overlapping special cases. Many of these models
> will rely on amateurs as researchers and writers. Many
> of these models will rely on sponsorship or grants or
> endowments instead of revenues. Many of these models
> will rely on excitable 14-year-olds distributing the
> results. Many of these models will fail. . . . [O]ver time,
> the collection of new experiments that do work might
> give us the journalism we need. ("Newspapers" 29)

Both the Pew Research Center and Shirky suggest that, in

order to survive, traditional news outlets need to learn from

the success of bloggers. Similarly, in their comprehensive study

comparing the purpose of citizen journalism Web sites to that

of newspaper Web sites, journalism experts Stephen Lacy,

Margaret Duffy, Daniel Riffe, Esther Thorson, and Ken Fleming

conclude that citizen journalism sites cannot sufficiently replace,

but should instead accompany, newspaper sites (42). Clearly, a

partnership between traditional and new media is essential for

the future of journalism.

Annotations (left margin):

Source cited: online interview.

Block quotation introduced by a sentence ending in a colon.

Period followed by three ellipsis points indicates omission in the quotation. Capitalization of the first word following the ellipses is adjusted with brackets (see p. 546). Parenthetical citation follows the period.

Synthesis of material from two sources, followed by integrated summary.

Restatement of thesis.

Hollingsworth 8

The relationship between traditional and new media outlets will continue to develop as people continue to demand up-to-the-minute reporting on a vast array of issues. Like Lacy and his colleagues, Shirky, and the Pew Research Center, technology writer Stephen Cass argues that the two forms of media are mutually dependent: new media outlets depend on traditional media to provide authoritative content, and older, established media are turning to the newer forms to increase their ratings and, sometimes, provide up-to-the-minute stories (63). As bloggers and amateur reporters recognize the need for increased reliability, mainstream media corporations also understand that bloggers and amateur reporters are plentiful and influential enough to both create and spread the news.

Synthesis of material from a number of sources, with a para-phrase from one source.

Although blogs and other forms of citizen journalism cannot produce news that is as trustworthy as traditionally researched news, they can raise immediate and widespread awareness about issues that might otherwise go unreported. Mass communication experts David D. Perlmutter and Misti McDaniel argue that bloggers are exceptionally good at reporting on issues in a way that creates mass appeal (60). In an interview conducted for the *State of the Blogosphere 2009* report published by the blog search engine Technorati, Mathew Ingram, a technology journalist and blogger, responds to a question about the blogosphere's impact on journalism as a whole: "I think the more people there are writing, and the easier it is to publish writing of all kinds, the more likely we are to find the information we need and the more likely we are to get a clearer picture of an event or a situation." Shirky agrees: "The mass amateurization of publishing undoes

Development by contrast (see p. 56).

Paraphrase integrated into sentence, with signal phrase that gives the source's credentials.

Source cited: interview published online.

Hollingsworth 9

the limitations inherent in having a small number of traditional press outlets" (*Here Comes Everybody* 65). In fact, Shirky compares new forms of media, like blogging, to fundamental advances in human literacy, such as the printing press (*Here Comes Everybody* 66). As Ingram and Shirky suggest, blogging has had an impact on human knowledge, communication, and interactions and has led to improvements in our daily lives. We are not only more up to date on the latest goings-on in the world, but are also connected to other informed citizens like never before.

Note use of transitional expression (see p. 74).

The evolution of journalism toward citizen-driven news has opened doors for those who both produce and consume the news. Blogs have been instrumental in this shift toward a freer, more immediate, more widespread, and, some would argue, more compelling experience of world issues and events. In the waning years of the newspaper, traditional news outlets have learned a harsh reality: Consumers want the news now, and they want it in an interactive format. With the availability of blogging and other forms of new media, we want to participate, right now, in the news we consume. We want to choose the stories we read, write, and respond to. We still depend on traditional news outlets to deliver reliable reporting, but we also have a say in what is reported and how it is delivered. We ourselves have become, essentially, the greatest news story of all time.

Conclusion with quali- fied version of thesis.

Hollingsworth 10

Notes

1. Former librarian and public administrator Will Manley notes that, in contrast to face-to-face audiences or print media audiences, his blogging audience is "solid and real" because of the sheer volume of daily traffic on his blog.

2. The editors of the *New Atlantis* point out in "Blogs Gone Bad" that because online content has an immediate and widespread impact, bloggers and other Web writers need to be especially careful in what they post online (106).

3. Jon Meacham argues that media outlets need to shift their attention to digital over print content and delivery in order to thrive.

New page, title centered; first line of each note indented one-half inch.

Cites by author additional source that provides supplemental information.

Cites by title additional source that provides supplemental information.

Paraphrases supplemental information from key source.

Hollingsworth 11

One inch to top of page — 1"

Works Cited

"Blog." *Encyclopaedia Britannica Online.* Encyclopaedia
Britannica, 2010. Web. 25 Apr. 2011.

"Blogs Gone Bad." Editorial. *New Atlantis* 8 (2005): 106-09.
Print.

Cass, Stephen. "Mainstream News Taps into Citizen
Journalism." *Technology Review* Jan.-Feb. 2010: 62-63.
Print.

Gillmor, Dan. Interview by Eric Olsen. *State of the Blogosphere
2009.* Technorati, 2009. Web. 21 Apr. 2011.

Goldhammer, Gary. *The Last Newspaper: Reflections on the
Future of News.* N.p.: Lulu, 2009. Print.

Ingram, Mathew. Interview by Eric Berlin. *State of the
Blogosphere 2009.* Technorati, 2009. Web. 21 Apr. 2011.

Lacy, Stephen, et al. "Citizen Journalism Web Sites
Complement Newspapers." *Newspaper Research Journal*
31.2 (2010): 34-46. *Academic Search Elite.* Web. 21 Apr.
2011.

Manley, Will. "My Favorite Medium." *American Libraries*
Apr. 2010: 64. *Academic Search Elite.* Web. 21 Apr. 2011.

Meacham, Jon. Interview by Jon Stewart. *The Daily Show with
Jon Stewart.* Comedy Central. 5 May 2010. Television.

Perlmutter, David D., and Misti McDaniel. "The Ascent of
Blogging." *Nieman Reports* Fall 2005: 60-64. Print.

Pew Research Center. Project for Excellence in Journalism.
*The State of the News Media 2010: An Annual Report on
American Journalism. Journalism.org.* Project for Excellence
in Journalism, 2010. Web. 22 Apr. 2011.

Title centered; entries in alphabetical order by author's last name or, if no author, by first important word in the title.

Source: online encyclopedia.

Source: journal editorial.

Source: magazine article.

Source: online interview.

Source: whole book (no place of publication).

Source: online interview.

Source: journal article by more than three authors, in online database.

Source: one-page magazine article in online database.

Source: broadcast interview

Source: magazine article by two authors

Source: Online report by corporate author.

½"

Hollingsworth 12

Rosen, Jay. "The New News." *Technology Review* Jan.-Feb.

    2010: 15. Print.

Shirky, Clay. *Here Comes Everybody: The Power of Organizing*

    without Organizations. New York: Penguin, 2008. Print.

---. "Newspapers and Thinking the Unthinkable." *Risk*

    Management May 2009: 24-29. *Academic Search Elite.*

    Web. 21 Apr. 2011.

Source: one-page magazine article.

Source: entire book.

Source: magazine article in online database; 3 hyphens are used instead of repeating author's name.

This detail of a Mayan vase shows a scribe at work. Scribes—who documented the deeds of rulers—were esteemed in the great Mayan cities that flourished on the Yucatan Peninsula from around 100 to 900 CE.

PART
5

Take the whole range of imaginative literature, and we are all wholesale borrowers. In every matter that relates to invention, to use, or beauty or form, we are borrowers.

—WENDELL PHILLIPS

APA
Documentation
Style

5 APA Documentation Style

APA style requires writers to provide bibliographic information about their sources in a list of references. To format entries for the list of references correctly, it is important to know what kind of source you are citing. The directory on pages 328–29 will help you find the appropriate sample to use as a model. Alternatively, you can use the charts on the foldout pages that follow. Answering the questions in the charts on the reverse side of the foldout will usually lead you to the sample entry you need. If you cannot find what you are looking for, consult your instructor.

WRITING OUTCOMES

Part 5 APA Documentation Style

This section will help you answer questions such as the following:

Rhetorical Knowledge

- Which disciplines use APA style? (26)

Critical Thinking, Reading, and Writing

- Why do I need to document my sources? (26, 27)

Processes

- How should I position and label visuals? (28)
- What information should an abstract contain? (28)

Knowledge of Conventions

- How should I cite sources in the text of my paper? (26)
- How do I create a list of references? (27)
- What kind of spacing and margins should my paper have? (28)

Composing in Electronic Environments

- What is a digital object identifier (DOI), and how is it used? (27)
- How do I cite electronic sources, such as Web sites, podcasts, and online articles with DOIs? (27)

For a general introduction to writing outcomes, see Id, page 5.

Entries in a List of References:

Books or Other Print Sources

❓ IS YOUR SOURCE A COMPLETE BOOK?

NO **YES** Go to this entry *on page*

❓ IS YOUR SOURCE PART OF A BOOK?

NO **YES** Go to this entry *on page*

Check the next panel or the directory on pages 328–29 or consult your instructor.

Short Work on a Web Site

Organization as author

Date of publication or last update

Corporation for National and Community Service, (2010, June 15).

→ *What is service learning?* Retrieved from http://www.
learnandserve.gov/about/service_learning/index.asp

Title

URL

Sponsor

URL

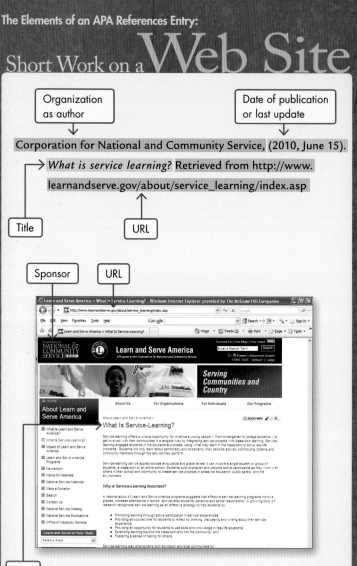

Title

The above citation derives from the APA model for an online report.
You may need to search on a site to find author, date, and other
information. List an individual author's last name first. If no date
is given, include *n.d.* Supplemental information about format may
follow the title. Here, the author is also the Web site sponsor
(Corporation for National and Community Service). When the
author is not the sponsor, name the sponsor after "Retrieved
from" (*see no. 56 on p. 340*). Include the home page URL for
magazine, newspaper, and journal articles (lacking a DOI). Give
the full URL for other sources.

Resources for Writers

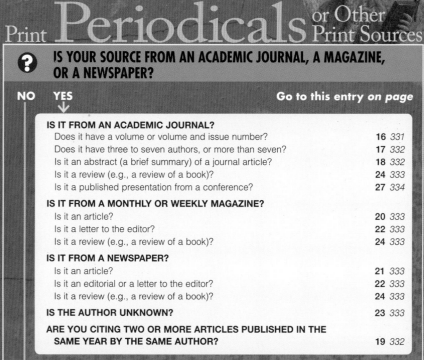

Entries in a List of References:

Print Periodicals or Other Print Sources

❓ IS YOUR SOURCE FROM AN ACADEMIC JOURNAL, A MAGAZINE, OR A NEWSPAPER?

NO | **YES** | Go to this entry *on page*

	Go to this entry *on page*

IS IT FROM AN ACADEMIC JOURNAL?

Does it have a volume or volume and issue number?	**16**	*331*
Does it have three to seven authors, or more than seven?	**17**	*332*
Is it an abstract (a brief summary) of a journal article?	**18**	*332*
Is it a review (e.g., a review of a book)?	**24**	*333*
Is it a published presentation from a conference?	**27**	*334*

IS IT FROM A MONTHLY OR WEEKLY MAGAZINE?

Is it an article?	**20**	*333*
Is it a letter to the editor?	**22**	*333*
Is it a review (e.g., a review of a book)?	**24**	*333*

IS IT FROM A NEWSPAPER?

Is it an article?	**21**	*333*
Is it an editorial or a letter to the editor?	**22**	*333*
Is it a review (e.g., a review of a book)?	**24**	*333*

IS THE AUTHOR UNKNOWN?	**23**	*333*

ARE YOU CITING TWO OR MORE ARTICLES PUBLISHED IN THE SAME YEAR BY THE SAME AUTHOR?	**19**	*332*

❓ IS IT A PRINT SOURCE BUT NOT A BOOK, A PART OF A BOOK, OR AN ARTICLE IN AN ACADEMIC JOURNAL, A MAGAZINE, OR A NEWSPAPER?

NO | **YES** | Go to this entry *on page*

IS IT PUBLISHED BY THE GOVERNMENT OR A NONGOVERNMENT ORGANIZATION?

Is it a government document?	**25**	*333*
Is it a report or a working paper?	**26**	*334*
Is it a brochure, pamphlet, fact sheet, or press release?	**29**	*335*
Is it from the *Congressional Record*?	**64**	*341*

IS IT AN UNPUBLISHED CONFERENCE PRESENTATION?	**27**	*334*
IS IT A DISSERTATION OR DISSERTATION ABSTRACT?	**28**	*334*

Check directory on pages 328–29 or consult your instructor.

The Elements of an APA References Entry:

Online Journal Article with DOI Assigned

Journal title · Authors · Year of publication · Article title

Plummer, C. A., Ai, A. L., Lemieux, C., Richardson, R., Dey, S., Taylor, P., . . . Hyun-Jun, K. (2008). Volunteerism among social work students during Hurricanes Katrina and Rita. *Journal of Social Service Research, 34*(3), 55–77. doi:10.1080/01488370802086328

DOI · Volume · Issue number · Page numbers

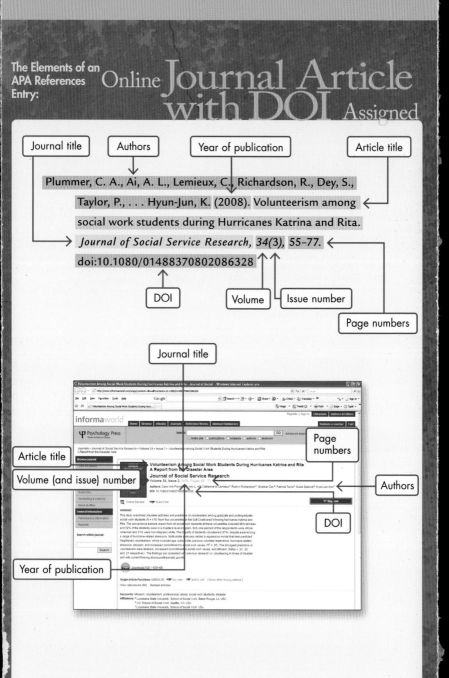

Journal title · Article title · Volume (and issue number) · Year of publication · Page numbers · Authors · DOI

If the article has a DOI (Digital Object Identifier), the citation does not require a URL. This article lists the DOI beneath the journal and citation information. For journals paginated by issue, include the issue number in parentheses after the volume number. For an article with more than seven authors, list the first six, followed by an ellipsis mark (three spaced periods) and the last author's name.

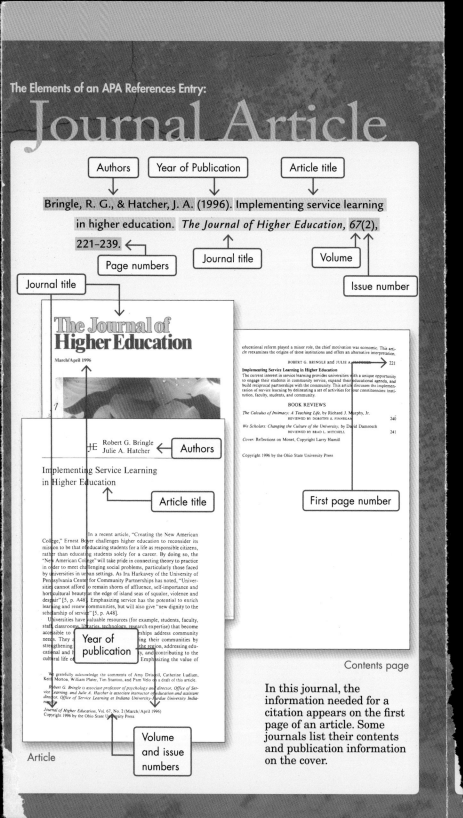

The Elements of an APA References Entry:

Journal Article

Authors → **Year of Publication** → **Article title** →

Bringle, R. G., & Hatcher, J. A. (1996). Implementing service learning in higher education. *The Journal of Higher Education, 67*(2), 221–239.

Page numbers — **Journal title** — **Volume** — **Issue number**

Journal title

The Journal of Higher Education

March/April 1996

JHE   Robert G. Bringle   Julie A. Hatcher   ← **Authors**

Implementing Service Learning in Higher Education   ← **Article title**

In a recent article, "Creating the New American College," Ernest Boyer challenges higher education to reconsider its mission to be that of educating students for a life as responsible citizens, rather than educating students solely for a career. By doing so, the "New American College" will take pride in connecting theory to practice in order to meet challenging social problems, particularly those faced by universities in urban settings. As Ira Harkavey of the University of Pennsylvania Center for Community Partnerships has noted, "Universities cannot afford to remain shores of affluence, self-importance and horticultural beauty at the edge of island seas of squalor, violence and despair" [5, p. A48]. Emphasizing service has the potential to enrich learning and renew communities, but will also give "new dignity to the scholarship of service" [5, p. A48].

Universities have valuable resources (for example, students, faculty, staff, classrooms, libraries, technology, research expertise) that become accessible to [...] rships address community needs. They a[...] **Year of publication** [...]ing their communities by strengthening [...] the region, addressing educational and h[...]ty, and contributing to the cultural life of [...] Emphasizing the value of

We gratefully acknowledge the comments of Amy Driscoll, Catherine Ludlum, Keith Morton, William Plater, Tim Stanton, and Pam Velo on a draft of this article.

Robert G. Bringle is associate professor of psychology and director, Office of Service Learning, and Julie A. Hatcher is associate instructor of education and assistant director, Office of Service Learning at Indiana University-Purdue University Indianapolis.

Journal of Higher Education, Vol. 67, No. 2 (March/April 1996)
Copyright 1996 by the Ohio State University Press

Article   **Volume and issue numbers**

educational reform played a minor role, the chief motivation was economic. This article reexamines the origins of these institutions and offers an alternative interpretation.

ROBERT G. BRINGLE and JULIE A. HATCHER → 221

Implementing Service Learning in Higher Education
The current interest in service learning provides universities with a unique opportunity to engage their students in community service, expand their educational agenda, and build reciprocal partnerships with the community. This article discusses the implementation of service learning by delineating a set of activities for four constituencies: institution, faculty, students, and community.

BOOK REVIEWS

The Calculus of Intimacy: A Teaching Life, by Richard J. Murphy, Jr.
REVIEWED BY DOROTHY E. FINNEGAN   240

We Scholars: Changing the Culture of the University, by David Damrosch
REVIEWED BY BRAD L. MITCHELL   241

Cover: Reflections on Monet, Copyright Larry Hamill

Copyright 1996 by the Ohio State University Press

First page number

Contents page

In this journal, the information needed for a citation appears on the first page of an article. Some journals list their contents and publication information on the cover.

Entries in a List of References:

Electronic or Other Nonprint

❓ DID YOU FIND YOUR NONPRINT SOURCE ONLINE?

NO **YES**   **Go to this entry *on page***

Go to next panel.

Instructors of courses in psychology, sociology, political science, communications, education, and business usually prefer a documentation style that emphasizes the author and the year of publication.

The information in Chapters 26–29 is based on the sixth edition of the American Psychological Association's *Publication Manual* (Washington: APA, 2010). For updates, check the APA-sponsored Web site at <www.apastyle.org>.

APA documentation style has two mandatory parts:

- In-text citations
- List of references

26 APA Style: In-Text Citations

In-text citations let readers know that they can find full information about the source of an idea you have paraphrased or summarized, or the source of a quotation, in the list of references at the end of your project.

1. Author named in sentence   Follow the author's name with the year of publication (in parentheses).

signal phrase
In her book *Generation Me*, Jean M. Twenge (2006) explains that Americans of current college age are preoccupied with amassing wealth and achieving material goals, but claims these aims and giving back to others aren't mutually exclusive.

2. Author named in parentheses   If you do not name the source's author in your sentence, then you must include the name in the parentheses, followed by the date and, if you are giving a quotation or a specific piece of information, the page number. Separate the name, date, and page number with commas.

This trend, which counters the stereotype of the self-centered college student, is expected to continue (Jaschik, 2006).

3. Two to five authors   If a source has five or fewer authors, name all of them the first time you cite the source.

Policy professors Bruce L. R. Smith and A. Lee Fritschler (2009) argue that service learning requires context: volunteering itself does not guarantee that students learn the lessons intended about citizenship or social policies.

If you put the names of the authors in parentheses, use an ampersand *(&)* instead of *and.*

Similarly, a study conducted for the Higher Education Research

Institute found that "students develop a heightened sense of civic

responsibility and personal effectiveness through participation

in service-learning courses" because they connect the academic

discussions of the classroom to the practical application of providing

ampersand used within parentheses
service in the community (Astin, Vogelgesang, Ikeda, & Yee, 2000, p. 2).

After the first time you cite a work by three or more authors, use the first author's name plus et al. (as an abbreviation, the *al.* has a period following it): (Astin et al., 2000). Always use both names when citing a work by two authors.

4. Six or more authors   For in-text citations of a work by six or more authors, always give the first author's name plus *et al.* In the reference list, however, list up to seven author names. For more than seven authors, list the first six authors' names, followed by an ellipsis mark (three spaced periods) and the last author's name *(see p. 332).*

APA IN-TEXT CITATIONS: DIRECTORY to SAMPLE TYPES

(See pp. 326–57 for examples of references entries.)

APA IN-TEXT CITATIONS

- Identify the author(s) of the source, either in the sentence or in a parenthetical citation.
- Indicate the year of publication of the source following the author's name, either in parentheses if the author's name is part of the sentence or, if the author is not named in the sentence, after the author's name and a comma in the parenthetical citation.
- Include a page reference for a quotation or specific piece of information. Put "p." before the page number. If the author is named in the text, the page number appears in the parenthetical citation following the borrowed material. Page numbers are not necessary when you are summarizing the source as a whole or paraphrasing an idea found throughout a work. *(For more on summary, paraphrase, and quotation, see Chapter 19: Working with Sources and Avoiding Plagiarism, pp. 246–58.)*
- If the source does not have page numbers (as with many online sources), do your best to direct readers. If the source has no page or paragraph numbering or easily identifiable headings, just use the name and date. *(See no. 13 and the note on p. 325.)*

As Barbre et al. (1989) have argued, using personal narratives enables researchers to connect the individual and the social.

5. Organization as author   Treat the organization as the author, and spell out its name the first time the source is cited. If the organization is well known, you may use an abbreviation thereafter.

According to the Pew Research Center for the People and the Press (2007), the roles food bank workers, role models for children in single-parent households, and youth drug counselors—to name a few— occupy today provide critical support, yet they were not as necessary to society years ago.

Public service announcements were used to inform parents of these findings (National Institute of Mental Health [NIMH], 1991).

In subsequent citations, only the abbreviation and the date need to be given: (NIMH, 1991).

6. Unknown author   Give the first one or two important words of the title. Use quotation marks for titles of articles, chapters, or Web pages and italics for titles of books, periodicals, or reports.

**26
APA**

The transformation of women's lives has been hailed as "the single most

important change of the past 1,000 years" ("Reflections," 1999, p. 77).

7. Two or more authors with the same last name   If the authors of two or more sources have the same last name, always include their first initial, even if the year of publication differs.

M. Smith (1988) showed how globalization has restructured both

cities and states.

8. Two or more works by the same author in the same year   Alphabetize the works by their titles in your reference list and assign a letter in alphabetical order (for example, *2006a, 2006b*). Use that same year-letter designation in your in-text citation.

J. P. Agarwal (1996b) described the relationship between trade and

foreign direct investment (FDI).

9. Two or more sources cited at one time   Cite the authors in the order in which they appear in the list of references, separated by a semicolon.

They contribute to the continual efforts to improve society without

expecting that significant change will occur; they expect to make a

difference in society locally, one citizen at a time; and they hope to

gain personally while doing so (Astin & Sax, 1998; Friedman, 2007).

10. E-mails, letters, and conversations   To cite information received from unpublished forms of personal communication—such as conversations, letters, notes, and e-mail messages—give the source's first initial or initials and last name, and provide as precise a date as possible. Because readers do not have access to them, do not include personal communications in your reference list.

According to scholar T. Williams (personal communication, June 10,

2010), many students volunteer because they believe in giving back to

the community they grew up in.

11. Specific part of a source   Include the chapter *(Chapter)*, page *(p.)*, figure, or table number.

Despite the new law, the state saw no drop in car fatalities involving

drivers ages 16–21 (Johnson, 2006, Chapter 4).

12. Indirect (secondary) source When referring to a source that you know only from reading another source, use the phrase *as cited in,* followed by the author of the source you actually read and its year of publication.

> Peter Levine, director of the Center for Information and Research on
>
> Civic Learning and Engagement at the University of Maryland, credits
>
> students with utilizing the Internet to effect change, "relying less on
>
> street protests and more on lobbying and volunteering" (as cited in
>
> Koch, 2008, p. 3a).

The work by Koch would be included in the references list, but the work by Peter Levine would not.

13. Electronic source Cite the author's last name or the name of the site's sponsor (if an author's name is not available) and the publication date. If the document is a PDF (portable document format) file with stable page numbers, cite the page number. If the source has paragraph numbers instead of page numbers, use *para.* instead of *p.*

> CNCS (2010) defines *service learning* as a practice that "engages
>
> students in the educational process, using what they learn in the
>
> classroom to solve real-life problems."

Note: If the specific part lacks page or paragraph numbering, cite the heading and the number of the paragraph under that heading where the information can be found. If the heading is long, use a short version in quotation marks. If you cannot determine the date, use the abbreviation *n.d.* in its place: (CNCS, n.d.).

---

14. Two or more sources in one sentence Include a parenthetical reference after each fact, idea, or quotation you have cited.

> As *New York Times* columnist Thomas L. Friedman (2007) has
>
> observed, while this generation might be less politically motivated
>
> than generations past, it does work quietly toward its own idealistic
>
> goals, which according to Bringle and Hatcher (1996) aligns with the
>
> motivation that students volunteer so that they can be a part of a
>
> community.

**26
APA**

15. Sacred or classical text Cite within your text only, and include the version you consulted as well as any standard book, part, or section numbers.

> The famous song sets forth a series of opposites, culminating in "a time to love, and a time to hate; a time of war, and a time of peace" (Eccles. 3:8, King James Bible).

27 APA Style: References

APA documentation style requires a list of references where readers can find complete bibliographical information about the sources referred to in your project. The list should appear at the end of your research project, beginning on a new page titled "References."

BOOKS

1. Book with one author

> Twenge, J. M. (2006). *Generation me: Why today's young Americans are more confident, assertive, entitled—and more miserable—than ever before.* New York, NY: Free Press.

2. Book with two or more authors
The final name should be preceded by an ampersand (&).

> Astin, A. W., Vogelgesang, L. J., Ikeda, E. K., & Yee, J. A. (2000). *How service learning affects students.* Los Angeles, CA: Higher Education Research Institute.

For more than seven authors, list the first six, an ellipsis mark (three spaced periods), and the final author *(see no. 17).*

3. Organization as author
When the publisher is the author, use *Author* instead of repeating the organization's name as the publisher.

Corporation for National and Community Service. (2010). *What is service learning?* Washington, DC: Author.

4. Two or more works by the same author   List the works in publication order, with the earliest one first. If a university publisher's name includes the state (note the second example), do not repeat it.

Eller, C. (2003). *Am I a woman? A skeptic's guide to gender.* Boston, MA: Beacon Press.

Eller, C. (2011). *Gentlemen and amazons: The myth of matriarchal prehistory, 1861–1900.* Berkeley: University of California Press.

If the works were published in the same year, put them in alphabetical order by title and add a letter *(a, b, c)* to the year to distinguish each entry in your in-text citations *(see no. 19).*

5. Book with editor(s)   Add *(Ed.)* or *(Eds.)* after the name. If a book lists an author and an editor, treat the editor like a translator *(see no. 9).*

Ferrari, J. & Chapman, J. G. (Eds.). (1999). *Educating students to make a difference: Community-based service learning.* New York, NY: Haworth Press.

6. Selection in an edited book or anthology   The selection's author, year of publication, and title come first, followed by the word *In* and information about the edited book. The page numbers of the selection go in parentheses after the book's title.

Primavera, J. (1999). The unintended consequences of volunteerism: Positive outcomes for those who serve. In Ferrari, J. & Chapman, J. G. (Eds.), *Educating students to make a difference: Community-based service learning* (pp. 125–140). New York, NY: Haworth Press.

7. Selection from a work already listed in References   Be sure to include all information for the larger work (see second example) preceded by that for the specific selection. Note that the first word of a title within a title should be capitalized.

Brodkey, L. (2003). On the subjects of class and gender in "The literacy letters." In V. Villanueva (Ed.), *Cross-talk in comp theory: A reader* (pp. 677–696). Urbana, IL: National Council of Teachers of English Press.

27 APA

APA REFERENCE ENTRIES: DIRECTORY to SAMPLE TYPES

(See pp. 321–26 for examples of in-text citations.)

APA REFERENCE ENTRIES: DIRECTORY to SAMPLE TYPES *(continued)*

27 APA

Villanueva, V. (Ed). (2003). *Cross-talk in comp theory: A reader.* Urbana, IL: National Council of Teachers of English.

8. Introduction, preface, foreword, or afterword   List the author and the section cited. If the book has a different author, write *In* next, followed by the book's author and the title.

Bellow, S. (1987). Foreword. In A. Bloom, *The closing of the American mind: How higher education has failed democracy and impoverished the souls of today's students.* New York, NY: Simon & Schuster.

9. Translation   After the title of the translation, put the name(s) of the translator(s) in parentheses, followed by the abbreviation *Trans.*

APA LIST of REFERENCES

- Begin on a new page with the centered title "References."
- Include a reference for every in-text citation except personal communications and sacred or classical texts *(see in-text citations no. 10 and no. 15)*.
- Put references in alphabetical order by author's last name.
- Give the last name and first or both initials for each author. If the work has more than one author, see no. 2 *(p. 326)* or no. 17 *(p. 332)*.
- Put the publication year in parentheses following the author or authors' names.
- Capitalize only the first word and proper nouns in titles. Also capitalize the first word following the colon in a subtitle.
- Use italics for titles of books, but not articles. Do not enclose titles of articles in quotation marks.
- Include the city and publisher for books. Give the state or country. If a university publisher's name includes the state, do not repeat it.
- Include the periodical name and volume number (both in italics) as well as the page numbers for a periodical article.
- End with the DOI, if any *(see nos. 16 and 43 and the box on p. 336)*.
- Separate the author's or authors' name(s), date (in parentheses), title, and publication information with periods.
- Use a hanging indent: Begin the first line of each entry at the left margin, and indent all subsequent lines of an entry (five spaces).
- Double-space within and between entries.

Jarausch, K. H., & Gransow, V. (1994). *Uniting Germany: Documents and debates, 1944–1993* (A. Brown & B. Cooper, Trans.). Providence, RI: Berg.

10. Article in an encyclopedia or another reference work
Begin with the author of the selection, if given. If no author is given, begin with the selection's title.

title of the selection
Arawak. (2000). In *The Columbia encyclopedia* (6th ed., p. 2533). New York, NY: Columbia University Press.

11. Entire dictionary or reference work   Unless an author or editor is indicated on the title page, list dictionaries by title, with the edition number in parentheses. (The in-text citation should include the title or a portion of the title.) *(See no. 10 on citing an article in a reference book and no. 12 on alphabetizing a work listed by title.)*

The American heritage dictionary of the English language (4th ed.). (2000). Boston, MA: Houghton Mifflin.

Hinson, M. (2004). *The pianist's dictionary.* Bloomington: Indiana University Press.

12. Unknown author or editor
Start with the title. When alphabetizing, use the first important word of the title (excluding articles such as *The, A,* or *An*).

Give me liberty. (1969). New York, NY: World.

13. Edition other than the first

Smyser, W. R. (1993). *The German economy: Colossus at crossroads* (2nd ed.). New York, NY: St. Martin's Press.

14. One volume of a multivolume work
If the volume has its own title, put it before the title of the whole work. No period separates the title and parenthetical volume number.

Google (2003). The ultimate online learning resource. In *E.enyclopedia* (Vol. 1). New York, NY: D. K. Publishing.

15. Republished book
In-text citations should give both years: "As Le Bon (1895/1960) pointed out. . . ."

Le Bon, G. (1960). *The crowd: A study of the popular mind.* New York, NY: Viking. (Original work published 1895)

PERIODICALS

16. Article in a journal (paginated by volume or issue)
Italicize the periodical title and the volume number. Provide the issue number—*not* italicized—in parentheses after the volume number, with no space between them. A DOI ends the entry if available *(also see no. 43).*

Inzlicht, M., & Kang, S. K. (2010). Stereotype threat spillover: How coping with threats to social identity affects aggression, eating, decision making, and attention. *Journal of Personality and Social Psychology, 99*(3), 467–481. doi:10.1037/a0018951

17. Article with three to seven authors, or with more than seven authors If a work has up to seven authors, list them all (see first example); if it has more than seven authors, list the first six followed by a comma, three ellipses, and the final author's name (see the second example).

> Hilgers, T., Hussey, E., & Stitt-Bergh, M. (1999). As you're writing, you
>
> have these epiphanies. *Written Communication, 16*(3), 317–353.

> Plummer, C. A., Ai, A. L., Lemieux, C., Richardson, R., Dey, S.,
>
> Taylor, P., . . . Hyun-Jun, K. (2008). Volunteerism among
>
> social work students during Hurricanes Katrina and
>
> Rita. *Journal of Social Service Research, 34*(3), 55–71.
>
> doi:10.1080/01488370802086328

18. Abstract For an abstract that appears in the original source, add the word *Abstract* in brackets after the title. If the abstract appears in a printed source that is different from the original publication, first give the original publication information for the article, followed by the publication information for the source of the abstract. If the dates of the publications differ, cite them both, with a slash between them, in the in-text citation: Murphy (2003/2004).

> Burnby, J. G. L. (1985, June). Pharmaceutical connections: The Maw's
>
> family [Abstract]. *Pharmaceutical Historian, 15*(2), 9–11.

> Murphy, M. (2003). Getting carbon out of thin air. *Chemistry &*
>
> *Industry, 6,* 14–16. Abstract retrieved from *Fuel and Energy*
>
> *Abstracts, 45*(6), 389.

19. Two or more works in one year by the same author Alphabetize by title, and attach a letter to each entry's year of publication, beginning with *a*. In-text citations must use the letter as well as the year.

> Agarwal, J. P. (1996a). *Does foreign direct investment contribute to*
>
> *unemployment in home countries? An empirical survey* (Discussion
>
> Paper No. 765). Kiel, Germany: Institute of World Economics.

> Agarwal, J. P. (1996b). Impact of Europe agreements on FDI in
>
> developing countries. *International Journal of Social Economics,*
>
> *23*(10/11), 150–163.

20. Article in a magazine After the year, add the month for magazines published monthly or the month and day for magazines published weekly. Note that the volume and issue numbers are also included.

> Gross, P. (2001, February). Exorcising sociobiology. *New Criterion,*
> *19*(6), 24.

21. Article in a newspaper Use *p.* or *pp.* (not italicized) with the section and page number. List all page numbers, separated by commas, if the article appears on discontinuous pages: pp. C1, C4, C6. If there is no identified author, begin with the title of the article.

> Smith, T. (2003, October 8). Grass is green for Amazon farmers. *The*
> *New York Times,* p. W1.

22. Editorial or letter to the editor

> Krugman, P. (2011, January 28). Their own private Europe [Editorial].
> *The New York Times,* p. A31.

23. Unsigned article Begin the entry with the title, and alphabetize it by the first important word (excluding articles such as *The, A,* or *An*).

> Four contestants pitch variety of film styles for competition. (2011,
> January 13). *The Lantern,* p. 6.

24. Review If the review is untitled, use the bracketed description in place of a title.

> Dargis, M. (2011, March 4). Creepy people with a plan, and a couple
> on the run [Review of the motion picture *The adjustment bureau,*
> 2011]. *The New York Times,* pp. C1, C10.

> MacFarquhar, Roderick (2011, February 10). The worst man-made
> catastrophe, ever [Review of the book *Mao's great famine: The*
> *history of China's most devastating catastrophe* by F. Dikotter]. *The*
> *New York Review of Books, 58*(2), pp. 26–28.

OTHER PRINT AND AUDIOVISUAL SOURCES

25. Government document When no author is listed, use the government agency as the author.

U.S. Bureau of the Census. (1976). *Historical statistics of the United States: Colonial times to 1970*. Washington, DC: Government Printing Office.

For an enacted resolution or piece of legislation, see no. 63.

26. Report or working paper If the issuing agency numbered the report, include that number in parentheses after the title.

Agarwal, J. P. (1996a). *Does foreign direct investment contribute to unemployment in home countries? An empirical survey* (Discussion Paper No. 765). Kiel, Germany: Institute of World Economics.

27. Conference presentation Treat published conference presentations as a selection in a book *(no. 6)*, as a periodical article *(no. 16)*, or as a report *(no. 26)*, whichever applies. For unpublished conference presentations, provide the author, the year and month of the conference, the italicized title of the presentation, and the presentation's form, forum, and place.

Desantis, R. (1998, June). *Optimal export taxes, welfare, industry concentration and firm size: A general equilibrium analysis*. Poster session presented at the First Annual Conference in Global Economic Analysis, West Lafayette, IN.

Markusen, J. (1998, June). *The role of multinationals in global economic analysis*. Paper presented at the First Annual Conference in Global Economic Analysis, West Lafayette, IN.

28. Dissertation or dissertation abstract Use this format for an unpublished dissertation. For a published dissertation accessed via a database, see no. 48.

Luster, L. (1992). *Schooling, survival and struggle: Black women and the GED* (Unpublished doctoral dissertation). Stanford University, Palo Alto, CA.

If you used an abstract from *Dissertation Abstracts International*, treat the entry like a periodical article.

Weinbaum, A. E. (1998). Genealogies of "race" and reproduction in

transatlantic modern thought. *Dissertation Abstracts International,*

58, 229.

29. Brochure, pamphlet, fact sheet, or press release If there is no date of publication, put *n.d.* in place of the date. If the publisher is an organization, list it first, and name the publisher as *Author* (not italicized).

U.S. Postal Service. (1995). *A consumer's guide to postal services and*

products [Brochure]. Washington, DC: Author.

Union College. (n.d.). *The Nott Memorial: A national historic landmark*

at Union College [Pamphlet]. Schenectady, NY: Author.

30. Published letter Begin with the letter writer's name, treating the addressee as part of the title *(Letter to . . .).* The following example is published in a collection of letters, so it is also treated as a selection within a larger book.

Lewis, C. S. (1905). Letter to his brother. In Walter Hooper (Ed.),

The collected letters of C. S. Lewis: Vol 1. Family letters, 1905–1931

(pp. 2–3). New York, NY: HarperCollins.

31. Film or DVD Begin with the cited person's name and, if appropriate, a parenthetical notation of his or her role. After the title, identify the medium, followed by the country and name of the distributor. *(For online video, see no. 75.)*

Rowling, J. K., Kloves, S. (Writers), Yates, D. (Director), & Barron, D.

(Producer). (2009). *Harry Potter and the half-blood prince* [Motion

picture]. United States: Warner Brothers Pictures.

32. CD or audio recording See no. 72 for an MP3 or no. 73 for an audio podcast.

title of piece

Corigliano, J. (2007). Red violin concerto [Recorded by J. Bell].

title of album

On *Red violin concerto* [CD]. New York: Sony Classics.

33. Radio broadcast See no. 73 for an audio podcast.

Adamski, G., & Conti, K. (Hosts). (2007, January 16). *Legally speaking*

[Radio broadcast]. Chicago, IL: WGN Radio.

27
APA

34. TV series For an entire TV series or specific news broadcast, treat the producer as author.

> Simon, D., & Noble, N. K. (Producers). (2002). *The wire* [Television
>
> series]. New York, NY: HBO.

35. Episode from a TV series Treat the writer as the author and the producer as the editor of the series. See no. 74 for a podcast TV series episode.

> Burns, E., Simon, D. (Writers), & Johnson, C. (Director). (2002).
>
> The target [Television series episode]. In D. Simon & N. K. Noble
>
> (Producers), *The wire*. New York, NY: HBO.

36. Advertisement Include the word *Advertisement* within brackets.

> Geek Squad. (2007, December 10). [Advertisement]. Minneapolis/St.
>
> Paul, MN: WCCO-TV.

37. Image, photograph, or work of art If you have reproduced a visual, give the source information with the caption. See no. 57 for online visuals.

> Smith, W. E. (1950). *Guardia Civil, Spain* [Photograph]. Minneapolis,
>
> MN: Minneapolis Institute of Arts.

38. Map or chart If you have reproduced a visual, give the source information with the caption *(for an example, see p. 357)*. Also include a reference-list entry. See no. 57 for online visuals.

> *Colonial Virginia* [Map]. (1960). Richmond: Virginia Historical Society.

39. Live performance

> Ibsen, H. (Author), Bly, R. (Translator), & Carroll, T. (Director). (2008,
>
> January 12). *Peer Gynt* [Theatrical performance]. Guthrie Theater,
>
> Minneapolis, MN.

40. Musical composition

> Rachmaninoff, S. (1900). *Piano concerto no. 2, opus 18* [Musical
>
> composition].

41. Lecture, speech, or address List the speaker; the year, month, and date (if available); and the italicized title of the presentation. Include location information when available (for online versions, add "Retrieved from," the Web site sponsor, and the URL).

> Cicerone, R. (2007, September 22). *Climate change in the U.S.* George S. Benton Lecture given at Johns Hopkins University, Baltimore, MD.

42. Personal interview Like other unpublished personal communications, personal interviews are not included in the reference list. See in-text citation entry no. 10 *(p. 324)*.

ELECTRONIC SOURCES

43. Online journal article with a Digital Object Identifier (DOI) If your source has a DOI, include it at the end of the entry; URL and access date are not needed.

> Ray, R., Wilhelm, F., & Gross, J. (2008). All in the mind's eye? Anger rumination and reappraisal. *Journal of Personality and Social Psychology, 94,* 133–145. doi:10.1037/0022-3514.94.1.133

44. Online journal article without a DOI Include the URL of the journal's home page.

> Chan, L. (2004). Supporting and enhancing scholarship in the digital age: The role of open access institutional repository. *Canadian Journal of Communication, 29,* 277–300. Retrieved from http://www.cjc-online.ca

45. Abstract from an online journal article Treat much like a journal article, but include the word *Abstract* before retrieval information.

> Plummer, C.A., Ai, A.L., Lemieux, C., Richardson, R., Dey, S., Taylor, P., . . .Hyun-Jun, K. (2008). Volunteerism among social work students during Hurricanes Katrina and Rita. *Journal of Social Service Research, 34*(3), 55–71. Abstract retrieved from Refdoc.fr

**27
APA**

APA ELECTRONIC REFERENCES

- Many print and online books and articles have a Digital Object Identifier (DOI), a unique alphanumeric string. Citations of online documents with DOIs do not require the URL. Do not place a period after a DOI.
- Include a retrieval date only for items that probably will change (such as a wiki).
- Do not include information about a database or library subscription service in the citation unless the work is difficult to find elsewhere (for example, archival material).
- Include the URL of the home page for journal, magazine, and newspaper articles lacking a DOI.
- Include the full URL for all other items lacking a DOI. Do not place a period after a URL.
- For nonperiodicals, name the site sponsor in the retrieval statement unless the author is the sponsor *(see no. 51)*. This format derives from the APA model for an online report.

> author
> Butler, R. A. (2008, July 31). *Future threats to the Amazon rain forest.*
> Web site sponsor
> Retrieved from Mongabay.com website: http://news.mongabay
>
> .com/2009/0601-brazil_politics.html

> author as Web site sponsor
> Sisters in Islam. (2007). *Mission.* Retrieved from http://sistersinislam
>
> .org.my/

---

46. Journal article from an online subscription or library database

Include database information only if the article is rare or found in just a few databases. *(Otherwise, see nos. 43 and 44.)* Give the URL of the database's home page.

> Gore, W. C. (1916). Memory, concept, judgment, logic (theory).
>
> *Psychological Bulletin, 13,* 355–358. Retrieved from PsycARTICLES
>
> database: http://psycnet.apa.org

47. Abstract from database as original source

> O'Leary, A., & Wolitski, R. J. (2009). Moral agency and the sexual
>
> transmission of HIV. *Psychological Bulletin, 135,* 478–494. Abstract
>
> retrieved from PsycINFO database: http://psycnet.apa.org

48. Published dissertation from a database Include the dissertation file number at the end of the entry.

> Gorski, A. (2007). *The environmental aesthetic appreciation of cultural landscapes* (Doctoral dissertation). Available from ProQuest Dissertations and Theses database. (UMI No. 1443335)

49. Newspaper or magazine article from a database Include database information for archival material not easily found elsewhere. Give the URL of the database's home page. *(Otherwise, see no. 51 for an online newspaper article or no. 52 for an online magazine article.)*

> Culnan, J. (1927, November 20). Madison to celebrate arrival of first air mail plane. *Wisconsin State Journal*, p. A1. Retrieved from Wisconsin Historical Society database: http://www.wisconsinhistory.org/WLHBA

50. Article in an online newspaper

> Rohter, L. (2004, December 12). South America seeks to fill the world's table. *The New York Times*. Retrieved from http://www.nytimes.com

51. Article in an online magazine Include the volume and issue numbers after the magazine title.

> Biello, D. (2007, December 5). Thunder, hail, fire: What does climate change mean for the U.S.? *Scientific American, 297*(6). Retrieved from http://www.sciam.com

52. Supplemental online magazine content A description in brackets such as *online exclusive* indicates that the material is distributed only in online venues.

> Perry, A. (2004, January 26). The future lies in democracy [Online exclusive]. *Time*. Retrieved from http://www.time.com

53. Review from an online publication

> Goodsell, C. T. (1993, January/February). Reinvent government or rediscover it? [Review of the book *Reinventing government: How the*

27
APA

entrepreneurial spirit is transforming the public sector, by T. Gaebler &
D. Osborne]. *Public Administration Review, 53*(1), 85–87. Retrieved
from JSTOR database.

54. In-press article Include the designation *in press* (not italicized) in place of a date.

Husky, M. M., Sheridan, M., McGuire, L., & Olfson, M. (in press).
Mental health screening and follow-up care in public high
schools. *Journal of the American Academy of Child & Adolescent
Psychiatry.* Retrieved from http://www.jaacap.org/inpress

55. Article in an online newsletter Give the full URL.

Gray, L. (2008, February). Corn gluten meal. *Shenandoah Chapter
Newsletter, Virginia Native Plant Society.* Retrieved from http://
www.vnps.org/chapters/shenandoah/Feb2008.pdf

56. Document or report on a Web site Include the Web site
sponsor in the retrieval statement unless the author of the work is
also the sponsor. Here, the author is the World Health Organization,
and the sponsor is BPD Sanctuary.

World Health Organization. (1992). *ICD-10 criteria for borderline
personality disorder.* Retrieved from BPD Sanctuary website: http://
www.mhsanctuary.com/borderline/icd10.htm

57. Visual on a Web site If you have used a graph, chart, map,
or image, give the source information following the figure caption *(for
an example, see p. 357).* Also include a reference-list entry.

Seattle [Map]. (2008). Retrieved from http://www.mapquest.com

58. Document on a university's Web site Include relevant
information about the university and department in the retrieval
statement.

Tugal, C. (2002). Islamism in Turkey: Beyond instrument and meaning.
Economy and Society, 31, 85–111. Retrieved from University of
California–Berkeley, Department of Sociology website: http://
sociology.berkeley.edu/public_sociology_pdf/tugal.pps05.pdf

59. Electronic version of a print book Provide a DOI if it is available instead of the URL.

> Mill, J. S. (1869). *On liberty.* (4th ed.). Retrieved from http://books
> .google.com/books

> Shariff, S. (2009). Confronting cyber-bullying: What schools need
> to know to control misconduct and avoid legal consequences.
> [Cambridge Books Online]. doi:10/1017/CBO9780511551260

60. Chapter from an electronic book

> Owen, S., & Kearns, R. (2006). Competition, adaptation and resistance:
> (Re)forming health organizations in New Zealand's third sector. In
> Milligan, C., & Conradson, D. (Eds.), *Landscapes of voluntarism: New
> spaces of health, welfare and governance* (pp. 115–134). Retrieved from
> http://books.google.com.proxy.lib.fsu.edu

61. Electronic book, no print edition

> Stevens, K. (n.d.). *The dreamer and the beast.* Retrieved from http://
> www.onlineoriginals.com/showitem.asp?itemID=321

62. Online brochure

> Corporation for National & Community Service. (2010). *A guide to
> working with the media* [Brochure]. Retrieved from http://www
> .nationalservice.gov/pdf/Media_Guide.pdf

63. Online government document other than the *Congressional Record*

> National Commission on Terrorist Attacks Upon the United States.
> (2004). *The 9/11 Commission report.* Retrieved from Government
> Printing Office website: http://www.gpoaccess.gov/911/index.html

64. *Congressional Record* (online or in print) For enacted resolutions or legislation, give the number of the Congress after the number of the resolution or legislation, the *Congressional Record* volume number, the page number(s), and year, followed by *(enacted)*.

**27
APA**

H. Res. 2408, 108th Cong., 150 Cong. Rec. 1331–1332 (2004)

(enacted).

Give the full name of the resolution or legislation when citing it within your sentence, but abbreviate the name when it appears in a parenthetical in-text citation: *(H. Res. 2408, 2004)*.

65. Online policy brief or white paper

Cramer, K., Shelton, L., Dietz, N., Dote, L., Fletcher, C., Jennings, S.,

. . . Silsby, J. (2010). *Volunteering in America 2010: National, state,*

and city information. Retrieved from Corporation for National and

Community Service website: http://www.volunteeringinamerica

.gov/assets/resources/IssueBriefFINALJune15.pdf

66. Online document lacking either a date or an author
Place the title before the date if no author is given. Use the abbreviation *n.d.* (no date; do not italicize) for any undated document.

Center for Science in the Public Interest. (n.d.). *Food additives to avoid.*

Retrieved from Mindfully.org website: http://www.mindfully.org

/Food/Food-Additives-Avoid.htm

67. Article in an online reference work   Begin with the author's name, if given, followed by the publication date. If no author is given, place the title before the date. Include the full URL.

Attribution theory. (2009). In *Encarta.* Retrieved from http://encarta

.msn.com/encyclopedia_761586848 /Attribution_Theory.html

68. Wiki article   Wikis are collaboratively written Web sites. Most are updated regularly, so include the access date in your citation. Check with your instructor before using a wiki article as a source.

Demographic transition. (2007, October 8). Retrieved from Citizendium

website: http://en.citizendium.org/wiki/Demographic_transition

69. Blog posting   This model is for a blog post. For an example of a video blog post, see the second example; use the description "video

file." For a comment, use the same format but substitute "Web log comment" for "Web log post."

> Eggers, A. (2009, May 20). Debates on government transparency websites [Web log post]. Retrieved from Social Science Statistics Blog website: http://www.iq.harvard.edu/blog/sss

> Underwood, Elizabeth. (2010, May 17). Audubon oil spill response volunteer. [Video file]. Retrieved from BirdLife International website: http://www.birdlife.org/community/2010/05 /audubon-oil-spill-response-volunteer-liz-video/

70. Post to an electronic mailing list, newsgroup, or discussion forum Provide the message's author, its date, and its subject line as the title. For a post to a mailing list, provide the description *Electronic mailing list message* in brackets. For a post to a newsgroup or discussion forum, give the identifying information *Online forum comment* in brackets. Conclude either entry with the words *Retrieved from,* followed by the URL of the archived message.

> Glick, D. (2007, February 10). Bio-char sequestration in terrestrial ecosystems—A review [Electronic mailing list message]. Retrieved from http://bioenergylists.org/newsgroup-archive /terrapreta_bioenergylists.org/2007-February/000023.html

> Jones, D. (2001, February 3). California solar power [Online forum comment]. Retrieved from http://yarchive.net/space/politics /california_power.html

71. E-mail or instant message (IM) E-mail, instant messages, or other nonarchived personal communication should be cited in the body of your text but not given in the references list *(see in-text citation entry no. 10 on p. 324).*

72. MP3 or other digital audio file Use brackets to identify the file type.

> Hansard, G., & Irglova, M. (2006). Falling slowly. On *The swell season* [MP3]. Chicago, IL: Overcoat Recordings.

27
APA

73. Audio podcast

Glass, I. (Host). (2008, June 30). Social engineering. *This American life* [Audio podcast]. Retrieved from http://www.thisamericanlife.org

74. Video podcast

Reitman, J. (Director), & Novak, B. J. (Writer). (2007). Local ad [Television series episode]. In S. Carrell, M. Kaling, L. Eisenberg, & G. Stupnitsky (Producers), *The office* [Video podcast]. Retrieved from http://www.nbc.com/the_office /video/episodes.shtml

75. Online video   For an online speech, see no. 39.

Wesch, M. (2007, March 8). The machine is us/ing us [Video file]. Retrieved from http://mediatedcultures.net/ksudigg/?p=84

76. Online advertisement

Lexus. (2011, January). [Advertisement]. Retrieved from http://www .pandora.com.

77. Computer software or video game   Cite only specialized software. Familiar software such as Microsoft Word doesn't need to be cited.

L.A. noire. (2011). [Video game]. New York, NY: Rockstar Games.

78. Presentation slides

Volunteering Australia Inc. (2009). Volunteering: What's it all about? [PowerPoint slides]. Retrieved from http://www .volunteeringaustralia.org/files/WZ7K0VWICM/Volunteering %20what_s%20it%20all%20about.ppt

28 APA Style: Format

The following guidelines are recommended by the *Publication Manual of the American Psychological Association,* sixth edition. For an example of a research paper that has been prepared using APA style, see pages 347–57.

Materials Back up your final draft. Use a high-quality printer and high-quality white 8½-by-11-inch paper. Do not justify your text or hyphenate words at the right margin; it should be ragged.

Title page The first page of your research report should be a title page. Center the title between the left and right margins in the upper half of the page, and put your name, the name of your course, your instructor's name, and the date on separate lines below the title. *(See p. 347 for an example.)*

Margins and spacing Use one-inch margins all around, except for the upper right-hand corner, where the page number goes, and the upper left-hand corner, where the running head goes.

Double-space lines throughout, including in the abstract, within any notes or captions, and in the list of references. Indent the first word of each paragraph one-half inch (or five spaces).

For quotations of more than forty words, use block format and indent five spaces from the left margin. Double-space the quoted lines.

Page numbers and abbreviated titles All pages, including the title page, should have a short version of your title in uppercase letters. On the title page, preface this with the words "Running head" and a colon. Put this information in the upper left-hand corner of each page, about one-half inch from the top. Put the page number in the upper right-hand corner.

Abstract Instructors sometimes require an abstract—a summary of your paper's thesis, major points or lines of development, and conclusions. The abstract appears on its own numbered page, entitled "Abstract," right after the title page. It should not exceed 150 to 250 words.

Headings Primary headings should be boldfaced and centered. All key words in the heading should be capitalized.

APA APA APA APA APA APA APA APA APA APA APA APA APA APA

Secondary headings should be boldfaced and appear flush against the left-hand margin. Do not use a heading for your introduction, however. *(For more on headings, see Chapter 5: Designing Academic Texts and Portfolios, pp. 92–93.)*

Visuals   Place each visual (table, chart, graph, or image) on its own page following the reference list and any content notes. Tables precede figures. Label each visual as a table or a figure, and number each kind consecutively (Table 1, Table 2). Provide an informative caption for each visual. Cite the source of the material, and provide explanatory notes as needed. *(For more on using visuals effectively, see Chapter 2: Planning and Shaping, pp. 43–45.)*

29 Sample Research Project in APA Style

Tina Schwab researched the topic of student volunteerism and wrote a report about it for her introductory sociology course. Her sources included books, journal articles, and Web documents.

CONSIDER YOUR SITUATION

Author: Tina Schwab

Type of writing: Research report

Purpose: To report on motivations for student volunteerism

Stance: Objective

Audience: Students, instructors, sociologists

Medium: Print, part of e-portfolio

Schwab writes: As I did my research for this topic, I was surprised about the mix of motivations that students have for volunteering.

Running head: THE NEW VOLUNTEER   1

All pages: short title and page number; on title page only: "Running head."

The New Volunteer:

College Students' Involvement in Community Giving Grows

Tina Schwab

Sociology 101

Professor Morgan

May 15, 2010

Title appears in full and centered on separate page with student's name, course information, and date.

THE NEW VOLUNTEER   2

Abstract appears on a new page after the title page. The first line is not indented.

Abstract

College students today are volunteering in record numbers. Research indicates that today's youth are just as committed to community service as the young Americans of the 1960s, who are often perceived as the most civic-minded of American generations. However, current college students have reasons for volunteering beyond the desire to do good. Today, volunteerism is built into the academic curriculum, aids career development, and provides a sense of community. While the motivations for and methods of volunteering may vary from one generation to another, the fact remains that today's students are committed to serving their communities and making their world a better place for all.

Research report is concisely and objectively summarized—key points are included, but not details or statistics.

Abstract should not exceed 150 to 250 words.

THE NEW VOLUNTEER

½"

3

1"

½"

½"

The New Volunteer: College Students'

Involvement in Community Giving Grows

Are college students today concerned with helping others? It may not seem so to older generations, to whom today's students may appear obsessed with social networking, text messaging, and materialistic values. In her book, *Generation Me,* Jean M. Twenge (2006) explains that Americans of current college age are preoccupied with amassing wealth and achieving material goals, but claims these aims and giving back to others aren't mutually exclusive. "As long as time spent volunteering does not conflict with other goals, GenMe finds fulfillment in helping others" (Twenge, 2006, p. 5). Attitudes and perceptions aside, today's college students actively help others in their communities, in ways that make a collective impact on the world. Their approach, however, differs from that of the previous generation. Today's college students tend to volunteer for at least one of three reasons: to satisfy a curricular requirement, to prepare for the financial success they hope to achieve professionally, and to be active members of their communities.

Volunteering in America and

Historical Changes in Motivation

According to the Corporation for National and Community Service (CNCS) (2009), volunteering is on the rise today, with one million more total volunteers in the United States than there were in 2002. Many of those volunteers are college students. In a 1998 report, researchers for the Higher Education Research Institute found that the most important predictor of volunteer service among college students is whether or not they volunteered in high

---

Full title is repeated on first page only.

Paraphrase from a source; the author is named in the text, so date follows her name in parentheses.

Direct quote from a source; page number is included in parenthetical citation.

Thesis statement.

Heading in bold type, centered.

Source is a corporation, spelled out at first mention with abbreviation in parentheses.

THE NEW VOLUNTEER   4

school (Astin & Sax, 1998). Among all volunteers in America, the percentage of those aged 16 to 24 increased from 20.8% in 2007 to 21.9% in 2008, adding over 441,000 volunteers from this age range (CNCS, 2009). This trend, which counters the stereotype of the self-centered college student, is expected to continue (Jaschik, 2006). As Penn State's president Graham Spanier (2008) notes, the number of postcollege applicants to both the Peace Corps and Teach for America is increasing. "Although some may write off today's postgraduate volunteerism as a reflection of a weak job market, I am among those who see it as a continuation of the habit of community service that students developed as teenagers" (p. A35).

Historically, college students planning to enter service professions such as nursing or social work have always volunteered their time as part of their professional development. They can make an especially valuable contribution in disastrous circumstances such as the aftermath of Hurricane Katrina (Plummer et al., 2008). However, today students from all disciplines volunteer to work at food banks, with youth service organizations, and as mentors, filling some of the most in-demand volunteer positions in the country (CNCS, 2009). There is little doubt that the current generation is doing its part to make the world a better place (see Figure 1).

At the same time, the ways that generations volunteer differ. Students volunteered in the past to change the status quo and to have an impact on social conditions in our country (Astin, 1998). Today's students also seek to effect change but with perhaps more practicality than idealism. They volunteer less for abstract,

Two names in source, separated by an ampersand (&); because there are only two names, both names are included in subsequent citations.

Quotation from authority is provided as support.

Page number for quotation.

Paraphrase, with source provided in parenthetical citation; *et al.* is used after the first author's name because there are more than six.

Development by illustration (see p. 48); figure reference is provided. Figure appears after the list of references.

THE NEW VOLUNTEER   5

altruistic reasons than for concrete, personal ones. They
contribute to the continual efforts to improve society without
expecting that significant change will occur; they expect to make
a difference in society locally, one citizen at a time, and they hope
to gain personally while doing so (Astin & Sax, 1998; Friedman,
2007). However, students' desire to combine their own interests
with their volunteer efforts does not diminish the fact that they
are having a positive effect on others.

Today it is easier for volunteers to have an impact at the
community level than at a national or regional level. According to
a report by the Pew Research Center for the People and the Press
(2007), the roles food bank workers, role models for children in
single-parent households, and youth drug counselors—to name
a few—occupy today provide critical support, yet they were not
as necessary to society years ago. Rather than effecting sweeping
change, today's volunteer tends to have an impact on one life
at a time. This difference may contribute to perceptions that
today's young people are not as involved as members of previous
generations when they were young, but these perceptions are
incorrect: volunteering looks and feels different now than it did
previously, but it has just as great an impact (Spanier, 2008).

Current College Students' Motivations for Volunteering

One reason that students volunteer today is that it is a
familiar behavior reinforced in the college environment. Many
colleges offer service learning courses and service initiatives
through campus organizations. These forms of volunteering,
especially service learning courses, often help students learn and
improve their grades (Bringle & Hatcher, 1996).

Summary
of informa-
tion in two
sources;
the two
sources are
separated by
semicolon.

The first
motivation
for volunteer-
ing, from the
thesis.

THE NEW VOLUNTEER   6

Service learning courses have two objectives: (1) learning in a given content area and (2) learning about citizenship and social policies. CNCS (2010) defines *service learning* as a practice that "engages students in the educational process, using what they learn in the classroom to solve real-life problems." Similarly, a study conducted for the Higher Education Research Institute found that "students develop a heightened sense of civic responsibility and personal effectiveness through participation in service-learning courses" because they connect the academic discussions of the classroom to the practical application of providing service in the community (Astin, Vogelgesang, Ikeda, & Yee, 2000, p. 2). The formal structure of service learning is designed to make student volunteering beneficial not only for the community but also for the students who perform it, increasing their academic development, leadership skills, and community awareness. George Mason University's School of Public Policy professors Bruce L. R. Smith and A. Lee Fritschler (2009) argue that service learning requires context so that students learn the lessons intended:

> Students can learn the wrong lessons about the roles of leaders and followers, partisanship, and the nature of civil society from a volunteer experience. Therefore, an intellectual framework, supplied by the appropriate faculty members, should be part of the student's experience as a volunteer. (p. 9)

Astin et al. (2000) maintain that service-learning courses are academically effective simply because they enhance students' critical thinking and writing skills, boosting grade point averages. Even after they are concluded, however, service learning courses are also believed to influence students positively; if a student

Source has four names, so all four are included in the first parenthetical citation.

Two names in a source are joined by *and* in running text, not by an ampersand (&).

Quotation of more than 40 words is indented one-half inch. Authors' names and the date are given, so only the page reference follows the quotation.

Source with four names has already been cited once, so *et al.* is used after first name for all subsequent citations.

has a good experience in a service learning initiative, he or she is more inclined to choose a service-related career (for example, a healthcare profession), continue community service postgraduation, and volunteer additional service hours outside of any academic commitment (Astin et al., 2000).

A second motivation is market driven. Differences in the way today's students volunteer reflect the unique challenges they face. Entering the job market has become much more difficult than it was for previous generations, so today's students often target their volunteer efforts strategically by seeking opportunities to develop skills and experience that can translate to future employment or financial success (Astin & Sax, 1998). This extracurricular form of volunteering is endorsed by many educators, and in fact college students do most of their volunteering through campus organizations.

In fact, the economic realities of our society have much to do with the perceptions of how volunteering is different for today's student than it was in times past. Students today volunteer for their own personal benefit, motivated partly by the desire for money or fame. One study of college-aged Americans, for instance, reported that for 81% of participants, getting rich was their highest priority in life, and 51% sought fame as a primary goal (Pew Research Center for the People and the Press, 2007). People who are working for a cause today usually integrate the common good with their own personal aspirations.

A third motivation for volunteering is the desire for community, which may particularly motivate college students looking to establish connections within peer groups at their

---

The second motivation for volunteering, from the thesis.

Name of corporate author is included in its entirety in parenthetical citation.

The third motivation for volunteering, from the thesis.

THE NEW VOLUNTEER   8

school, students who want to integrate their daily lives with their academic work, and new students seeking to establish a sense of belonging in a new place (Bringle & Hatcher, 1996). As *New York Times* columnist Thomas L. Friedman (2007) has observed, while this generation might be less politically motivated than generations past, it does work quietly toward its own idealistic goals.

Online collaboration also fulfills the desire for community interaction. Students often use the Internet to organize support for a cause; for example, students have used MySpace and Facebook to urge assistance for victims of Hurricane Katrina and survivors of terrorist attacks. These efforts at raising awareness might not seem like much when conducted individually, but when considered collectively, they have a significant impact. Since MySpace began in 2004, more than 22,000 nonprofit groups have signed up to engage supporters (Koch, 2008). For example, students can find initiatives online such as the Pay It Forward Movement.org, named for the book by Catherine Ryan Hyde and started by four University of Minnesota first-year students. Student volunteers who participate in Pay It Forward tours spend school breaks on community service projects like cleaning up a city park or helping to set up a homeless shelter. Peter Levine, director of the Center for Information and Research on Civic Learning and Engagement at the University of Maryland, credits students with utilizing the Internet to effect change, "relying less on street protests and more on lobbying and volunteering" (as cited in Koch, 2008, p. 03a). The Pay It Forward Movement, which relies exclusively on online communication, also hosts web-a-thons designed to raise awareness and generate volunteers (Tehven & Fernandez, 2009).

Development by illustration (see p. 48).

Secondary source; page number is given for the location of the quotation in the Koch article.

THE NEW VOLUNTEER   9

An Assessment of College Volunteerism

Friedman (2007) thinks the current generation of college students is too quiet, however. He resists the idea that projects like Pay It Forward can bring about the change that is needed and maintains that more engaged activity is required, that "virtual politics is just that—virtual." He urges college students to set their sights higher: to organize "in a way that will force politicians to pay attention rather than just patronize them." Regardless of motivation and how others perceive their efforts, there is no doubt that college students today are making a difference. Today's students represent many voices working together to enrich their communities in myriad ways. Their efforts are relevant to their career goals, and they give their time in ways that also benefit their own lives. What matters is that their commitment to enriching the lives of others and to enhancing the communities in which we live is as strong as that of any previous generation.

Quotation is integrated effectively into the text of the report; page number is not included because the source is a Web site.

Restatement of thesis at conclusion.

THE NEW VOLUNTEER   10

References

Astin, A. W. (1998). The changing American college student: Thirty-year trends, 1966–1996. *The Review of Higher Education, 21*(2), 115–135. Retrieved from http://www.press.jhu.edu/journals/review_of_higher_education

Astin, A. W., & Sax, L. J. (1998). How undergraduates are affected by service participation. *Journal of College Student Development, 39*(3), 251–263.

Astin, A. W., Vogelgesang, L. J., Ikeda, E. K., & Yee, J. A. (2000). *How service learning affects students.* Los Angeles, CA: Higher Education Research Institute.

Bringle, R. G., & Hatcher, J. A. (1996). Implementing service learning in higher education. *Journal of Higher Education, 67*(2), 221–239.

Corporation for National and Community Service. (2009, July). *Volunteering in America research highlights.* Retrieved from http://www.volunteeringinamerica.gov/assets/resources/VolunteeringInAmericaResearchHighlights.pdf

Corporation for National and Community Service. (2010, June 15). *What is service learning?* Retrieved from http://www.learnandserve.gov/about/service_learning/index.asp

Friedman, T. (2007, October 10). Generation Q. *The New York Times.* Retrieved from http://www.nytimes.com

Jaschik, S. (2006, October 17). Student volunteerism is up. *Inside Higher Ed.* Retrieved from http://www.insidehighered.com

New page, title centered; entries are in alphabetical order by author's last name or, if no author, by first important word in the title.

Source: journal article with volume and issue number, retrieved online.

Source: entire book by four authors.

Source: report by a corporate author, retrieved online.

Source: online newspaper article.

Source: online magazine article.

THE NEW VOLUNTEER   11

Koch, W. (2008, March 13). Internet spurs upswing in
    volunteerism. *USA Today*. Retrieved from http://www
    .usatoday.com/

Pew Research Center for the People and the Press. (2007,
    January 9). *A portrait of "Generation Next": How young people
    view their lives, futures and politics* [Summary of findings].
    Retrieved from http://people-press.org/report/300
    /a-portrait-of-generation-next

Plummer, C. A., Ai, A. L., Lemieux, C., Richardson, R., Dey,
    S., Taylor, P., . . . Hyun-Jun, K. (2008). Volunteerism
    among social work students during Hurricanes Katrina
    and Rita. *Journal of Social Service Research, 34*(3), 55–71.
    doi:10.1080/01488370802086328

Smith, B. L. R., & Fritschler, A. L. (2009, Fall). Engagement in civic
    education remains weak. *Phi Kappa Phi Forum, 89*(3), 8–10.

Spanier, G. (2008, October 17). Is campus activism dead—or
    just misguided? A president wonders where the radicals are
    now. *The Chronicle of Higher Education*. Retrieved from http://
    chronicle.com

Tehven, G., & Fernandez, I. (2009). *Pay It Forward movement*.
    Retrieved from http://www.payitforward.org/groups
    /PayItForwardTour.htm

Twenge, J. M. (2006). *Generation me: Why today's young Americans
    are more confident, assertive, entitled—and more miserable—than
    ever before*. New York, NY: Free Press.

Source: journal article with volume and issue number, as well as a digital object identifier (DOI); because there are at least eight authors, three ellipsis points appear between the sixth and last authors' names.

Source: information from a Web site.

THE NEW VOLUNTEER   12

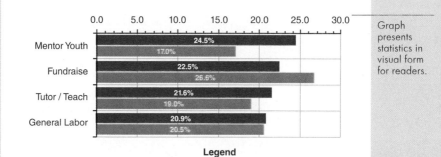

Graph presents statistics in visual form for readers.

Figure 1. Top four volunteering activities in which college students engage. Adapted from *Volunteering in America research highlights: College student profile,* by Corporation for National and Community Service, 2009. Retrieved from http://www .volunteeringinamerica.gov/special/College-Students

Figure number in italics, followed by figure title and source information, appears below the figure.

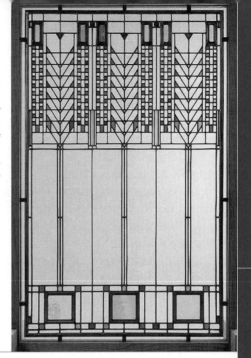

Frank Lloyd Wright's Darwin D. Martin House features Wright's famous "Tree of Life" window. Sunlight brings out the clarity of each window's design; in turn, the design—a variety of geometric, colorful patterns—transforms the light.

I . . . believe that words *can* help us move or keep us paralyzed, and that our choices of language and verbal tone have something—a great deal—to do with how we live our lives and whom we end up speaking with and hearing. . . .

—ADRIENNE RICH

Editing
for Clarity

6 Editing for Clarity

WRITING OUTCOMES

This section will help you learn to do the following:

Rhetorical Knowledge

- Is my writing too formal or too informal for college assignments? **(39b)**

- How can I avoid sexist language such as *mankind* and the general use of *he?* **(39e)**

Critical Thinking, Reading, and Writing

- How can subordination clarify relationships between ideas? **(36b)**

- How can I choose between two words with similar meanings? **(39a, 40a, b)**

Processes

- Can my word processor's grammar checker help me edit for clarity? **(30–38)**

Knowledge of Conventions

- What's wrong with the comparison *I like texting more than John?* **(31c)**

- What's wrong with saying *the reason . . . is because?* **(32c)**

- Should I use *their, there,* or *they're* in this sentence? **(41)**

Writing in Online Environments

- Can a grammar checker help me find mixed constructions, shifts, and misplaced and dangling modifiers in my writing? **(40a, 41, 43a, e)**

For a general introduction to writing outcomes, see Id, page 5.

30 Avoiding Wordiness

A sentence does not have to be short and simple to be concise, but every word in it must count.

Wordiness and Grammar Checkers

Most computer grammar checkers recognize many wordy structures, but inconsistently so. One style checker flagged most passive verbs and some *it is* and *there are* (expletive) constructions, but not others. It also flagged the redundant expression *true fact* but missed *round circle* and the empty phrase *it is a fact that.*

30a Eliminating redundancies and unnecessary modifiers

Be on the lookout for redundancies such as *first and foremost, full and complete, final result, past histories, round in shape,* and *refer back.*

▶ Students living ~~in close proximity~~ in the dorms need to cooperate ~~together if they want~~ to live in harmony.

Usually, modifiers such as *very, rather,* and *really* and intensifiers such as *absolutely, definitely,* and *incredibly* can be deleted.

▶ The ending ~~definitely~~ shocked us ~~very much.~~

30b Replacing wordy phrases

Make your sentences more concise by replacing wordy phrases with appropriate alternatives.

                                    Tests must now
▶ ~~It is necessary at this point in time that tests~~ be run
                                            ^
              to measure
~~for the purposes of measuring~~ the switch's strength.
                              ^

Wordy Phrases	**Concise Alternatives**
at that point in time	then
at this point in time	now
due to the fact that	because
for the reason that	because
in close proximity to	near
in order to	to
in spite of the fact that	although
in the event that	if
in the final analysis	finally
in the not-too-distant future	soon
is able to	can
is necessary that	must

Exercise 30.1 Identifying and editing wordy or empty phrases and unnecessary repetition

Eliminate wordy or empty phrases and unnecessary repetition to make the following sentences concise.

EXAMPLE

The
~~The truth is that the time of the~~ rainy season in Hawaii is
                                          ^

from ~~the month of~~ November to ~~the month of~~ March.

1. Charlotte Perkins Gilman was first and foremost known as a woman who was a champion of women's rights.
2. She was born on the date July 3, 1860, in the city of Hartford, which is in the state of Connecticut.
3. Gilman's "The Yellow Wallpaper," a novella about the holy matrimony of marriage and a state of madness, still speaks to contemporary readers in this present day and age.
4. The leading female heroine in Gilman's story is diagnosed by her physician husband as having an illness that is mental in origin.
5. Gilman wrote and published her book *Women and Economics* in the year 1898 and then published her book *Concerning Children* in the year 1900.

30c Editing roundabout sentences

Eliminate expletive constructions like *there is, there are,* and *it is;* replace the static verbs *be* and *have* with active verbs; and beware of overusing nouns derived from verbs.

▶ ~~There are~~ *The* stylicstic similarities between "This Lime-Tree

Bower" and "Tintern Abbey," ~~which are indications of the~~ *indicate*

~~influence~~ *influenced* that Coleridge ~~had on~~ Wordsworth.

For conciseness and clarity, simplify your sentence structure by turning modifying clauses into phrases.

▶ The film *The Social Network*, ~~which was~~ directed by David

Fincher, portrays the turbulent founding of Facebook.

Often, you can reduce phrases to single words.

▶ David Fincher's film *The Social Network* portrays the

turbulent founding of Facebook.

You can combine short, repetitive sentences.

▶ Hurricane Ike~~'s~~ *'s torrential rains devastated* ~~had a devastating effect on~~ our town,

~~The destruction resulted from torrential rains. Flooding~~

submerg~~ed~~ *ing* Main Street under eight feet of water. ~~The rain~~ *and*

~~also~~ trigger~~ed~~ *ing* mudslides that destroyed two nearby towns.

30c

w

Exercise 30.2 Writing straightforward sentences

Use the techniques described in this chapter to make each of the following passages into a single concise sentence.

EXAMPLE

The play opened on October 1. There were many reviews in which critics gave it a pan. The public loathed it too, which is why it closed after a run of less than two weeks.

The play opened on October 1, but critics panned it, the public loathed it, and it closed after a run of less than two weeks.

1. There are many concerns that environmentalists have about whether genetically modified food products are absolutely safe for the environment.

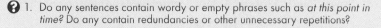

IDENTIFY AND EDIT | Wordy Sentences

W

Ask yourself these questions as you edit:

❓ 1. Do any sentences contain wordy or empty phrases such as *at this point in time?* Do any contain redundancies or other unnecessary repetitions?

> ▪ ~~The fact is that at this point in time more~~ women than men ^More^ attend college. ^now^
>
> ▪ College enrollments have increased steadily ~~upward~~ since the 1940s, but since the 1970s women have enrolled in greater numbers than men ~~have~~.

❓ 2. Can any clauses be reduced to phrases, or phrases to single words? Can any sentences be combined to reduce repetitive information?

> ▪ ~~Reports that come from college~~ officials ^College^ indicate that more women are applying than men./~~This pattern indicates~~ that ^and^ women will outnumber men in college for some time to come.

❓ 3. Do any sentences include *there is,* or *there are,* or *it is* expressions; weak verbs; or nouns derived from verbs?

> ▪ In 1970, ~~there were~~ more than 1.5 million. ^men outnumbered women in college by^ ~~more men in college than women.~~
>
> ▪ This trend ~~is a reflection of~~ broad changes in gender roles ^reflects^ throughout U.S. society.

---

2. Soybeans that are genetically engineered are very resistant to certain artificially made herbicides. These beans are also very resistant to certain artificially made insecticides.

3. These soybeans, which are resistant, permit the use of larger quantities of herbicides by farmers than before.

4. The herbicides kill surrounding plants. They also kill insects that are not considered pests, such as the monarch butterfly.

5. There are also concerns from consumers about the handling of genetically modified soy crops. One of these concerns is that the genetically modified soy crops are not segregated from soy crops that have not been genetically modified.

Exercise 30.3 Chapter review: Revising wordy sentences

Use the techniques described in this chapter to make the following passage concise.

In this day and age, people definitely should take preventive precautions to prevent identity theft from happening to them. Identity thieves have the ability to use someone else's personal information to commit fraud or theft, such as opening a fraudulent credit card account. Identity thieves also have the capacity to create counterfeit checks. This type of theft is often done in such a clever manner that often the victim of identity theft never realizes that his or her identity has been stolen. People whose identity has been stolen should first and foremost contact the Federal Trade Commission (FTC) for the purpose of disputing fraudulent charges. There is also the fact that people should learn how they can minimize the chance that they will face the risk of becoming a victim of this type of crime.

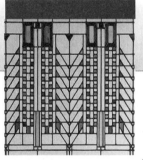

31 Adding Missing Words

Do not omit words the reader needs to understand your sentence.

31a
miss

✓ **31a** Adding needed words to compound structures

For conciseness, words can sometimes be omitted from compound structures: *His anger is extreme and his behavior [is] violent.* But do not leave out part of a compound structure unless both parts of the compound are the same.

> *with*
► **The gang members neither cooperated nor listened to**
  ^

  the authorities.

31b Adding the word *that*

Add the word *that* if doing so makes the sentence clearer.

> *that*
> ► The attorney argued＾men and women should receive equal
>
> pay for equal work.

31c Making comparisons clear

To be clear, comparisons must be complete. Check comparisons to make sure your meaning is clear. In the following example, does the writer mean that she loved her grandmother more than her sister did—or more than she loved her sister? To clarify, add the missing words.

> *did*
> ► I loved my grandmother more than my sister＾.
>
> *I loved*
> ► I loved my grandmother more than＾my sister.

When you use *as* to compare people or things, be sure to use it twice.

> *as*
> ► Napoleon's temper was＾volatile as a volcano.

Include *other* or *else* to indicate that people or things belong to the group with which the subject is being compared.

> ► High schools and colleges stage *The Laramie Project* more
>
> than any *other* play.

> ► Professor Koonig wrote more books than anyone *else* in the
>
> department.

Use a possessive form when comparing attributes or possessions.

> *Aristotle's.*
> ► Plato's philosophy is easier to read than＾~~that of Aristotle.~~

Complex comparisons may require more than one addition to be clear.

> *than Jones's book*
> ► Smith's book is longer,＾but his account of the war is
>
> *Jones's account.*
> more interesting than ~~Jones's.~~＾

31d Adding the articles *a, an,* or *the*

Omitting an article usually sounds odd, unless the omission occurs in a series of nouns.

the
▶ He gave me ˄ books he liked best.

▶ He gave me books, CDs, and games.

If the articles in a series are not all the same, each one must be included.

▶ I have a fish tank, birdcage, and rabbit hutch.

          a   *a*
I have *an* aquarium, ˄birdcage, and ˄rabbit hutch.

(For more information about the use of articles, multilingual writers should consult Chapter 48, pp. 489–90.)

Exercise 31.1 Chapter review: Editing for missing words

Read the following paragraphs carefully, and supply any missing words.

    Most early scientists thought the speed of light was infinite. The Italian scientist Galileo never agreed nor listened to arguments of his contemporaries. He set up experiment to measure the speed of light between two hills that were a known distance apart. Although its results were ambiguous, Galileo's experiment was more influential than any experiment of his day.

    Almost one hundred years later, the Danish astronomer Olaus Roemer devised a sophisticated experiment to measure speed of light. Roemer hypothesized the farther away planet Jupiter is from Earth, the longer its light will take. Knowing Jupiter's distance from Earth at various times of the year, Roemer calculated the speed of light at 141,000 miles per second. Roemer's result was closer than that of any earlier scientist to the actual speed of light, which is now known to be 186,281.7 miles per second in a vacuum.

    According to Albert Einstein's theory of relativity, the speed of light has never and will never be exceeded. The speed of light is variable, however. For instance, it travels about twenty-five percent slower through water.

**31d
miss**

32 Unscrambling Mixed Constructions

Sentences that do not fit together grammatically or logically can be confusing and must be revised.

✓ 32a Untangling mixed-up grammar

A sentence should not start one way and then midway through change grammatical direction.

> *Family*
> ► ~~For family~~ members who enjoy one another's
>   ^
>
> company often choose a vacation spot together.

A prepositional phrase cannot be the subject of a sentence. Eliminating the preposition *for* makes it clear that *family members* is the subject of the verb *choose*.

>   *can be*
> ► In Mexican culture, ~~when~~ a curandero ~~is~~ consulted
>   ^
>   *for*
> ~~can address~~ spiritual or physical illness.
>   ^

The dependent clause *when a curandero is consulted* cannot serve as the subject of the sentence. Transforming the dependent clause into an independent clause with a subject and predicate fixes the problem.

Mixed Constructions and Grammar Checkers

Computer grammar checkers are unreliable at detecting mixed constructions. For example, a grammar checker failed to high-light the two examples of mixed-up sentences in Section 32a.

32b Repairing illogical predicates

A sentence's subject and verb must match both logically and grammatically. When they do not, the result is faulty predication.

>   *A*
> ► ~~The best kind of education for me would be a~~ university
>   ^
>   *would be best for me*
> with both a school of music and a school of government.
>   ^

A university is an institution, not a type of education.

The phrases *is when, is where,* and *the reason is . . . because* may sound logical, but they usually result in faulty predication.

    the production of carbohydrates from the interaction of

► **Photosynthesis is ~~where~~ carbon dioxide, water, and**
                     ^

chlorophyll. ~~interact in the presence of sunlight to form~~
          ^

~~carbohydrates.~~

Photosynthesis is a process, not a place, so *is where* is illogical.

                                  that

► **The reason the joint did not hold is ~~because~~ the coupling**
                                     ^

bolt broke.

or

► **The ~~reason the~~ joint did not hold ~~is~~ because the coupling**

bolt broke.

Exercise 32.1 Chapter review: Eliminating mixed constructions

Edit the following paragraph to eliminate mixed constructions. Some sentences may not need correction, and there may be several acceptable options for editing those that do need it.

32b
mix

    Electrons spin around the nucleus of an atom according to definite rules. The single electron of a hydrogen atom occupies a kind of spherical shell around a single proton. According to the discoveries of quantum physics, says that we can never determine exactly where in this shell the electron is at a given time. The indeterminacy principle is a rule where we can only know the probability that the electron will be at a given point at a given moment. The set of places where the electron is most likely to be is called its orbital. By outlining a set of rules for the orbitals of electrons, the Austrian physicist Wolfgang Pauli developed the concept of the quantum state. Through using this concept permits scientists to describe the energy and behavior of any electron in a series of four numbers. The first of these, or principal quantum number, is where the average distance of the electron from the nucleus is specified. For the other quantum numbers describe the shape of the orbital and the "spin" of the electron. That no two electrons can ever be in exactly the same quantum state, according to Pauli's basic rule. The reason chemists use the four quantum numbers as a shorthand for each electron in an atom is because they can calculate the behavior of the atom as a whole.

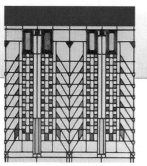

33 Fixing Confusing Shifts

Revise confusing shifts in point of view, tense, mood, or voice.

Confusing Shifts and Grammar Checkers

Computer grammar checkers rarely flag confusing shifts. Consider this blatant example:

▶   **The teacher entered the room, and then roll is called.**

Although the sentence shifts confusingly from past to present tense and from active to passive voice, at least one grammar checker failed to highlight it.

✓ **33a**   Fixing shifts in point of view

A writer has three points of view to choose from: first person *(I* or *we),* second person *(you),* and third person *(he, she, it, one,* or *they).* Once you choose a point of view, use it consistently.

                                                                    they
▶   **Students will have no trouble getting a good seat if ~~you~~**
                                                                     ^

arrive at the theater before 7 o'clock.

Note: When making a general statement about what people should or should not do, use the third person, not the second person.

Do not switch from singular to plural or plural to singular for no reason. When correcting such shifts, choose the plural to avoid using *his or her* or introducing gender bias. *(See Chapter 39, pp. 403–6.)*

▶ A person is *often surprised when they are complimented.*
      People are

✓ **33b** Fixing shifts in tense

Verb tenses show the time of an action in relation to other actions. Choose a time frame—present, past, or future—and use it consistently, changing tense only when the meaning of your text requires you to do so.

▶ **The wind was blowing a hundred miles an hour when**

    was   *fell*
suddenly there is a big crash, and a tree falls into the

living room.

▶ **She has admired many strange buildings at the university**

   thinks   *looks*
but thought that the new Science Center looked completely

out of place.

**33b
shift**

NAVIGATING THROUGH COLLEGE AND BEYOND

Present Tense and Literary Works

By convention—because as long as a book is read, it is "alive"—we use the present tense to write about the content of literary works.

▶ **David Copperfield describes villains such as Mr.**

Murdstone and heroes such as Mr. Micawber in

                         is
unforgettable detail. But Copperfield was not himself an

especially interesting person.

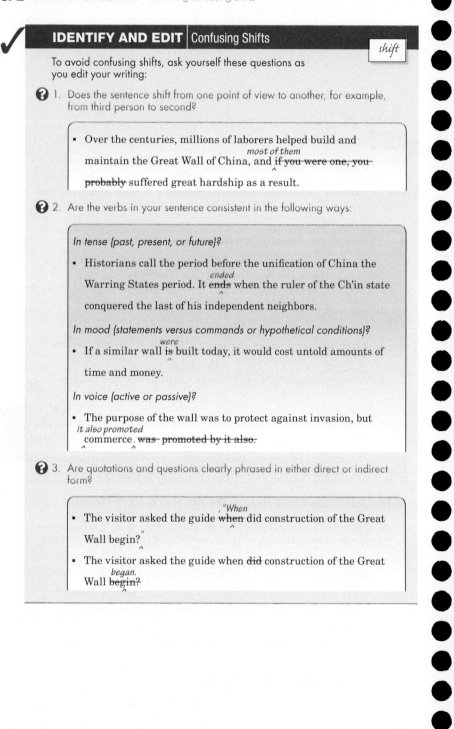

✓ **IDENTIFY AND EDIT** | Confusing Shifts

shift

To avoid confusing shifts, ask yourself these questions as you edit your writing:

❷ 1. Does the sentence shift from one point of view to another, for example, from third person to second?

> - Over the centuries, millions of laborers helped build and
>   *most of them*
>   maintain the Great Wall of China, and ~~if you were one, you probably~~ suffered great hardship as a result.

❷ 2. Are the verbs in your sentence consistent in the following ways:

> *In tense (past, present, or future)?*
>
> - Historians call the period before the unification of China the
>   *ended*
>   Warring States period. It ~~ends~~ when the ruler of the Ch'in state conquered the last of his independent neighbors.
>
> *In mood (statements versus commands or hypothetical conditions)?*
>
> *were*
> - If a similar wall ~~is~~ built today, it would cost untold amounts of time and money.
>
> *In voice (active or passive)?*
>
> - The purpose of the wall was to protect against invasion, but
>   *it also promoted*
>   commerce. ~~was promoted by it also.~~

❷ 3. Are quotations and questions clearly phrased in either direct or indirect form?

> *, "When*
> - The visitor asked the guide ~~when~~ did construction of the Great
>   *"*
>   Wall begin?
> - The visitor asked the guide when ~~did~~ construction of the Great
>   *began.*
>   Wall ~~begin?~~

Exercise 33.1 Making point of view consistent

Edit the following sentences so that they are consistent in person and number.

EXAMPLE

they
When people vote, ~~you~~ participate in government.
                  ^

or

you
When ~~people~~ vote, you participate in government.
      ^

1. On November 30, 1974, archeologists discovered the 3.5 million-year-old skeleton of an early hominid (or human ancestor) you call Lucy.
2. If you consider how long ago Lucy lived, one might be surprised so many of her bones remained intact.
3. When an early hominid like Lucy reached full height, they were about three and a half feet tall.
4. When these early hominids were born, she could expect to live about thirty years.
5. Lucy and the other hominids who lived with her in what is to-day Ethiopia, Africa, all walked upright and could manipulate a tool with their dextrous hands.

33c Avoiding unnecessary shifts in mood and voice

Verbs have a mood and a voice. There are three basic moods: the **in-dicative,** used to state or question facts, acts, and opinions; the **im-perative,** used to give commands or advice; and the **subjunctive,** used to express wishes, conjectures, and hypothetical conditions. Unnecessary shifts in mood can confuse and distract your readers.

could go
▶ If he ~~goes~~ to night school, he would take a course in
        ^

accounting.

▶ The sign says that in case of emergency passengers should

should not
follow the instructions of the train crew and ~~don't~~ leave the
                                                ^

train unless instructed to do so.

33c
shift

Most verbs have two voices. In the **active voice,** the subject does the acting; in the **passive voice,** the subject is acted on. Do not shift abruptly from one voice to the other.

They favored violet,
▶ The Impressionist painters hated black. ~~Violet,~~ green, blue,
                                            ^

pink, and red. ~~were favored by them.~~
             ^

The revision uses *they* to make "the Impressionist painters" the subject of the second sentence as well as the first.

Exercise 33.2 Keeping verbs consistent in tense, mood, and voice

Edit the following sentences so that the verbs are consistent in tense, mood, and voice unless meaning requires a shift. If a sentence is correct as is, circle its number.

EXAMPLE

The Silk Road, the famous trade route that linked Asia
                  followed
and Europe, ~~follows~~ the Great Wall of China for much
              ^

of its length.

1. Many visitors who have looked with amazement at the Great Wall of China did not know that its origins reached back to the seventh century BCE.

2. In 221 BCE, the ruler of the Ch'in state conquered the last of its independent neighbors and unifies China for the first time.

3. The Ch'in ruler ordered the walls the states had erected between themselves to be torn down, but the walls on the northern frontier were combined and reinforced.

4. Subsequent Chinese rulers extended and improved the wall until the seventeenth century CE, when it reached its present length of more than four thousand miles.

5. History shows that as a defense against invasion from the north, the wall was not always effective.

6. China was conquered by the Mongols in the thirteenth century, and the Manchus took control of the empire in the seventeenth century.

7. The wall, however, also served as a trade route and had helped open new regions to farming.
8. As a result, was it not for the wall, China's prosperity might have suffered.

33d Avoiding shifts between direct and indirect quotations and questions

Indirect quotations report what others wrote or said without repeating their words exactly. **Direct quotations** report the words of others exactly and should be enclosed in quotation marks. *(For more on punctuating quotations, see Chapter 53, pp. 538–39.)* Do not shift from one form of quotation to the other within a sentence.

▶ **In his inaugural speech, President Kennedy called on**

Americans not to ask what their country could do for them

       to   *they could*   *their*

but instead ⸢ask what ~~you can~~ do for ~~your~~ country.⸣

The writer could have included the quotation in its entirety: *In his inaugural speech, President Kennedy said, "My fellow Americans, ask not what your country can do for you; ask what you can do for your country."*

Similarly, do not shift from an indirect to a direct question.

                                         whether

▶ **The performance was so bad the audience wondered ~~had~~**

      had

the performers ever rehearsed.

As an alternative, the writer could ask the question directly: *Had the performers ever rehearsed? The performance was so bad the audience wasn't sure.*

33d
shift

Exercise 33.3 Chapter review: Eliminating confusing shifts

Edit the following passage, changing words as necessary to avoid confusing shifts.

From about the first to the eighth century CE, the Moche civilization dominated the north coast of what is now Peru.

The people of this remarkable civilization, which flourished nearly a thousand years before the better-known Inca civilization, are sophisticated engineers and skilled artisans. They built enormous adobe pyramids and a vast system of irrigation canals was created and maintained. Moche smiths forged spectacular gold ornaments as well as copper tools and weapons. The Moche potter sculpted realistic-looking portraits and scenes of everyday life onto clay vessels; they also decorated vessels with intricate drawings of imposing and elaborately garbed figures involved in complex ceremonies. One such scene, which appeared on many Moche vessels, depicted a figure archeologists call the Warrior Priest engaged in a ceremony that involves the ritual sacrifice of bound prisoners.

A question is what do these drawings represent. You wonder whether they depict Moche gods and mythological events, or do they represent actual figures from Moche society conducting actual Moche rituals? A dramatic discovery in 1987 provided an answer to these questions. In that year, archeologists have uncovered a group of intact Moche tombs at a site called Sipán. In one of the tombs were the remains of a man who had been buried clothed in stunningly rich regalia. As this outfit was carefully removed by the archeologists, they realized that it corresponded to the outfit worn by the Warrior Priest depicted on Moche pottery. If the warrior priest was just a mythological figure, then this tomb should not exist, but it did. In other words, the archeologists realized, the man in the tomb was an actual Moche Warrior Priest.

34 Using Parallel Constructions

Parallel constructions present equally important ideas in the same grammatical form.

▶ **At Gettysburg in 1863, Lincoln said that the Civil War was being fought to make sure that government *of the people, by the people,* and *for the people* might not perish from the earth.**

Correct items in a series or paired ideas that do not have the same grammatical form by making them parallel. Put items at the same level in an outline or items in a list in parallel form.

✓ **34a** Making items in a series parallel

A list or series of equally important items should be parallel in grammatical structure.

▶ **The Census Bureau classifies people as employed if they receive payment for any kind of labor, are temporarily absent from their jobs, or ~~working~~ at least fifteen hours as**
 work
unpaid laborers in a family business.

Parallel construction can make a sentence more forceful and memorable.

▶ **My sister obviously thought that I was too young, ̰ignorant,**
 too
and ~~a troublemaker.~~
 too troublesome

Exercise 34.1 Identifying effective parallelism

Underline the parallel elements in the following passage.

I believe this government cannot endure permanently half slave and half free. I do not expect the Union to be dissolved—I do not expect the house to fall—but I do expect

34a
//

377

it will cease to be divided. It will become all one thing, or all the other. Either the opponents of slavery will arrest the further spread of it, and place it where the public mind shall rest in the belief that it is in the course of ultimate extinction; or its advocates will push it forward till it shall become alike lawful in all the states, old as well as new, North as well as South.

—ABRAHAM LINCOLN, speech at the Republican State Convention, Springfield, Illinois, June 16, 1858

34b Making paired ideas parallel

Paired ideas connected with a coordinating conjunction *(and, but, or, nor, for, so, yet)*, a correlative conjunction *(not only . . . but also, both . . . and, either . . . or, neither . . . nor)*, or a comparative expression *(as much as, more than, less than)* must have parallel grammatical form.

▶ Successful teachers must inspire ~~students~~ *both* students and ~~challenging them is also important.~~ *challenge their students*

▶ I dreamed not only of getting the girl but also of the *winning* gold medal.

▶ Many people find that having meaningful work is more important than *earning* high pay.

Exercise 34.2 Correcting faulty parallelism

Revise the following sentences to eliminate any faulty parallelism.

EXAMPLE

Newlywed couples need to learn to communicate effectively and budget in a wise manner.

Newlywed couples need to learn to communicate effectively and budget wisely.

1. *Impressionism* is a term that applies primarily to an art movement of the late nineteenth century, but the music of some composers of the era is also considered Impressionist.

IDENTIFY AND EDIT | Faulty Parallelism

// ✓

To avoid faulty parallelism, ask yourself these questions as you edit your writing:

? 1. Are the items in a series in parallel form?

> - The senator stepped to the podium, ~~an angry glance shooting toward~~ *glanced angrily at* her challenger, and began to refute his charges.

? 2. Are paired items in parallel form?

> - Her challenger, she claimed, ~~had~~ not only *had* accused her falsely of accepting illegal campaign contributions, but ~~his contributions were from illegal sources also.~~ *had accepted illegal contributions himself.*

? 3. Are the items in outlines and lists in parallel form?

FAULTY PARALLELISM	She listed four reasons for voters to send her back to Washington: 1. Ability to protect the state's interests 2. Her seniority on important committees 3. Works with members of both parties to get things done 4. Has a close working relationship with the President
REVISED	She listed four reasons for voters to send her back to Washington: 1. *Her ability* to protect the state's interests 2. *Her seniority* on important committees 3. *Her ability* to work with members of both parties to get things done 4. *Her* close working *relationship* with the President

34b
//

2. The early Impressionists include Edouard Manet, Claude Monet, and Mary Cassatt, and also among them are Edgar Degas and Camille Pissarro.

3. Impressionist composers include Claude Debussy, and Maurice Ravel is considered an Impressionist also.

4. Just as Impressionism in art challenged accepted conventions of color and line, in music the challenge from Impressionism was to accepted conventions of form and harmony.

5. Critics at first condemned both Impressionist artists and Impressionist music.

6. Women Impressionist painters included Mary Cassatt from the United States and Berthe Morisot, who was French.

7. Among Monet's goals were to observe the changing effects of light and color on a landscape, and he recorded his observations quickly.

8. To accomplish these goals he would create not just one painting but painted a series of them over the course of a day.

34c Repeating function words as needed

Function words such as prepositions *(to, for, by)* and subordinating conjunctions *(although, that)* give information about a word or indicate the relationships among words in a sentence. Although they can sometimes be omitted, include them whenever they signal a parallel structure that might be missed by readers.

▶ **The project has three goals: to survey the valley for**

 to
Inca-period sites, excavate a test trench at each site,
 ^

 to
and excavate one of those sites completely.
 ^

The writer added *to* to make it clear where one goal ends and the next begins.

Exercise 34.3 Chapter review: Correcting faulty parallelism

Edit the following passage so that parallel ideas are presented in parallel structures.

People can be classified as either Type A or Type B personalities depending on their competitiveness, how perfectionistic they are, and ability to relax. Type A people are often workaholics who not only drive themselves hard but also are driving others hard. In the workplace, employers often like Type A personalities because they tend to work quickly, punctually, and are efficient. However, because Type A people can characteristically also be impatient, verbally aggressive, or show hostility, they tend not to rise to top management positions as often as Type B people. Type A people also tend to be acutely aware of time, talking quickly, they interrupt when others are speaking, and try to complete other people's sentences. A Type B person in contrast takes the world in stride, walking and talking more slowly, and listens attentively. Type B people are better at dealing with stress and keep things in perspective, rather than being worried the way Type A people do.

People with traits that put them clearly on either end of the continuum between Type A and Type B should try to adopt characteristics of the opposite type. For example, to moderate some of their characteristic behaviors and reduce their risk of high blood pressure and heart disease, Type A people can use exercise, relaxation techniques, diet, and meditate. Understanding one's personality is half the battle, but implementing change takes time, discipline, and patience is needed.

35 Fixing Misplaced and Dangling Modifiers

For a sentence to make sense, its parts must be arranged appropriately. When a modifying word, phrase, or clause is misplaced or dangling, readers get confused.

35a mm

35a Fixing misplaced modifiers

Modifiers should usually come immediately before or after the words they modify. In the following sentence, the clause *after the police arrested them* modifies *protesters,* not *property.*

▶ *After the police had arrested them, the*
~~The~~ protesters were charged with destroying college
    ^

property. ~~after the police had arrested them.~~
        ^

Prepositional phrases used as adverbs are easy to misplace.

▶ *From the cabin's porch, the*
~~The~~ hikers watched the storm gathering force. ~~from the~~
    ^   ^

~~cabin's porch.~~

Misplaced Modifiers and Grammar Checkers

Some grammar checkers will reliably highlight split infinitives *(see 35d),* but they will only occasionally highlight other types of misplaced modifiers. One grammar checker, for example, missed the misplaced modifier *with a loud crash* in this sentence.

▶ **The valuable vase *with a loud crash* fell to the floor and broke into hundreds of pieces.**

35b Clarifying ambiguous modifiers

Adverbs can modify words that precede or follow them. When they are ambiguously placed, they are called **squinting modifiers**. The following revision shows that the objection is vehement, not the argument.

        vehemently
▶ **Historians who object to this account ~~vehemently~~ argue that**
                      ^

the presidency was never endangered.

Problems occur with limiting modifiers such as *only, even, almost, nearly,* and *just.* Check every sentence that includes one of these modifiers.

AMBIGUOUS   The restaurant *only offers* seafood for dinner.

REVISED   The restaurant *offers only* seafood for dinner.

     or

     The restaurant *offers* seafood *only* for dinner.

35c Moving disruptive modifiers

Separating grammatical elements that belong together, such as a subject and verb, with a lengthy modifying phrase or clause disrupts the connection between the two sentence elements.

    Despite their similar conceptions of the self,
▶ **Descartes and Hume, ~~despite their similar conceptions of the~~**
  ^

~~self,~~ deal with the issue of personal identity in different ways.

IDENTIFY AND EDIT | Misplaced Modifiers

mm

To avoid misplaced modifiers, ask yourself these questions:

? 1. Are all the modifiers close to the expressions they modify?

> *At the beginning of the Great Depression, people*
> ▪ ~~People~~ panicked and all tried to get their money out of the banks
>   ^
>
> at the same time, forcing many banks to close. ~~at the beginning~~
>
> ~~of the Great Depression.~~

? 2. Are any modifiers placed in such a way that they modify more than one expression? Pay particular attention to limiting modifiers such as *only, even,* and *just*.

>   *quickly*
> ▪ President Roosevelt declared a bank holiday, ~~quickly~~ helping to
>   ^   ^
>
> restore confidence in the nation's financial system.
>
> ▪ Congress enacted many programs to combat the Depression ~~only~~
>   *only*
> within the first one hundred days of Roosevelt's presidency.
>   ^

? 3. Do any modifiers disrupt the relationships among the grammatical elements of the sentence?

> *Given how entrenched segregation was at the time, the*
> ▪ ~~The~~ president's wife, Eleanor, was a surprisingly strong~~, given~~
>
> ~~how entrenched segregation was at the time,~~ advocate for racial
>
> justice in Roosevelt's administration.

35d

mm

35d Avoiding split infinitives

An **infinitive** couples the word *to* with the base form of a verb. In a **split infinitive,** one or more words intervene between *to* and the verb form. Avoid splitting infinitives with a modifier unless keeping them together results in an awkward or ambiguous construction.

In the example that follows, the modifier *successfully* should be moved. The modifier *carefully* should probably stay where it is, however, even though it splits the infinitive *to assess.*

                        successfully,

▸   To ~~successfully~~ complete this assignment, students have to
                                          ^

  carefully assess projected economic benefits.

Exercise 35.1 Repositioning misplaced modifiers

Edit the following sentences to correct any misplaced modifiers. If a sentence is acceptable as written, circle its number.

EXAMPLE

Although
~~Global warming has received, although~~ long a cause for
^

global warming has received
concern among scientists and environmentalists, scant
^

attention from some governments.

1. R. Buckminster Fuller developed during his career as an architect and engineer some of the most important design innovations of the twentieth century.
2. Fuller, a weak student, was expelled from Harvard.
3. Fuller resolved to dedicate his life to improving people's lives after suffering from a period of severe depression at the age of thirty-two.
4. Fuller intended his efficient designs to not waste precious resources.
5. Those who doubted Fuller often were proved wrong.
6. Fuller is known as the inventor of the geodesic dome to most people today.
7. The geodesic dome is a spherical structure that is both lightweight and economical, which Fuller developed in the late 1940s.
8. Today there are more than 300,000 domes around the world based on Fuller's designs.
9. His contention that wind generators on high-voltage transmission towers could supply much of the electricity the United States needs, policy makers have largely ignored.
10. His twenty-eight books have sold more than a million copies, in which he wrote about a range of social, political, cultural, and economic issues.

✓ 35e Fixing dangling modifiers

A **dangling modifier** is a descriptive phrase that implies an actor different from the sentence's subject. When readers try to connect the modifying phrase with the subject, the result may be humorous as well as confusing.

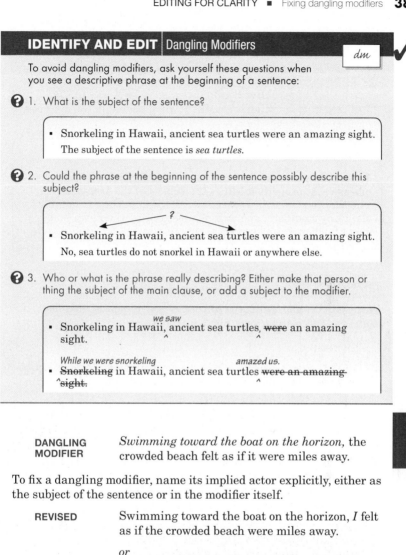

IDENTIFY AND EDIT | Dangling Modifiers

dm ✓

To avoid dangling modifiers, ask yourself these questions when you see a descriptive phrase at the beginning of a sentence:

❓ 1. What is the subject of the sentence?

> • Snorkeling in Hawaii, ancient sea turtles were an amazing sight.
> The subject of the sentence is *sea turtles*.

❓ 2. Could the phrase at the beginning of the sentence possibly describe this subject?

> ?
> • Snorkeling in Hawaii, ancient sea turtles were an amazing sight.
> No, sea turtles do not snorkel in Hawaii or anywhere else.

❓ 3. Who or what is the phrase really describing? Either make that person or thing the subject of the main clause, or add a subject to the modifier.

> _we saw_
> • Snorkeling in Hawaii, ancient sea turtles, ~~were~~ an amazing sight.
>
> _While we were snorkeling_ _amazed us._
> • ~~Snorkeling~~ in Hawaii, ancient sea turtles ~~were an amazing~~ _sight._

35e mm

DANGLING MODIFIER	*Swimming toward the boat on the horizon,* the crowded beach felt as if it were miles away.

To fix a dangling modifier, name its implied actor explicitly, either as the subject of the sentence or in the modifier itself.

REVISED	Swimming toward the boat on the horizon, *I* felt as if the crowded beach were miles away.

or

As *I swam* toward the boat on the horizon, the crowded beach seemed miles away.

Simply moving a dangling modifier won't fix the problem. To make the meaning clear, you must make the implied actor in the modifying phrase explicit.

DANGLING MODIFIER	*After struggling for weeks in the wilderness,* the town pleased them mightily.

REVISED   After struggling for weeks in the wilderness, *they* were pleased to come upon the town.

or

After *they had struggled* for weeks in the wilderness, the town appeared in the distance.

Dangling Modifiers and Grammar Checkers

Computer grammar checkers cannot distinguish a descriptive phrase that properly modifies the subject of the sentence from one that implies a different actor. As a result, they do not flag dangling modifiers, and writers must rely on their own judgment to identify and correct them.

Exercise 35.2   Correcting dangling modifiers

Edit the following sentences to correct any dangling modifiers. If a sentence is acceptable as is, circle its number.

EXAMPLE

Passengers   *that was entering the station*
~~Entering the station, passengers~~ waited to board the train.

1. Admired by many women artists as a pioneer in the mostly male art world, Georgia O'Keeffe lived and worked without regard to social conventions or artistic trends.
2. One of the most admired American artists of the twentieth century, her color-saturated images of cactus flowers, bleached bones, and pale skies are widely reproduced.
3. Growing up in Wisconsin, art was always important to her.
4. Defending her gifted student to the principal, one of her teachers said, "When the spirit moves Georgia, she can do more in a day than you or I can do in a week."
5. Without informing her, some of O'Keeffe's drawings were exhibited by Alfred Steiglitz at his 291 Gallery.
6. Marrying in 1924, O'Keeffe and Steiglitz enjoyed one of the most fruitful collaborations of the modernist era.
7. Despite critical and financial success in the 1920s, New York City did not provide suitable subject matter for her paintings.
8. Vacationing with a friend in the summer of 1929, O'Keeffe discovered the stark natural beauty of Taos, New Mexico.

Exercise 35.3 Chapter review: Editing for misplaced and dangling modifiers

Edit the following passage to eliminate any misplaced or dangling modifiers.

Henri Matisse and Pablo Picasso are considered often to have been the formative artists of the twentieth century. Although rivals for most of their careers, a traveling exhibit called "Matisse Picasso" exhibited their work side by side in museums in London, Paris, and New York.

Picasso's work may in comparison to Matisse's be more disturbing, and some say it is, in addition, more daring and experimental. Yet Matisse, too, with his use of vivid colors and distorted shapes, was a daring innovator.

Looking for similarities, the works of both artists suggest an underlying anxiety. Yet each in different ways responded to this anxiety. Matisse painted tranquil yet often emotionally charged domestic scenes, whereas Picasso fought his inner fears with often jarringly disquieting images, by contrast.

36 Using Coordination and Subordination Effectively

Coordination and subordination allow you to combine and develop ideas in ways that readers can follow and understand.

Coordination gives two or more ideas equal weight. To coordinate parts within a sentence, join them with a coordinating conjunction *(and, but, or, for, nor, yet,* or *so)*. To coordinate two or more sentences, use a comma plus a coordinating conjunction, or insert a semicolon.

▶ **The auditorium was huge, *and* the acoustics were terrible.**

▶ **The tenor bellowed the aria, *but* no one in the back could hear him.**

▶ **The student was *both* late for class *and* unprepared.**

▶ **Jones did not agree with her position on health care; *nevertheless,* he supported her campaign for office.**

Note: When a semicolon is used to coordinate two sentences, it is often followed by a conjunctive adverb such as *moreover, nevertheless, however, therefore,* or *subsequently.*

Subordination makes one idea depend on another. Less important ideas belong in subordinate clauses. Subordinate clauses start with a relative pronoun *(who, whom, that, which, whoever, whomever, whose)* or a subordinating conjunction such as *after, although, because, if, since, when,* or *where.*

▶ The blue liquid, *which will be added to the beaker later,* must be kept at room temperature.

▶ Christopher Columbus discovered the New World in 1492, *although he never understood just what he had found.*

▶ *After writing the opening four sections,* Wordsworth put the work aside for two years.

Note: Commas often set off subordinate ideas, especially when the subordinate clause or phrase opens the sentence. *(For more on using commas, see Chapter 49, pp. 509–22.)*

If you do not fix the following problems with coordination and subordination, your readers will have difficulty following your train of thought.

36a Using subordination, not coordination, for ideas of unequal importance

Coordination should be used only when two or more ideas deserve equal emphasis: *Smith supports bilingual education, but Johnson does not.* Subordination, not coordination, should be used to indicate information of secondary importance and to show its logical relation to the main idea.

                   When the
▶ ~~The~~ police arrived, ~~and~~ the burglars ran away.
    ^

36b Keeping major ideas in main clauses

Major ideas belong in main clauses, not in subordinate clauses or phrases. The writer revised the following sentence because the subject of the paper was definitions of literacy, not those who value literacy.

Highly valued by businesspeople as well as academics, literacy
▶ ~~Literacy, which~~ has been defined as the ability to talk
      ^

intelligently about many topics, ~~is highly valued by~~
                              ^

~~businesspeople as well as academics.~~

Exercise 36.1 | Using coordination and subordination

Combine the following sets of sentences, using coordination, subordination, or both to clarify the relationships among ideas.

EXAMPLE

France was a major player in Europe's late-nineteenth-century imperial expansion. It began the conquest of Vietnam in 1858. By 1883 it controlled the entire country.

France, a major player in Europe's late-nineteenth-century imperial expansion, began its conquest of Vietnam in 1858 and controlled the entire country by 1883.

1. France divided Vietnam into three administrative regions. This was before World War II.
2. Most Vietnamese opposed French rule. Many groups formed to regain the country's independence.
3. Vietnam remained a French-administered colony during World War II. It was under Japanese control, however, from 1940 to 1945.
4. By the end of the war, a Communist group called the Viet Minh had emerged as Vietnam's dominant nationalist organization. Ho Chi Minh (1890–1969) was the leader of the Viet Minh.
5. In 1945, the Viet Minh declared independence. They took control of northern Vietnam. The French, however, regained control of the south. The British helped the French.
6. The French reached an agreement with Ho Chi Minh in 1946. The agreement would have made Vietnam an autonomous country tied to France.
7. The agreement broke down. War started. The French wanted to reassert colonial control over all of Vietnam. Ho Chi Minh wanted total independence.
8. The United States supported the French. Russia and China supported the Viet Minh.

**36b
coord/sub**

9. The French suffered a major defeat at Dien Bien Phu in 1954.
    After that they realized they could not defeat the Viet Minh.
10. An agreement reached in Geneva left Vietnam divided into
    two regions. One region was the Communist-controlled north.
    The other region was the non-Communist south.

36c   Avoiding excessive subordination

When a sentence seems overloaded, separate it into two or more
sentences.

▶   **Big-city mayors, ~~who are supported by public funds,~~ should**

   be cautious about spending taxpayers' money for personal

   needs, ~~such as furnishing official residences,~~ especially

   when municipal budget shortfalls have caused extensive job

   They risk   by using public funds for furnishing official residences.
   layoffs, angering city workers and the general public.

Exercise 36.2   Avoiding inappropriate or excessive coordination
                    and subordination

Rewrite the numbered passages that follow to eliminate inappropriate or excessive coordination or subordination. Do not hesitate to
break up long strings of clauses into two or more sentences when it
seems appropriate to do so.

EXAMPLE

The Industrial Revolution triggered economic and social
upheavals, including changes in family structure, patterns
of work, and the distribution of wealth, and in 1848, in the
wake of these upheavals, the governments of France, Italy,
and several central European countries were all threatened
with revolution.

The Industrial Revolution triggered economic and social upheavals, including
changes in family structure, patterns of work, and the distribution of wealth.
In 1848, in the wake of these upheavals, the governments of France, Italy, and
several central European countries were all threatened with revolution.

1. During the early years of the Industrial Revolution, the many
    thousands of people who had left the countryside to move to Eu-

rope's fast-growing cities in search of work encountered poverty, disease, lack of sanitation, and exhausting, dangerous factory jobs, making cities breeding grounds for insurrection, and this threat of unrest increased after an international financial crisis in 1848 and the epidemic of bankruptcies and unemployment that followed it.

2. France's King Louis-Phillippe, hopelessly unpopular, abdicated the throne in February, and the country was thrown into a revolution in which citizens set up barricades in the narrow streets of Paris, restricting the movement of government troops.

3. Revolutionary fervor also took hold in Vienna, the capital of the Austrian Empire, and at the same time, nationalist forces gained strength in Hungary and other regions of the empire, prompting Hungarian nationalists to demand autonomy from Vienna and radicals in Prague to demand greater autonomy for the Empire's Slavic peoples.

4. By the middle of 1848, however, events had begun to turn against the revolutionaries, and the rulers of the Austrian Empire used divisions among the revolutionaries to reassert their power, and the Empire provided supplies and encouragement to Romanian nationalists who feared persecution in an independent Hungary.

36d Combining short, choppy sentences

Short sentences are easy to read, but several of them in a row can become so monotonous that meaning gets lost.

**36d
coord/sub**

CHOPPY   My cousin Jim is not an accountant. But he does my taxes every year. He suggests various deductions. These deductions reduce my tax bill considerably.

Put the idea you want to emphasize in the main clause, and use subordinate clauses and phrases for the other ideas. In this revision, the main clause is italicized.

REVISED   Even though he is not an accountant, *my cousin Jim does my taxes every year,* suggesting various deductions that reduce my tax bill considerably.

If a series of short sentences includes two major ideas of equal importance, use coordination for the two major ideas and subordinate the secondary information.

CHOPPY   Bilingual education is designed for children. The native language of these children is not English. Smith supports expanding bilingual education. Johnson does not support expanding bilingual education.

REVISED   Smith supports bilingual education for children
whose native language is not English; Johnson,
however, does not.

Exercise 36.3 Chapter review: Editing for coordination and
subordination

Edit the following passage to correct faulty coordination and subordination, eliminate choppy sentences, and reduce excessive coordination and subordination.

Germany and Italy were not always unified nations. For centuries they were divided into many city-states. They were also divided into many kingdoms, dukedoms, fiefdoms, and principalities. These city-states, kingdoms, dukedoms, fiefdoms, and principalities had maintained their autonomy for centuries.

Largely responsible for the unifications of Italy and Germany were two men. These men were Camillo di Cavour and Otto von Bismarck. Cavour became prime minister of the republic of Piedmont in 1852. Bismarck became chancellor of Prussia in 1862. Cavour was a practitioner of *realpolitik,* and *realpolitik* is a political policy based on the ruthless advancement of national interests. Bismarck was also a practitioner of *realpolitik.*

Cavour hoped to govern Piedmont in a way that would inspire other Italian states to join it to form a unified nation. Increasing the power of parliament, modernizing agriculture and industry, and building a railroad that encouraged trade with the rest of Europe, he also modernized the port of Genoa, updated the court system and installed a king, Victor Emmanuel, all of which made hopes for nationhood center on Piedmont. With the help of Napoleon III, Cavour engaged in a crafty political maneuver. Napoleon III was the emperor of France. Cavour induced Austria to attack Piedmont and then with French help defeated the Austrian armies, thus inspiring Modena and Tuscany to join Piedmont.

Bismarck used similar tactics in pursuit of unification as he prearranged French neutrality, and then he attacked and destroyed the Austrian army at Sadowa, and he eliminated Austrian influence in Prussia, and he paved the way for Prussian control of a large north German federation by 1867. Both men continued to use these tactics until they succeeded with the unification of Germany in 1871 and of Italy in 1879.

37 Varying Your Sentences

Enliven your prose by using a variety of sentence patterns.

Sentence Variety and Grammar Checkers

A computer grammar checker might flag a very long sentence, but it cannot decide whether the sentence is too long.

37a Varying sentence openings

When all the sentences in a passage begin with the subject, you risk losing your readers' attention. Vary your sentences by moving a modifier to the beginning. The modifier may be a single word, a phrase, or a clause.

▶ *Eventually,* Louis Armstrong's innovations on the trumpet ~~eventually~~ became the standard.

▶ *In at least two instances, this* ~~Armstrong's~~ money-making strategy backfired. ~~in at least two instances.~~

▶ *After Glaser became his manager,* Armstrong no longer had to worry about business. ~~after Glaser became his manager.~~

A **participial phrase** begins with an *-ing* verb *(driving)* or a past participle *(moved, driven)* and is used as a modifier. You can often move it to the beginning of a sentence for variety, but make sure that the phrase describes the explicit subject of the sentence, or you will end up with a dangling modifier *(see pp. 384–86).*

▶ *Pushing the other children aside,* Joseph~~, pushing the other children aside,~~ demanded that the teacher give him a cookie first.

393

Stunned by the stock market crash in 1929, many
▶ ~~Many~~ brokers, ~~stunned by the stock market crash in 1929,~~
  ^

committed suicide.

37b Varying sentence length and structure

Short, simple sentences (under ten words) will keep your readers alert
if they occur in a context that also includes longer, complex sentences.

As you edit your work, check to see if you have overused one kind
of sentence structure. Are most of your sentences short and simple?
If so, use subordination to combine some of them *(see p. 391).* However, if most of your sentences are long and complex, put at least one
of your ideas into a short, simple sentence. Your goal is to achieve a
good mix.

DRAFT   I dived quickly into the sea. I peered through my
        mask at the watery world. It turned darker. A
        school of fish went by. The distant light glittered
        on their bodies, and I stopped swimming. I waited
        to see if the fish might be chased by a shark. I was
        satisfied that there was no shark and continued
        down.

REVISED I dived quickly into the sea, peering through my
        mask at a watery world that turned darker as I de-
        scended. A school of fish went by, the distant light
        glittering on their bodies. I stopped swimming and
        waited. Perhaps the fish were being chased by a
        shark? Satisfied that there was no shark, I contin-
        ued down.

(For more on coordination and subordination, see pp. 387–92.)

Exercise 37.1 Varying sentence openings

Rewrite each sentence so that it does not begin with the subject.

EXAMPLE   **He would ask her to marry him in his own
          good time.**

          In his own good time, he would ask her to marry him.

1. Germany entered World War II better prepared than the Allies,
   as it had in World War I.
2. The Germans, gambling on a quick victory, struck suddenly in
   both 1914 and 1939.

3. The United States entered World War II in 1941.
4. World War II, fought with highly mobile armies, never developed into the kind of prolonged stalemate that had characterized World War I.
5. The productive power of the United States, swinging into gear by the spring of 1943, contributed to the Allied victory.

37c Including a few cumulative and periodic sentences

Cumulative sentences, which add a series of descriptive participial or absolute phrases to the basic subject-plus-verb pattern, make writing more forceful. They work best in personal essays and in writing in the humanities.

► **The motorcycle spun out of control,** *plunging down the ravine, crashing through the fence,* **and** *coming to rest on its side.*

Cumulative sentences can also add details.

► **Wollstonecraft headed for France,** *her soul determined to be free, her mind committed to reason, her heart longing for love.*

Another way to increase the force of your writing is to use a few periodic sentences. In a **periodic sentence,** the key word, phrase, or idea appears at the end.

► **In 1946 and 1947, young people turned away from the horrors of World War II and fell in love—with the jukebox.**

37c
vary

Exercise 37.2 Constructing cumulative sentences

Combine the sentences in each numbered item that follows to create cumulative sentences.

EXAMPLE

Europe suffered greatly in the fourteenth century. The Hundred Years War consumed France and England. Schism weakened Europe's strongest unifying institution, the Church. The Black Death swept away one-third of the population.

Europe suffered greatly in the fourteenth century, with the Hundred Years War consuming France and England; schism weakening the Church, Europe's strongest unifying institution; and the Black Death sweeping away one-third of the population.

1. The Black Death started in China around 1333. It spread to Europe over trade routes. It killed one-third of the population in two years. It proved to be one of the worst natural disasters in history.
2. It was a horrible time. Dead bodies were abandoned on the streets. People were terrified of one another. Cattle and livestock were left to roam the countryside.
3. It was everyone for him- or herself. Friends deserted friends. Husbands left wives. Parents even abandoned children.

Exercise 37.3 Constructing periodic sentences

Rewrite the sentences that follow so that the key words (underlined) appear at the end.

EXAMPLE

Prince Gautama achieved enlightenment while sitting in deep meditation under a Bo-tree after a long spiritual quest.

Sitting in deep meditation under a Bo-tree after a long spiritual quest, Prince Gautama achieved enlightenment.

1. The Indus River in Pakistan was home to one of the earliest civilizations in the world, as were the Nile River in Egypt, the Tigris and Euphrates rivers in Iraq, and the Yellow River in China.
2. In 1921, archeologists discovered the remains of Harappa, one of the two great cities of the Indus civilization, which until then was unknown to modern scholars.
3. The Indus civilization, which flourished from about 2500 to 1700 BCE, had two main centers, Harappa and another city, Mohenjo-Daro.

37d Trying an occasional inversion, a rhetorical question, or an exclamation

Most sentences are declarative and follow the normal sentence pattern of subject plus verb plus object. Occasionally, though, you might try using an inverted sentence pattern or another sentence type, such as a rhetorical question or an exclamation.

You can create an **inversion** by putting the verb before the subject.

▶ **Characteristic of Issey Miyake's work are bold design and original thinking.**

Because many inversions sound odd, they should be used infrequently and carefully.

Asking a question invites your readers to participate more actively in your work. Because you do not expect your audience to answer, this kind of question is called a **rhetorical question.**

▶ **Athletes injured at an early age too often find themselves without a job, a college degree, or their health. Is it any wonder that a few turn to drugs and alcohol?**

Rhetorical questions work best in the middle or at the end of a long, complicated passage. Sometimes they can help make a transition from one topic to another. Use them selectively, however, and avoid using them to begin an essay.

In academic writing, **exclamations** are rare. If you decide to use one, be sure that strong emotion is appropriate and worth risking a loss of credibility.

▶ **Wordsworth completed the thirteen-book *Prelude* in 1805, after seven years of hard work. Instead of publishing his masterpiece, however, he devoted himself to revising it—for forty-five years! The poem, in a fourteen-book version, was finally published in 1850, after he had died.**

Exercise 37.4 Chapter review: Revising for sentence variety

Revise the following passage for variety and emphasis using the strategies presented in this chapter.

> The United Nations was established in 1945. It was intended to prevent another world war. It began with twenty-one members. Nearly every nation in the world belongs to the United Nations today.
>
> The United Nations has four purposes, according to its charter. One purpose is to maintain international peace and security. Another is to develop friendly relations among nations. Another is to promote cooperation among nations in solving international problems and in promoting respect for human rights. Last is to provide a forum for harmonizing the actions of nations.
>
> All of the members of the United Nations have a seat in the General Assembly. The General Assembly considers numerous topics. These topics include globalization, AIDS, and pollution. Every member has a vote in the General Assembly.
>
> A smaller group within the United Nations has the primary responsibility for maintaining international peace and

37d
vary

security. This group is called the Security Council. The Security Council has five permanent members. They are China, France, the Russian Federation, the United Kingdom, and the United States. The Security Council also has ten elected members. The General Assembly elects the members of the Security Council. The elected members serve for two-year terms.

38 Choosing Active Verbs

Active verbs such as *run, shout, write,* and *think* are more direct and forceful than forms of the verb *be (am, are, is, was, were, been, being)* or passive-voice constructions. The more active your verbs, the stronger and clearer your writing will be.

Active Verbs and Grammar Checkers

Computer grammar checkers generally do not flag weak uses of the *be* verb. Some grammar checkers do flag most passive-voice sentences *(see Section 38b),* but their suggestions for revising them can sometimes make the sentence worse.

38a Considering alternatives to *be* verbs

Be does a lot of work in English.

BE AS A LINKING VERB

Germany *is* relatively poor in natural resources.

BE AS HELPING VERB

Macbeth *was* returning from battle when he met the three witches.

Be verbs are so useful that they get overworked. Watch for weak, roundabout sentences with *be* verbs, and consider replacing those verbs with active verbs.

demonstrates
▶ The mayor's refusal to meet with our group ~~is a~~
^

~~demonstration of~~ his lack of respect for us, as well as

for the environment.

Exercise 38.1 Editing for overuse of *be* verbs

In the following sentences, replace the *be* verbs with active verbs.

EXAMPLE
puzzled
The contradictory clues ~~were a puzzle to~~ the detective.
^

1. Historians are generally in agreement that the Egyptians were the inventors of sailing around 3000 BCE.
2. Many years passed before mariners were to understand that boats could sail upwind.
3. The invention of the keel was an improvement in sailboat navigation.
4. Steamships and transcontinental railroads were contributing factors in the disappearance of commercial sailing ships.
5. Today, either diesel or steam engines are the source of power for most ships.

38b Preferring the active voice when writing for a general audience

38b
act

Verbs can be in the active or passive voice. In the **active voice,** the subject of the sentence acts; in the **passive voice,** the subject is acted on.

ACTIVE The Senate finally passed the bill.

PASSIVE The bill was finally passed by the Senate.

The passive voice downplays the actors as well as the action, so much so that the actors are often left out of the sentence.

PASSIVE The bill was finally passed.

The active voice is more forceful, and readers usually want to know who or what does the acting.

PASSIVE Polluting chemicals were dumped into the river.

ACTIVE Industrial Products Corporation dumped polluting chemicals into the river.

NAVIGATING THROUGH COLLEGE AND BEYOND

Passive Voice

The passive voice is often used in scientific reports to keep the focus on the experiment and its results rather than on the experimenters.

▶ **The bacteria were treated carefully with nicotine and stopped reproducing.**

However, when the recipient of the action is more important than the doer of the action, the passive voice is appropriate.

▶ **After her heart attack, my mother was taken to the hospital.**

Mother and the fact that she was taken to the hospital are more important than who took her to the hospital.

Exercise 38.2 Editing to avoid the passive voice

Change the verbs in the following sentences from passive to active voice. In some cases, you may have to give an identity to an otherwise unidentified actor. Circle the number of any sentence that is already in the active voice or that is better left in its passive-voice form.

> EXAMPLE **The milk was spilled.**
>
> *Someone spilled the milk.*

1. The remote islands of Oceania were settled by Polynesian sailors beginning in the early first millennium CE.
2. Around 500, Hawaii was reached.
3. By about 900, settlers had reached Easter Island, the most remote island in Polynesia.
4. New Zealand, the largest Polynesian island, was also the last to be settled.
5. These immensely long voyages were probably made by families of settlers in open, double-hulled sailing canoes.

Exercise 38.3 Chapter review: Using active verbs

Minimize the use of the passive voice and the *be* verbs in the following paragraph.

> The idea of a lighter-than-air balloon was first conceived by inventors in the Middle Ages. Not until October 15, 1783, however, was Pilâtre de Rozier successful in ascending in a

hot-air balloon. Five weeks later, he and a companion were makers of history again, accomplishing the world's first aerial journey with a five-mile trip across the city of Paris. For the next century, lighter-than-air balloons were considered the future of human flight. Balloonists were able to reach heights of up to three miles and made long, cross-country journeys. In 1859, for instance, a balloonist was carried from St. Louis to Henderson, New York. Balloonists were unable, however, to control the movement of their craft. To overcome this deficiency, efforts were made to use hand-cranked propellers and even giant oars. The invention of the internal-combustion engine was what finally made it possible to create controllable, self-propelled balloons, which are known as airships. Hot air was replaced by hydrogen in the earliest airships. Hydrogen gas catches fire easily, however, and this was the doom of the airship as a major means of travel. In 1937, the German airship *Hindenburg* exploded as it was landing in New Jersey, a tragedy that was described by a radio announcer in a live broadcast. As a result, helium has replaced hydrogen in today's airships.

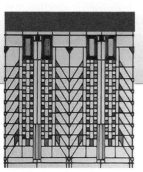

39 Using Appropriate Language

39a d

Language is appropriate when it fits your writing situation: your topic, purpose, and audience. You can develop a sense of audience through reading how other writers in the field handle your topic.

39a Avoiding slang, regional expressions, and nonstandard English

In college writing, slang terms and the tone that goes with them should be avoided.

SLANG   In *Heart of Darkness,* we hear a lot about a *dude* named Kurtz, but we don't see the *guy* much.

REVISED   In *Heart of Darkness,* Marlow, the narrator, talks continually about Kurtz, but we meet Kurtz himself only at the end.

Like slang, regional and nonstandard expressions such as *y'all, hisself,* and *don't be doing that* may work fine in conversation but not in college writing.

39b Using an appropriate level of formality

College writing assignments usually call for a style that avoids the extremes of the stuffy and the casual, the pretentious and the chatty. Revise passages that veer toward one extreme or the other.

PRETENTIOUS	Romantic lovers are characterized by a preoccupation with a deliberately restricted set of qualities in the love object that are viewed as means to some ideal end.
REVISED	People in love see what they want to see, usually by idealizing the beloved.

39c Avoiding jargon

When specialists communicate with each other, they often use technical language. **Jargon** is the inappropriate use of specialized or technical language. You should not use language that is appropriate for specialists when you are writing for a general audience.

JARGON	Pegasus Technologies developed a Web-based PSP system to support standard off-line brands in meeting their loyalty-driven marketing objectives via the social networking space.
REVISED	Pegasus Technologies developed a system that helps businesses create networking sites to run promotions for their customers.

If you must use technical terms when writing for nonspecialists, be sure to provide definitions.

▶ **Armstrong's innovative singing style featured "scat," a technique that combines "nonsense syllables [with] improvised melodies" (Robinson 515).**

39d Avoiding euphemisms and doublespeak

Euphemisms substitute nice-sounding words like *correctional facility* and *passing away* for such harsh realities as *prison* and *death.* **Doublespeak** is used to obscure facts and evade responsibility.

DOUBLESPEAK   Pursuant to the environmental protection
regulations enforcement policy of the Bureau
of Natural Resources, special management
area land use permit issuance procedures have
been instituted.

REVISED   The Bureau of Natural Resources has established procedures for issuing land use permits.

Avoid using words that evade or deceive.

Exercise 39.1 Editing for informal language, pretentious language,
jargon, and euphemisms

Edit the following sentences so that they are suitable for college writing.

1. With the invention of really cool steel engraving and mechanical printing presses in the nineteenth century, publishers could
make tons of books like practically overnight.

2. France was the womb of nineteenth-century realism, a fecund
literary land that gave birth to those behemoths of realism
Stendhal, Balzac, and Flaubert.

3. Flaubert really hated the bourgeoisie because he thought they
never thought about anything but cash, stuff, and looking good
in front of others.

4. Flaubert's *Madame Bovary* is the story of this really bored pro-
vincial chick who dreams of being a fancy lady, cheats on her
husband, and then does herself in.

5. Intense class antagonisms, combined with complex currents of
historical determinism, extending back into the ancient traditions of serfdom and the czar, may precisely index the factors
constitutive of the precipitant flowering of the Russian novel in
the nineteenth century.

6. The present writer's former belief that nineteenth-century literature is incomprehensible is no longer operational.

39e

39e Avoiding biased or sexist language

Biased or sexist language can undermine your credibility with readers.

1. Biased language

Always review your writing to see if it is unintentionally biased. Be
on the lookout for stereotypes, rigid, unexamined generalizations
that demean, ignore, or patronize people on the basis of gender, race,

religion, national origin, ethnicity, physical ability, sexual orientation, occupation, or any other human condition. Revise for inclusiveness.

For example, do not assume that Irish Catholics have large families.

>   *The*   *an*   *Catholic family with*
> ▶ ~~Although the~~ Browns are Irish ~~Catholics, there are only~~ two
>
> children. ~~in the family.~~

In addition, remember that a positive stereotype is still an overgeneralization, which listeners hear as patronizing, that is, as coming from someone who believes she or he is superior.

>   *We*
> ▶ ~~Because Asian students are whizzes at math, we~~ all wanted
>
> *math whizzes*
>   ~~them~~ in our study group.

2. The generic use of *he* or *man*

Traditionally, the pronoun *he* and the noun *man* have been used to represent either gender. Today, however, the use of *he* or *man* or any other masculine noun to represent people in general is considered offensive.

BIASED	Everybody had his way.
REVISED	We all had our way.
BIASED	It's every man for himself.
REVISED	All of us have to save ourselves.

Follow these simple principles to avoid gender bias in your writing:

- Replace terms that indicate gender with their gender-free equivalents:

No	Yes
chairman	chair, chairperson
congressman	representative, member of Congress
forefathers	ancestors
man, mankind	people, humans, humankind
man-made	artificial
policeman	police officer
spokesman	spokesperson

- Refer to men and women in parallel ways: *ladies and gentlemen, men and women, husband and wife.*

> **BIASED**   D. H. Lawrence and Mrs. Woolf met each other, but Lawrence did not like the Bloomsbury circle that revolved around Virginia.

> **REVISED**   D. H. Lawrence and Virginia Woolf met each other, but Lawrence did not like the Bloomsbury circle that revolved around Woolf.

- Replace the masculine pronouns *he, him, his,* and *himself* when they are being used generically to refer to both women and men. One way to replace masculine pronouns is to use the plural.

> ▶ ~~Each~~ **Senators** ~~senator~~ returned to ~~his district~~ **their districts** during the break.

> ▶ ~~A lawyer needs~~ **Lawyers need** to be frank with ~~his~~ **their** clients.

Some writers alternate *he* and *she,* and *him* and *her.* This strategy is effective but distracting. The constructions *his or her* and *he or she* are acceptable as long as they are not used more than once in a sentence.

> ▶ **Each student in the psychology class was to choose a book, ~~according to his or her interests, to~~ read ~~the book~~ it overnight, ~~to~~ do without ~~his or her normal~~ sleep, ~~to~~ write a short summary of ~~what he or she had read,~~ the book the next morning, and then ~~to~~ see whether he or she dreamed about the book the following night.**

The constructions *his/her* and *s/he* are not acceptable.

39e
d

Note: Using the neuter impersonal pronoun *one* can sometimes help you avoid masculine pronouns, but it can make your writing sound stuffy.

STUFFY The American creed holds that if *one* works hard, *one* will succeed in life.

REVISED The American creed holds that those who work hard will succeed in life.

(For more on editing to avoid the generic use of he, him, his, *or* himself, *see Chapter 46, pp. 466–68.)*

3. Sexist language

Avoid language that demeans or stereotypes women and men. Women are usually the explicit targets. For example, many labels and clichés imply that women are not as able or mature as men. Consider the meaning of words and phrases like *the fair sex, acting like a girl, poetess,* and *coed.*

Exercise 39.2 Editing to eliminate biased language

Identify the biased language in each of the following sentences, and rewrite each sentence using the suggestions in Section 39e.

EXAMPLE

    flight attendants
Because ~~stewardesses~~ travel so much, child care is an issue
        ^
for them.

1. Man is fast approaching a population crisis.
2. Each of us must do his part to reduce the production of greenhouse gases.
3. Every housewife should encourage her children to make recycling a habit, and every corporate chief executive officer should encourage his employees to carpool or take mass transit whenever possible.
4. Congressmen should make conservation and environmental protection legislative priorities.
5. If he tried, the average motorist could help reduce our dependence on oil.

Exercise 39.3 Chapter review: Editing for appropriate language

Edit the following passage to make the language appropriate for college writing.

The writer of novels Henry James had many illustrious forefathers. His grandfather William traversed the Atlantic in 1789 with little more than a Latin grammar book and a desire to see the battlefields of the Revolutionary War. When William James met his maker in 1832, he left an estate worth $3 million, or about $100 million in today's cash. This little something was to be divided among eleven children and his better half, Catherine Barber James. William's fourth kid, Henry, who is often referred to as the elder Henry James so's that he is not confused with the novelist, became a lecturer and writer on metaphysics. His big thing was the doctrines of the Swedish mystic Emanuel Swedenborg. Although some thought the elder Henry James a few plates short of a picnic, his work was very well known and influential during his lifetime.

40 Using Exact Language

To convey your meaning clearly, you need to choose the right words. Is your choice of words as precise as it should be?

40a d

40a Choosing words with suitable connotations

Words have denotations and connotations. **Denotations** are the primary meanings of the word. **Connotations** are the feelings and images associated with a word.

As you revise, replace any word whose connotation does not fit what you want to say.

> *demand*
> ► The players' union should ~~request~~ that the NFL amend its
> ^
> pension plan.

If you cannot think of a more suitable word, consult a print or online thesaurus for **synonyms**—words with similar meanings. Keep in mind, however, that most words have connotations that allow them to work in some contexts but not in others. To find out more about a synonym's connotations, look the word up in a dictionary. *(For help using the dictionary, see pp. 412–14.)*

Exercise 40.1 Choosing words with suitable connotations

Use a dictionary or thesaurus to list as many synonyms as you can for each of the underlined words in the passages that follow. Discuss why you think the authors chose the underlined words.

1. Space and time capture the imagination like no other scientific subject. . . . They form the arena of reality, the very fabric of the cosmos. Our entire existence—everything we do, think, and experience—takes place in some region of space during some interval of time. Yet science is still struggling to understand what space and time actually are.

   —BRIAN BREENE, *The Fabric of the Cosmos*

2. On Waverly Street, everybody knew everybody else. It was only one short block, after all—a narrow strip of patched and repatched pavement, bracketed between a high stone cemetery wall at one end and the commercial clutter of Govans Road at the other. The trees were elderly maples with lumpy, bulbous trunks. The squat clapboard houses seemed mostly front porch.

   —ANNE TYLER, *Saint Maybe*

40b Including specific and concrete words

Specific words name particular kinds of things or items, such as *pines* or *college sophomores*.

Concrete words name things we can sense by touch, taste, smell, hearing, and sight, such as *velvet* or *sweater*.

By creating images that appeal to the senses, specific and concrete words make writing more precise.

VAGUE The trees were affected by the bad weather.

PRECISE The tall pines shook in the gale.

As you edit, develop specific and concrete details. Also check for overused, vague terms—such as *factor, thing, good, nice,* and *interesting*—and replace them with more specific and concrete words.

               crimes   committed.
▶ The protesters were charged with ~~things~~ they never ~~did.~~

| **Exercise 40.2** | Including specific and concrete words |

Draw on your own knowledge, experience, and imagination to re-write the following paragraph with invented details described in specific and concrete language.

EXAMPLE

Niagara Falls is an awe-inspiring sight.

The waters of the Niagara River flow over the edge of the half-mile-wide, crescent-shaped Horseshoe Falls and plunge with a roar to the bottom of the cataract two hundred feet below.

    Last summer I worked as an intern at a company in a field that interests me. The work was hard and the hours were long, but I gained a lot of experience. At first I was assigned only routine office work. As I learned more about the business, however, my employers began to give me more interesting tasks. By the end of the summer I was helping out on several high-priority projects. My employers liked my work and offered me another internship for the following summer.

40c Using standard idioms

Idioms are customary forms of expression. They are not always logical and are hard to translate. Often they involve selecting the right preposition. If you are not sure which preposition to use, look up the main word in a dictionary.

    Some verbs, called **phrasal verbs,** include a preposition to make their idiomatic meaning complete:

- Henry *made up* with Gloria.
- Henry *made off* with Gloria.
- Henry *made out* with Gloria.

(For a list of common idiomatic expressions, see Chapter 48, pp. 502–3. For more help with phrasal verbs and idiomatic expressions, see Chapter 48, pp. 500–1.)

40d Avoiding clichés

A **cliché** is an overworked expression that no longer creates a vivid picture in a reader's imagination. Rephrase clichés in plain language.

                                    made some good observations.

▶   **The speaker at our conference ~~hit the nail on the head.~~**
                                             ^

**40d
d**

The list that follows gives some clichés to avoid.

Examples of Clichés

agony of suspense	depths of despair	rise to the
beat a hasty	few and far	occasion
retreat	between	sadder but wiser
beyond the	flat as a pancake	sink or swim
shadow of a	green with envy	smart as a whip
doubt	heave a sigh of	sneaking
blind as a bat	relief	suspicion
calm, cool, and	hit the nail on the	straight and
collected	head	narrow
cold, hard facts	last but not least	tired but happy
cool as a	the other side of	tried and true
cucumber	the coin	ugly as sin
dead as a	pass the buck	untimely death
doornail	pretty as a	white as a sheet
deep, dark	picture	worth its weight
secret	quick as a flash	in gold

40e Using suitable figures of speech

Figures of speech make writing vivid by supplementing the literal meaning of words. A **simile** is a comparison that contains the word *like* or *as*.

► **Hakim's smile was like sunshine after a rainstorm.**

A **metaphor** is an implied comparison. It treats one thing or action as if it were something else.

► **The senator's speech rolled along a familiar highway, past the usual landmarks: taxes and foreign policy.**

Because it is compressed, a metaphor is often more forceful than a simile.

Only compatible comparisons make prose vivid. Be careful not to mix metaphors.

MIXED His presentation of the plan was such a *well-constructed tower of logic* that we immediately decided *to come aboard*.

REVISED His clear presentation of the plan immediately convinced us to come aboard.

| **Exercise 40.3** | Recognizing figures of speech |

Identify and explain the figures of speech (simile or metaphor) in the following passages.

EXAMPLE

A miss is as good as a mile.

This expression is a simile suggesting that an error is an error, whether small ("a miss") or large ("a mile").

1. Her voice is full of money.
   —F. SCOTT FITZGERALD, *The Great Gatsby*

2. America is woven of many strands; I would recognize them and let it so remain. . . . Our fate is to become one, and yet many.
   —RALPH ELLISON, *Invisible Man*

3. Our military forces are one team—in the game to win regardless of who carries the ball.
   —OMAR BRADLEY, testimony to the Committee on Armed Services, House of Representatives, October 19, 1949

4.   We are such stuff
   As dreams are made on, and our little life
   Is rounded with a sleep.
   —WILLIAM SHAKESPEARE, *The Tempest,* IV, i, 149

✓ **40f** Avoiding the misuse of words

**40f
d**

Avoid mistakes in your use of new terms and unfamiliar words. Consult a dictionary whenever you include an unfamiliar word in your writing.

exhibited
The aristocracy ~~exuded~~ numerous vices, including greed
^

licentiousness.
and ~~license.~~
^

| **Exercise 40.4** | Avoiding the misuse of words |

In the following sentences, replace any of the underlined words that are misused with a word with an appropriate denotation, and circle those that are properly used. For help, consult a dictionary or the Glossary of Usage *(pp. 414–24).*

EXAMPLE

           complement
Computer software and computer hardware ~~compliment~~
                   ^
each other.
~~one another.~~
  ^

1. The nineteenth-century Englishman Charles Babbage was probably the first person to conceive of a general-purpose computing machine, but the ability to build one <u>alluded</u> him.

2. Because she was able to <u>imply</u> the kinds of instructions that would work with Babbage's machine, some historians <u>cite</u> Ada Lovelace, daughter of the poet Byron, as the first computer programmer.

3. <u>Incredulous</u> as it may seem, the first general-purpose digital electronic computer was 100 feet long and 10 feet high, but it had less computing power than one of today's inexpensive laptop computers.

4. The U.S. government was the <u>principle</u> source of funding for some of the most important advances in computing after World War II.

5. Without the invention of the transistor, today's small, powerful computing devices would not have been <u>plausible</u>.

6. Each year a new <u>devise</u> comes on the market with amazing capabilities.

40g Using the dictionary

A standard desk dictionary provides definitions of words as well as information about usage, the correct spellings of important place names, the official names of countries with their areas and populations, the names of capital cities, biographical entries, lists of abbreviations and symbols, names and locations of colleges and universities, titles and correct forms of address, and conversion tables for weights and measures. Dictionaries of varying size also appear in most word-processing software and on Web sites. *(For ESL dictionaries, see Chapter 48, p. 488.)*

  An entry from the *Random House Webster's College Dictionary* follows. The labels point to the kinds of information discussed in the following sections.

Phonetic symbols showing pronunciation.

Word endings and grammatical abbreviations.

Dictionary entry.

com•pare (kəmpâr´), *v.*, **-pared, -par • ing,** *n.* —*v.t.* **1.** to examine (two or more objects, ideas, people, etc.) in order to note similarities and differences. **2.** to consider or describe as similar; liken: "*Shall I compare thee to a summer's day?*" **3.** to form or display the degrees of comparison of (an adjective or adverb). —*v.i.* **4.** to be worthy of comparison: *Whose plays can compare with Shakespeare's?* **5.** to be in similar standing; be alike: *This recital compares with the one he gave last year.* **6.** to appear in quality, progress, etc., as specified: *Their development compares poorly with that of neighbor nations.* **7.** to make comparisons. —*n.* **8.** comparison: *a beauty beyond compare.* —*Idiom.* **9. compare notes,** to exchange views, ideas, or impressions. [1375–1425; late ME < OF *comperer* < L *comparāre* to place together, match, v. der. of *compar* alike, matching (see COM-, PAR)] —**com•par´er,** *n.* —**Usage.** A traditional rule states that COMPARE should be followed by *to* when it points out likenesses between unlike persons or things: *she compared his handwriting to knotted string.* It should be followed by *with,* the rule says, when it examines two entities of the same general class for similarities or differences: *She compared his handwriting with mine.* This rule, though sensible, is not always followed, even in formal speech and writing. Common practice is to use *to* for likeness between members of different classes: *to compare a language to a living organism.* Between members of the same category, both *to* and *with* are used: *Compare the Chicago of today with* (or *to*) *the Chicago of the 1890s.* After the past participle COMPARED, either *to* or *with* is used regardless of the type of comparison.

Definition as noun (*n.*).

Etymology.

Definitions as transitive verb (*v.t.*).

Definitions as intransitive verb (*v.i.*).

Special meaning.

Usage note.

1. Spelling, word division, and pronunciation

Entries in a dictionary are listed in alphabetical order according to their standard spelling. In the *Random House Webster's College Dictionary,* the verb *compare* is entered as **com•pare.** The dot separates the word into its two syllables.

Phonetic symbols in parentheses following the entry show its correct pronunciation. The second syllable of *compare* receives the greater stress when you pronounce the word correctly: you say "com-PARE." In this dictionary, an accent mark (´) appears after the syllable that receives the primary stress.

Plurals of nouns are usually not given if they are formed by adding an *s,* unless the word is foreign *(gondolas, dashikis).* Irregular plurals—such as *children* for *child*—are noted.

Some dictionaries list alternate spellings, always giving the preferred spelling first or placing the full entry under the preferred spelling only.

40g d

2. Word endings and grammatical labels

The abbreviation *v.* immediately after the pronunciation tells you that *compare* is most frequently used as a verb. The next abbreviation, *n.,* indicates that *compare* can sometimes function as a noun, as in the phrase *beyond compare.* Other common abbreviations for grammatical terms include *adj.* (adjective), *adv.* (adverb), *pron.* (pronoun), *pl.* (plural), *sing.* (singular), and *poss.* (possessive).

The **-pared** shows the simple past and past participle form of the verb; the present participle form, **-par • ing**, follows, indicating that *compare* drops the final *e* when *-ing* is added.

3. Definitions and word origins
In the sample entry on page 413, the definitions begin after the abbreviation *v.t.,* which indicates that the first three meanings relate to *compare* as a transitive verb. A little further down in the entry, *v.i.* introduces definitions of *compare* as an intransitive verb. Next, after *n.,* comes the definition of *compare* as a noun. Finally, the word *Idiom* signals a special meaning not included in the previous definitions.

Included in most dictionary entries is an **etymology**—a brief history of the word's origins—set off in brackets. There we see the date of the first known use of the word in English together with the earlier words from which it is derived. *Compare* came into English between 1375 and 1425 and was derived from the Old French word *comperer,* which came from Latin.

4. Usage
Some main entries in the dictionary conclude with examples of and comments about the common usage of the word.

41 Glossary of Usage

The following words and expressions are often confused, misused, or considered nonstandard. This list will help you use these words precisely.

a, an   Use *a* with a word that begins with a consonant sound: *a cat, a dog, a one-sided argument, a house.* Use *an* with a word that begins with a vowel sound: *an apple, an X-ray, an honor* (*h* is silent).

accept, except   *Accept* is a verb meaning "to receive willingly": *Please accept my apologies. Except* is a preposition meaning "but": *Everyone except Julie saw the film.*

adapt, adopt   *Adapt* means "to adjust or become accustomed to": *They adapted to the customs of their new country. Adopt* means "to take as one's own": *We adopted a puppy.*

advice, advise   *Advice* is a noun; *advise* is a verb: *I took his advice and deeply regretted it. I advise you to disregard it, too.*

affect, effect   As a verb, *affect* means "to influence": *Inflation affects our sense of security.* As a noun, *affect* means "a feeling or an emotion": *To study affect, psychologists probe the unconscious.* As a noun, *effect* means "result": *Inflation is one of the many effects of war.* As a verb, *effect* means "to make or accomplish": *Inflation has effected many changes in the way we spend money.*

agree to, agree with   *Agree to* means "consent to"; *agree with* means "be in accord with": *They will agree to a peace treaty, even though they do not agree with each other on all points.*

ain't   A slang contraction for *is not, am not,* or *are not, ain't* should not be used in formal writing or speech.

all ready, already   *All ready* means "fully prepared"; *already* means "previously": *We were all ready to go out when we discovered that Jack had already ordered a pizza.*

all right, alright   *Alright* is nonstandard. Use *all right. He told me it was all right to miss class tomorrow.*

all together, altogether   *All together* expresses unity or common location; *altogether* means "completely," often in a tone of ironic understatement: *At the casino, it was altogether startling to see so many kinds of gambling all together in one place.*

allude, elude, refer to   *Allude* means "to refer indirectly": *He alluded to his miserable adolescence. Elude* means "to avoid" or "to escape from": *She eluded the police for nearly two days.* Do not use *allude* to mean "to refer directly": *The teacher referred* [not *alluded*] *to page 468 in the text.*

almost, most   *Almost* means "nearly." *Most* means "the greater part of." Do not use *most* when you mean *almost: He wrote to me about almost* [not *most*] *everything he did. He told his mother about most things he did.*

a lot   *A lot* is always two words. Do not use *alot.*

A.M., AM, a.m.   These abbreviations mean "before noon" when used with numbers: *6 A.M., 6 a.m.* Be consistent, and do not use the abbreviations as a synonym for *morning: In the morning* [not *a.m.*], *the train is full.*

among, between   Generally, use *among* with three or more nouns, and *between* with two: *The distance between Boston and Knoxville is a thousand miles. The desire to quit smoking is common among those who have smoked for a long time.*

amoral, immoral   *Amoral* means "neither moral nor immoral" and "not caring about moral judgments"; *immoral* means "morally wrong": *Unlike such amoral natural disasters as earthquakes and hurricanes, war is intentionally violent and therefore immoral.*

amount, number   Use *amount* for quantities you cannot count; use *number* for quantities you can count: *The amount of oil left underground in*

41
usage

the United States is a matter of dispute, but the number of oil companies losing money is tiny.

an *See* a, an.

anxious, eager *Anxious* means "fearful": *I am anxious before a test.* *Eager* signals strong interest or desire: *I am eager to be done with that exam.*

anymore, any more *Anymore* means "no longer." *Any more* means "no more." Both are used in negative contexts: *I do not enjoy dancing anymore. I do not want any more peanut butter.*

anyone/any one, anybody/any body, everyone/every one, everybody/every body *Anyone, anybody, everyone,* and *everybody* are indefinite pronouns: *Anybody can make a mistake.* When the pronoun *one* or the noun *body* is modified by the adjective *any* or *every,* the words should be separated by a space: *A good mystery writer accounts for every body that turns up in the story.*

as Do not use *as* as a synonym for *since, when,* or *because: I told him he should visit Alcatraz since* [not *as*] *he was going to San Francisco. When* [not *as*] *I complained about the meal, the cook said he did not like to eat there himself. Because* [not *as*] *we asked her nicely, our teacher decided to cancel the exam.*

as, like In formal writing, avoid the use of *like* as a conjunction: *He sneezed as if* [not *like*] *he had a cold. Like* is perfectly acceptable as a preposition that introduces a comparison: *She handled the reins like an expert.*

at Avoid the use of *at* to complete the notion of *where:* not *Where is Michael at?* but *Where is Michael?*

awful, awfully Use *awful* and *awfully* to convey the emotion of terror or wonder (awe-full): *The vampire flew out the window with an awful shriek.* In writing, do not use *awful* to mean "bad" or *awfully* to mean "very" or "extremely."

awhile, a while *Awhile* is an adverb: *Stay awhile with me* [but not *for awhile with me*]. *A while* consists of an article and a noun and can be used with or without a preposition: *A while ago I found my red pencil. I was reading under the tree for a while.*

bad, badly *Bad* is an adjective used after a linking verb such as feel; *badly* is an adverb: *She felt bad about playing the piano badly at the recital.*

being as, being that Do not use *being as* or *being that* as synonyms for *since* or *because: Because* [not *being as*] *the mountain was there, we had to climb it.*

belief, believe *Belief* is a noun meaning "conviction"; *believe* is a verb meaning "to have confidence in the truth of": *Her belief that lying was often justified made it hard for us to believe her story.*

beside, besides *Beside* is a preposition meaning "next to" or "apart from": *The ski slope was beside the lodge. She was beside herself with joy.* Be-

sides is both a preposition and an adverb meaning "in addition to" or "except for": *Besides a bicycle, he will need a tent and a pack.*

better   Avoid using *better* in expressions of quantity: *Crossing the continent by train took more than* [not *better than*] *four days.*

between   *See* among, between.

bring, take   Use *bring* when an object is being moved toward you, and *take* when it is being moved away: *Please bring me a new disk, and take the old one home with you.*

but that, but what   In expressions of doubt, avoid writing *but that* or *but what* when you mean *that: I have no doubt that* [not *but that*] *you can learn to write well.*

can, may   *Can* refers to ability; *may* refers to possibility or permission: *I see that you can Rollerblade without crashing into people; nevertheless, you may not Rollerblade on the promenade.*

can't hardly   This double negative is ungrammatical and self-contradictory: *I can* [not *can't*] *hardly understand algebra. I can't understand algebra.*

capital, capitol   *Capital* can refer to wealth or resources or to a city; *capitol* refers to a building where lawmakers meet: *Protesters traveled to the state capital to converge on the capitol steps.*

censor, censure   *Censor* means "to remove or suppress material"; *censure* means "to reprimand formally": *The Chinese government has been censured by the U.S. Congress for censoring Web access.*

cite, sight, site   The verb *cite* means "to quote or mention": *Be sure to cite all your sources in your bibliography.* As a noun, the word *sight* means "view": *It was love at first sight. Site* is a noun meaning "a particular place" as well as "a location on the Internet."

compare to, compare with   Use *compare to* to point out similarities between two unlike persons or things: *She compared his singing to the croaking of a wounded frog.* Use *compare with* for differences or likenesses between two things in the same general category: *Compare Shakespeare's* Antony and Cleopatra *with Dryden's* All for Love.

complement, compliment   *Complement* means "to go well with": *I consider sauerkraut the perfect complement to sausages. Compliment* means "praise": *She received many compliments on her thesis.*

conscience, conscious   The noun *conscience* means "a sense of right and wrong": *His conscience bothered him.* The adjective *conscious* means "awake" or "aware": *I was conscious of a presence in the room.*

continual, continuous   *Continual* means "repeated regularly and frequently": *She continually checked her computer for new e-mail. Continuous* means "extended or prolonged without interruption": *The car alarm made a continuous wail in the night.*

41 usage

could care less *Could care less* is nonstandard; use *does not care at all* instead: *She does not care at all about her physics homework.*

could of, should of, would of Avoid these ungrammatical forms of *could have, should have,* and *would have.*

criteria, criterion *Criteria* is the plural form of the Latin word *criterion,* meaning "standard of judgment": *The criteria are not very strict. The most important criterion is whether you can do the work.*

data *Data* is the plural form of the Latin word *datum,* meaning "fact." Although *data* is often used informally as a singular noun, in writing, treat *data* as a plural noun: *The data indicate that recycling has gained popularity.*

differ from, differ with *Differ from* expresses a lack of similarity; *differ with* expresses disagreement: *The ancient Greeks differed less from the Persians than we often think. Aristotle differed with Plato on some important issues.*

different from, different than Use *different from: The east coast of Florida is very different from the west coast.*

discreet, discrete *Discreet* means "tactful" or "prudent"; *discrete* means "separate" or "distinct": *What's a discreet way of telling them that these are two discrete issues?*

disinterested, uninterested *Disinterested* means "impartial": *We expect members of a jury to be disinterested. Uninterested* means "indifferent" or "unconcerned": *Most people today are uninterested in alchemy.*

don't, doesn't *Don't* is the contraction for *do not* and is used with *I, you, we, they,* and plural nouns; *doesn't* is the contraction for *does not* and is used with *he, she, it, one* and singular nouns: *You don't know what you're talking about. He doesn't know what you're talking about either.*

each and every Use one of these words or the other but not both: *Every cow came in at feeding time. Each one had to be watered.*

each other, one another Use *each other* in sentences involving two subjects and *one another* in sentences involving more than two: *Husbands and wives should help each other. Classmates should share ideas with one another.*

eager *See* anxious, eager.

effect *See* affect, effect.

either, neither Both *either* and *neither* are singular: *Neither of the two girls has played the game. Either of the two boys is willing to show you the way home. Either* has an intensive use that *neither* does not, and when it is used as an intensive, *either* is always negative: *She told him she would not go either.* (For [either . . . or] *and* [neither . . . nor] *constructions, see p. 446.*)

elicit, illicit The verb *elicit* means "to draw out"; the adjective *illicit* means "unlawful": *The detective was unable to elicit any information about other illicit activities.*

elude *See* allude, elude, refer to.

emigrate, immigrate *Emigrate* means "to move away from one's country": *My father emigrated from Vietnam in 1980. Immigrate* means "to move to another country and settle there": *Father immigrated to the United States.*

eminent, imminent, immanent *Eminent* means "celebrated" or "well known": *Many eminent Victorians were melancholy. Imminent* means "about to happen" or "about to come": *In August 1939, many Europeans sensed that war was imminent. Immanent* refers to something invisible but dwelling throughout the world: *Medieval Christians believed that God's power was immanent through the universe.*

etc. The abbreviation *etc.* stands for the Latin *et cetera,* meaning "and others" or "and other things." Because *and* is included in the abbreviation, do not write *and etc.* In a series, a comma comes before *etc.,* just as it would before the coordinating conjunction that closes a series: *He brought string, wax, paper, etc.* In most college writing, it is better to end a series of examples with a final example or the words *and so on.*

everybody/every body, everyone/every one *See* anyone/any one. . . .

except *See* accept, except.

expect, suppose *Expect* means "to hope" or "to anticipate": *I expect a good grade on my final paper. Suppose* means "to presume": *I suppose you did not win the lottery on Saturday.*

explicit, implicit *Explicit* means "stated outright"; *implicit* means "implied, unstated": *Her explicit instructions were to go to the party without her, but the implicit message she conveyed was disapproval.*

farther, further *Farther* describes geographical distances: *Ten miles farther on is a hotel. Further* means "in addition" when geography is not involved: *He said further that he didn't like my attitude.*

fewer, less *Fewer* refers to items that can be counted individually; *less* refers to general amounts: *Fewer people signed up for indoor soccer this year than last. Your argument has less substance than you think.*

firstly *Firstly* is common in British English but not in the United States. *First, second, third,* and so on are the accepted forms.

flaunt, flout *Flaunt* means "to wave" or "to show publicly" with a delight tinged with pride and even arrogance: *He flaunted his wealth by wearing many gold chains. Flout* means "to scorn" or "to defy," especially in a public way, seemingly without concern for the consequences: *She flouted the traffic laws by running through red lights.*

former, latter *Former* refers to the first and *latter* to the second of two things mentioned previously: *Mario and Alice are both good cooks; the former is fonder of Chinese cooking, the latter of Mexican.*

further *See* farther, further.

41
usage

get   In formal writing, avoid colloquial uses of *get,* as in *get with it, get it all together, get-up-and-go, get it,* and *that gets me.*

good, well   *Good* is an adjective and should not be used in place of the adverb *well: He felt good about doing well on the exam.*

half, a half, half a   Write *half, a half,* or *half a* but not *half of, a half a,* or *a half of: Half the clerical staff went out on strike. I want a half-dozen eggs to throw at the actors. Half a loaf is better than none, unless you are on a diet.*

hanged, hung   People are *hanged* by the neck until dead. Pictures and all other things that can be suspended are *hung.*

hopefully   *Hopefully* means "with hope." It is often misused to mean "it is hoped": *We waited hopefully for our ship to come in* [not *Hopefully, our ship will come in,* but *We hope our ship will come in*].

if . . . then   Avoid using these words in tandem. Redundant: *If I get my license, then I can drive a cab.* Better: *If I get my license, I can drive a cab. Once I get my license, I can drive a cab.*

if, whether   Use *whether* instead of *if* when expressing options: *If we go to the movies, we don't know whether we'll see a comedy or a drama.*

illicit   *See* elicit, illicit.

immigrate   *See* emigrate, immigrate.

imminent   *See* eminent, imminent, immanent.

immoral   *See* amoral, immoral.

implicit   *See* explicit, implicit.

imply, infer   *Imply* means "to suggest something without stating it directly": *By putting his fingers in his ears, he implied that she should stop singing. Infer* means "to draw a conclusion from evidence": *When she dozed off in the middle of his declaration of eternal love, he inferred that she did not feel the same way about him.*

in, in to, into   *In* refers to a location inside something: *Charles kept a snake in his room. In to* refers to motion with a purpose: *The resident manager came in to capture it. Into* refers to movement from outside to inside or from separation to contact: *The snake escaped by crawling into a drain.*

incredible, incredulous   *Incredible* stories and events cannot be believed; *incredulous* people do not believe: *Kaitlyn told an incredible story of being abducted by a UFO over the weekend. We were all incredulous.*

infer   *See* imply, infer.

inside of, outside of   The "of " is unnecessary in these phrases: *He was outside the house.*

ironically   *Ironically* means "contrary to what was or might have been expected" in a sense that implies the unintentional or foolish: *Ironically, the peace activists were planning a "War against Hate" campaign.* It should not be confused with *surprisingly* ("unexpectedly") or with *coincidentally* ("occurring at the same time or place").

irregardless This construction is a double negative because both the prefix *ir-* and the suffix *-less* are negatives. Use *regardless* instead.

it's, its *It's* is a contraction, usually for *it is* but sometimes for *it has: It's often been said that English is a difficult language to learn. Its* is a possessive pronoun: *The dog sat down and scratched its fleas.*

kind(s) *Kind* is singular: *This kind of house is easy to build. Kinds* is plural and should be used only to indicate more than one kind: *These three kinds of toys are better than those two kinds.*

kind of, sort of These constructions should not be used to mean *somewhat* or *a little: I was somewhat tired after the party.*

lay, lie *Lay* means "to place." Its main forms are *lay, laid,* and *laid.* It generally has a direct object, specifying what has been placed: *She laid her book on the steps and left it there. Lie* means "to recline" and does not take a direct object. Its main forms are *lie, lay,* and *lain: She often lay awake at night.*

less *See* fewer, less.

like *See* as, like.

literally *Literally* means "actually" or "exactly as written": *Literally thousands gathered along the parade route.* Do not use *literally* as an intensive adverb when it can be misleading or even ridiculous, as here: *His blood literally boiled.*

loose, lose *Loose* is an adjective that means "not securely attached"; *lose* is a verb that means "to misplace": *Better tighten that loose screw before you lose the whole structure.*

may *See* can, may.

maybe, may be *Maybe* is an adverb meaning "perhaps": *Maybe he can get a summer job as a lifeguard. May be* is a verb phrase meaning "is possible": *It may be that I can get a job as a lifeguard, too.*

moral, morale *Moral* means "lesson," especially a lesson about standards of behavior or the nature of life: *The moral of the story is do not drink and drive. Morale* means "attitude" or "mental condition": *Employee morale dropped sharply after the president of the company was arrested.*

more/more of *See* all/all of. . . .

more important, more importantly Use *more important.*

most *See* almost, most.

myself (himself, herself, and so on) Pronouns ending with *-self* refer to or intensify other words: *Jack hurt himself. Standing in the doorway was the man himself.* When you are unsure whether to use *I* or *me, she* or *her,* or *he* or *him* in a compound subject or object, you may be tempted to substitute

41

usage

one of the -*self* pronouns. Don't do it: *The quarrel was between her and me* [not *myself*]. (*For more on pronouns, see Part 7, starting on p. 465.*)

neither   *See* either, neither.

nohow, nowheres   These words are nonstandard for *anyway, in no way, in any way, in any place,* and *in no place.* Do not use them in formal writing.

number   *See* amount, number.

off of   Omit the *of*: *She took the painting off the wall.*

one another   *See* each other, one another.

outside of   *See* inside of, outside of.

plus   Avoid using *plus* as a coordinating conjunction (use *and*) or a transitional expression (use *moreover*): *He had to walk the dog, do the dishes, empty the garbage, and* [not *plus*] *write a term paper.*

precede, proceed   *Precede* means "come before"; *proceed* means "go forward": *Despite the heavy snows that preceded us, we managed to proceed up the hiking trail.*

previous to, prior to   Avoid these wordy and somewhat pompous substitutions for *before*.

principal, principle   *Principal* is an adjective meaning "most important" or a noun meaning "the head of an organization" or "a sum of money": *Our principal objections to the school's principal are that he is a liar and a cheat. Principle* is a noun meaning "a basic standard or law": *We believe in the principles of honesty and fair play.*

proceed   *See* precede, proceed.

raise, rise   *Raise* means "to lift or cause to move upward." It takes a direct object—someone raises something: *I raised the windows in the classroom. Rise* means "to go upward." It does not take a direct object—something rises by itself: *We watched the balloon rise to the ceiling.*

real, really   Do not use the word *real* or *really* when you mean *very*: *The cake was very* [not *real* or *really*] *good.*

reason . . . is because, reason why   These are redundant expressions. Use either *the reason is that* or *because*: *The reason he fell on the ice is that he cannot skate. He fell on the ice because he cannot skate.*

refer to   *See* allude, elude, refer to.

respectfully, respectively   *Respectfully* means "with respect": *Treat your partners respectfully. Respectively* means "in the given order": *The three Williams she referred to were Shakespeare, Wordsworth, and Yeats, respectively.*

rise   *See* raise, rise.

set, sit   *Set* is usually a transitive verb meaning "to establish" or "to place." It takes a direct object, and its principal parts are *set, set,* and *set: DiMaggio* *set the standard of excellence in fielding. She set the box down in the corner. Sit* is usually intransitive, meaning "to place oneself in a sitting position." Its principal parts are *sit, sat,* and *sat: The dog sat on command.*

shall, will   Today, most writers use *will* instead of *shall* in the ordinary future tense for the first person: *I will celebrate my birthday by throwing a big party. Shall* is still used in questions. *Shall we dance?*

should of   *See* could of, should of, would of.

site   *See* cite, sight, site.

some   Avoid using the adjective *some* in place of the adverb *somewhat: He felt somewhat* [not *some*] *better after a good night's sleep.*

some of   *See* all/all of. . . .

somewheres   Use *somewhere* or *someplace* instead.

sort of   *See* kind of, sort of.

suppose   *See* expect, suppose.

sure   Avoid confusing the adjective *sure* with the adverb *surely: The dress she wore to the party was surely bizarre.*

sure and   *Sure and* is often used colloquially. In formal writing, *sure to* is preferred: *Be sure to* [not *be sure and*] *get to the wedding on time.*

take   *See* bring, take.

than, then   *Than* is a conjunction used in comparisons: *I am taller than you. Then* is an adverb referring to a point in time: *We will sing and then dance.*

that, which   Many writers use *that* for restrictive (that is, essential) clauses and *which* for nonrestrictive (that is, nonessential) clauses: *The bull that escaped from the ring ran through my china shop, which was located in the square. (Also see Chapter 49, pp. 513–15.)*

**41
usage**

their, there, they're   *Their* is a possessive pronoun: *They gave their lives. There* is an adverb of place: *She was standing there. They're* is a contraction of *they are: They're reading more poetry this semester.*

this here, these here, that there, them there   When writing, avoid these nonstandard forms.

to, too, two   *To* is a preposition; *too* is an adverb; *two* is a number: *The two of us got lost too many times on our way to his house.*

try and   *Try to* is the standard form: *Try to* [not *try and*] *understand.*

uninterested   *See* disinterested, uninterested.

unique   *Unique* means "one of a kind." Do not use any qualifiers with it.

use, utilize   *Use* is preferable because it is simpler: *Use five sources in your project.*

verbally, orally To say something *orally* is to say it aloud: *We agreed orally to share credit for the work, but when I asked her to confirm it in writing, she refused.* To say something *verbally* is to use words: *His eyes flashed anger, but he did not express his feelings verbally.*

wait for, wait on People *wait for* those who are late; they *wait on* tables.

weather, whether The noun *weather* refers to the atmosphere: *She worried that the weather would not clear up in time for the victory celebration.* *Whether* is a conjunction referring to a choice between alternatives: *I can't decide whether to go now or next week.*

well *See* good, well.

whether *See* if, whether, *and* weather, whether.

which, who, whose *Which* is used for things, and *who* and *whose* for people: *My fountain pen, which I had lost last week, was found by a child who had never seen one before, whose whole life had been spent with ballpoints.*

who, whom Use *who* with subjects and their complements. Use *whom* with objects (of verbs). *The person who will fill the post is Janelle, whom you met last week.* (Also see Chapter 46, pp. 478–79.)

will *See* shall, will.

would of *See* could of, should of, would of.

your, you're *Your* is a possessive pronoun: *Is that your new car? You're* is a contraction of *you are: You're a lucky guy.*

PART
7

There is a core simplicity to the English language and its American variant, but it's a slippery core.

—Stephen King

Editing
for Grammar
Conventions

7 Editing for Grammar Conventions

WRITING OUTCOMES

Part 7 Editing for Grammar Conventions

This section will help you answer questions such as the following:

Rhetorical Knowledge

- Are sentence fragments ever acceptable in any kind of writing? **(42b)**

Critical Thinking, Reading, and Writing

- What's wrong with *A student should enjoy their college experience?* How can I fix it without sounding sexist? **(46a)**

Processes

- How can I recognize and fix sentence fragments when I edit? **(42a)**

Knowledge of Conventions

- When should I use *lie* or *lay?* **(45b)**
- Is it ever correct to say *I feel good?* **(47b)**

Writing in Online Environments

- Can my word processor's grammar checker help me edit for grammar conventions? **(42–47)**

For a general introduction to writing outcomes, see Id, page 5.

42 Fixing Sentence Fragments

A word group that begins with a capital letter and ends with a period may not be a complete sentence. A complete sentence meets all three of the following requirements:

- **A sentence names a *subject*,** the *who* or *what* that the sentence addresses.
- **A sentence has a complete *verb* that indicates tense, person, and number.**
- **A sentence includes at least one independent *clause*.** An independent clause has a subject and a complete verb and does not begin with a subordinating word such as *although, because, that,* or *which.*

In the following example, the first word group meets all three requirements and is a complete sentence. Although the second word group has a subject and a complete verb, they are part of a dependent clause that begins with the subordinating word *because.* Therefore, it is not a complete sentence.

POSSIBLE Many people feel threatened by globalization.
FRAGMENT *Because they think it will undermine their cultural traditions.*

You can fix fragments in one of two ways: either transform them into sentences or attach them to a nearby independent clause.

▶ Many people feel threatened by globalization. ~~Because~~ They ~~they~~

think it will undermine their cultural traditions.

▶ Many people feel threatened by globalization/ because ~~Because~~ they

think it will undermine their cultural traditions.

Fragments and Grammar Checkers

Grammar checkers identify some fragments, but they will not tell you what the fragment is missing or how to edit it. Grammar checkers can also miss fragments without subjects that could be interpreted as commands, such as this fragment from a passage about the ancient Maya: *Develop the concept of zero, for example.*

✓ **IDENTIFY AND EDIT** | Sentence Fragments

frag

❓ 1. *Do you see a complete verb?*

Yes | **No → FRAGMENT**

| FRAGMENT | For example, the concept of zero. |
| SENTENCE | For example, they were among the first to develop the concept of zero. |

subj | verb (above "they were")

❓ 2. *Do you see a subject?*

Yes | **No → FRAGMENT**

| FRAGMENT | Developed the concept of zero, for example. |
| SENTENCE | They developed the concept of zero, for example. |

subj | verb (above "They developed")

❓ 3. *Do you see only a dependent clause?*

No | **Yes → FRAGMENT**

| FRAGMENT | Because they were among the earliest people to develop the concept of zero. |
| SENTENCE | Because they were among the earliest people to develop the concept of zero, the Maya deserve a place in the history of mathematics. |

SENTENCE

NAVIGATING THROUGH COLLEGE AND BEYOND

Intentional Fragments

Advertisers often use attention-getting fragments: "Hot deal! Big savings! Because you're worth it." Occasionally, you may want to use a sentence fragment for stylistic reasons. Keep in mind, however, that advertising and college writing have different contexts and purposes. In formal writing, use deliberate sentence fragments sparingly.

42a Repairing dependent-clause fragments

Fragments that begin with a subordinating word such as *although, even though,* or *whenever* can usually be attached to a nearby independent clause.

▶ **None of the thirty-three subjects indicated any concern**

about the amount or kind of fruit the institution served⌄,

even
E̶v̶e̶n̶ though all of them identified diet as an important
   ^

issue for those with diabetes.

It is sometimes better to transform such a fragment into a complete sentence by deleting the subordinating word.

▶ **The harmony of our group was disrupted in two ways.**

Members
W̶h̶e̶n̶ ̶m̶e̶m̶b̶e̶r̶s̶ either disagreed about priorities or
   ^

advocated different political strategies.

Exercise 42.1   Editing to repair dependent-clause fragments

Correct the dependent-clause fragments in the following items by attaching them to a sentence or by eliminating or replacing the subordinating word.

EXAMPLE

The most commonly traded stone in Mesopotamia was

     which
obsidian⌄, W̶h̶i̶c̶h̶ is black, volcanic, and glasslike.
    ^   ^

1. Ancient people traded salt. Which is an important nutrient.
2. Some groups resorted to war and conquest. Because they wanted to gain control over valuable goods and resources.
3. When they could, people transported large stones by river. Since doing so required less effort than other means of moving them.
4. Obsidian is hard and makes a sharp edge. Even though it is brittle.

**42a
frag**

5. After a while, a type of currency developed. When traders began exchanging silver bars or rings.

6. The earliest writing appeared in Mesopotamia. After people there began living in cities.

7. Agriculture thrived in Egypt. Because the Nile flooded regularly.

8. Although the Egyptians had abundant crops and large supplies of limestone. They imported many goods.

9. Egypt added gold objects to its lengthy list of exports. After its artisans began to work the precious metal in about 4000 BCE.

10. Egypt's first king was Menes. Who united the country by conquest in about 3150 BCE.

42b Repairing phrase fragments

Often unintentional fragments are **phrases,** word groups that lack a subject or a complete verb or both and usually function as modifiers or nouns. Phrase fragments frequently begin with **verbals**—words derived from verbs, such as *putting* or *to put.* They do not change form to reflect tense and number. *(For more on verbals, see pp. 592–93.)*

> FRAGMENT   That summer, we had the time of our lives. *Swimming in the mountain lake each day and exploring the nearby woods.*

One way to fix this fragment is to transform it into an independent clause with its own subject and verbs:

▶ That summer, we had the time of our lives. ~~Swimming~~ *We swam* in the

mountain lake each day and ~~exploring~~ *explored* the nearby woods.

Another way to fix the problem is to attach the fragment to the part of the previous sentence that it modifies (in this case, *the time of our lives*).

▶ That summer, we had the time of our lives., ~~Swimming~~ *swimming*

in the mountain lake each day and exploring the nearby

woods.

Phrase fragments can also begin with one-word prepositions such as *as, at, by, for, from, in, of, on,* or *to.* Attach these fragments to a nearby sentence.

▶ **Impressionist painters often depicted their subjects in**

$$at$$

everyday situations, At a restaurant, perhaps, or by the

seashore.

Exercise 42.2 | Identifying fragments

Underline the fragments in the following passage, and identify each as either a phrase (without a subject or verb) or a dependent clause.

EXAMPLE **I am headed to the library tonight.**
dependent clause
Because I have a paper due.

Pool hustlers deceive their opponents in many ways. Sometimes appearing unfamiliar with the rules of the game. They may try acting as if they are drunk. Or pretend to be inept. For example, they will put so much spin on the ball that it jumps out of the intended pocket. So that their opponents will be tricked into betting. Some other ways to cheat. When their opponents are not looking, pool hustlers may remove their own balls from the table. Then change the position of the balls on the table. Because today's pool balls have metallic cores. Hustlers can use electromagnets to affect the path of the balls. Be aware of these tricks!

Exercise 42.3 | Editing to repair phrase fragments

Repair the phrase fragments in the items that follow by attaching them to a sentence or adding words to turn them into sentences.

EXAMPLE

$$such$$

Film music can create a mood, Such as romantic,

lighthearted, or mysterious.

1. The ominous music prepares us for a shocking scene. And confuses us when the shock does not come.

**42b
frag**

2. Filmmakers may try to evoke nostalgic feelings. By choosing songs from a particular era.

3. The musical producer used a mix of traditional songs and new compositions. In the Civil War drama *Cold Mountain.*

4. Usually, filmmakers edit the images first and add music later. To be sure that the music supports the visual elements.

5. Music can provide transitions between scenes. Marking the passage of time, signaling a change of place, or foreshadowing a shift in mood.

6. Exactly matching the rhythms of the music to the movement on screen is known as "Mickey Mousing." After the animated classic.

7. To create atmosphere, filmmakers sometimes use sounds from nature. Such as crashing waves, bird calls, and moaning winds.

8. Do not underestimate the effect of a short "dead track," the complete absence of sound. Forcing us to look intently at the image.

42c Repairing other types of fragments

Word groups that start with transitions or with words that introduce examples, appositives, lists, and compound predicates can also cause problems.

1. Word groups that start with transitions

Some fragments start with two- or three-word prepositions that function as transitions, such as *as well as, as compared with,* or *in addition to.*

► For sixty-five years, the growth in consumer spending

in
has been both steep and steady. ~~In~~ contrast to the growth

in gross domestic product (GDP), which has fluctuated

significantly.

2. Words and phrases that introduce examples

It is always a good idea to check word groups beginning with *for example, like, specifically,* or *such as.*

▶ **Elizabeth I of England faced many dangers as a princess.**

she fell
For example, ~~falling~~ out of favor with her sister, Queen
                     ^

was
Mary, and ~~being~~ imprisoned in the Tower of London.
            ^

3. Appositives

An **appositive** is a noun or noun phrase that renames a noun or pronoun.

▶ **In 1965, Lyndon Johnson increased the number of troops in**

a
Vietnam,, A former French colony in Southeast Asia.
         ^ ^

4. Lists

You can connect a list to the preceding sentence using a colon or a dash.

▶ **In the 1930s, three great band leaders helped popularize**

jazz,: Louis Armstrong, Benny Goodman, and Duke
      ^

Ellington.

5. Compound predicates

A **compound predicate** is made up of at least two verbs as well as their objects and modifiers, connected by a coordinating conjunction such as *and, but,* or *or.* The parts of a compound predicate have the same subject and should be together in one sentence.

▶ **The group gathered at dawn at the base of the mountain,**

and
~~And~~ assembled their gear in preparation for the morning's
         ^

climb.

42c frag

Exercise 42.4 Chapter review: Editing for sentence fragments

Edit the following passage to repair fragments.

According to the United States Constitution, which was ratified in 1788, the president and vice president of the United States were not to be elected directly by the people in a popular election. But elected indirectly by an "electoral college," made up of "electors." Who were at first often chosen by the state legislatures. In the early nineteenth century, the population of the United States grew rapidly, and electors were increasingly chosen by statewide popular vote. Gradually making the electoral college system more democratic. Nonetheless, in the elections of 1824, 1876, 1888, and 2000, the elected candidate won the vote in the electoral college. But not a majority of the popular vote.

43 Repairing Comma Splices and Run-on Sentences

A **comma splice** is a sentence with at least two independent clauses joined by only a comma. Recall that an independent clause has a subject and a complete verb and can stand on its own as a sentence. *(See page 427.)*

COMMA SPLICE	The media influence people's political views, the family is another major source of ideas about the proper role of government.

A **run-on sentence,** sometimes called a **fused sentence,** does not even have a comma between the independent clauses, making it difficult for readers to tell where one clause ends and the next begins.

RUN-ON	Local news shows often focus on crime stories network and cable news broadcasts cover national politics in detail.

Comma splices and run-ons often occur when clauses are linked with a transitional expression such as *as a result, for example, in addition, in other words,* or *on the contrary* or a conjunctive adverb such as *however, consequently, moreover,* or *nevertheless. (See p. 437 for a list of conjunctive adverbs and transitional expressions.)*

COMMA
SPLICE
Rare books can be extremely valuable, *for example,* an original edition of Audubon's *Birds of America* is worth more than a million dollars.

RUN-ON
Most students complied with the new policy *however* a few refused to do so.

Run-ons may also occur when a sentence's second clause either specifies or explains its first clause.

RUN-ON
The economy is still recovering from the financial crisis that began in 2007 Bear Stearns was the first large investment bank to experience problems that year.

Comma Splices, Run-on Sentences, and Grammar Checkers

Computer grammar checkers are unreliable at distinguishing between properly and improperly joined independent clauses. One grammar checker, for example, correctly flagged this sentence for incorrect comma usage: *Many history textbooks are clear, some are hard to follow.* It failed, however, to flag this longer alternative: *Many history textbooks are clear and easy to read, some are dense and hard to follow.*

You can repair comma splices and run-on sentences in one of five ways:

- Join the two clauses with a comma and a coordinating conjunction *(and, but, or, nor, for, so, yet).*
- Join the two clauses with a semicolon.
- Separate the clauses into two sentences.
- Turn one of the independent clauses into a dependent clause.
- Transform the two clauses into a single independent clause.

**43
cs/run-on**

Exercise 43.1   Identifying comma splices and run-on sentences

Bracket the comma splices and run-on sentences in the following passage. For each error, note if it is a comma splice (CS) or a run-on sentence (RO).

EXAMPLE
[**The Gutenberg Bible is one of the first printed**
                  CS
books, copies are extremely rare.]

Rare books can be extremely valuable. Most books have to be in good shape to fetch high prices nevertheless some remain valuable no matter what. A first edition of Audubon's *Birds of America* can be worth more than a million dollars however it must be in good condition. On the other hand, even without a cover, an early edition of Cotton Mather's *An Ecclesiastical History of New England* will be worth at least three thousand dollars. Generally speaking, the newer a book is the more important its condition, even a book from the 1940s will have to be in excellent condition to be worth three figures. There are other factors that determine a book's value, certainly whether the author has signed it is important. Even students can collect books for instance they can search for bargains and great "finds" at yard and garage sales. In addition, used-book and author sites on the Internet offer opportunities for beginning collectors.

43a Joining two clauses with a comma and a coordinating conjunction such as *and* or *but*

Be sure to choose the coordinating conjunction that most clearly expresses the logical relationship between the clauses. A comma *must* precede the conjunction, or the sentence remains a run-on.

► John is a very stubborn person, _{so} I had a hard time convincing him to let me take the wheel.

► My stepmother teaches at Central State _{, but} I go to Eastern Tech.

43b Joining two clauses with a semicolon

A semicolon tells readers that two closely related clauses are logically connected. However, a semicolon does not spell out the logic of the connection.

► Most students complied with the new policy_; a few refused.

To show the logic of the connection, you can add a conjunctive adverb or transitional expression.

► Most students complied with the new policy_{; however,} a few refused to do so.

Conjunctive Adverbs and Transitional Expressions

also	incidentally	now
as a result	indeed	nonetheless
besides	in fact	of course
certainly	in other words	on the contrary
consequently	instead	otherwise
finally	in the meantime	similarly
for example	likewise	still
for instance	meanwhile	then
furthermore	moreover	therefore
however	nevertheless	thus
in addition	next	undoubtedly

The conjunctive adverb or transitional expression is usually followed by a comma when it appears at the beginning of the second clause. It can also appear in the middle of a clause, set off by two commas, or at the end, preceded by a comma.

, however,

▶ **Most students complied with the new policy,; a few refused.**

, however

▶ **Most students complied with the new policy,; a few refused.**

When the first independent clause introduces or expands on the second one, you can use a colon instead of a semicolon.

▶ **Professor Kim then revealed his most important point: the**

paper would count for half my grade.

Exercise 43.2 Editing to repair comma splices and run-on sentences

Some of the sentences below contain comma splices, and some are run-ons. Circle the number of each sentence that is correct. Edit those that are not correct using either (1) a semicolon and, if appropriate, a conjunctive adverb or transitional expression or (2) a comma with a coordinating conjunction.

EXAMPLE   **Slavery has always been an oppressive**

but

institution, its severity has varied from society

to society throughout history.

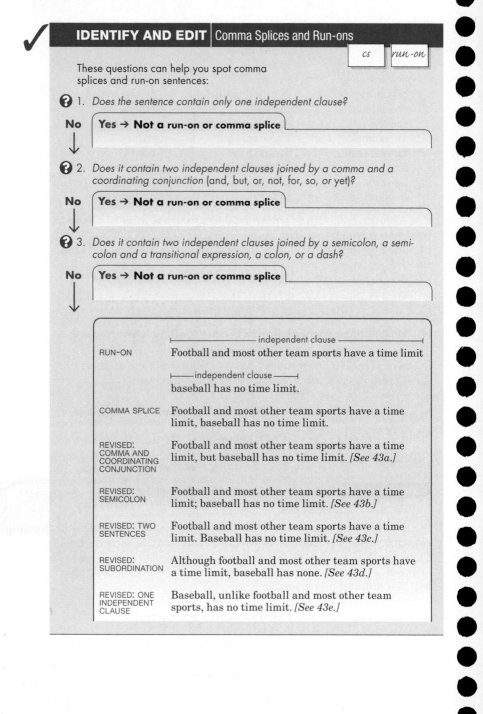

✓ **IDENTIFY AND EDIT** | Comma Splices and Run-ons

cs run-on

These questions can help you spot comma splices and run-on sentences:

? 1. *Does the sentence contain only one independent clause?*

No ↓ | Yes → **Not a run-on or comma splice**

? 2. *Does it contain two independent clauses joined by a comma and a coordinating conjunction (and, but, or, not, for, so, or yet)?*

No ↓ | Yes → **Not a run-on or comma splice**

? 3. *Does it contain two independent clauses joined by a semicolon, a semicolon and a transitional expression, a colon, or a dash?*

No ↓ | Yes → **Not a run-on or comma splice**

RUN-ON	├───── independent clause ─────┤ Football and most other team sports have a time limit ├── independent clause ──┤ baseball has no time limit.
COMMA SPLICE	Football and most other team sports have a time limit, baseball has no time limit.
REVISED: COMMA AND COORDINATING CONJUNCTION	Football and most other team sports have a time limit, but baseball has no time limit. *[See 43a.]*
REVISED: SEMICOLON	Football and most other team sports have a time limit; baseball has no time limit. *[See 43b.]*
REVISED: TWO SENTENCES	Football and most other team sports have a time limit. Baseball has no time limit. *[See 43c.]*
REVISED: SUBORDINATION	Although football and most other team sports have a time limit, baseball has none. *[See 43d.]*
REVISED: ONE INDEPENDENT CLAUSE	Baseball, unlike football and most other team sports, has no time limit. *[See 43e.]*

1. The earliest large societies probably did not depend on slave labor, but the people in them were not necessarily free to work where and how they pleased.
2. All early civilizations were autocratic in a sense all people in them were slaves.
3. No one knows when slavery began, it was common in many ancient agricultural civilizations.
4. The ancient Egyptians enslaved thousands of people from Nubia and other parts of Africa, some of these people were then sent to Mesopotamia.
5. Egypt's kings also used slaves to build some of the country's most famous monuments, for example, the pyramids were almost entirely the work of slaves.
6. Some stones in the Great Pyramid at Giza weigh nearly one hundred tons they could never have been set in place without the effort of thousands of workers.
7. In ancient Mesopotamia, slavery was not necessarily a lifelong condition, in fact slaves could sometimes work their way to freedom.
8. In both Egypt and Mesopotamia, slaves could sometimes own property.

43c Separating clauses into two sentences

The simplest way to correct comma splices and run-on sentences is to turn the clauses into separate sentences.

▶ I realized that it was time to choose, ~~either~~ I had to learn
   . Either

   how to drive, or I had to move back to the city.

When the two independent clauses are part of a quotation, with a phrase such as *he said* or *she noted* between them, each clause should be a separate sentence.

▶ "This was the longest day of my life," she said,

   ~~"unfortunately,~~ it's not over yet."
   "Unfortunately,

43c
cs/run-on

43d Turning one of the independent clauses into a dependent clause

In editing the following sentence, the writer chose to make the clause about *a few* her main point and the clause about *most* a subordinate idea. Remember that readers will expect subsequent sentences to tell them more about the subject of the main clause.

► *Although most*
~~Most~~ students complied with the new policy~~,~~ ~~however~~ a few

refused to do so.

43e Transforming two clauses into one independent clause

Transforming two clauses into one clear and correct independent clause is often worth the work.

► I realized that it was time ~~to choose,~~ either ~~I had~~ to learn

how to drive or ~~I had~~ to move back to the city.

Sometimes you can change one of the clauses to a phrase and place it next to the word it modifies.

► *, first printed in the nineteenth century,*
Baseball cards are an obsession among some collectors~~.~~

~~The cards were first printed in the nineteenth century.~~

Exercise 43.3 Editing to repair comma splices and run-on sentences

Some of the sentences below contain comma splices, and some are run-ons. Circle the number of each sentence that is correct. Edit those that are not correct by (1) separating the clauses into two sentences, (2) changing one clause into a dependent clause introduced by a subordinating word, or (3) combining the clauses into one independent clause.

EXAMPLE

► The human population of the world~~,~~ ~~was~~ no more than about

10 million at the beginning of the agricultural revolution

10,000 years ago, ~~it~~ had increased to about 800 million

by the beginning of the Industrial Revolution in the

eighteenth century.

1. Globally, population has increased steadily particular regions have suffered sometimes drastic declines.
2. For example, Europe lost about one-third of its population when the bubonic plague struck for the first time in the fourteenth century.
3. The plague was not the only catastrophe to strike Europe in the fourteenth century, a devastating famine also slowed population growth at the beginning of the century.
4. Images of death and destruction pervade the art of the time these images reflect the demoralizing effect of the plague.
5. The native population of Mexico collapsed in the wake of European conquest and colonization in the sixteenth century, it dropped from perhaps as many as 25 million in 1500 to little more than 1 million by 1600.
6. Hernando Cortés used diplomacy and superior military technology—horses and cannons—to conquer the Aztecs, whose forces vastly outnumbered his.
7. These were not the only reasons for Spanish success, however, at least as important was the impact of a smallpox epidemic on Aztec population and morale.
8. The population decline had many causes, these included the conquerors' efforts to destroy native culture and exploit native labor as well as the devastating effect of disease.

Exercise 43.4   Chapter review: Editing for comma splices
and run-ons

Turn back to Exercise 43.1 *(p. 435)*. Edit the paragraph to eliminate comma splices and run-ons using the methods described in this chapter.

**43e
cs/run-on**

Exercise 43.5   Chapter review: Editing for comma splices
and run-ons

Edit the passage that follows to eliminate comma splices and run-on sentences.

> The economy of the United States has always been turbulent. Many people think that the Great Depression of the 1930s was the only economic cataclysm this country has suffered the United States has had a long history of financial panics and upheavals. The early years of the nation were no exception.

Before the Revolution, the American economy was closely linked with Britain's, during the war and for many years after it, Britain barred the import of American goods. Americans, however, continued to import British goods with the loss of British markets the new country's trade deficit ballooned. Eventually, this deficit triggered a severe depression social unrest followed. The economy began to recover at the end of the 1780s with the establishment of a stable government, the opening of new markets to American shipping, and the adoption of new forms of industry. Exports grew steadily throughout the 1790s, indeed the United States soon found itself in direct competition with both England and France.

The American economy suffered a new setback beginning in 1803 England declared war on France. France and England each threatened to impound any American ships engaged in trade with the other. President Thomas Jefferson sought to change the policies of France and England with the Embargo Act of 1807, it prohibited all trade between the United States and the warring countries. Jefferson hoped to bring France and England to the negotiating table, the ploy failed. The economies of France and England suffered little from the loss of trade with the United States, meanwhile the U.S. shipping industry came almost to a halt.

44 Maintaining Subject-Verb Agreement

Verbs must agree with their subjects in **person** (first, second, or third—*I, we; you; he, she, it, they*) and **number** (singular or plural). For regular verbs, the present tense *-s* or *-es* ending is added to the verb if its subject is third-person singular; otherwise, the verb has no ending.

Note, however, that the verb *be* has irregular forms in both the present and the past tense. The irregular verbs *be, have,* and *do* have the following forms in the present and past tenses.

Verb Tenses (Present and Past)

	READ (REGULAR)	BE	HAS	DO
SINGULAR				
First person *(I)*	read *(read)*	am *(was)*	have *(had)*	do/don't *(did/didn't)*
Second person *(you)*	read *(read)*	are *(were)*	have *(had)*	do/don't *(did/didn't)*
Third person *(he, she, it)*	reads *(reads)*	is *(was)*	has *(had)*	does/doesn't *(did/didn't)*
PLURAL				
First person *(we)*	read *(read)*	are *(were)*	have *(had)*	do/don't *(did/didn't)*
Second person *(you)*	read *(read)*	are *(were)*	have *(had)*	do/don't *(did/didn't)*
Third person *(they)*	read *(read)*	are *(were)*	have *(had)*	do/don't *(did/didn't)*

Exercise 44.1   Identifying subject-verb agreement

In each sentence, underline the subject, and circle the verb that goes with it.

> **EXAMPLE**   Graphic design <u>studios</u> (⟨require⟩/requires)
>
> their designers to be trained in the use of
>
> design software.

1. Nowadays, computers (gives/give) graphic designers a great deal of freedom.
2. Before computers, a design (was/were) produced mostly by hand.
3. Alternative designs (is/are) produced much faster on the computer than by hand.
4. With computers, a designer (is/are) able to reduce or enlarge text in seconds.
5. Page layout programs (takes/take) some of the drudgery out of combining images with text.
6. Designers (has/have) the option of removing blemishes and other imperfections from photographs.
7. They (doesn't/don't) have to make special prints to show their work to others.
8. Designs (is/are) e-mailed as attachments all the time.

44
sv agr

9. Still, the design professional (doesn't/don't) feel that the computer is anything more than just another tool.

10. Nonetheless, to be a graphic designer today, you (needs/need) to be ready to spend a lot of time staring at a screen.

✓ | **IDENTIFY AND EDIT** | Problems with Subject-Verb Agreement

agr

❋ 1. *Find the verb.*

> | | verb |
> | PROBLEM SENTENCE | Hamlet and Claudius *brings* down the Danish royal family. |
>
> Verbs specify action, condition, or state of being.

❋ 2. *Ask the who or what question to identify the subject.*

> | | ⊢——— subject ———⊣ ⊢verb⊣ |
> | PROBLEM SENTENCE | *Hamlet and Claudius brings* down the Danish royal family. |
>
> The answer to the question "What brings?" is *Hamlet and Claudius.*

❋ 3. *Determine the person (first, second, or third) and number (singular or plural) of the subject.*

> | | ⊢———subject———⊣ |
> | PROBLEM SENTENCE | *Hamlet and Claudius* brings down the Danish royal family. |
>
> The subject of the sentence—*Hamlet and Claudius*—is a compound joined by *and* and is third-person plural.

❋ 4. *If necessary, change the verb to agree with the subject.*

> | | bring |
> | EDITED PROBLEM SENTENCE | Hamlet and Claudius ~~brings~~ down the Danish royal family. |
>
> *Bring* is the third-person plural form of the verb.

44a When a word group separates the subject from the verb

To locate the subject of a sentence, find the verb, and then ask the *who* or *what* question about it ("Who is?" "What is?"). Does that subject match the verb in number?

> oppose
> ▶ The ~~leaders of the trade union~~ o̶p̶p̶o̶s̶e̶s̶ the new law.

The answer to the question "Who opposes?" is *leaders,* a plural noun, so the verb should be in the plural form: *oppose.*

If a word group beginning with *as well as, along with,* or *in addition to* follows a singular subject, the subject does not become plural.

> opposes
> ▶ My ~~teacher,~~ as well as other faculty members, o̶p̶p̶o̶s̶e̶ the
>
> new school policy.

Subject-Verb Agreement and Grammar Checkers

A grammar checker failed to flag this sentence for correction: *The candidate's position on foreign policy issues trouble some voters.* The subject is the singular noun *position,* so the verb should be *troubles.* Apparently, however, the grammar checker interpreted the word *issues* as the subject.

44b Compound subjects

Compound subjects are made up of two or more parts joined by either a coordinating conjunction *(and, or, nor)* or a correlative conjunction *(both . . . and, either . . . or, neither . . . nor).*

**44b
sv agr**

- **Most compound subjects are plural.**

  PLURAL *The king and his advisers were* shocked by this turn of events.

  PLURAL This poem's *first line and last word have* a powerful effect on the reader.

- **Some compound subjects are singular.** Compound subjects should be treated as singular in the following circumstances:

- When they are considered as a single unit:

  ▶ **In some ways, forty acres and a mule continues to be what is needed.**

- When they are preceded by the word *each* or *every:*

  ▶ **Each man, woman, and child deserves respect.**

- When they refer to the same entity:

  ▶ **My best girlfriend and most dependable adviser is my mother.**

- **Some compound subjects can be either plural or singular.** Compound subjects connected by *or, nor, either . . . or,* or *neither . . . nor* can take either a singular or a plural verb, depending on the subject that is closest to the verb.

  SINGULAR **Either the children or *their mother is* to blame.**

  PLURAL **Neither the experimenter nor *her subjects were* aware of the takeover.**

Sentences often sound less awkward with the plural subject closer to the verb.

44c Collective subjects

A **collective noun** names a unit made up of many persons or things, treating it as an entity, such as *audience, family, group,* and *team.*

- **Most often, collective nouns are singular.** Words such as *news, athletics, physics,* and *statistics* are usually singular as well, despite their *-s* ending. Units of measurement used collectively, such as *six inches* or *20 percent,* are also treated as singular.

  ▶ **The *audience is* restless.**

  ▶ **That *news leaves* me speechless.**

  ▶ **One-fourth of the liquid *was* poured into test tube 1.**

- **Some collective subjects are plural.** When the members of a group are acting as individuals, the collective subject can be considered plural.

▶ The *group were* passing around a bottle of beer.

You may want to add a modifying phrase that contains a plural noun to make the sentence clearer and avoid awkwardness.

▶ The *group of troublemakers were* passing around a bottle of beer.

- When units of measurement refer to people or things, they are plural.

▶ *One-fourth* of the students in the class *are* failing the course.

44d Indefinite subjects

Indefinite pronouns do not refer to a specific person or item.

- **Most indefinite pronouns are singular.** The following indefinite pronouns are always singular: *anybody, anyone, anything, each, either, everybody, everyone, everything, neither, nobody, no one, none, nothing, one, somebody, someone,* and *something.*

▶ *Everyone* in my hiking club *is* an experienced climber.

None and *neither* are always singular.

▶ In the movie, five men set out on an expedition,

but *none returns.*

▶ *Neither sees* a way out of this predicament.

- **Some indefinite pronouns are always plural.** A handful of indefinite pronouns *(both, few, many, several)* are always plural because by definition they mean more than one. *Both,* for example, always indicates two.

▶ *Both* of us *want* to go to the rally for the environment.

44d
sv agr

► *Several* of my friends *were* very happy about the outcome of the election.

▪ **Some indefinite pronouns can be either plural or singular.** Some indefinite pronouns *(some, any, all, most)* can be either plural or singular, depending on whether they refer to a plural or singular noun in the sentence.

► *Some* of the *book is* missing, but *all* of the *papers are* here.

44e When the subject comes after the verb

In most English sentences, the verb comes after the subject. Sometimes, however, a writer will switch this order. In the following sentence, you can locate the subject by asking, "*Who* or *what* stand?" The answer is the sentence's subject: *an oak and a weeping willow.* Because the subject is a compound subject (two subjects joined by *and*), the verb must be plural.

► Out back behind the lean-to *stand an old oak tree and a weeping willow.*

In sentences that begin with *there is* or *there are,* the subject always follows the verb.

► There *is* a worn wooden *bench* in the shade of the two trees.

Exercise 44.2 Editing for subject-verb agreement

Underline the simple subjects and verbs in each of the following sentences, and then check for subject-verb agreement. Circle the number of each correct sentence. Repair the other sentences by changing the verb form.

EXAMPLE   The <u>audience</u> for new productions of

  appears
Shakespeare's plays ~~appear~~ to be growing.
  ^

1. Designers since the invention of printing has sought to create attractive, readable type.
2. A layout shows the general design of a book or magazine.

3. Half of all ad pages contains lots of white space.
4. The size of the page, width of the margins, and style of type is some of the things that concern a designer.
5. China and Japan were centers for the development of the art of calligraphy.
6. Neither a standard style of lettering nor a uniform alphabet were prevalent in the early days of the printing press.
7. A pioneering type designer and graphic artist were Albrecht Dürer.
8. A number of contemporary typefaces show the influence of Dürer's designs.
9. A design committee approve any changes to the look of a publication.
10. Each letter and punctuation mark are designed for maximum readability.

44f Subject complement

A **subject complement** renames and specifies the sentence's subject. It follows a **linking verb**—a verb, often a form of *be,* that joins the subject to its description or definition: *children are innocent.* In the following sentence, the verb has been changed to agree with *gift,* the subject, instead of *books,* the subject complement.

▶ One gift that gives her pleasure ~~are~~ books.
        is

(For more information on linking verbs and subject complements, see Chapter 61, p. 581, and Chapter 62, p. 588.)

44g Relative pronouns *(who, which,* or *that)*

When a relative pronoun such as *who, which,* or *that* is the subject of a dependent clause, it is taking the place of a noun that appears earlier in the sentence—its **antecedent.** The verb that goes with *who, which,* or *that* must agree with this antecedent. In the following sentence, the relative pronoun *that* is the subject of the dependent clause *that has dangerous side effects. Disease,* a singular noun, is the antecedent of *that;* therefore, the verb in the dependent clause is singular.

▶ Measles is a childhood *disease that has* dangerous side effects.

44g
sv agr

The phrase *one of the* implies more than one and so is plural. *Only one of the* implies just one, however, and is singular. Generally, use the plural form of the verb when the phrase *one of the* comes before the antecedent. Use the singular form of the verb when *only one of the* comes before the plural noun.

PLURAL	Tuberculosis is *one of the* diseases *that have* long, tragic histories in many parts of the world.
SINGULAR	Barbara is the *only one of the* scientists *who has* a degree in physics.

Exercise 44.3 Editing for subject-verb agreement problems

In some of the sentences below, the verb does not agree with the subject. Circle the number of each sentence in which subject and verb agree. In the others, change verbs as needed to bring subjects and verbs into agreement.

EXAMPLE The best part of the play ~~are~~ *is* her soliloquies.

1. The Guerrilla Girls are a group of women who acts on behalf of female artists.
2. One of their main concerns are to combat the underrepresentation of women artists in museum shows.
3. No one knows how many Guerrilla Girls there are, and none of them have ever revealed her true identity.
4. The Guerrilla Girls maintain their anonymity by appearing only in gorilla masks.
5. Some people claim that a few famous artists is members of the Guerrilla Girls.
6. Their story begin in 1985, when the Museum of Modern Art in New York exhibited a major survey of contemporary art.
7. Fewer than 10 percent of the artists represented was women.
8. Not everyone is amused by the protests of the Guerrilla Girls.
9. They often shows up in costume at exhibits dominated by the work of male artists.
10. Several of the Guerrilla Girls have coauthored a book.

44h Phrases beginning with *-ing* verbs

A **gerund phrase** is an *-ing* verb form followed by objects, complements, or modifiers. When a gerund phrase is the subject in a sentence, it is singular.

► *Experimenting with drugs* is a dangerous practice.

44i Titles of works, names of companies, and words considered as words

is
► *The Two Gentlemen of Verona* ~~are~~ considered the weakest of
Shakespeare's comedies.

includes
► Kraft Foods ~~include~~ many different brands.

has
► In today's highly partisan politics *moderates* ~~have~~ come to
mean "wishy-washy people."

Exercise 44.4 Chapter review: Editing for subject-verb agreement
Edit the passage to correct subject-verb agreement errors.

The end of the nineteenth century saw the rise of a new
kind of architecture. Originating in response to the development of new building materials, this so-called modern architecture characterizes most of the buildings we sees around
us today.

Iron and reinforced concrete makes the modern building
possible. Previously, the structural characteristics of wood
and stone limited the dimensions of a building. Wood-frame
structures becomes unstable above a certain height. Stone
can bear great weight, but architects building in stone con-
fronts severe limits on the height of a structure in relation
to the width of its base. The principal advantage of iron and
steel are that they reduce those limits, permitting much
greater height than stone.

At first the new materials was used for decoration. However, architects like Hermann Muthesius and Walter Gropius began to use iron and steel as structural elements
within their buildings. The designs of Frank Lloyd Wright
also shows how the development of iron and steel technology
revolutionized building interiors. When every wall do not
have to bear weight from the floors above, open floor plans
is possible.

44i
sv agr

45 Recognizing Problems with Verbs

Verbs report action and show time. They change form to indicate person and number, voice and mood.

45a Learning the forms of regular and irregular verbs

English verbs have five main forms, except for the verb *be,* which has eight:

- The **base form** is the form found in a dictionary. *(For irregular verbs, other forms are given as well. See pp. 453–54 for a list.)*

- The **present tense** form indicates an action occurring at the moment, habitually, or at a set future time and also introduces quotations, literary events, and scientific facts *(pp. 458–60 and pp. 461–62).* The third-person singular present tense is the *-s* form.

- The **past tense** indicates an action completed at a specific time in the past *(pp. 458–60).*

- The **past participle** is used with *have, has,* or *had* to form the perfect tenses *(pp. 458–60);* with a form of the *be* verb to form the passive voice *(Chapter 38, pp. 399–400);* and as an adjective (the *polished* silver).

- The **present participle** is used with a form of the *be* verb to form the progressive tenses *(pp. 458–60).* It can also be used as a noun (the *writing* is finished) and as an adjective (the *smiling* man).

Regular verbs always add *-d* or *-ed* to the base verb to form the past tense and past participle. **Irregular verbs,** by contrast, do not form the past tense or past participle in a consistent way. Here are the five principal forms of the regular verb *walk* and the irregular verb *begin* as well as the eight forms of the verb *be.*

Principal Forms of *Walk* and *Begin*

BASE	PRESENT TENSE (THIRD PERSON)	PAST TENSE	PAST PARTICIPLE	PRESENT PARTICIPLE
walk	walks	walked	walked	walking
begin	begins	began	begun	beginning

Principal Forms of *Be*

BASE	PRESENT TENSE	PAST TENSE	PAST PARTICIPLE	PRESENT PARTICIPLE
be	I *am*. He, she, it *is*. We, you, they *are*.	I *was*. He, she, it *was*. We, you, they *were*.	I have *been*.	I am *being*.

1. A list of common irregular verbs

You can also find the past tense and past participle forms of irregular verbs by looking up the base form in a standard dictionary.

Forms of Common Irregular Verbs

BASE	PAST TENSE	PAST PARTICIPLE
arise	arose	arisen
awake	awoke	awoke/awakened
be	was/were	been
beat	beat	beaten
become	became	become
begin	began	begun
blow	blew	blown
break	broke	broken
bring	brought	brought
buy	bought	bought
catch	caught	caught
choose	chose	chosen
cling	clung	clung
come	came	come
do	did	done
draw	drew	drawn
drink	drank	drunk
drive	drove	driven
eat	ate	eaten
fall	fell	fallen
fight	fought	fought
fly	flew	flown
forget	forgot	forgotten/forgot
forgive	forgave	forgiven
freeze	froze	frozen
get	got	gotten/got
give	gave	given
go	went	gone
grow	grew	grown
hang	hung	hung (for things)
hang	hanged	hanged (for people)

45a
vb

BASE	PAST TENSE	PAST PARTICIPLE
have	had	had
hear	heard	heard
know	knew	known
lay	laid	laid
lie	lay	lain
lose	lost	lost
pay	paid	paid
raise	raised	raised
ride	rode	ridden
ring	rang	rung
rise	rose	risen
say	said	said
see	saw	seen
set	set	set
shake	shook	shaken
sit	sat	sat
spin	spun	spun
steal	stole	stolen
spend	spent	spent
strive	strove/strived	striven/strived
swear	swore	sworn
swim	swam	swum
swing	swung	swung
take	took	taken
tear	tore	torn
tread	trod	trod/trodden
wear	wore	worn
weave	wove	woven
wring	wrung	wrung
write	wrote	written

2. *Went* and *gone, saw* and *seen*

Went and *saw* are the past tense forms of the irregular verbs *go* and *see*. *Gone* and *seen* are the past participle forms. These verb forms are sometimes confused.

▶ I had ~~went~~ there yesterday.
        gone

▶ We ~~seen~~ the rabid dog and called for help.
      saw

3. Irregular verbs such as *drink (drank/drunk)*

For a few irregular verbs, such as *swim (swam/swum), drink (drank/drunk),* and *ring (rang/rung),* the difference between the past tense form and the past participle is only one letter. Be careful not to mix up these forms in your writing.

> *drunk*
► I had ~~drank~~ more than eight bottles of water that day.
    ^

> *rung*
► The church bell had ~~rang~~ five times before she heard it.
    ^

Exercise 45.1 Using irregular verb forms

Use the past participle or past tense form of the verb in parentheses, whichever is appropriate, to fill in the blanks in the following sentences.

> **EXAMPLE** **Today, a woman's right to vote is** *taken* **for granted. (take)**

1. Elizabeth Cady Stanton and Lucretia Mott _____ two of the founders of the women's rights movement in the United States. (be)

2. The movement had _____ out of the abolitionist movement. (grow)

3. Stanton and Mott hoped to address the inequalities between men and women that they _____ in American society. (see)

4. In 1848, hundreds of people, both men and women, _____ to Seneca Falls in upstate New York for the first convention on women's rights. (go)

5. Many of the words in the convention's Declaration of Sentiments were _____ directly from the Declaration of Independence. (draw)

6. With the Declaration of Sentiments' demand for a woman's right to vote, the women's suffrage movement had _____. (begin)

45b Distinguishing between *lay* and *lie, sit* and *set,* and *rise* and *raise*

45b
vb

Even experienced writers confuse the verbs *lay* and *lie, sit* and *set,* and *rise* and *raise.* The correct forms are given in the following table.

Often-Confused Verbs and Their Principal Forms

BASE	-S FORM	PAST	PAST PARTICIPLE	PRESENT PARTICIPLE
lay (to place)	lays	laid	laid	laying
lie (to recline)	lies	lay	lain	lying
lie (to speak an untruth)	lies	lied	lied	lying
rise (to go/get up)	rises	rose	risen	rising
sit (to be seated)	sits	sat	sat	sitting
set (to put on a surface)	sets	set	set	setting

One verb in each of these groups *(lay, set, raise)* is **transitive,** which means that an object receives the action of the verb. The other verbs *(lie, sit, rise)* are **intransitive** and cannot take an object. You should use a form of *lay, raise,* or *set* if you can replace the verb with *place* or *put.*

direct object
▶ The dog *lays a bone* at your feet, then *lies* down and closes his eyes.

direct object
▶ As the flames *rise,* the heat *raises the temperature* of the room.

direct object
▶ The technician *sits* down and *sets the samples* in front of her.

Lay (to place) and *lie* (to recline) are also confusing because the past tense of the irregular verb *lie* is *lay (lie, lay, lain).* Always double-check the verb *lay* when it appears in your writing.

laid
▶ He washed the dishes carefully and ~~lay~~ them on a clean towel.
                                           ^

Exercise 45.2 Distinguishing commonly confused verbs

Some of the sentences that follow have the wrong choice of verb. Edit the incorrect sentences, and circle the number of each sentence that is already correct.

lying
EXAMPLE   She was ~~laying~~ down after nearly fainting.
                    ^

1. Humans, like many other animals, usually lay down to sleep.
2. We found the manuscript lying on the desk where he left it.
3. The restless students had been setting at their desks all morning.
4. The actor sat the prop on the wrong table.
5. The archeologists rose the lid of the tomb.
6. The Wright brothers' contraption rose above the sands of Kitty Hawk.

45c Adding an *-s* or *-es* ending

In the present tense, almost all verbs add an *-s* or *-es* ending if the subject is third-person singular. *(See Chapter 44, pp. 442–51, for more on standard subject-verb combinations.)* Third-person singular subjects can be nouns *(woman, Benjamin, desk)*, pronouns *(he, she, it)*, or indefinite pronouns *(everyone)*.

> *rises*
> ► The stock market ~~rise~~ when economic news is good.
> ^

If the subject is in the first person *(I)*, the second person *(you)*, or the third-person plural *(people, they)*, the verb does *not* add an *-s* or *-es* ending.

> ► You invest~~s~~ your money wisely.

> ► People need~~s~~ to learn about companies before buying their stock.

Verb Forms and Grammar and Spelling Checkers

A grammar checker flagged the incorrect form in this sentence: *She had chose to go to the state college.* It also suggested the correct form: *chosen*. However, the checker missed the misuse of *set* in this sentence: *I am going to set down for a while.*

Spelling checkers will not highlight a verb form that is used incorrectly in a sentence.

45d Adding a *-d* or an *-ed* ending

These endings should be included on all regular verbs in the past tense and all past participles of regular verbs.

> *asked*
> ► The driving instructor ~~ask~~ the student driver to pull over to
> ^
> the curb.

> *mixed*
> ► After we had ~~mix~~ the formula, we let it cool.
> ^

Also check for missing *-d* or *-ed* endings on past participles used as adjectives.

> *concerned*
> ► The ~~concern~~ parents met with the school board.
> ^

45d vb

Exercise 45.3 Editing for verb form

Underline the verbs in each sentence. Then check to ensure that the correct verb forms are used, using the advice in Sections 45a–e. Circle the number of each correct sentence. Edit the remaining sentences.

EXAMPLE   The dentist has ~~forgave~~ *forgiven* Maya for biting his finger.

1. Humans are tremendously adaptable creatures.
2. Desert peoples have learn that loose, light garments protects them from the heat.
3. They have long drank from deep wells that they digged for water.
4. Arctic peoples have developed cultural practices that keeps them alive in a region where the temperature rarely rise above zero for months at a time.
5. Many people in mountainous areas have long builded terraces on steep slopes to create more land for farming.
6. Anthropologists and archeologists have argued about whether all cultural practices have an adaptive purpose.
7. Some practices may have went from adaptive to destructive.
8. For example, in ancient times, irrigation canals increased food production in arid areas.
9. After many centuries passed, however, the canals had deposit so much salt on the irrigated fields that the fields had became unfarmable.
10. By then, much of the population had fleed.

45e Using tenses accurately

Tenses show the time of a verb's action. English has three basic time frames—present, past, and future—and each tense has simple, perfect, and progressive verb forms to indicate the time span of the actions taking place. *(For a review of the present tense forms of a typical verb and of the verbs* be, have, *and* do, *see p. 443; for a review of the principal forms of regular and irregular verbs, which are used to form tenses, see pp. 452–54.)*

1. The simple present and past tenses

These two tenses do not use a helping verb or verbs. The **simple present tense** describes actions occurring at the moment, habitually, or at a set future time. The **simple past tense** is used for actions completed at a specific time in the past.

SIMPLE PRESENT

Every May, she *plans* next year's marketing strategy.

SIMPLE PAST

In the early morning hours before the office opened, she *planned* her marketing strategy.

2. The simple future tense

The **simple future tense** takes *will* plus the verb. It is used for actions that have not yet begun.

SIMPLE FUTURE

In May, I *will plan* next year's marketing strategy.

3. The perfect tenses

The **perfect tenses** take a form of *have (has, had)* plus the past participle. They indicate actions that were or will be completed by the time of another action or a specific time. The present perfect also describes actions that continue into the present.

PRESENT PERFECT

She *has* already *planned* next year's marketing strategy.

PAST PERFECT

By the time she resigned, Maria *had* already *planned* next year's marketing strategy.

FUTURE PERFECT

By May 31, she *will have planned* next year's marketing strategy.

When the verb in the past perfect is irregular, be sure to use the proper form of the past participle.

▶ **By the time the week was over, both plants had ~~grew~~ five inches.** *grown*

4. Progressive tenses

The **progressive tenses** take a form of *be (am, are, was, were)* plus the present participle. The progressive forms of the simple and perfect tenses indicate ongoing action.

**45e
vb**

PRESENT PROGRESSIVE

She *is planning* next year's marketing strategy now.

PAST PROGRESSIVE

She *was planning* next year's marketing strategy when she started to look for another job.

FUTURE PROGRESSIVE

During the month of May, she *will be planning* next year's marketing strategy.

References to planned events that didn't happen take *was*/*were going to* plus the base form.

▶ She *was going to plan* the marketing strategy, but she left the company.

5. Perfect progressive tenses

The **perfect progressive tenses** take *have* plus *be* plus the verb. These tenses indicate an action that takes place over a specific period of time. The present perfect progressive tense describes actions that start in the past and continue to the present; the past and future perfect progressive tenses are used for actions that ended or will end at a specified time or before another action.

PRESENT PERFECT PROGRESSIVE

She *has been planning* next year's marketing strategy since the beginning of May.

PAST PERFECT PROGRESSIVE

She *had been planning* next year's marketing strategy when she was offered another job.

FUTURE PERFECT PROGRESSIVE

By May 18, she *will have been planning* next year's marketing strategy for more than two weeks.

45f Using the past perfect tense

When a past event was ongoing but ended before a particular time or another past event, use the past perfect rather than the simple past.

▶ Before the Johnstown Flood occurred in 1889, people in the

    had

area expressed their concern about the safety of the dam on
    ^

the Conemaugh River.

People expressed their concern before the flood occurred.

If two past events happened simultaneously, however, use the simple past, not the past perfect.

▶ When the Conemaugh flooded, many people in the area ~~had~~ lost their lives.

NAVIGATING THROUGH COLLEGE AND BEYOND

Reporting Research Findings

Although we see a written work as always existing in the present, we think of research findings as having been collected at one time in the past. Use the past or present perfect tense to report the results of research:

► Three of the compounds (nos. 2, 3, and 6) ~~respond~~ *responded* positively by turning purple.

► Clegg (1990) ~~reviews~~ *has reviewed* studies of workplace organization focused on struggles for control of the labor process.

45g Using the present tense

If the conventions of a discipline require you to state what your paper does, do so in the present, not the future, tense.

► In this paper, I *describe* the effects of increasing NaCl concentrations on the germination of radish seeds.

Here are some other special uses of the present tense:

- By convention, events in a novel, short story, poem, or other literary work are described in the present tense.

  ► Even though Huck's journey down the river ~~was~~ *is* an escape from society, his relationship with Jim ~~was~~ *is* a form of community.

- Like events in a literary work, scientific facts are considered to be perpetually present, even though they were discovered in the past. (Theories that have been disproved should appear in the past tense.)

  ► Mendel discovered that genes ~~had~~ *have* different forms, or alleles.

45g vb

- The present tense is also used to introduce a quotation, paraphrase, or summary of someone else's writing.

  writes
► William Julius Wilson ~~wrote~~ that "the disappearance of
  ^

  work has become a characteristic feature of the inner-city

  ghetto" (31).

Note: When using APA style, introduce others' writing or research findings with the past tense (for example, Wilson *wrote*) or past perfect tense (Johnson *has found*).

Exercise 45.4   Using verb tenses

Underline the verb that best fits the sentence.

EXAMPLE   Marlow (<u>encounters</u>/encountered) Kurtz in the climax of Conrad's *Heart of Darkness.*

1. Newton showed that planetary motion (followed/follows) mathematical laws.
2. In *Principia Mathematica,* Newton (states/stated), "To every action there is always opposed an equal reaction."
3. Newton (publishes/published) the *Principia* in 1675.
4. With the *Principia,* Newton (had changed/changed) the course of science.
5. By the time of his death, Newton (had become/became) internationally famous.
6. Scientists and philosophers (were absorbing/absorbed) the implications of Newton's discoveries long after his death.

45h Using complete verbs

With only a few exceptions, all English sentences must contain a **complete verb,** which consists of the main verb along with any helping verbs that are needed to express the tense *(see pp. 458–60)* or voice *(see pp. 399–400).* **Helping verbs** include forms of *be, have,* and *do* and the modal verbs *can, could, may, might, shall, should, will, ought to, must,* and *would.* Helping verbs can be part of contractions *(he's running, we'd better go),* but they cannot be left out of the sentence entirely.

  will
► **They be going on a field trip next week.**
  ^

Do not use *of* in place of *have*.

> *have*
> ► I could ~~of~~ finished earlier.
>   ^

A **linking verb,** often a form of *be,* connects the subject to a description or definition of it: *Cats are mammals.* Linking verbs can be part of contractions *(she's a student),* but they should not be left out entirely.

> *is*
> ► Montreal a major Canadian city.
>   ^

Exercise 45.5   Editing for verb tense

Edit the following passage, replacing or deleting verb parts so that the tenses reflect the context of the passage.

> EXAMPLE   **Returning to the area, the survivors ~~had~~ found massive destruction.**

For some time, anthropologists are being puzzled by the lack of a written language among the ancient Incas of South America. The Incas, who had conquered most of Andean South America by about 1500, had sophisticated architecture, advanced knowledge of engineering and astronomy, and sophisticated social and political structures. Why aren't they having a written language as well?

Ancient Egypt, Iraq, and China, as well as early Mexican civilizations such as the Aztec and Maya, had all been having written language. It is seeming strange that only the Incas will have lacked a written language.

Anthropologists now think that the Incas have possessed a kind of written language after all. Scholars will believe that the Incas used knots in multicolored strings as the medium for their "writing." The Incas called these strings *khipu.*

45i
vb

45i   Using the subjunctive mood

The **mood** of a verb indicates the writer's attitude. Use the **indicative mood** to state or to question facts, acts, and opinions *(Our collection is on display. Did you see it?).* Use the **imperative mood** for commands, directions, and entreaties. The subject of an imperative sentence is always *you,* but the *you* is usually understood, not written out *(Shut the door!)*. Use the **subjunctive mood** to express a wish or a demand or to make a statement contrary to fact *(I wish I were a millionaire)*. The mood that writers have the most trouble with is the subjunctive.

Verbs in the subjunctive mood may be in the present tense, past tense, or perfect tense. Present tense subjunctive verbs do not change form to signal person or number. The only form used is the verb's base form: *accompany* or *be,* not *accompanies* or *am, are, is.* Also, the verb *be* has only one past tense form in the subjunctive mood: *were.*

WISH

I wish I *were* more prepared for this test.

Note: In everyday conversation, most speakers use the indicative rather than the subjunctive when expressing wishes *(I wish I was more prepared for this test).*

Words such as *ask, insist, recommend, request,* and *suggest* indicate the subjunctive mood; the verb in the *that* clause that follows should be in the subjunctive.

DEMAND

I insist that all applicants *find* their seats by 8:00 A.M.

CONTRARY-TO-FACT STATEMENT

He would not be so irresponsible if his father *were* [not *was*] still alive.

Contrary-to-fact statements often contain a subordinate clause that begins with *if:* the verb in the *if* clause should be in the subjunctive mood.

Note: Some common expressions of conjecture are in the subjunctive mood, including *as it were, come rain or shine, far be it from me,* and *be that as it may.*

Exercise 45.6   Using the subjunctive

Fill in each blank with the correct form of the base verb in parentheses. Some of the sentences are in the subjunctive; others are in the indicative or imperative mood.

> EXAMPLE   **We ask that everyone _bring_ pencils to the exam.
> (bring)**

1. The stockholders wish the company _____ run more profitably. (be)

2. The board demanded that the CEO _____. (resign)

3. "If I _____ you," said the board chairperson, "I would take a long vacation." (be)

4. Judging from the stock's recent rise, the management change _____ investors. (please)

5. _____ share value or face the consequences! (increase)

(For more on the use of speculation and the subjunctive, see Chapter 48, pp. 505–6.)

46 Fixing Problems with Pronouns

A **pronoun** *(he/him, it/its, they/their)* takes the place of a noun. The noun that the pronoun replaces is called its **antecedent.** In the following sentence, *snow* is the antecedent of the pronoun *it.*

▶ The *snow* fell all day long, and by nightfall *it* was three feet deep.

**46
pn agr**

Like nouns, pronouns are singular or plural.

SINGULAR The *house* was dark and gloomy, and *it* sat in a grove of tall cedars.

PLURAL The *cars* swept by on the highway, all of *them* doing more than sixty-five miles per hour.

A pronoun needs an antecedent to refer to and agree with, and a pronoun must match its antecedent in number (plural/singular) and gender *(he/his, she/her, it/its).* A pronoun must also be in a form, or case, that matches its function in the sentence.

Pronoun Problems and Grammar Checkers

Do not rely on grammar checkers to alert you to problems in pronoun-antecedent agreement or pronoun reference. One grammar checker, for example, missed the case error in the following sentence: *Ford's son Edsel,* who [*should be* whom] *the auto magnate treated very cruelly, was a brilliant automotive designer. (See pp. 478–79 for a discussion of the proper use of* who *and* whom.*)*

✓ **46a** Making pronouns agree with their antecedents

Problems with pronoun-antecedent agreement tend to occur when a pronoun's antecedent is an indefinite pronoun, a collective noun, or a compound noun. Problems may also occur when writers are trying to avoid the generic use of *he.*

1. Indefinite pronouns

Indefinite pronouns such as *someone, anybody,* and *nothing* refer to nonspecific people or things. They sometimes function as antecedents for other pronouns. Most indefinite pronouns are singular *(anybody, anyone, anything, each, either, everybody, everyone, everything, much, neither, nobody, none* [meaning *not one*], *no one, nothing, one, somebody, something).*

ALWAYS **Did *either* of the boys lose *his* bicycle?**
SINGULAR

A few indefinite pronouns—*both, few, many,* and *several*—are plural.

ALWAYS **Both of the boys lost *their* bicycles.**
PLURAL

The indefinite pronouns *all, any, more, most,* and *some* can be either singular or plural, depending on the noun to which they refer.

PLURAL **The students debated, *some* arguing that *their* positions on the issue were in the mainstream.**

SINGULAR **The bread is on the counter, but *some* of *it* has already been eaten.**

Problems arise when writers attempt to make indefinite pronouns agree with their antecedents without introducing gender bias. There are three ways to avoid gender bias when correcting a pronoun agreement problem such as the following.

FAULTY   **None of the great Romantic writers believed that their achievements equaled their aspirations.**

■ If possible, change a singular indefinite pronoun to a plural pronoun, editing the sentence as necessary.

All
▶ ~~None~~ of the great Romantic writers believed that their
   ^

         fell short of
achievements ~~equaled~~ **their aspirations.**
        ^

■ Reword the sentence to eliminate the indefinite pronoun.

The
▶ ~~None of the~~ great Romantic writers believed that their
   ^

         did not equal
achievements ~~equaled~~ **their aspirations.**
        ^

■ Substitute *he or she* or *his or her* (but never *his/her*) for the singular pronoun. Change the sentence as necessary to avoid using this construction more than once.

▶ **None of the great Romantic writers believed that**

                 his or her   *had been realized*
~~their achievements equaled their~~ **aspirations.**
              ^   ^

2. Generic nouns

A **generic noun** represents anyone and everyone in a group—a typical doctor, the average voter. Because most groups consist of both males and females, using male pronouns to refer to generic nouns is usually considered sexist. To fix agreement problems with generic nouns, use one of the three options suggested in the preceding section.

> **46a**
> **pn agr**

College students   *s*
▶ ~~A college student~~ **should have a̶ mind of their own.**
       ^   ^

                   an independent point of view.
▶ **A college student should have** ~~a mind of their own.~~
                          ^

                   his or her
▶ **A college student should have a mind of** ~~their~~ **own.**
                           ^

✓ | **IDENTIFY AND EDIT** | Problems with Gender Bias and Pronoun-Antecedent Agreement | *agr*

Try these three strategies for avoiding gender bias when an indefinite pronoun or generic noun is the antecedent in a sentence:

❋ 1. *If possible, change the antecedent to a plural indefinite pronoun or a plural noun.*

> *All*   *our*
> - ~~Each~~ of us should decide ~~their~~ vote on issues, not personality.
>   ^   ^
>
> *Responsible citizens decide*
> - ~~The responsible citizen decides~~ their vote on issues, not
>   ^
>
>   personality.

❋ 2. *Reword the sentence to eliminate the pronoun.*

> - Each of us should ~~decide their~~ vote on issues, not personality.
>
>   *votes*
> - The responsible citizen ~~decides their vote~~ on issues, not
>   ^
>
>   personality.

❋ 3. *Substitute* he or she *or* his or her *(but never his/her) for the singular pronoun to maintain pronoun-antecedent agreement.*

>   *his or her*
> - Each of us should decide ~~their~~ vote on issues, not personality.
>   ^
>
>   *his or her*
> - The responsible citizen decides ~~their~~ vote on issues, not
>   ^
>
>   personality.
>
> **Caution:** Use this strategy sparingly. Using *he or she* or *his or her* several times in quick succession makes for tedious reading.

3. Collective nouns

Collective nouns such as *team, family, jury, committee,* and *crowd* are singular unless the people in the group are acting as individuals.

▶ All together, the crowd surged through the palace gates,

                 its
trampling over everything in ~~their~~ path.
           ^

The phrase *all together* indicates that this crowd is acting as a collection of individuals.

► **The committee left the conference room and returned to**

their

~~its~~ **offices.**
 ^

In this case, the members of the committee are acting as individuals: each is returning to an office.

If you are using a collective noun that has a plural meaning, consider adding a plural noun to clarify the meaning: *The committee members returned to their offices.*

4. Compound antecedents

Compound antecedents joined by *and* are almost always plural.

► **To remove all traces of the crime, James put the book and**

their places.
the magnifying glass back in ~~its place.~~
 ^

When a compound antecedent is joined by *or* or *nor,* the pronoun should agree with the closest part of the compound antecedent. If one part is singular and the other is plural, the sentence will be smoother and more effective if the plural antecedent is closest to the pronoun.

PLURAL   **Neither *the child nor the parents* shared *their* food.**

When the two parts of the compound antecedent refer to the same person, or when the word *each* or *every* precedes the compound antecedent, use a singular pronoun.

SINGULAR   **Being *a teacher and a mother* keeps *her* busy.**

SINGULAR   ***Every* poem and letter by Keats has *its* own special power.**

46a
pn agr

Exercise 46.1   Editing for pronoun-antecedent agreement

Some of the sentences that follow contain errors in pronoun-antecedent agreement. Circle the number of each correct sentence, and edit the others so that the pronouns agree with their antecedents. Rewrite sentences as necessary to avoid gender bias; you may eliminate pronouns or change words. There will be several possible answers for rewritten sentences.

their
EXAMPLE   **Neither the dog nor the cats ate ~~its~~ chow.**
                                              ^

1. Everybody at the displaced-persons camp had to submit his medical records before boarding the ships to the United States.
2. Many were forbidden to board because they had histories of tuberculosis and other illnesses.
3. This news was always devastating because no one wanted to be separated from their family.
4. Some immigrants resorted to forging his medical records.
5. After all, a mother could not be separated from their children, and the family had to get to America.
6. Immigrants had heard that a doctor in America takes good care of their patients and felt they had a chance for a better life there.
7. Even so, was it fair to expose others to illness just to bring parents and a child to its new surroundings?
8. Every difficulty and ethical dilemma presented its own challenge for displaced persons trying to find a home with a future after World War II.

✓ **46b** Making pronoun references clear

If a pronoun does not clearly refer to a specific antecedent, readers can become confused. Two common problems are ambiguous references and implied references.

1. Ambiguous references

If a pronoun can refer to more than one noun in a sentence, the reference is ambiguous. To clear up the ambiguity, eliminate the pronoun, and use the appropriate noun.

► **The friendly banter between Hamlet and Horatio eventually**

Hamlet
provokes ~~him~~ to declare that his worldview has changed.
            ^

Sometimes the ambiguous reference can be cleared up by rewriting the sentence.

When   *was in London, she*   *with Cassandra.*
► **Jane Austen ~~and Cassandra~~ corresponded regularly ~~when~~**
      ^   ^   ^

~~she was in London.~~

2. Implied references

The antecedent that a pronoun refers to must be present in the sentence, and it must be a noun or another pronoun, not a word that modifies a noun. Possessives and verbs cannot be antecedents in college writing, although this usage is common in speech and informal contexts.

> *his*   *Wilson*
> ► In ~~Wilson's~~ essay "When Work Disappears," ~~he~~ proposes a
>
> four-point plan for the revitalization of blighted inner-city
>
> communities.

Replacing *he* with *Wilson* gives the pronoun *his* an antecedent that is stated explicitly, not just implied. Note that in the revised sentence, the antecedent follows the pronoun.

> ► Every weekday afternoon, my brothers skateboard home
>
>   *their skateboards*
> from school, and then they leave ~~them~~ in the driveway.

In the original sentence, *skateboard* is a verb, not a noun, and cannot act as a pronoun antecedent.

3. *This, that,* and *which*

The pronouns *this, that,* and *which* often refer vaguely to ideas expressed in preceding sentences. To make the sentence containing the pronoun clearer, either change the pronoun to a specific noun or add a specific antecedent or clarifying noun.

> ► As government funding for higher education decreases,
>
>   *these higher costs*
> tuition increases. Are we students supposed to accept ~~this~~
>
> without protest?

> ► As government funding for higher education decreases,
>
> tuition increases. Are we students supposed to accept
>
> *situation*
> this without protest?

46b
ref

4. *You, they,* and *it*

The pronouns *you, they,* and *it* should refer to definite, explicitly stated antecedents. If the antecedent is unclear, replace the pronoun with an appropriately specific noun, or rewrite the sentence to eliminate the pronoun.

the government pays
► In some countries such as Canada, ~~they pay~~ for such

medical procedures.

students
► According to college policy, ~~you~~ must have a permit to park

a car on campus.

The
► ~~In the~~ textbook, ~~it~~ states that borrowing to fund the

purchase of financial assets results in a double-counting

of debt.

In college writing, use *you* only to address the reader: *Turn left when you reach the corner.*

Note: Writers sometimes use *one* as a generic pronoun. This practice usually seems pompous, however, and is best avoided.

Exercise 46.2 Editing to clarify pronoun reference

Rewrite each sentence to eliminate unclear pronoun references. Some sentences have several possible correct answers.

EXAMPLE   **You are not allowed to drive if you are a woman in Saudi Arabia.**

Women in Saudi Arabia are not allowed to drive.

1. The historic race between Barack Obama and Hillary Clinton for the Democratic nomination in 2008 was not resolved until late spring. This was a worrisome development for campaign strategists.

2. After John McCain's selection of Alaska governor Sarah Palin as his running mate, he expected to gain more votes from women.

3. When candidates Barack Obama and John McCain debated for the first time in the general election campaign, he managed to avoid making any major mistakes.

4. With Obama as president, they promised to work on strengthening the faltering economy with a stimulus package.

5. Because of all the polling, you had little doubt that Obama would win the election on Tuesday, November 4, 2008.

6. In this article, it notes that the tables were turned two years later in 2010 when the Republicans won control of the House of Representatives.

✓ **46c** Choosing the correct pronoun case: for example, *I* vs. *me*

When a pronoun's form, or **case,** does not match its function in a sentence, readers will feel that something is wrong:

- Pronouns in the subjective case are used as subjects or subject complements: *I, you, he, she, it, we, they, who, whoever.*

- Pronouns in the objective case are used as objects of verbs or prepositions: *me, you, him, her, it, us, them, whom, whomever.*

- Pronouns in the possessive case show ownership: *my, mine, your, yours, his, hers, its, our, ours, their, theirs, whose.* Adjective forms (*her* room, *our* office) appear before nouns. Noun forms stand alone (that room is *hers; mine* is on the left). When noun forms act as subjects, the verb agrees with the antecedent *(room).*

1. Pronouns in compound structures

Compound structures (words or phrases joined by *and, or,* or *nor*) can appear as subjects or objects. If you are not sure which form of a pronoun to use in a compound structure, treat the pronoun as the only subject or object, and note how the sentence sounds.

46c
case

SUBJECT **Angela and *I* [not *me*] were cleaning up the kitchen.**

If you treat the pronoun as the only subject, the original sentence is clearly wrong: *Me [was] cleaning up the kitchen.*

OBJECT **My parents waited for an explanation from John and *me* [not *I*].**

If you treat the pronoun as the only object, the original sentence is clearly wrong: *My parents waited for an answer from I.*

2. Subject complements

A **subject complement** renames and specifies the sentence's subject. It follows a **linking verb**—a verb, often a form of *be,* that links the subject to its description or definition: *Children* <u>are</u> *innocent.*

> SUBJECT **Mark's best friends are Jane and *I* [not *me*].**
> COMPLEMENT

You can also switch the order to make the pronoun into the subject: *Jane and I are Mark's best friends.*

3. Appositives

Appositives are nouns or noun phrases that rename nouns or pronouns. They appear right after the word they rename and have the same function in the sentence that the word has.

> SUBJECTIVE **The two weary travelers, Ramon and *I* [not *me*], found shelter in an old cabin.**

> OBJECTIVE **The police arrested two protesters, Jane and *me* [not *I*].**

4. *We* or *us*

When *we* or *us* comes before a noun, it has the same function in the sentence as the noun it precedes.

> SUBJECTIVE ***We* [not *Us*] students never get to decide such things.**

We renames the subject: *students.*

> OBJECTIVE **Things were looking desperate for *us* [not *we*] campers.**

Us renames the object of the preposition *for: campers.*

5. Comparisons with *than* or *as*

In comparisons, words are often left out of the sentence because the reader can guess what they would be. When a pronoun follows *than* or *as,* make sure you are using the correct form by mentally adding the missing word or words.

► **Meg is quicker than she [is].**

► **We find ourselves remembering Maria as often as [we remember] her.**

IDENTIFY AND EDIT | Problems with Pronoun Case | *case* ✓

Follow these steps to decide on the proper form of pronouns in compound structures:

❋ 1. *Identify the compound structure (a pronoun and a noun or other pronoun joined by and, but, or, or nor) in the problem sentence.*

> compound structure
>
> PROBLEM
> SENTENCE
> [Her or her roommate] should call the campus technical support office and sign up for broadband Internet service.
>
> compound structure
>
> PROBLEM
> SENTENCE
> The director gave the leading roles to [my brother and I].

❋ 2. *Isolate the pronoun that you are unsure about, then read the sentence to yourself without the rest of the compound structure. If the result sounds wrong, change the case of the pronoun, and read the sentence again.*

> PROBLEM
> SENTENCE
> [Her ~~or her roommate~~] should call the campus technical support office and sign up for the broadband Internet service.
>
> *Her should call the campus technical support office* sounds wrong. The pronoun should be in the subjective case: *she.*
>
> PROBLEM
> SENTENCE
> The director gave the leading roles to [~~my brother and~~ I].
>
> *The director gave the leading role[s] to I* sounds wrong. The pronoun should be in the objective case: *me.*

❋ 3. *If necessary, correct the original sentence.*

> *She*
> • ~~Her~~ or her roommate should call the campus technical support
>   ^
>   office and sign up for broadband Internet service.
>   *me*
> • The director gave the leading roles to my brother and ~~I~~.
>   ^

46c
case

Sometimes the correct form depends on intended meaning:

▶ **My brother likes our dog more than I [do].**

▶ **My brother likes our dog more than [he likes] me.**

If a sentence with a comparison sounds too awkward or formal, add the missing words: *Meg is quicker than she is.*

6. Pronouns as the subject or the object of an infinitive

An **infinitive** is *to* plus the base verb *(to breathe, to sing, to dance).* Whether a pronoun functions as the subject or the object of an infinitive, it should be in the objective case.

infinitive   infinitive
subject   object

▶ **We wanted our lawyer and *her* to defend *us* against this unfair charge.**

7. Pronouns in front of an *-ing* noun (a gerund)

- When a noun or pronoun appears before a **gerund** (an *-ing* verb form functioning as a noun), it should usually be treated as a possessive.

animals'
▶ **The ~~animals~~ fighting disturbed the entire neighborhood.**
      ^

their
▶ **Because of ~~them~~ screeching, no one could get any sleep.**
       ^

When the *-ing* word is functioning as a modifier, not a noun, use the subjective or objective case for the pronoun that precedes it. Consider these two sentences.

▶ **The teacher punished their cheating.**

Cheating is the object of the sentence, modified by the possessive pronoun *their.*

▶ **The teacher saw them cheating.**

Them is the object of the sentence, modified by *cheating.*

Exercise 46.3 Choosing pronoun case

Underline the pronoun in parentheses that is appropriate to the sentence.

EXAMPLE   **Michael and (I/me) grew up in Philadelphia.**

1. The first person to receive a diploma was (I/me). Matt and Lara followed behind me.

2. Throughout the ceremony, I joked with Lara and (he/him), enjoying my last official college event with them.

3. Lara joked that the people least likely to succeed after college were Matt and (her/she).

4. That outcome is highly unlikely, however, because Lara and (he/him) were tied for valedictorian.

5. Graduation was a bittersweet day for my friends and (I/me).

Exercise 46.4   Choosing pronoun case with appositives

Underline the pronoun in parentheses that is appropriate to the sentence.

EXAMPLE   **(We/Us) players are ready to hit the field.**

1. (We/Us) Americans live in a cultural melting pot.

2. My parents, for example, have passed on Finnish and Spanish cultural traditions to their children, my two brothers and (I/me).

3. Our grandparents have told fascinating stories about our ancestors to (we/us) grandchildren.

4. On New Year's Eve, the younger family members, my brothers and (I/me), tell fortunes according to a Finnish custom, and then, following a Spanish tradition, the whole family eats grapes.

5. My grandmother gave her oldest grandchild, (I/me), a journal with her observations of our family's varied cultural traditions—our own melting pot.

Exercise 46.5   Choosing pronoun case with comparisons, infinitives, and gerunds

Underline the pronoun in parentheses that is appropriate to the sentence.

EXAMPLE   **Troy is a better driver than (she/her).**

1. Robert Browning, an admirer of Elizabeth Barrett, started to court (she/her) in 1844, thus beginning one of the most famous romances in history.

2. Barrett's parents did not want Browning and (she/her) to marry, but the couple wed secretly in 1846.

3. (Their/Them) moving to Italy from England helped Barrett improve her poor health.

4. Even though Browning also had great talent, Barrett was recognized as a poet earlier than (he/him).

5. Today, however, he is considered as prominent a poet as (she/her).

46c
case

Exercise 46.6   Editing for pronoun case

Edit the following passage, substituting the correct form of the pronoun for any pronoun in the wrong case.

EXAMPLE   **The winning points were scored by Hatcher**
me
and ~~I~~.
         ^

Sociolinguists investigate the relationship between linguistic variations and culture. They spend a lot of time in the field to gather data for analysis. For instance, them might compare the speech patterns of people who live in a city with those of people who reside in the suburbs. Sociolinguists might discover differences in pronunciation or word choice. Their researching helps us understand both language and culture.

Us laypeople might confuse sociolinguistics with sociology. Sociolinguists do a more specialized type of research than do most sociologists, who study broad patterns within societies. Being concerned with such particulars as the pronunciation of a single vowel, sociolinguists work at a finer level of detail than them.

46d   Choosing between *who* and *whom*

The relative pronouns *who, whom, whoever,* and *whomever* are used to introduce dependent clauses and in questions. Their case depends on their function:

- **Subjective:** *who, whoever*
- **Objective:** *whom, whomever*

1. Pronouns in dependent clauses

If the pronoun is functioning as a subject and is performing an action, use *who* or *whoever*. If the pronoun is the object of a verb or preposition, use *whom* or *whomever*. (Note that *whom* usually appears at the beginning of the clause.)

SUBJECT   Henry Ford, *who* started the Ford Motor Company, was autocratic and stubborn.

OBJECT   Ford's son Edsel, *whom* the auto magnate treated cruelly, was a brilliant automobile designer.

2. Pronouns in questions

To choose the correct form for the pronoun, answer the question with a personal pronoun.

SUBJECT   **Who founded the General Motors Corporation?**

The answer could be *He founded it. He* is in the subjective case, so *who* is correct.

OBJECT   **Whom did the Chrysler Corporation turn to for leadership in the 1980s?**

The answer could be *It turned to him. Him* is in the objective case, so *whom* is correct.

Exercise 46.7   Choosing between *who* and *whom*

Underline the pronoun that is appropriate to the sentence.

EXAMPLE   **Arlia is the one (who/whom) people say will have the top sales results.**

1. (Who/Whom) invented the light bulb? Thomas Edison did.
2. He was a scientist and inventor (who/whom) also invented the phonograph and improved the telegraph, telephone, and motion picture technology.
3. Edison, (who/whom) patented 1,093 inventions in his lifetime, was nicknamed the "Wizard of Menlo Park."
4. The hardworking Edison, (who/whom) everyone greatly admired, believed that "genius is one percent inspiration and ninety-nine percent perspiration."
5. (Who/Whom) should we remember the next time we switch on the light? Thomas Edison.

Exercise 46.8   Chapter review: Fixing problems with pronouns

Edit the following passage so that all pronouns have clear antecedents, agree with their antecedents, and are in the appropriate case.

46d
case

Margaret Mead was probably the best-known anthropologist of the twentieth century. It was she whom wrote *Coming of Age in Samoa,* a book well known in the 1930s and still in print today. It was her who gave us the idea that Melanesian natives grow up free of the strictures and repressions that can characterize adolescence in our society. Her writings found an audience just as the work of Sigmund Freud was becoming widely known in the United States.

In his work, he argued for "an incomparably freer sexual life," saying that rigid attitudes toward sexuality contributed to mental illness among we Westerners. Her accessible and gracefully written account of life among the Samoans showed them to be both relatively free of pathology and relaxed about sexual matters. Their work both provoked and contributed to a debate over theories about the best way to raise children.

47 Recognizing Problems with Adjectives and Adverbs

Adjectives and **adverbs** are words that qualify— or modify—the meanings of other words. Adjectives modify nouns and pronouns. Adverbs modify verbs, adjectives, and other adverbs.

47a Using adverbs correctly

Adverbs modify verbs, adjectives, other adverbs, and even whole clauses. They tell where, when, why, how, how often, how much, or to what degree.

▶   The authenticity of the document is *hotly* contested.

▶   The water was *brilliant* blue and *icy* cold.

▶   Dickens mixed humor and pathos *better* than any other

English writer after Shakespeare.

▶   *Consequently,* Dickens is still read by millions.

Do not substitute an adjective for an adverb. Watch especially for the adjectives *bad, good,* and *real,* which sometimes substitute for the adverbs *badly, well,* and *really* in casual speech.

▶ He plays the role so ~~bad~~ *badly* that it is an insult to Shakespeare.

▶ At times, he gets ~~real~~ *really* close to the edge of the stage.

▶ I've seen other actors play the role ~~good~~ *well*, but they were

classically trained.

Adjectives, Adverbs, and Grammar Checkers

Computer grammar checkers are sensitive to some problems with adjectives and adverbs but miss far more than they catch. A grammar checker failed to flag the errors in the following sentences: *The price took a suddenly plunge* [should be *sudden*], and *The price plunged sudden* [should be *suddenly*].

47b Using adjectives correctly

Adjectives modify nouns and pronouns; they do not modify any other kind of word. Adjectives tell what kind or how many and may come before or after the noun or pronoun they modify.

▶ The *looming* clouds, *ominous* and *gray*, frightened the

children.

Some proper nouns have adjective forms. Proper adjectives, like the proper nouns they are derived from, are capitalized: *Victoria/Victorian, Britain/British, America/American, Shakespeare/Shakespearean.*

In some cases, a noun is used as an adjective without a change in form.

▶ *Cigarette* smoking harms the lungs and is banned in offices.

Occasionally, descriptive adjectives function as if they were nouns.

▶ The *unemployed* should not be equated with the *lazy*.

Watch out for some common problem areas with the use of adjectives:

- ▪ **Adjectives treated as adverbs.** In common speech, we sometimes treat adjectives as adverbs. In writing, avoid this informal usage.

47b
ad

really well
▶ He hit that ball ~~real good~~.

Both *real* and *good* are adjectives, but they are used as adverbs in the original sentence, with *real* modifying *good* and *good* modifying the verb *hit*.

Note that *well* can function as an adjective and subject complement with a linking verb to describe a person's health.

▶ After the treatment, the patient felt *well* again.

certainly
▶ She ~~sure~~ made me work hard for my grade.

In the original sentence, the adjective *sure* tries to do the work of an adverb modifying the verb *made*.

▪ **Adjectives with linking verbs.** Use adjectives after linking verbs to describe the subject. Descriptive adjectives that modify a sentence's subject but appear after a linking verb are called **subject complements**.

▶ During the winter, both Emily and Anne *were sick*.

    Linking verbs are related to states of being and the five senses: *appear, become, feel, grow, look, smell, sound,* and *taste*. Verbs related to the senses can be either linking or action verbs, depending on the meaning of the sentence.

LINKING   The dog smelled *bad* [adjective].

ACTION   The dog smelled *badly* [adverb].

▪ **Adjectives and adverbs that are spelled alike.** In most instances, *-ly* endings indicate adverbs; however, words with *-ly* endings can sometimes be adjectives *(the lovely girl)*. In standard English, many adverbs do not require the *-ly* ending, and some words are both adjectives and adverbs: *fast, only, hard, right,* and *straight*. Note that *right* also has an *-ly* form as an adverb: *rightly*. When in doubt, consult a dictionary.

Exercise 47.1   Identifying adjectives and adverbs

In the sentences that follow on the next page, underline and label all adjectives (adj), nouns used as adjectives (n), and adverbs (adv). Then draw an arrow from each modifier to the word or words it modifies.

EXAMPLE   The water was **chillingly cold.**

1. The spread of destructive viruses to computers around the world is a serious problem with potentially deadly consequences.
2. Carried by infected e-mails, the viruses spread fast, moving from computer to computer at the click of a mouse.
3. Viruses have hit businesses badly in the past, disrupting railroads, delaying flights, and closing stores and offices.
4. Because viruses are so harmful, computer users should install antivirus software and update it regularly.
5. Other precautions include maintaining a good firewall and screening e-mail well to avoid opening suspicious messages.

Exercise 47.2   Editing adjectives and adverbs

Edit the sentences that follow so that adjectives are not used where adverbs belong and adverbs are not used where adjectives belong. Circle the number of any sentence that is already correct.

well

EXAMPLE   **She hid the money so ~~good~~ that she could not**
           ^
           find it when she needed it.

1. Sociology, the scholarly study of human society, is well and thriving today.
2. The discipline's intellectual roots reach real far back, to the eighteenth century.
3. Auguste Comte (1798–1857) invented the word _sociology,_ and mostly sociologists would probable agree that he founded the discipline.
4. According to Comte, scientific laws control human social behavior as sure as they control the motion of planets around the sun.
5. Comte believed his scientific approach was good because it would further human progress.
6. Emile Durkheim (1858–1917) helped place modern sociology on a well foundation.
7. Durkheim argued that societies can be good understood only if analyzed on their own terms, apart from the individuals who constitute them.
8. He proposed that society shapes the individual more than the other way around and that the individual fares bad without a sense of social belonging.

**47b
ad**

47c Using positive, comparative, and superlative adjectives and adverbs

Most adjectives and adverbs have three forms: positive *(dumb)*, comparative *(dumber)*, and superlative *(dumbest)*. The simplest form of the adjective is the positive form.

1. Comparatives and superlatives

Use the comparative form to compare two things and the superlative form to compare three or more things.

▶ In total area, New York is a *larger* state than Pennsylvania.

▶ Texas is the *largest* state in the Southwest.

2. *-er/-est* endings and *more/most*

To form comparatives and superlatives of short adjectives, add the suffixes *-er* and *-est (brighter/brightest)*. With longer adjectives (three or more syllables), use *more* or *less* and *most* or *least (more dangerous/ most dangerous)*.

                    nearest
▶ Mercury is the ~~most near~~ planet to the sun.

A few short adverbs have *-er* and *-est* endings in their comparative and superlative forms *(harder/hardest)*. Most adverbs, however, including all adverbs that end in *-ly,* use *more* or *less* and *most* or *least* in their comparative and superlative forms.

▶ She sings *more loudly* than we expected.

Two common adjectives—*good* and *bad*—form the comparative and superlative in an irregular way: *good, better, best* and *bad, worse, worst.*

           worse
▶ He felt ~~badder~~ as his illness progressed.

3. Double comparatives and superlatives

Use either an *-er* or an *-est* ending or *more/most* to form the comparative or superlative, as appropriate; do not use both.

▶ Since World War II, Britain has been the ~~most~~ closest ally of the United States.

4. Concepts that cannot be compared

Do not use comparative or superlative forms with adjectives such as *unique, infinite, impossible, perfect, round, square,* and *destroyed.* These concepts are *absolutes.* If something is unique, for example, it is the only one of its kind, making comparison impossible.

▶ You will never find ~~a more unique~~ restaurant ~~than~~ this one.

another ... *like*

47d Avoiding double negatives

The words *no, not,* and *never* can modify the meaning of nouns and pronouns as well as other sentence elements.

NOUN	You are *no* friend of mine.
ADJECTIVE	The red house was *not* large.
VERB	He *never* ran in a marathon.

However, it takes only one negative word to change the meaning of a sentence from positive to negative. When two negatives are used together, they cancel each other, resulting in a positive meaning. Unless you want your sentence to have a positive meaning (*I am not unaware of your feelings in this matter*), edit by changing or eliminating one of the negative words.

▶ They don't have ~~no~~ reason to go there.

any

▶ He ~~can't~~ hardly do that assignment.

can

Note that *hardly* has a negative meaning and cannot be used with *no, not,* or *never.*

Exercise 47.3 Editing comparisons

Edit the sentences that follow so that adjectives and adverbs are used correctly in comparisons. Some of the sentences are already correct; circle their numbers.

EXAMPLE He felt ~~badder~~ as his illness progressed.

worse

1. Biotechnology, perhaps the controversialest application of science in recent decades, is the basis of genetic engineering, cloning, and gene therapy.
2. Some of these fields are more popular than others.

47d
ad

3. Ethicists find it more easy to defend the genetic engineering of plants than the cloning of animals.

4. Gene therapy is often a last resort for people suffering from the worser types of cancer.

5. Gene therapy, one of the more newer forms of biotechnology, involves introducing cells containing specialized genetic material into the patient's body.

6. Cloning, a way of creating an exact duplicate of an organism, is probably more hard to justify than any other biotechnological procedure.

7. A female lamb cloned in Scotland in 1997 seemed no different from others of her breed.

8. Despite the successes that have been achieved with animal cloning, most people do not want no humans to be cloned.

9. The Raelians, a fringe group, claimed they had cloned a human infant.

10. Many people cannot hardly believe that the Raelians really cloned an infant.

Exercise 47.4   Fixing problems with adjectives and adverbs

Edit the following passage to correct any problems with adjectives and adverbs.

Although there are many approaches to sociology, the two most commonest ones are functionalism and conflict theory. The functionalist view, usual associated with Harvard sociologist Talcott Parsons, sees society as a whole that tries to maintain equilibrium, or stasis. No proponent of conflict theory is most famous than Karl Marx, who invented the concept of class warfare. Promoted in the United States by the African-American sociologist W. E. B. Du Bois, among others, conflict theory sees society as made up of groups that cannot hardly avoid being in conflict or competition with one another.

For a functionalist like Parsons, societies are best understood according to how good they maintain stability. On the other hand, for a conflict theorist like Du Bois, a society is more better analyzed in terms of how its various groups compete for power.

48 Special Editing Topics for Multilingual Writers

Your native language or even the language of your ancestors may influence the way you use English. The following sections will help you with some common problems encountered by writers whose first language is not English. These sections might help native speakers as well.

48a Learning in English as a second language

To some extent, college presents everyone with an unfamiliar culture and its languages. If you spoke another language before learning English, you already have experience trying to feel at home in a new culture and working to acquire a new language.

1. Becoming aware of cultural differences in communication

Because you are familiar with at least two languages and cultures, you already know that there is more than one way to interact politely and effectively with other people. The introduction to this text discusses the process of joining the academic conversation and offers suggestions for doing so *(see pp. 10–13)*. Communication is your first priority, so gather up your confidence, and join the conversation:

- Participate actively in small-group discussions.
- Ask and answer questions during class discussions.
- Approach instructors and fellow students outside class when you need additional help.

2. Using writing to learn more about English

To develop fluency in English, get into the habit of writing in English every day:

- **Write a personal journal.** Explore your thoughts and feelings about your studies and college life.
- **Keep a writer's notebook.** Write down a quotation from something you have read, and then either comment on it or put the idea into your own words. Write down bits of dialogue you overhear. Make lists of words and phrases that are new to you. Go over these lists with your writing group, a friend, or a tutor in the writing center.
- **Write letters and e-mail in English.** Letters and e-mail are a good way to practice the informal style used in conversation.

3. Using learning tools that are available for multilingual students

The following kinds of reference books can help you as you write for your college courses.

ESL dictionary A good dictionary designed especially for ESL students can be a useful source of information about word meanings. Like all standard English dictionaries, an ESL dictionary includes instructions that explain the abbreviations used in the entries. They also list the special notations used for words classified as *slang, vulgar, informal, nonstandard,* or another category worthy of special attention. In the ESL/Learner's Edition of the *Random House Webster's Dictionary of American English* (1997), you will find "pig out" as the sixth entry under the word *pig:*

> **Pig out** (no obj) Slang. to eat too much food: *We pigged out on pizza last night.*

The entry tells you that "pig out" does not take a direct object ("no obj") and that its use is very informal ("Slang"), appropriate in talking with classmates but not in writing papers.

The dictionary will help you with spelling, syllabication, pronunciation, definitions, word origins, and usage *(see Chapter 40, pp. 412–14).*

Dictionary of American idioms An idiom is an expression that is peculiar to a particular language and cannot be understood by looking at the individual words. "To catch a bus" is an idiom.

Desk encyclopedia In the reference section of your college library, you will find one-volume encyclopedias on every subject from U.S. history to classical or biblical allusions. Look up people, places, and events that are new to you for a quick identification.

COUNT AND NONCOUNT NOUNS

A common noun that refers to something specific that can be counted is a **count noun.** Count nouns can be singular or plural, like *cup* or *suggestion (four cups, several suggestions).* **Noncount nouns** are nonspecific; these common nouns refer to categories of people, places, or things and cannot be counted. They do not have a plural form *(the pottery is beautiful, his advice was useful).*

Count Nouns	**Noncount Nouns**
cars	transportation
computers	Internet
facts	information

Count Nouns	Noncount Nouns
clouds	rain
stars	sunshine
tools	equipment
machines	machinery
suggestions	advice
earrings	jewelry
tables	furniture
smiles	happiness

Following is a list of some quantifiers (words that tell how much or how many) for count nouns and for noncount nouns, as well as a few quantifiers that can be used with both:

- **With count nouns only:** *several, many, a couple of, a number of, a few, few*
- **With noncount nouns only:** *a great deal of, much, not much, little, a little, less,* a word that indicates a unit *(a bag of sugar)*
- **With either count or noncount nouns:** *all, any, some, a lot of*

48b Using articles *(a, an,* and *the)* appropriately

Some languages do not use articles at all, and most languages do not use articles in the same way as English. Therefore, articles often cause problems for multilingual writers. In English, there are only three articles: *a, an,* and *the.*

1. Using *a* or *an*

A or *an* refers to one nonspecific person, place, or thing. *A* is used before words that begin with consonant sounds, whether or not the first letter is a vowel *(a European vacation, a country),* and *an* is used before words that begin with vowel sounds, whether or not the first letter is a consonant *(an hour, an opener).*

48b
ESL

Count nouns that are singular and refer to a nonspecific person, place, or thing take *a* or *an.* Noncount nouns and plural nouns do not take *a* or *an.* For a list of count and noncount nouns, see the box on pages 488–89.

an
▶ The manager needs to hire assistant.
    ^

▶ We needed to buy a̶ furniture for our apartment.

2. Using *the*

The refers to a specific person, place, or thing and can be used with singular or plural nouns. A person, place, or thing is specific if it has already been referred to in a preceding sentence, if it is specified within the sentence itself, or if it is commonly known.

The problem
▶ We are trying to solve a difficult problem. ~~Problem~~ started
⌃

    when we planned two meetings for the same day.

The girl
▶ ~~Girl~~ you have been waiting for is here.
⌃

The moon
▶ ~~Moon~~ is shining brightly this evening.
⌃

Exception: When a noun represents all examples of something, *the* should be omitted.

Dogs
▶ ~~The dogs~~ were first domesticated long before recorded
⌃

    history.

Common nouns that refer to a specific person, place, or thing take *the*. Most proper nouns do not use articles unless they are plural, in which case they take the article *the*. There are some exceptions, however:

- Proper nouns that include a common noun and *of* as part of the title: *the Museum of Modern Art, the Fourth of July, the Statue of Liberty*
- Parts of the globe, names of oceans and seas, deserts, land and water formations: *the West, the Equator, the North Pole, the Mediterranean, the Sahara, the Bering Strait*
- Countries with more than one word in their names: *the Dominican Republic*
- Names of highways: *the Santa Monica Freeway*
- Landmark buildings: *the Eiffel Tower*
- Hotels: *the Marriott Hotel*
- Cultural and political institutions: *the Metropolitan Opera, the Pentagon*

Exercise 48.1 Using articles in context

Correct the errors in article use in the following passage.

     In his book *Travels with Charley,* John Steinbeck describes the journey he took that helped him discover his country. The Hurricane Donna struck New York State and delayed the beginning of the long-planned trip. While author was traveling in the New England, weather became cold, and leaves turned their fall colors. On his way, he met farmer who had a Yankee face and the Yankee accent. Steinbeck discovered that the best way to learn about local population was to visit local bar or church. He also saw many people fleeing New England to escape winter. Many shops were closed, and some had signs saying they would be closed until following summer. As he traveled through states, he noticed the changes in the language. These differences were apparent in road signs. A trouble arose when he was not allowed to cross Canadian border because he did not have vaccination certificate for his dog, Charley. Steinbeck and his companion were later able to resume their trip without the further problems.

48c   Using helping verbs with main verbs

Verbs change form to indicate person, number, tense, voice, and mood. *(For a detailed discussion of verbs, see Chapter 45.)* To do all this, a **main verb** is often accompanied by one or more **helping verbs** in a **verb phrase.** Helping verbs include forms of *do, have,* and *be* as well as modal verbs, such as *may, must, should,* and *would.*

1. Do, Does, Did

The helping verb *do* and its forms *does* and *did* combine with the base form of a verb to ask a question or to emphasize something. *Do, does,* or *did* can also combine with the word *not* to create an emphatic negative statement.

QUESTION	*Do* you hear those dogs barking?
EMPHATIC STATEMENT	I *do* hear them barking.
EMPHATIC NEGATIVE	I *do not* want to have to call the police about those dogs.

48c
ESL

2. *Have, Has, Had*

The helping verb *have* and its forms *has* and *had* combine with a past participle (usually ending in *-d, -t,* or *-n*) to form the *perfect tenses.* Do not confuse the simple past tense with the present perfect tense (formed with *have* or *has*), which is distinct from the simple past because the action can continue in the present. *(For a review of perfect tense forms, see Chapter 45, pp. 459–60.)*

SIMPLE PAST	Those dogs *barked* all day.
PRESENT PERFECT	Those dogs *have barked* all day.
PAST PERFECT	Those dogs *had barked* all day.

3. *Be*

Forms of *be* combine with a present participle (ending in *-ing*) to form the **progressive tenses,** which express continuing action. Do not confuse the simple present tense or the present perfect with these progressive forms. Unlike the simple present, which indicates an action that occurs frequently and might include the present moment, the present progressive form indicates an action that is going on right now. In its past form, the progressive tense indicates actions that are going on simultaneously. *(For a review of progressive tense forms, see Chapter 45, pp. 459–60.)*

SIMPLE PRESENT	Those dogs *bark* all the time.
PRESENT PROGRESSIVE	Those dogs *are barking* all the time.
PAST PROGRESSIVE	Those dogs *were barking* all day while I *was trying* to study.

Note: A number of verbs that are related to thoughts, preferences, and ownership are seldom used in the progressive tense in English. These include *appear, believe, know, like, need, own, seem, understand,* and *want.*

Forms of *be* combine with the past participle (which usually ends in *-d, -t,* or *-n*) to form the passive voice, which is often used to express a state of being instead of an action.

BE + PAST PARTICIPLE	
PASSIVE	The dogs *were scolded* by their owner.
PASSIVE	I *was satisfied* by her answer.

Intransitive verbs such as *happen* and *occur* cannot appear in the passive voice because they do not take direct objects.

▶ The accident ~~was~~ happened after he returned from his trip.

4. Modals

Other helping verbs, called **modals,** signify the manner, or mode, of an action. Unlike *be, have,* and *do,* one-word modals such as *may, must,* and *will* are almost never used alone as main verbs, nor do they change form to show person or number. Modals do not add *-s* endings, two modals are never used together (such as *might could*), and modals are always followed by the base form of the verb without *to.*

▶ **We must ~~to~~ study now.**

The one-word modals are *can, could, may, might, will, would, shall, should,* and *must.*

hv mv

▶ **Contrary to press reports, she *will* not *run* for political office.**

Note that a negative word such as *not* may come between the helping and the main verb.

Phrasal modals, however, do change form to show time, person, and number. Here are some phrasal modals: *have to, have got to, used to, be supposed to, be going to, be allowed to, be able to.*

hv mv

▶ **Yesterday, I *was going to study* for three hours.**

hv mv

▶ **Next week, I *am going to study* three hours a day.**

Exercise 48.2   Using modals and other helping verbs

Correct any errors in the use of modals and other helping verbs in the following sentences.

EXAMPLE

had
▶ **We been hoping that we could ~~to~~ visit California before we**
    ^

graduated.

1. Do you know where you and Erica will to go on vacation this summer?
2. You should to look online. You can to find great deals there.
3. I have been looking all over the Internet, but I not found any cheap hotels.

48c
ESL

4. Have you thought about camping? My sister did able to save a lot of money by camping when she traveling around Europe last summer.

5. That is a great idea! Are there any campsites she can suggests in Spain and Portugal?

6. I am not sure if she went to Portugal, but she must been to Spain. Let me ask her.

7. That is excellent. I just hope I will not have buy too much camping gear.

8. I have a lot of gear, and I am sure Erica coulds borrow some of my sister's things.

48d Using verbs followed by gerunds or infinitives

Verbs in English differ as to whether they can be followed by a gerund, an infinitive, or either. Some verbs, like *avoid,* can be followed by a gerund but not an infinitive.

           climbing
► We avoided ~~to climb~~ the mountain during the storm.

Other verbs, like *attempt,* can be followed by an infinitive but not a gerund.

           to reach
► We attempted ~~reaching~~ the summit when the weather

cleared.

Others can be followed by either a gerund or an infinitive with no change in meaning.

► We began climbing.

► We began to climb.

Still others have a different meaning when followed by a gerund than they do when followed by an infinitive. Compare these examples.

► She stopped eating.

   She was eating but she stopped.

► She stopped to eat.

   She stopped what she was doing before in order to eat.

The following lists provide common examples of each type of verb.

Some Verbs That Take Only an Infinitive

afford	hurry	promise
appear	intend	refuse
attempt	learn	request
choose	manage	seem
claim	mean	tend
decide	need	threaten
expect	offer	want
fail	plan	wish
hope	prepare	would like

Some Verbs That Take Only a Gerund

admit	finish	recommend
advise	forgive	regret
avoid	imagine	resist
consider	look forward to	risk
defend	mention	suggest
deny	mind	support
discuss	practice	tolerate
enjoy	propose	understand
feel like	quit	urge

Some Verbs That Can Take Either a Gerund or an Infinitive

An asterisk (*) indicates those verbs for which the choice of gerund or infinitive affects meaning.

begin	love	start
continue	prefer	*stop
hate	*remember	*try
like		

Note: For some verbs, such as *allow, cause, encourage, have, persuade, remind,* and *tell,* a noun or pronoun must precede the infinitive: *I reminded my sister to return my sweater.* For a few verbs, such as *ask, expect, need,* and *want,* the noun may either precede or follow the infinitive, depending on the meaning you want to express: *I want to return my sweater to my sister. I want my sister to return my sweater.*

Make, let, and *have* are followed by a noun or pronoun plus the base form without *to: Make that boy come home on time.*

**48d
ESL**

Exercise 48.3 Using gerunds versus infinitives after verbs

Underline the correct choice—gerund or infinitive—in each pair in parentheses.

EXAMPLE

Most people hope <u>(to work/working)</u> in rewarding jobs.

1. In the past, people were expected (to stay/staying) in the same job for a long time, ideally for their whole career.
2. Today, people tend (to change/changing) careers several times before retiring.
3. People who are not happy with their careers attempt (to find/finding) other jobs that interest them more.
4. Others, who regret (not to get/not getting) undergraduate or graduate degrees when they were younger, go back to school.
5. Some people even look forward to (change/changing) jobs every few years to avoid boredom.
6. So if you do not like your job, stop (to complain/complaining), and do something about it.

48e Using complete subjects and verbs

1. Using a complete subject

Every clause in English has a subject, even if it is only a stand-in subject like *there* or *it*. Check your clauses to make sure that each one has a subject.

> No one thought the party could end, but _^ *it* ended abruptly
>
> when the stock market crashed.

> *There is*
> ~~Is~~ general agreement that the crash helped bring on the
> _^
> Great Depression.

2. Including a complete verb

Verb structure, as well as where the verb is placed within a sentence, varies dramatically across languages, but in English each sentence needs to include at least one complete verb. The verb cannot be an infinitive—the *to* form of the verb—or an *-ing* form without a helping verb.

NOT COMPLETE	The caterer *to bring* dinner.
COMPLETE VERBS	The caterer *brings* dinner.
	The caterer *will bring* dinner.
	The caterer *is bringing* dinner.

NOT COMPLETE	Children *running* in the park.
COMPLETE VERBS	Children *are running* in the park.
	Children *have been running* in the park.
	Children *will be running* in the park.

48f Using only one subject or object

Watch out for repeated subjects in your clauses.

▶ **The celebrity ~~he~~ signed my program.**

Watch out as well for repeated objects in clauses that begin with relative pronouns *(that, which, who, whom, whose)* or relative adverbs *(where, when, how)*.

▶ **Our dog guards the house where we live ~~there~~.**

Even if the relative pronoun does not appear in the sentence but is only implied, you should still omit repeated objects.

▶ **He is the man I need to talk to ~~him~~.**

The relative pronoun *whom* (he is the man *whom* I need to talk to) is implied, so *him* is not needed.

48g Using adjectives correctly

English adjectives do not change form to agree with the form of the nouns they modify. They stay the same whatever the number or gender of the noun. *(For more on adjectives, see Chapter 47, pp. 480–86, and Chapter 61, pp. 580–81.)*

▶ **Juan is an *attentive* father. Alyssa is an *attentive* mother. They are *attentive* parents.**

Adjectives usually come before a noun, but they can also occur after a linking verb.

▶ **The food at the restaurant was *delicious*.**

The position of an adjective can affect its meaning, however. The phrase *my old friend,* for example, can refer to a long friendship *(a friend I have known for a long time)* or an elderly friend *(my friend who is eighty years old).* In the sentence *My friend is old,* by contrast, *old* has only one meaning—elderly.

48g ESL

1. Adjective order

When two or more adjectives modify a noun cumulatively, they follow a sequence—determined by their meaning—that is particular to English logic:

1. Adjectives of size and shape: *big, small, huge, tiny, tall, short, narrow, thick, round, square*
2. Adjectives that suggest subjective evaluation: *cozy, intelligent, outrageous, elegant, original*
3. Adjectives of color: *yellow, green, pale*
4. Adjectives of origin and type: *African, Czech, gothic*
5. Nouns used as adjectives: *brick, plastic, glass, stone*
6. NOUN

► **the tall, African, stone statues**

2. Present and past participles used as adjectives

Both the present and past participle forms of verbs can function as adjectives. To use them properly, keep the following in mind:

- Present participle adjectives usually modify nouns that are the agent of an action.
- Past participle adjectives usually modify nouns that are the recipient of an action.

► **This problem is *confusing*.**

> The present participle *confusing* modifies *problem,* which is the agent, or cause of the confusion.

► **The students are *confused* by the problem.**

> The past participle *confused* modifies *students,* who are the recipients of the confusion the problem is causing.

The following are some other present and past participle pairs that often cause problems:

amazing/amazed
annoying/annoyed
boring/bored
depressing/depressed
embarrassing/embarrassed
exciting/excited
fascinating/fascinated

frightening/frightened
interesting/interested
satisfying/satisfied
shocking/shocked
surprising/surprised
tiring/tired

Exercise 48.4 Working with English adjectives

Correct any errors in adjective placement or agreement in the following sentences. Some of the sentences may be correct as written; circle their numbers.

EXAMPLE

huge brick
The houses in the development were all ~~brick huge~~
mansions.
                                              ^

1. Many house hunters look for a comfortable big place to live near a school.
2. Real estate agents describe properties in glowing terms such as "brick spacious prewar building."
3. Multiple bedrooms, bathrooms fully equipped, and gardens landscaped are becoming standard features of suburban new properties.
4. The kitchens are filled with shiny surfaces and hi-tech numerous gadgets.
5. Many American young families cannot afford those expensive properties.

Exercise 48.5 Choosing the correct participle

Underline the correct participle from each pair in parentheses.

EXAMPLE

The (tiring/<u>tired</u>) students celebrated the end of final exams.

1. The review material for the art history final is very (boring/bored).
2. The term paper I am writing for the class is on a (challenging/challenged) topic: twentieth-century painting.
3. The paintings of Picasso are especially (interesting/interested).
4. Most students have already submitted their (completing/completed) papers.
5. After a week of studying, I am (prepared/preparing) for the exam.

48h
ESL

48h Putting adverbs in the correct place

Although adverbs can appear in almost any position within a sentence, they should not separate a verb from its direct object. *(For more on adverbs, see Chapter 47, pp. 480–86, and Chapter 61, pp. 581–83.)*

quickly
► Juan found ~~quickly~~ his cat.
  ^

The negative word *not* usually precedes the main verb and follows the first helping verb in a verb phrase.

not
► I have been ~~not~~ sick lately.
  ^

48i Using prepositions

Every language uses prepositions idiomatically in ways that do not match their literal meaning, which is why prepositional phrases can be difficult for multilingual writers. In English, prepositions combine with other words in such a variety of ways that the combinations can only be learned with repetition and over time *(see Chapter 61, pp. 583–84). (For a list of common prepositions, see p. 583.)*

1. Idiomatic uses of prepositions indicating time and location

The prepositions that indicate time and location are often the most idiosyncratic in a language. The following are some common ways in which the prepositions *at, by, in,* and *on* are used.

TIME

AT The wedding ceremony starts *at two o'clock.* [a specific clock time]

BY Our honeymoon plans should be ready *by next week.* [a particular time]

IN The reception will start *in the evening.* [a portion of the day]

ON The wedding will take place *on May 1.* The rehearsal is *on* Tuesday. [a particular date or day of the week]

LOCATION

AT I will meet you *at the zoo.* [a particular place]

You need to turn right *at the light.* [a corner or an intersection]

We took a seat *at the table.* [near a piece of furniture]

BY Meet me *by the fountain.* [a familiar place]

IN Park your car *in the parking lot,* and give the money to the attendant *in the booth.* [on a space of some kind or inside a structure]

I enjoyed the bratwurst *in Chicago.* [a city, state, or other geographic location]

I found that article *in this book.* [a print medium]

ON An excellent restaurant is located *on Mulberry Street.* [a street, avenue, or other thoroughfare]

I spilled milk *on the floor.* [a surface]

I watched the report *on television.* [an electronic medium]

2. Prepositions plus gerunds *(-ing)*

A gerund is the *-ing* form of a verb acting as a noun. A gerund can occur after a preposition *(thanks for coming),* but when the preposition is *to,* be careful not to confuse it with the infinitive form of a verb.

> ▸ I look forward to ~~win~~ *winning* at Jeopardy.

The box on pages 502–3 contains a list of common idiomatic expressions in English. These often cause problems for multilingual writers, who must study and memorize them.

48j Using direct objects with two-word verbs

If a two-word verb has a direct object, the preposition (also called a particle) may be either separable *(I filled the form out)* or inseparable *(I got over the shock).* If the verb is separable, the direct object can also follow the preposition if it is a noun *(I filled out the form).* If the direct object is a pronoun, however, it must appear between the verb and preposition.

> ▸ I filled out ~~it~~ *it.*

48k Using coordination and subordination appropriately

48k
ESL

Do not use both subordination and coordination together to combine the same two clauses, even if the subordinating and coordinating words are similar in meaning. Some examples include *although* or *even though* with *but* and *because* with *therefore.*

> ▸ Although I came early, ~~but~~ the tickets were already sold out.

or

> ▸ ~~Although~~ I came early, but the tickets were already sold out.

(For more on coordination and subordination, see Chapter 36, pp. 387–92.)

COMMON IDIOMATIC EXPRESSIONS in ENGLISH

COMMON ADJECTIVE + PREPOSITION COMBINATIONS

afraid of: fearing someone or something

anxious about: worried

ashamed of: embarrassed by someone or something

aware of: know about

content with: having no complaints about; happy about

fond of: having positive feelings for

full of: filled with

grateful to (someone) (for something): thankful; appreciative

interested in: curious; wanting to know more about

jealous of: feeling envy toward

proud/suspicious of: pleased about/distrustful of

tired of: had enough of; bored with

responsible to (someone) (for something): accountable; in charge

satisfied with: having no complaints about

COMMON VERB + PREPOSITION COMBINATIONS

apologize to: express regret for actions

arrive in (a place): come to a city/country *(I arrived in Paris.)*

arrive at (an event at a specific location): come to a building or a house *(I arrived at the Louvre at ten.)*

blame for: hold responsible; accuse

complain about: find fault; criticize

concentrate on: focus; pay attention

consist of: contain; be made of

congratulate on: offer good wishes for success

depend on: trust

explain to: make something clear to someone

insist on: be firm

laugh at: express amusement

rely on: trust

smile at: act friendly toward

take care of: look after; tend

thank for: express appreciation

throw at: toss an object toward someone or something

throw to: toss something to someone to catch

throw (something) away: discard
throw (something) out: discard; present an idea for consideration
worry about: feel concern; fear for someone's safety or well-being

COMMON PARTICIPLES

These verb + preposition combinations create **verb phrasals,** expressions with meanings that are different from the meaning of the verb itself. An asterisk (*) indicates a separable participle *(I called the meeting off).*

break down: stop functioning
*call off: cancel
*fill out: complete
*find out: discover
get over: recover
*give up: surrender; stop work on
*leave out: omit
look forward to: anticipate
look into: research
*look up: check a fact
look up to: admire
put up with: endure
run across: meet unexpectedly
run out: use up
stand up for: defend
turn down: reject

---

481 Putting sentence parts in the correct order for English

**481
ESL**

In some languages (such as Spanish), it is acceptable to omit subjects. In others (such as Arabic), it is acceptable to omit certain kinds of verbs. Other languages (such as Japanese) place verbs last, and still others (such as Hebrew) allow verbs to precede the subject. English, however, has its own distinct order for sentence parts. *(See also Chapter 62, pp. 588–91.)*

MODIFIERS + SUBJECT → VERB + OBJECTS, COMPLEMENTS, MODIFIERS
   mod   subj   verb   mod   obj   obj comp

▶ **The playful kitten batted the crystal glasses on the shelf.**

Changing a **direct quotation** (someone else's exact words) to an **indirect quotation** (a report on what the person said or wrote) often requires changing many sentence elements. When the quotation is a declarative sentence, however, the subject-before-verb word order does not change.

DIRECT QUOTATION The instructor said, "You have only one more week to finish your papers."

INDIRECT QUOTATION The instructor told the students that they had only one more week to finish their papers.

Note: In the indirect quotation, the verb tense changes from present to past.

Changing a direct question to an indirect question, however, does require a word order change—from the verb-subject pattern of a question to the subject-verb pattern of a declarative sentence.

DIRECT QUESTION The instructor always asks, "Are you ready to begin?"

INDIRECT QUESTION The instructor always asks *[us]* if we are ready to begin.

In an indirect quotation of a command, a pronoun or noun takes the place of the command's omitted subject, *you,* and is followed by the infinitive *(to)* form of the verb.

DIRECT QUOTATION COMMAND The instructor always says *"[you]* Write down the assignment before you leave."

INDIRECT QUOTATION COMMAND The instructor always tells *us* to write down the assignment before we leave.

Exercise 48.6 Using English word order

Find and correct the errors in the following sentences. Some sentences have more than one error.

EXAMPLE

Because they worry about food so much, ~~therefore~~ Americans may have more eating-related problems than people in other developed countries.

1. As Michael Pollan in the *New York Times Magazine* writes, Americans have become the world's most anxious eaters.
2. Researchers have found that Americans they worry more about what they eat than people do in other developed countries.

3. Therefore, tend to enjoy their food less and associate a good meal with guilty pleasure.

4. Paradoxically, this worrying does not stop regularly many Americans from overeating.

5. The report also tells to readers that it is not uncommon for people to visit the gym after overeating.

6. The people of many other nations take pleasure in eating and turn often a meal into a festive occasion.

7. Although they relish their meals, but they are less prone to obesity or eating disorders than Americans.

8. Some scientists speculate that the people of these nations therefore are less obese because they cook with more healthful ingredients than Americans.

9. The question arises, however, whether might people's attitude toward eating be as important to good health as what they eat?

48m Understanding the purposes and constructions of *if* clauses

If clauses (also called **conditional clauses**) state facts, make predictions, and speculate about unlikely or impossible events. These conditional constructions most often begin with *if,* but *when, unless,* or other words can introduce conditional constructions as well:

- Use the present tense for facts. When the relationship you are describing is usually true, the verbs in both clauses should be in the same tense.

STATES FACTS

If people *practice* doing good consistently, they *have* a sense of satisfaction.

When Meg *found* a new cause, she always *talked* about it incessantly.

- In a sentence that predicts, use the present tense in the *if* clause. The verb in the independent clause is a modal plus the base form of the verb.

PREDICTS POSSIBILITIES

If you *practice* doing good through politics, you *will have* a greater effect on your community.

**48m
ESL**

- If you are speculating about something that is unlikely to happen, use the past tense in the *if* clause and *could, should,* or *would* plus the base verb in the independent clause.

SPECULATES ON THE UNLIKELY

If you *were* less overcommitted, you *would volunteer* for that good cause.

- Use the past perfect tense in the *if* clause if you are speculating about an event that did not happen. In the independent clause, use *could have, might have,* or *would have* plus the past participle.

SPECULATES ON SOMETHING THAT DID NOT HAPPEN

If you *had volunteered* for the Peace Corps when you were young, you *would have been* a different person today.

- Use *were* in the *if* clause and *could, might,* or *would* plus the base form in the main clause if you are speculating about something that could never happen.

SPECULATES ABOUT THE IMPOSSIBLE

If Lincoln *were* alive today, he *would fight* for equal protection under the law.

PART

8

It wasn't a matter of rewriting but simply of tightening up all the bolts.

—MARGUERITE YOURCENAR

Editing
for Correctness
Punctuation, Mechanics, and Spelling

8

Editing for Correctness

WRITING OUTCOMES

Part 8 Editing for Correctness

This section will help you answer questions such as the following:

Rhetorical Knowledge

- Should I use contractions such as *can't* or *don't* in my college work? **(52c)**
- Which numbers should be spelled out in my technical report? **(57a)**

Critical Thinking, Reading, and Writing

- How should I set off words I have added to a quotation? **(54f)**
- How do I use ellipses ethically to indicate omissions from quotations? **(54g)**

Processes

- What are some strategies for proofreading my work? **(60)**

Knowledge of Conventions

- When should I set off a word or phrase with commas? **(49e, f)**
- What is the difference between *its* and *it's*? **(52c)**

Writing in Online Environments

- What are the strengths and limitations of my word processor's spelling checker? **(52, 60)**
- Can my word processor's grammar checker help me edit for punctuation and mechanics? **(49–51, 53–59)**

For a general introduction to writing outcomes, see Id, page 5.

49 Commas

You may have been told that commas are used to mark pauses, but that is not an accurate general principle. To clarify meaning, commas are used in the following situations:

- Following introductory elements *(pp. 509–10)*
- After each item in a series and between coordinate adjectives *(pp. 510–11)*
- Between coordinated independent clauses *(pp. 511–12)*
- To set off interruptions or nonessential information *(pp. 513–18)*
- To set off direct quotations *(pp. 518–19)*
- In dates, addresses, people's titles, and numbers *(pp. 519–20)*
- To replace an omitted word or phrase or to prevent misreading *(p. 520)*

✓ **49a** Using a comma after an introductory word group

A comma both attaches an introductory word, phrase, or clause to and distinguishes it from the rest of the sentence.

► **Finally, the car careened to the right.**

► **Reflecting on her life experiences, Washburn attributed her successes to her own efforts.**

► **Until he noticed the handprint on the wall, the detective was frustrated by the lack of clues.**

When the introductory phrase is shorter than five words and there is no danger of confusion without a comma, the comma can be omitted.

► **For several hours we rode on in silence.**

Do not add a comma after a word group that functions as the subject of the sentence. Be especially careful with word groups that begin with *-ing* words.

► **Persuading constituents/ is one of a politician's most important tasks.**

Commas and Grammar Checkers

Computer grammar checkers usually will not highlight missing commas following introductory elements or between independent clauses joined by a coordinating conjunction such as *and,* and they cannot decide whether a sentence element is essential or nonessential.

Exercise 49.1 Using commas with introductory word groups

Edit the following sentences, adding commas as needed after introductory word groups. Some sentences may be correct; circle their numbers.

EXAMPLE   **During the early Middle Ages, Western Europeans**
                                        ʌ
remained fairly cut off from the East.

1. After the year 1000 CE Europeans became less isolated.
2. To the Holy Lands traveled Western pilgrims and merchants in a steady stream.
3. Increasingly aware of the rich civilizations beyond their borders Europeans began to enter into business relationships with the cities and countries in the East.
4. Establishing contact with the principal ports of the eastern Mediterranean and Black seas allowed merchants to develop a vigorous trade.
5. As this trade expanded across the Mediterranean world Western Europeans were able to enjoy spices and other exotic products.
6. In the thirteenth and fourteenth centuries European missionaries and merchants traveled to China, India, and the Near East.

49b Using commas between items in a series

A comma should appear after each item in a series.

▶ **Three industries that have been important to New England**

are shipbuilding, tourism, and commercial fishing.
                         ʌ   ʌ

Commas clarify which items are part of the series. In the following example, the third comma clarifies that the hikers are packing lunch *and* snacks, not chocolate and trail mix meant for lunch.

CONFUSING	For the hiking trip, we needed to pack lunch, chocolate and trail mix.
CLEAR	For the hiking trip, we needed to pack lunch, chocolate, and trail mix.

Note: If you are writing for a journalism course, you may be required to leave out the final comma that precedes *and* in a series, just as magazines and newspapers usually do. Follow the convention that your instructor prefers.

✓ **49c** Using a comma in front of a coordinating conjunction that joins independent clauses

When a coordinating conjunction *(and, but, for, nor, or, so,* or *yet)* is used to join clauses that could each stand alone as a sentence, put a comma before the coordinating conjunction.

▶ **Injuries were so frequent that he began to worry, and his**
                                                       ^

   style of play became more cautious.

If the word groups you are joining are not independent clauses, do not add a comma *(see p. 521).*

Exception: If you are joining two short clauses, you may leave out the comma unless it is needed for clarity.

▶ **The running back caught the ball and the fans cheered.**

Exercise 49.2 Combining sentences with commas and coordinating conjunctions

Use a comma and a coordinating conjunction to combine each set of sentences into one sentence. Vary your choice of conjunctions.

EXAMPLE   **The experiment did not support our**

                  , yet we
  hypothesis. ~~We~~ considered it a success.
          ^

49c
^

1. Asperger's syndrome and autism, although they are both classified as autism spectrum disorders, are not the same. Asperger's syndrome is often confused with autism.
2. People with Asperger's syndrome have normal IQs. They experience difficulty interacting with others in a social setting.

3. Children with this disorder often engage in solitary, repetitive routines. In school they may have difficulty working in groups.
4. People with Asperger's syndrome also have a difficult time with nonverbal communication. They may be unable to read other people's body language.
5. The public has only recently become aware of Asperger's syndrome. Drugs that can cure this neurobiological disorder have yet to be developed.

49d   Adding a comma between coordinate adjectives

A comma is used between **coordinate adjectives** because these adjectives modify a noun independently.

▶ **This brave, intelligent, persistent woman was the first**

   female to earn a PhD in psychology.

If you cannot add *and* between the adjectives or change their order, they are **cumulative adjectives,** with each one modifying the ones that follow it, and should not be separated with a comma or commas *(see p. 521).*

▶ **Andrea Boccelli, the world-famous Italian tenor, has performed in concerts and operas.**

   World-famous modifies *Italian tenor,* not just the noun *tenor.* You could not add *and* between the adjectives (world-famous *and* Italian tenor) or change their order (*Italian world-famous tenor*).

Exercise 49.3   Using commas with series of nouns and adjectives

Edit the following sentences, adding commas as needed to separate items in a series and coordinate adjectives. Some sentences may be correct; circle their numbers.

   EXAMPLE   **One part of the wall was covered with pictures**

            of leaping, prancing animals.

1. Scholars have studied prehistoric cave paintings for almost a century.
2. Paintings have been found in North America Europe Africa and Australia.
3. Paintings found in southeastern France contain images of animals birds and fish.

4. Some scholars believe that the cave painter may have been a rapturous entranced shaman.

5. We can picture the flickering dazzling torchlight that guided the painter's way through dank dark passageways.

6. Mixing colors with their saliva and blowing the paint onto the wall with their breath must have given the cave painters feelings of creative power supernatural control and expressive glory.

✓ 49e Using commas to set off nonessential elements

Nonessential, or **nonrestrictive,** words, phrases, and clauses add information to a sentence but are not required for its basic meaning to be understood. Nonrestrictive additions are set off with commas.

▶ **Mary Shelley's best-known novel** ͜ *Frankenstein or the*

Modern Prometheus ͜ **was first published in 1818.**

The sentence would have the same basic meaning without the title.

Restrictive words, phrases, and clauses are essential to a sentence because they identify exactly who or what the writer is talking about. Restrictive additions are not set off with commas.

▶ **Mary Shelley's novel** *Frankenstein or the Modern Prometheus* **was first published in 1818.**

Without the title, the reader would not know which novel the sentence is referring to.

Three types of additions to sentences often cause problems: adjective clauses, adjective phrases, and appositives.

1. Adjective clauses

Adjective clauses begin with a relative pronoun or an adverb—*who, whom, whose, which, that, where,* or *when*—and modify a noun or pronoun within the sentence.

NONRESTRICTIVE

With his tale of Odysseus, *whose journey can be traced on modern maps,* Homer brought accounts of alien and strange creatures to the ancient Greeks.

RESTRICTIVE

The contestant *whom he most wanted to beat* was his father.

49e
͜

Note: Use *that* only with restrictive clauses. *Which* can introduce either restrictive or nonrestrictive clauses. Some writers prefer to use *which* only with nonrestrictive clauses.

2. Adjective phrases

Like an adjective clause, an adjective phrase also modifies a noun or pronoun in a sentence. Adjective phrases begin with a preposition (for example, *with, by, at,* or *for*) or a verbal (a word formed from a verb). Adjective phrases can be either restrictive or nonrestrictive.

NONRESTRICTIVE

Some people, *by their faith in human nature or their general good will,* bring out the best in others.

The phrase is nonessential because it does not specify which people are being discussed.

RESTRICTIVE

People *fighting passionately for their rights* can inspire others to join a cause.

The phrase indicates which people the writer is talking about.

3. Appositives

Appositives are nouns or noun phrases that rename nouns or pronouns and appear right after the word they rename.

NONRESTRICTIVE

One researcher, *the widely respected R. S. Smith,* has shown that a child's performance on IQ tests can be inconsistent.

Because the word *one* already restricts the word *researcher,* the researcher's name is not essential to the meaning of the sentence.

RESTRICTIVE

The researcher *R. S. Smith* has shown that a child's performance on IQ tests can be inconsistent.

The name *R. S. Smith* tells readers which researcher is meant.

Exercise 49.4 Using commas with nonrestrictive elements

Edit the following sentences, adding commas as needed to set off nonrestrictive clauses, adjective phrases, and appositives. Some sentences may be correct; circle their numbers.

EXAMPLE   The brain, connected by nerves to all the other

parts of the body, seems to be the seat of the

mind, an abstract term for the workings of the

brain.

1. The mind-body problem under debate for centuries concerns the relationship between the mind and the body.
2. Prehistoric peoples must have observed that when a person died the body remained and the mind departed.
3. Since the time of the ancient Greeks the prevailing opinion has been that the mind and the body are separate entities.
4. Plato the Greek philosopher is often credited with originating the concept of mind-body dualism.
5. The French philosopher René Descartes described the mind and the body as independent.
6. Descartes' influential theories helped lay the foundation for scientific rationalism which views nature as a vast machine.

49f Using a comma or commas with transitional and parenthetical expressions, contrasting comments, and absolute phrases

1. Transitional expressions

Conjunctive adverbs *(however, therefore, moreover)* and other transitional phrases *(for example, on the other hand)* are usually set off by commas. *(For a list of transitional expressions, see Chapter 43, p. 437.)*

▶ Brian Wilson, for example, was unable to cope with the

pressures of touring with the Beach Boys.

When a transitional expression connects two independent clauses, use a semicolon before and a comma after it.

▶ The Beatles were a phenomenon when they toured the

United States in 1964; subsequently, they became the most

successful rock band of all time.

Short expressions such as *also, at least, certainly, instead, of course, then, perhaps,* and *therefore* do not always need to set off with commas.

▶ I found my notes and *also* got my story in on time.

49f
∧
？

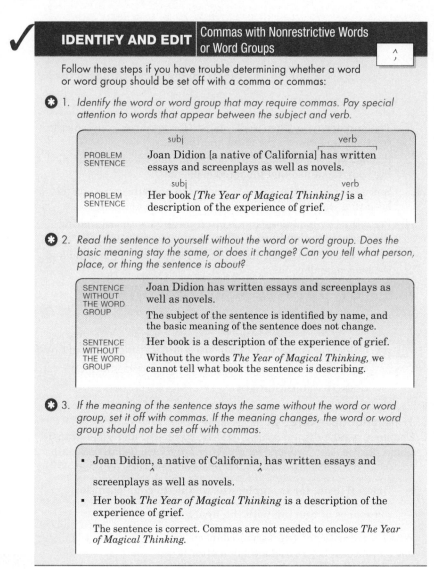

✓ **IDENTIFY AND EDIT** | Commas with Nonrestrictive Words or Word Groups

Follow these steps if you have trouble determining whether a word or word group should be set off with a comma or commas:

❋ 1. *Identify the word or word group that may require commas. Pay special attention to words that appear between the subject and verb.*

> PROBLEM SENTENCE
> subj — verb
> Joan Didion [a native of California] has written essays and screenplays as well as novels.
>
> PROBLEM SENTENCE
> subj — verb
> Her book *[The Year of Magical Thinking]* is a description of the experience of grief.

❋ 2. *Read the sentence to yourself without the word or word group. Does the basic meaning stay the same, or does it change? Can you tell what person, place, or thing the sentence is about?*

> SENTENCE WITHOUT THE WORD GROUP
> Joan Didion has written essays and screenplays as well as novels.
> The subject of the sentence is identified by name, and the basic meaning of the sentence does not change.
>
> SENTENCE WITHOUT THE WORD GROUP
> Her book is a description of the experience of grief.
> Without the words *The Year of Magical Thinking*, we cannot tell what book the sentence is describing.

❋ 3. *If the meaning of the sentence stays the same without the word or word group, set it off with commas. If the meaning changes, the word or word group should not be set off with commas.*

> • Joan Didion, a native of California, has written essays and screenplays as well as novels.
>
> • Her book *The Year of Magical Thinking* is a description of the experience of grief.
> The sentence is correct. Commas are not needed to enclose *The Year of Magical Thinking*.

2. Parenthetical expressions

The information that parenthetical expressions provide is relatively insignificant and could easily be left out. Therefore, they are set off with a comma or commas.

▶ **Human cloning, so they say, will be possible within a decade.**

3. Contrasting comments

Contrasting comments beginning with words such as *not, unlike,* or *in contrast to* should be set off with commas.

▶ Adam Sandler is famous as a comedian, not a tragedian.

4. Absolute phrases

Absolute phrases usually include a noun *(sunlight)* followed by a participle *(shining)* and are used to modify whole sentences.

▶ The snake slithered through the tall grass, the sunlight

shining now and then on its green skin.

49g Using a comma or commas to set off words of direct address, *yes* and *no,* mild interjections, and tag questions

▶ Thank you, Mr. Rao, for your help.

▶ Yes, I will meet you at noon.

▶ Of course, if that's what you want, we'll do it.

▶ We can do better, don't you think?

Exercise 49.5 Using commas to set off other nonessential
sentence elements

Edit the following sentences, adding commas where they are needed to set off nonessential elements.

EXAMPLE Yes, I will go with you to dinner; however, I

must leave by ten, not a minute later.

1. Millions of viewers watch reality-based television shows. Cultural critics however argue that shows such as *The Amazing Race, Survivor,* and *Jersey Shore* exploit human greed and the desire for fame.
2. These shows so the critics say take advantage of our insecurities.
3. The participants who appear on these shows are average, everyday people not actors.
4. *The Amazing Race* follows its subjects contestants hoping to beat out their competitors by traveling around the world and solving puzzles.

49g
∧/

5. The message is always the same: You too can be rich and famous Average Jane or Joe.
6. Yes many of these shows hold the promise that anyone can win
   a million dollars or gain instant celebrity.
7. These shows of course are extremely enjoyable.
8. Their entertainment value explains why we watch them don't
   you think?

49h Using a comma or commas to separate a direct
quotation from the rest of the sentence

▶ Irving Howe declares, "Whitman is quite realistic about the

place of the self in an urban world" (261).

▶ "Whitman is quite realistic about the place of the self in an

urban world," declares Irving Howe (261).

If the quoted sentence is interrupted, use commas to set off the interrupting words.

▶ "When we interpret a poem," DiYanni says, "we explain it to

ourselves in order to understand it."

If you are quoting more than one sentence and interrupting the
quotation between sentences, the interrupting words should end with
a period.

▶ "But it is not possible to give to each department an equal

power of self defense," James Madison writes in *The*

Federalist No. 51. "In republican government the legislative

authority, necessarily, predominates."

A comma is not needed to separate an indirect quotation or a
paraphrase from the words that identify its source.

▶ Irving Howe notes/ that Whitman realistically depicts the

urban self as free to wander (261).

Note: A comma is not needed if the quotation ends with a question mark
or an exclamation point: *"Where is my sunscreen?" she asked in a panic.
(For more on using quotations, see Chapter 53, pp. 534–41.)*

Exercise 49.6 Using commas to set off direct quotations

Edit the following sentences to correct problems with the use of commas. Some sentences may be correct; circle their numbers.

EXAMPLE **"Nothing I studied was on the test⌄" she moaned**

to her friends.

1. Professor Bartman entered the room and proclaimed "Today we will examine Erikson's eight stages of human development."
2. "Who may I ask has read the assignment" he queried.
3. "Patricia" he hissed "please enlighten the rest of the class."
4. "What would you like to know?" she asked.
5. Now smiling, he replied "Begin by telling us what the eight stages are."
6. She explained that the first stage occurs when infants must learn to trust that their needs will be met.

49i Using commas with dates, addresses, titles and numbers

- **Dates.** Use paired commas in dates when the month, day, and year are included. Do not use commas when the day of the month is omitted or when the day appears before the month.

  ▶ **On March 4, 1931, she traveled to New York.**

  ▶ **She traveled to New York in March 1931.**

  ▶ **She traveled to New York on 4 March 1931.**

- **Addresses.** Use commas to set off the parts of an address or the name of a state, but do not use a comma preceding a zip code.

  ▶ **At Cleveland, Ohio, the river changes direction.**

  ▶ **My address is 63 Oceanside Drive, Apt. 2A, Surf City, New Jersey 08008.**

- **People's titles or degrees.** Put a comma between the person's name and the title or degree when it comes after the name, followed by another comma.

  ▶ **Luis Mendez, MD, gave her the green light to resume her exercise regimen.**

49i
⋀

▪ **Numbers.** When a number has more than four digits, use commas to mark off the numerals by hundreds—that is, by groups of three beginning at the right.

▶ **Andrew Jackson received 647,276 votes in the 1828 presidential election.**

▪ If the number is four digits long, the comma is optional.

▶ **The survey had 1856 [or 1,856] respondents.**

Exceptions: Street numbers, zip codes, telephone numbers, page numbers (p. 2304), and years (1828) do not include commas.

49j Using a comma to take the place of an omitted word or phrase or to prevent misreading

When a writer omits one or more words from a sentence to create an effect, a comma is often needed to make the meaning of the sentence clear for readers.

▶ **Under the tree he found his puppy, and under the car, his cat.**
                                                            ∧

Commas are also used to keep readers from misunderstanding a writer's meaning when words are repeated or might be misread.

▶ **Many birds that sing, sing first thing in the morning.**
                        ∧

It is often better, however, to revise the sentence to avoid the need for the clarifying comma: *Many songbirds sing first thing in the morning.*

49k Common errors in using commas

A comma used incorrectly can confuse readers. Commas should *not* be used in the following situations:

▪ To separate major elements in an independent clause.

▶ **Reflecting on your life,/ is necessary for emotional growth.**

The subject, *reflecting on your life,* should not be separated from the verb, *is.*

▶ **Clarkson decided,/ that her own efforts were the key to her success.**

The verb *decided* should not be separated from its direct object, the subordinate clause *that her own efforts were the key to her success.*

- Before the first or after the final item in a series.

    ▶ **Americans work longer hours than/ German, French, or British workers/ are expected to work.**

    Note: Commas should never be used after *such as* or *like (see p. 522).*

- To separate compound word groups that are not independent clauses.

    ▶ **Injuries were so frequent that he became worried/ and started to play more cautiously.**

- To set off restrictive elements.

    ▶ **The applicants/ who had studied for the admissions test/ were restless and eager for the exam to begin.**

    ▶ **The director/ Alfred Hitchcock/ was responsible for many classic thrillers and horror films, including *Psycho*.**

Adverb clauses beginning with *after, as soon as, before, because, if, since, unless, until,* or *when* are usually essential to a sentence's meaning and therefore are not usually set off with commas when they appear at the end of a sentence.

RESTRICTIVE   I am eager to test the children's IQ again *because significant variations in a child's test score indicate that the test itself may be flawed.*

Clauses beginning with *although, even though, though,* or *whereas* present a contrasting thought and are usually nonrestrictive.

NONRESTRICTIVE   IQ tests can be useful indicators of a child's abilities, *although they should not be taken as the definitive measurement of a child's intelligence.*

- Between cumulative adjectives (*see p. 511*).

    ▶ **Three/ well-known/ U.S. writers visited the artist's studio.**

- Between adjectives and nouns.

    ▶ **An art review by a celebrated, powerful/ writer would be guaranteed publication.**

- Between adverbs and adjectives.

    ▶ **The artist's studio was delightfully/ chaotic.**

49k
no ⌃

▪ After coordinating conjunctions *(and, but, or, nor, for, so, yet).*

▶ **The *duomo* in Siena was begun in the thirteenth century, and,/ it was used as a model for other Italian cathedrals.**

▪ After *although, such as,* or *like.*

▶ **Stage designers can achieve many unusual effects, such as,/ the helicopter that landed onstage in *Miss Saigon.***

▪ Before a parenthesis.

▶ **When in office cubicles,/ (a recent invention), workers need to be considerate of others.**

▪ With a question mark or an exclamation point.

▶ **"Where are my glasses?,/" she asked.**

Exercise 49.7 | Chapter review: Editing for comma use

Edit the following passage, adding and deleting commas as needed.

Every society has families but the structure of the family varies from, society to society. Over time the function of the family, has changed so that in today's postindustrial society for instance the primary function of the family is to provide "emotional gratification" according to Professor Paula Stein noted sociologist of Stonehall University New Hampshire. In a recent interview Stein also said "Images of the family tend to be based on ideals not realities." To back up this claim Stein pointed to, a survey of more than 10000 married American couples, that she and her staff conducted. Released in the October 17 2008 edition of the *Weekly Sociologist,* the survey indicates that the biggest change has been the increase in the variety of family arrangements including singles single parents and childless, couples. Most Americans marry for love they say, but research portrays courtship as an analysis of costs benefits assets and liabilities, not unlike a business deal.

Virtually all children, are upset by divorce, but most recover in a few years while others suffer lasting serious, problems. Despite the high rate of divorce which reached its height in 1979, Americans still believe in the institution of marriage as indicated by the high rate of remarriages that form *blended families.* "Yes some see the breakup of the family as a social problem or the cause of other problems but, others see changes in the family as adaptations to changing social conditions as I do" concluded the professor.

50 Semicolons

Semicolons are used to join ideas that are closely related and grammatically equivalent.

Semicolons and Grammar Checkers

Grammar checker programs will catch some comma splices that can be corrected by adding a semicolon between the two clauses. They will also catch some incorrect uses of the semicolon. They will not tell you when a semicolon *could* be used for clarity, however, nor whether the semicolon is the best choice.

50a Using a semicolon to join independent clauses

A semicolon should join two related independent clauses when they are not joined by a comma and a coordinating conjunction *(and, but, or, nor, for, so, yet)*.

► Before 8000 BCE wheat was not the luxuriant plant it is today; it was merely a wild grass that spread throughout the Middle East.

Sometimes, the close relationship is a contrast.

► Philip had completed the assignment; Lucy had not.

Note: If a comma is used between two clauses without a coordinating conjunction, the sentence is a comma splice, a serious error. If no punctuation appears between the two clauses, the sentence is a run-on. One way to correct a comma splice or a run-on is with a semicolon. *(For more on comma splices and run-on sentences, see Chapter 43, pp. 434–42.)*

50b Using semicolons with transitional expressions that connect independent clauses

Transitional expressions, including transitional phrases *(for example, in addition, on the contrary)* and conjunctive adverbs *(consequently, however),* indicate the relationship between two clauses. When a transitional expression appears between two clauses, it is preceded by a semicolon and usually followed by a comma. Using a comma instead of a semicolon creates a comma splice. *(For a list of*

50b

;

523

transitional expressions, see Chapter 43, p. 437. For help with correcting comma splices, see pp. 434–42.)

▶ **Sheila had to wait until the plumber arrived; consequently, she was late for the exam.**

The semicolon always appears between the two clauses, even when the transitional expression appears in another position within the second clause. Wherever it appears, the transitional expression is usually set off with a comma or commas.

▶ **My friends are all taking golf lessons; my roommate and I, however, are more interested in tennis.**

50c Using a semicolon to separate items or clauses in a series when the items or clauses contain commas

Because the following sentence contains a series with internal commas, the semicolons are needed for clarity.

▶ **The committee included Dr. Curtis Youngblood, the county medical examiner; Roberta Collingwood, the director of the bureau's criminal division; and Darcy Coolidge, the chief of police.**

If two independent clauses are joined by a coordinating conjunction *(and, but, for, nor, or, so, yet)* and at least one of them already contains several internal commas, a semicolon can help readers locate the point where the clauses are separated.

▶ **The closing scenes return to the English countryside, recalling the opening; but these scenes are bathed in a different, cooler light, suggesting that memories of her marriage still haunt her.**

Exercise 50.1 Editing using semicolons

Use semicolons to correct any comma splices and run-on sentences in the following items. *(See Chapter 43 for a detailed discussion of comma splices and run-ons.)* Also add semicolons in place of commas in sentences that contain a series with internal commas.

EXAMPLE   The witness took the stand/; the defendant,

meanwhile, never looked up from her notepad.

1. The Pop Art movement flourished in the United States and in Britain in the 1960s it was a reaction to the abstract art that had dominated the art scene during the 1950s.
2. Pop artists were inspired by popular culture and consumerism, for example, they painted advertisements, comic strips, supermarket products, and even dollar bills!
3. The artists' goal was to transform ordinary daily experiences into art, they also wanted to comment on the modern world of mass production.
4. Pop artist Andy Warhol used silkscreening techniques to create identical, mass-produced images on canvas, so the result was repeated images of Campbell's soup cans and Coca-Cola bottles, as well as famous people like Marilyn Monroe, Elvis Presley, and Jacqueline Kennedy.
5. Other pop artists include Roy Lichtenstein, who is best known for his depiction of cartoons, Richard Hamilton, who is famous for his collages of commercial art, and David Hockney, whose trademark theme is swimming pools.
6. These artists all attained great fame in the art world however, many people did not accept their work as real art.

50d   Common errors in using semicolons

Watch out for and correct common errors in using the semicolon:

- To join a dependent clause or a phrase to an independent clause.

  ▶ **Professional writers need to devote time every day to**

  their writing/, although doing so takes discipline.

  ▶ **Seemingly tame and lovable/, housecats can actually be**

  fierce hunters.

- To join most independent clauses linked by a coordinating conjunction *(and, but, or, nor, for, so,* or *yet).*

  ▶ **Nineteenth-century women wore colorful clothes/,**

  but their attire looks drab in the black-and-white

  photographs of the era.

50d

;

▪ To introduce a series, an explanation, or a quotation.

▶ **My day was planned/: a morning walk, an afternoon in the library, dinner with friends, and a great horror movie.**

▶ **The doctor finally diagnosed the problem/: a severe sinus infection.**

▶ **Boyd warns of the difficulty in describing Bach/: "Even his physical appearance largely eludes us."**

Exercise 50.2 Combining sentences with semicolons

Use a semicolon to combine each set of sentences into one sentence. Add, remove, or change words as necessary. Use a semicolon and a transitional expression between clauses for at least two of your revised sentences. More than one answer is possible for each item.

EXAMPLE **A recent *New York Times* article discusses new discoveries/ These discoveries are about**
the
personality in animals/; Some scientists are quoted in the article. The scientists are studying personality traits in hyenas and wild birds.

1. Some scientists are studying a European bird related to the chickadee. The scientists are at the Netherlands Institute of Ecology. They are conducting experiments with this bird.

2. Another scientist has studied hyena populations. His name is Dr. Samuel Gosling. Dr. Gosling asked handlers to rate the hyenas using a questionnaire. He adapted a version of a questionnaire used for humans.

3. These studies and others indicate that animals display personality traits. These traits include boldness and shyness. Bold birds quickly investigate new items in their environment. Shy birds take more time.

4. Bold birds have an advantage over shy birds in some situations. They do not have an advantage in other situations.

5. Some experts on human personality are skeptical. They doubt that animals have the same personality traits that humans do.

Scientists who study personality in animals need to be careful to avoid anthropomorphism. That is the tendency to attribute human characteristics to animals.

51 Colons

A colon draws attention to what it is introducing. It also has other conventional uses.

Colons and Grammar Checkers

A grammar checker may point out when you have used a colon incorrectly, but since colons are usually optional, most of the time you must decide whether a colon is your best choice in a sentence.

51a Using colons to introduce lists, appositives, or quotations

Colons are almost always preceded by complete sentences (independent clauses).

LIST	**Several majors interest me: biology, chemistry, and art.**
APPOSITIVE	**She shared with me her favorite toys: a spatula and a pot lid.**
QUOTATION	**He said the dreaded words: "Let's just be friends."**

51b Using a colon when a second independent clause elaborates on the first one

The colon can be used to link independent clauses when the second clause restates or elaborates on the first. Use it when you want to emphasize the second clause.

51b
:

▶ **I can predict tonight's sequence of events: My brother will arrive late, talk loudly, and eat too much.**

Note: When a complete sentence follows a colon, the first word may begin with either a capital or a lowercase letter. Be consistent throughout your document.

51c Using colons in business letters and memos, in ratios and expressions of times of day, for city and publisher citations in bibliographies, and between titles and subtitles

▶ **Dear Mr. Worth: To:**

▶ **The ratio of armed to unarmed members of the gang was 3:1.**

▶ **He woke up at 6:30 in the morning.**

▶ **New York: McGraw, 2010**

▶ *Possible Lives: The Promise of Public Education in America*

Note: Colons are often used to separate biblical chapters and verses (John 3:16), but the Modern Language Association (MLA) recommends using a period instead (John 3.16).

51d Common errors in using the colon

▪ Between a verb and its object or complement.

   ▶ **The elements in a good smoothie are/ yogurt, fresh fruit, and honey.**

▪ Between a preposition and its object or objects.

   ▶ **Many feel that cancer can be prevented by a diet of/ fruit, nuts, and vegetables.**

▪ After *such as, for example,* or *including.*

   ▶ **I am ready for a change, such as/ a vacation.**

Exercise 51.1 Chapter review: Editing for colons

Edit the following passage by adding or deleting colons.

EXAMPLE   The director of the soup kitchen is considering
           ways to raise funds, for example/ a bake sale,
           car wash, or readathon.

Ciguatera is a form of food poisoning, humans are poisoned when they consume reef fish that contain toxic substances called ciguatoxins. These toxins accumulate at the end of the food chain: large carnivorous fish prey on smaller herbivorous fish. These smaller fish feed on ciguatoxins, which are produced by microorganisms that grow on the surface of marine algae. Ciguatoxins are found in certain marine fish, snapper, mackerel, barracuda, and grouper. People should avoid eating fish from reef waters, including: the tropical and subtropical waters of the Pacific and Indian oceans and the Caribbean Sea.

Some people think that ciguatera can be destroyed by: cooking or freezing the fish. People who consume reef fish should avoid eating: the head, internal organs, or eggs. People who eat contaminated fish experience gastrointestinal and neurological problems: vomiting, diarrhea, numbness, and muscle pains. Most physicians offer the same advice, "Eat fish only from reputable restaurants and dealers."

52 Apostrophes

Apostrophes show possession and indicate omitted letters in contractions. Apostrophes are used in such a variety of ways that they can be confusing. The most common confusion is between plurals and possessives.

52
v̌

Apostrophes and Grammar Checkers

A spelling checker will sometimes highlight *its* used incorrectly (instead of *it's*) or an error in a possessive (for example, *Englands' glory*). You should double-check all words that end in -*s* in your work, however.

52a Using apostrophes to indicate possession

For a noun to be possessive, two elements are usually required: someone or something is the possessor, and someone, something, or some attribute or quality is possessed.

1. Forming the possessive of singular nouns

To form the possessive of all singular nouns, add an apostrophe plus *-s* to the noun: *baby's.* Even singular nouns that end in *-s* form the possessive by adding *-'s: bus's.*

If a singular noun with more than two syllables ends in *-s,* and adding *-'s* would make the word sound awkward, it is acceptable to use only an apostrophe to form the possessive: *Socrates'.*

2. Forming the possessive of plural nouns

- To form the possessive of a plural noun that ends in *-s,* add only an apostrophe: *subjects', babies'.*
- To form the possessive of a plural noun that does not end in *-s,* add an apostrophe plus *-s: men's, cattle's.*

3. Showing joint possession

To express joint ownership by two or more people, use the possessive form for the last name only; to express individual ownership, use the possessive form for each name.

▶ **Felicia and Elias's report**

▶ **The city's and the state's finances**

4. Forming the possessive of compound nouns

For compound words, add an apostrophe plus *-s* to the last word in the compound to form the possessive: *my father-in-law's job.*

52b Using an apostrophe and *-s* with indefinite pronouns

Indefinite pronouns such as *no one, everyone, everything,* and *something* do not refer to a specific person or a specific item. Use *-'s* to form the possessive.

▶ **Well, it is anybody's guess.**

Exercise 52.1 Using apostrophes to form the possessive

Write the possessive form of each word. The first one has been done for you.

Word(s)	**Possessive**
the press	*the press's*
nobody	
newspapers	
Monday and Tuesday classes (individual ownership)	
deer	
women	
someone	
Edward	
trade-off	
well-worn footpath	
United States	
this year and last year combined population (joint ownership)	

52c Using apostrophes to mark contractions

In a contraction, the apostrophe substitutes for omitted letters:

it's	for *it is* or *it has*
weren't	for *were not*

Apostrophes can also substitute for omitted numbers in a year *(the class of '11)*.

Note: Although the MLA and APA style manuals allow contractions in academic writing, some instructors think they are too informal. Check with your instructor before using contractions.

52d Forming plural letters, words used as words, numbers, and abbreviations

An apostrophe plus *-s* *('s)* can be used to show the plural of a letter. Underline or italicize single letters but not the apostrophe or the *-s*.

▶ ***Committee*** **has two *m*'s, two *t*'s, and two *e*'s.**

If a word is used as a word rather than as a symbol of the meaning it conveys, it can be made plural by adding an apostrophe plus -*s*. The word should be italicized or underlined, but the -*s* should not be.

▶ **There are twelve *no*'s in the first paragraph.**

MLA and APA style now recommend against using an apostrophe to form plurals of numbers and abbreviations.

▶ **He makes his 2s look like 5s.**

▶ **Professor Morris has two PhDs.**

✓ 52e Common errors in using apostrophes

Do not use an apostrophe in the following situations:

- **With a plural noun.** Most often, writers misuse the apostrophe by adding it to a plural noun that is not possessive. The plurals of most nouns are formed by adding -*s*: *boy/boys, girl/girls, teacher/teachers*. Possessives are formed by adding an apostrophe plus -*s* (*'s*): *boy/boy's, girl/girl's, teacher/teacher's*. The possessive form and the plural form are not interchangeable.

  teachers   girls   boys
  ▶ **The ~~teacher's~~ asked the ~~girl's~~ and ~~boy's~~ for their attention.**

- **With possessive pronouns and contractions.** Be careful not to use a contraction when a possessive is called for, and vice versa. Personal pronouns and the relative pronoun *who* have special possessive forms, which never require apostrophes *(my/mine, your/yours, his, her/hers, it/its, our/ours, their/theirs,* and *whose)*. When an apostrophe appears with a pronoun, the apostrophe usually marks omissions in a contraction, unless the pronoun is indefinite *(see p. 530)*.

  ours
  ▶ **That cat of ~~our's~~ is always sleeping!**

  its
  ▶ **The dog sat down and scratched ~~it's~~ fleas.**

  Its is a possessive pronoun. *It's* is a contraction for *it is* or *it has: It's [It + is] too hot*.

  their
  ▶ **They gave ~~they're~~ lives.**

  Their is a possessive pronoun; *they're* is a contraction of *they are*. Both are also confused with the adverb *there: She was standing there*.

Exercise 52.2 Distinguishing between contractions and pronouns

Underline the correct word choice in each sentence.

EXAMPLE **Transcendentalists have had a strong influence on American thought; (there/they're/their) important figures in our literary history.**

1. In the essay "The Over-soul," Ralph Waldo Emerson describes the unity of nature by cataloging (it's/its) divine, yet earthly, expressions, such as waterfalls and well-worn footpaths.

2. Emerson states that you must have faith to believe in something that supersedes or contradicts (your/you're) real-life experiences.

3. (Who's/Whose) the author of the poem at the beginning of Emerson's "Self-Reliance"?

4. Emerson believes that (there/they're/their) are ways to live within a society without having to give in to its pressures.

5. According to Emerson, people should occasionally silence the noise of (there/they're/their) inner voices and learn to listen to the world's unconscious voice.

6. Emerson also believes that, in the end, (it's/its) the individual— and the individual alone—who must decide his or her own fate.

Exercise 52.3 Chapter review: Editing for apostrophes

Edit the following passage by adding and deleting apostrophes and correcting any incorrect word choices.

Transcendentalism was a movement of thought in the mid-to-late 1800s that was originated by Ralph Waldo Emerson, Henry David Thoreau, and several other's who's scholarship helped to shape the democratic ideals of their day and usher America into it's modern age. Emerson, a member of New Englands' elite, was particularly interested in spreading Transcendentalist notion's of self-reliance; he is probably best known for his essay "Self-Reliance," which is still widely read in todays' universities. Most people remember Thoreau, however, not only for what he wrote but also for how he lived: its well known that—for a while, at least—he chose to live a simple life in a cabin on Walden Pond. Altogether, one could say that Emerson's and Thoreau's main accomplishment was to expand the influence of literature and philosophy over the development of the average Americans' identity. With a new national literature forming, people's interest in they're self-development quickly increased as they began to read more and more about what it meant to be American. In fact, one

52e

∨

could even say (perhaps half-jokingly) that, today, the success of home makeovers on TV and the popularity of self-help books might have a lot to do with Emerson's and Thoreau's ideas about self-sufficiency and living simply—idea's that took root in this nation more than a hundred years ago.

53 Quotation Marks

Quotation marks enclose words, phrases, and sentences that are quoted directly; titles of short works such as poems, articles, songs, and short stories; and words and phrases used in a special sense.

Note: Citations in this chapter follow MLA style. See Part 5 for examples of APA style.

Quotation Marks and Grammar Checkers

A grammar checker can alert you to the lack of an opening or closing quotation mark, but it cannot determine where a quotation should begin and end. Grammar checkers also may not point out errors in the use of quotation marks with other punctuation marks. For example, a grammar checker did not highlight the error in the placement of the period at the end of the following sentence *(see p. 538).*

| INCORRECT | **Barbara Ehrenreich observes, "There are no Palm Pilots, cable channels, or Web sites to advise the low-wage job seeker".** |

53a Using quotation marks to indicate direct quotations

Direct quotations from written material may include whole sentences or only a few words or phrases.

▶ In *Angela's Ashes,* Frank McCourt writes, "Worse than the ordinary miserable childhood is the miserable Irish childhood" (11).

▶ Frank McCourt believes that being Irish worsens what is all too "ordinary"—a "miserable childhood" (11).

Use quotation marks to enclose everything a speaker says in written dialogue. If the quoted sentence is interrupted by a phrase like *he said,* enclose just the quotation in quotation marks.

Do not use quotation marks to set off an indirect quotation, which reports what a speaker said but does not use the exact words.

▶ He said that ⁊he didn't know what I was talking about.⁊

Exception: If you are using a quotation that is longer than four typed lines, set it off from the text as a **block quotation.** A block quotation is *not* surrounded by quotation marks. The following long quotes follow MLA style. *(For examples of APA style, see Part 5.)*

> As Carl Schorske points out, the young Freud was passionately
> interested in classical archeology:
>> He cultivated a new friendship in the Viennese professional
>> elite—especially rare in those days of withdrawal—with
>> Emanuel Loewy, a professor of archeology. "He keeps me up
>> till three o'clock in the morning," Freud wrote appreciatively
>> to Fliess. "He tells me about Rome." (273)

Longer verse quotations (four lines or more) are indented block style, like long prose quotations. If you cannot fit an entire line of poetry on a single line of your typescript, you may indent the turned line an extra quarter inch (three spaces).

> In the following lines from "Crossing Brooklyn Ferry," Walt Whitman
> celebrates the beauty of the Manhattan skyline and his love for that city:
>> Ah, what can ever be more stately and
>>> admirable to me than mast-hemm'd
>> Manhattan?
>> River and sunset and scallop-edg'd waves of
>> flood-tide?
>> The sea-gulls oscillating their bodies, the
>>> hay-boat in the twilight, and the belated lighter?

53a
" "

> What gods can exceed these that clasp me by
>
> the hand, and with voices I love call me
>
> promptly and loudly by my nighest name as
>
> I approach? (lines 92–95)

Use single quotation marks to set off a quotation within a quotation.

▶   **In response to alumni, the president of the university said, "I know you're saying to me, 'We want a winning football team.' But I'm telling you that I want an honest football team."**

53b Using quotation marks to enclose titles of short works

The titles of long works, such as books, are usually put in italics or underlined *(see Chapter 58, p. 561).* The titles of book chapters, essays, most poems, and other short works are usually put in quotation marks. Quotation marks are also used for titles of unpublished works, including student papers, theses, and dissertations.

▶   **"The Girl in Conflict" is Chapter 11 of *Coming of Age in Samoa.***

Note: If quotation marks are needed within the title of a short work, use single quotation marks: "The 'Animal Rights' War on Medicine."

53c Using quotation marks to indicate that a word or phrase is being used in a special way

Put quotation marks around a word or phrase that someone else has used in a way that you or your readers may not agree with. These quotation marks function as raised eyebrows do in conversation and should be used sparingly.

▶   **The "worker's paradise" of Stalinist Russia included slave-labor camps.**

Words cited as words can also be put in quotation marks, although the more common practice is to italicize them.

▶   **The words "compliment" and "complement" sound alike but have different meanings.**

Exercise 53.1   Using double and single quotation marks

Following is a passage from the Seneca Falls Declaration (1848) by Elizabeth Cady Stanton, followed by a series of quotations from this passage. Add, delete, or replace quotation marks to quote from the passage accurately. Some sentences may be correct; circle their numbers.

> The history of mankind is a history of repeated injuries and usurpations on the part of man toward woman, having in direct object the establishment of an absolute tyranny over her. To prove this, let facts be submitted to a candid world.
>
> WHEREAS, The great precept of nature is conceded to be that "man shall pursue his own true and substantial happiness." Blackstone in his *Commentaries* remarks that this law of Nature being coeval with mankind, and dictated by God himself, is of course superior in obligation to any other. It is binding over all the globe, in all countries and at all times; no human laws are of any validity if contrary to this, and such of them as are valid, derive all their force, and all their validity, and all their authority, mediately and immediately, from this original; therefore,
>
> RESOLVED, That such laws as conflict, in any way, with the true and substantial happiness of woman, are contrary to the great precept of nature and of no validity, for this is "superior in obligation to any other."

EXAMPLE   As Elizabeth Cady Stanton points out, "The

great precept of nature is conceded to be that

'man shall pursue his own true and substantial

happiness.' "

1. "The history of mankind is a history of repeated injuries and usurpations on the part of man toward woman," Elizabeth Cady Stanton asserts, "having in direct object the establishment of an absolute tyranny over her."
2. To prove this, writes Stanton, let facts be submitted to a candid world.
3. Stanton argues that men have oppressed women throughout history.
4. Stanton contends "that all laws are subject to natural laws."
5. Stanton resolves "that such laws as conflict, in any way, with the true and substantial happiness of woman, are contrary to the great precept of nature and of no validity, for this is "superior in obligation to any other." "

53c

" "

53d Other punctuation with quotation marks

As you edit, check all closing quotation marks and the marks of punctuation that appear next to them to make sure that you have placed them in the right order.

1. Periods and commas

Always place the period or comma before the final quotation mark even when the quotation is brief.

▶ **"Instead of sharing an experience the spectator must come to grips with things," Brecht writes in "The Epic Theatre and Its Difficulties."**

Exception: A parenthetical citation in either MLA or APA style always appears between the closing quotation mark and the period: *Brecht wants the spectator to "come to grips with things" (23).*

2. Question marks and exclamation points

Place a question mark or an exclamation point after the final quotation mark unless the quoted material is itself a question or an exclamation.

▶ **How does epic theatre make us "come to grips with things"?**

▶ **Brecht was asked, "Are we to see science in the theatre?"**

3. Colons and semicolons

Place colons and semicolons after the final quotation mark.

▶ **Dean Wilcox cited the items he called his "daily delights": a free parking space for his scooter at the faculty club, a special table in the club itself, and friends to laugh with after a day's work.**

4. Dashes

Place a dash outside either an opening or a closing quotation mark if the dash precedes or follows the quotation, or outside both if two dashes are used to set off the quotation.

▶ **One phrase—"time is running out"—haunted me throughout my dream.**

Place a dash inside either an opening or a closing quotation mark if it is part of the quotation.

▶ **"Where is the—" she called. "Oh, here it is. Never mind."**

(For more in integrating quotations into your sentences, see Chapter 19, Working with Sources and Avoiding Plagiarism, pp. 253–57.)

Exercise 53.2 Using quotation marks with other punctuation

Edit the following sentences to correct problems with the use of quotation marks with other punctuation. Some sentences may be correct; circle their numbers.

> **EXAMPLE** **In June 1776, Richard Henry Lee proposed that the Continental Congress adopt a resolution that "these united Colonies are, and of right ought to be, free and independent States."/**

1. "We hold these truths to be self-evident", wrote Thomas Jefferson in 1776.
2. Most Americans can recite their "unalienable rights:" "life, liberty, and the pursuit of happiness."
3. According to the Declaration of Independence, "whenever any form of government becomes destructive to these ends, it is the right of the people to alter or to abolish it."!
4. The signers of the Declaration of Independence contended that the "history of the present King of Great Britain is a history of repeated injuries and usurpations, all having in direct object the establishment of an absolute tyranny over these states."
5. What did the creators of this document mean by a "candid world?"
6. Feminists and civil rights advocates have challenged the Declaration's most famous phrase "—all men are created equal"—on the grounds that these "unalienable rights" were originally extended only to white men who owned property.

53e Common errors in using quotation marks

Watch out for and correct common errors in using quotation marks:

- **To distance yourself from slang, clichés, or trite expressions.** It is best to avoid overused or slang expressions altogether in college writing. If your writing situation permits slang, however, do not enclose it in quotation marks.

  WEAK Californians are so "laid back."

  REVISED Many Californians have a carefree style.

53e
" "

- **For indirect quotations.** Do not use quotation marks for indirect quotations. Watch out for errors in pronoun reference as well. *(See Chapter 46, pp. 470–73.)*

  INCORRECT   He wanted to tell his boss that "he needed a vacation."

  CORRECT   He told his boss that his boss needed a vacation.

  CORRECT   He said to his boss, "You need a vacation."

- **In quotations that end with a question.** Only the question mark that ends the quoted sentence is needed, even when the entire sentence that includes the quotation is also a question.

  ▶   **What did Juliet mean when she cried, "O Romeo, Romeo! Wherefore art thou Romeo?"?**

- **To enclose the title of your own paper.** Do not use quotation marks around the title of your own essay at the beginning of your paper.

  ▶   **"Edgar Allan Poe and the Paradox of the Gothic"**

Exercise 53.3   Chapter review: Editing for quotation marks

Edit the following passage to correct problems with the use of quotation marks.

On August 28, 1963, Dr. Martin Luther King Jr. delivered his famous 'I Have a Dream' speech at the nation's Lincoln Memorial. According to King, "When the architects of our republic wrote the magnificent words of the Constitution and the Declaration of Independence, they were signing a promissory note to which every American was to fall heir". King declared that "this note was a promise that all men, yes, black men as well as white men, would be guaranteed the unalienable rights of life, liberty, and the pursuit of happiness." This promissory note, however, came back "marked "insufficient funds."" King's speech, therefore, was designed to rally his supporters to "make justice a reality."

Unlike the more militant civil rights leaders of the 1950s, King advocated nonviolence. This stance is why King said that the 'Negro community' should not drink "from the cup of bitterness and hatred" and that they should not use physical violence.

King's dream was uniquely American: "I have a dream that one day this nation will rise up and live out the true meaning of its creed: 'We hold these truths to be self-evident: that all men are created equal.'" King challenged all Americans to fully embrace racial equality. Nearly fifty years later, we must ask ourselves if King's dream has in fact become a reality. Are "all of God's children, black men and white men, Jews and Gentiles, Protestants and Catholics . . . able to join hands and sing in the words of the old Negro spiritual, "Free at last! free at last! thank God Almighty, we are free at last!?""

54 Other Punctuation Marks

Punctuation and Grammar Checkers

Your grammar checker might highlight a period used instead of a question mark at the end of a question. However, grammar checkers will not tell you when you might use a pair of dashes or parentheses to set material off in a sentence or when you need a second dash or parenthesis to enclose parenthetical material.

54a The period

Use a period to end all sentences except direct questions or exclamations. Statements that ask questions indirectly end in a period.

► **She asked me where I had gone to college.**

A period is conventionally used with the following common abbreviations, which end in lowercase letters:

Mr.	Mrs.	i.e.	Mass.
Ms.	Dr.	e.g.	Jan.

If the abbreviation is made up of capital letters, however, the periods are optional:

RN (or R.N.)	BA (or B.A.)
MD (or M.D.)	PhD (or Ph.D.)

54a

Periods are omitted in abbreviations for organizations, famous people, states in mailing addresses, and acronyms (words made up of initials):

FBI	JFK	MA	NATO
CIA	LBJ	TX	NAFTA

When in doubt, consult a dictionary.

54b The question mark

Use a question mark after a direct question.

▶ **Who wrote *The Old Man and the Sea*?**

Occasionally, a question mark changes a statement into a question.

▶ **You expect me to believe a story like that?**

Do not use a question mark after an indirect quotation, even if the words being indirectly quoted were originally a question.

▶ **He asked her if she would be at home later?.**

Note: When questions follow one another in a series, each one can be followed by a question mark even if the questions are not complete sentences. Each question in the series can begin with either a capital or a lowercase letter.

▶ **What will you contribute? Your time? Your talent? Your money? [*or* your time? your talent? your money?]**

54c The exclamation point

Use exclamation points sparingly to convey shock, surprise, or some other strong emotion.

▶ **Stolen! The money was stolen! Right before our eyes, somebody snatched my purse and ran off with it.**

Using numerous exclamation points throughout a document actually weakens their force. Try to convey emotion with your choice of words and your sentence structure instead.

▶ **Jefferson and Adams both died on the same day in 1826, exactly fifty years after the signing of the Declaration of Independence!.**

The fact that the sentence reports is surprising enough without the addition of an exclamation point.

Exercise 54.1	Editing for end punctuation

Insert periods, question marks, and exclamation points in the following passage. Delete any unnecessary commas *(see Chapter 49, pp. 520–22).*

Do you realize that there is a volcano larger than Mt St Helens Mt Vesuvius Mt Etna Mauna Loa is the largest volcano on Earth, covering at least half the island of Hawaii The summit of Mauna Loa stands 56,000 feet above its base This is why Native Hawaiians named this volcano, the "Long Mountain" Mauna Loa is also one of the most active volcanoes on the planet, having erupted thirty-three times since 1843 Its last eruption occurred in 1984 Most people associate a volcanic eruption with red lava spewing from the volcano's crater, but few people realize that the lava flow, and volcanic gases are also extremely hazardous Tourists like to follow the lava to where it meets the sea, but this practice is dangerous because of the steam produced when the lava meets the water So the next time you visit an active volcano, beware

54d Dashes

Use a dash or dashes to set off words, phrases, or clauses that deserve special attention. A typeset dash, sometimes called an *em dash,* is a single, unbroken line about as wide as a capital *M.* Most word-processing programs provide the em dash as a special character or will convert two hyphens to an em dash as an automatic function. Otherwise, you can make a dash by typing two hyphens in a row with no space between them. Do not put a space before or after the dash.

1. To set off parenthetical material, a series, or an explanation

▶ **All finite creations—including humans—are incomplete and contradictory.**

▶ **Coca-Cola, potato chips, and brevity—these are the marks of a good study session in the dorm.**

▶ **I think the Comets will win the tournament for one reason—their goalie.**

54d

Sometimes, a dash is used to set off an independent clause within a sentence. In such sentences, the set-off clause provides interesting information but is not essential to the main assertion.

▶ **The first rotary gasoline engine—it was made by Mazda—burned 15 percent more fuel than conventional engines.**

2. To indicate a sudden change in tone or idea

▶ Breathing heavily, the archaeologist opened the old chest in wild anticipation and found—an old pair of socks and an empty soda can.

Note: Used sparingly, the dash can be an effective mark of punctuation, but if it is overused, it can make your writing disjointed.

▶ After we found the puppy—shivering under the porch—, we

brought her into the house—into the entryway, actually—

and wrapped her in an old towel— to warm her up.

Exercise 54.2 Using dashes

Insert or correct dashes where needed in the following sentences.

EXAMPLE   Women once shut out of electoral office

altogether have made great progress in

recent decades.

1. Patsy Mink, Geraldine Ferraro, Antonia Novello, Madeleine Albright, Hillary Clinton, and Sarah Palin all are political pioneers in the history of the United States.
2. Patsy Mink the first Asian-American woman elected to the U.S. Congress served for twenty-four years in the U.S. House of Representatives.
3. Geraldine Ferraro congresswoman from Queens, New York became the first female vice presidential candidate when she was nominated by the Democratic Party in 1984.
4. Antonia Novello—former U.S. surgeon general—was the first woman—and the first Hispanic—to hold this position.
5. Madeleine Albright, the first female secretary of state, has observed, "To understand Europe, you have to be a genius-or French."
6. In 2008 two strong women candidates Hillary Clinton and Sarah Palin ran for the Democratic presidential nomination and as the Republican vice presidential nominee, respectively.

54e Parentheses

Parentheses should be used infrequently and only to set off supplementary information, a digression, or a comment that interrupts the flow of thought within a sentence or paragraph.

▶ **The tickets (ranging in price from $10 to $50) go on sale Monday.**

When parentheses enclose a whole sentence, the sentence begins with a capital letter and ends with a period before the final parenthesis. A sentence that appears inside parentheses *within a sentence* should neither begin with a capital letter nor end with a period.

▶ **Folktales and urban legends often reflect the concerns of a particular era. (The familiar tale of a cat accidentally caught in a microwave oven is an example of this phenomenon.)**

▶ **Angela Merkel (she is the first female chancellor of Germany) formed a coalition government following her election in 2005.**

If the material in parentheses is at the end of an introductory or nonessential word group followed by a comma, place the comma after the closing parenthesis. A comma should never appear before the opening parenthesis.

▶ **As the soloist walked onstage/ (carrying her famous violin), the audience rose to its feet.**

Parentheses enclose numbers or letters that label items in a list.

▶ **He says the argument is nonsense because (1) university presidents don't work as well as machines, (2) university presidents don't do any real work at all, and (3) universities should be run by faculty committees.**

Parentheses also enclose in-text citations in many systems of documenting sources. *(For more on documenting sources, see Parts 4 and 5.)*

Note: Too many parentheses are distracting to readers. If you find that you have used a large number of parentheses in a draft, go over it carefully to see if any of the material within parentheses really deserves more emphasis.

54e

Exercise 54.3 Using parentheses

Insert parentheses where needed in the following sentences, and correct any errors in their use.

EXAMPLE **During leap year, February has twenty-nine**

( )
29 days.
^   ^

1. German meteorologist Alfred Wegener he was also a geo-physicist proposed the first comprehensive theory of continental drift.
2. According to this geological theory, 1 the earth originally contained a single large continent, 2 this land mass eventually separated into six continents, and 3 these continents gradually drifted apart.
3. Wegener contended that continents will continue to drift. They are not rigidly fixed. The evidence indicates that his predictions are accurate.
4. The continents are moving at a rate of one yard .09144 meters per century.
5. The movement of the continents, (slow though this movement may be), occasionally causes earthquakes along fault lines such as the famous San Andreas Fault in California.

54f Brackets

Brackets set off information you add to a quotation that is not part of the quotation itself.

▶ **Samuel Eliot Morison has written, "This passage has attracted a good deal of scorn to the Florentine mariner [Verrazano], but without justice."**

Morison's sentence does not include the name of the "Florentine mariner," so the writer places the name in brackets.

Use brackets to enclose the word *sic* (Latin for "thus") after a word in a quotation that was incorrect in the original. If you are following MLA style, the word *sic* should not be underlined or italicized.

▶ **The critic noted that "the battle scenes in *The Patriot* are realistic, but the rest of the film is historically inacurate [sic]."**

54g Ellipses

Use three spaced periods, called ellipses or an ellipsis mark, to show readers that you have omitted words from a passage you are quoting.

FULL QUOTATION FROM A WORK BY WILKINS

In the nineteenth century, railroads, lacing their way across continents, reaching into the heart of every major city in Europe and America, and bringing a new romance to travel, added to the unity of nations and fueled the nationalist fires already set burning by the French Revolution and the wars of Napoleon.

EDITED QUOTATION

In his account of nineteenth-century society, Wilkins argues that "railroads . . . added to the unity of nations and fueled the nationalist fires already set burning by the French Revolution and the wars of Napoleon."

If you are omitting the end of a quoted sentence, the three ellipsis points are preceded by a period to end the sentence.

EDITED QUOTATION

In describing the growth of railroads, Wilkins pictures them "lacing their way across continents, reaching into the heart of every major city in Europe and America. . . ."

When you need to add a parenthetical reference after the ellipses at the end of a sentence, place it after the quotation mark but before the final period: . . ." (253).

Ellipses are usually not needed to indicate an omission when only a word or phrase is being quoted.

▶ **Railroads brought "a new romance to travel," according to Wilkins.**

To indicate the omission of an entire line or more from the middle of a poem, insert a line of spaced periods.

Note: Ellipses should be used only as a means of shortening a quotation, never as a device for changing its fundamental meaning or emphasis.

54h Slashes

Use the slash to show divisions between lines of poetry when you quote more than one line of a poem as part of a sentence. Add a space on either side of the slash. When you are quoting four or more lines of poetry, use a block quotation instead *(see pp. 535–36).*

54h

▶ **In "The Tower," Yeats makes his peace with "All those things whereof / Man makes a superhuman / Mirror-resembling dream" (163–165).**

The slash is sometimes used between two words that represent choices or combinations. Do not add spaces around the slash when you use it in this way.

▶   **The college offers three credit/noncredit courses.**

Slashes mark divisions in online addresses (URLs): *http://www .georgetown.edu/crossroads/navigate.html.*

Some writers use the slash as a marker between the words *and* and *or* or between *he* and *she* or *his* and *her* to avoid sexism. Most writers, however, consider such usage awkward. It is usually better to rephrase the sentence.

Exercise 54.4   Using brackets, ellipses, and slashes

Insert brackets, ellipses, and slashes where needed in the following sentences, and correct any errors in their use. Refer to the following excerpts from a poem and an essay.

> The lights begin to twinkle from the rocks;
> The long day wanes; the slow moon climbs, the deep
> Moans round with many voices. Come, my friends.
> 'T is not too late to seek a newer world. (54–57)
>
> —ALFRED, LORD TENNYSON, *Ulysses*

> Now when I had mastered the language of this water and had come to know every trifling feature that bordered the great river as familiarly as I knew the letters of the alphabet, I had made a valuable acquisition. But I had lost something, too. I had lost something which could never be restored to me while I lived. All the grace, the beauty, the poetry had gone out of the majestic river!
>
> MARK TWAIN, "Two Views of the Mississippi"

EXAMPLE   **The speaker in the poem *Ulysses* is looking for**

"*/ / /* **a newer world" (57).**

1.   Ulysses is tempted as he looks toward the sea: "The lights begin to twinkle from the rocks; The long day wanes . . ." (54–55).

2.   In "Two Views of the Mississippi," Mark Twain writes that "when I had mastered the language of this water, I had made a valuable acquisition."

3. Twain regrets that he "has lost something"—his sense of the beauty of the river.

4. In Tennyson's poem, "the deep the ocean / moans round with many voices" (55–56).

5. In *Ulysses* the ocean beckons with possibilities; in "Two Views of the Mississippi," the river has become too familiar: "All the grace had gone out of the majestic river!"

Exercise 54.5 Chapter review: Editing for dashes, parentheses, and other punctuation marks

Edit the following passage by adding or deleting dashes, parentheses, brackets, ellipses, and slashes. Make any other additions, deletions, or changes that are necessary for correctness and sense. Refer to the following excerpt as necessary.

> This is a book about that most admirable of human virtues—courage.
>
> . . . .
>
> Some of my colleagues who are criticized today for lack of forthright principles—or who are looked upon with scornful eyes as compromising "politicians"—are simply engaged in the fine art of conciliating, balancing and interpreting the forces and factions of public opinion, an art essential to keeping our nation united and enabling our Government to function.
>
> —JOHN F. KENNEDY, *Profiles in Courage,* pp. 1, 5

John Fitzgerald Kennedy—the youngest man to be elected U.S. president—he was also the youngest president to be assassinated. He was born on May 29, 1917, in Brookline, Massachusetts. Kennedy was born into a family with a tradition of public service; his father, Joseph Kennedy, served as ambassador to Great Britain. (his maternal grandfather, John Frances Fitzgerald, served as the mayor of Boston.)

Caroline, John Fitzgerald Jr., and Patrick B. (Who died in infancy) are the children of the late John F. Kennedy. Kennedy's background, a Harvard education, military service as a lieutenant in the navy, and public service as Massachusetts senator—helped provide John F. Kennedy with the experience, insight, and recognition needed to defeat Richard Nixon in 1960.

54h

Even before being elected U.S. president, Kennedy received the Pulitzer Prize for his book *Profiles in Courage* 1957. According to Kennedy, "This *Profiles in Courage* is a book about that most admirable of human virtues—courage" 1. "Some of my colleagues," Kennedy continues, "who are criticized today for lack of forthright principles / are simply engaged in the fine art of conciliating . . ." 5.

During Kennedy's presidency, Americans witnessed 1 the Cuban missile crisis, 2 the Bay of Pigs invasion, and 3 the Berlin crisis. Most Americans—we hope—are able to recognize Kennedy's famous words—which were first delivered during his Inaugural Address: "Ask not what your country can do for you—ask what you can do for your country."

55 Capitalization

Many rules for the use of capital letters have been fixed by custom, such as the convention of beginning each sentence with a capital letter, but the rules change all the time. A recent dictionary is a good guide to capitalization.

✓ 55a Proper nouns

Proper nouns are the names of specific people, places, or things. Capitalize proper nouns, words derived from proper nouns, brand names, abbreviations of capitalized words, and call letters of radio and television stations:

Ronald Reagan
Reaganomics
Apple computer
FBI (government agency)
WNBC (television station)

Note: Although holidays and the names of months and days of the week are capitalized, seasons, such as *summer,* are not. Neither are the days of the month when they are spelled out *(the seventh of March).*

TYPES and EXAMPLES of PROPER NOUNS

- **People:** Helena Bonham Carter, Sonia Sotomayor, Bill Gates
- **Nationalities, ethnic groups, and languages:** English, Swiss, African Americans, Arabs, Chinese, Turkish
- **Places:** the United States of America, Tennessee, the Irunia Restaurant, the Great Lakes, *but* my state, the lake
- **Organizations and institutions:** Phi Beta Kappa, Republican Party (Republicans), Department of Defense, Cumberland College, the North Carolina Tarheels, *but* the department, this college, our hockey team
- **Religious bodies, books, and figures:** Jews, Christians, Baptists, Hindus, Roman Catholic Church, the Bible, the Koran or Qur'an, the Torah, God, Holy Spirit, Allah, *but* a Greek goddess, a biblical reference
- **Scientific names and terms:** *Homo sapiens, H. sapiens, Acer rubrum, A. rubrum,* Addison's disease (*or* Addison disease), Cenozoic era, Newton's first law, *but* the law of gravity
- **Names of planets, stars, and other astronomical bodies:** Earth (as a planet) *but* the earth, Mercury, Polaris *or* the North Star, Whirlpool Galaxy, *but* a star, that galaxy, the solar system
- **Computer terms:** the Internet, the World Wide Web *or* the Web, *but* search engine, a network, my browser
- **Days and months:** Monday, Veterans Day, August, the Fourth of July, *but* yesterday, spring and summer, the winter term, second-quarter earnings
- **Historical events, movements, and periods:** World War II, Impressionism, the Renaissance, the Jazz Age, the Declaration of Independence, the Magna Carta, *but* the last war, a golden age, the twentieth century, the amendment
- **Academic subjects and courses:** English 101, Psychology 221, a course in Italian, *but* a physics course, my art history class

---

Capitalization and Grammar Checkers

Grammar checkers will flag some words that should be capitalized or lowercase by convention, but they won't flag proper nouns unless the noun is stored in the program's dictionary, and they may not flag a noun that can be either proper or common depending on the context, such as the capitalization error *buffalo* in the sentence *I used to live in buffalo, New York.*

55a
cap

55b Personal titles

Family members: Aunt Lou, *but* my aunt, Father (name used alone) or my father

Political Figures: Governor Andrew Cuomo, Senator Olympia Snowe, *but* the governor, my senator

Most writers do not capitalize the title *president* unless they are referring to the President of the United States: *The* president *of this university has seventeen honorary degrees.*

55c Titles of creative works

Capitalize the important words in titles and subtitles. Do not capitalize articles *(a, an, the)*, the *to* in infinitives, or prepositions and conjunctions unless they begin or end the title or subtitle. Capitalize both parts of a hyphenated word. In MLA style, capitalize subordinating conjunctions *(because)*. Capitalize the first word after a colon or semicolon in a title. Capitalize titles of major divisions of a work, such as chapters:

- **Book:** *Water for Elephants*
- **Play:** *The Importance of Being Earnest*
- **Building:** the Eiffel Tower
- **Ship or aircraft:** *Titanic* or *Concorde*
- **Painting:** the *Mona Lisa*
- **Article or essay:** "Next-Generation Scientists"
- **Poem:** "Stopping by Woods on a Snowy Evening"
- **Music:** "The Star-Spangled Banner"
- **Document:** the Bill of Rights
- **Course:** Economics 206: Macroeconomic Analysis
- **Chapter:** "Capitalization" in *The Brief McGraw-Hill Handbook*

55d Names of areas and regions

Names of geographical regions are generally capitalized if they are well established, like *the Midwest* and *Central Europe.* Names of directions, as in the sentence *Turn south,* are not capitalized.

CORRECT   *East* meets *West* at the summit.

CORRECT   You will need to go *west* on Sunset.

The word *western,* when used as a general direction or the name of a genre, is not capitalized (*the western* High Noon*).* It is capitalized when it is part of the name of a specific region: *I visited Western Europe last year.*

55e Names of races, ethnic groups, and sacred things

The words *black* and *white* are usually not capitalized when they are used to refer to members of racial groups because they are adjectives that substitute for the implied common nouns *black person* and *white person.* However, names of ethnic groups and races are capitalized: *African Americans, Italians, Asians, Caucasians.*

Note: In accordance with current APA guidelines, most social scientists capitalize the terms *Black* and *White,* treating them as proper nouns.

Many religious terms, such as *sacrament, altar,* and *rabbi,* are not capitalized. The word *Bible* is capitalized (though *biblical* is not), but it is never capitalized when it is used as a metaphor for an essential book.

▶ **His book *Winning at Stud Poker* used to be the *bible* of gamblers.**

55f First word of a sentence or quoted sentence

A capital letter is used to signal the beginning of a new sentence. Capitalize the first word of a quoted sentence but not the first word of a quoted phrase.

▶ **Jim, the narrator of *My Ántonia,* concludes, "Whatever we had missed, we possessed together the precious, the incommunicable past" (324).**

▶ **Jim took comfort in sharing with Ántonia "the precious, the incommunicable past" (324).**

If you need to change the first letter of a quotation to fit your sentence, enclose the letter in brackets.

▶ **The lawyer noted that "[t]he man seen leaving the area after the blast was not the same height as the defendant."**

If you interrupt the sentence you are quoting with an expression such as *he said,* the first word of the rest of the quotation should not be capitalized.

55f
cap

▶ **"When I come home an hour later," she explained, "the trains are usually less crowded."**

55g First word after a colon

If the word group that follows a colon is not a complete sentence, do not capitalize it. If it is a complete sentence, you may capitalize it or not, but be consistent throughout your document. (See whether your instructor or style guide prefers one option.)

▶ **The question is serious: do you think peace is possible?**

or

▶ **The question is serious: Do you think peace is possible?**

Exercise 55.1 Chapter review: Editing for capitalization

Edit the following passage, changing letters to capital or lowercase as necessary.

Perhaps the most notable writer of the 1920s is F. Scott Fitzgerald. He was born on September 24, 1896, in St. Paul, Minnesota, to Edward Fitzgerald and Mary "mollie" McQuillan, who were both members of the catholic church. After attending Princeton university and embarking on a career as a writer, Fitzgerald married southern belle Zelda Sayre from Montgomery, Alabama. Together, he and his Wife lived the celebrated life of the roaring twenties and the jazz age. Fitzgerald wrote numerous short stories as well as four novels: *This Side of Paradise, The Beautiful and Damned, The Great Gatsby,* and *Tender is the night.* The Great Gatsby, which he finished in the Winter of 1924 and published in 1925, is considered Fitzgerald's most brilliant and critically acclaimed work. readers who have read this novel will remember the opening words spoken by Nick Carraway, the narrator in the story: "in my younger and more vulnerable years my father gave me some advice that i've been turning over in my mind ever since. 'Whenever you feel like criticizing anyone,' he told me, 'Just remember that all the people in this world haven't had the advantages that you've had.'"

Unless you are writing a scientific or technical report, spell out most terms and titles, except in the following cases.

56a Titles that always precede or follow a person's name

Some abbreviations appear before a person's name *(Mr., Mrs., Dr.),* and some follow a proper name *(Jr., Sr., MD, Esq., PhD).* When an abbreviation follows a person's name, a comma is placed between the name and the abbreviation:

> Mrs. Jean Bascom
> Elaine Less, CPA, LL.D.

Many writers consider the comma before *Jr.* and *Sr.* to be optional.
Do not use two abbreviations that represent the same thing: *Dr. Peter Joyce, MD.* Use either *Dr. Peter Joyce* or *Peter Joyce, MD.*
Spell out titles used without proper names.

doctor
Mr. Carew asked if she had seen the ~~dr.~~

Abbreviations and Grammar Checkers

Computer grammar or spelling checkers may flag an abbreviation, but they generally will not tell you if your use of it is acceptable or consistent within a piece of writing.

56b Familiar abbreviations

If you use a technical term or the name of an organization in a report, you may abbreviate it as long as your readers are likely to be familiar with the abbreviation. For example, a medical writer might use *PT (physical therapy)* in a medical report or professional newsletter. Abbreviations of three or more capital letters generally do not use periods.

FAMILIAR ABBREVIATION	The *EPA* has had a lasting impact on the air quality in this country.
UNFAMILIAR ABBREVIATION	After you have completed them, take these forms to the *Human Resources and Education Center* [not *HREC*].

56b
abbr

555

Write out an unfamiliar term or name the first time you use it, and give the abbreviation in parentheses.

► **The Student Nonviolent Coordinating Committee (SNCC) was far to the left of other civil rights organizations. However, SNCC quickly burned itself out and disappeared.**

Abbreviations or symbols associated with numbers should be used only when accompanying a number: *3 p.m.*, not *in the p.m.*; *$500*, not *How many $ do you have?* The abbreviation *BC* ("Before Christ") follows a date; *AD* ("in the year of our Lord") precedes the date. The alternative abbreviations *BCE* ("Before the Common Era") and *CE* ("Common Era") can be used instead of *BC* or *AD*, respectively; both of these follow the date.

6:00 p.m. or 6:00 P.M. or 6:00 PM
9:45 a.m. or 9:45 A.M. or 9:45 AM
498 B.C. or 498 B.C.E. or 498 BC or 498 BCE or 498 BCE
A.D. 275 or 275 C.E. or AD 275 or 275 CE or 275 CE
6,000 rpm
271 cm

Note: Be consistent. If you use *A.M.* in one sentence, do not switch to *A.M.* in the next sentence. If an abbreviation is made up of capital letters, the periods are optional: *B.C.* or *BC*. *(For more on using periods with abbreviations, see Chapter 54, pp. 541–42.)*

In charts and graphs, abbreviations and symbols such as = for *equals, in.* for *inches,* % for *percent,* and $ with numbers are acceptable because they save space.

NAVIGATING THROUGH COLLEGE AND BEYOND

Scientific Abbreviations

Most abbreviations used in scientific or technical writing, such as those related to measurement, should be given without periods: *mph, lb, dc, rpm.* If an abbreviation looks like an actual word, however, you can use a period to prevent confusion: *in., Fig.*

56c Latin abbreviations

Latin abbreviations can be used in notes or works-cited lists, but in formal writing, it is usually a good idea to avoid even common Latin abbreviations *(e.g., et al., etc.,* and *i.e.).* Instead of *e.g.,* use *such as* or *for example.* Reword or omit constructions that use *etc.:*

cf.	compare *(confer)*
e.g.	for example, such as *(exempli gratia)*
et al.	and others *(et alia)*
etc.	and so forth, and so on *(et cetera)*
i.e.	that is *(id est)*
N.B.	note well *(nota bene)*
viz.	namely *(videlicet)*

56d Inappropriate abbreviations and symbols

Days of the week *(Sat.)*, places *(TX* or *Tex.)*, the word *company (Co.)*, people's names *(Wm.)*, disciplines and professions *(econ.)*, parts of speech *(v.)*, parts of written works *(ch., p.)*, symbols *(@)*, and units of measurement *(lb.)* are all spelled out in formal writing.

▶ The *environmental* [not *env.*] **engineers from the Paramus**
   Water *Company* [not *Co.*] are arriving in *New York City* [not
   ***NYC*] this *Thursday* [not *Thurs.*] to correct the problems in**
   the *physical education* [not *phys. ed.*] building in time for
   ***Christmas* [not *Xmas*].**

Exceptions: If an abbreviation such as *Inc., Co.,* or *Corp.* is part of a company's official name, then it can be included in formal writing: *Apple Inc. announced these changes in late December.* The ampersand symbol *(&)* can also be used, but only if it is part of an official name: *Church & Dwight.* Symbols such as @ may also appear within a URL.

Exercise 56.1 Chapter review: Editing for abbreviations
                    and symbols

Spell out any inappropriate abbreviations in this passage of nontechnical writing.

In today's digital-savvy world, a person who has never used a computer with access to the WWW and a Motion Pictures Experts Group Layer 3 (MP3) player would be surprised to find that anyone can download and groove to the sounds of "Nights in White Satin" by the 1960s rock band the Moody Blues at 3 AM without ever having to have spent $ for the album *Days of Future Past.* However, such file sharing, commonly known as "file swapping," is illegal and surrounded by controversy. The Recording Industry Association of America (RIAA), which represents the U.S. recording industry, has taken aggressive legal action against such acts of online piracy. E.g., in a landmark case in 2004, U.S. District Judge

56d
abbr

Denny Chin ruled that ISPs must identify those subscribers who share music online, at least in the states of NY, NJ, and CT. As the nature of music recordings changes with the proliferation of digital music services & file formats, this controversy is far from being resolved. In recent yrs companies such as Apple & Microsoft as well as celluar phone carriers have set up online music stores. Consumers can buy downloadable music files for very little $.

57 Numbers

57a Numbers versus words

In nontechnical writing, spell out numbers up to one hundred, and round numbers greater than one hundred.

▶ Approximately *two hundred fifty* students passed the exam, but *twenty-five* students failed.

When you are using a great many numbers or when a spelled-out number would require more than three or four words, use numerals.

▶ This regulation affects nearly *10,500* taxpayers, substantially more than the *200* originally projected. Of those affected, *2,325* filled out the papers incorrectly, and another *743* called the office for help.

Round numbers larger than one million are expressed in numerals and words: *8 million, 2.4 trillion.* Use all numerals rather than mixing numerals and spelled-out words for the same type of item in a passage.

▶ We wrote to 132 people, but only 16 responded.

Exception: When two numbers appear together, spell out one and use numerals for the other: *two 20-pound bags.*

Punctuation tip: Use a hyphen with two-word numbers from twenty-one through ninety-nine, whether they appear alone or within a larger number: *fifty-six, one hundred twenty-eight.* A hyphen also appears in two-word fractions *(one-third, five-eighths)* and in compound words made up of a spelled-out number or numeral and another word *(forty-hour work week, 5-page paper).*

In technical and business writing, use numerals for exact measurements and all numbers greater than ten.

► **The endosperm halves were placed in each of 14 small glass test tubes.**

► **Sample solutions with GA$_3$ concentrations ranging from 0 g/mL to 10^5 g/mL were added, one to each test tube.**

Note: In nontechnical writing, spell out the names of units of measurement *(inches, liters)* in text. Use abbreviations *(in., L)* and symbols *(%)* in charts and graphs to save space.

57b Numbers that begin sentences

If a number begins a sentence, reword the sentence or spell out the numeral.

► *Three hundred twelve* **children are in each elementary grade.**

57c Conventional uses of numerals

- **Dates:** October 9, 2002; A.D. 1066 *(or* AD 1066); *but* October ninth, May first
- **Time of day:** 6 A.M. *(or* AM *or* a.m.), a quarter past eight in the evening, three o'clock in the morning
- **Addresses:** 21 Meadow Road, Apt. 6J; Grand Island, NY 14072
- **Percentages:** 73 percent, 73%
- **Fractions and decimals:** 21.84, 6½, two-thirds, a fourth
- **Measurements:** 100 miles per hour *(or* 100 mph), 9 kilograms *(or* 9 kg), 38°F, 15°Celsius, 3 tablespoons *(or* 3 T), 4 liters *(or* 4 L), 18 inches *(or* 18 in.)
- **Volume, page, chapter:** volume 4, chapter 8, page 44
- **Scenes in a play:** *Hamlet,* act 2, scene 1, lines 77–84
- **Scores and statistics:** 0 to 3, 98–92, an average age of 35
- **Amounts of money:** 10¢ *(or* 10 cents), $125, $2.25, $2.8 million
- **Serial or identification numbers:** batch number 4875, 105.5 on the AM dial
- **Surveys:** 9 of 10
- **Telephone numbers:** (716) 555-2174

To make a number plural, add -*s.*

57c
num

Exercise 57.1   Chapter review: Editing for numbers

Edit the sentences that follow to correct errors in the use of numbers. Some sentences are correct; circle their numbers.

$546
EXAMPLE   **I have ~~five hundred forty-six dollars~~ in my bank**
                                           ∧

account.

1. The soccer team raised one thousand sixty seven dollars by selling entertainment booklets filled with coupons, discounts, and special promotions.
2. 55% of the participants in the sociology student's survey reported that they would lie to a professor in order to have a late assignment accepted.
3. In one year alone, 115 employees at the company objected to their performance appraisals, but only twenty-four filed formal complaints.
4. When preparing a professional letter, set the margins at 1 inch.
5. Eighty-five applicants hoped to win the four-year scholarship, but only one person was awarded full tuition and living expenses.
6. Four out of 5 children who enter preschool in Upper East County already know the alphabet.
7. The motorcycle accident occurred at a half past 4 in the morning on the interstate highway, but paramedics did not arrive until six thirty AM.
8. The horticulturist at the nursery raises more than 200 varieties of orchids.

58 Italics (Underlining)

Italics, characters in a typeface that slants to the right, are used to set off certain words and phrases. If italics are not available, you may underline words that would be typeset in italics. MLA style, however, requires italics.

TEXTCONNEX

Italics and Underlining

Italics may not be available in online environments. To indicate underlining, put an underscore mark or an asterisk before and after what you would italicize in a manuscript: Daniel Day-Lewis gives one of his best performances in _There Will Be Blood_.

On the Web, underlining indicates a hypertext link. If your work is going to be posted online, use italics, if available, instead of underlining for titles to avoid confusion.

58a Titles of works or separate publications

Italicize (or underline) titles of books, magazines, journals, newspapers, comic strips, plays, films, television series, musical compositions, choreographic works, artworks, Web sites, software, long poems, pamphlets, and other long works. In titles of lengthy works, *a, an,* or *the* is capitalized and italicized (underlined) if it is the first word, but *the* is not generally treated as part of the title in names of newspapers and periodicals: the *New York Times.*

▶ Picasso's *Guernica* captures the anguish and despair of violence.

▶ Plays by Shakespeare provide details and story lines for Verdi's opera *Falstaff,* Cole Porter's musical comedy *Kiss Me, Kate,* and Baz Luhrmann's film *Romeo and Juliet.*

Court cases may also be italicized or underlined.

▶ In *Brown v. Board of Education of Topeka* (1954), the U.S. Supreme Court ruled that segregation in public schools is unconstitutional.

Exception: Do not use italics or underlining when referring to the Bible and other sacred books.

Quotation marks are used for the titles of short works—essays, newspaper and magazine articles and columns, short stories, individual episodes of television and radio programs, short poems, songs, and chapters or other book subdivisions. Quotation marks are also used for titles of unpublished works, including student papers, theses, and dissertations. *(See Chapter 53, p. 536, for more on quotation marks with titles.)*

58a
ital

58b Names of ships, trains, aircraft, and spaceships

► The commentators were stunned into silence when the space shuttle *Challenger* exploded.

58c Foreign terms

► In the Paris airport, we recognized the familiar no smoking sign: *Défense de fumer.*

Many foreign words have become accepted as part of the English language—rigor mortis, pasta, and sombrero, for example—and therefore require no italics or underlining. (These words appear in English dictionaries.)

58d Scientific names

The scientific (Latin) names of organisms are always italicized.

► Most chicks are infected with *Cryptosporidium baileyi*, a parasite typical of young animals.

Note: Although the whole name is italicized, only the genus part of the name is capitalized.

58e Words, letters, and numbers referred to as themselves

For clarity, italicize words or phrases used as words rather than for the meaning they convey. (You may also use quotation marks for this purpose.) Letters and numbers used alone should also be italicized.

► The term *romantic* does not mean the same thing to the Shelley scholar that it does to the fan of Danielle Steel's novels.

► Add a *3* to that column.

58f For emphasis

An occasional word in italics helps you make a point. Too much emphasis, however, may mean no emphasis at all.

WEAK   You don't *mean* that your *teacher* told the whole *class* that *he* did not know the answer *himself?*

REVISED Your teacher admitted that he did not know the answer? That is amazing.

If you add italics or underlining to a quotation, indicate the change in parentheses following the quotation.

▶ **Instead of promising that no harm will come to us, Blake only assures us that we "need not *fear* harm" (emphasis added).**

Exercise 58.1 Chapter review: Editing for italics

Edit the following passage, underlining the words that should be italicized and circling the italicized words that should be roman.

Today, thousands of people in the United States practice *yoga* for its physical, spiritual, and mental benefits. The word *yoga,* originating from the Sanskrit root yuj, means the union of the body, spirit, and mind. Although there are many styles of *yoga,* people who want a gentle introduction to *yoga* should practice Iyengar yoga, a style developed by B. K. S. Iyengar of India, which uses props such as blocks, belts, and pillows to help the body find alignment in asanas (poses) and pranayama (breathing). Those people who want to learn more about Iyengar yoga are encouraged to read the following books written by the master himself: *Light on Yoga, Light on Pranayama,* The *Art of Yoga,* The *Tree of Yoga,* and *Light on the Yoga Sutras of Patanjali.* Those who want to learn about the general benefits of *yoga* can find numerous articles, such as *"Yoga and Weight Loss,"* by doing a general online search. All forms of *yoga* promise the *diligent* and *faithful* practitioner increased *strength, flexibility,* and *balance.*

59 Hyphens

59a To form compound words

A hyphen joins two nouns to make one compound word. Scientists speak of a *kilogram-meter* as a measure of force, and professors of literature talk about the *scholar-poet.* The hyphen lets us know that the two nouns work together as one.

59a hyph

A dictionary is the best resource when you are unsure about whether to use a hyphen. If you cannot find a compound word in the dictionary, spell it as two separate words.

59b To create compound adjective or noun forms

A noun can also be linked with an adjective, an adverb, or another part of speech to form a compound adjective:

> accident-prone
> quick-witted

Hyphens are also used in nouns designating family relationships and compounds of more than two words:

> brother-in-law
> stay-at-home

Compound nouns with hyphens generally form plurals by adding *-s* or *-es* to the most important word: *mother-in-law/mothers-in-law.*

Some proper nouns that are joined to make an adjective are hyphenated: the *Franco-Prussian war.*

Hyphens often help clarify adjectives that come before the word they modify. Modifiers that are hyphenated when they are placed *before* the word they modify are usually not hyphenated when they are placed *after* the word they modify.

▶ It was a *bad-mannered* reply.

▶ The reply was *bad mannered.*

Do not use a hyphen to connect *-ly* adverbs to the words they modify.

▶ They explored the newly⁄discovered territories.

In a pair or series of compound nouns or adjectives, add suspended hyphens after the first word of each item.

▶ The child care center accepted three-, four-, and five-year-olds.

59c To spell out fractions and compound numbers

Use a hyphen when writing out fractions or compound numbers from twenty-one to ninety-nine:

three-fourths of a gallon
thirty-two

Note: In MLA style, use a hyphen to show inclusive numbers: *pages 100-40.*

59d To attach some prefixes and suffixes

Use a hyphen to join a prefix and a capitalized word.

▶ **Skipping the parade on the Fourth of July is positively *un-American!***

A hyphen is sometimes used to join a capital letter and a word: *T-shirt, V-six engine.*

The prefixes *ex-, self-,* and *all-* and the suffixes *-elect, -odd,* and *-something* generally take hyphens. However, most prefixes are not attached by hyphens, unless a hyphen is needed to show pronunciation or to reveal a special meaning that distinguishes the word from the same word without a hyphen: *recreate* versus *re-create.* Check a dictionary to be certain you are using the standard spelling.

▶ **Because he was an *ex-convict,* he was a *nonjudgmental coworker.***

▶ **They were *self-sufficient, antisocial* neighbors.**

59e To divide words at the ends of lines

When you must divide words, do so between syllables. However, pronunciation alone cannot always tell you where to divide a word. If you are unsure about how to break a word into syllables, consult your dictionary.

▶ **My writing group had a very fruitful *collab-oration* [not *colla-boration*].**

Note: Never leave just one or two letters on a line.

Exercise 59.1 Chapter review: Editing for hyphens

Edit the following passage, adding and deleting hyphens as necessary.

We need only to turn on the television or pick up a recent issue of a popular fashion or fitness magazine to see evidence of modern society's obsession with images of thinness. Few actors, models, or celebrities fail to flaunt their thinly-trimmed waist-lines, regardless of their gender. Not surprisingly, more

**59e
hyph**

than ten million females and almost one million males in the United States are currently battling eating disorders such as anorexia nervosa and bulimia nervosa. A person who is anorexic fears gaining weight, and thus engages in self starvation and excessive weight loss. A person who is bulimic binges and then engages in self-induced purging in order to lose weight. Although we are often quick to assume that those with eating disorders suffer from low self-esteem and have a history of family or peer problems, we cannot ignore the role of the media in encouraging eating disorders, particularly when thinness is equated with physical attractiveness, health and fitness, and success over-all. We need to remember the threat of these eating disorders the next time we hear a ten year old girl tell her mommy that she "can't afford" to eat more than one half of her peanut butter and jelly sandwich.

60 Spelling

Proofread your writing carefully. Misspellings creep into the prose of even the best writers. Use the following strategies to help you improve your spelling:

- Become familiar with major spelling rules and commonly misspelled words.
- Use your dictionary whenever you are unsure about the spelling of a specific word.

Spelling Checkers

Computer spell checkers are helpful tools. Remember, however, that a spell checker cannot tell *how* you are using a particular word. If you write *their* but mean *there,* a spell checker cannot point out your mistake. Spell checkers also cannot point out many misspelled proper nouns.

60a Basic spelling rules

1. Use *i* before *e* except after *c* or when sounded like *a,* as in *neighbor* and *weigh.*

- *i* **before** *e:* believe, relieve, chief, grief, wield, yield
- **Except after** *c:* receive, deceive, ceiling, conceit
- *Exceptions:* seize, caffeine, codeine, weird, height

2. Prefixes do not change a word's spelling when attached.

Examples: preview, reconnect, unwind, deemphasize

3. Suffixes change a word's spelling depending on the suffix or the final letter(s) of the root word.

- **Final silent** *e:*
  Drop it if the suffix begins with a vowel: *force/forcing, remove/ removable, surprise/surprising*
  Keep it if the suffix begins with a consonant: *care/careful.*

  Exceptions: argue/argument, true/truly, change/changeable, judge/judgment, acknowledge/acknowledgment

  Note: Keep the silent *e* if it is needed to clarify the pronunciation or if the word would be confused with another word without the *e:*

  dye/dyeing (to avoid confusion with *dying*)
  hoe/hoeing (to avoid mispronunciation)

- **Final** *y:*
  Keep it when adding the suffix *-ing: enjoy/enjoying, cry/crying*
  Keep or change it when adding other suffixes:
  - **When** *y* **follows a consonant, change to** *i* **or** *ie:* happy/ happier, marry/married
  - **When** *y* **follows a vowel, keep it:** defray/defrayed, enjoy/ enjoying

- **Final consonant:**
  Double it if the root word ends in a single vowel + a consonant and is only one syllable long or has an accent on the final syllable: *grip/gripping, refer/referred*

  For other types of root words, do not double the consonant: *crack/ cracking, laundering*

  Exceptions: bus/busing, focus/focused

60a
sp

- **-*ly* with words that end in -*ic*:**
  Add -*ally*: logic/logically, terrific/terrifically

  Exception: public/publicly

- **Words ending in -*able*/-*ible*, -*ant*/-*ent*, and -*ify*/-*efy*:**
  Consult a dictionary for the correct spelling of words ending in these frequently confused suffixes.

3. Forming plurals

Most plurals are formed by adding -*s*. Some are formed by adding -*es*.

- **Words ending in -*s*, -*sh*, -*x*, -*z* "soft" -*ch* (add -*es*):** bus/buses, bush/bushes, fox/foxes, buzz/buzzes, peach/peaches

- **Words ending in a consonant + *o* (add -*es*):** hero/heroes, tomato/tomatoes, *but* solo/solos

- **Words ending in a consonant + *y* (change *y* to *i* and add -*es*):** beauty/beauties, city/cities, *but* the Kirbys (a family's name)

- **Words ending in -*f* or -*fe* (change *f* to *v* and add -*s* or -*es*):** leaf/leaves, knife/knives, wife/wives, *but* staff/staffs, roof/roofs

Most plurals follow standard rules, but some have irregular forms *(child/children, tooth/teeth),* and some words with foreign roots create plurals in the pattern of the language they come from, as do these words:

analysis/analyses	medium/media
crisis/crises	stimulus/stimuli
datum/data	thesis/theses

Some nouns with foreign roots have regular and irregular plural forms *(appendix/appendices/appendixes).* Be consistent in the spelling you choose.

> ***Note:*** Some writers now treat *data* as though it were singular, but the preferred practice is still to recognize that *data* is plural and takes a plural verb: *The data are clear on this point: the pass/fail course has become outdated by events.* Scientists are particularly strict about plural usage.

Compound nouns with or without hyphens generally form plurals by adding -*s* or -*es* to the most important word: *sister-in-law/ sisters-in-law, attorney general/attorneys general.*

For some compound words that appear as one word, the same rule applies *(passersby);* for others, it does not *(cupfuls).* Consult a dictionary if you are not sure.

If both words in the compound are equally important, add -*s* to the second word: *singer-songwriters.*

For MULTILINGUAL WRITERS

American and British Spelling

Standard British spelling differs from American spelling for some words—among them *color/colour, canceled/cancelled, theater/theatre, realize/realise,* and *judgment/judgement.*

A few words such as *fish* and *sheep* have the same forms for singular and plural.

Exercise 60.1 Practicing spelling

Write the correct plural form for each of the following words. Consult the preceding rules or a dictionary, as needed.

Bentley	hoof	trophy
president-elect	potato	index
life	fungus	Sidney
box	brother-in-law	self
appendix	stereo	nucleus

Exercise 60.2 Practicing spelling

Some words in the following list are misspelled. Circle each of the misspelled words, and write the correct spelling next to it.

either	boxxing	hopping
hygiene	supplyed	nieghbor
dealer	neither	worried
buying	divorced	tring
exced	receipt	

✓ **60b** Words pronounced alike but spelled differently

60b
sp

Homonyms sound alike but have different meanings and different spellings. The following is a list of common homonyms as well as words that are almost homonyms.

accept: to take willingly
except: to leave out (verb); but for (preposition)

affect: to influence (verb); a feeling or an emotion (noun)
effect: to make or accomplish (verb); result (noun)

all ready: prepared
already: by this time

cite: to quote or refer to
sight: spectacle, sense
site: place

it's: contraction for *it is* or *it has*
its: possessive pronoun

loose: not tight
lose: to misplace

precede: to come before
proceed: to go forward

principal: most important (adjective); the head of an
    organization or a sum of money (noun)
principle: a basic standard or law (noun)

their: possessive pronoun
there: adverb of place
they're: contraction for *they are*

to: indicating movement
too: also
two: number

who's: contraction for *who is*
whose: possessive of *who*

your: possessive pronoun
you're: contraction for *you are*

Exercise 60.3   Fixing commonly misspelled words

In a list or spelling log, write down words you often misspell. Try to group your errors. Do they fall into patterns—errors with suffixes or plurals, for example? Errors with silent letters or doubled consonants?

Leucaena leucocephala, *or white leadtree,* is widely used in reforestation, land reclamation, and erosion prevention programs. It enriches the soil as well. Just as trees require soil to grow, language is "rooted" in basic grammar.

Grammar and rhetoric are complementary. . . .
Grammar maps out the possible;
rhetoric narrows the possible down to the
desirable or effective.

—Francis Christensen

Basic
Grammar

9 Basic Grammar

WRITING OUTCOMES

Part 9: Basic Grammar

This section will help you answer questions such as the following:

Rhetorical Knowledge

- How does sentence structure in some other languages differ from that of English? **(62)**
- How does a sentence's purpose affect its type? **(64b)**

Critical Thinking, Reading, and Writing

- How do I find the subject and predicate of a sentence? **(62a, b)**

Processes

- During editing, should I add a comma after an *-ing* verb phrase? **(63b)**

Knowledge of Conventions

- How do nouns function in a sentence? What are count and noncount nouns? **(61b)**
- What are the five common sentence patterns in English? **(62b)**
- How do verb tenses work with *if* (conditional) clauses? **(63e)**

For a general introduction to writing outcomes, see Id, p. 5.

Written language, although based on the grammar of spoken language, has its own logic and rules. The chapters that follow explain the basic rules of standard written English. *(Non-native speakers of standard American English should see Chapter 48 as well.)*

61 Parts of Speech

English has eight primary **parts of speech:** verbs, nouns, pronouns, adjectives, adverbs, prepositions, conjunctions, and interjections. All English words belong to one or more of these categories. Particular words can belong to different categories, depending on the role they play in a sentence. For example, the word *button* can be a noun *(the button on a coat)* or a verb *(Button your jacket now).*

61a Verbs

Verbs carry a lot of information. They report action *(run, write),* condition *(bloom, sit),* or state of being *(be, seem).* Verbs also change form to indicate person, number, tense, voice, and mood. To do all this, a **main verb** is often preceded by one or more **helping verbs,** thereby becoming a **verb phrase.**

► The play *begins* at eight.
      _{mv}

    _{hv mv}   _{hv mv}
► I *may change* seats after the play *has begun.*

1. Main verbs

Main verbs change form **(tense)** to indicate when something has happened. If a word does not indicate tense, it is not a main verb. All main verbs have five forms, except for *be,* which has eight.

BASE FORM	*(talk, sing)*
PAST TENSE	Yesterday I *(talked, sang).*
PAST PARTICIPLE	In the past, I have *(talked, sung).*

61a
gram

573

PRESENT PARTICIPLE	Right now I am *(talking, singing)*.
THIRD PERSON SINGULAR (OR *-S* FORM)	Usually, he/she/it *(talks, sings)*.

(For more on subject-verb agreement and verb tense, see Chapter 44, pp. 442–51, and Chapter 45, pp. 451–65, as well as the list of common irregular verbs on pp. 453–54. For information on using verbs followed by infinitives or gerunds, see Chapter 48, pp. 494–96.)

2. Helping verbs that show time

Some helping verbs—mostly forms of *be, have,* and *do*—function to signify time *(will have been playing, has played)* or emphasis *(does play)*. Forms of *do* are also used to ask questions *(Do you play?)*. Here are other such helping **(auxiliary)** verbs:

be, am, is	being, been	do, does, did
are, was, were	have, has, had	

(For information on matching helping verbs with the appropriate tense of the main verb, see Chapter 48, pp. 491–93.)

3. Modals

Other helping verbs, called **modals,** express an attitude toward the action or circumstance of a sentence:

can	must	should
could	ought to	will
may	shall	would
might		

Modal verbs share several characteristics:

- They do not change form to indicate person or number.
- They do not change form to indicate tense.
- They are followed directly by the base form of the verb without *to*.

► We must ~~to~~ study now.

► He *must* have studied hard to do so well.

Some verbal expressions ending in *to* also function as modals, including *have to, be able to,* and *be supposed to*. These **phrasal modals** behave more like ordinary verbs than true modals, changing form to indicate tense and agree with the subject.

Exercise 61.1 Identifying verbs

Underline the main verb in each sentence, and circle any helping verbs.

EXAMPLE **Government of the people, by the people, for the**

people (shall) not perish from the earth.

1. An increasing number of Americans, both men and women, undergo cosmetic surgery for aesthetic rather than medical reasons.

2. A decade ago, the average American believed that only Hollywood celebrities underwent face-lifts and tummy tucks.

3. Do you think that you need to improve your physical appearance?

4. Men, often in their mid-forties, are choosing a variety of surgical procedures, including hair replacement and chin augmentation.

5. For a lean, flat abdomen, a cosmetic surgeon may suggest both abdominoplasty and liposuction.

6. People are now able to achieve their ideal body image, not through exercise and diet but through elective cosmetic surgery.

61b Nouns

Nouns name people *(Shakespeare, actors, Englishman)*, places *(Manhattan, city, island)*, things *(Kleenex, handkerchief, sneeze, cats)*, and ideas *(Marxism, justice, democracy, clarity)*.

▶ *Shakespeare* lived in *England* and wrote *plays* about the human *condition.*

1. Proper and common nouns

Proper nouns name specific people, places, and things and are always capitalized: *Aretha Franklin, Hinduism, Albany, Microsoft.* All other nouns are **common nouns:** *singer, religion, capital, corporation.*

2. Count and noncount nouns

A common noun that refers to something specific that can be counted is a **count noun.** Count nouns can be singular or plural, like *cup* or *suggestion (four cups, several suggestions).* **Noncount nouns** are nonspecific; these common nouns refer to categories of people, places, or things and cannot be counted. They do not have a plural form *(the orange juice is delicious; his advice was useful). (For use of articles and quantifiers with count and noncount nouns, see Chapter 48, pp. 489–90.)*

**61b
gram**

3. Concrete and abstract nouns

Nouns that name things that can be perceived by the senses are called **concrete nouns:** *boy, wind, book, song.* **Abstract nouns** name qualities and concepts that do not have physical properties: *charity, patience, beauty, hope. (For more on using concrete and abstract nouns, see Chapter 40, p. 408.)*

4. Singular and plural nouns

Most nouns name things that can be counted and are singular or plural. Singular nouns typically become plural by adding *-s* or *-es: boy/boys, ocean/oceans, church/churches, agency/agencies.* Some have irregular plurals, such as *man/men, child/children,* and *tooth/teeth.* Noncount nouns like *intelligence* and *electricity* do not form plurals. *(See Chapter 60, pp. 568–69, for help forming plurals.)*

5. Collective nouns

Collective nouns such as *team, family, herd,* and *orchestra* are treated as singular. They are not noncount nouns, however, because collective nouns can be counted and can be made plural: *teams, families. (Also see Chapter 44, pp. 446–47, and Chapter 46, pp. 468–69.)*

6. Possessive nouns

When nouns are used in the **possessive case** to indicate ownership, they change their form. To form the possessive case, singular nouns add an apostrophe plus *s* *('s),* whereas plural nouns ending in *-s* just add an apostrophe *(').* *(Also see Chapter 52, pp. 529–32.)*

SINGULAR	insect	insect's sting
PLURAL	neighbors	neighbors' car

7. Determiners used with nouns

Determiners precede and specify nouns: *a* desk, *five* books. They include articles *(a, an, the),* possessives *(my, neighbors'),* demonstrative pronouns used as adjectives *(this, that, these, those),* and numbers as well as quantifiers (words that tell how much or how many). A singular count noun must have a determiner.

61c Pronouns

A **pronoun** takes the place of a noun. The noun that the pronoun replaces is called its **antecedent.** *(For more on pronoun-antecedent agreement, see Chapter 46, pp. 466–70.)*

▶ The *snow* fell all day long, and by nightfall *it* was three feet deep.

The box on pp. 578–79 summarizes the different kinds of pronouns.

1. Personal pronouns

The **personal pronouns** *I, me, you, he, his, she, her, it, we, us, they,* and *them* refer to specific people or things and vary in form to indicate person, number, gender, and case. *(For more on pronoun reference and case, see Chapter 46, pp. 470–79.)*

▶ *You* told *us* that *he* gave Jane a lock of *his* hair.

2. Possessive pronouns

Like possessive nouns, **possessive pronouns** indicate ownership. However, unlike possessive nouns, possessive pronouns do not add apostrophes: *my/mine, your/yours, her/hers, his, its, our/ours, their/theirs.*

▶ Brunch is at *her* place this Saturday.

3. Reflexive and intensive pronouns

Pronouns ending in *-self* or *-selves* are either reflexive or intensive. **Reflexive pronouns** refer to the subject and are necessary for sentence sense.

▶ Many of the women blamed *themselves* for the problem.

Intensive pronouns add emphasis to the nouns or pronouns they follow and are grammatically optional.

▶ President Harding *himself* drank whiskey during Prohibition.

4. Relative pronouns

The **relative pronouns** *who, whom, whose, that,* and *which* relate a dependent clause—a word group containing a subject and verb and a subordinating word—to an antecedent noun or pronoun in the sentence.

dependent clause

▶ In Kipling's story, Dravot is the man *who* would be king.

The form of a relative pronoun varies according to its **case**—the grammatical role it plays in the sentence. *(For more on pronoun case, see Chapter 46, pp. 473–79.)*

5. Demonstrative pronouns

The **demonstrative pronouns** *this, that, these,* and *those* point out nouns and pronouns that come later.

▶ *This* is the book literary critics have been waiting for.

61c
gram

PRONOUNS

Personal (Including Possessive)

SINGULAR	PLURAL
I, me, my, mine	we, us, our, ours
you, your, yours	you, your, yours
he, him, his	they, them, their, theirs
she, her, hers	
it, its	

Reflexive and Intensive

SINGULAR	PLURAL
myself	ourselves
yourself	yourselves
himself, herself, itself	themselves
oneself	

Relative

who	whoever	what	whatever	that
whom	whomever	whose	whichever	which

Demonstrative

this, that, these, those

Sometimes these pronouns function as adjectives: *This book won the Pulitzer.* Sometimes they are noun equivalents: *This is my book.*

6. Interrogative pronouns

Interrogative pronouns such as *who, whatever,* and *whom* are used to ask questions.

► *Whatever* **happened to you?**

The form of the interrogative pronouns *who, whom, whoever,* and *whomever* indicates the grammatical role they play in a sentence. *(See Chapter 46, pp. 478–79.)*

7. Indefinite pronouns

Indefinite pronouns such as *someone, anybody, nothing,* and *few* refer to a nonspecific person or thing and do not change form to indicate person, number, or gender.

Interrogative

who	what	which
whoever	whatever	whichever
whom	whomever	whose

Indefinite

SINGULAR		PLURAL	SINGULAR/PLURAL
anybody	nobody	both	all
anyone	no one	few	any
anything	none	many	either
each	nothing	several	more
everybody	one		most
everyone	somebody		some
everything	someone		
much	something		
neither			

Reciprocal

each other, any other

▶ *Anybody* who cares enough to come and help may take *some* home.

Most indefinite pronouns are always singular *(anybody, everyone).* Some are always plural *(many, few),* and a handful can be singular or plural *(any, most). (See Chapter 44, pp. 447–48, and Chapter 46, pp. 466–67.)*

8. Reciprocal pronouns

Reciprocal pronouns such as *each other* and *one another* refer to the separate parts of their plural antecedent.

▶ My sister and I are close because we live near *each other.*

Exercise 61.2 Identifying nouns and pronouns

Underline the nouns and circle the pronouns in each sentence.

EXAMPLE (We) have (nothing) to fear but fear (itself.)

61c
gram

1. Following World War I, the nation witnessed an unprecedented explosion of African-American fiction, poetry, drama, music, art, social commentary, and political activism.

2. Many African-American intellectuals, artists, cultural critics, and political leaders during the 1920s and 1930s were drawn to Harlem, a vibrant section of upper Manhattan in New York City.

3. Sociologist and intellectual Alain Locke, author of *The New Negro,* is best known as the New Negro Movement's founder.

4. W. E. B. Du Bois was the author of *The Souls of Black Folk,* and he was also a cofounder of the National Association for the Advancement of Colored People (NAACP), a prominent civil rights organization.

5. These intellectuals of the Harlem Renaissance profoundly influenced each other.

6. They spoke about the effect of marginality and alienation on themselves and on the shaping of their consciousness as African Americans.

7. Zora Neale Hurston was herself a cultural anthropologist who studied the folklore of the rural South, which is reflected in her novel *Their Eyes Were Watching God.*

8. Nella Larsen, author of *Quicksand* and *Passing,* was awarded a Guggenheim fellowship for her creative writing in 1929.

9. Who among the visual artists during the Harlem Renaissance did not use Africa as a source of inspiration?

Exercise 61.3 Identifying types of nouns and pronouns

On a separate sheet of paper, list each noun and pronoun that you identified in Exercise 61.2. For each noun, label it proper or common, count or noncount, concrete or abstract, and singular or plural. Also identify the one collective noun and the one possessive noun. For each pronoun, label it personal, possessive, reflexive, intensive, relative, demonstrative, interrogative, indefinite, or reciprocal. Note if the pronoun is singular or plural.

61d Adjectives

Adjectives modify nouns and pronouns by answering questions like *Which one? What kind? How many? What size? What color? What condition?* and *Whose?* They can describe, enumerate, identify, define, and limit *(one person, that person)*. When articles *(a, an, the)* identify nouns, they function as adjectives.

Sometimes proper nouns are treated as adjectives; the proper adjectives that result are capitalized: *Britain/British.* Pronouns can also function as adjectives *(his green car)*, and adjectives often have forms that allow you to make comparisons *(great, greater, greatest)*.

▶ The *decisive* and *diligent* king regularly attended meetings of the council. [What kind of king?]

▶ *These four artistic* qualities affect how an advertisement is received. [Which, how many, what kind of qualities?]

▶ *My little blue* Volkswagen died *one icy winter* morning. [Whose, what size, what color car? Which, what kind of morning?]

Like all modifiers, adjectives should be close to the words they modify. Most often, adjectives appear before the noun they modify, but **descriptive adjectives**—adjectives that designate qualities or attributes—may come before or after the noun or pronoun they modify for stylistic reasons. Adjectives that describe the subject and follow linking verbs *(be, am, is, are, was, being, been, appear, become, feel, grow, look, make, prove, taste)* are called subject complements.

BEFORE SUBJECT

The *sick* and *destitute* poet no longer believed that love would save him.

AFTER SUBJECT

The poet, *sick* and *destitute,* no longer believed that love would save him.

AFTER LINKING VERB

No longer believing that love would save him, the poet was *sick* and *destitute.*

(For more on adjectives, see Chapter 47. For common problems multilingual writers have with adjectives, see Chapter 48, p. 497.)

61e   Adverbs

Adverbs often end in *-ly (beautifully, gracefully, quietly)* and usually answer such questions as *When? Where? How? How often? How much? To what degree?* and *Why?*

▶ The authenticity of the document is *hotly* contested. [How is it contested?]

Adverbs modify verbs, other adverbs, and adjectives. Like adjectives, adverbs can be used to compare *(less, lesser, least)*. In addition to modifying individual words, they can be used to modify whole clauses. Adverbs can be placed at the beginning or end of a sentence or before the verb they modify, but they should not be placed between the verb and

61e

gram

its direct object. Generally, they should appear as close as possible to the words they modify.

▶ The water was *brilliant* blue and *icy* cold. [The adverbs intensify the adjectives *blue* and *cold*.]

▶ Dickens mixed humor and pathos *better* than any other English writer after Shakespeare. [The adverb compares Dickens with other writers.]

▶ *Consequently,* he is still read by millions.

Consequently is a conjunctive adverb that modifies the independent clause that follows it and shows how the sentence is related to the preceding sentence. *(For more on conjunctive adverbs, see the material on conjunctions, pp. 584–85. For issues multilingual writers have with adverbs, see Chapter 48, pp. 497–99.)*

No, not, and *never* are among the most common adverbs. *Never* should not appear at the end of a sentence.

It takes only one negator *(no/not/never)* to change the meaning of a sentence from positive to negative. In fact, when two negatives are used together, they cancel each other.

any
▶ They don't have ~~no~~ reason to go there.
⌃

Exercise 61.4   Identifying adjectives and adverbs

Underline the adjectives and circle the adverbs in each sentence.

EXAMPLE   Peter Piper (patiently) picked a peck of pickled peppers.

1. A growing number of Americans are overweight or clinically obese.

2. Obesity increases a person's risk for type 2 diabetes, heart disease, high blood pressure, stroke, liver damage, cancer, and premature death.

3. Fad diets promise Americans rapid but temporary weight loss, not weight management.

4. Robert C. Atkins, M.D., author of *Dr. Atkins' New Diet Revolution,* best explains a low-carbohydrate, high-protein diet.

5. Other fad diets, such as the Sugar Busters diet, work on the premise that high glycemic carbohydrates are primarily responsible for weight gain.

6. In the best seller *Eat Right for Your Type,* naturopath Peter J. D'Adamo argues that certain foods should be avoided based on a person's blood type.

7. Many other fad diets, such as the grapefruit diet and the cabbage diet, promise quick weight loss.
8. Many fad diets inevitably drive dieters to carbohydrate cravings and binge eating.
9. Few fad diets emphasize the need for dieters to increase their metabolic rate significantly with regular aerobic exercise.

61f Prepositions and prepositional phrases

Prepositions *(on, in, at, by)* usually appear as part of a **prepositional phrase.** Their main function is to allow the noun or pronoun in the phrase to modify another word in the sentence. Prepositional phrases always begin with a preposition and end with a noun, pronoun, or other word group that functions as the **object of the preposition** (in *time,* on the *table*).

A preposition can be one word *(about, despite, on)* or a word group *(according to, as well as, in spite of)*. Place prepositional phrases as close as possible to the words they modify. Adjectival prepositional phrases usually appear right after the noun or pronoun they modify and answer questions like *Which one?* and *What kind of?* Adverbial phrases answer questions like *When? Where? How?* and *Why?*

AS ADJECTIVE   Many species *of birds* nest there.

AS ADVERB   The younger children stared *out the window.*

COMMON PREPOSITIONS and COMPOUND PREPOSITIONS

about	behind	in addition to	through
above	below	in case of	to
according to	beside	including	toward
across	between	in front of	under
after	beyond	in place of	underneath
against	by	in regard to	until
along	by means of	inside	up
along with	by way of	instead of	upon
among	down	into	up to
apart from	during	like	via
as	except	near	with
as to	except for	of	within
as well as	excluding	on	without
at	following	on account of	with reference to
because of	from	over	with respect to
before	in	since	

61f
gram

Multilingual writers often have difficulty with the idiomatic use of prepositions *(see Chapter 48, pp. 500–1, 502–3).*

61g Conjunctions

Conjunctions join words, phrases, or clauses and indicate their relation to each other.

1. Coordinating conjunctions

The common **coordinating conjunctions** (or **coordinators**) are *and, but, or, for, nor, yet,* and *so.* Coordinating conjunctions join elements of equal weight or function.

▶   She was strong *and* healthy.

▶   The war was short *but* devastating.

▶   They must have been tired, *for* they had been climbing all day long.

2. Correlative conjunctions

Correlative conjunctions also link sentence elements of equal value, but they always come in pairs: *both . . . and, either . . . or, neither. . . nor, not only . . . but also,* and *whether . . . or.*

▶   *Neither* the doctor *nor* the police believe his story.

3. Subordinating conjunctions

Common **subordinating conjunctions** (or **subordinators**) link sentence elements that are not of equal importance. They include the following words and phrases:

Subordinating Words

after	once	until
although	since	when
as	that	whenever
because	though	where
before	till	wherever
if	unless	while

Subordinating Phrases

as if	even though	in that
as soon as	even when	rather than
as though	for as much as	sooner than
even after	in order that	so that
even if	in order to	

Because subordinating conjunctions join unequal sentence parts, they are used to introduce dependent, or subordinate, clauses in a sentence.

▶ **The software will not run properly *if* the computer lacks sufficient memory.**

(For help in punctuating sentences with conjunctions, see p. 511 and pp. 520–21. Help for multilingual writers appears in Chapter 48, p. 501.)

4. Conjunctive adverbs

Conjunctive adverbs indicate the relation between two clauses, but unlike conjunctions *(and, but)*, they are not grammatically strong enough on their own to hold the clauses together. A period or semicolon is also needed.

▶ **Swimming is an excellent exercise for the heart and for the muscles; *however,* swimming does not help a person control weight as well as jogging does.**

Common Conjunctive Adverbs

accordingly	incidentally	otherwise
also	indeed	similarly
as a result	instead	specifically
besides	likewise	still
certainly	meanwhile	subsequently
consequently	moreover	suddenly
finally	nevertheless	then
furthermore	next	therefore
hence	nonetheless	thus
however	now	

61h   Interjections

Interjections are forceful expressions that often occur alone (as in the first example following). They are rarely used in academic writing except in quotations of dialogue.

▶ ***"Wow!"* Davis said. "Are you telling me that there's a former presidential adviser who hasn't written a book?"**

Exercise 61.5   Chapter review: Identifying parts of speech

In the following sentences, label each word according to its part of speech: verb (v), noun (n), pronoun (pn), adjective (adj), adverb (adv), preposition (prep), conjunction (conj), or interjection (interj).

                adj   n   v   interj adj   adj   n

EXAMPLE   **Tell-all books are, alas, the biggest sellers.**

**61h
gram**

1. Cancer begins when your body's cells divide abnormally and form a malignant growth or tumor.
2. Many types of cancer, alas, can attack parts of your body imperceptibly, including your body's skin, organs, and blood.
3. One of the most commonly diagnosed types of cancer in the United States, however, is skin cancer.
4. People who are fair-skinned and freckled are more prone to develop skin cancer if they are exposed often to ultraviolet radiation.
5. Many people are relieved to discover that most skin cancers can usually be treated successfully if detected early.

62 Parts of Sentences

Every complete sentence contains at least one **subject** (a noun and its modifiers) and one **predicate** (a verb and its objects, complements, and modifiers) that fit together to make a statement, ask a question, or give a command.

```
       subj  ┌──── pred ────┐
```
▶ The *children solved* the puzzle.

62a Subjects

The **simple subject** is the word or words that name the topic of the sentence; it is always a noun or pronoun. To find the subject, ask who or what the sentence is about. The **complete subject** is the simple subject plus its modifiers.

```
          simple subj
```
▶ Did *Sir Walter Raleigh* give Queen Elizabeth I complete obedience? [Who gave the queen obedience?]

```
┌──── complete subj ────┐
          simple subj
```
▶ *Three 6-year-old children* solved the puzzle in less than five minutes. [Who solved the puzzle?]

A **compound subject** contains two or more simple subjects connected with a conjunction such as *and, but, or,* or *neither . . . nor.*

```
                 compound
      ┌─────────────────────────────┐
      simple              simple
```
▶ *Original thinking* and *bold design* characterize her work.

In **imperative sentences,** which give directions or commands, the subject *you* is usually implied, not stated. A helping verb is needed to transform an imperative sentence into a question.

▶ [*You*] **Keep this advice in mind.**

▶ *Would* **you keep this advice in mind?**

In sentences beginning with *there* or *here* followed by some form of *be,* the subject comes after the verb.

```
                 simple subj
```
▶ **Here are the *remnants* of an infamous empire.**

For more on subjects, multilingual writers should see Chapter 48, pp. 496–97.

62b Verbs and their objects or complements

In a sentence, the **predicate** says something about the subject. The verb constitutes the **simple predicate.** The verb plus its object or complement make up the **complete predicate.**

Exercise 62.1 Identifying the subject and predicate

Place one line under the complete subject and two lines under the complete predicate in each sentence. Circle the simple subject and simple predicate. If the subject is implied, write "implied subject" instead.

EXAMPLE   Little Jack Horner sat in a corner.

1. Did Gene Roddenberry, the creator and producer of *Star Trek,* anticipate that his science fiction television series would be watched by people of all ages for more than thirty years?

2. Both Captain James T. Kirk from *Star Trek: The Original Series* and Captain Jean-Luc Picard from *Star Trek: The Next Generation* command a ship called the *Enterprise.*

3. Do not forget that the captain in *Star Trek: Voyager* is a woman, Kathryn Janeway.

4. There are six *Star Trek* series: *The Original Series, The Next Generation, Deep Space Nine, Voyager, Enterprise,* and *The Animated Adventures.*

62b
gram

5. Captain Benjamin Sisko commanded Starfleet's Deep Space Nine station and served as the emissary for the Bajoran people.

1. Understanding verb functions in sentences

Based on how they function in sentences, verbs are linking, transitive, or intransitive. The kind of verb determines what elements the complete predicate must include and therefore determines the correct order of sentence parts. Most meaningful English sentences use one of five basic sentence patterns:

- ■ SUBJECT + LINKING VERB + SUBJECT COMPLEMENT
  New Yorkers are busy people.
- ■ SUBJECT + TRANSITIVE VERB + DIRECT OBJECT
  The police officer caught the jaywalker.
- ■ SUBJECT + TRANSITIVE VERB + INDIRECT OBJECT + DIRECT OBJECT
  The officer gave the jaywalker a ticket.
- ■ SUBJECT + TRANSITIVE VERB + DIRECT OBJECT + OBJECT COMPLEMENT
  The ticket made the jaywalker unhappy.
- ■ SUBJECT + INTRANSITIVE VERB
  She sighed.

Questions and commands have different word orders *(see p. 591). (To learn how word order changes from direct to indirect quotations, see Chapter 48, pp. 503–4.)*

Linking verbs and subject complements A **linking verb** joins a subject to information about the subject that follows the verb. That information is called the **subject complement.** The subject complement may be a noun, a pronoun, or an adjective.

subj   lv   comp

▶ **Ann Yearsley was *a milkmaid.***

The most frequently used linking verb is the *be* verb *(is, are, was, were),* but verbs such as *seem, look, appear, feel, become, smell, sound,* and *taste* can also function as links between a sentence's subject and its complement.

subj   lv   comp

▶ **That new hairstyle *looks* beautiful.**

Transitive verbs and direct objects A **transitive verb** identifies an action that the subject performs or does to somebody or something else—the receiver of the action, or **direct object.** To complete its meaning, a transitive verb needs a direct object, usually a noun, pronoun, or word group that acts like a noun or pronoun.

NOUN I threw *the ball*.

PRONOUN I threw *it* over a fence.

WORD GROUP I put *what I needed* into my backpack.

Most often, the subject is doing the action, the direct object is being acted on, and the transitive verb is in the **active voice.**

ACTIVE *Parents* sometimes *consider* their *children* unreasonable.

If the verb in a sentence is transitive, it can be in the **passive voice.** In the following revised sentence, the direct object *(children)* has become the subject; the original subject *(parents)* is introduced with the preposition *by* and is now part of a prepositional phrase.

PASSIVE Children are considered unreasonable by their parents.

(For more on the active and passive voices, see Chapter 38, pp. 398–401.)

Exercise 62.2 Using active and passive voice

Rewrite each sentence, changing the verb from the passive to the active voice.

EXAMPLE

A new nation was brought forth on this continent by our fathers four score and seven years ago.

Four score and seven years ago our fathers brought forth on this continent a new nation.

1. The first national convention on women's rights was organized by Lucretia Mott and Elizabeth Cady Stanton.
2. The convention was held by them in 1848 at Seneca Falls, a town in upstate New York.
3. The Declaration of Sentiments, which included a demand that women be granted the right to vote, was issued by the convention.
4. The Declaration of Sentiments was modeled by the leaders who drafted it on the Declaration of Independence.

62b
gram

Transitive verbs, indirect objects, and direct objects **Indirect objects** name to whom an action was done or for whom it was completed and are most commonly used with verbs such as *give, ask, tell, sing,* and *write.*

>   subj   v   ind obj   dir obj
> ▶ **Coleridge wrote *Sara* a heartrending letter.**

Note that indirect objects appear after the verb but before the direct object.

Transitive verbs, direct objects, and object complements In addition to a direct object and an indirect object, a transitive verb can take another element in its predicate: an **object complement.** An object complement describes or renames the direct object it follows.

>   dir obj   obj comp
> ▶ **His investment in a plantation made Johnson *a rich man.***

Intransitive verbs An **intransitive verb** describes an action by a subject that is not done directly to anything or anyone else. Therefore, an intransitive verb cannot take an object or a complement. However, adverbs and adverb phrases often appear in predicates built around intransitive verbs. In the sentence that follows, the complete predicate is in italics and the intransitive verb is underlined.

> ▶ **As a recruit, I *<u>complied</u> with the order mandating short hair.***

Some verbs, such as *cooperate, assent, disappear,* and *insist,* are always intransitive. Others, such as *increase, grow, roll,* and *work,* can be either transitive or intransitive.

> **TRANSITIVE**   I *grow* carrots and celery in my victory garden.
>
> **INTRANSITIVE**   My son *grows* taller every week.

NAVIGATING THROUGH COLLEGE AND BEYOND

Using the Dictionary to Determine Prepositions and Transitive and Intransitive Verbs

Your dictionary will note if a verb is intransitive *(v.i.),* transitive *(v.t.),* or both. It will also tell you—or show by example—the appropriate preposition to use when you are modifying an intransitive verb with an adverbial phrase. For example, we may *accede to* a rule, but if and when we *comply,* it has to be *with* something or someone.

2. Understanding word order in questions

In most questions, the verb, or part of it, precedes the subject:

▪ For simple forms of the verb *be,* put the subject before the verb.

She *was* on time for the
meeting.

Was she on time for
the meeting?

▪ For other simple verbs, begin the question with a form of *do*
followed by the subject and then the main verb.

You *noticed* the change
in the report.

Did you *notice* the change
in the report?

▪ For verbs consisting of a main verb with one or more helping
verbs, put the subject after the first (or only) helping verb.

He *is pleased* with the
results.

Is he *pleased* with the
results?

▪ For questions that begin with question words like *how, what,
who, when, where,* or *why,* follow the same patterns.

When did the guests *arrive?*

Where have you *been* hiding?

▪ When the question word is the subject, however, the question
follows the S-V word order of a declarative sentence.

What happened last night?

3. Understanding word order in commands

In commands, or imperative sentences, the subject, which is always
you, is omitted.

▶ **[You] Read the instructions before using this machine.**

▶ **[You] Do not enter.**

▶ **[You] Do not touch this chemical—it is hazardous.**

Exercise 62.3 Identifying objects and complements of verbs

Underline the verb in each sentence, and label it transitive (trans),
intransitive (intrans), or linking (link). If the verb is transitive, circle
and label the direct object (DO) and label any indirect object (IO) or
object complement (OC). If the verb is linking, circle and label the
subject complement (SC).

	trans	*DO*
EXAMPLE	The ancient Mayas deserve a ⬭place⬭ in the	

history of mathematics.

**62b
gram**

1. Hybrid cars produce low tailpipe emissions.
2. Automakers promise consumers affordable gasoline-electric cars.
3. Hybrid cars are desirable alternatives to gasoline-powered vehicles.
4. Their two sources of power make hybrid cars fuel efficient.
5. Consumers agree that automakers should design and manufacture more hybrid models.

63 Phrases and Dependent Clauses

A **phrase** is a group of related words that lacks either a subject or a predicate or both. Phrases function within sentences but not on their own. A **dependent clause** has a subject and a predicate but cannot function as a complete sentence because it begins with a subordinating word.

63a Noun phrases

A **noun phrase** consists of a noun or noun substitute plus all of its modifiers. Noun phrases can function as a sentence's subject, object, or subject complement.

SUBJECT   *The old, dark, ramshackle house* collapsed.

OBJECT   Greg cooked *an authentic, delicious haggis* for the Robert Burns dinner.

SUBJECT   Tom became *an accomplished and well-known*
COMPLEMENT   *cook.*

63b Verb phrases and verbals

A **verb phrase** is a verb plus its helping verbs. It functions as the predicate in a sentence: *Mary should have photographed me.* **Verbals** are words derived from verbs. They function as nouns, adjectives, or adverbs, not as verbs.

VERBAL AS NOUN	*Crawling* comes before walking.
VERBAL AS ADJECTIVE	Chris tripped over the *crawling* child.
VERBAL AS ADVERB	The child began *to crawl*.

Verbals may take modifiers, objects, and complements to form **verbal phrases.** There are three kinds of verbal phrases: participial, gerund, and infinitive.

1. Participial phrases

A **participial phrase** begins with either a present participle (the *-ing* form of a verb) or a past participle (the *-ed* or *-en* form of a verb). Participial phrases always function as adjectives. They can appear before or after the word they modify.

▶ *Working in groups,* **the children solved the problem.**

▶ *Insulted by his remark,* **Elizabeth refused to dance.**

▶ **His pitching arm,** *broken in two places by the fall,* **would never be the same again.**

2. Gerund phrases

A **gerund phrase** uses the *-ing* form of the verb, just as some participial phrases do. But gerund phrases always function as nouns, not adjectives.

subj
▶ *Walking one hour a day* **will keep you fit.**

dir obj
▶ **The instructor praised** *my acting in both scenes.*

3. Infinitive phrases

An **infinitive phrase** is formed using the infinitive, or *to* form, of a verb: *to be, to do, to live.* It can function as an adverb, an adjective, or a noun and can be the subject, subject or object complement, or direct object in a sentence. In constructions with *make, let,* or *have,* the *to* is omitted.

noun/subj
▶ *To finish his novel* **was his greatest ambition.**

adj/obj comp
▶ **He made many efforts** *to finish his novel* **for his publisher.**

adv/dir obj
▶ **He needed** *to finish his novel.*

adv/dir obj
▶ **Please let me** *finish my novel.*

**63b
gram**

63c Appositive phrases

Appositives rename nouns or pronouns and appear right after the word they rename.

noun   appositive

▶ One researcher, *the widely respected R. S. Smith,* has shown that a child's performance on such tests can be very inconsistent.

63d Absolute phrases

Absolute phrases modify an entire sentence. They include a noun or pronoun, a participle, and their related modifiers, objects, or complements. They may appear almost anywhere in a sentence.

▶ The sheriff strode into the bar, *his hands hovering over his pistols.*

Exercise 63.1   Identifying phrases

For the underlined words in the following sentences, identify what kind of phrase each is and how it functions in the sentence.

> EXAMPLE   **Raking leaves is a seasonal chore for many American teenagers.** *[verbal phrase, gerund, functioning as the subject of the sentence]*

1. The earliest of the little-known ancient civilizations of the Andes emerged more than four thousand years ago.
2. The Chavin culture, the earliest Andean culture with widespread influence, dates to between 800 and 200 BCE.
3. The distinctive art style of the Chavin culture probably reflects a compelling and influential religious movement.
4. The Paracas and Nazca cultures appear to have been the regional successors to the Chavin culture on Peru's south coast.
5. The Moche culture, encompassing most of Peru's north coast, flourished from about 200 to 700 CE.
6. The primary function of Moche warfare was probably to secure captives for sacrifice.
7. Interpreting the silent remnants of past cultures is the archeologist's challenge.
8. To see the magnificent objects buried with the Moche lord at Sipan is an awe-inspiring experience.

9. Hiram Bingham, <u>an American archeologist</u>, set out for Peru in 1911.

10. Bingham discovered the spectacular ruins of the Inca city of Machu Picchu, <u>securing for himself an enduring place in the history of Andean archeology</u>.

63e Dependent clauses

Although **dependent clauses** (also known as **subordinate clauses**) have a subject and predicate, they cannot stand alone as complete sentences. They are introduced by subordinators—either a subordinating conjunction such as *after, in order to,* or *since (for a more complete listing, see p. 584)* or a relative pronoun such as *who, which,* or *that (for more, see the box on p. 578).* They function in sentences as adjectives, adverbs, or nouns.

1. Adjective clauses

An **adjective clause** modifies a noun or pronoun. Relative pronouns *(who, whom, whose, which, that)* or relative adverbs *(where, when)* are used to connect adjective clauses to the nouns or pronouns they modify. The relative pronoun usually follows the word that is being modified and also points back to the noun or pronoun. *(For help with punctuating restrictive and nonrestrictive clauses, see Chapter 49, pp. 513–14 and 521.)*

▶ Odysseus's journey, *which can be traced on modern maps,* has inspired many works of literature.

In adjective clauses, the direct object sometimes comes before rather than after the verb.

▶ The contestant *whom he most wanted to beat* was his father.

2. Adverb clauses

An **adverb clause** modifies a verb, an adjective, or an adverb and answers the same questions adverbs answer: *When? Where? What? Why?* and *How?* Adverb clauses are often introduced by subordinators *(after, when, before, because, although, if, though, whenever, where, wherever).*

▶ *After we had talked for an hour,* he began to get nervous.

▶ He reacted *as if he already knew.*

3. Noun clauses

A **noun clause** is a dependent clause that functions as a noun. In a sentence, a noun clause may serve as the subject, object of a verb or preposition, or complement and is usually introduced by a relative pronoun *(who, which, that)* or a relative adverb *(how, what, where, when, why)*.

> SUBJECT   *What he saw* shocked him.
>
> OBJECT   The instructor found out *who had skipped class.*
>
> COMPLEMENT   The book was *where I had left it.*

As in an adjective clause, in a noun clause the direct object or subject complement can come first, violating the typical sentence order.

dir obj subj

The doctor wondered *to whom he* should send the bill.

Exercise 63.2   Identifying dependent clauses

Underline any dependent clauses in the following sentences. Identify each one as an adjective, adverb, or noun clause.

> EXAMPLE   **Because they were among the first to develop the concept of zero, the ancient Mayas deserve a prominent place in the history of mathematics.**
> *[adverb clause]*

1. During the 1970s and 1980s, Asian-American writers, who often drew on their immigrant experiences, gained a wide readership.

2. Because these writers wrote about their struggles and the struggles of their ancestors, readers were able to learn about the Chinese Exclusion Act of 1892 and the internment of Japanese Americans during World War II.

3. Many readers know Amy Tan as the Chinese-American novelist who wrote *The Joy Luck Club,* which was adapted into a feature film, but are unfamiliar with most of her other novels, such as *The Kitchen God's Wife, The Hundred Secret Senses,* and *The Bonesetter's Daughter.*

64 Types of Sentences

Classifying by how many clauses they contain and how those clauses are joined, we can categorize sentences into four types: simple, compound, complex, and compound-complex. We can also classify sentences by purpose: declarative, interrogative, imperative, and exclamatory.

64a Sentence structures

A clause is a group of related words that includes a subject and a predicate. **Independent clauses** can stand on their own as complete sentences. **Dependent, or subordinate, clauses** cannot stand alone. They function in sentences as adjectives, adverbs, or nouns. The presence of one or both of these two types of clauses, and their relation to each other if there is more than one, determines whether the sentence is simple, compound, complex, or compound-complex.

1. Simple sentences

A simple sentence has only one independent clause. Simple does not necessarily mean short, however. Although a simple sentence does not include any dependent clauses, it may have several embedded phrases, a compound subject, and a compound predicate.

INDEPENDENT CLAUSE

The bloodhound is the oldest known breed of dog.

INDEPENDENT CLAUSE: COMPOUND SUBJ + COMPOUND PRED

Historians, novelists, short-story writers, and playwrights write about characters, design plots, and usually seek the dramatic resolution of a problem.

2. Compound sentences

A compound sentence contains two or more independent clauses but no dependent clause. The independent clauses may be joined by a comma and a coordinating conjunction or by a semicolon with or without a conjunctive adverb.

▶ **The police arrested him for drunk driving, *so* he lost his car.**

▶ **The sun blasted the earth; *therefore*, the plants withered and died.**

3. Complex sentences

A complex sentence contains one independent clause and one or more dependent clauses.

　　　　　independent clause　　　　　　　　　dependent clause

▶ **He consulted the dictionary** *because he did not know how to*

pronounce the word.

4. Compound-complex sentences

A compound-complex sentence contains two or more coordinated independent clauses and at least one dependent clause (italicized in the example).

▶ **She discovered a new world of international finance, but she worked so hard investing other people's money** *that she had no time to invest any of her own.*

Exercise 64.1　Classifying sentences

Identify each sentence as simple, compound, complex, or compound-complex.

　　EXAMPLE　　**Biotechnology promises great benefits for humanity, but it also raises many difficult ethical issues.** *[compound]*

1. Rock and roll originated in the 1950s.
2. Chuck Berry, Jerry Lee Lewis, and Elvis Presley were early rock-and-roll greats.
3. Teenagers loved the new music, but it disturbed many parents.
4. As much as the music itself, it was the sexually suggestive body language of the performers that worried the older generation.
5. The social turmoil that marked the 1960s influenced many performers, and some began to use their music as a vehicle for protest.

64b　Sentence purposes

When you write a sentence, your purpose helps you decide which sentence type to use. If you want to provide information, you usually use a declarative sentence. If you want to ask a question, you usually use an interrogative sentence. To make a request or give an order (a command), you use the imperative. An exclamatory sentence emphasizes a point or expresses strong emotion.

DECLARATIVE	He watches *Seinfeld* reruns.
INTERROGATIVE	Does he watch *Seinfeld* reruns?
IMPERATIVE	Do not watch reruns of *Seinfeld.*
EXCLAMATORY	I'm really looking forward to watching *Seinfeld* reruns with you!

Exercise 64.2 Chapter review: Sentence basics

Place one line under each independent clause and two lines under each dependent clause. (Recall that an independent clause can stand on its own as a complete sentence.) Label each sentence as simple, compound, complex, or compound-complex.

Many argue that the blues and jazz are the first truly American musical forms. With its origins in slave narratives, the blues took root during the 1920s and 1930s as African-American composers, musicians, and singers performed in the cabarets and clubs of Harlem. Jazz, however, has its origins in New Orleans. Today, we can still appreciate the music of Bessie Smith, Duke Ellington, and B. B. King.

Rock and roll is also a distinctively American form of music. Our country's first "rock star" was without a doubt Elvis Presley, who emerged on the nation's airwaves in the mid-1950s with such hits as *Heartbreak Hotel, Don't Be Cruel,* and *All Shook Up.* A decade later, Americans were expressing themselves musically through rhythm and blues, pop, folk rock, and protest music, and today, thanks to recording technology, we have easy access to our country's rich musical history.

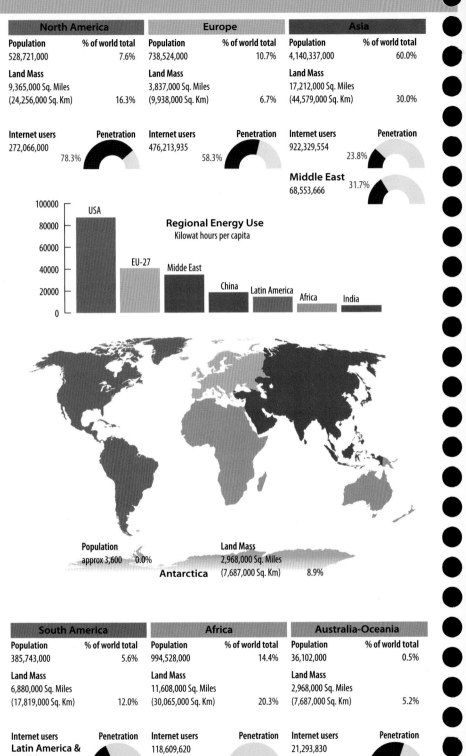

North America		Europe		Asia	
Population	**% of world total**	**Population**	**% of world total**	**Population**	**% of world total**
528,721,000	7.6%	738,524,000	10.7%	4,140,337,000	60.0%
Land Mass		**Land Mass**		**Land Mass**	
9,365,000 Sq. Miles		3,837,000 Sq. Miles		17,212,000 Sq. Miles	
(24,256,000 Sq. Km)	16.3%	(9,938,000 Sq. Km)	6.7%	(44,579,000 Sq. Km)	30.0%
Internet users	**Penetration**	**Internet users**	**Penetration**	**Internet users**	**Penetration**
272,066,000	78.3%	476,213,935	58.3%	922,329,554	23.8%

Middle East
68,553,666   31.7%

Regional Energy Use
Kilowat hours per capita

USA
EU-27
Midde East
China
Latin America
Africa
India

100000
80000
60000
40000
20000
0

Population
approx 3,600   0.0%

Land Mass
2,968,000 Sq. Miles
(7,687,000 Sq. Km)   8.9%

Antarctica

South America		Africa		Australia-Oceania	
Population	**% of world total**	**Population**	**% of world total**	**Population**	**% of world total**
385,743,000	5.6%	994,528,000	14.4%	36,102,000	0.5%
Land Mass		**Land Mass**		**Land Mass**	
6,880,000 Sq. Miles		11,608,000 Sq. Miles		2,968,000 Sq. Miles	
(17,819,000 Sq. Km)	12.0%	(30,065,000 Sq. Km)	20.3%	(7,687,000 Sq. Km)	5.2%
Internet users	**Penetration**	**Internet users**	**Penetration**	**Internet users**	**Penetration**
Latin America & Caribbean		118,609,620	11.4%	21,293,830	60.1%
215,939,400	36.2%				

Answers
to Tutorials and Selected Exercises

Note to instructors: answers to all exercises appear in the Instructor's Manual on the instructor version of **www.mhhe.com/bmhh.**

Answers to Tutorial A, page viii

1. Students today face many pressures that can lead to plagiarism. [52e]
2. If students paraphrase another writer's work too closely without giving the source, they have plagiarized. *Or* If a student paraphrases another writer's work too closely without giving the source, he or she has plagiarized. [46a]
3. Although many students do not realize it, they can plagiarize by using their own words in another writer's sentence structure. [42a]
4. Colleges deal with plagiarism in different ways. Some expel students caught plagiarizing; others give warnings first. *Or* Colleges deal with plagiarism in different ways. Some expel students caught plagiarizing, while others give warnings first. [43]
5. The Internet has made a variety of sources available to students. [44]
6. No error. [49c]
7. Plagiarism-detection software (can *or* may) be helpful to teachers. [45h]

Answers to Tutorial B, page viii

1. Look up *the reason . . . is because* and go to section 32b (Illogical Predicates). You'll see that *because* is incorrect. *The reason* is a noun and can't take *is because* as its predicate. (*A student is because . . .* doesn't make sense, does it?) Corrected sentence: The reason some students plagiarize is that they feel pressured to keep a high GPA.
2. Find *none* and go to section 44d to find that indefinite subjects such as *none, every,* and *each* are always singular. *Have* should be *has.*
3. In the index, the entry for *it* directs you to section 46b (Pronoun reference). In this case, *it* does not refer clearly to an antecedent, so the sentence must be changed. Corrected sentence: Our honor code says students must report others who plagiarize.
4. Look up *his/her* and go to section 39e (Biased or sexist language). Although *his/her* avoids the sexism of using *his* to refer to both men and women, it is considered clunky and unacceptable in academic writing. Instead, make the subject plural and use *their.* Corrected sentence:

   Students who let other students turn in their work for a paper are guilty of plagiarism.
5. The entry for *I vs. me* leads you to section 46c (Pronoun case), which tells you *my friend and me* is correct. You wouldn't say *A teacher accused I.* Corrected sentence: A teacher once accused my friend and me of copying material from Wikipedia.
6. The entry for *different from, different than* leads you to the Glossary of Usage (41), which tells you to avoid *different than.* Corrected sentence: Turning in someone else's writing as your own is no different from any other type of cheating.
7. Look up *except* and you will find a reference to the Glossary of Usage (41), which tells you *accepts (receives willingly* or *tolerates)* should be used in this sentence. Corrected sentence: Many students do not understand plagiarism because our society accepts many forms of borrowing, such as music samples and Web site mashups.

A-1

Answers to Tutorial C, page ix

1. The *number* of prominent authors accused of plagiarism has increased recently.
2. Instructors must ensure that *every one* of their students knows how to use sources appropriately.
3. Schools should *adopt* a program of educational seminars about integrating and documenting sources.
4. Students who *flout* school policy by failing to document sources must be *censured* [*censured* is correct].
5. Even when unintentional, plagiarism has a negative *effect* on the academic community.
6. When writing research papers, students have to *cite* their sources.

Answers to Tutorial D, page ix

Hulbert, Ann. "How Kaavya Got Packaged and Got into Trouble." *Slate.* 27 Apr. 2006. Web. 15 Mar. 2007.

Lathrop, Ann, and Kathleen Foss. *Student Cheating and Plagiarism in the Internet Era: A Wake-Up Call.* Englewood: Libraries Unlimited, 2000. Print.

Read, Brock. "Are Professors to Blame for Plagiarism?" *The Wired Campus.* 18 Oct. 2006. Web. 5 Mar. 2007.

Answers to Tutorial E, page x

1. Section 5c (Thinking intentionally about design) recommends using a common font such as Courier, Times New Roman, or Bookman, in an eleven- or twelve-point size.
2. Section 2e (Using visuals) states that line graphs effectively demonstrate change over time.
3. Scan the detailed Contents inside the back cover to find the listing for section 11d (Creating and interacting with blogs and wikis). The section includes a checklist for setting up a wiki.
4. Turn to Chapter 14, Finding and Managing Print and Online Sources. The title of section 14g (Using your library's catalog to find books) answers this question.
5. Section 16b (Questioning Internet sources) indicates that a Web site that ends in .com and sells a product probably has a strong bias. Joe should be skeptical of any claims made by this site, particularly those not supported by evidence.

Answers to Exercise 2.5, page 45

1. Pie chart
2. Bar graph
3. Line graph

Answers to Exercise 4.2, page 74

Answers will vary.

1. During his prime, Vivaldi was an acclaimed violin virtuoso and an influential composer. As has happened to many famous musicians, however, his popularity eventually waned, and he died in poverty and obscurity. He remained forgotten for two hundred years until the baroque revival of the 1950s brought his music back to the public's attention.

2. People thinking about adopting an exotic pet should know the consequences of doing so—and think again. Baby snakes and reptiles, for example, may seem easy to manage, but many require carefully controlled environments, and some of them can grow very large. Similarly, lion and tiger cubs may seem as playful, friendly, and harmless as kittens, but once full grown, they can revert to a wild state quite easily. They can also escape, posing a danger to themselves and others. Most exotic animals need the kind of professional care that is available in zoos and wild-animal

parks, not in people's homes. The best environment for an exotic animal, however, is in the wild.

Answers to Exercise 4.5, page 80

Answers will vary.

Answers to Exercise 8.1, page 124

Answers will vary.

1. Possible warrant: College students can decide for themselves what constitutes a good education.
2. Possible warrant: Those who are eligible to vote and to serve in the military should be able to decide for themselves whether to consume alcohol.
3. Possible warrant: The strongest country in the world has an obligation to set an example.

Answers to Exercise 30.1, page 362

Answers may vary.

1. Charlotte Perkins Gilman was a champion of women's rights.
2. She was born on July 3, 1860, in Hartford, Connecticut.
3. Gilman's "The Yellow Wallpaper," a novella about marriage and madness, still speaks to readers.

Answers to Exercise 30.2, page 363

Answers may vary.

1. Environmentalists worry about the environmental safety of genetically modified food products.
2. Genetically engineered soybeans resist certain herbicides and insecticides.
3. These genetically altered soybeans encourage farmers to use larger quantities of herbicides.

Answer to Exercise 30.3, page 365

Responses may vary.

People today should take measures to prevent identity theft. Identity thieves use someone else's personal information to commit fraud or theft, such as opening a fraudulent credit card account or creating counterfeit checks. Often the victim of identify theft never realizes that his or her identity has been cleverly stolen. Victims of identity theft should contact the Federal Trade Commission (FTC) to dispute fraudulent charges. People should also learn how to minimize their risk of falling victim to this type of crime.

Answer to Exercise 31.1, page 367

Most early scientists thought that the speed of light was infinite. The Italian scientist Galileo never agreed with or listened to the arguments of his contemporaries. He set up an experiment to measure the speed of light between two hills that were a known distance apart. Although its results were ambiguous, Galileo's experiment was more influential than any other experiment of his day.

Almost one hundred years later, the Danish astronomer Olaus Roemer devised a sophisticated experiment to measure the speed of light. Roemer hypothesized that the farther away the planet Jupiter is from Earth, the longer its light will take to reach Earth. Knowing Jupiter's distance from Earth at various times of the year, Roemer calculated the speed of light to be 141,000 miles per second. Roemer's result was closer than any earlier scientist's to the actual speed of light, which is now known to be 186,281.7 miles per second in a vacuum.

According to Albert Einstein's theory of relativity, the speed of light has never been and will never be exceeded. The speed of light is variable, however. For instance, it travels about 25 percent slower through water than through a vacuum.

Answer to Exercise 32.1, page 369

Responses may vary.

Electrons spin around the nucleus of an atom according to definite rules. The single electron of a hydrogen atom occupies a kind of spherical shell around a single proton. According to the discoveries of quantum physics, we can never determine exactly where in this shell the electron is at a given time. The Indeterminacy Principle states that we can only know the probability that the electron will be at a given point at a given moment. The set of places where the electron is most likely to be is called its orbital. By outlining a set of rules for the orbitals of electrons, the Austrian physicist Wolfgang Pauli developed the concept of the quantum state. Using this concept, scientists can describe the energy and behavior of any electron in a series of four numbers. The first of these, or principal quantum number, specifies the average distance of the electron from the nucleus. The other quantum numbers describe the shape of the orbital and the "spin" of the electron. According to Pauli's basic rule, no two electrons can ever be in exactly the same quantum state. Using the four quantum numbers as a shorthand for each electron in an atom, chemists can calculate the behavior of the atom as a whole.

Answers to Exercise 33.1, page 373

1. On November 30th, 1974, archeologists discovered the 3.5-million-year-old skeleton of an early hominid (or human ancestor) they call Lucy.

2. If you consider how long ago Lucy lived, you might be surprised so many of her bones remained intact. *Or* Considering how long ago Lucy lived, one might be surprised so many of her bones remained intact.

3. When early hominids like Lucy reached full height, they were about three and a half feet tall.

Answers to Exercise 33.2, page 374

1. Many visitors who have looked with amazement at the Great Wall of China do not know that its origins reach back to the seventh century BCE.

2. In 221 BCE, the ruler of the Ch'in state conquered the last of its independent neighbors and unified China for the first time.

3. The Ch'in ruler ordered the walls the states had erected between themselves to be torn down, but he ordered the walls on the northern frontier to be combined and reinforced.

Answer to Exercise 33.3, page 375

Responses will vary.

From about the first to the eighth century CE the Moche civilization dominated the north coast of what is now Peru. The people of this remarkable civilization, which flourished nearly a thousand years before the better-known Inca civilization, were sophisticated engineers and skilled artisans. They built enormous adobe pyramids and created and maintained a vast system of irrigation canals. Moche smiths forged spectacular gold ornaments as well as copper tools and weapons. Moche potters sculpted realistic-looking portraits and scenes of everyday life onto clay vessels; they also decorated vessels with intricate drawings of imposing and elaborately garbed figures involved in complex ceremonies. One such scene, which appears on many Moche vessels, depicts a figure archeologists call the Warrior Priest engaged in a ceremony that involves the ritual sacrifice of bound prisoners.

What do these drawings represent? Do they depict Moche gods and mythological events, or do they depict actual figures from Moche society conducting actual Moche rituals? A dramatic discovery in 1987 provided an answer to these questions. In that year, archeologists uncovered a group of intact Moche tombs at a site called Sipán. In one of the tombs were the remains of a man who had been buried clothed in stunningly rich regalia. As archeologists carefully removed the parts of this outfit, they realized that it corresponded to the outfit worn by the Warrior Priest depicted on Moche pottery. If the Warrior Priest were just a mythological figure, then this tomb should not exist, but it did. In other words, the archeologists realized, the man in the tomb was an actual Moche Warrior Priest.

Answer to Exercise 34.1, page 377

I believe this government cannot endure permanently half slave and half free. I do not expect the Union to be dissolved—I do not expect the house to fall—but I do expect it will cease to be divided. It will become all one thing, or all the other. Either the opponents of slavery will arrest the further spread of it, and place it where the public mind shall rest in the belief that it is in the course of ultimate extinction; or its advocates will push it forward till it shall become alike lawful in all the states, old as well as new, North as well as South.

Answers to Exercise 34.2, page 378

1. *Impressionism,* a term that applies primarily to an art movement of the late nineteenth century, also applies to the music of some composers of the era.

2. The early Impressionists include Edouard Manet, Claude Monet, Mary Cassat, Edgar Degas, and Camille Pissarro. *Or* The early Impressionists include Edouard Manet, Claude Monet, and Mary Cassat, as well as Edgar Degas and Camille Pissarro.

3. Impressionist composers include both Claude Debussy and Maurice Ravel.

Answer to Exercise 34.3, page 380

Responses will vary.

People can be classified as either Type A or Type B personalities depending on their level of competitiveness, degree of perfectionism, and ability to relax. Type A people are often workaholics who not only drive themselves hard but also drive others hard. In the workplace, employers often like Type A personalities because they tend to be punctual and to work quickly and efficiently. However, because Type A people also tend to be impatient, verbally aggressive, or hostile, they do not rise to top management positions as often as Type B people. Type A people also tend to be acutely aware of time, to talk quickly, and either to interrupt others or to complete their sentences for them. Type B people, in contrast, take the world in stride, walk and talk more slowly, and listen attentively. Type B people are better at dealing with stress and keeping things in perspective than Type A people, who, in contrast, tend to worry more than Type B people.

People with traits that put them clearly on either end of the continuum between Type A and Type B should try to adopt characteristics of the opposite type. For example, to moderate some of their characteristic behaviors and reduce their risk of high blood pressure and heart disease, Type A people can use exercise, relaxation techniques, diet, and meditation. Understanding one's personality is half the battle, but implementing change takes time, discipline, and patience.

Answers to Exercise 35.1, page 384

1. During his career as an architect and engineer, R. Buckminster Fuller developed some of the most important design innovations of the twentieth century.

2. Correct

3. After suffering from a period of severe depression at the age of thirty-two, Fuller resolved to dedicate his life to improving people's lives.

Answers to Exercise 35.2, page 386

Answers may vary.

1. Correct

2. O'Keefe is one of the most admired American artists of the twentieth century, and her color-saturated images of cactus flowers, bleached bones, and pale skies are widely reproduced.

3. Art was always important to O'Keefe while she was growing up in Wisconsin.

Answer to Exercise 35.3, page 387

Responses may vary.

Henri Matisse and Pablo Picasso, often considered to have been the formative artists of the twentieth century, were also rivals for most of their careers. Both artists were the subject of a travelling exhibit called "Matisse Picasso," which exhibited their works side by side in museums in London, Paris, and New York.

Picasso's work may be more disturbing than Matisse's, and some say it is also more daring and experimental. Yet Matisse, too, with his use of vivid colors and distorted shapes, was a daring innovator.

Looking for similarities, viewers can see that the works of both artists suggest an underlying anxiety. Yet each artist responded differently from the other to this anxiety. Matisse painted tranquil yet often emotionally charged domestic scenes, whereas Picasso fought his inner fears with often jarringly disquieting images.

Answers to Exercise 36.1, page 389

Answers may vary.

1. Before World War II, France divided Vietnam into three administrative regions.

2. Most Vietnamese opposed French rule, and many groups formed to regain the country's independence.

3. Although it was under Japanese control from 1940 to 1945, Vietnam remained a French-administered colony during World War II.

Answers to Exercise 36.2, page 390

Answers may vary.

1. During the early years of the Industrial Revolution, many thousands of people left the countryside in search of work in Europe's fast-growing cities. There they encountered poverty, disease, lack of sanitation, and exhausting, dangerous factory jobs. These conditions made the cities breeding grounds for insurrection. After an international financial crisis in 1848 and the epidemic of bankruptcies and unemployment that followed it, the threat of unrest increased.

2. Louis-Philippe, France's hopelessly unpopular king, abdicated in February, throwing the country into revolution. Citizens set up barricades in the narrow streets of Paris, restricting the movement of government troops.

3. Revolutionary fervor also took hold in Vienna, the capital of the Austrian Empire. At the same time, nationalist forces gained strength in Hungary and other regions of the empire. Hungarian nationalists demanded autonomy from Vienna, and radicals in Prague demanded autonomy for the Empire's Slavic peoples.

Answer to Exercise 36.3, page 392

Responses will vary.

Germany and Italy were not always unified nations. On the contrary, they were divided for centuries into many city-states, kingdoms, dukedoms, fiefdoms, and principalities, all of them intent on maintaining their autonomy.

Two men, Camillo di Cavour in Italy and Otto von Bismarck in Germany, were largely responsible for the unification of each country. Cavour, who became prime minister of the republic of Piedmont in 1852, and Bismarck, who was named chancellor of Prussia in 1862, were both practitioners of *realpolitik,* a political policy based on the ruthless advancement of national interests.

Cavour hoped to govern Piedmont in a way that would make it the focus of national aspirations throughout Italy and inspire other Italian states to join it to form a unified nation. He increased the power of Piedmont's parliament, modernized its agriculture and industry, built a railroad that opened the country to trade with the rest of Europe, and installed Victor Emmanuel as king. Modena and Tuscany joined Piedmont after Piedmont, with the help of Napoleon III of France, defeated an Austrian invasion that Cavour had craftily provoked.

Bismarck used similar tactics in pursuit of Germany's unification. For example, after arranging for French neutrality, he attacked and destroyed the Austrian army at Sadowa, eliminating Austrian influence in Prussia and paving the way for Prussian control of a large north German federation by 1867. Both men continued to use these tactics until they succeeded with the unification of Germany in 1871 and of Italy in 1879.

Answers to Exercise 37.1, page 394

Answers may vary.

1. As it had in World War I, Germany entered World War II better prepared than the Allies.
2. Gambling on a quick victory, the Germans struck suddenly in both 1914 and 1939.
3. In 1941, the United States entered World War II.

Answers to Exercise 37.2, page 395

Answers may vary.

1. The Black Death, one of the worst natural disasters in history, started in China around 1333, spread to Europe over trade routes, and killed one third of Europe's population in two years.
2. It was a horrible time, with dead bodies abandoned on the streets, people terrified of one another, and cattle and livestock left to roam the countryside.
3. It was everyone for him- or herself, friends deserting friends, husbands leaving wives, parents even abandoning children.

Answers to Exercise 37.3, page 396

1. As were the Nile River in Egypt, the Tigris and Euphrates Rivers in Iraq, and the Yellow River in China, the Indus River in Pakistan was home to one of the earliest civilizations in the world.
2. The Indus civilization was unknown to modern scholars until 1921, when archeologists discovered the remains of one of its two great cities, Harappa.
3. Harappa and another city, Mohenjo-Daro, were the two main centers of the Indus civilization, which flourished from about 2500 to 1700 BCE.

Answer to Exercise 37.4, page 397

Responses will vary.

Established in 1945, the United Nations was intended to prevent another world war. Only twenty-one nations belonged to the United Nations when it began, but today nearly every nation in the world is a member.

According to its charter, the United Nations has four purposes: to maintain international peace and security, to develop friendly relations among nations, to promote cooperation among nations for the solution of international problems and the protection of human rights, and to provide a forum for coordinating international action.

All members of the United Nations have a seat and a vote in the General Assembly, which considers a variety of topics such as globalization, AIDS, and pollution. Primary responsibility for maintaining international peace and security, however, rests with the Security Council, a much smaller body within the United Nations. The Security Council has fifteen members. Five of them—China, France, Russia, the United Kingdom, and the United States—are permanent. The other ten are elected by the General Assembly for two-year terms.

Answers to Exercise 38.1, page 399

1. Historians generally agree that the Egyptians invented sailing around 3000 BCE.
2. Many years passed before mariners learned to sail upwind.
3. The invention of the keel improved sailboat navigation.

Answers to Exercise 38.2, page 400

1. Polynesian sailors settled the remote islands of Oceania beginning in the early first millennium CE.
2. Polynesian settlers reached Hawaii around 500 CE.
3. By about 900, settlers had reached Easter Island, the most remote island in Polynesia. [already in active voice]

Answer to Exercise 38.3, page 400

Responses will vary.

Inventors first conceived of the idea of a lighter-than-air balloon in the Middle Ages. However, not until October 15, 1783, did Pilatre de Rosier successfully ascend in a hot-air balloon. Five weeks later, he and a companion made history again, accomplishing the world's first aerial journey with a five-mile trip across the city of Paris. For the next century, many people considered lighter-than-air balloons the future of human flight. Balloonists reached heights of up to three miles and made long, cross-country journeys. In 1859, for instance, the wind carried a balloonist from St. Louis to Henderson, New York. Balloonists couldn't, however, control the movement of their craft. Some tried to use hand-cranked propellers and even giant oars to overcome this deficiency. The invention of the internal-combustion engine finally made possible controllable, self-propelled balloons, which are known as airships. Hydrogen gas replaced hot air in the earliest airships. Hydrogen gas catches fire easily, however, a fact that doomed the airship as a major means of travel. In 1937, the German airship *Hindenburg* exploded as it was landing in New Jersey, a tragedy that an announcer described in a live radio broadcast. As a result, helium has replaced hydrogen in today's airships.

Answers to Exercise 39.1, page 403

Answers will vary.

1. With the invention of steel engraving and mechanical printing presses in the nineteenth century, publishers could print books in far greater quantities than before.
2. Nineteenth-century realism began in France, which produced such notable realists as Stendhal, Balzac, and Flaubert.
3. Flaubert thought the bourgeoisie were materialistic and vain.

Answers to Exercise 39.2, page 406

1. Humanity is fast approaching a population crisis.
2. We must all do our part to reduce the production of greenhouse gasses.
3. Families should make recycling a habit, and employers should encourage commuters to carpool or take mass transit whenever possible.

Answer to Exercise 39.3, page 406

Responses may vary.

Novelist Henry James had many famous ancestors. His grandfather William crossed the Atlantic in 1789 with little more than a Latin grammar book and a desire to see the battlefields of the Revolutionary War. When William James died in 1832, he left an estate of $3 million, equivalent to about $100 million today. This amount was to be divided among eleven children and his wife, Catherine Barber James. Henry, William's fourth child, often referred to as the elder Henry James to distinguish him from the novelist, became a lecturer and writer on metaphysics. He was interested in the doctrines of the Swedish mystic Emanuel Swedenborg. Although some thought the older Henry James an eccentric, his work was well known and influential during his lifetime.

Answers to Exercise 40.1, page 408

Answers will vary.

Answers to Exercise 40.2, page 409

Answers will vary.

Answers to Exercise 40.3, page 411

1. Metaphor
2. Metaphor
3. Metaphor

Answers to Exercise 40.4, page 411

1. eluded
2. infer; cite is correct
3. incredible

Answers to Exercise 42.1, page 429

1. Ancient people traded salt, which is an important nutrient.
2. Some groups resorted to war and conquest because they wanted to gain control over valuable goods and resources.
3. When they could, people transported large stones by river since doing so required less effort than other means of moving them.

Answer to Exercise 42.2, page 431

Pool hustlers deceive their opponents in many ways. Sometimes appearing unfamiliar with the rules of the game (phrase). They may try acting as if they are drunk. Or pretend to be inept (phrase). For example, they will put so much spin on the ball that it jumps out of the intended pocket. So that their opponents will be tricked into betting (dep. clause). Some other ways to cheat (phrase). When their opponents are not looking, pool hustlers may remove their own balls from the table. Then change the position of the balls on the table (phrase). Because today's pool balls have metallic cores (dep. clause). Hustlers can use electromagnets to affect the path of balls. Be aware of these tricks!

Answers to Exercise 42.3, page 431

1. The ominous music prepares us for a shocking scene and confuses us when the shock does not come.
2. Filmmakers may try to evoke nostalgic feelings by choosing songs from a particular era.
3. The musical producer used a mix of traditional songs and new compositions in the Civil War drama *Cold Mountain*.

Answer to Exercise 42.4, page 433

Responses may vary.

According to the United States Constitution, which was ratified in 1788, the president and vice president of the United States were not to be elected directly by the people in a popular election. Instead they were to be elected indirectly by an "electoral college," made up of "electors" who at first were often chosen by the state legislatures. In the early nineteenth century, the population of the United States grew rapidly, and electors were increasingly chosen by statewide popular vote, gradually making the electoral college system more democratic. Nonetheless, in the elections of 1824, 1876, 1888, and 2000, the elected candidate won the vote in the electoral college but not a majority of the popular vote.

Answer to Exercise 43.1, page 435

Rare books can be extremely valuable. [Most books have to be in good shape to fetch high prices nevertheless some remain valuable no matter what] (RO). [A first edition of Audubon's *Birds of America* can be worth more than a million dollars however it must be in good condition] (RO). On the other hand, even without a cover, an early edition of Cotton Mather's *An Ecclesiastical History of New England* will be worth at least three thousand dollars. [Generally speaking, the newer a book is the more important its condition, even a book from the 1940s will have to be in excellent condition to be worth three figures] (CS). [There are other factors that determine a book's value, certainly whether the author has signed it is important] (CS). [Even students can collect books for instance they can search for bargains and great "finds" at yard and garage sales] (RO). In addition, used-book and author sites on the Internet offer opportunities for beginning collectors.

Answers to Exercise 43.2, page 437

Answers may vary.

1. Correct
2. All early civilizations were autocratic; in a sense, all people in them were slaves.
3. No one knows when slavery began, but it was common in many ancient agricultural civilizations.

Answers to Exercise 43.3, page 440

Answers may vary.

1. Although globally population has increased steadily, particular regions have suffered sometimes drastic declines.
2. Correct
3. The plague was not the only catastrophe to strike Europe in the fourteenth century. A devastating famine also slowed population growth at the beginning of the century.

Answer to Exercise 43.4, page 441

Responses will vary.

Rare books can be extremely valuable. Although most books have to be in good shape to fetch high prices, some remain valuable no matter what. For example, a first edition of Audubon's *Birds of America* can be worth more than a million dollars, but it must be in good condition. On the other hand, even without a cover, an early edition of Cotton Mather's *An Ecclesiastical History of New England* will be worth at least three thousand dollars. Generally speaking, the newer a book is the more important its condition; even a book from the 1940s will have to be in excellent condition to be worth three figures. Other important factors that determine a book's value include, certainly, whether the author has signed it. Even students can collect books, for instance by searching for bargains and great "finds" at yard and garage sales. In addition, used-book and author sites on the Internet offer opportunities for beginning collectors.

Answer to Exercise 43.5, page 441

Responses will vary.

The economy of the United States has always been turbulent. Many people think that the Great Depression of the 1930s was the only economic cataclysm this country has suffered, but the United States has had a long history of financial panics and upheavals. The early years of the nation were no exception.

Before the Revolution, the American economy was closely linked with Britain's, but during the war and for many years after it, Britain barred the import of

American goods. Americans, however, continued to import British goods, but with the loss of British markets the new country's trade deficit ballooned. Eventually, this deficit triggered a severe depression, and social unrest followed. The economy began to recover at the end of the 1780s with the establishment of a stable government, the opening of new markets to American shipping, and the adoption of new forms of industry. Exports grew steadily throughout the 1790s; indeed, the United States soon found itself in direct competition with both England and France.

Beginning in 1803, when England declared war on France, the American economy suffered a new setback. France and England each threatened to impound any American ships engaged in trade with the other. President Thomas Jefferson sought to change the policies of France and England with the Embargo Act of 1807, which prohibited all trade between the United States and the warring countries. Jefferson hoped to bring France and England to the negotiating table, but the ploy failed. The economies of France and England suffered little from the loss of trade with the United States; the U.S. shipping industry, however, came almost to a halt.

Answers to Exercise 44.1, page 443

1. Nowadays, <u>computers</u> (gives / give) graphic designers a great deal of freedom.
2. Before computers, a <u>design</u> (was / were) produced mostly by hand.
3. Alternative <u>designs</u> (is / are) produced much faster on the computer than by hand.

Answers to Exercise 44.2, page 448

1. <u>Designers</u> since the invention of printing <u>have</u> sought to create attractive, readable type.
2. Correct; subject is <u>layout</u>, verb is <u>shows</u>.
3. Correct; subject is <u>half</u>, verb is <u>contains</u>.

Answers to Exercise 44.3, page 450

1. The Guerilla Girls is a group of women who act on behalf of female artists.
2. One of their main concerns is to combat the underrepresentation of women artists in museum shows.
3. No one knows how many Guerilla Girls there are, and none of them has ever revealed her true identity.

Answer to Exercise 44.4, page 451

The end of the nineteenth century saw the rise of a new kind of architecture. Originating in response to the development of new building materials, this so-called modern architecture characterizes most of the buildings we see around us today.

Iron and reinforced concrete make the modern building possible. Previously, the structural characteristics of wood and stone limited the dimensions of a building. Wood-frame structures become unstable above a certain height. Stone can bear great weight, but architects building in stone confront severe limits on the height of a structure in relation to the width of its base. The principal advantage of iron and steel is that they reduce those limits, permitting much greater height than stone.

At first the new materials were used for decoration. However, architects like Hermann Muthesius and Walter Gropius began to use iron and steel as structural elements within their buildings. The designs of Frank Lloyd Wright also show how the development of iron and steel technology revolutionized building interiors. When every wall does not have to bear weight from the floors above, open floor plans are possible.

Answers to Exercise 45.1, page 455

1. were
2. grown
3. saw

Answers to Exercise 45.2, page 456

1. Humans, like many other mammals, usually lie down to sleep.
2. Correct
3. The restless students had been sitting at their desks all morning.

Answers to Exercise 45.3, page 457

1. Correct
2. Desert peoples have learned that loose, light garments protect them from the heat.
3. They have long drunk from deep wells that they dug for water.

Answers to Exercise 45.4, page 462

1. follows
2. states
3. published

Answer to Exercise 45.5, page 463

For some time, anthropologists were puzzled by the lack of a written language among the ancient Incas of South America. The Incas, who had conquered most of Andean South America by about 1500, had sophisticated architecture, advanced knowledge of engineering and astronomy, and sophisticated social and political structures. Why didn't they have a written language as well?

Ancient Egypt, Iraq, and China, as well as early Mexican civilizations such as the Aztec and Maya, all had written language. It seems strange that only the Incas lacked a written language.

Anthropologists now think that the Incas possessed a kind of written language after all. Scholars believe that the Incas used knots in multicolored strings as the medium for their "writing." The Incas called these knotted strings *khipu*.

Answers to Exercise 45.6, page 464

1. were
2. resign
3. were

Answers to Exercise 46.1, page 469

Answers may vary.

1. All the people at the displaced-persons camp had to submit their medical records before boarding the ships to the United States.
2. Correct
3. This news was always devastating because families wanted to stay together.

Answers to Exercise 46.2, page 472

Answers will vary.

1. The historic race between Barack Obama and Hillary Clinton for the Democratic nomination in 2008 was not resolved until late spring. This development made Obama's campaign strategists very worried.
2. After he selected Alaska governor Sarah Palin as his running mate, John McCain expected to gain more votes from women.
3. When Barack Obama and John McCain debated for the first time in the general election campaign, both candidates managed to avoid making any major mistakes.

Answers to Exercise 46.3, page 476

1. I
2. him
3. she

Answers to Exercise 46.4, page 477
1. We
2. me
3. us

Answers to Exercise 46.5, page 477
1. her
2. her
3. Their

Answer to Exercise 46.6, page 478

Sociolinguists investigate the relationship between linguistic variations and culture. They spend a lot of time in the field to gather data for analysis. For instance, they might compare the speech patterns of people who live in a city with those of people who reside in the suburbs. Sociolinguists might discover differences in pronunciation or word choice. Their researching helps us understand both language and culture.

We laypeople might confuse sociolinguistics with sociology. Sociolinguists do a more specialized type of research than do most sociologists, who study broad patterns within societies. Being concerned with such particulars as the pronunciation of a single vowel, sociolinguists work at a finer level of detail than they.

Answers to Exercise 46.7, page 479
1. Who
2. who
3. who

Answer to Exercise 46.8, page 479
Responses may vary.

Margaret Mead was probably the best-known anthropologist of the twentieth century. It was she who wrote *Coming of Age in Samoa*, a book well known in the 1930s and still in print today. It was she who gave us the idea that Melanesian natives grow up free of the strictures and repression that can characterize adolescence in our society. Her writings found an audience just as the work of Sigmund Freud was becoming widely known in the United States.

In his work, Freud argued for "an incomparably freer sexual life," saying that rigid attitudes toward sexuality contributed to mental illness among us Westerners. Mead's accessible and gracefully written account of life among the Samoans showed them to be both relatively free of pathology and relaxed about sexual matters. The work of both Mead and Freud provoked and contributed to a debate over theories about the best way to raise children.

Answers to Exercise 47.1, page 482

1. The spread of destructive (adj) viruses to computers around the world is a serious (adj) problem with potentially (adv) deadly (adj) consequences.

2. Carried by infected (adj) e-mails, the viruses spread fast (adv), moving from computer to computer at the click of a mouse.

3. Viruses have hit businesses badly (adv) in the past, disrupting railroads, delaying flights, and closing stores and offices.

Answers to Exercise 47.2, page 483

1. Correct
2. The discipline's intellectual roots reach really far back, to the eighteenth century. (*Very* is preferable.)
3. Auguste Comte (1798–1857) invented the word *sociology,* and most sociologists would probably agree that he founded the discipline.

Answers to Exercise 47.3, page 485

1. Biotechnology, perhaps the most controversial application of science in recent decades, is the basis of genetic engineering, cloning, and gene therapy.
2. Correct
3. Ethicists find it easier to defend the genetic engineering of plants than the cloning of animals.

Answer to Exercise 47.4, page 486

Although there are many approaches to sociology, the two most common are functionalism and conflict theory. The functionalist view, usually associated with Harvard sociologist Talcott Parsons, sees society as a whole that tries to maintain equilibrium, or stasis. No proponent of conflict theory is more famous than Karl Marx, who invented the concept of class warfare. Promoted in the United States by the African-American sociologist W. E. B. Du Bois, among others, conflict theory sees society as made up of groups that cannot avoid being in conflict or competition with one another.

For a functionalist like Parsons, societies are best understood according to how well they maintain stability. On the other hand, for a conflict theorist like Du Bois, a society is best analyzed in terms of how its various groups compete for power.

Answer to Exercise 48.1, page 491

In his book *Travels with Charley,* John Steinbeck describes a journey he took that helped him discover his country. Hurricane Donna struck New York State and delayed the beginning of the long-planned trip. While the author was traveling in New England, the weather became cold and leaves turned their fall colors. On his way, he met a farmer who had a Yankee face and Yankee accent. Steinbeck discovered that the best way to learn about the local population was to visit a local bar or a church. He also saw many people fleeing New England to escape the winter. Many shops were closed, and some had signs saying they would be closed until the following summer. As he traveled through the states, he noticed changes in the language. These differences were apparent in road signs. Trouble arose when he was not allowed to cross the Canadian border because he did not have a vaccination certificate for his dog, Charley. Steinbeck and his companion were later able to resume their trip without further problems.

Answers to Exercise 48.2, page 493

1. Do you know where you and Erica will go on vacation this summer?
2. You should look online. You can find great deals there.
3. I have been looking all over the Internet, but I have not found any cheap hotels.

Answers to Exercise 48.3, page 495

1. In the past, people were expected (to stay/staying) at the same job for a long time, ideally for their whole career.
2. Today, people tend (to change/changing) careers several times before retiring.
3. People who are not happy with their careers attempt (to find/finding) other jobs that interest them more.

Answers to Exercise 48.4, page 499

1. Many house hunters look for a big comfortable place to live near a school.
2. Real estate agents describe properties in glowing terms such as "spacious prewar brick building."
3. Multiple bedrooms, fully equipped bathrooms, and landscaped gardens are becoming standard features of new suburban properties.

Answers to Exercise 48.5, page 499

1. The review material for the art history final is very (boring/bored).
2. The term paper I am writing for the class is on a (challenging/challenged) topic: twentieth-century painting.
3. The paintings of Picasso are especially (interesting/interested).

Answers to Exercise 48.6, page 504

1. As Michael Pollan writes in the *New York Times Magazine,* Americans have become the world's most anxious eaters.
2. Researchers have found that Americans worry more about what they eat than people in other developed countries do.
3. Therefore, they tend to enjoy their food less and associate a good meal with guilty pleasure.

Answers to Exercise 49.1, page 510

1. After the year 1000 CE, Europeans became less isolated.
2. Correct
3. Increasingly aware of the rich civilizations beyond their borders, Europeans began to enter into business relationships with the cities and countries in the East.

Answers to Exercise 49.2, page 511

1. Asperger syndrome is not the same as autism, yet it is often confused with autism.
2. People with Asperger syndrome have normal IQs, but they have difficulty interacting with others in a social setting.
3. In school, students afflicted with this disorder may have difficulty working in groups, for they prefer solitary, repetitive routines.

Answers to Exercise 49.3, page 512

1. Correct
2. Paintings have been found in North America, Europe, Africa, and Australia.
3. Paintings found in southeastern France contain images of animals, birds, and fish.

Answers to Exercise 49.4, page 514

1. The mind-body problem, under debate for centuries, concerns the relationship between the mind and the body.
2. Correct
3. Since the time of the ancient Greeks, the prevailing opinion has been that the mind and body are separate entities.

Answers to Exercise 49.5, page 517

1. Millions of viewers watch reality-based television shows. Cultural critics, however, argue that shows such as *The Amazing Race, Survivor,* and *Jersey Shore* exploit human greed and the desire for fame.
2. These shows, so the critics say, take advantage of our insecurities.
3. The participants who appear on these shows are average, everyday people, not actors.

Answers to Exercise 49.6, page 519

1. Professor Bartman entered the room and proclaimed, "Today we will examine Erikson's eight stages of human development."
2. "Who may I ask has read the assignment?" he queried.
3. "Patricia," he hissed, "please enlighten the rest of the class."

Answer to Exercise 49.7, page 522

Every society has families, but the structure of the family varies from society to society. Over time the function of the family has changed so that in today's postindustrial society, for instance, the primary function of the family is to provide "emotional gratification," according to Professor Paula Stein, noted sociologist of Stonehall University, New Hampshire. In a recent interview, Stein [or In a recent interview Stein . . .] also said, "Images of the family tend to be based on ideals, not realities." To back up this claim, Stein pointed to a survey of more than 10,000 married American couples that she and her staff conducted. Released in the October 17, 2008, edition of the *Weekly Sociologist,* the survey indicates that the biggest change has been the increase in the variety of family arrangements, including singles, single parents, and childless couples. Most Americans marry for love, they say, but research portrays courtship as an analysis of costs, benefits, assets, and liabilities, not unlike a business deal.

Virtually all children are upset by divorce, but most recover in a few years while others suffer lasting, serious problems. Despite the high rate of divorce, which reached its height in 1979, Americans still believe in the institution of marriage, as indicated by the high rate of remarriages that form *blended families.* "Yes, some see the breakup of the family as a social problem or cause of other problems, but others see changes in the family as adaptations to changing social conditions, as I do," concluded the professor.

Answers to Exercise 50.1, page 524

1. The Pop Art movement flourished in the United States and in Britain in the 1960s; it was a reaction to the abstract art that had dominated the art scene during the 1950s.
2. Pop artists were inspired by popular culture and consumerism; for example, they painted advertisements, comic strips, supermarket products, and even dollar bills!
3. The artists' goal was to transform ordinary daily experiences into art; they also wanted to comment on the modern world of mass production.

Answers to Exercise 50.2, page 526

1. Some scientists are studying a European bird related to the chickadee; these scientists, at the Netherlands Institute of Ecology, are conducting experiments with this bird.
2. Another scientist, Dr. Samuel Gosling, has studied hyena populations; he asked handlers to rate the hyenas using a questionnaire that was adapted from a questionnaire used for humans.
3. These studies and others indicate that animals display personality traits like boldness and shyness; bold birds quickly investigate new items in their environment while shy birds take more time.

Answer to Exercise 51.1, page 528

Ciguatera is a form of food poisoning: humans are poisoned when they consume reef fish that contain toxic substances called ciguatoxins. These toxins accumulate at the end of the food chain: large carnivorous fish prey on smaller herbivorous fish. These smaller fish feed on ciguatoxins, which are produced by microorganisms that grow on the surface of marine algae. Ciguatoxins are found in certain marine fish: snapper, mackerel, barracuda, and grouper. People should avoid eating fish from reef waters, including the tropical and subtropical waters of the Pacific and Indian Oceans, and the Caribbean Sea.

Some people think that ciguatera can be destroyed by cooking or freezing the fish. People who consume reef fish should avoid eating the head, internal organs, or eggs. People who eat contaminated fish experience gastrointestinal and neurological problems: vomiting, diarrhea, numbness, and muscle pains. Most physicians offer the same advice: "Eat fish only from reputable restaurants and dealers."

Answers to Exercise 52.1, page 531

WORD(S)	POSSESSIVE
the press	the press's
nobody	nobody's
newspapers	newspapers'

Answers to Exercise 52.2, page 533

1. In the essay "The Over-soul," Ralph Waldo Emerson describes the unity of nature by cataloging (it's/<u>its</u>) divine, yet earthly, expressions, such as waterfalls and well-worn footpaths.

2. Emerson states that you must have faith to believe in something that supersedes or contradicts (<u>your</u>/you're) real-life experiences.

3. (<u>Who's</u>/Whose) the author of the poem at the beginning of Emerson's "Self-Reliance"?

Answer to Exercise 52.3, page 533

Transcendentalism was a movement of thought in the mid-to-late 1800s that was originated by Ralph Waldo Emerson, Henry David Thoreau, and several others whose scholarship helped to shape the democratic ideals of their day and usher America into its modern age. Emerson, a member of New England's elite, was particularly interested in spreading Transcendentalist notions of self-reliance; he is probably best known for his essay "Self-Reliance," which is still widely read in today's universities. Most people remember Thoreau, however, not only for what he wrote but also for how he lived: it's well known that—for a while, at least—he chose to live a simple life in a cabin on Walden Pond. Altogether, one could say that Emerson and Thoreau's main accomplishment was to expand the influence of literature and philosophy over the development of the average American's identity. With a new national literature forming, people's interest in their self-development quickly increased as they began to read more and more about what it meant to be American. In fact, one could even say (perhaps half-jokingly) that, today, the success of home makeovers on TV and the popularity of self-help books might have a lot to do with Emerson's and Thoreau's ideas about self-sufficiency and living simply—ideas that took root in this nation more than a hundred years ago.

Answers to Exercise 53.1, page 536

1. Correct
2. "To prove this," writes Stanton, "let facts be submitted to a candid world."
3. Correct

Answers to Exercise 53.2, page 539

1. "We hold these truths to be self-evident," wrote Thomas Jefferson in 1776.
2. Most Americans can recite their "unalienable rights": "life, liberty, and the pursuit of happiness."
3. According to the Declaration of Independence, "whenever any form of government becomes destructive to these ends, it is the right of the people to alter or to abolish it."

Answer to Exercise 53.3, page 540

On August 28, 1963, Dr. Martin Luther King Jr. delivered his famous "I Have a Dream" speech at the nation's Lincoln Memorial. According to King, "When the architects of our republic wrote the magnificent words of the Constitution and the Declaration of Independence, they were signing a promissory note to which every American was to fall heir." King declared that "this note was a promise that all men, yes, black men as well as white men, would be guaranteed the unalienable rights of life, liberty, and the pursuit of happiness. This promissory note, however, came back marked 'insufficient funds.'" King's speech, therefore, was designed to rally his supporters to "make justice a reality."

Unlike the more militant civil rights leaders of the 1950s, King advocated nonviolence. This stance is why King said that the "Negro community" should not drink "from the cup of bitterness and hatred," and that they should not use physical violence.

King's dream was uniquely American: "I have a dream that one day this nation will rise up and live out the true meaning of its creed: 'We hold these truths to be self-evident: that all men are created equal.'" King challenged all Americans to fully embrace racial equality. Nearly fifty years later, we must ask ourselves if King's dream has in fact become a reality. Are "all of God's children, black men and white men, Jews and Gentiles, Protestants and Catholics . . . able to join hands and sing in the words of the old Negro spiritual, 'Free at last! Free at last! Thank God Almighty, we are free at last!'"?

Answer to Exercise 54.1, page 543

Do you realize that there is a volcano larger than Mt. St. Helens? Mt. Vesuvius? Mt. Etna? Mauna Loa is the largest volcano on Earth, covering at least half the island of Hawaii. The summit of Mauna Loa stands 56,000 feet above its base. This is why Native Hawaiians named this volcano the "Long Mountain." Mauna Loa is also one of the most active volcanoes on the planet, having erupted thirty-three times since 1843. Its last eruption occurred in 1984. Most people associate a volcanic eruption with red lava spewing from the volcano's crater, but few people realize that the lava flow and volcanic gases are also extremely hazardous. Tourists like to follow the lava to where it meets the sea, but this practice is dangerous because of the steam produced when the lava meets the water. So, the next time you visit an active volcano, beware!

Answers to Exercise 54.2, page 544

1. Patsy Mink, Geraldine Ferraro, Antonia Novello, Madeline Albright, Hillary Clinton, and Sarah Palin—all are political pioneers in the history of the United States.
2. Patsy Mink—the first Asian-American woman elected to the U.S. Congress—served for twenty-four years in the U.S. House of Representatives.
3. Geraldine Ferraro—congresswoman from Queens, New York—became the first female vice presidential candidate when she was nominated by the Democratic Party in 1984.

Answers to Exercise 54.3, page 545

1. German meteorologist Alfred Wegener (he was also a geophysicist) proposed the first comprehensive theory of continental drift.
2. According to this geological theory, (1) the earth originally contained a single large continent, (2) this land mass eventually separated into six continents, and (3) these continents gradually drifted apart.
3. Wegener contended that continents will continue to drift (they are not rigidly fixed), and the evidence indicates that his predictions are accurate.

Answers to Exercise 54.4, page 548

1. Ulysses is tempted as he looks toward the sea: "The lights begin to twinkle from the rocks; / The long day wanes; . . ." (54–55).

2. In "Two Views of the Mississippi," Mark Twain writes that "when I had mastered the language of this water, . . . I had made a valuable acquisition."

3. Twain regrets that he "[has] lost something"—his sense of the beauty of the river.

Answer to Exercise 54.5, page 549

Responses will vary.

John Fitzgerald Kennedy—the youngest man to be elected U.S. President—was also the youngest President to be assassinated. He was born on May 29, 1917, in Brookline, Massachusetts. Kennedy was born into a family with a tradition of public service—his father, Joseph Kennedy, served as ambassador to Great Britain. (His maternal grandfather, John Frances Fitzgerald, served as the mayor of Boston.)

Caroline, John Fitzgerald Jr., and Patrick B. (who died in infancy) are the children of the late John F. Kennedy. Kennedy's background—a Harvard education, military service as a lieutenant in the navy, and public service as Massachusetts senator—helped provide him with the experience, insight, and recognition needed to defeat Richard Nixon in 1960.

Even before being elected U.S. President, Kennedy received the Pulitzer Prize for his book *Profiles in Courage* (1957). According to Kennedy, "This [*Profiles in Courage*] is a book about that most admirable of human virtues—courage" (1). "Some of my colleagues," Kennedy continues, "who are criticized today for lack of forthright principles . . . are simply engaged in the fine art of conciliating . . ." (5).

During Kennedy's presidency, Americans witnessed (1) the Cuban Missile Crisis, (2) the Bay of Pigs Invasion, and (3) the Berlin Crisis. Most Americans, we hope, are able to recognize Kennedy's famous words, which were first delivered during his Inaugural Address: "Ask not what your country can do for you—ask what you can do for your country."

Answer to Exercise 55.1, page 554

Perhaps the most notable writer of the 1920s is F. Scott Fitzgerald. He was born on September 24, 1896, in St. Paul, Minnesota, to Edward Fitzgerald and Mary "Mollie" McQuillan, who were both members of the Catholic Church. After attending Princeton University and embarking on a career as a writer, Fitzgerald married southern belle Zelda Sayre from Montgomery, Alabama. Together, he and his wife lived the celebrated life of the Roaring Twenties and the Jazz Age. Fitzgerald wrote numerous short stories as well as four novels: *This Side of Paradise, The Beautiful and Damned, The Great Gatsby,* and *Tender Is the Night. The Great Gatsby,* which he finished in the winter of 1924 and published in 1925, is considered Fitzgerald's most brilliant and critically acclaimed work. Readers who have read this novel will remember these opening words spoken by Nick Carraway, the narrator in the story: "In my younger and more vulnerable years my father gave me some advice that I've been turning over in my mind ever since. 'Whenever you feel like criticizing anyone,' he told me, 'just remember that all the people in this world haven't had the advantages that you've had.'"

Answer to Exercise 56.1, page 557

In today's digital-savvy world, a person who has never used a computer with access to the World Wide Web (WWW) and a Motion Pictures Experts Group Layer 3 (MP3) player would be surprised to find that anyone can download and groove to the sounds of "Nights in White Satin" by the 1960s rock band the Moody Blues at 3 AM without ever having to have spent money for the album *Days of Future Past.* However, such file sharing, commonly known as "file swapping," is illegal and surrounded by controversy. The Recording Industry Association of America (RIAA), which represents the U.S. recording industry, has taken aggressive legal action against such acts of online piracy. For example, in a landmark case in 2004, U.S. District Judge Denny Chin ruled that Internet service providers must identify those subscribers who share music online, at least in the states of New York, New Jersey, and Connecticut. As the nature of music recordings changes with the proliferation of digital music services and file formats, this controversy is far from being resolved. In recent years, companies such as Apple and Microsoft as well as cellular phone carriers have set up online music stores. Consumers can buy downloadable music files for very little money.

Answers to Exercise 57.1, page 560

1. The soccer team raised $1,067 by selling entertainment booklets filled with coupons, discounts, and special promotions.
2. Fifty-five percent of the participants in the sociology student's survey reported that they would lie to a professor in order to have a late assignment accepted.
3. In one year alone, 115 employees at the company objected to their performance appraisals, but only 24 filed formal complaints.

Answer to Exercise 58.1, page 563

Today, thousands of people in the United States practice yoga for its physical, spiritual, and mental benefits. The word *yoga,* originating from the Sanskrit root *yuj,* means the union of the body, spirit, and mind. Although there are many styles of yoga, people who want a gentle introduction to yoga should practice Iyengar Yoga, a style developed by B. K. S. Iyengar of India, which uses props such as blocks, belts, and pillows to help the body find alignment in *asanas* (poses) and *pranayana* (breathing). Those people who want to learn more about Iyengar Yoga are encouraged to read the following books written by the master himself: *Light on Yoga, Light on Pranayama, The Art of Yoga, The Tree of Yoga,* and *Light on the Yoga Sutras of Patanjali.* Those who want to learn about the general benefits of yoga can find numerous articles, such as "Yoga and Weight Loss," by doing a general online search. All forms of yoga promise the diligent and faithful practitioner increased strength, flexibility, and balance.

Answer to Exercise 59.1, page 565

We need only to turn on the television or pick up a recent issue of a popular fashion or fitness magazine to see evidence of modern society's obsession with images of thinness. Few actors, models, or celebrities fail to flaunt their thinly trimmed waistlines, regardless of their gender. Not surprisingly, more than ten million females and almost one million males in the United States are currently battling eating disorders such as anorexia nervosa and bulimia nervosa. A person who is anorexic fears gaining weight and thus engages in self-starvation with excessive weight loss. A person who is bulimic binges and then engages in self-induced purging in order to lose weight. Although we are often quick to assume that those with eating disorders suffer from low self-esteem and have a history of family or peer problems, we cannot ignore the role of the media in encouraging eating disorders, particularly when thinness is equated with physical attractiveness, health and fitness, and success overall. We need to remember the threat of these eating disorders the next time we hear a ten-year-old girl tell her mommy that she "can't afford" to eat more than one-half of her peanut-butter-and-jelly sandwich.

Answers to Exercise 60.1, page 569

Bentleys
presidents-elect
lives

Answers to Exercise 60.2, page 569

either (correct)
hygiene (correct)
dealer (correct)

Answers to Exercise 60.3, page 570

Answers will vary.

Answers to Exercise 61.1, page 575

1. undergo (mv)
2. believed (mv)
3. think (mv); Do (hv)

Answers to Exercise 61.2 and Exercise 61.3, pages 579 and 580

1. Following <u>World War I</u>, the <u>nation</u> witnessed an unprecedented <u>explosion</u> of <u>African-American</u> <u>fiction</u>, <u>poetry</u>, <u>drama</u>, <u>music</u>, <u>art</u>, social <u>commentary</u>, and political <u>activism</u>.

   Nouns:
   World War I—proper, concrete, singular (count/noncount not applicable)
   nation—common, count, concrete, singular
   explosion—common, count, concrete, singular
   fiction—common, noncount, concrete, singular
   poetry—common, noncount, concrete, singular
   drama—common, noncount, concrete, singular
   music—common, noncount, concrete, singular
   art—common, noncount, concrete, singular
   commentary—common, count, concrete, singular
   activism—common, noncount, concrete, singular

2. Many African-American <u>intellectuals</u>, <u>artists</u>, cultural <u>critics</u>, and political <u>leaders</u> during the <u>1920s</u> and <u>1930s</u> were drawn to <u>Harlem</u>, a vibrant <u>section</u> of upper <u>Manhattan</u> in <u>New York City</u>.

   Nouns: intellectuals—common, count, concrete, plural
   artists—common, count, concrete, plural
   critics—common, count, concrete, plural
   leaders—common, count, concrete, plural
   1920s—either common or proper could be correct, count, concrete, plural
   1930s—either common or proper could be correct, count, concrete, plural
   Harlem—proper, concrete, singular (count/noncount not applicable)
   section—common, count, concrete, singular
   Manhattan—proper, concrete, singular (count/noncount not applicable)
   New York City—proper, concrete, singular (count/noncount not applicable)

3. <u>Sociologist</u> and <u>intellectual</u> <u>Alain Locke</u>, <u>author</u> of <u>The New Negro</u>, is best known as the <u>New Negro Movement's</u> <u>founder</u>.

   Nouns:
   Sociologist—common, count, concrete, singular
   intellectual—common, count, concrete, singular
   Alain Locke—proper, concrete, singular (count/noncount not applicable)
   author—common, count, concrete, singular
   The New Negro—proper, concrete, singular (count/noncount not applicable)
   New Negro Movement's (as a whole)—possessive proper noun, concrete, singular (count/noncount not applicable)
   founder—common, count, concrete, singular

Answers to Exercise 61.4, page 582

1. Adj: growing, overweight, obese; adv: clinically
2. Adj: Type 2, heart, high, blood, liver, premature
3. Adj: fad, rapid, temporary, weight, weight

Answers to Exercise 61.5, page 585

1. Cancer (n) begins (v) when (conj) your (pron/adj) body's (noun/adj) cells (n) divide (v) abnormally (adv) and (conj) form (v) a (adj) malignant (adj) growth (n) or (conj) tumor (n).
2. Many (adj) types (n) of (prep) cancer (n) alas (interj) can (v) attack (v) parts (n) of (conj) your (pron/adj) body (n) imperceptibly (adv), including (prep) your (pron/adj) body's (n/adj) skin (n), organs (n), and (conj) blood (n).

3. One (n) of (prep) the (adj) most (adv) commonly (adv) diagnosed (adj) types (n) of (prep) cancer (n) in (prep) the (adj) United States (n), however (adv), is (v) skin (n/adj) cancer (n).

Answers to Exercise 62.1, page 587

1. Did Gene Roddenberry, the creator and producer of *Star Trek*, anticipate that his science fiction television series would be watched by people of all ages for more than thirty years?

2. Both Captain James T. Kirk from *Star Trek: The Original Series* and Captain Jean-Luc Picard from *Star Trek: The Next Generation* command a ship called the *Enterprise.*

3. Do not forget that the captain in *Star Trek: Voyager* is a woman, Kathryn Janeway. [implied subject]

Answers to Exercise 62.2, page 589

1. Lucretia Mott and Elizabeth Cady Stanton organized the first national convention on women's rights.
2. They held the convention in 1848 at Seneca Falls, a town in upstate New York.
3. The convention issued the Declaration of Sentiments, which included a demand that women be granted the right to vote.

Answers to Exercise 62.3, page 591

1. Hybrid cars produce (trans) low tailpipe emissions (DO).
2. Automakers promise (trans) consumers (IO) affordable gasoline-electric cars (DO).
3. Hybrid cars are (link) desirable alternatives (SC) to gasoline-powered vehicles.

Answers to Exercise 63.1, page 594

1. Noun phrase functioning as the subject of the sentence
2. Noun phrase, appositive
3. Noun phrase functioning as the object of the sentence

Answers to Exercise 63.2, page 596

1. During the 1970s and 1980s, Asian-American writers, who often drew on their immigrant experiences, gained a wide readership. [adj. clause]
2. Because these writers wrote about their struggles and the struggles of their ancestors, readers were able to learn about the Chinese Exclusion Act of 1892 and the internment of Japanese Americans during World War II. [adv. clause]
3. Many readers know Amy Tan as the Chinese-American novelist who wrote *The Joy Luck Club*, which was adapted into a feature film, but are unfamiliar with most of her other novels, such as *The Kitchen God's Wife, The Hundred Secret Senses,* and *The Bonesetter's Daughter.* [two adj. clauses, the first modifying "Amy Tan," the second modifying "The Joy Luck Club"]

Answers to Exercise 64.1, page 598

1. Simple
2. Simple
3. Compound

Credits

Text/Line Art Credits

Introduction: Fig. 1.2: From *A Writer's Resource,* 3ed, by Elaine Maimon and Janice Peritz. Copyright © 2010 by The McGraw-Hill Companies, Inc. Reprinted with permission of the McGraw-Hill Companies, Inc. **p. 4:** From *P.O.W.E.R. Learning: Strategies for Success in College and Life,* 2ed, by Robert S. Feldman. Copyright © 2003 by The McGraw-Hill Companies, Inc. Reprinted with permission of the McGraw-Hill Companies, Inc.
Chapter 1: p. 21: Hentoff, Nat. "Misguided Multiculturalism" *The Village Voice,* July 19-25, 2000, pp. 29-30. Copyright © 2000 by Nat Hentoff. Reprinted by permission of the author.
Chapter 2: p. 43 bar graphs: From *A More Perfect Union,* 1ed, by Brigid Harrison and Jean Harris, p. 369. Copyright © 2011 by The McGraw-Hill Companies, Inc. Reprinted with permission of the McGraw-Hill Companies, Inc. **p. 44 pie chart:** From *Sociology in Modules,* 1ed, by Richard T. Schaefer, p. 353. Copyright © 2011 by The McGraw-Hill Companies, Inc. Reprinted with permission of the McGraw-Hill Companies, Inc. **p. 44 line graph:** From *Sociology in Modules,* 1ed, by Richard T. Schaefer, p. 78. Copyright © 2011 by The McGraw-Hill Companies, Inc. Reprinted with permission of the McGraw-Hill Companies, Inc. **p. 44 diagram:** From "Modeling Offenders' Decisions: A Framework for Research and Policy" by R.V. Clark and D.B. Cornish. *Crime and Justice,* Vol. 6, by M. Tonry and N. Morris (eds), p. 169. Copyright © 1985 by University of Chicago Press. Reprinted with permission. **p. 45 map:** From Brigid Harrison, *A More Perfect Union,* 1st Ed. Copyright © 2011 McGraw-Hill. Reprinted with permission from The McGraw-Hill Companies, Inc.
Chapter 3: pp. 49–50: Ducharme, Michelle M. From "A Lifetime in Production." *Newsweek,* September 9, 1996, p. 17. All rights reserved. Reprinted by permission of the author. **pp. 51–52:** Reich, Robert. From "The Future of Work," *Harper's,* April 1989, 26+. Copyright © 1989 by Robert Reich. Reprinted by permission of the author. **Fig 3.4:** From Galle, *Business Communication: A Technology-Based Approach,* 1st ed., 1996, Fig. 8.4, p. 240. Copyright © 1996 The McGraw-Hill Companies. Reprinted with permission. **pp. 52–53:** Wordiq.com. **Fig 3.6:** From *Understanding Psychology,* 9ed, by Robert S. Feldman, Module 11, Figure 2. Copyright © 2009 by The McGraw-Hill Companies, Inc. Reprinted with permission. **pp. 54–55:** From *Understanding Psychology* 10ed, by Richard T. Schaefer, p. 29. Copyright © 2007 by The McGraw-Hill Companies, Inc. Reprinted with permission. **Fig 3.7:** From *Sociology* 10ed, by Richard T. Schaefer. Copyright © 2007 by The McGraw-Hill Companies, Inc. Reprinted with permission. **pp. 55-56:** From "Heat Wave of 1995" by Eric Klineberg. *The Electronic Encyclopedia of Chicago.* © 2005 Chicago Historical Society. **p. 58:** Jonathan Fast, "After Columbine: How People Mourn Sudden Death," *Social Work,* Vol. 48, No. 4, p. 485. Copyright © National Association of Social Workers. Reprinted with permission from the National Association of Social Workers, Inc. **p. 59:** Robinson, Damian, "Riding into the Afterlife," *Archaeology,* Vol. 57, No. 2, March/April 2004. © 2004 by The Archaeological Institute of America. Reprinted with permission. **p. 59:** From "Students Must Focus on Degree Completion" by Elaine Maimon. *The Times of Northwest Indiana,* Nov. 7, 2010. Reprinted with permission. **p. 60:** Chapell,

Photo Credits

Index

Index for Multilingual Writers

CHECKLISTS

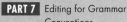

THE MOST COMMON ERRORS

SECTIONS ON VISUAL RHETORIC

Contents